ECONOMIC POLICY

48

October
2006

budget deficits and current accounts
Openness and fiscal persistence
CORSETTI and MÜLLER

fiscal policy and trade
Spillovers in the EU
BEETSMA, GIULIODORI and KLAASSEN

fiscal discipline
Budget institutions and politics
FABRIZIO and MODY

antitrust policy
The influence of economics
NEVEN

ECONOMIC POLICY

Editorial address: Centre for Economic Policy Research, 90–98 Goswell Road, London EC1V 7RR, UK; Center for Economic Studies, University of Munich, Schackstr. 4, 80539 Munich, GERMANY; Paris-Jourdan Sciences Economiques, ENS, 48 Boulevard Jourdan, 75014 Paris, FRANCE. URL: http://www.economic-policy.org

Publisher: *Economic Policy* is published by Blackwell Publishing, 9600 Garsington Road, Oxford OX4 2DQ, UK and 350 Main Street, Malden, MA 02148, USA.

Information for subscribers: *Economic Policy* is published in four issues per year. Subscription prices for 2006 are:

	Europe	The Americas	ROW
Premium Institutional:	£308	US$468	£308
Personal:	€68	US$67	£45
Student:	€33	US$36	£22

Customers in the UK should add VAT at 5%; customers in the EU should also add VAT at 5%, or provide a VAT registration number or evidence of entitlement to exemption. Customers in Canada should add 7% GST or provide evidence of entitlement to exception. The Premium institutional price includes online access to the current and all available previous year electronic issues. For other pricing options or more information about online access to Blackwell Publishing journals, including access information and terms and conditions, please visit www.blackwellpublishing.com/ecop.

EEA members: Subscriptions are available now at 40 euro. Apply to the European Economic Association, Voie du Roman Pays, 34, B-1348 Louvain-la-Neuve, Belgium (tel: +32 10 472 012, fax: +32 10 474 021/474 301, email: eea@core.ucl.ac.be, URL: http://www.eeassoc.org).

Available online: This journal is available online at *Blackwell Synergy*. Visit www.blackwell-synergy.com to search the articles and register for table of contents e-mail alerts.

Journal Customer Services: For ordering information, claims and any enquiry concerning your journal subscription please contact your nearest office:

UK: Email: customerservices@blackwellpublishing.com; Tel: +44 (0) 1865 778315; Fax: +44 (0) 1865 471775

USA: Email: customerservices@blackwellpublishing.com; Tel: +1 781 388 8206 or 1 800 835 6770 (Toll free in the USA); Fax: +1 781 388 8232 or Fax: +44 (0) 1865 471775

Asia: Email: customerservices@blackwellpublishing.com; Tel: +65 6511 8000; Fax: +44 (0) 1865 471775

Production Editor: Caroline Clamp (email: caroline.clamp@oxon.blackwellpublishing.com).

Back issues: Single issues from current and recent volumes are available at the current single issue price from Blackwell Publishing Journals. Earlier issues may be obtained from Periodicals Service Company, 11 Main Street, Germantown, NY 12526, USA. Tel: +1 518 537 4700, Fax: +1 518 537 5899, Email: psc@periodicals.com.

Advertising: Andy Patterson (email: andy@patads.co.uk).

Abstracting and Indexing Services: Contents of Recent Economics Journals; Current Contents/Social and Behavioural Sciences; Economic Literature Index; Geographical Abstracts; Human Geography; International Bibliography of the Social Sciences; International Development Abstracts; Journal of Economic Literature; PAIS International in Print; Research Alert; Sage Public Administration Abstracts; Social Science Citation Index; Social Scisearch.

Disclaimer: The Publisher, Centre for Economic Policy Research, Center for Economic Studies, Maison des Sciences de l'Homme and Editors cannot be held responsible for errors or any consequences arising from the use of information contained in this journal; the views and opinions expressed do not necessarily reflect those of the Publisher, Centre for Economic Policy Research, Center for Economic Studies, Maison des Sciences de l'Homme and Editors, neither does the publication of advertisements constitute any endorsement by the Publisher, Centre for Economic Policy Research, Center for Economic Studies, Maison des Sciences de l'Homme and Editors of the products advertised.

Paper: Blackwell Publishing's policy is to use permanent paper from mills that operate a sustainable forestry policy, and which has been manufactured from pulp that is processed using acid-free and elementary chlorine-free practices. Furthermore, Blackwell Publishing ensures that the text paper and cover board used in all our journals has met acceptable environmental accreditation standards.

Printed in Great Britain.

For submission instructions, subscription and all other information visit: www.blackwellpublishing.com/ecop

ISSN: 0266-4658 (print); ISSN: 1468-0327 (online)

ISBN: 1-4051-4511-0; ISBN-13: 9781405145114

48

October
2006

ECONOMIC POLICY

SENIOR EDITORS
GEORGES DE MÉNIL
RICHARD PORTES
HANS-WERNER SINN

MANAGING EDITORS
GIUSEPPE BERTOLA
PHILIPPE MARTIN
PAUL SEABRIGHT

Published in association with the European Economic Association

Blackwell Publishing Ltd for Centre for Economic Policy Research,
Center for Economic Studies of the University of Munich, and
Paris-Jourdan Sciences Economiques (PSE)
in collaboration with the Maison des Sciences de l'Homme.

STATEMENT OF PURPOSE

Economic Policy provides timely and authoritative analyses of the choices which confront policy-makers. The subject matter ranges from the study of how individual markets can and should work to the broadest interactions in the world economy.

Economic Policy is a joint activity of the Centre for Economic Policy Research (CEPR), the Munich-based Center for Economic Studies (CES) and the Paris-based Maison des Sciences de l'Homme (PSE). It offers an independent, non-partisan, European perspective on issues of worldwide concern. It emphasizes problems of international significance, either because they affect the world economy directly or because the experience of one country contains important lessons for policy-makers elsewhere.

All the articles are specifically commissioned from leading professional economists. Their brief is to demonstrate how live policy issues can be illuminated by the insights of modern economics and by the most recent evidence. The presentation is incisive and written in plain language accessible to the wide audience which participates in the policy debate.

Prior to publication, the contents of each volume are discussed by a Panel of distinguished economists from Europe and elsewhere. The Panel rotates annually. Inclusion in each volume of a summary of the highlights of the Economic Policy Panel discussion provides the reader with alternative interpretations of the evidence and a sense of the liveliness of the current debate.

Economic Policy is owned by the Maison des Sciences de l'Homme, CEPR and CES. The 43rd Panel meeting was held in Vienna and was hosted by the Österreichische Nationalbank. We gratefully acknowledge this support, without implicating any of these organizations in the views expressed here, which are the sole responsibility of the authors.

48
October 2006

CONTENTS

Editors' introduction

Three of the papers published in this issue were presented in draft form at the Panel meeting hosted in April 2006 by the Austrian National Bank in Vienna, and followed the normal commissioning and review process. We conclude the issue – and the first of the new four-issue volume years of *Economic Policy* – with the fourth of the special essays, commissioned to review twenty years of policy-oriented economic research in celebration of the journal's 20th anniversary, that were presented at the Panel hosted in London by the Bank of England in October 2005.

BUDGET DEFICITS AND CURRENT ACCOUNTS: OPENNESS AND FISCAL PERSISTENCE

When a government's expenditures exceed its receipts, does the whole country also spend more than it earns? If so, the government's budget deficit and the country's current account deficit are 'twins', and concerns with the sustainability of a country's accumulation of external debt and of public debt have tightly related policy implications. The link between a country's external and public deficits is not so simple, however, both because the private sector's income and expenditure can react to fiscal shocks, and because international adjustments occur via price changes as well as through changes in the volume of income and expenditure.

In their paper, Giancarlo Corsetti and Gernot J. Müller identify sensible and policy relevant ways in which shock characteristics and structural features may affect the transmission of fiscal policy developments to either or both deficits. Their theoretical model indicates that public and external deficits may or may not be 'twins', depending on the persistence of fiscal shocks and on the degree of openness to international influences of countries' economic structure, and suggests that cross-country comparative work can offer important new insights to a literature dominated by single-country (chiefly the US) or panel studies. As is often the case in macroeconomics, empirical work on unavoidably limited data cannot do justice to the implications of dynamic, general equilibrium

Economic Policy October 2006 pp. 593–596 Printed in Great Britain
© CEPR, CES, MSH, 2006.

594					EDITORS' INTRODUCTION

frameworks of analysis. The data support the paper's theoretical argument, in that the extent to which 'twin' deficit dynamics are observed appears related to openness and persistence indicators across the four countries where suitable fiscal information is available.

While the evidence is much more mixed as regards the role of international relative price changes in affecting the profitability of country-specific investment, the Panel appreciated the empirical potential of the paper's novel approach, and engaged the authors in a lively discussion of their theoretical approach's relationship to simpler textbook derivations on the one hand, and to even more sophisticated and debatable models on the other hand. The paper's original approach to a vexed question will undoubtedly spur much further work by both empirical and theoretical macroeconomists.

FISCAL POLICY AND TRADE: SPILL-OVERS IN THE EU

Policy concerns with the effects of fiscal policy are probably nowhere stronger than in the European Union and in the Eurozone, where some large countries have violated the deficit limits imposed by the Stability and Growth Pact. There are many important reasons why individual countries' fiscal developments may concern other countries, individually and collectively. One of the relevant channels of international interaction is carefully analysed by Roel Beetsma, Massimo Giuliodori and Franc Klaassen, who focus on how a country's fiscal policy influences not only its own, but also its trading partners' economic activity.

Combining the information contained in each country's fiscal and income time series with that provided by cross-country trade flows, their paper offers precise and non-negligible estimates of cross-border fiscal shocks in the European Union. Like every empirical exercise, this one needs to abstract from a variety of issues. Its results are remarkably robust in a variety of respects, but are derived under restrictive maintained assumptions regarding the scope of real and financial interactions between different countries' fiscal and monetary policies. As the Panel discussion made clear, this makes it difficult to formulate detailed policy implications, which would need to rely on a more structural approach to policies' welfare implications. The methodological and empirical contributions of this paper, however, provide a solid basis for all further work in this area.

Depending on the underlying structural relationships, spill-overs may be beneficial or detrimental. But this paper's measurement of their intensity must be relevant for the character of optimal fiscal policy rules, for the severity of the consequences of misguided discretionary policies, and for any other analysis of policy issues in an economic area as closely interconnected as the European Union.

FISCAL DISCIPLINE: BUDGET INSTITUTIONS AND POLITICS

Not only the consequences, but also the origins of fiscal policy developments deserve close attention and scrutiny by policymakers and researchers. A recent literature has argued that fiscal performance is importantly influenced by countries' constitutional provisions and electoral rules, which are in turn likely to reflect deeper societal structures (such as divisions along ethnic or religious lines). In the next article of this issue, Stefania Fabrizio and Ashoka Mody cleverly exploit the rich diversity of Central and Eastern European countries' experiences to disentangle the role of budget institutions from that of structural and political factors in explaining fiscal performance.

In preparation for European Union accession, all the 10 countries analysed by Fabrizio and Mody committed to budgetary discipline. Between 1997 and 2003, however, their fiscal outcomes were quite different. The paper confirms that politics played a crucial role in shaping these outcomes, but also provides evidence that fiscal institutions (in the form of checks and balances in the budgetary process, hierarchical rules and collegiality) did improve budgetary discipline. The scope for indiscipline is greatest on the expenditure side of the budget, and the paper finds that institutional features can be most important in preventing undesirable expenditure developments. Overall, the paper offers an optimistic message to benevolent policymakers: fiscal reforms can control fiscal outcomes even when the politics work in favour of fiscal indiscipline.

Some panel members were surprised by the speed with which changes in fiscal institutions affected fiscal outcomes, suspected that endogeneity of fiscal reforms may be an issue, and wondered whether the results could be generalized beyond the specific and very special group of countries analyzed. But the Panel found the paper to be a stimulating and carefully crafted contribution to a key issue in the debate about European political and institutional process: the experience of institutional reform in Central and Eastern European countries has produced new and valuable empirical results that will need to be referenced by all related future work.

ANTITRUST POLICY: THE INFLUENCE OF ECONOMICS

In the last of the four papers specially commissioned for the 20th anniversary of *Economic Policy*, Damien J. Neven seeks to assess the influence that economic analysis has had on competition policy in the European Union over the last twenty years. Economists are increasingly used as experts in antitrust cases: the annual turnover of the main economic consultancy firms has increased by a factor of 20 since the early 1990s and currently exceeds £20 million. This is about 15% of the aggregate fees earned on antitrust cases, a proportion close to that in the US. However, the economic resources mobilized by the EU Commission are an order of magnitude smaller, an imbalance that is a significant source of concern. The legal framework and the case decisions have also been influenced by economic analysis in important ways. For instance, the analysis of agreements between firms has increasingly focused on effects; the analysis of the factors that determine effective competition has become more sophisticated; the concept of collective dominance has been progressively developed in terms of the theory of collusion in repeated interactions, and quantitative methods have become more important. However, enforcement has sometimes appealed to economic reasoning in flawed or speculative ways; the paper discusses procedural reasons why this may have occurred. Neven assesses the system of evidence gathering implemented by the Commission in the light of the law and economics literature, concluding that while the reforms recently implemented by the Commission do address the main weaknesses of this system, they may still not allow for the most effective development of economic theory and evidence in actual cases.

The paper provoked much discussion at the panel, with some differences over how to assess the undoubted advances in EU anti-trust policy in recent years – should the focus be more upon its sophistication compared to other areas of EU economic policy such as agricultural and commercial policy, or its shortcomings compared to the challenges still ahead? Some panellists were unconvinced that statistics charting the involvement of economists as experts in cases were a reliable indicator of the influence of economic ideas. The revised paper we publish offers more articulate and convincing evidence of the fact that, in anti-trust policymaking, economic arguments and modelling are now taken much more seriously than was the case twenty years ago. The more important question of whether and to what extent economic outcomes have improved as a result is much harder to answer, and the Lisbon Agenda's focus on the microeconomic determinants of macroeconomic dynamism guarantees that these issues will capture the attention of researchers and policymakers in the twenty years to come.

Budget deficits and current accounts

OPENNESS AND FISCAL PERSISTENCE

SUMMARY

Simple accounting suggests that shocks to the government budget move the current account in the same direction, and this 'twin deficits' intuition leads many observers to call for fiscal consolidation in the US as a necessary measure to reduce the large external imbalance of this country. The response of other macroeconomic variables to budget developments, however, has important implications for 'twin deficits' and for this policy prescription. Focusing on the international transmission of fiscal policy shocks via terms of trade changes, we show that the likelihood and magnitude of twin deficits increases with the degree of openness of an economy, and decreases with the persistence of fiscal shocks. We take this insight to the data and investigate the transmission of fiscal shocks in a vector autoregression (VAR) model estimated for Australia, Canada, the UK and the US. We find that in less open countries the external impact of shocks to either government spending or budget deficits is limited, while private investment responds in line with our theoretical prediction. These results suggest that a fiscal retrenchment in the US may have a limited impact on its current external deficit.

— *Giancarlo Corsetti and Gernot J. Müller*

Twin deficits: squaring theory, evidence and common sense

Giancarlo Corsetti and Gernot J. Müller

European University Institute, University of Rome III and CEPR; Goethe University Frankfurt

1. INTRODUCTION

The fiscal deterioration in the US during the first George W. Bush administration, coupled with persistent US trade deficits, focused renewed attention on the twin deficit hypothesis. According to this hypothesis, fiscal shocks which cause a deterioration of the government's budget also worsen a country's current account balance. As this argument is supposed to apply symmetrically to the case of fiscal retrenchments, policy circles and institutions strongly advocate domestic fiscal consolidation as a necessary measure to correct the US current account deficit, and as a crucial contribution to resolving global imbalances (e.g. IMF, 2004, 2005; *The Economist*, 2005). But how strong is the evidence for the twin deficit hypothesis, and the theoretical case for it? While fiscal consolidation may be desirable in the US regardless of its external

We are grateful for comments to four anonymous referees, the participants of the *Economic Policy* panel and the conference on Current Account Sustainability in Major Advanced Economies in Madison-Wisconsin (April 2006) and seminar participants at the European University Institute and Goethe University Frankfurt. In particular we thank our discussant Anne Sibert, as well as Keith Küster, Rick van der Ploeg, Morten Ravn, Hélène Rey and Frank Warnock for helpful comments and Larry Schembri for help with the Canadian data. Zeno Enders provided excellent research assistance, Lucia Vigna invaluable help with the text. Corsetti's work on this project is part of the Pierre Werner Chair Programme on Monetary Union of the Robert Schuman Centre at the European University Institute. Financial support by the programme is gratefully acknowledged. The usual disclaimer applies.

The Managing Editor in charge of this paper was Giuseppe Bertola.

Economic Policy October 2006 pp. 597–638 Printed in Great Britain implications, recent work has strengthened doubts about the quantitative relevance of budget policy for the current account, at least in the short run (e.g. Kim and Roubini, 2003; Erceg *et al.*, 2005a; Bussière *et al.*, 2005). The results are to some extent consistent with a larger body of evidence that suggests a weakening of the overall macroeconomic effects of fiscal policy in the last two decades (Perotti, 2005).

This paper reconsiders the twin deficits hypothesis both theoretically and empirically. Since the external effects of a fiscal shock to deficits ultimately depend on the response of private saving and investment, analysing the twin deficits is tantamount to analysing the international transmission mechanism of fiscal policy. Using standard general equilibrium analysis, we identify a transmission channel via changes in the terms of trade (the relative price of imports and exports) that has been neglected in the literature but has very important implications. We show that, because of this channel, the likelihood and magnitude of twin deficits increase with the degree of openness of an economy, and decrease with the persistence of fiscal shocks. This theoretical argument explains why fiscal expansions or contractions may have a smaller impact on external balance (and a larger impact on investment) in countries which are large and relatively closed to trade, such as the US, and when the shock is temporary. We take this 'refined twin deficit hypothesis' to the data, finding some empirical evidence consistent with it.

Our argument starts from the observation that, by national accounting, a fall in national saving due to a government deficit translates – other things equal – into a fall in the current account balance. However, there are different channels through which the response by the private sector may magnify, or partially offset, the consequences of fiscal loosening on the external account. On the one hand, insofar as a fiscal expansion appreciates the domestic currency, net exports fall, causing twin deficits. On the other hand, private savings will typically increase in response to fiscal shocks raising public debt, as a higher debt generates expectations of higher taxes in the future. The strength of this effect depends on the extent to which households internalize the government's intertemporal budget constraint (a point stressed by proponents of Ricardian equivalence). Moreover, to the extent that a loosening of fiscal policy raises interest rates, a fall in public saving may crowd out investment.

These channels are well understood in the literature: it is usually thought that their off-setting effects cannot fully 'undo' the negative impact of budget deficits on the external account and that therefore fiscal shocks induce twin deficits. Yet, these channels do not characterize the international transmission of fiscal shocks in all its dimensions. An additional, important channel through which fiscal shocks affect the external balance is via the impact of terms of trade and real exchange rate movements on relative (domestic vs. foreign) investment. Recent contributions – most notably Obstfeld and Rogoff (2001) – argue that, despite globalization, national economies remain quite 'insular', in the sense that international real and financial markets remain segmented along national borders for a variety of reasons. These include trade costs, distribution, price discrimination, and preferences generating a substantial degree of home bias in consumption and portfolio decisions. As a result, production, consumption and investment decisions respond to a set of prices that may be quite different from the set of prices abroad – although the two are related in general equilibrium at the world level. We focus on the fact that, by making domestic goods more expensive in the world market, a persistent domestic fiscal expansion raises the expected return of domestic investment projects in terms of domestic consumption, balancing conventional crowding out effects of changes in interest rates.

The main features of this transmission channel have traditionally been analysed in isolation within two distinct ways of thinking about the link between fiscal policy and the current account. According to the Mundell–Fleming model, with flexible exchange rates, fiscal deficits appreciate the currency: a higher relative price of domestic goods crowds out net export. If fiscal deficits also raise the interest rate, the resulting external imbalance may be mitigated because of a simultaneous fall in domestic investment. This model stresses changes in terms of trade and interest rates, but abstracts from intertemporal consumption smoothing and treats the rate of return to investment as exogenous. Conversely, models following the so-called intertemporal approach to the current account emphasize consumption smoothing and optimal intertemporal investment decisions, but typically posit a high degree of world market integration. Most contributions in this area either assume only one homogenous tradable good or disregard the equilibrium implications of relative price changes for the return to investment and the real interest rate. This is where our general equilibrium analysis brings in most novel insights.

If goods are not homogenous and government spending falls mostly on domestically produced goods, a persistent government spending shock causes a lasting terms of trade appreciation: the current and future prices of domestic goods rise relative to imported goods. Such a terms of trade appreciation will raise the price of domestically produced goods in terms of consumption and investment goods, which usually have a non-negligible import content. As a result, the present discounted value of output from domestic investment projects rises relative to the price of investment, driving up its real rate of return. This effect on the rates of return counteracts crowding out effects of fiscal policy on investment via higher interest rates.

The relative strength of both effects depends on how much an economy is integrated into world markets. In a *relatively open economy* (i.e. an economy where the import content of both consumption and investment is high) domestic interest rates are not much affected by a fiscal expansion, while an appreciation of the terms of trade increases the real return to investment substantially. As a result investment is – *ceteris paribus* – encouraged. Conversely, in a *relatively closed economy* domestic interest rates are more strongly affected by a fiscal expansion, while an appreciation of the terms of trade has little effect on the real return to investment. As a result investment is – *ceteris paribus* – discouraged. In addition, the overall impact crucially depends on shock persistence: the longer the shock is expected to last, the more persistent the improvement of the terms of trade. Our theoretical analysis establishes that the degree of 'insularity' (reflected in low openness) has significant effects on the international spillovers from fiscal policy, and should be taken into account by policy analysts.

The main empirical prediction of our analysis can thus be stated as a refined twin deficit hypothesis: twin deficits are more likely if (1) the economy is relatively open, i.e. highly integrated into world markets, and (2) fiscal expansions are persistent. Conversely, if an economy is sufficiently closed and fiscal expansions are relatively short-lived, the fiscal deficit resulting from a temporary fiscal expansion is less likely to be accompanied by significant, contemporaneous external trade deterioration. Our empirical analysis builds on a recent vector autoregression (VAR) study by Kim and Roubini (2003) on the US, which identifies spending and budget shocks by restricting their short-run effects on output. In order to assess the refined twin deficit hypothesis, we revisit the main findings of these authors in a comparative perspective: in addition to the US, which is a large and relatively closed economy, we include in our sample three medium-sized OECD economies – the UK, Canada and Australia – which differ with respect to their degree of openness. For the US we corroborate earlier findings that a typical fiscal expansion has a negligible or even positive effect on the external balance. We thus do not find twin deficits. At the same time spending shocks substantially depress investment. Conversely, for Canada and the UK, economies which are considerably more open than the US, we find that the effects of fiscal shocks on investment are small, while the external balance declines substantially. For these relatively open economies we thus do find twin deficits. The evidence for Australia, which is less open than Canada and the UK, is instead similar to the US. We also compute different measures for the persistence of the fiscal shocks identified in the estimated VAR models. Our estimates suggest that a typical government spending shock is relatively persistent in Canada and much less so in Australia.

Our empirical results on investment and the trade balance response to fiscal shocks underscore our theoretical argument, that the magnitude of twin deficits depends crucially on the degree of openness and the persistence of unexpected fiscal expansions or contractions. The empirical model, however, works less well as regards the dynamics of relative prices and interest rates – adding to the list of pricing puzzles in the literature.

Nonetheless, our findings do provide a way to reconcile the existing empirical evidence with the received wisdom and common sense in policy making, according to which prudent budget policies are desirable when the external deficit is excessive. Even for the US, where we find that fiscal shocks have a small contemporaneous quantitative effect on the external balance on average, a fiscal correction is likely to crowd in domestic capital. By raising the stock of capital, a fiscal correction will increase the ability of the US to generate the resources required to meet its external obligations in the future.

This paper is organized as follows. In Section 2 we start with a short discussion of the joint behaviour of the budget balance and the trade balance for the four countries in our sample. In Section 3 we develop our theoretical argument for why openness and shock persistence are key determinants for the response of private investment.

We also state conditions under which twin deficits are likely to result from temporary increases in government spending. In Section 4 we investigate to what extent fiscal shocks drive trade movements in our sample of OECD countries. We specify and estimate a VAR model where spending shocks are identified following the approach suggested by Blanchard and Perotti (2002), and deficit shocks are identified following Kim and Roubini (2003). In Section 5 we discuss the policy implications of our result. Section 6 concludes. Two boxes provide analytical and technical details on our quantitative and empirical models. The Appendix provides details on the data, while the Web Appendix contains formal derivations and a description of the quantitative experiments underlying our argument.

2. A FIRST LOOK AT THE EVIDENCE

2.1. Basic accounting

Virtually all analyses of the twin deficit hypothesis begin with a review of a basic national accounting identity. We stick to this well-established tradition, and begin by relating the external deficit to the difference between national investment and national saving, which in turn is the sum of private and public saving. By definition, the current account balance, hereafter CA, is equal to the value of net exports, NX, plus the interest payments earned on net foreign assets. Equivalently, the CA balance equals private disposable income (the sum of GDP, Y, plus income on net foreign assets, less taxes net of transfers, T) minus private consumption and investment expenditures (denoted C and I, respectively), plus taxes net of transfers, T, less government spending denoted G:

$$CA = NX + rB = (Y + rB - T) - C - I + (T - G)$$

where B denotes the stock of net foreign assets and r denotes the average interest rate earned on them. Now, define private saving as disposable income net of consumption expenditure, i.e. $(Y + rB - T) - C$; by the same token define government saving as $T - G$, in practice, the negative of the budget deficit. After changing sign, we can rewrite the basic identity above as:

  Current Account Deficit = Investment − Private Saving + Budget Deficit.

From an accounting perspective, holding investment and private saving constant, a deterioration of the fiscal position (an increase in the budget deficit) worsens the external balance. From an economic perspective, however, private saving and investment will also adjust in response to changes in the fiscal stance.

The twin deficit hypothesis is formulated with reference to policy innovations whereby a government changes its fiscal stance; say, by reforming the tax code and/or by altering spending policies which generate an increase in the budget deficit. The fiscal initiatives by the George W. Bush administration upon coming to power in 2000 provide a good example of the kind of shocks proponents of the hypothesis have in mind. Naturally, fiscal policy innovations are likely to affect households' consumption and firms' investment behaviour. Tax cuts may stimulate domestic demand via their effects on disposable income, or the price of consumption (e.g. the government implements a temporary reduction in indirect taxes), or via their effects on investment. However, forward-looking households may also react to temporary tax reduction by increasing private saving, as they forecast higher tax liabilities in the future. The literature has long made clear that, if there are no financial frictions, if taxes are not distortionary, and if higher future taxes entirely fall on those who benefit from the current tax cuts (in other words, if Ricardian equivalence holds), private saving will completely offset any change in public saving resulting from changes in tax policies. Similarly, an unexpected increase in government spending may raise households' disposable income in the short run, but lower their permanent income in proportion to the present discounted value of the additional spending. Government spending also affects relative prices, including the real interest rate, the real exchange rate, and the terms of trade. In a nutshell, the twin deficit hypothesis stipulates that, whatever the fiscal transmission channel, the endogenous response of the private sector to fiscal shocks will not completely offset the effect of public dissaving on the external balance: the current account ends up deteriorating together with the government budget.

Before proceeding, we state upfront that, in our theoretical and empirical analysis below, we will mostly use the trade balance (or net exports), instead of the current account, as a measure of a country's external position. Using the definitions reported above, net exports (NX) differ from the current account because they do not include interest payments on national debt (rB). Early literature, (e.g. Baxter, 1995), argues that, at business cycle frequencies, the two measures tend to move closely together since the stock of debt adjusts very slowly. Hence, unless interest rates are very volatile, the difference between net exports and the current account can be observed mostly in the low-frequency components of the data.[1] For the purpose of this paper, focusing on the trade balance rather than the current account has the advantage that net exports always have a well-defined counterpart in theoretical models, independently of specific assumptions regarding the structure of international financial markets. Consequently, in our analysis below we will exclude interest payments also from our measure of a country's fiscal position. In other words, we will use the primary budget balance.[2]

---

[1] With the rapid growth of the stock of foreign assets and liabilities in countries' portfolios, capital gains and losses on these assets, including those attributable to exchange rate movements, can be quite sizeable. Hence, the effective return on net foreign assets may be quite volatile, even when the official balance of payment statistics, which record only payments of dividends and coupons, are not. A reconsideration of twin deficits using a dataset allowing for capital gains and losses is an interesting direction of research that we intend to pursue in the future. For the time being, however, data availability on a cross-country basis limits our ability to do so.

[2] We normalize both the primary budget balance and net exports by GDP to allow cross-country comparisons. To the extent that fiscal shocks raise the risk premium on sovereign debt, twin deficits may emerge from rising costs of internal and external borrowing.

2.2. A systematic co-movement of budget and trade deficits?

In specific episodes of fiscal loosening, e.g. following the Reagan 1980s tax cuts, budget policies have been accompanied by substantial external trade deterioration. These episodes are often taken as evidence in support of the twin deficit hypothesis. Figure 1 displays the *primary budget balance* and the *trade balance* for the US, the UK, Australia and Canada.[3]

The reason why the twin deficit hypothesis gained popularity at certain times, and less so in others, is apparent. The US budget balance and trade balance move closely together in the mid-1980s and after the year 2000. As both periods are characterized

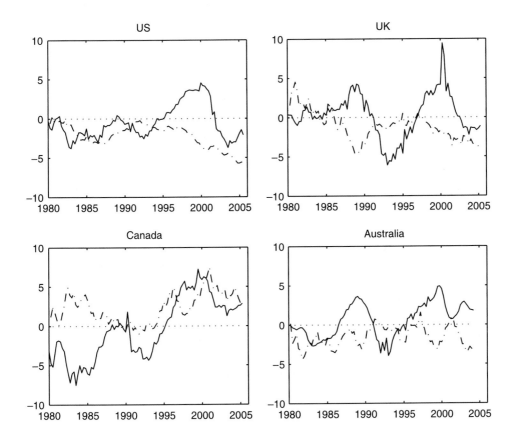

Figure 1. Four OECD countries; 1980 to date

Notes: Straight line is Primary Budget Balance; broken line is Trade Balance, both measured in percentage of GDP.

Source: OECD *Economic Outlook* database.

[3] While the joint evolution of the budget and the trade deficit in the US has traditionally been the focus of the policy debate, we analyse the time series of three additional countries. Here, our sample choice is largely determined by considerations regarding the feasibility of the VAR analysis in Section 4 below. For each country the sample ends on the latest available record (see Appendix).

by considerable fiscal expansions, many observers have pointed to these policies as an important factor driving the US trade deficit. However, there is also a remarkable divergence of the two time series during the late 1990s. The pattern is even less clear-cut for the UK and Australia, for which one can spot several periods of twin divergence. In Canada the two time series appear to move closely together since the early 1990s.

The main lesson from Figure 1 is that the correlation between the budget balance and the trade balance is not necessarily positive. To explore this issue further, we isolate the short-run fluctuations at business cycle frequency from long-run movements by applying the Hodrick-Prescott-filter to the series displayed in Figure 1. We then compute the correlation of budget and trade balances using their cyclical components. The correlation coefficient turns out to be negative in all four countries: −0.24 in the US, −0.26 in the UK, −0.16 in Canada and −0.37 in Australia – meaning that budget deficits are systematically associated with trade surpluses, that is, the opposite of twin deficits.

This statistical result is sometimes used as the basis for a crude argument, stating that 'twin deficits do not exist in the data'. Such argument is faulty, since it fails to recognize the obvious cyclical nature of the fiscal stance and the trade balance. Typically, an economic boom will improve the budget balance: for given fiscal rules, tax revenues rise with income and some categories of spending fall with the level of economic activity. At the same time the external position deteriorates as the trade balance is generally found to be countercyclical. This argument applies whether the expansion is associated with a supply (technological) shock or a nominal shock. To the extent that these shocks (other than of a fiscal nature) can account for most macro-economic fluctuations,[4] a negative correlation between government budgets and external trade at business cycle frequencies may not tell us much about the response of these two aggregates to spending and tax shocks – which is the essence of twin deficits.

To explore further the joint cyclical behaviour of the trade and the budget balance, we also compute the correlation between the budget balance and future realizations of the trade balance as a synthetic representation of the joint dynamics of these two variables. The results are shown in Figure 2. For each country, we plot the correlation between the current value of the primary government balance, bb, and current and future realizations of the trade balance, nx, for up to two years. All countries display a broadly similar pattern: the contemporaneous correlation is negative, but the cor-relation between future realizations of the trade balance and the current budget balance becomes positive at some point. The pattern turns out to be quite robust to changes in the sample size and to the filter applied to the raw data,[5] as well as to the inclusion of more countries in the analysis.

---

[4] This interpretation is also supported by results in Kollmann (1998) and Freund (2000), which suggest that the trade balance is mostly driven by technology shocks or, more generally, moves with the business cycle.

[5] When applying the HP filter, we use a smoothing parameter of 1600. We also applied the Band Pass Filter suggested by Christiano and Fitzgerald (2003) instead of the HP filter, and extended our analysis by using data from the earliest available data point, 1964Q1, without significant effect on the shapes of the cross-correlation functions. By the same token, using current account instead of net exports does not affect the results.

The correlation patterns displayed in Figure 2 provide a summary of the joint dynamics of the budget balance and the trade balance over the business cycle, in response to the many factors, which drive a typical business cycle movement. This is novel evidence that we explore further in related work (Corsetti and Müller, 2005). For the purpose of this paper, the main conclusion from Figure 2 is that evidence in support of the twin deficit hypothesis is not easy to detect. It requires identifying fiscal shocks, isolating these from other shocks which generate cyclical movements of the economy, and testing whether these shocks move the two deficits in the same direction, thus overturning the typical correlation pattern detected at business cycle frequencies.

A large body of empirical literature has addressed this problem by using single equation techniques (see, e.g., Summers, 1986; Bernheim, 1988; or Roubini, 1988). Within this strand of the literature there is considerable disagreement on the quantitative

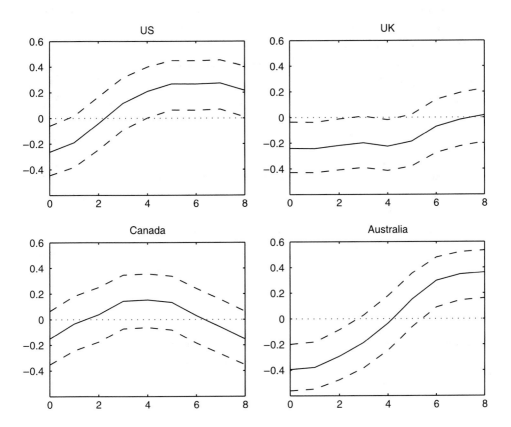

Figure 2. Cross-correlation of primary budget balance and trade balance

Notes: Correlation is calculated for business cycle components between primary budget balance (*t*) and trade balance at varying horizon (*t* + *k*) measured in quarters on the horizontal axes. Dashed lines give 95% confidence intervals.

Source: Own calculations on OECD *Economic Outlook* database.

effect of fiscal deficits on trade deficits. Nonetheless, some studies have succeeded in establishing the notion that about one-third of the increase in the budget deficit is reflected in the trade deficit (e.g. Chinn and Prasad, 2003). More recent studies have reported somewhat lower estimates for the twin deficit relationship. Bussière *et al.* (2005), Gruber and Kamin (2005) and Chinn and Ito (2005) find that only some 1–20% of the increase in the public deficit is reflected in the trade deficit, whereas the effect is statistically significant only according to the last study.

These results suggest that the response of private saving and investment to changes in fiscal stance are substantial, motivating a careful reconsideration of the different channels through which fiscal policy affects the private sector's consumption and investment decisions. This is the task we pursue in the next section.

3. A NEW PERSPECTIVE ON FISCAL POLICY TRANSMISSION IN OPEN ECONOMIES: THE ROLE OF OPENNESS

The twin deficit hypothesis raises fundamental issues regarding the transmission of fiscal policy in the open economy: how do saving and investment rates respond to a domestic fiscal shock in the domestic economy and abroad? In this section we reconsider this question in detail, taking a specific angle. Namely, starting from the empirical evidence on the import content of national expenditure, we explore the implications of varying the degree of a country's openness and fiscal shock persistence for the international transmission of fiscal policy. We proceed as follows. First, we review the traditional debate on fiscal transmission and on twin deficits, highlighting an area where we find traditional analyses insufficiently developed; second, we provide some evidence on the import content of GDP, motivating our assumption of home bias in spending; third, we develop our main theoretical argument shedding light on how home bias affects the international transmission mechanism via investment decisions, and support our analytical results with quantitative experiments. We close this section with an extension of our results to the case of tax shocks and a summary.

3.1. The traditional focus of the debate

The traditional debate on the fiscal transmission mechanism and twin deficits emphasizes two distinct channels. One stresses relative price movements, the other intertemporal (borrowing and lending) decisions. The first transmission channel is central to the Mundell–Fleming model. In this model, an expansionary fiscal shock raises disposable income and internal demand and causes a trade deficit for two reasons. On the one hand, part of the higher consumption demand 'leaks abroad' in the form of higher imports, independently of price movements. On the other hand, with flexible exchange rates a stronger domestic demand appreciates the exchange rate, crowding out foreign demand. Because of differences in the multiplier, the external impact is stronger for spending hikes than for tax cuts. The deterioration of the external deficit is somewhat mitigated to the extent that the upsurge in domestic demand raises the domestic interest rate, and thus crowds out domestic investment. Overall, however, the emphasis is on a static transmission channel, linking fiscal deficits to excess demand and relative price movements.

In contrast, the so-called intertemporal approach to the current account emphasizes shock persistence. Consider the baseline dynamic small open-economy model with infinite-horizon identical agents, where the interest rate is assumed to be constant and labour supply is fixed. When the level of government spending increases unexpectedly but permanently, households lower their consumption by the same amount. Here the basic principle is that, irrespectively of the timing of the tax incidence, households will have to carry the burden of the increase in public spending. So, even if the increase in government spending is initially financed through debt, private saving rises enough to offset entirely the government's budget deficit: there is no impact on the current account. Conversely, when the increase in government spending is transitory, permanent income and thus consumption plans of domestic households are hardly affected. So, if the upsurge in spending is financed through debt, domestic private saving will not rise much, and the current account will fall almost one-for-one with the increase in the government budget deficit: transitory increases in government spending induce twin deficits.[6] For later reference, we note that allowing for elastic labour supply strengthens the external effects of fiscal shocks: in response to a lasting government spending shock (which eventually lowers household wealth) households supply more labour, affecting total private saving but also raising the marginal product of capital (under standard assumptions about the production function). A higher return on capital drives up investment and therefore tends to lower the trade balance. This mechanism runs counter to possible changes in the real interest rate, which tend to discourage investment.[7]

The static and intertemporal channels identified by the traditional debate on the transmission of fiscal policy are essential building blocks for an analysis of twin deficits. We will draw extensively on them below. However, traditional explanations miss an important element: they disregard the interaction between relative price movements and intertemporal investment and saving decisions. This interaction constitutes a distinct channel of the international transmission mechanism of fiscal policy; and – as we show in this paper – its relative importance crucially depends on the degree of openness of the economy, that is, the degree to which good markets are integrated across national borders.

---

[6] If the government follows a balanced-budget rule, one will, by construction, not observe literal twin deficits. The fiscal expansion will nevertheless lower the external position.

[7] See Ahmed (1986) for an exploration of government spending shocks in the baseline intertemporal small open-economy model and Baxter (1995) and Kollmann (1998) for an extensive numerical analysis within the one-good two-country model.

3.2. Globalization and insularity of national economies

In a well-known contribution, Obstfeld and Rogoff (2001) present a host of theoretical and empirical arguments showing that despite ongoing 'globalization' there are many dimensions in which markets remain quite 'insular' along national borders. For instance, the literature has provided ample evidence on persistent cross-border price differentials for identical goods, suggesting barriers to trade and frictions of different nature. Perhaps thanks to *The Economist*'s regular reporting on the price of the Big Mac in different markets, there is wide awareness of the importance and pervasiveness of such price differentials.

Barriers and frictions in international trade may be expected to play an important role in explaining why the import content of consumption and investment expenditure remains quite limited. Table 1 shows the import content of GDP and its components for the four countries in our sample. In one of the more open of our countries, the UK, imports account for over 30% of investment and more than 40% of the change in inventories, but the import content in private consumption is only 20%.[8] In the least open of our economies, the US, the import content of different categories of spending is approximately one half of the corresponding figures for the UK.

As a way to capture the economic factors determining a low import content in domestic expenditure in an analytically tractable way, the literature often refers to the idea that domestic spending is 'biased towards home goods'. Other things equal, households and firms have a preference for domestically produced goods. As home bias is reflected in the import content of private expenditures and thus in the share of imports in total GDP, it is closely related to the degree of openness of an economy. In our standard model of the global economy outlined in Box 1 below, home bias is just the negative of openness (measured by the import–GDP ratio): the same parameter determines both. In what follows we will use either term to refer to the same phenomenon: that the typical consumption and investment basket contains more domestically produced than imported goods.

Table 1. Import content of GDP and GDP components (in %)

	US	UK	Canada	Australia
GDP	11.7	27.3	30.4	19.0
Government spending	5.8	11.5	10.9	10.4
Private consumption	11.6	20.3	8.7–20.3	16.9
Private investment	15.8	35.9	21.0–71.7	25.8
Change in inventories	21.8	45.6	35.0	35.7

Notes: This table displays the import content in GDP and its components. Import content in is average import–GDP ratio from 1980:1 to date. Calculation of import content of GDP components is detailed in the Appendix.
Source: OECD *Economic Outlook* database and own calculations drawing on various sources, see Appendix.

[8] Erceg *et al.* (2005b) argue that the high import content in investment relative to private consumption should be taken into account in assessing different scenarios of trade adjustment. Our analysis, in contrast, focuses on the fact that the import content of government spending is particularly low and that the import content in overall private absorption remains limited.

In the presence of home bias, the price of national consumption baskets typically differs across countries (the purchasing power parity condition does not hold), even if the law of one price holds for all individual goods. This is because the consumer price index (CPI) in each country gives a large weight to the prices of domestically produced goods. Because of home bias, inflation rates are not necessarily the same, and the domestic real interest rate (which by definition is the price of consumption at different dates) needs not be equal across borders.

While the evidence in Table 1 shows that domestically produced goods clearly dominate imports in investment and consumption expenditure, it also suggests that the strongest home bias is in government spending. The question as of whether and to which extent government demand falls on foreign produced goods, rather than domestic goods, is important for understanding twin deficits. To the extent that government spending falls on foreign goods, a positive fiscal shock would have a direct and immediate effect on imports. For instance, if the import content of public spending were as high as 20%, other things equal, a one dollar increase in spending would deteriorate the trade balance by 20 cents. In our four countries, however, this direct transmission channel is not very strong, as the import content is everywhere below 12%.

Home bias in public and private spending and the resulting differentials of CPI-inflation and the real interest rates, are two characteristics of the world economy which are crucial for the purpose of understanding the effects of fiscal expansion on the trade deficits. We will explain the reason why in the next subsection.

3.3. Fiscal policy, terms of trade, and the return on investment in partially integrated economies

We are now ready to reconsider the international transmission of fiscal shocks, specifically focusing on the consequences of fiscal expansions for the trade balance. Taking a new perspective relative to models assuming an idealized one-good world, we place limited good markets integration at the heart of our argument: because of home bias, fiscal shocks drive a wedge between the return on domestic investment and the return earned on investment in the rest of the world, as well as a wedge between domestic and foreign interest rates. These wedges govern domestic investment decisions relative to those abroad and eventually drive the response of the domestic trade balance.

To illustrate how this works, consider an unexpected increase in fiscal spending, which, in light of the evidence in the previous subsection, falls mostly on domestically produced goods (or domestic labour services). To the extent that a sustained increase in public demand has a lasting, positive effect on the price of these goods relative to foreign goods, this leads to a lasting terms of trade appreciation. In the tradition of the Mundell–Fleming analysis reviewed above, a terms-of-trade appreciation crowds out net exports via a static, relative-price effect: consumers switch away from domestic goods which are now more expensive. However, the Mundell–Fleming model ignores the repercussions of this relative price change on the rate of return to capital, which drive investment dynamics in general equilibrium.

Because of these repercussions, a lasting terms-of-trade appreciation raises the present discounted value of output from domestic investment projects relative to the cost of investment, as investment goods consists of both local and imported goods. As a result, the terms of trade appreciation raises the real return to domestic investment by domestic investors.

Formally, consider the determinants of the real return to investment in domestic capital from the perspective of a domestic agent. Let P_d denote the price of domestically produced goods, as opposed to import prices P_f, and let P denote the price of domestic consumption. To focus sharply on our main point, it is analytically convenient to consider the case in which investment and consumption have the same composition in terms of domestic and imported goods (so that the price of investment in terms of consumption is identically equal to one), and to abstract from depreciation and uncertainty. Under these simplifying assumptions, the return to investment in real terms (i.e. in terms of consumption goods) is a simple product of two terms:

$$\text{Real return to investment} = (\text{marginal product in units domestic goods})\, \frac{P_d}{P}$$

For a given marginal product of capital in physical terms, a rise in the price of domestic goods relative to consumption increases the real rate of return. To see the role of terms of trade movements and openness, recall that the price of consumption P is a weighted average of domestic good prices P_d and import prices P_f. Denote the corresponding weights with ω and $1 - \omega$, respectively, ω is the measure of home bias and $1 - \omega$ provides a measure for openness, that is, the share of spending that falls on imported goods. Then, any change in the P_d to P ratio can be approximated by the following expression, involving only changes in the terms of trade (P_f/P_d):

$$\text{Change in } \frac{P_d}{P} = (1 - \omega)\, \text{Change in } \frac{P_d}{P_f}$$

This expression emphasizes that an increase in the price of domestic goods which appreciates the terms of trade, raises the real value of domestic output in proportion to the degree of home bias. Thus, we can rephrase our conclusion above as follows: for a given marginal product of capital in units of domestic goods, an appreciation of the terms of trade (P_d increases relative to P_f) improves the rate of return on domestic investment by $(1 - \omega)$: the more open an economy, the stronger the improvement of the real return on investment. Put differently, the larger the home bias (ω going to 1), the weaker the improvement of the real return on investment. Clearly, the degree of home bias will also influence the magnitude of the terms-of-trade response to shocks. In our quantitative analysis (see below), however, we find that the overall return on capital systematically falls with ω.[9]

[9] If the composition of investment is different from that of consumption, the expression for the rate of return should be multiplied by the inverse of the lagged price of investment in terms of consumption. When the import content of investment is larger than consumption, as is in the data, this factor is smaller than one: the positive effect of a terms-of-trade appreciation on the real rate of return is magnified. Conversely, if the import content of investment is counterfactually low, the improvement in the rate of return from terms-of-trade movements becomes smaller, or may even change sign. See the Web Appendix for details.

We have seen above that the effect of the terms of trade on the return to capital is decreasing in the degree of home bias (i.e. the effect is stronger in more open economies). In addition to home bias, a second crucial element in our analysis is the degree of persistence of fiscal shocks. As is well known, the tax burden on the private sector rises with shock persistence. For our argument, however, there is another effect which is relevant. If the shock to government spending is long lasting, the public demand for domestic goods is expected to remain relatively high in the future, and so is the increase in the relative price of domestic goods, raising the expected return on domestic capital. All else equal, domestic investment increases in the degree of persistence of the fiscal shock.

Note that the above arguments apply to foreign investment demand as well, but with the opposite sign. A fiscal expansion in the domestic country worsens the terms of trade abroad and reduces the return to foreign capital in terms of foreign consumption, thus discouraging capital accumulation abroad.

In addition to affecting the expected real return to investment, a fiscal expansion is also likely to raise the real interest rate in both the domestic and the foreign economy. In each country, the real interest rate measures the relative price of consumption in the future relative to consumption today. With no home bias and no deviation from the law of one price, the price of consumption and therefore the real interest rate is equalized across countries: via the interest rate channel, a fiscal shock would affect investment symmetrically in all countries. With home bias, instead, an appreciation of the terms of trade will drive the domestic and foreign real interest rate apart. Fiscal shocks thus generate positive differentials in the real rate of interest, which discourages investment in the domestic economy more than abroad. For the same reasons discussed above, these differentials will depend on the degree of shock persistence.

In equilibrium the expected rate of return to investment must be equal to the real interest rate. To solve for the equilibrium allocation in the incomplete market version of our model, we assume that domestic capital is entirely owned by domestic residents, and discount future revenues on the basis of their marginal utility of consumption for those agents. So, what matters for the rate of return is the relative price of domestic goods in terms of consumption, and a terms-of-trade appreciation increases the value of investment in domestic capital.[10]

The overall effects of a domestic fiscal expansion on capital accumulation will depend on the relative strength of terms of trade and the interest rate effect. In this respect, home bias and shock persistence are key. A stronger home bias tends to decrease the equilibrium impact of terms-of-trade movements on the return to capital and to increase the differentials in the real rate of interest. For a given degree of shock persistence, crowding out effects of fiscal shocks are therefore larger in economies

---

[10] If we write the rate of return from the perspective of the foreign agents, the variables will be expressed in terms of foreign consumption (recall that, with deviations from purchasing power parity, the price of domestic and foreign consumption is in general not equalized across countries).

which are less integrated in the world markets. In more open economies, instead, fiscal shocks improve the return to capital, while having a small effect on real interest differentials. In the next section, we show that investment differentials are quantitatively relevant in driving the response of the external balance to fiscal shocks.

3.4. Openness and shock persistence: quantitative results

In this section, we use a general equilibrium model to quantify the insights on the transmission channel discussed above. Our quantitative assessment is based on the two-country, two-good model described in detail in Box 1. Note that, as a way to focus on the transmission of fiscal shocks to net exports via changes in consumption and investment, we abstract from the import content in government spending and assume that government demand falls entirely on domestically produced goods.[11]

To start with, reconsider the definition of the current account (given in Section 2). In a world economy consisting of two countries, the deficit in the home country is equal to the current account surplus by the other country. Denoting the latter ROW for 'rest of the world' and assuming that the two countries are of the same size we can write:

Current account deficit = $0.5*$[(Investment − Investment$_{ROW}$) − (Private Saving − Private Saving$_{ROW}$) + (Budget Deficit − Budget Deficit$_{ROW}$)]

The home current account deficit results from a difference between home and foreign in (a) investment, (b) private saving, and (c) the government budget deficit. To quantify the interaction of openness and the degree of shock persistence in shaping the international transmission of fiscal shocks, we focus on the *differential* between home investment and investment in the rest of the world, the first term on the right-hand side of the above identity.

Figure 3 plots the combinations of openness (measured by the import content of GDP) and shock persistence which would generate *no change* in domestic investment relative to foreign investment. The different lines in Figure 3 correspond to different assumptions about international financial markets and the elasticity of labour supply. In the baseline case we assume that international financial markets are complete and labour supply is inelastic (dotted line); in the two other cases we assume that international financial markets are incomplete: the straight line corresponds to the case of inelastic labour supply; the dashed line corresponds to the case of elastic labour supply.[12] For

---

[11] Backus *et al.* (1994) analyse the transmission of fiscal shocks in a two-country model where the import content is assumed to be 15%. Therefore, this model provides a suitable starting point for our analysis of how goods market fragmentation affects the private sector's response to government spending shocks. More recently, Erceg *et al.* (2005a) analyse fiscal transmission in a two-good model which also features nominal frictions and non-Ricardian households.

[12] Formally, the assumption that international financial markets are complete can be implemented by assuming that there exists a complete set of state-contingent securities which are traded across countries. As a consequence, country-specific shocks such as a shock to government spending are fully insured and their financial burden is equally shared between domestic households and the households in the rest of the world. Under incomplete international financial markets, in contrast, only trade in non-contingent bonds is assumed to take place across countries.

Box 1. Theoretical framework

Our theoretical discussion of the international transmission of fiscal policy is based on a stylized intertemporal two-country two-good model. In what follows, we outline the basic structure of the model, which is similar to those analysed in Backus et $al.$ (1994) or Heathcote and Perri (2002). More details on the model and the computational details are provided in the Web Appendix.

The world economy consists of two countries, labelled country 1 and 2. In the main text, we refer to country 1 as the home country and to country 2 as the rest of the world. Through the allocation of consumption expenditure, c_1, and labour, n_1, the representative household in country 1 maximizes:

$$E_0 \sum_{t=0}^{\infty} \beta_{1t} \frac{1}{1-\gamma} \left[c_{1t}^{\mu} (1 - n_{1t}^{1-\mu}) \right]^{1-\gamma}$$

where β_{1t} is a so-called endogenous time discount factor, which ensures the stationarity of bond holdings in case international financial markets are assumed to be incomplete. The same applies to the representative household in country 2. Regarding production, each country specializes in a single intermediate good – good a in country 1 and good b in country 2. Government spending, g_{1t}, falls entirely on the intermediate domestic good. Total private absorption (by both countries) of home intermediate goods, $a_{1t} + a_{2t}$, is equal to home GDP, y_{1t}, net of government spending. Similarly, total absorption of the foreign intermediate goods, $b_{1t} + b_{2t}$, is equal to GDP net of government spending in the rest of the world:

$$a_{1t} + a_{2t} = y_{1t} - g_{1t}$$
$$b_{1t} + b_{2t} = y_{2t} - g_{2t}$$

In each country, intermediate goods are produced by combining capital, k, and labour. In the home country, we have $y_{1t} = k_{1t}^{\theta} n_{1t}^{1-\theta}$. Production functions are identical in the two countries. Consumption and investment, x, are composites of the domestic and foreign intermediate goods:

$$c_{1t} + x_{1t} = \left[\omega^{\frac{1}{\sigma}} a_{1t}^{\frac{\sigma-1}{\sigma}} + (1-\omega)^{\frac{1}{\sigma}} b_{1t}^{\frac{\sigma-1}{\sigma}} \right]^{\sigma/(\sigma-1)}$$

$$c_{2t} + x_{2t} = \left[(1-\omega)^{\frac{1}{\sigma}} a_{2t}^{\frac{\sigma-1}{\sigma}} + \omega^{\frac{1}{\sigma}} b_{2t}^{\frac{\sigma-1}{\sigma}} \right]^{\sigma/(\sigma-1)}$$

The parameters σ and ω measure the intratemporal elasticity of substitution between the domestic and foreign intermediate good and the home bias in private expenditure, respectively. At the same time $1 - \omega$ measures the degree of openness, i.e. the ratio of imports to net output.

The dynamic behaviour of the economy is determined by the evolution of the capital stock. Let δ denote the depreciation rate of capital. The capital stock grows with investment net of depreciation. For the home country, we can write $k_{1t+1} = (1 - \delta)k_{1t} + x_{1t}$.

We are interested in the dynamic adjustment of the world economy to a country-specific temporary increase in government spending. We assume that home spending shocks follow an AR(1) process: $g_{1t} = \gamma g_{1t-1} + \varepsilon_{1t}$, while foreign government spending remains constant. To close the model, we need to specify the structure of international asset markets. In our numerical experiments, we will analyse our model both under complete and incomplete asset markets.

each of these lines, the area above the line is one of *relative crowding in* of domestic investment, the area below the line one of *relative crowding out*.[13]

Consider first the line drawn for the baseline case of complete markets and inelastic labour supply. Start from a point *on* the dotted line: raising shock persistence for a given degree of openness leads to relative crowding in; conversely, lowering the degree of openness, that is, increasing home bias, for a given degree of shock persistence, leads to a fall in domestic investment relative to foreign investment.

In order to gain insight in the logic of the argument, consider the extreme case of fiscal shocks with no persistence at all: if government spending is raised exclusively in the current period, and there is no home bias in private consumption and investment (imports account for 50% of private spending but for only 40% of GDP since government spending falls entirely on domestic goods and services), there will be no change in relative investment. This is so because a temporary shock has no lasting sizeable effects on the terms of trade, so that there is little or no impact on expected return to capital. The interest rate will increase. However, with no home bias in private spending, the interest rate will be identical at home and abroad. As a result, investment will respond negatively, but symmetrically, in the two countries. If, with temporary shocks, we allow for some home bias in private spending (the import share in GDP is less than 40%), we are located somewhere in the area below the dotted line. The real interest rate increases more in the domestic economy than abroad: investment thus falls more at home than abroad (corresponding to relative crowding out).

Now, start again from the extreme case of no home bias, and consider a lasting spending shock. As argued above, without home bias, the real interest rate increases identically in both countries. However, the expected return on domestic investment

---

[13] We omit from the main text an analysis of consumption and saving. In our model the overall tax burden from the expanded government spending (irrespectively of when lump-sum taxes are levied) lowers current consumption. For given taxes, this raises private saving, offsetting in part the fall in public saving. The magnitude of the impact on private wealth and thus on consumption depends on the degree to which households share idiosyncratic risk across countries. Under complete international financial markets, households in the home and foreign country would equally share the burden of the domestic fiscal expansion. However, we should observe here that, even in the absence of efficient portfolio diversification, a terms-of-trade improvement in response to government spending shocks would tend to transfer some of the burden from the domestic fiscal shock onto foreign households. This is because a home appreciation reduces the value of foreign output relative to the domestic one, depressing foreign consumption. Overall, consumption falls in both countries.

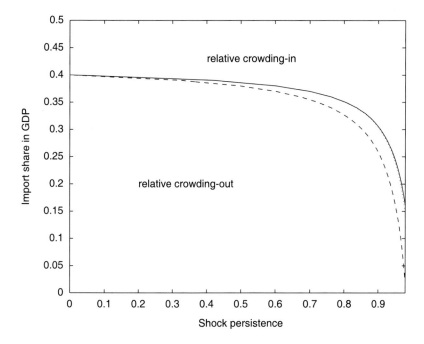

Figure 3. Relative investment response

Notes: Lines indicate locus where impact response of relative investment is zero. Dotted line: complete financial markets and inelastic labour supply. Straight line: incomplete financial markets and inelastic labour supply. Dashed line: incomplete financial markets with elastic labour supply.

Source: Own calculations on the basis of the model outlined in Box 1.

is now higher, because a lasting fiscal shock at home induces a lasting terms of trade appreciation which raises the return to domestic capital. This is why domestic investment increases relative to foreign, that is, there is *relative* crowding in.

Figure 3 suggests that the degree of risk-sharing does not impinge on the main transmission mechanism discussed above. The locus of 'no-relative investment changes' is almost identical in the cases of complete and incomplete markets. When calibrating the model, we set the elasticity of substitution between domestic and foreign goods equal to 1.5 – a standard value in the literature used, for instance, in the baseline calibration of Backus *et al.* (1994). It is well known that, for values of such elasticity close to unity, terms-of-trade movements reduce the consumption risk of technology shocks (see Cole and Obstfeld, 1991; Corsetti and Pesenti, 2001; and Corsetti *et al.*, 2004). Further experiments, however, established the robustness of results regarding the 'no-relative investment changes' with respect to variations of this parameter.[14]

[14] We consider values for the intratemporal elasticity of substitution between domestic and foreign goods between 0.3 and 3. Details are provided in the Web Appendix. In all experiments we confirm our main conclusions regarding the role of openness in determining the magnitude and sign of twin deficits. Moreover, we do not find any economically significant difference in the response of relative investment to a fiscal shock. However, we detect differences in the response of the trade balance, because of different valuation effects on imports and exports (see Müller, 2006). For an analysis of the model with low price elasticities of import demand, see Corsetti *et al.* (2004).

Relative to the baseline scenario (inelastic labour supply), the results obtained under the assumption of endogenous labour supply are particularly interesting. As shown in the graph (dashed line), allowing for elastic labour supply raises the area of relative crowding in of domestic investment: the locus corresponding to 'no-relative investment changes' shifts inwards. We have already discussed the reason for such a result in Section 3.1. A lasting government spending shock corresponds to a negative wealth shock to households: facing a higher tax burden, they reduce their consumption of goods and leisure (thus work more). Insofar as labour and capital are complements in production, a higher labour supply raises the marginal return to capital and hence the incentive to invest. To capture this consideration, we amend our formulation of the return to capital above by writing the marginal product of capital in physical units, MPC, explicitly as a function of employment:

$$\text{Real return to investment} = (MPC[\text{employment}]) \, \frac{P_d}{P}$$

A positive labour supply response to fiscal shocks tends to work in favour of twin deficits, as it raises the incentive to invest in domestic capital and thus partially offsets the increase in the domestic interest rate.

We close this subsection by emphasizing that our results on the *relative* crowding in of investment (which is the relevant variable to assess the transmission of fiscal shocks to the external trade) should not be confused with an increase in the *level* of investment in the home country. Figure 4 shows impulse responses to a government spending shock, generated by our model under the assumption of incomplete markets and elastic labour supply. The figure presents two sets of impulse responses, one for an economy with a relatively small import content of spending where imports account for only 10% of GDP, the other for a more open economy where imports account for 30% of GDP.

In response to a shock to domestic government spending, the stock of domestic capital falls in both simulations, but the fall is much more marked in the case of high home bias (imports 10% of GDP). In this case, domestic investment falls also relative to foreign investment. As a consequence, net exports are hardly affected by the fiscal expansion. This is not true for the relatively more open economy: here domestic investment increases relative to foreign, and a trade deficit results.[15] Figure 4 thus illustrates that (the sign of) the response of the external balance depends very much on the sign of the investment response in *relative* terms.

[15] In addition to their effects on the demand level, terms-of-trade movements will also determine the composition of spending. A domestic appreciation temporarily raises the import content of domestic consumption and investment, while the reverse occurs in the foreign country. This composition effect tends to lower the domestic trade balance, depending on the price elasticity of imports. At the same time, there is a 'valuation effect': the domestic appreciation will tend to improve the trade balance, by raising the value of exports relative to imports. In our numerical analysis, the substitution effect dominates the valuation effect: *ceteris paribus* an appreciation (of the terms of trade) will reduce the trade balance as the equivalent of the Marshall–Lerner–Robinson (MLR) conditions is assumed to hold in general equilibrium (see Tille, 2001 and Müller, 2006 for further analysis).

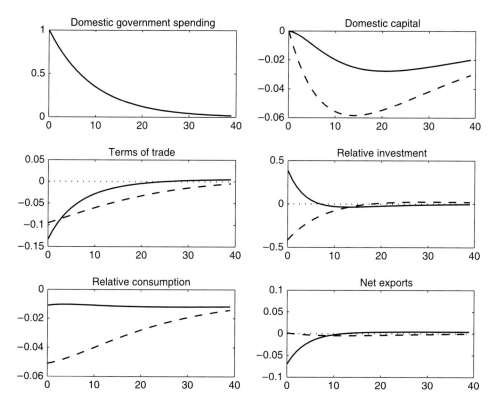

Figure 4. Selected impulse responses to a government spending shock

Notes: Straight line gives responses of economy with import share of 30%. Dashed line gives responses of economy with import share of 10%. Vertical axes indicate percentage deviations from steady state; horizontal axes indicate quarters.

Source: Own calculations on the basis of the model outlined in Box 1.

Finally, recall that in our baseline theoretical model we distinguish between domestically produced and imported goods and assume that government spending falls entirely on domestically produced goods. Following Finn (1998) we have also investigated the effects of an exogenous increase in the government wage bill which accounts for approximately 50% of government expenditure.[16] This specification of the model assumes an additional sector in the economy, where labour produces the goods and services demanded by the government.[17] The result of this experiment, reported in the Web Appendix, confirms our main conclusions regarding the role of openness in determining the magnitude and sign of twin deficits.

[16] According to the OECD *Economic Outlook* database the average wage consumption expenditure of the government is about 10% of GDP in our sample (1980:1 to date) for Canada, the UK and the US (mnemonic CGW) and thus accounts for approximately one-half of government expenditures.

[17] Relative to our baseline case (which can be interpreted as government services produced using the same production function as the private sector), this new specification introduces a strong asymmetry in capital intensity across sectors (the government sector does not use capital at all).

3.5. An extension of the argument to tax cuts

Would the same transmission mechanism generalize to the case of a tax cut? To answer this question, we distinguish between the wealth effects of a cut, and the effects of altering tax rates on labour and capital income, which may directly affect agents' incentive to work and save. To analyse the former, consider an economy similar to the one in our model (Box 1), but in which infinite-horizon households are replaced with overlapping generations of finite-horizon agents with no inter-generational altruism, so that Ricardian equivalence does not hold. Although we do not perform a formal analysis of this case, in what follows we sketch an answer to our question by drawing on the main building blocks of our argument. A reduction of lump-sum taxes increases the permanent income of currently active households (at the expense of future generations) and thus raises domestic consumption. This has a direct negative implication for the trade balance proportional to the import content in private spending. So, if the import content of consumption is 20%, other things equal, a tax cut would worsen the trade balance by 20% of the change in consumption. In equilibrium, however, the external balance will also reflect the indirect effects of the reduction of lump-sum taxes, via adjustment in saving and investment rates. In particular, the degree of home bias in domestic spending and the persistence of the shock would still determine the strength and dynamics of the terms-of-trade appreciation induced by the increase in domestic consumption expenditure, and thus the return to domestic capital. By the same token, they will determine the movements in real interest rates at home and abroad. The transmission mechanism is identical to the one discussed in the previous section. Hence, we expect openness to be an important feature also for the international transmission of a reduction of domestic lump-sum taxes: the stronger the home bias in private spending, the smaller the deterioration of the trade balance.

The mechanism underlying the international transmission of a tax cut via a reduction of distortionary tax rates is somewhat different. Using the model in Box 1 appropriately amended, we nonetheless find that openness matters also in this case. For simplicity, we consider a temporary reduction in income taxes, financed through Ricardian debt, that is, debt that will be repaid by an increase in (future) lump-sum taxes.[18] A temporary reduction in the domestic tax rate on income from labour and capital directly raises the incentives for households and firms to work and invest. But the resulting increase in domestic output over time *depreciates* the terms of trade of the country: this reduces the incentive to invest. This effect is relatively stronger, the smaller the home bias. In our quantitative experiments, however, we find that the terms of trade response to a

---

[18] Specifically, we assume that steady state government spending is financed through taxing a fixed proportion of labour and capital income or, equivalently, intermediate goods. Shocks to government spending or temporary changes in the tax rate induce an increase (fall) in tax revenues relative to government spending. To balance the budget, the government adjusts lump-sum transfers (taxes) accordingly. Following Baxter (1995), these lump-sum transfers (taxes) can be interpreted as a surplus (deficit) of the government budget. Results from this experiment are displayed in the Web Appendix.

temporary cut in tax rates is small relative to their response (with an opposite sign) to an increase in government spending (driving up demand for domestic goods). What drives the relative investment change is mainly the short-run real rate differential, whose size is a function of home bias. Higher domestic interest rates counteract the positive effect of a country-specific tax rate cut on investment decisions: domestic investment (relative to foreign) increases less in economies where home bias is pervasive than in very open economies. Hence, the effect of a tax cut on the trade balance is small in relatively closed economies.[19]

3.6. Summing up

In this section, we have analysed in detail a novel channel through which fiscal shocks which reduce public savings translate into changes in private investment and saving and thus ultimately affect the external balance (see the accounting identity in Section 2.1). A useful way to synthesize this channel consists of emphasizing the trade-offs between borrowing from abroad, involving some degree of substitution away from domestic goods into foreign goods, and reducing the rate of capital accumulation. Intuitively, borrowing from abroad is attractive when there is no strong preference for the home good, so that the economy is relatively open to trade. By raising their demand for foreign goods, domestic households can prevent a fall in consumption below their permanent income, as well as a fall in the domestic capital stock. If the government spending shock is persistent enough, it is efficient to *raise* the domestic capital stock, against higher future demand for domestic output, as well as to service foreign debt incurred in response to the shock. This is clearly the scenario underlying twin deficits.

When there is a strong preference for the home goods instead, the economy is relatively closed: in response to fiscal shocks which reduce the amount of domestic goods available for private use, borrowing from abroad is less attractive, as it implies consuming foreign goods instead of the much preferred domestic goods. A temporary contraction of investment is an efficient strategy to prevent a fall in consumption. This is true as long as the fiscal shock is not too persistent. If the shock is persistent, however, running down domestic capital may not be efficient vis-à-vis the need to sustain high future government claims on domestic output.

These insights are useful in addressing differing results in the literature. The net effect of a fiscal expansion on the external trade of a country depends on several factors, many of which oppose each other. Among these we have singled out home bias and shock persistence, as factors shaping not only the size, but even the sign of the trade response to shocks.

---

[19] Erceg *et al.* (2005a) consider another failure of Ricardian equivalence by assuming that a fraction of the population spends its disposable income in each period. However, Erceg *et al.* (2005a) calibrate a Dynamic Stochastic General Equilibrium (DSGE) model with such non-Ricardian households to the US and find that the effect of fiscal shocks on the trade balance is only mildly affected by the share of non-Ricardian households in the population.

4. TIME SERIES EVIDENCE

As discussed above, the idea of twin deficits is traditionally illustrated by pointing to historical episodes of fiscal easing. The question we address in this section is whether one can find any statistical evidence in support of the hypothesis that fiscal innovations systematically move the budget deficit and the trade deficit in the same direction. To address this question, we employ structural VAR techniques. These techniques are well established in the analysis of monetary policy and have been recently extended to analyse the dynamic effects of fiscal policy (see e.g. Blanchard and Perotti, 2002; and Fatás and Mihov, 2001). Within this literature, a few studies have focused on the effects of fiscal policy on foreign trade, including Clarida and Prendergast (1999), who analyse the effects of budget deficits on the real exchange rate, Canzoneri *et al.* (2003), who focus on output spillovers of US fiscal policies on foreign GDP and Giuliodori and Beetsma (2004) as well as Beetsma *et al.* (2006), who use European data to investigate the effects of government spending on imports, and especially Kim and Roubini (2003).

Kim and Roubini (2003) is the first study to address the twin deficit issue explicitly within a VAR framework. Using US data they find that a negative innovation to the budget balance increases the current account. That is, they find 'twin divergence' instead of twin deficits. This finding is shown to be qualitatively similar in response to tax and spending shocks, in addition to budget shocks (i.e. when they identify tax and spending innovations, instead of innovations to the budget balance). Twin divergence is also obtained by Müller (2006), who identifies spending innovations in US time series. In what follows, we will build on the same approach.

In contrast to Kim and Roubini, we will analyse possible cross-country variations in the external effects of fiscal policy by extending the analysis to a sample of four countries: Australia, Canada, the UK and the US. The composition of this sample is the same as in Perotti (2005), who applies the VAR approach to the fiscal policy of Blanchard and Perotti (2002) to closed-economy issues.[20]

We proceed as follows. We first outline the basic ideas underlying the application of VAR techniques. Second, we motivate our comparative study on four countries in light of the main results from our theoretical analysis. Next, we focus on innovations to government spending as possible sources of budget deficits and their transmission through the global economy via investment and net exports. Finally, we also consider the international transmission of deficit shocks, that is, the effects of negative innovations on the budget balance.

---

[20] In contrast to Perotti (2005), we focus on external trade, rather than pursuing a complete and exhaustive characterization of the macroeconomic effects of fiscal policy. We should note here that Perotti also considers time series for West Germany up to 1989.

4.1. Structural vector autoregressions

Adopting a structural VAR model allows us to capture the dynamic interdependence of macroeconomic aggregates within a linear model, where the value of each variable is expressed in terms of its own past values, past values of all the other variables in the VAR and an error term. While serially uncorrelated, the error terms associated with each variable are likely to be mutually correlated, as long as contemporaneous relationships between variables are not taken into account. Structural VAR models therefore are explicit about contemporaneous relationships between variables in order to ensure identification.

In light of the transmission mechanism analysed in the previous section, we proceed by identifying government spending shocks. Following Blanchard and Perotti (2002), we assume that government spending does not contemporaneously respond to changes in the other variables. These other variables, however, can be immediately affected by government spending. In a later subsection, we will also consider the fiscal transmission mechanism focusing on deficit shocks directly. As in Kim and Roubini (2003), we will then assume that the budget balance responds contemporaneously to changes in output, but not to changes in the other variables; at the same time we will posit that changes in the budget balance possibly affect output only after one quarter.

Once we have identified a typical fiscal innovation (either to spending or directly to the deficit), we track the dynamic effects of such an innovation on the other variables in the VAR controlling for other changes in the economic environment which may also induce co-movements between fiscal and other macroeconomic variables. Like all statistical techniques, the quality of our results depends on their correct application. An important issue in identification is that fiscal policy changes are usually announced before effective implementation and therefore may affect behaviour through expectations before the fiscal shock shows up in fiscal data – one of the points stressed by Mountford and Uhlig (2004). Perotti (2005) takes up this and other possible complications, providing arguments to support the application of structural VAR models to identify the effects of fiscal policy. We discuss technical aspects of our approach in Box 2.

4.2. From theory to data

Before turning to our estimated VAR model, we emphasize the benefits of carrying out our empirical analysis of twin deficits in a comparative perspective, focusing on four countries which differ in the degree of openness. In light of our theoretical analysis in the previous section, we bring to the data a *refined twin deficit prediction*: the extent to which a temporary increase in government spending reduces the trade balance depends on the degree of (1) openness of the economy and (2) persistence of fiscal shocks. Provided that shocks are persistent enough, and/or the economy is quite open, a temporary increase in government spending will have a limited effect on

Box 2. Structural vector autoregressions

Our empirical results are based on estimated structural VAR models. We estimate two specifications on quarterly time series, one identifying shocks to government spending (which in turn generate a budget deficit), the other identifying shocks to the government budget directly. In the first specification, we set up a VAR model including seven variables: government spending, g_t, and output, y_t, both in logs of real per capita terms; the primary budget balance scaled by GDP, bb_t, inflation, π_t, the long-term nominal interest rate, r_t, the log of terms of trade, p_t, and the trade balance scaled by GDP, nx_t. In the second specification, we drop real government spending, and replace the trade balance with the current account scaled by GDP, ca_t. The Appendix provides further details on the construction of the variables. In both specifications, we allow for linear and quadratic terms in time as well as for quarterly dummies in each equation, but omit them in the discussion below.

Letting Z denote a vector which contains these variables in the same order as they were introduced above, i.e. in the first specification $Z_t = [g_t y_t\, bb_t\, \pi_t\, r_t\, p_t\, nx_t]'$ while in the second specification $Z_t = [y_t\, bb_t\, \pi_t\, r_t\, p_t\, ca_t]'$, we consider the following structural model

$$A_0 Z_t = \sum_{i=1}^{4} A_i Z_{t-i} + \varepsilon_t$$

where ε_t is a vector of mutually uncorrelated innovations. The coefficient matrix A_0 reflects contemporaneous relationships among the variables in Z_t. It is not possible to estimate A_0 and therefore identify the innovations ε_t without further assumptions. Therefore we assume that A_0 is a lower triangular matrix. This is equivalent to estimating a reduced form VAR model and computing the Choleski factorization of the VAR covariance matrix (see Stock and Watson, 2001). In the first specification, given that government spending is the first variable in Z_t, this boils down to the assumption that government spending responds to the other variables with a delay of one quarter. In the second specification, given that the budget balance is the second variable in Z_t, this boils down to the assumption that the budget does respond to changes of y_t, but not to changes in the other variables – *within* a quarter. Under these assumptions, we can estimate both specifications of the VAR consistently by applying OLS recursively.

Once the structural VAR is estimated, we generate impulse response functions on the basis of its reduced form. These responses provide a convenient way to summarize the macroeconomic dynamics triggered by fiscal innovations. More precisely, an impulse response at horizon k is the difference between the expected value of a variable in period $t + k$ conditional on a spending innovation in period t and its expected value in the period before the shock. We also report cumulative impulse responses at time horizon k by simply adding up the impulse responses up to this horizon. We compute standard errors for the impulse response functions by bootstrapping based on 1000 replications.

Finally, we re-estimate the VAR models, replacing the trade balance, in turn, with investment, x_t, and private consumption, c_t, both in logs of real per capita terms (first specification); and the current account balance with the household savings ratio, s_t (second specification). Thereby we try to gain further insights into the transmission of fiscal shocks, while keeping dimensions manageable. We report the impulse responses of these additional variables together with the results for our baseline specifications.

investment, but a relatively strong effect on net exports. On the other hand, when shocks are not very persistent, and/or the economy is rather closed, investment will fall strongly and mute the effects of the fiscal expansion on the trade balance.

The empirical counterpart of openness can be easily computed from the data and is displayed in the first row of Table 1 above. We observe a considerable degree of heterogeneity: while Canada and the UK are characterized by a high degree of openness (the ratio of imports to output is 0.30 and 0.27, respectively), the weight of US imports in output is only 0.12. Australia, with a value of 0.19, is characterized by an intermediate degree of openness.

The degree of persistence of fiscal shocks cannot be observed directly. However, as we identify fiscal shocks using our VAR model, we can use the same model to compute a measure of their persistence. Specifically, we approximate the response of government spending to a one-time impulse to government spending by an AR(1) process.[21] We find that a typical government spending shock displays the highest persistence in Canada (0.93) and the lowest persistence in Australia (0.69). For the US (0.85) and the UK (0.77) we find intermediate values.[22]

Overall, Canada and the UK are the countries with the highest degree of openness in our sample; Canada is also the country where we find the highest degree of fiscal shock persistence. In light of our theory, for these countries we expect that a typical expansionary fiscal shock would have a relatively large negative impact on external trade, and a relatively low crowding out effect on domestic investment. Conversely, Australia and the US are relatively closed, and, according to our estimates, have a low or intermediate degree of fiscal shock persistence. In the case of these countries, we expect a relatively strong negative effect on investment, and only a mild effect on the trade balance.

---

[21] Letting ρ denote the degree of autocorrelation of government spending following an exogenous AR(1) process, we proceed by computing ρ for each horizon k. If the shock occurs at horizon zero, then ρk is the response of government spending at horizon k to the power $(1/k)$, and we compute ρ as the average over ρk for $k = 1 \ldots 10$.

[22] Other measures of persistence lead to a similar ordering, e.g. adding up the coefficients on the coefficients on the lagged values of government spending obtained from estimating the first equation of our VAR model also gives the highest persistence for Canada and the lowest for Australia.

4.3. The international transmission of spending shocks

We begin our empirical study by analysing the dynamic effects of a government spending innovation equal to 1% of GDP. We thus rely on the first specification of the VAR model discussed in Box 2. Specifically, we focus on the dynamic adjustment process, that is, the impulse responses of the variables of interest triggered by these shocks. Figure 5 displays the responses of the budget balance and the trade balance together with the response of investment in the four countries in our sample. In this figure, impulse responses are measured in percentage points of trend output (vertical axis), while the horizontal axis gives the time horizon in quarters. Each straight line displays the point estimate, while the broken lines indicate the two symmetric one standard error bands, computed by bootstrapping based on 1,000 replications.

The first column of Figure 5 shows the response of the budget balance to a spending innovation. Spending innovations lead to a budget deficit in all countries: to a considerable extent government spending innovations are thus debt financed everywhere in our sample. However, the magnitude of the effect differs across countries. The effect of the spending shock on the budget deficit is particularly strong for Canada and the UK but quite limited for Australia (where it changes sign over time), in line with the results reported by Perotti (2005) for a post-1980s sample.

The second column of Figure 5 displays the response of the trade balance. The figure shows significant effects of fiscal loosening on the trade balance for the UK and Canada: in the UK the impact effect is about −0.5% of trend output and a maximum effect of −0.8 is reached after five quarters; in Canada the impact effect is about −0.17 and the trade balance remains depressed for an extended period (reaching 1% of trend output). Given that the spending innovation is 1% of trend output, these effects are quantitatively substantial if compared with results reported in the empirical literature adopting a single equation approach (see Section 2.2).

Turning to the response of the trade balance in the US and Australia, there are, in fact, no significant effects. While for the US the point estimates are negative between the third and the eight quarter after the shock, in both countries the trade response is mildly positive at some point over time. This confirms earlier findings by Kim and Roubini (2003) and Müller (2006) for the US. Relative to these studies, we find a somewhat weaker response of the trade balance.[23]

The last column of Figure 5 shows the response of investment. In our sample, the economies with a relatively high degree of openness are Canada and the UK. Consistent with our hypothesis, the capital stock of these countries does not fall nearly as much as in the US. In fact, investment is found to increase for an extended period in Canada, the country where we find the highest degree of fiscal shock persistence. In contrast, the US, which is less open to international trade, experiences less persistent fiscal shocks. As suggested

[23] Further experiments (not reported) suggest that these differences are likely to result from different sample periods, notably, from changing the starting date. Kim and Roubini start in 1975, Müller in 1973. Perotti (2005) suggests a break date in fiscal policy transmission around 1980. Consistently, we use 1980Q1 as the first observation for the dependent variable.

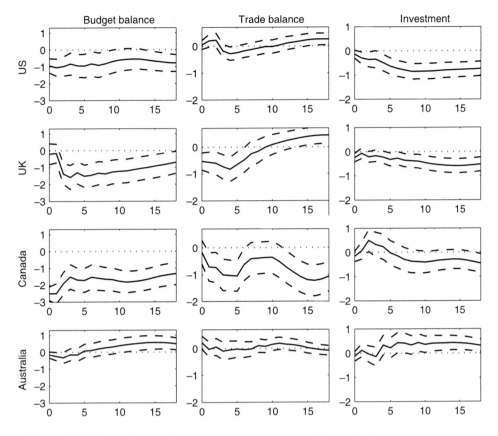

Figure 5. Selected responses to government spending shock

Notes: Sample is 1980:1 to date. The solid line gives the point estimate. Broken lines indicate bootstrapped two one-standard error bands. Vertical axis indicate deviations from unshocked path measured in percentage points of GDP. Horizontal axis indicate quarters.

Source: Own calculations on OECD *Economic Outlook* database, see Box 2.

by our hypothesis we see a substantial decline in US investment: it falls by about 0.8% of trend output. In the case of Australia, on the other hand, we find neither a decline in investment nor a decline in the trade balance. Note that also the budget balance seems to be hardly affected by the spending shock – it even improves over time.

The three columns of Figure 5 together suggest that, consistent with our refined twin deficit hypothesis, spending shocks generate twin deficits in countries which are quite open to trade, especially when spending shocks are relatively persistent. In more closed economies, instead, there is no systematic evidence in favour of twin deficits. Actually, one may even observe twin divergence.

We complete our analysis by briefly discussing the responses of the other variables included in our VAR model. To give a concise summary of our results, we compute cumulated impulse responses for the first year and for three years after the spending shock. Table 2 displays the results for all nine variables included subsequently in our VAR model.

The first line reports the cumulative response of government spending to an innovation in government spending. It therefore provides yet another measure of how long a fiscal expansion lasts in each country; again, we find the highest persistence for Canada and the lowest for Australia. The second line reports the response of output: hardly any significant effect is observed – broadly in line with the results by Perotti (2005), who argues that the overall macroeconomic effect of fiscal policy tends to fall in the post-1980 period relative to a pre-1980s sample.

As shown in the fourth and fifth line the responses of inflation and interest rates are either positive or negative depending on the horizon and the country which one considers. This evidence is similar to that of other contributions (e.g. Mountford and Uhlig, 2004 and Perotti, 2005), and is puzzling because theory would generally predict a positive response of inflation and interest rates.[24]

The sixth line of the table shows that the terms of trade generally tend to increase, that is, to depreciate, following a fiscal shock, although they initially appreciate in the case of the US and three years after the shock in the case of Canada. The response of the terms of trade does not square well with our theoretical model, according to

Table 2. Cumulative response to a government spending shock

	Horizon	US	UK	Canada	Australia
Government spending	4	0.72*	0.64*	0.82*	0.55*
	12	1.6*	1.15*	2.55*	0.85*
GDP	4	0.53	0.00	0.32	0.42*
	12	0.07	0.08	1.37	0.91
Budget balance	4	−0.95*	−0.83*	−2.11*	−0.22
	12	−2.53*	−3.51*	−5.46*	0.19
Inflation	4	0.01	−0.37*	−1.29*	−0.29
	12	0.50	0.71*	−0.37	0.91*
Nominal interest rate	4	−0.09	−0.18	−0.45*	0.21
	12	−0.95*	0.04	0.04	0.64
Terms of trade	4	−0.79*	1.13*	0.85	0.22
	12	1.97*	2.17*	−0.86	2.94*
Trade balance	4	0.07	−0.61*	−0.65*	0.04
	12	−0.15	−1.15*	−1.84*	0.14
Investment	4	−0.28*	−0.17	0.18	−0.04
	12	−1.78*	−0.9*	−0.26	0.69
Consumption	4	0.24	−0.06	0.11	0.00
	12	0.47	−0.12	0.68	−0.38*

Notes: Annualized responses – cumulative responses are expressed in yearly rates (i.e. cumulative responses are divided by 4); all quantities are expressed in percentage of GDP; Horizon is in quarters. Sample starts in 1980:1 (dependent variable), see Box 2 for details. An asterisk (*) indicates that zero is outside the region between the two one-standard error bands obtained by bootstrap based on 1000 replications.

Source: Own calculations on OECD *Economic Outlook* database.

---

[24] Regarding the effects of fiscal policy on interest rates, a large literature has documented difficulties in detecting a positive effect of fiscal innovations on interest rates. A recent counterexample is Laubach (2005) who finds a substantial and significant effect of the debt-to-GDP ratio on interest rates using data on expectations of future long-term interest rates as well as on debt and deficit projections.

which an appreciation of the terms of trade is an important component of the international transmission of fiscal shocks. However, we should note here that the terms of trade response is not very robust across various specifications of our empirical VAR analysis.[25] In this sense, our empirical analysis of the international transmission of fiscal shocks adds a new dimension to the list of open issues in related analyses of fiscal transmission in closed economies. Further analysis is needed to understand not only the response of inflation and the interest rate, but also the behaviour of the terms of trade.[26] Finally, the last row of Table 2 gives the cumulative response of private consumption. This is insignificant in almost all cases, and in none of the countries we find a strong response of consumption to the spending shock. This finding confirms the importance of focusing on investment in understanding the heterogeneity in the response of net exports to a shock to government spending in the four countries.

4.4. The international transmission of deficit shocks

In the subsection above, we have analysed expansionary government spending shocks as a cause of twin deficits/twin divergence. Clearly, tax cuts are likely to also play an important role in determining the joint dynamics of the budget balance and the external balance. However, identifying tax shocks raises technical difficulties, in particular with respect to the estimation of the elasticity of tax revenues to output, see Blanchard and Perotti (2002). Leaving the analysis of tax shocks to future research, and for the sake of comparison with the results reported by Kim and Roubini (2003), we prefer to conclude our empirical investigation by looking at shocks to budget deficits. This corresponds to the second specification of the VAR model discussed in Box 2.

Specifically, we consider deficit shocks, defined as an unanticipated fall in the budget balance by 1% of GDP. Different from the analysis above, we follow Kim and Roubini and analyse the current account balance rather than the trade balance.[27] Figure 6 displays the results for the variables of interest (in percentage points of trend output). As in Figure 5, straight lines correspond to point estimates, while broken lines indicate the two symmetric one-standard error bands, computed by bootstrapping based on 1,000 replications.

The first column of Figure 6 shows the response of the budget deficit, which displays a similar shape and persistence in all countries. In contrast, the response of the current account (second column) is markedly different across our countries. On impact, the current account improves in the US and Australia, which are the least open economies

---

[25] Müller (2006) finds an appreciation of the terms of trade in the US using data from 1973–2003 and a similar identification scheme than the one employed in the present paper.

[26] Several empirical and quantitative contributions have emphasized that trade elasticities are quite low in the short run, see the discussion by Corsetti et al. (2004). In the Web Appendix we show numerically that if markets are incomplete, with a low trade elasticity it is possible that a positive shock to government spending leads to a depreciation of the terms of trade. At the same time, our experiments with a low elasticity confirm our main predictions regarding the role of openness for the response of relative investment to fiscal shocks.

[27] Using the trade balance instead of the current account gives very similar results.

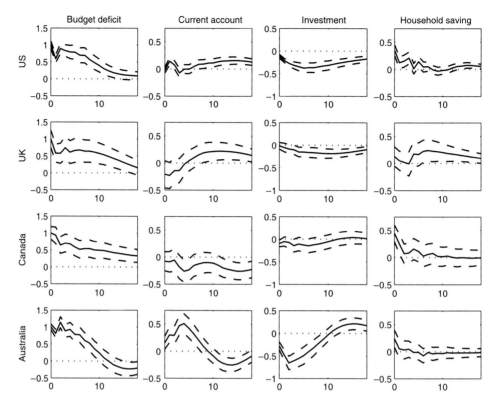

Figure 6. Selected responses to deficit shock

Notes: Sample is 1980:1 to date. The solid line gives the point estimate. Broken lines indicate bootstrapped two one-standard error bands. Vertical axis indicate deviations from unshocked path measured in percentage points of GDP. Horizontal axis indicate quarters.

Source: Own calculations on OECD *Economic Outlook* database, see Box 2.

in our sample; it deteriorates in Canada and the UK, which are the most open economies in our sample. In line with our theoretical discussion we find that investment falls markedly in the case of the US and Australia (third column). It falls much less, or insignificantly, in the case of Canada and the UK.

Figure 6 also reports the responses of household saving (fourth column), which follow a remarkably similar pattern across countries: household savings increase on impact. While the response is not negligible, it is, however, insufficient to offset the negative shock to public savings.[28] A summary of the dynamic effects of a deficit shock for our second VAR specification is given by Table 3. Overall, the results in this subsection suggest that the transmission mechanism identified in the case of a government spending shock is also at work in the case of direct shocks to the budget deficit.

[28] In the analysis we use gross investment. Thus the response shown in the graph abstracts from changes in the depreciation rate. Household savings, on the other hand, are net savings, i.e. disposable income less consumption expenditure. As a result, we are not in a position to analyse the proper components of the current account in isolation.

5. FISCAL AND GLOBAL IMBALANCES

For relatively closed economies such as the US, our study confirms an important policy-related finding of the literature, namely, that the effects of fiscal shocks on external trade are small. Does it follow that fiscal policy would not play any significant role in correcting the unprecedented stream of large current account deficits run by the US in recent years? In other words, can the US fiscal authorities be relieved from the responsibility of contributing to rebalancing the US external account, simply because fiscal instruments would not have a strong effect on net exports? We believe that such a conclusion would be a severe misreading of our results.

Our theoretical analysis and empirical evidence both show that the fiscal transmission mechanism has either an external or an internal intertemporal component. Facing an increasing claim by the government on domestic resources, households can choose to sustain their consumption plans at their optimal level by either borrowing from abroad, or by reducing investment. The second option is more attractive, the more domestic households prefer domestic goods over foreign goods and the more persistent the fiscal shock. In this case, the contemporaneous impact of fiscal shocks on the current account is limited.

Hence, even if the external balance does not deteriorate on impact, fiscal expansions are by no means irrelevant for external solvency, because of their crowding out effects on investment. Everything else equal, a lower capital stock in the future means that the US is pledging future resources at the expense of future consumption. Unless the differential in the rate of growth of productivity between the US and the rest of

Table 3. Cumulative response to a deficit shock

	Horizon	US	UK	Canada	Australia
GDP	4	−0.14*	−0.02	0.01	−0.5*
	12	−0.69*	−0.45*	0.13	−1.47*
Budget deficit	4	0.83*	0.72*	0.82*	0.96*
	12	2*	1.96*	1.9*	2.04*
Inflation	4	0.12*	0.08	−0.37*	−0.07
	12	0.42*	0.31*	−0.25	−0.71*
Nominal interest rate	4	−0.19*	0.09	−0.07	−0.13*
	12	−0.47*	0.25*	−0.05	−0.57*
Terms of trade	4	−0.02	0.17	0.25	0.36
	12	1.6*	0.16	−0.05	2.49*
Current account	4	0.03	−0.18*	−0.10	0.3*
	12	0.17*	0.09	−0.41*	0.62*
Investment	4	−0.23*	−0.06	−0.09	−0.5*
	12	−0.91*	−0.4*	−0.29	−1.03*
Household savings	4	0.21*	0.05	0.21*	0.09
	12	0.26*	0.46*	0.34	0.04

Notes: Annualized responses – cumulative responses are expressed in yearly rates (i.e. cumulative responses are divided by 4); all quantities are expressed in percentage of GDP; horizon is in quarters. Sample starts in 1980:1 (dependent variable), see Box 2 for details. An asterisk (*) indicates that zero is outside the region between the two one-standard error bands obtained by bootstrap based on 1,000 replications.

Source: Own calculations.

the world is bound to remain large, delaying a fiscal correction may create macroeconomic and political risk.

In addition, there may be reasons for a large fiscal correction in the US to have
stronger effects than we find in our study. One cannot exclude that when fiscal
authorities take drastic measures the macroeconomic impact of fiscal shocks is larger
than the average impact picked up by VAR estimates.[29]

In conclusion, our analysis suggests that a US fiscal correction is called for in light
of sustained global imbalances. According to our results, however, the transmission
mechanism is mainly intertemporal via investment, rather than intratemporal through
foreign trade.

6. CONCLUSIONS

The budget balance and the trade balance have a very strong cyclical component,
which induces a negative correlation between the two variables over the business cycle:
economic expansions tend to improve the budget balance, but worsen the trade balance.
However, according to the twin deficit hypothesis, fiscal innovations which are not
systematically related to the cyclical conditions of the economy reverse the sign of this
correlation. Namely, fiscal shocks generating budget deficits also worsen external trade.

In this paper we reconsider the twin deficit hypothesis both from a theoretical
point of view and by analysing data for Australia, Canada, the UK and the US. At
the theoretical level, we show why openness and the persistence of fiscal shocks are
major determinants of the magnitude (or even the sign) of the response of the trade
balance to fiscal shocks. Our emphasis is on international relative price movements,
and their repercussion on the rate of return and real rate of interest across borders.
We have shown that, for a given persistence of the fiscal shock, the crowding out
effect on investment is stronger in a relatively closed economy. In this case, the
deterioration of the trade balance is not very pronounced. Given openness, crowding
out of investment is stronger when the fiscal shock is persistent. We can thus qualify
the twin deficit hypothesis by relating the effects of fiscal shocks on the external
balance to (1) openness and (2) shock persistence. The mechanism underlying our
result highlights a macroeconomic trade-off of great policy relevance – we find that
fiscal expansions either reduce domestic capital or the external balance.

At the empirical level, we assess our analytical and quantitative insights by investigating the transmission of fiscal shocks in a VAR framework in four OECD countries,
differing in their degree of openness. Our empirical findings regarding the dynamic
response of trade and investment to fiscal shocks support our argument's predictions.
In the US and Australia, which are relatively less open than Canada and the UK,

---

[29] Would this argument rescue a strong version of the twin deficit hypothesis for large spending corrections? An element raising
doubts regarding this possibility is that previous studies analysing substantial current account adjustments fail to find any
significant impact of fiscal policy, see e.g. Freund (2000).

and where government spending shocks are less persistent, we find that the current account impact of fiscal policy is rather limited. Instead, private investment responds substantially. The reverse is true for Canada and the UK. These findings confirm and put into perspective earlier results, whereby fiscal expansions in the US have on average a negligible effect on the country's trade balance. The data's support is not as strong for the specific transmission channel we focus on, however, as the response of the terms of trade to fiscal shocks does not square well with theory. The results suggest that further theoretical and empirical work along this paper's lines could be very fruitful.

We emphasize that our main result, that twin deficit effects may be small in relatively closed economies, are by no means a critique of the call for a US fiscal retrenchment to address global imbalances. Our main point is that the impact of budget cuts on the current US external balance is going to be muted by their positive effects on domestic investment. Building a higher capital stock cannot but strengthen the ability of the US to generate the resources required to service this country's external liabilities in the future.

Discussion

Anne Sibert
Birkbeck College, London

A US government budget deficit of nearly 5 per cent of GDP in 2003 and 2004 was associated with a small increase in government spending as a share of GDP between 2000 and 2003, coupled with a sizable decline in current receipts. The United States has run current account deficits every year but one since 1982 and its deficit in 2005, measured as a share of GDP, was probably the largest in US history. The magnitude of the US external imbalances and the size of the concurrent US government budget deficits have sparked renewed interest in the 'twin deficit' hypothesis and the purported purpose of this paper is to examine whether fiscal shocks that have a particular effect on the government budget balance also have a systematic effect on the current account deficit.

The authors focus on changes in government spending and employ an intertemporal optimizing equilibrium model that allows them to focus on three ways that shocks are transmitted. The first is a standard static terms-of-trade effect. A temporary increase in home government spending on the domestic good increases the price of the domestic good relative to the foreign good and the trade balance deteriorates. The second is an intertemporal effect. The increased tax liability associated with an increase in home government spending causes the representative home household to be worse off. Thus, the household decreases both its consumption of the domestic consumption good and its consumption of leisure. The resulting decrease in the capital–labour ratio causes the marginal product of capital to rise and puts upward pressure on the return to home investment. Investment rises to restore equality between the return to investment at home and the return to investment in the rest of the world. This tends to worsen the current account.

The third channel is a more unusual 'home bias' effect. The authors assume that each country has a single domestically produced final good that can be used either for consumption or as a capital good. The final good is produced with both a home and a foreign intermediate good. Each country's intermediate good is produced with the capital good and with labour. The authors assume extreme home-biasedness. The technology for producing each country's final good is intensive in that country's intermediate good. Government spending is assumed to be solely purchases of the domestic intermediate good. Each country consumes solely its own final good and it uses only its own capital in the production of the intermediate good. Because the final good is produced with both countries' intermediate goods, an increase in the home country's domestic spending increases the price of the home intermediate good relative to the price of its final good. Since the final good is used as capital in the production of the intermediate good, this increases the return to investment at home and this effect also worsens the current account. The authors view the degree to which the intermediate good technology is intensive in the home good as an inverse measure of 'openness'. Although the relationship between the intensity and openness is not completely obvious this allows the authors to claim that increased openness increases the home-bias effect.

While the authors have identified an interesting and plausible way in which government spending can affect the trade balance and the current account, numerous other stories are possible as well. For example, if the increase in government spending is associated with increased fears of insolvency then capital outflows may occur, improving the current account deficit. Much of actual government spending is spending on wages. If the government spending entails the withdrawal of labour – but not capital – from the private sector, then the capital–labour ratio will rise in the private sector tending to cause the return to capital to fall below world levels. Capital will flow out until the marginal product of capital is equated to the marginal product of capital in the rest of the world and the current account will increase.

In its most basic form, fiscal policy has two components: the amount of government spending, which the authors analyse, and how that spending is financed. If government spending is fixed, then fiscal shocks that affect the government budget deficit are shocks that affect the timing of taxes. In this case the idea behind the twin deficits hypothesis is that if output remains unchanged, a decrease in current taxes that leads to a budget deficit also causes households to believe that they are wealthier and, hence, to consume more and save less. Thus, the current account worsens.

To international economists reared on the Mundell–Fleming model this story is appealing in that it is consistent with the prediction of that framework: an expansionary fiscal policy causes upward pressure on the home interest rate; the exchange rate appreciates and the current account balance declines. The authors of this paper cite the Mundell–Fleming model repeatedly in their discussion of fiscal policy. However, as the Mundell–Fleming model does not contain either optimizing households or

explicit intertemporal budget constraints it would be a peculiar framework for analysing either the intertemporal pattern of taxes or the timing and intertemporal
effects of government spending.

The simple story behind the fiscal deficits may be flawed. When current tax
decreases are financed by borrowing, then the principal and interest must be repaid
by increasing taxes in the future. In the canonical frictionless optimizing representative agent model the household internalizes the government's budget constraint and,
realizing that the discounted present value of its tax obligations has not changed, it
does not alter its consumption path in response to the lower current taxes. Hence,
there is no increase in its consumption. If the tax is to have an effect on consumption
there must be some departure from this Ricardian equivalence.

There will be a departure from Ricardian equivalence if the tax burden is borne
by a future generation and households are not altruistically linked; increasing their
bequests to offset future higher taxes. In this case a current tax decrease does increase
the wealth of current households and their consumption will rise. Alternatively, there
will also be a departure from Ricardian equivalence if taxes are distortionary or costly
to administer and collect. In this case a fall in current taxes and a rise in future taxes
increases real resources available today relative to the future. A rise in current consumption may be associated with a *lower* real interest rate and a rise in domestic savings.
It appears likely that both types of departures from Ricardian equivalence occur and
the relative magnitudes of the effects are uncertain. Efforts to test them empirically
are fraught with problems. For example, taxes, interest rates, consumption and savings
are all endogenous and any apparent relationship may be due to the influence of
other variables, such as factors affecting or associated with the business cycle. Perhaps
because of these problems, despite the title, the authors devote little space to considering
the relationship between the timing of taxes – that is, the budget deficit *per se* – and
external balances. Indeed, the main background model – with its infinite-lived representative agents and obviously distortionary taxes – appears to be Ricardian.

Panel discussion

Allan Drazen was concerned with the possible endogeneity of government spending,
which can respond to current account developments. Ashoka Mody thought that the
occurrence of twin deficits does not appear to depend on country characteristics in
the real world. Rather, it may depend on liquidity conditions in the international
capital market, which may in turn interact with the openness of the economy. Richard
Portes liked Mody's story but felt that it couldn't explain why the deficits behaved
so differently in the US in the late 1990s compared to the other periods (1980s,
2000s) when the characteristics of the economy had not changed. Portes suggested
that it would be useful to consider a range of economies to tease out any differences

between them. Wendy Carlin pointed out that the paper did not investigate the movement of the nominal exchange rate and thought that it may have played different roles in periods with different monetary policy regimes. This is because when the central bank reacts more strongly to stabilize inflation, the exchange rate has less work to do. Similarly, a more open economy will have similar qualitative results, but a lower multiplier–interest rates will increase less so there is less crowding out and the real exchange rate has to work less too.

APPENDIX: DATA SOURCES AND DEFINITIONS

Except for Table 1, all data are obtained from the OECD *Economic Outlook* database. OECD mnemonics are given in capital letters. Our sample is based on quarterly data for Australia, Canada, the UK and the US, starting in the first quarter of 1979 and ranging up to the third quarter of 2005 for the US, to the second quarter of 2005 for Canada and the UK, and to the second quarter of 2004 for Australia.

While the budget balance is already scaled by GDP (NLGXQ: Primary government balance, percentage of GDP), we calculate the net export–GDP ratio by scaling FBGS (Net exports of goods and services, value) by GDP (Gross Domestic Product, market prices, value). Also the current account is available as a percentage of GDP (CBGDPR: current account, as a percentage of GDP).

Real government spending is CGV (Government final consumption expenditure, volume) plus IGV (Government fixed capital formation, volume). Real private investment is IPV (private total fixed capital formation, volume). Real private consumption expenditures is CPV (private final consumption expenditure, volume).

The savings ratio is SRATIO (Household savings ratio, percent). The interest rate is IRL (long-term interest rate on government bonds, percent). To compute inflation rates, we compute the GDP deflator, dividing GDP by GDPV (Gross Domestic Product, volume) and take four times the log difference of the GDP deflator (to obtained annualized inflation rates). To compute the terms of trade we take the log of the ratio of the deflator for imports to the deflator for exports, i.e. PMGS (Imports of goods and services, deflator) and PXGS (Exports of goods and services, deflator), respectively. In the VAR model we scale quantity variables by POPT (population, total between 15 and 64 years old).

Table 1

The data used to calculate the import content of GDP and its components reported in Table 1 are drawn from various sources. For all four countries we compute the import content of GDP on the basis of OECD data by taking the mean of the ratio of imports (MGSV: imports of goods and services, national accounts basis, value) to GDP. To compute the import content of GDP components we use different sources.

For the US: computations are based on the assumption that the import content of a particular (intermediate and final) commodity for all final uses is equal to the economy wide average for this commodity. Direct imports are added from the supplementary 1997 Benchmark NAICS Import Matrix (Source: Bureau of Economic Analysis (2002). *Survey of Current Business Bureau*, December, Table 2, on p. 107). Government spending consists of consumption and investment of the federal and state governments.

For the UK: Import content in GDP components is taken directly from Herzberg *et al.* (2002, p. 204). The data refer to the year 1995.

For Canada: Import content in GDP components is taken directly from Dion *et al.* (2005, table 7, p. 13). The data refer to the year 2000.

For Australia: Own calculations based on Australian Bureau of Statistics, cat. no. 5209.0.55.001 Australian National Accounts: Input-Output Tables – Electronic Publication, Table 18. The data refer to 1998–99.

We conclude by noting that, in Table 1, government spending is public consumption and investment, except for UK and Canada where it is only government consumption.

WEB APPENDIX

Available at http://www.economic-policy.org

REFERENCES

Ahmed, S. (1986). 'Temporary and permanent government spending in an open economy: some evidence for the United Kingdom', *Journal of Monetary Economics*, 17, March, 197–224.

Backus, D.K., P.J. Kehoe and F.E. Kydland (1994). 'Dynamics of the trade balance and the terms of trade: the J-curve?', *American Economic Review*, 84(1), 84–103.

Baxter, M. (1995). 'International trade and business cycles', in G. Grossmann and K. Rogoff (eds.), *Handbook of International Economics*, Volume 3, North-Holland, Amsterdam, 1801–64.

Beetsma, R., M. Giuliodori and F. Klaassen (2006). 'Trade spill-overs of fiscal policy in the European Union: a panel analysis', *Economic Policy*, this volume.

Bernheim, B.D. (1988). 'Budget deficits and the balance of trade', in L.H. Summers (eds.), *Tax Policy and the Economy*, Volume 2, MIT Press, Cambridge, MA, 1–32.

Blanchard, O. and R. Perotti (2002). 'An empirical characterization of the dynamic effects of changes in government spending and taxes on output', *Quarterly Journal of Economics*, 117(4), November, 1329–68.

Bussière, M., M. Fratzscher and G.J. Müller (2005). 'Productivity shocks, budget deficits and the current account', *ECB Working Paper Series*, 509, August.

Canzoneri, M.B., R.E. Cumby and B. Diba (2003). 'New views on the transatlantic transmission of fiscal policy and macroeconomic policy coordination', in M. Buti (eds.), *Monetary and Fiscal Policies in EMU: Interactions and Coordination*, Cambridge University Press, Cambridge, 283–314.

Chinn, M.D. and E.S. Prasad (2003). 'Medium-term determinants of current accounts in industrial and developing countries: an empirical exploration', *Journal of International Economics*, 59(1), 47–76.

Chinn, M.D. and H. Ito (2005). 'Current account balances, financial development and institutions: assaying the world "savings glut" ', mimeo, NBER Working Paper, No. 11761, November.

Christiano, L.J. and T.J. Fitzgerald (2003). 'The band pass filter', *International Economic Review*, 44(2), 435–65.

Clarida, R. and J. Prendergast (1999). 'Fiscal stance and the real exchange: some empirical estimates', NBER Working Paper, No. 7077, April.

Cole, H.L. and M. Obstfeld (1991). 'Commodity trade and international risk sharing: how much do financial markets matter?', *Journal of Monetary Economics*, 28(1), 3–24.

Corsetti, G. and G. Müller (2005). 'Dynamics of the fiscal balance and the trade balance: twins?', mimeo.

Corsetti, G., L. Dedola and S. Leduc (2004). 'International risk sharing and the transmission of productivity shocks', *ECB Working Paper Series*, 308, February.

Corsetti, G. and P. Pesenti (2001). 'Welfare and macroeconomic interdependence', *Quarterly Journal of Economics*, 116(2), 421–46.

Dion, R., M. Laurence and Y. Zheng (2005). 'Exports, imports, and the appreciation of the Canadian dollar', *Bank of Canada Review*, Autumn, 5–18.

Erceg, C.J., L. Guerrieri and C. Gust (2005a). 'Expansionary Fiscal Shocks and the Trade Deficit, Board of Governors of the Federal Reserve System', International Finance Discussion Papers, 825, January.

—— (2005b). 'Trade adjustment and the composition of trade', Board of Governors of the Federal Reserve System, mimeo, November.

Fatás, A. and I. Mihov (2001). 'The effects of fiscal policy on consumption and employment: theory and evidence', INSEAD mimeo, CEPR Discussion Paper, No. 2760, April.

Finn, M.G. (1998). 'Cyclical effects of government's employment and goods purchases', *International Economic Review*, 39(3), 635–57.

Freund, C.L. (2000). 'Current account adjustment in industrialized countries', Board of Governors of the Federal Reserve System, *International Finance Discussion Papers*, No. 692, December.

Giuliodori, M. and R. Beetsma (2004). 'What are the spill-overs from fiscal shocks in Europe? An empirical analysis', *ECB Working Paper Series*, 325, March.

Gruber, J.W. and S.B. Kamin (2005). 'Explaining the global pattern of current account imbalances', Board of Governors of the Federal Reserve System, International Finance Discussion Papers, No. 846, November.

Heathcote, J. and F. Perri (2002). 'Financial autarky and international business cycles', *Journal of Monetary Economics*, 49(3), 601–27.

Herzberg, V., M. Sebastia-Barriel and S. Whitaker (2002). 'Why are UK imports so cyclical?', *Bank of England Quarterly Bulletin*, 42(2), 203–208.

International Monetary Fund (2004). *World Economic Outlook*, April.

—— (2005). *World Economic Outlook*, September.

Kim, S. and N. Roubini (2003). 'Twin deficits or twin divergence? Fiscal policy, current account, and real exchange rate in the US', NYU Stern mimeo.

Kollmann, R. (1998). 'US trade balance dynamics: the role of fiscal policy and productivity shocks and of financial market linkages', *Journal of International Money and Finance*, 17(4), 637–69.

Laubach, T. (2003). 'New evidence on the interest rate effects of budget deficits and debt', Board of Governors of the Federal Reserve System, *Finance and Economics Discussion Series*, 2003–12, May.

—— (2005). 'New evidence on the interest rate effects of budget deficits and debt', Board of Governors of the Federal Reserve System, mimeo.

Mountford, A. and H. Uhlig (2004). 'What are the effects of fiscal policy shocks', Humboldt University mimeo.

Müller, G.J. (2006). 'Understanding the dynamic effects of government spending on foreign trade', *Journal of International Money and Finance*, forthcoming.

Obstfeld, M. and K. Rogoff (2001). 'The six major puzzles in international macroeconomics: is there a common cause?', in B. Bernanke and K. Rogoff (eds.), *NBER Macroeconomics Annual 2000*, MIT Press, Cambridge, MA, 339–90.

Perotti, R. (2005). 'Estimating the effects of fiscal policy in OECD countries', CEPR Discussion Paper, No. 4842, January.

Roubini, N. (1988). 'Current account and budget deficits in an intertemporal model of consumption and taxation smoothing. A solution to the "Feldstein-Horioka puzzle"?', NBER Working Paper Series, No. 2773, November.

Stock, J.H. and M.W. Watson (2001). 'Vector autoregressions', *Journal of Economic Perspectives*, 15(4), 101–15.

Summers, L.H. (1986). 'Debt problems and macroeconomic policies', NBER Working Paper Series, No. 2061, October.

The Economist (2005). Various issues.

Tille, C. (2001). 'The role of consumption substitutability in the international transmission of monetary shocks', *Journal of International Economics*, 53(2), 421–44.

Spill-overs in the EU

SUMMARY

We explore international spill-overs from fiscal policy shocks via trade in Europe. To assess and quantify the channels through which a fiscal expansion stimulates domestic activity, foreign exports, and foreign output, we estimate a dynamic empirical model of government spending, net taxes, and output, and combine its estimates with a panel model of trade linkages across European countries. The baseline estimates of both models are quite robust and statistically significant. Our results indicate that trade spill-overs of fiscal shocks should be taken into account when assessing the character and intensity of economic integration in the European Union.

— *Roel Beetsma, Massimo Giuliodori and Franc Klaassen*

Economic Policy October 2006 Printed in Great Britain
© CEPR, CES, MSH, 2006.

Trade spill-overs of fiscal policy in the European Union: a panel analysis

Roel Beetsma, Massimo Giuliodori and Franc Klaassen

University of Amsterdam

1. INTRODUCTION

Cross-border integration of national economies is progressing steadily in the European Union (EU). As a result, policy changes in one country may have potentially important effects on other countries in the EU. In this paper, we shall explore the relevance of international trade for the cross-border transmission of fiscal shocks within the EU. The importance of such spill-overs helps to determine the interdependence of national macroeconomic policies and the interest that governments might have in each others' policy stances. To the best of our knowledge, the empirical literature has hardly given any attention to fiscal spill-overs via trade and, hence, it is not clear to what extent

We thank Volker Wieland (our discussant), Peter Boswijk, Maurice Bun, Peter Claeys, Hugo Rojas-Romagosa, Evi Pappa, Jan in't Veld, four anonymous referees, the participants of the *Economic Policy* Panel, seminar participants at the University of Amsterdam, CPB Netherlands Bureau for Economic Policy Analysis, University of Zurich, and participants of the third MAPMU-RTN Conference (London Business School), the third Quantitative Macroeconomics Workshop (University of Cologne) and the fourth TAXBEN workshop on 'Macroeconomic Modeling of Tax Policies' (CEPII, Paris) for helpful comments and discussions. Part of this paper was written while Beetsma was visiting the Robert Schuman Centre of the European University Institute in Florence. He thanks the RSC for its hospitality and its excellent research environment. This research is part of the RTN project 'Macroeconomic Policy Design for Monetary Unions', funded by the European Commission (contract number HPRN-CT-2002-00237). The usual disclaimer applies.

The Managing Editor in charge of this paper was Giuseppe Bertola.

Economic Policy October 2006 pp. 639–687 Printed in Great Britain
© CEPR, CES, MSH, 2006.

policymakers should be concerned with foreign fiscal policy changes. One reason for this lack of attention might be that in the past it has proved hard to find statistically significant effects of such spill-overs (e.g., see McKibbin, 1997). Therefore, some authors, such as Gros and Hobza (2001) and In't Veld (2004), simulate calibrated models to assess the trade spill-overs from fiscal policy.

Our empirical analysis is based on the conjecture that a fiscal expansion stimulates domestic activity, which leads to more domestic imports and thus more exports by other countries. This, in turn, boosts foreign income. Our quantification of these effects is innovative. In particular, we combine a panel vector auto-regression (VAR) model with a panel trade model to calculate the 'full' effect of a fiscal impulse on bilateral foreign exports. The panel VAR model allows us to identify the fiscal shocks and compute the output responses to these shocks, while the panel trade model, which is closely related to the well-known gravity model, enables us to calculate the effect of output on bilateral foreign exports. This allows us to (1) combine two models with different dimensionality, that is, a country panel VAR model and a country-pair trade model, (2) disentangle the contributions of the various steps leading to the overall trade spill-over of fiscal policy, and (3) exploit the similarities between the EU countries in the data set. Nevertheless, the approach also has potential disadvantages. By splitting the calculation of the fiscal spill-over in steps, we may forego the (presumably) greater flexibility of a fully integrated approach in terms of capturing the cross-border transmission of fiscal shocks. In addition, our panel analysis imposes homogeneity restrictions on a number of model parameters. However, our sensitivity analysis shows that the results are quite robust to extensions aimed at capturing both richer cross-border transmission processes and heterogeneity.

The panel VAR model shows that both an increase in government spending (i.e. government consumption plus investment) and a reduction in net taxes (i.e. revenues minus transfers) give a significant boost to domestic economic activity, which persists for some years. The panel trade estimates reveal a significantly positive impact effect of domestic output on foreign exports. Combining the baseline estimates of the two models, we find that, on average, over the first two years a German public spending increase equal to 1% of GDP implies a foreign exports gain of 2.2% of its annual level. The corresponding figure for an equal-size net tax reduction is 0.8%. Both estimates are statistically significant. As far as the direct effect of enhanced exports on average foreign activity is concerned, the corresponding gains from the two shocks are, respectively, 0.15% and 0.05% of annual GDP. Obviously, these numbers become smaller when the fiscal shock originates from other EU countries. The smallest effect is found for a fiscal stimulus in Greece, which raises average foreign GDP by only 0.01% in the case of a spending increase and 0.005% in the case of a net tax reduction. The numbers reported here provide only a first attempt at quantification and are intended to show that fiscal policy spill-overs via trade are potentially relevant, at least when they originate from large trading partners.

Obviously, we conduct our analysis under a number of simplifying assumptions. First, the baseline version of our panel VAR model implicitly assumes that neither monetary policy nor the exchange rate react to the fiscal shocks or the ensuing output changes. Our sensitivity analysis suggests that this simplification is reasonable here. Second, we impose that the output reaction to the fiscal shocks be proportional to the size of the shock and independent of the state of the public finances. The literature has pointed out that large fiscal adjustments (in particular, cuts in government spending) in periods of fiscal distress may have non-Keynesian effects (see, for example, Giavazzi and Pagano, 1990), which would contrast with the economy's reaction under 'normal' circumstances. We thus assume that the sample is dominated by 'normal' circumstances. Finally, we neglect potential anticipation effects of fiscal policy that would result in movements in macroeconomic variables taking place before the fiscal impulse actually takes place.[1]

By focusing on the trade spill-overs of fiscal policy, we thus largely ignore other potential spill-overs, in particular those that take place through changes in the interest rate.[2] There are several reasons to motivate this choice. First, the possibility of positive output spill-overs of fiscal expansions via trade has received much less attention in the discussions surrounding the European fiscal framework than the negative spill-overs on foreign activity through a rise in the common interest rate. Second, especially in the case of Europe, the trade channel may well be more important than the interest rate channel. Spill-overs via trade are mostly confined to Europe, because intra-European trade is substantially larger than trade with the rest of the world, while, to the extent that the European capital market is integrated with the capital market in the rest of the world, the interest rate increase following a debt-financed fiscal expansion in some European country is diluted.[3] Even so, we check for possible interest rate spill-overs by extending our baseline national panel VAR with the average foreign (*ex-post*) real interest rate. The effects of national fiscal impulses on this variable are either small or insignificant, while the responses of other variables are unaffected.

We believe that our findings may provide policymakers with potentially useful insights. First, better information on the quantitative importance and time profile of the effects of domestic fiscal expansions on the national economies should enable policymakers to design better-targeted measures for stabilizing their own economy. Further, the EU Ministers of Finance meet regularly in a formal capacity in the

[1] In their analysis of the effects of US fiscal policy, Blanchard and Perotti (2002) find only weak anticipation effects. Their analysis is conducted on quarterly data. With yearly data, we expect anticipation effects to become even weaker, because any anticipation of policy changes that are on average further into the future becomes less likely. Moreover, even when a policy change is anticipated, details of the change often remain obscure until close to the date of the change.

[2] Theoretically, a fiscal expansion can generate a spill-over both via the common short-run and the common long-run interest rate. If the expansion puts upward pressure on inflation, the European Central Bank (ECB) is forced to raise the short interest rate. If public debt rises, then the long-run interest rate may go up.

[3] If the rise in the interest rate is caused by an increase in the likelihood of debt default, then there is *a priori* no reason why the rise should be transmitted to other countries. However, if part of the rise is explained by crowding out because the additional debt generates an excessive demand for funds at the initial interest rate, then one might expect also an upward pressure on the foreign interest rate as funds are attracted from abroad.

ECOFIN and informally in the Euro-group (the Euro-area Finance ministers only). Insight into the national and cross-border effects of fiscal policy should help them form a judgment on each other's fiscal plans and evaluate the consequences for their own economy. A recent example is the stimulation package designed by the new German government under Merkel. Our results could help understand the consequences of this package for Germany and its trading partners. Even though the European fiscal authorities do not coordinate their macroeconomic policies, peer pressure and regular interaction in combination with better information on the spill-over effects should be conducive to a better alignment of national fiscal policies. Finally, more accurate information on the distribution of the costs and benefits of fiscal stimulation should create a better understanding of other countries' policy positions.

Our analysis could also shed some light on the suitability of the existing macroeconomic framework in Europe and, in particular, on the role of the Stability and Growth Pact (SGP). Our estimates can help policymakers to assess the short-run effects of a tight enforcement of the Pact's deficit limit, both for the economy for which the limit is binding but also for the economies of trading partners. Of course, a more comprehensive assessment of the functioning of the SGP requires taking into account not only these short-run effects but also the longer-run effects of reduced public debt under enforcement. Ironically, our results suggest that the positive trade benefits of a laxer fiscal policy of some EU countries could make it easier for others to obey the Pact's limits in the short run.

The remainder of the paper is structured as follows. Section 2 discusses in more detail the empirical strategy. Section 3 presents the baseline estimates (as well as a number of robustness checks) for the effects of fiscal policy in the panel VAR model, while Section 4 does the same for the panel trade model. Then, Section 5 combines the results from the previous two sections to produce estimates of domestic fiscal impulses on foreign trade and foreign output. Section 6 discusses some policy experiments based on the estimated models. Finally, Section 7 concludes the main body of this paper. Details on the data, procedures and some technicalities are contained in the Appendices, which are available from the web.

2. MOTIVATION FOR THE EMPIRICAL STRATEGY AND SAMPLE CHOICE

We obtain the overall effect of domestic fiscal impulses on exports by trading partners in Europe in two steps. In the first step, we estimate the link between a domestic fiscal impulse and domestic output. To fix terminology, we will refer to this step as the *fiscal block*. In the second step, we link foreign exports to domestic GDP. We shall refer to this step as the *trade block*. By combining the links established in the two blocks, we can quantify the overall effect of a domestic fiscal impulse on foreign exports. In an extra step, we can then translate the movements in exports into changes in foreign output.

Because we are most interested in the short- and medium-run economic effects of the fiscal impulses, the fiscal and trade blocks will be specified as dynamic rather than static. For the fiscal block, we estimate a panel VAR model in which the responses of output to the discretionary fiscal shocks are traced out. For the other block, we set up a panel trade model based on the gravity approach and estimate the dynamic responses of bilateral exports by the EU trading partners to domestic output.

By estimating the fiscal and trade blocks separately and then combining the respective outcomes, we circumvent the difficulty that the two models have different dimensions, because the fiscal block concerns the domestic economy only, whereas the trade block deals with the interactions between pairs of countries. An additional advantage of estimating these models separately is that this allows us to disentangle the sizes of both steps going from the fiscal impulse via domestic output to foreign exports. Such an approach buys extra transparency and, more importantly, the estimates of both blocks contribute to the respective fields of research and can be compared with what is found there.

Using a block approach rather than combining the transmission from fiscal shocks to foreign trade into a single panel VAR also has potential disadvantages. In particular, the block approach ignores possible direct effects of fiscal variables on foreign exports (although we will test for this in our approach) and it ignores possible feedback effects from these exports onto the real exchange rate.[4] Other recent empirical contributions, briefly reviewed in Box 1, adopt different approaches, with different advantages and disadvantages.

Our choice of countries is led by the fact that we want to explore the trade spill-overs of fiscal shocks within the EU. An advantage of focusing on EU countries only is that this helps to limit the potential heterogeneity, as the economies share many similarities. This is important, because the use of panels requires us to impose certain homogeneity restrictions. In principle, we could have considered including other European countries, such as Switzerland and Norway, but the availability of the fiscal data was too limited for these countries. Data limitations also force us to exclude Luxemburg for the fiscal block as well as the recent EU entrants. Including this latter group would in any case not be recommendable in view of the still substantial economic differences with the 14 current EU members that are now left in the sample.

As regards the time dimension of our panels, our sample period is 1965–2004. However, for some countries it is shorter (see Appendix A). In view of the potential remaining differences across the countries and the sub-periods in our sample, we allow for extensive deterministic heterogeneity across the observations. Moreover, we shall explore how our findings change with specific sub-samples of countries and sub-periods.

While many recent analyses of the effects of fiscal impulses rely either on relatively small samples or on quarterly fiscal data, in this paper we use panels over a relatively long period of time. This provides us with enough observations to use annual data for our fiscal block. Although with annual data we may miss potentially interesting

---

[4] In an earlier experiment, we combined the fiscal and trade blocks in a single, huge panel VAR. The responses of exports to fiscal policy shocks were very similar to those described below. This provides another reason to keep the two blocks separate.

Box 1. Related empirical literature

As an alternative to our block approach, one could link fiscal policy to trade directly. Lane and Perotti (1998) regress the trade balance, exports and imports directly on movements in different components of the budget. Their main finding is that higher wage government consumption in a country causes a fall in that country's exports (that is especially large under a flexible exchange rate), while imports are also negatively affected or unaffected, depending on the regression specification. Using a VAR analysis for the US, Kim and Roubini (2003) find that a fiscal expansion improves the current account. Following up on this, Müller (2004) finds that an increase in government spending improves the US trade balance, which may be rationalized if public spending increases fall entirely on domestic products (raising their relative price) and the substitutability between domestic and foreign goods is small. Corsetti and Müller (2006) extend the analysis to three other countries. For our purposes, it is important to note that European countries are very open, and high substitutability of domestic and foreign goods tends to imply that public spending worsens the trade balance in those papers' framework of analysis. Giuliodori and Beetsma (2005) is the closest antecedent to the present paper. It includes imports in a VAR (with fiscal and other macroeconomic variables) that is separately estimated for Germany, France and Italy. Imports are either aggregate imports or bilateral imports from EU countries. The effects of fiscal expansions on aggregate imports are significantly positive in half of the cases, while they are positive on bilateral imports in quite a large number of cases. Marcellino (2002) estimates VARs that include the German output gap and German fiscal policy together with the corresponding variables for other large European countries. He finds only small and insignificant effects of German fiscal shocks on the other economies. Canzoneri et al. (2003) employ a VAR to explore the effects of changes in US fiscal policy on output in France, Italy and the United Kingdom. They obtain quite large spill-over effects for each of these countries. Our analysis does not address the political economy aspects of fiscal behaviour, such as the possibility that discretionary fiscal shocks may be related to the colour of the government – for example, discretionary tax cuts could be larger or more likely under a right-wing government – and largely ignores the (potentially strategic) interactions of fiscal policy with monetary policy. Recent empirical work on that issue, based on a VAR approach, is found in Van Aarle et al. (2003), Muscatelli et al. (2004) and Claeys (2004, 2006). In contrast to almost the entire related literature (including the present paper) Claeys (2006) imposes long-term solvency restrictions on the government budget. The output effects of fiscal shocks reported by these papers vary substantially. Rather than focusing on the consequences of discretionary shocks as we do, Favero (2003) studies systematic monetary and fiscal policies in Europe.

dynamics and some of our identification assumptions become stronger, the use of annual rather than quarterly data also has advantages. One is statistical. With annual data, there is no (or less) need to be concerned with seasonal effects in the data or potential quarter dependence in the coefficients of the lagged variables in our regressions. Second, details about the institutional setting become more important with quarterly fiscal data and it is hard to properly capture these in an empirical model. Examples are tax collection lags and differences in payment methods across countries and over time (see Perotti, 2005, for a detailed description). Third, the economic interpretation of fiscal shocks may be difficult at the quarterly level. While budget revisions are generally possible within the fiscal year, their frequency is often less than quarterly and their size and scope are likely to be more modest than changes associated with the budget presented for the entire fiscal year. Fourth, the quality of quarterly fiscal series is often not clear, because only little may be known about the construction of the data and in many cases the quarterly time series are interpolated from annual or semi-annual data. An exception is the dataset constructed by Perotti (2005), which, however, is available only for a limited number of countries.

Our choice of the data frequency for the trade block is led by our choice for the fiscal block. In addition, as far as the trade block is concerned, it is useful to note that with the use of bilateral trade data we avoid potential biases caused by the aggregation of trade flows over the countries.

3. THE FISCAL BLOCK

In this section we estimate our baseline panel VAR. We find that discretionary fiscal shocks lead to Keynesian effects. Then, we put the identification of the baseline model under further scrutiny and submit the model to a number of robustness checks. In particular, we extend it by including the domestic interest rate to control for monetary policy responses or the (ex-post) real foreign interest rate to check for cross-border interest rate spill-overs. We also do some sub-sample analysis. Overall, the baseline model's performance is satisfactory.

3.1. Model set-up and baseline estimates

The baseline fiscal block (see Appendix B.1 for technical details) is modelled as a panel VAR that explains as follows the dynamics of real public spending (g_{it}, i.e. government consumption plus government investment), cyclically adjusted real net taxes (nt_{it}^{CA}, i.e. revenues minus transfers), and real total output (y_{it}), all in natural logarithms:

$$
\begin{pmatrix} 1 & 0 & 0 \\ -\alpha_{tg} & 1 & 0 \\ -\alpha_{yg} & -\alpha_{yt} & 1 \end{pmatrix} \begin{bmatrix} g_{it} \\ nt_{it}^{CA} \\ y_{it} \end{bmatrix} = A(L) \begin{bmatrix} g_{i,t-1} \\ nt_{i,t-1}^{CA} \\ y_{i,t-1} \end{bmatrix} + \begin{bmatrix} e_{it}^{g} \\ e_{it}^{nt,CA} \\ e_{it}^{y} \end{bmatrix}, \tag{1}
$$

where subscripts 'i' and 't' index the country and the year, respectively, and the matrix on the left-hand side captures the contemporaneous relations between the variables. Further, $A(L)$ is a matrix polynomial in the lag operator L, which captures the relation between the current values of the variables and their lags. Finally, e_{it}^g, $e_{it}^{nt,CA}$, and e_{it}^y are mutually uncorrelated structural shocks that we want to recover. The first two are discretionary shocks to government spending and cyclically adjusted net taxes, respectively. Our specification follows Blanchard and Perotti (2002). We set the lag length of the system to two and estimate it for 14 EU countries over the period 1965–2004.[5]

Equation (1) shows that public spending is allowed to depend on lagged public spending, lagged (cyclically adjusted) net taxes, lagged output and a discretionary shock. However, it does not depend on contemporaneous values of net taxes and income. In contrast, net taxes may depend on contemporaneous spending, but not on current income, and income is allowed to depend on the contemporaneous values of both other variables. Hence, the model restricts three contemporaneous effects to zero. With these assumptions we can estimate the model and identify the structural shocks.

To justify the restriction that cyclically adjusted net taxes do not respond to output, we follow Blanchard and Perotti (2002) and Perotti (2005) in using elasticities of the various components of net taxes with respect to output to purge each of these components of its cyclical part. These elasticities are available on a country-by-country basis from the OECD (2005). Adding up the cyclically adjusted components then yields the cyclically adjusted net taxes (see Appendix A for more details). This variable thus takes account of the fact that the tax elasticities differ across countries. By including cyclically adjusted rather than non-adjusted net taxes we can thus impose that the contemporaneous reaction of this variable to output is zero.

Another advantage of making these *country-specific* cyclical adjustments to net taxes is that this should enable us to more accurately identify the country-specific discretionary tax shocks. If the elasticities between net taxes and output indeed differ across countries, then imposing homogeneity on the reaction of unadjusted net taxes to output would lead us to identify as the net tax shocks combinations of the true shock and the country-specific part of the cyclical reaction of net taxes to output.

The other two restrictions implicit in Equation (1) are based on the assumption that public spending does not react to contemporaneous changes in (cyclically adjusted) net taxes and output. These assumptions seem reasonable given that spending plans are usually determined in a government budget that is presented before the new fiscal year starts. (Note that while government transfers, in particular unemployment benefits, may be sensitive to the cycle, these are not included in our measure

---

[5] We de-mean and de-trend each variable included in the panel VAR to control for country-fixed effects and country-specific linear time trend effects. Additionally, fixed time effects are included. With a panel that is large enough in the time dimension, ordinary least square (OLS) estimation yields consistent estimates. Alesina *et al.* (2002) and Ardagna *et al.* (2004) estimate panel VARs for similar country and period samples.

of government expenditure.) An alternative to the former restriction would be to assume that cyclically adjusted net taxes do not react to government spending.[6] As in Alesina *et al.* (2002), however, our results show that the specific restriction on the contemporaneous relation between the two fiscal variables has no bearing on the results.[7] Therefore, in what follows, we will always restrict the effect of cyclically adjusted net taxes on public spending to zero.

Column 1 of Table 1 reports the maximum likelihood estimates of the unrestricted left-hand-side coefficients in (1) over the full sample period 1965–2004. We take this as the baseline case for the panel VAR. The results indicate that government spending has no clear contemporaneous effect on cyclically adjusted net taxes. Further, a government spending increase and a net tax cut exert a highly significant positive effect on current output. We depict the impulse responses in Figure 1, where the size of both fiscal shocks is set to 1% of GDP. The impulse responses trace out the time path of the effect of the shock on output and the other variables contained in the VAR. In both instances, output rises significantly upon impact and the increase remains significant for three years after the net tax shock and for even longer after the spending impulse.

3.2. Comparison of the baseline with the literature

The scope for comparison with the literature of the size of the output responses to fiscal impulses is limited. Most of the literature focuses on the US rather than Europe (and thus employs single-country VARs rather than panel VARs). The IMF (2004) provides an overview of some studies for the US and shows that the magnitudes of the output responses to fiscal shocks vary quite widely. We find a peak response of output to a spending increase in the EU that is larger (but not much) than what Blanchard and Perotti (2002) find on the basis of full-sample estimation for the US and substantially larger than the (positive) effects found by Mountford and Uhlig (2002). The output response to a net tax reduction that we obtain for Europe lies between the positive responses obtained by Mountford and Uhlig (2002) and Blanchard and Perotti (2002) for the US. Canova and Pappa (2003) find for most Euro-countries output multipliers of government spending shocks that are larger than one. Perotti (2005) conducts a quarterly analysis on five countries, only two of which are also in our sample (Germany and the UK). He generally finds weak effects of fiscal impulses on output – we return to this in the next subsection.

---

[6] This ordering would thus allow government spending to react to net taxes. Such a reaction could, for example, be imagined when tax revenues are unexpectedly low and the SGP is considered as strictly binding, in which case a government would be forced to cut spending. However, an unexpected fall in taxes is usually caused by an unexpected slowdown of the economy, so that correct identification would point to a negative output shock as the source of the spending contraction. But there is no evidence of a contemporaneous reaction of government spending to output, the SGP applies only to a relatively small part of our sample, and it is unclear to what extent it is actually binding.

[7] Indeed, the correlation between the reduced-form residuals of the government spending and the net tax equations turns out to be insignificant, while the impulse responses are very similar to those for the baseline.

Table 1. Estimates of the contemporaneous coefficients of the fiscal block

	1	2	3
	Baseline	Baseline over 1985–2004	Baseline with private output
α_{tg}	−0.152	−0.122	−0.157
	(0.100)	(0.132)	(0.099)
α_{yg}	0.253***	0.252***	0.037
	(0.027)	(0.032)	(0.036)
α_{yt}	−0.072***	−0.052***	−0.095***
	(0.012)	(0.015)	(0.015)
Sample period	1965–2004	1985–2004	1965–2004
Panel size	14	14	14
Observations	493	278	493

Notes: The table shows the coefficient estimates (and their standard errors in parentheses) of the contemporaneous effects between the variables. Here, α_{tg} is the effect of government spending on net taxes, α_{yg} is the effect of government spending on output, while α_{yt} is the effect of net taxes on output. Finally, *, ** and *** indicate statistical significance at the 10%, 5% and 1% level, respectively.

Source: Authors' calculations.

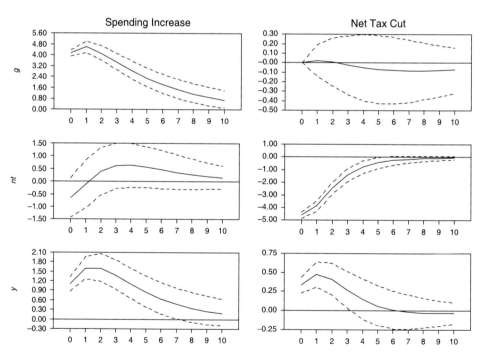

Figure 1. Impulse responses for the fiscal block (baseline panel VAR)

Notes: Confidence bands are the 5th and the 95th percentiles from Monte Carlo simulations based on 1000 replications.

3.3. Putting identification under further scrutiny

A priori, the assumption that fiscal variables are not affected by output within the year could be contentious. Government spending and net taxes may automatically react to business cycle movements that take place after the budget has been set for the fiscal year. Such automatic reaction is generally thought to be small for government spending, while for net taxes we have tried to correct for it with the cyclical adjustment described above. However, fiscal variables could also be subject to a discretionary reaction to output movements within the year. Such a reaction can, for example, be embedded in a mid-term revision of the budget. While within-year adjustments of tax rates, tax bases and transfer programs are likely to be limited due to the time it takes to prepare such measures and transfer them through the parliament, the renewal of public sector wage contracts could take into account changes in business cycle conditions that occur after the yearly budget has been set. If governments follow a counter-cyclical fiscal policy within the year by systematically reducing spending in response to unexpected increases in output, then our impulse responses would overstate the effect of a discretionary fiscal expansion on output. The opposite happens when governments pursue a within-year pro-cyclical spending policy.

To assess the potential importance of the within-year reaction of government spending to output movements, we exploit the fact that within-period reactions become less likely the shorter the period is. Following Perotti (2005), we assume that the reaction is zero within one quarter. Therefore, we estimate the baseline VAR for quarterly data for Germany (see Appendix C.1),[8] which is the only country for which we are confident that none of the variables is interpolated at the quarterly frequency. We check that seasonal patterns in the data are absent. Using the procedure described in Appendix D, we then transform the estimates of the quarterly model into respective estimates α_{gy}, α_{gt} and α_{ty} for the yearly VAR of the contemporaneous reactions of public spending to an output shock and a cyclically adjusted net tax shock and of the latter to an output shock. Although theory (see McCrorie and Chambers, 2003) indicates that if the true quarterly model is a VAR, then the annual model is a vector-autoregressive moving average (VARMA) model, our procedure should provide a reasonable compromise between accuracy and complexity. The procedure also yields 90% confidence bands on α_{gy}, α_{gt} and α_{ty}, which are (−0.22, 0.69), (−0.13, 0.23) and (−3.07, 3.76), respectively. Our baseline identifying restriction that all parameters are zero is thus not rejected. However, the interval on α_{gy} suggests that its true value may be positive. Using our *a priori* arguments discussed earlier, we will thus examine α_{gy} further, whereas we believe that the zero restrictions on α_{gt} and α_{ty} are acceptable.

The confidence band on α_{gy} is quite wide. This is mainly due to the limited number of observations. We can enhance the number of observations by excluding

---

[8] To construct cyclically adjusted net taxes at the quarterly frequency, we use the elasticity of net taxes with respect to output found by Perotti (2005) for West Germany (0.90).

net taxes from the VAR, as quarterly data on government spending and output are available for seven countries (Finland, France, Germany, Italy, the Netherlands, Sweden and the UK). For this sub-sample and on the basis of inspection of the series, we are quite confident that government spending (or at least government consumption) is not interpolated. Again, we order government spending first and impose that its within-quarter reaction to output shocks is absent. The resulting 90% confidence band on α_{gy} is now (−0.082, 0.168) and has become substantially narrower, while a zero within-year reaction of government spending to output is still contained in the band. To obtain a feeling about the consequences of the uncertainty around α_{gy}, we re-estimate the yearly panel VAR (1) on the entire sample, but with α_{gy} set at the bounds 0.168 or −0.082. The impact reactions of output to a 1% of GDP spending increase are 0.8% and 1.2%, respectively. These values are contained by the confidence interval around the baseline, which is roughly the average of the other two impact reactions. Hence, we believe that the baseline annual identification scheme will give reasonable approximations to the effects of interest for this paper.

As we mentioned earlier, in his analysis with quarterly data, Perotti (2005) found only weak effects of fiscal impulses on output. Quite interestingly, for the two-variable panel VAR in government spending and output estimated on our 7-country sub-sample for both quarterly and annual data, we find that the former case yields substantially weaker and less persistent effects of a spending shock on output than the latter. For the latter case, the results were very close to what we obtained for the three-variable VAR for the full sample of countries. Although this is speculation, a possible source of difference may be that what the model identifies as quarterly shocks consists of not only discretionary policy shocks but possibly also other shocks,[9] in which case we should not *a priori* expect economic activity to react.

3.4. Robustness analysis

To assess further the robustness of the baseline model, we have estimated a number of plausible variants of (1). Basically, all cases show that the baseline is robust. The rest of this section discusses a number of variants that we have considered.

3.4.1. Enlarging the baseline panel VAR.
We now extend the baseline model with the (log of the) price level, the short-run interest rate and the (log of the) real multilateral exchange rate. One cannot *a priori* exclude the possibility that fiscal shocks influence the dynamics of economic activity by affecting these variables. In particular, it could be important to include an exchange rate, because in a large part of the sample exchange rates were not fixed. Of course, by extending our panel VAR in this way, we still assume that the reaction of monetary policy and the exchange

---

[9] For example, depending on the specific accounting practices used, a cash disbursement could be recorded in a different quarter than when it takes place.

rate to macroeconomic developments is uniform across the sample.[10] We assume that the price level is contemporaneously unaffected by any of the other variables in the system. This restriction is motivated by the fact that prices tend to be sticky in the short run. Further, we allow for the real exchange rate to be contemporaneously affected by all other variables in the system, because (through the nominal exchange rate) it is expected to react instantaneously to changes in other macroeconomic variables. The interest rate is potentially contemporaneously affected by all other variables except for the exchange rate.[11] The impulse responses of output (and the fiscal variables) are very similar to the baseline responses (compare Figure 2 to Figure 1), which supports our choice to proceed with the baseline specification in the remainder of the analysis. The price rise is followed by a lagged increase in the interest rate that can presumably be explained by the desire of the central banks to counteract inflationary pressures. However, the increase in the interest rate is barely statistically significant. The real exchange rate is unaffected after the spending shock, but depreciates (i.e., increases) slightly for a brief period after the net tax reduction. We also estimated a version of the model with a long-run interest rate replacing the short-run interest rate and we estimated a version in which the short and the long interest rate were included together. The impulse responses are virtually unchanged, while the long interest rate behaves in much the same way as the short interest rate. This is not surprising given the strong empirical correlation that is usually found between the short and long end of the term structure.

In studying fiscal spill-overs, we limit ourselves to an assessment of the spill-overs through the trade channel. However, the panel VAR set up for the fiscal block can also be used to get an indication of potential spill-overs via the interest rate. In our extended panel VAR, we therefore replace the domestic nominal interest rate for each country with the GDP-weighted average *ex-post* long-term real interest rate of all *other* countries in the sample. This seems to be the most relevant variable for the measurement of interest spill-overs, because the long-term real interest rate is the basis for investment decisions or decisions about the purchase of durable consumption goods. To save space, we only report the relevant impulse responses in Appendix C.2. The impact effect of a fiscal impulse on the foreign real interest rate is zero, while it exhibits a significant peak one year after a spending increase and it becomes almost significant two years after a net tax reduction. However, these increases are short-lived, while their magnitudes are small with peaks of approximately nine, respectively one, basis points after a one-percent of GDP spending increase or an equal-size reduction in net taxes. The responses of the other

---

[10] The theoretical implications of fiscal impulses can differ widely according to the exchange rate regime, as exemplified in the standard Mundell–Fleming model. For a recent overview, see Hemming *et al.* (2002). Wieland (1996) simulates a German fiscal expansion in a macroeconometric model (based on Taylor, 1993) for the European Monetary System and shows that the spill-over effects on other countries depend substantially on the degree of symmetry or asymmetry in the exchange rate system.

[11] We have also experimented with a switch in the position of the interest rate and the exchange rate in the system. This left the results unchanged, however.

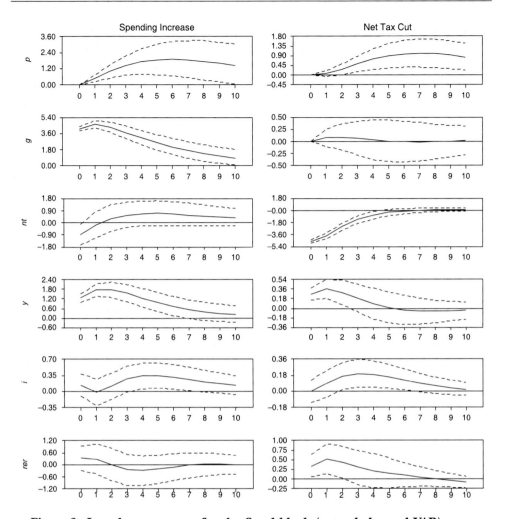

Figure 2. Impulse responses for the fiscal block (extended panel VAR)

Notes: In addition to the definitions already included in the main text, we have p = log of price level, i = short-run interest rate and *rer* = log of real multilateral exchange rate. In the figure, a rise in *rer* corresponds to a real *de*preciation. Further, see Notes to Figure 1.

variables remain very close to their baseline, which motivates us to retain our baseline specification.

We emphasize that there are several reasons why these results do not allow us to draw strong conclusions about the relevance of spill-overs via the interest rate. For example, a theoretically better measure of the relevant interest rate would have been the *ex-ante* rather than the *ex-post* real interest rate. This issue can be addressed by using data on inflation expectations, which is beyond the scope of the present analysis, however. Further, we have estimated the interest spill-over of fiscal impulses without differentiating over the originating countries. *Ceteris paribus*, we would expect a German fiscal impulse to have a larger spill-over effect than an equal-size (as a share of GDP) fiscal impulse in another country.

3.4.2. Potential heterogeneity. We have also estimated the baseline model only
for the second half of the sample period (i.e., for 1985–2004). Galí and Perotti (2003)
and Perotti (2005) find that fiscal policies and their effects might have changed over
time. Table 1, column 2, reports the results for this case, while Figure 3 shows the
impulse responses. However, both the effect of a government spending increase and
that of a net tax reduction on output are basically unchanged.

Another baseline assumption is that we force impulse responses to be the same
for all countries. Although the countries in our sample are all members of the EU,
which ensures that their economies are similar in some basic respects, and our panel
VAR allows for substantial deterministic heterogeneity (country and time effects and
country-specific time trends), it is important to put this homogeneity restriction
under further scrutiny.

Heterogeneity in the responses to shocks could in principle arise for many reasons.
For example, differences in the size and operation of the welfare system affect the
strength with which transfers and thus net taxes react to movements in the economy.
Further, the response of government consumption to the performance of the economy
may vary with differences in the wage-setting process for civil servants. Differences
in the political system could affect the speed with which decisions can be taken
in response to economic developments. While our data are too limited to test these
possibilities within our panel VAR setting, we shall now split the country sample in

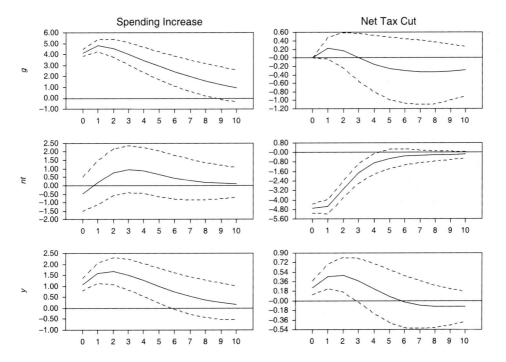

Figure 3. Impulse responses for the fiscal block (sample is 1985–2004)

Notes: See Notes to Figure 1.

some ways to focus on possible sources of heterogeneity that we can indeed test for with our data. Later on (Section 5), we shall explore the variation in the estimates of the fiscal block on individual countries.

A potential major source of heterogeneity that we can explore with our empirical framework concerns the differences in the size of the economies in our sample. Larger economies are generally more closed, suggesting that fiscal expansions are more effective, as less of the stimulus leaks abroad. To investigate the relevance of the country size for the impulse responses, we estimate the baseline model on a sub-sample with the five largest economies (Germany, France, UK, Italy and Spain) and a sub-sample with the nine remaining countries. The impulse responses are shown in Figures 4a and 4b, respectively. The output responses to the shocks are of a similar order of magnitude. The main difference concerns the net tax response after the initial spending impulse. The large countries react with a somewhat lagged tax increase after a spending increase, while the small countries react with a (barely) significant net tax cut on impact. We shall not speculate on an explanation for this difference, which may require a detailed look at differences in the budgetary processes in the various countries. Our main focus is on the output effects, in particular because the size of the trade spill-overs, assessed later on, is to a large extent linked to the output responses. These are rather similar, if somewhat shorter-lived after a public spending shock in the group of large countries. Thus, we continue to impose homogeneity on our panel VAR system.

As a further check for possible heterogeneity, we estimate the baseline model on the 'core' set of countries (France, Germany, Italy, Belgium and the Netherlands) that have been members of the EU (previously European Community) from the start. Therefore, trade linkages between these countries may be more intense than on average in the sample and a fiscal impulse originating in a core country may have a smaller effect on its economy, as a larger part of the shock leaks away. However, the stimulating effects of a spending increase or a net tax reduction on output hardly differ from those for the entire sample and we only report the impulse responses in Appendix C.3.

3.4.3. Miscellaneous robustness checks.   A potential problem with the baseline estimates could be that, because business cycles are on average positively correlated in Europe, countries tend to simultaneously expand (or contract) fiscal policy. When fiscal expansions have positive cross-border effects, we would then overestimate the effect of a domestic fiscal expansion on the national economy. However, inspecting the correlations of the estimated series of the structural shocks, we see that the average bilateral correlations of the government spending, net tax and output shocks are -0.070, -0.071 and -0.075, respectively (with standard deviations 0.20, 0.19 and 0.25, respectively). As these correlations are all negative and close to zero, the potential upward bias in the effect of fiscal expansions seems to be absent. Further inspection shows that our use of fixed time effects has been crucial in reducing the cross-country

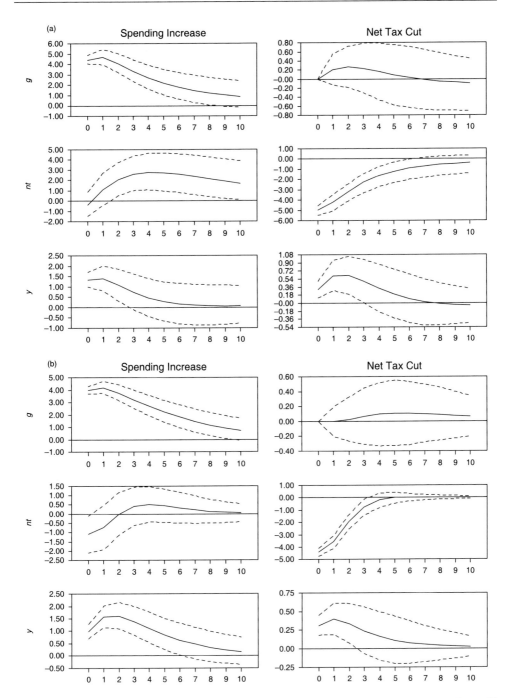

Figure 4. Impulse responses for (a) group of large countries; (b) group of small countries

Notes: The group of large countries consists of Germany, France, UK, Italy and Spain. The remaining countries in the sample together form the group of small countries. Further, see Notes to Figure 1.

correlations of the estimated structural shocks, indicating that these dummies absorb the common movements of fiscal and output variables across countries.

As a further robustness check, we have estimated Equation (1) in first differences, which leads to basically the same outcomes as under the baseline. In another variant, we replace output (GDP) in the panel VAR with (the log of) real private output, that is, GDP minus government expenditures. The objective is to see if a spending impulse causes significant multiplier effects on output. We realize that this approach is not entirely accurate, because we subtract from output also the component of government spending that falls on foreign products. However, this component is generally small, so that our measure of private output should be close to the conceptually correct one. We report the estimates in column 3 of Table 1 and the impulse responses in Appendix C.4. Not surprisingly, the response of private output to a spending increase is weaker than the response of total output, though it still becomes significant after one period. Hence, this indicates the presence of multiplier effects.[12]

The impulse response analysis conducted so far implicitly assumed that the composition of government spending is irrelevant. Figures 5a and 5b check whether this assumption is warranted. We return to the baseline specification, but replace total government spending with one of its components, government consumption (Figure 5a) or government investment (Figure 5b). For comparability, in each case, we depict the responses to a shock equal to one percent of GDP. With average government investment of roughly 3% of GDP, this implies a rise in investment close to 35%. While the output stimulus from the investment shock is slightly larger and more persistent than the stimulus produced by the government consumption shock, the differences are modest and from a statistical point of view the baseline model, which treats government consumption and investment symmetrically, is acceptable.

4. THE TRADE BLOCK

In this section, we estimate a baseline dynamic panel trade model and a number of extensions. We also estimate the baseline model for sub-samples. Increases in domestic income and a domestic real exchange rate appreciation lead to a significant boost in foreign bilateral exports. The stimulus is rather short-lived, especially after an income shock.

4.1. Model set-up and baseline estimates

The second step in our procedure is to estimate the trade block. We are interested in the effect of domestic output on foreign exports to the home country. These exports are also affected by the exchange rate, for which we want to control. A popular model

---

[12] Focusing on the US, Fatás and Mihov (2001) and Galí and Perotti (2003) find that private consumption goes up in response to a rise in public spending. This is consistent with our result that a positive spending shock raises private output, as the latter largely consists of private consumption.

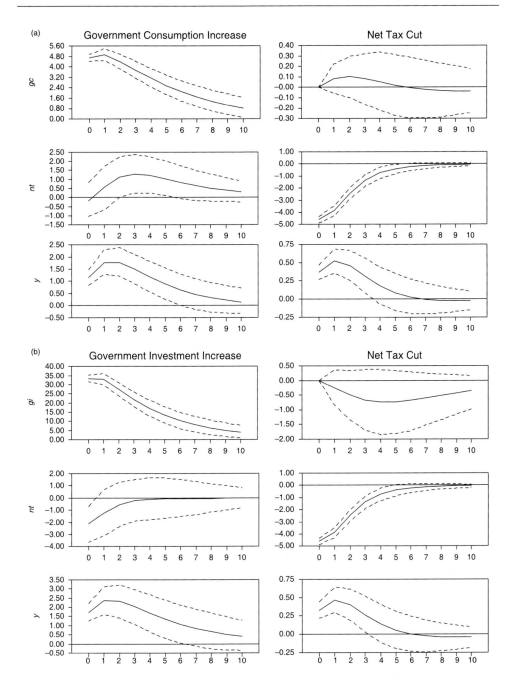

Figure 5. Decomposition of government spending: Impulse responses for fiscal block (a) with government consumption; (b) with government investment

Notes: See Notes to Figure 1. In addition to the definitions already included in the main text, we have *gc* = government consumption and *gi* = government investment.

that includes both income and the exchange rate as export determinants is the gravity model of trade – see Bergstrand (1989) for a description and theoretical motivation. Our model is closely related to that model. Nevertheless, to simplify the model, we leave out some typical gravity variables, such as the exporter's income and income per capita, because they turn out to be unimportant here – see Section 4.3.

Because we are ultimately interested in the short- and medium-run effects of fiscal impulses on foreign exports, we have to extend the standard gravity model by allowing for dynamics in the form of lagged responses of exports to income, the exchange rate and past exports. Therefore, we use the following autoregressive distributed lag (ADL) specification with $n = 2$ lags:

$$x_{ji,t} = \sum_{s=1}^{n} \beta_{1s} x_{ji,t-s} + \sum_{s=0}^{n} \beta_{2s} y_{i,t-s} + \sum_{s=0}^{n} \beta_{3s} rer_{ji,t-s} + \varepsilon_{ji,t}, \tag{2}$$

where $x_{ji,t}$ is (the log of) bilateral real exports at time t from country j (the foreign country) to i (the home country), $y_{i,t-s}$ is (the log of) real output in the home country, and $rer_{ji,t-s}$ is the (log of the) bilateral real exchange rate between country j and country i. It is defined such that, if $rer_{ji,t-s}$ rises, then the currency of country j (the exporting country) depreciates in real terms against the currency of country i. The model also contains – though not shown in Equation (2) – fixed effects for country-pair ji, which capture the impact of all time-invariant determinants of trade (such as distance, a common border, a common language, etc., as in the gravity model). Further, we include fixed time effects to control for, among other things, the general state of the European economy in a specific year, and country-pair specific linear time trends representing potentially omitted country-pair variation in trending determinants of exports (such as transportation costs and trade liberalization),[13] as motivated in Bun and Klaassen (2007) – see also below. Following standard practice in the trade literature (see, for example, Rose, 2000, and Glick and Rose, 2002), we add the dummies $EU_{ji,t}$ and $FTA_{ji,t}$. The former dummy scores one if at time t both j and i are members of the EU (or the European Community, before the ratification of the Maastricht Treaty), and zero otherwise. Similarly, $FTA_{ji,t}$ is a dummy equal to one if there is a free trade agreement between j and i at time t. For both dummies only contemporaneous values are included, because their lags turn out to be irrelevant. Finally, $\varepsilon_{ji,t}$ is a zero-mean random variable that may be heteroskedastic (over time and country pairs), but is assumed to be uncorrelated over time and country pairs.

We estimate the model by OLS (see Panopoulou and Pittis, 2004, for theoretical and empirical support). Again, the data set covers the period 1965–2004. It accounts for all bilateral trade relationships between the 14 EU countries used in the fiscal block, providing us with 182 country pairs (see Appendix A for further details).

---

[13] Barrell and Dées (2005) show that the growth of foreign direct investments may also be a potentially important determinant of the trend in imports (hence, exports).

Table 2, column 1, presents the estimates for the parameters of interest in Equation (2). Bilateral exports are highly correlated with bilateral exports one year earlier. A real depreciation of the exporting country's currency (i.e. a rise in $rer_{ji,t}$) has a strong positive effect on bilateral exports from j to i; the long-run effect (i.e. sum of the

Table 2. Estimates of the bilateral export panel model

	1	2	3	4	5	6
	Baseline	Adding spending shocks	Adding foreign output	EU5 (five largest countries)	EU9 (nine smallest countries)	EU5-core
$x_{ji,t-1}$	0.610***	0.598***	0.566***	0.729***	0.584***	0.746***
	(0.033)	(0.035)	(0.035)	(0.067)	(0.052)	(0.046)
$x_{ji,t-2}$	0.065**	0.070**	0.102***	−0.0052	0.065	−0.0011
	(0.030)	(0.032)	(0.033)	(0.055)	(0.047)	(0.040)
$rer_{ji,t}$	0.502***	0.510***	0.486***	0.359***	0.600***	0.435***
	(0.036)	(0.038)	(0.035)	(0.054)	(0.081)	(0.056)
$rer_{ji,t-1}$	−0.187**	−0.174***	−0.134***	−0.127	−0.404***	−0.195**
	(0.052)	(0.053)	(0.050)	(0.081)	(0.107)	(0.077)
$rer_{ji,t-2}$	−0.087**	−0.099***	−0.153***	−0.083	0.059	−0.130**
	(0.036)	(0.037)	(0.035)	(0.054)	(0.078)	(0.054)
$y_{i,t}$	1.747***	1.687***	1.723***	1.980***	1.644***	1.419***
	(0.137)	(0.146)	(0.131)	(0.269)	(0.252)	(0.172)
$y_{i,t-1}$	−1.300***	−1.167***	−1.191***	−1.876***	−1.221***	−1.815***
	(0.219)	(0.233)	(0.206)	(0.414)	(0.416)	(0.243)
$y_{i,t-2}$	−0.077	−0.155	−0.219*	0.147	0.107	0.589***
	(0.142)	(0.154)	(0.132)	(0.256)	(0.283)	(0.160)
e^g_{it}		0.089				
		(0.095)				
$e^g_{i,t-1}$		−0.113				
		(0.099)				
$e^g_{i,t-2}$		0.102				
		(0.086)				
$y_{j,t}$			0.097			
			(0.142)			
$y_{j,t-1}$			−0.171			
			(0.220)			
$y_{j,t-2}$			0.064			
			(0.131)			
EU	0.064***	0.063***	0.063***	0.108***	0.060***	
	(0.0082)	(0.0087)	(0.0084)	(0.023)	(0.019)	
FTA	0.064***	0.069***	0.051***	0.0042	0.071***	
	(0.011)	(0.011)	(0.011)	(0.021)	(0.023)	
Panel size	182	182	182	20	72	20
Observations	6409	6045	6012	760	2424	724

Notes: The table shows the estimates of the coefficients (and their respective standard errors in parentheses) in alternative specifications of Equation (2). *, ** and *** indicate statistical significance at the 10%, 5% and 1% level, respectively. Each model is estimated with time fixed effects, country-pair fixed effects and country-pair time trends. Observe that column 6 does not present estimates of the EU and FTA dummies. These are not identified, because the EU5-core are all EU (or European Community) members and had free trade among themselves over the whole sample period.

Source: Authors' calculations.

contemporaneous and all lagged effects) is 0.704 with a standard error of 0.070 (not reported in the table).[14] Similarly, an increase in real GDP of country i, the importing country, exerts a strong positive effect (the long-run effect is 1.133 with standard error 0.149). Finally, in the long run, membership of a free trade area leads to 20% (standard error 3.5%) more trade and membership of the EU stimulates trade also by an additional 20% (standard error 2.3%). Obviously, these effects are substantial.

To see how the long-run effects materialize over time, we plot the impulse responses of bilateral exports from the foreign to the domestic country to one-time shocks in bilateral exports, the real exchange rate and domestic output (see Figure 6). The size of the shock is a 1% increase in the variable under consideration. As expected, the effect of an increase in domestic output on bilateral exports is positive and statistically highly significant on impact. A 1% real depreciation of the foreign currency leads to a statistically significant 0.5% increase in foreign exports on impact. However, these effects die out quickly. The effect of the real exchange rate impulse has disappeared after two years, while the effect of the output shock vanishes already

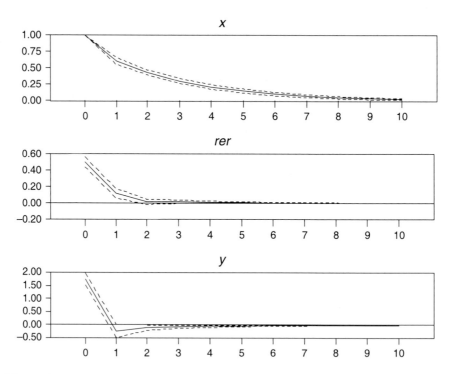

Figure 6. Impulse responses of bilateral foreign exports (baseline model of trade block)

Notes: This figure shows the impulse responses of bilateral exports from the foreign country to the domestic country, after, respectively, a positive shock (of size 1) to exports (x), a depreciation of the foreign real exchange rate (rer) and a shock to domestic GDP (y). Further, see Notes to Figure 1.

---

[14] This long-run effect is computed as $(\beta_{30} + \beta_{31} + \beta_{32})/(1 - \beta_{11} - \beta_{12})$.

after one year.[15] Note that the accumulation of the impulse responses over time gives the long-run estimates presented above.

4.2. Relation of the baseline with the literature

We can compare our baseline estimates for the trade block with the literature. Barrell and te Velde (2002) provide a recent survey of (long-run) income and price elasticities for European countries. Typically, the income elasticity is clearly positive and lies between one and two. Regarding the exchange rate effect on trade (the price elasticity), one usually reports significant estimates with values between zero and one. Our results are thus in line with what the literature finds. However, we should note that in contrast to the literature, we include country-pair specific time trends. In particular, if we leave these out, the long-run income elasticity rises, although it remains well within the range from one to two.

As the inclusion of country-pair specific time trends is not standard for gravity-type models such as Equation (2), we shall now clarify their relevance in more detail. Suppose that we estimate model (2) without country-pair trends and also leave out any dynamics (i.e., $n = 0$ in (2)). Further, let us divide all country pairs into two groups, namely those that have the euro now and the other pairs. The left graph of panel A1 in Figure 7 shows that the averaged residual series for each of the two groups (the solid line for the 110 Euro-country pairs and the dotted line for the 72 remaining pairs) exhibits strongly diverging trends, thereby invalidating standard inference.[16]

If we add the dynamics to the model, while still excluding the country-pair trends, we obtain the left graph of panel A2, which no longer exhibits trends. In fact, this is entirely due to the presence of lagged dependent variables.[17] However, the underlying estimates for lagged exports are substantially and significantly higher than in our benchmark model with country-pair trends: 0.746 and 0.145 instead of 0.610 and 0.065, respectively. As the latter model generalizes the former, the estimated coefficients of lagged exports are distorted if there is no correction for potential omitted trending trade determinants. Proper inference thus requires adjusting the model.[18]

There are two possible approaches in this regard. First, one could try to find regressors that fully explain the omitted determinants of exports. Although above we

---

[15] Notice that, although the estimated coefficient of one-year lagged domestic output is significantly negative, the impulse response to the shock is close to zero after one year. The reason is that the impulse response captures the total effect of the one-year output lag on current foreign exports. Hence, it captures also the positive effect via lagged foreign exports.

[16] The residuals capture a deviation from a general time trend. For each year, aggregated over all country-pairs they sum to zero, implying that whenever the solid line has a positive slope, the other line has a negative (and steeper, due to the difference in group size) slope.

[17] Leaving these out, while including lagged income and real exchange rate terms, results in a graph similar to panel A1.

[18] The residual trends may also be partly due to neglected country-pair heterogeneity of the parameters in specification (2). A model with fully heterogeneous regression parameters but no country-pair trends indeed shows no trends in the residuals. However, such a model does not correct for potential omitted trending trade determinants, so it would still be unclear to what extent the estimates would be biased. Hence, we prefer solving the trends problem first, and address the heterogeneity issue later on as another robustness check.

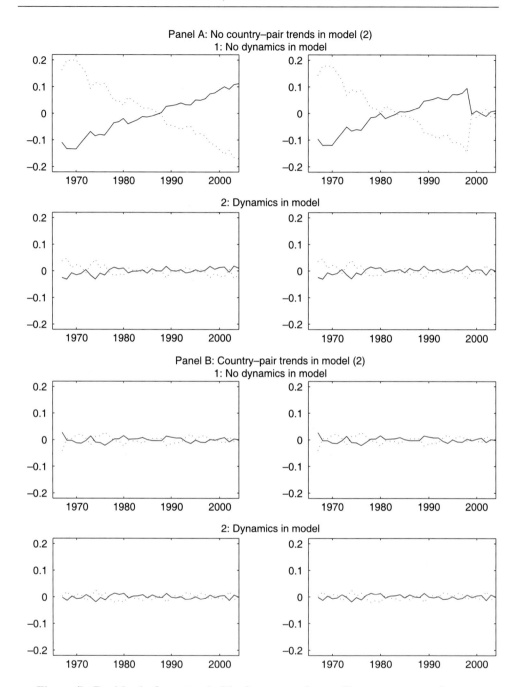

Figure 7. Residuals from trade block averaged over Euro country pairs versus other pairs

Notes: For each year, the solid line gives the average of the residuals over the 110 euro-country pairs (i.e., the pairs of countries that are now part of the Euro-area), while the dotted line is the average residual over all remaining country-pairs. The left figures are based on Equation (2), that is, without a euro dummy. The right figures include a Euro dummy as regressor.

discussed some potential determinants, it is difficult, if not impossible, to find the complete set of determinants. Second, as an approximate solution one can include deterministic trends to correct for the main signal of the omitted trending variables. As the left graph of panel B1 in Figure 7 shows, the problem of residual trends disappears for the static variant. In the dynamic variant, which is our baseline model (2), the lagged export coefficients then more cleanly represent the true export dynamics. Thus improved inference motivates our use of country-pair trends.

4.3. Robustness analysis

4.3.1. More explanatory variables. Column 2 in Table 2 reports the estimates when we add as explanatory variables in the panel trade model the domestic discretionary government spending shocks that we identified from the fiscal block. It is conceivable that the government buys part of a spending increase directly from abroad, in which case the discretionary government spending shock should enter with a positive coefficient in the trade equation. However, the estimates show that the discretionary spending impulse exerts no direct effect on bilateral exports from the foreign country. This is not surprising, because generally by far most of government spending falls on domestic goods and services. Incidentally, we note that the government spending shock is a generated regressor in the trade model. Hence, if correctly computed, the standard errors would exceed those reported in Table 2, which would reinforce our finding that the government spending shock has no significant direct effect on foreign exports.

We have estimated a number of additional variations on the baseline, motivated by trade model specifications elsewhere in the literature. First, we add the log of real GDP of the exporting country j. While this variable includes the bilateral export that is on the left-hand side of the regression equation, on average this bilateral export makes up only a small fraction of total exporter's income. Hence, any potential endogenous regressor problem is likely to be unimportant. Column 3 of Table 2 shows the estimates. We conclude that there is no indication that foreign output matters for foreign exports, which motivates us to retain our baseline specification. Second, we have also estimated specifications in which we added to the baseline the log of real GDP *per capita* of country i or country j (to control for the effect of the welfare level) or a measure of bilateral real exchange rate volatility. The estimates are not reported here, but none of these variables came out significantly. This result differs somewhat from what is usually found in the empirical trade literature. The reason is that we use a dynamic instead of a static model. Indeed, if we follow the usual procedure of estimating static models and not adjusting the standard errors for serial correlation in the residuals, then all the variables just mentioned become statistically significant. Because we find clear evidence of dynamics (see Table 2), again we prefer to stick to our baseline specification.

4.3.2. Euro area membership. We also explore a variation on the baseline in which we add a dummy for joint membership of the Euro area. This extension is motivated by the work of Rose and co-authors. They find evidence that, *ceteris paribus*, countries trade substantially more with each other when they share a common currency.[19] Although this conclusion is based on datasets in which the country-pairs forming a currency union tend to be very different from the Euro-area pairs in our data (the former pairs mostly involve smaller and poorer countries, while many of them are former colonies of industrialized countries), Micco *et al.* (2003) confirm the trade-enhancing impact of currency unions for the Euro-zone. Our estimates, however, show that the Euro dummy is insignificant and close to zero. As Bun and Klaassen (2007) explain, this is due to the fact that, in contrast to existing papers, we include country-pair specific time trends to control for omitted trending variables.

To show this more explicitly, recall the top left graph in Figure 7 based on the estimation of (2) in the absence of country-pair specific trends and dynamics. This resembles the specification typically used in the currency union trade literature. The diverging trends between the two groups of country pairs lead to a large difference in the residuals at the end of the sample period. If we then add the Euro dummy and plot the new average residual series, we obtain the top right panel. It shows that the Euro dummy, as it equals unity only towards the end of the sample, simply explains the difference in the residuals towards the end of the sample. Not surprisingly, the Euro effect estimated using this standard specification is 30% (on the log of exports), and this is thus driven by the diverging trends that started long before the Euro came into existence – see Bun and Klaassen (2007) for further analysis. As we have seen earlier, adding dynamics (but leaving out country-pair trends) removes the trends in the average residual series. However, it still leaves a distorted (long-run) Euro effect of 31% (standard error 2%), while our more general approach with heterogeneous trends included yields an estimate of 0% (standard error 3%). Hence, such trends are important for inference on the Euro effect.

Nevertheless, one should realize that our insignificant estimate of the Euro effect does not necessarily contradict the work by Rose and others. For instance, the trade-magnifying effect of the formation of a currency union may take time to materialize. The Euro has existed for only 5 years and that may be insufficient for finding strong trade increments. However, our result motivates us not to include a Euro dummy in our baseline model. In addition, interactions of joint Euro membership with year dummies, to allow for time-varying effects of the Euro, and interactions with the other variables in the regression were mostly insignificant. In particular, in one extension of the baseline model, we included additional interaction terms of domestic income

---

[19] See Rose (2000, 2001), Rose and van Wincoop (2001), Frankel and Rose (2002) and Glick and Rose (2002). A positive effect of monetary unification on trade is also found by Barro and Tenreyro (2004) who use an instrumental variables approach to control for the effect that trade intensity itself might have on the choice of forming a currency union. However, Persson (2001) argues that the characteristics of country-pairs in a union may systematically differ from the entire sample of country pairs. Moreover, he points to the relevance of potential non-linearities. He indeed finds much smaller, though still substantial, effects of a currency union on trade. However, the effects he estimates are statistically insignificant or only weakly significant.

(and its lags) with the Euro dummy. None of these terms came out significantly, while the long-run effect of the interaction of domestic income with the dummy was also insignificant. In the remainder, we shall thus also leave out interaction terms with the Euro dummy.

4.3.3. Potential heterogeneity.
As we also did for the fiscal block, we explore whether the results differ over sub-samples of countries or time. Again, this helps us to assess the homogeneity assumption. As before, we split the sample into the five large (EU5) and nine small (EU9) countries. The parameter estimates reported in columns 4 and 5 of Table 2 are reasonably similar, though there are some small differences. Column 6 of the table reports the corresponding estimates when the sample is limited to the EU5-core (Germany, Italy, France, Belgium and the Netherlands). Again, the differences with the baseline are limited. Given our focus on the income elasticity, we retain the baseline model. This is also confirmed by the impulse responses (not reported here).

How do the parameter estimates vary over time? We repeat the baseline regression, where we now allow the coefficients on lagged trade flows, home country income, the real exchange rate and EU membership to depend on the specific sub-period, 1965–84 or 1985–2004. (Because in the second sub-period all country pairs had free trade, the parameter for the FTA dummy over the second period is not identified, so we do not make that dummy time varying.) Table 3 shows the results. While the sign and significance are the same for all parameters for both sub-periods, the size of the impact effect of income is larger for the first sub-period: 2.13 versus 1.43. Not surprisingly, the impact effect of the baseline model, 1.75, is in between these numbers. Given the standard errors of the three estimates, and the fact that the long-run effects are very close for the two sub-periods (1.10 in both cases), we stick to the baseline model as a reasonable compromise. Nevertheless, because the income elasticity is important for our overall estimate of the effect of fiscal policy on foreign exports, we will further examine the consequence of the short-run sub-sample sensitivity of the income elasticity on this overall estimate in Section 5.1.

5. THE EFFECTS OF A FISCAL IMPULSE ON FOREIGN EXPORTS AND INCOME

We shall now combine the impulse responses from the fiscal block with the estimates of the trade block to calculate the effects of domestic fiscal impulses on foreign bilateral exports. We combine the baseline estimates as well as some alternative specifications of the two blocks. The foreign export responses are generally persistent and statistically and economically significant. We also combine individual country estimates of the two blocks. This also suggests an overall tendency towards spill-overs. Given the inaccuracy of the individual fiscal block estimates, there is no indication of strong heterogeneity. As a final step, we compute how domestic fiscal impulses affect

Table 3. Bilateral export panel model, with period-dependent coefficients

	Sub-period	
	1965–84	1985–2004
$x_{ji,t-1}$	0.593***	0.620***
	(0.048)	(0.037)
$x_{ji,t-2}$	0.073*	0.048
	(0.044)	(0.037)
$rer_{ji,t}$	0.559***	0.472***
	(0.053)	(0.040)
$rer_{ji,t-1}$	−0.258***	−0.117**
	(0.081)	(0.057)
$rer_{ji,t-2}$	−0.061	−0.112***
	(0.054)	(0.039)
$y_{i,t}$	2.127***	1.428***
	(0.216)	(0.141)
$y_{i,t-1}$	−1.553***	−0.937***
	(0.327)	(0.224)
$y_{i,t-2}$	−0.204	−0.124
	(0.236)	(0.141)
EU	0.111***	0.049***
	(0.013)	(0.0081)
FTA	0.044***	
	(0.012)	
Panel size	182	
Observations	6409	

Notes: The table shows the estimates of the coefficients (and their respective standard errors in parentheses) in alternative specifications of Equation (2). *, ** and *** indicate statistical significance at the 10%, 5% and 1% level, respectively. Each model is estimated with time fixed effects, country-pair fixed effects and country-pair time trends. These are held constant over the two sub-periods. We thus conduct a single estimation for the full sample period, interacting some of the coefficients with specific sub-periods.

Source: Authors' calculations.

foreign output. The effects vary substantially over country pairs, but are quantitatively important in a number of cases.

5.1. The overall effect on foreign exports

By combining the estimates for the trade block with those for the fiscal block, we can compute the overall effect of a domestic fiscal impulse on foreign bilateral exports to the domestic country. In principle, the effect can operate both through output and through the real exchange rate. In our baseline, we set the effect via this second channel to zero. The reason is that we want to assess the spill-overs of a fiscal impulse under the current regime of a monetary union in Europe. With a common currency and sticky prices, we can expect only limited short-run movements in real exchange rates.

Appendix B.2 shows that to obtain the impulse responses of foreign bilateral exports to a fiscal shock, we can simply multiply the impulse response function estimated for the fiscal block with the estimated distributed lag on home output for the

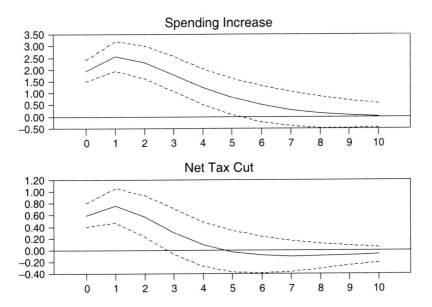

Figure 8. Impulse response of bilateral foreign exports to a domestic fiscal shock after combining the fiscal and trade blocks

Notes: In each case the size of the fiscal shock equals 1% of GDP. The estimates and the 90% confidence bands are based on Monte Carlo simulations, where we multiply 1000 draws for the impulse-response function from the fiscal model by 1000 draws for the distributed-lag function from the trade model.

trade block. Figure 8 shows the impulse responses obtained by combining the baseline estimates of the fiscal and the trade block. The effect of a domestic spending shock is significantly positive for several years and reaches its maximum after one year. A net-tax cut also produces a significant increase in net exports. However, the effect is smaller and shorter-lived than that of an equal-size spending increase.

Table 4 reports the corresponding cumulative effects on foreign exports of the domestic fiscal shock. A relevant question concerns the appropriate horizon for assessing the effects of the shock. As we explained earlier, we are primarily interested in the short- and medium-run consequences of fiscal impulses. Therefore, Table 4 reports the impact effects and cumulative responses after two and after five years. For a 1% of GDP spending increase, which amounts to an increase in public spending of slightly over 4%, the cumulative export effect after two years is a statistically significant gain of 6.8% of annual exports. For an equal-size net tax reduction, the (significant) gain in exports amounts to 1.9%.

A complication in assessing the gains from a fiscal impulse is that, after the shock, fiscal policy continues to deviate from its original value for some time (recall Figure 1). It can be reasonably argued that these subsequent deviations should be added to the initial spending shock in order to obtain the total budgetary cost of the cumulative export gain. Table 4 also reports the 'normalized' response, which divides the cumulative gain in exports by the cumulative deviation of government spending from its original level. Over a two-year horizon there is an export gain of 2.2% of annual

Table 4. Responses of foreign exports to domestic fiscal shocks – cumulative and normalized

Case		Cumulative			Normalized		
		Impact effect	After 2 years	After 5 years	Impact effect	After 2 years	After 5 years
Panel A: Spending increase (1% of GDP)							
Baseline	*Point estimate*	1.94	6.82	10.66	1.94	2.21	2.07
	Lower (5%)	1.49	5.20	7.26	1.49	1.64	1.35
	Upper (95%)	2.42	8.47	14.38	2.42	2.76	2.83
Extended VAR – *rer* channel shut	Point estimate	2.16	7.41	11.67	2.16	2.36	2.17
Extended VAR – *rer* channel open	Point estimate	2.00	7.07	11.76	2.00	2.25	2.19
1985–2004	Point estimate	1.54	5.96	10.31	1.55	1.84	1.83
Large EU-5	Point estimate	2.65	6.08	6.58	2.66	2.06	1.39
Small EU-9	Point estimate	1.63	6.26	11.10	1.63	2.09	2.22
EU5-core	Point estimate	1.97	3.65	4.60	1.98	1.23	0.98
Panel B: Net tax cut (1% of GDP)							
Baseline	*Point estimate*	0.59	1.92	2.30	0.59	0.81	0.79
	Lower (5%)	0.40	1.18	0.61	0.40	0.49	0.21
	Upper (95%)	0.80	2.73	4.14	0.80	1.16	1.42
Extended VAR – *rer* channel shut	Point estimate	0.47	1.47	1.61	0.47	0.63	0.57
Extended VAR – *rer* channel open	Point estimate	0.31	0.72	0.36	0.31	0.31	0.13
1985–2004	Point estimate	0.33	1.52	2.18	0.33	0.59	0.68
Large EU-5	Point estimate	0.59	2.56	3.29	0.59	1.04	0.95
Small EU-9	Point estimate	0.51	1.55	2.30	0.51	0.70	0.95
EU5-core	Point estimate	0.42	1.46	1.86	0.42	0.65	0.61

Notes: Numbers are in percentage of annual exports. They are based on 1000 Monte Carlo simulations. 'Point estimate' is the mean value of the simulations, 'Lower' and 'Upper' are respectively the 5th and the 95th percentiles. The fiscal shock that takes place at time 0 equals 1% of GDP. The 'cumulative' effect is the sum of the percentage deviations of exports from their original value. Specifically, after t years, it is given as $100 * \Sigma_{\tau=0}^{t} (X_\tau - \bar{X})/\bar{X}$, where $\bar{X}$ is the original value of the exports. The 'normalized' effect takes into account that the fiscal variable, after the initial shock, continues to deviate from its original value. Specifically, taking the case of a spending increase as an example, the normalized effect after t years is given by $[\Sigma_{\tau=0}^{t}(X_t - \bar{X})/\bar{X}]/[\Sigma_{\tau=0}^{t}(\bar{G}_\tau - \bar{G})/\bar{Y}]$, where $\bar{G}$ and $\bar{Y}$ are the original values of government spending and GDP. Hence, this number can be interpreted as the average over the period 0 to t of additional exports per percentage of output increase in public spending. For the computation we use average spending and net tax ratios of GDP over the whole sample. 'Baseline' combines the baselines of the panel VAR and the panel trade model. The other cases are variants described in the text.

Source: Authors' calculations.

exports for each 1% of GDP additional spending. The corresponding figure for a net tax reduction is 0.8%. Both figures are statistically significant.

To examine the robustness of these estimates, we also compute the responses of foreign exports to domestic fiscal shocks for some major variants of the baseline model. In particular, we consider the combination of (1) the extended panel VAR with the baseline trade model when we shut off the effect on trade via movements in the real exchange rate, (2) the extended panel VAR with the baseline trade model when we also include the effect on trade via changes in the real exchange rate (for details, see Appendix B.2), (3) the panel VAR and the trade model both for the most relevant sub-period, 1985–2004, (4) the panel VAR and the trade model each for the group of the five largest EU countries, (5) the panel VAR and the trade model each for the group of the nine smallest EU countries and (6) the panel VAR and the trade model each for the EU-5 core (Germany, France, Italy, Belgium and the Netherlands). The numbers are again found in Table 4. In most instances the responses remain reasonably close to those for the baseline combination, while in a few instances the responses are outside the confidence band for the baseline combination. In virtually all cases we consider, the effect of the fiscal shock on trade is significant and quite sizeable, with the effects for government spending being larger than for the net tax cut. The exception is case (2) when the fiscal shock is a net tax reduction. As Figure 2 already showed, a net tax reduction leads to a real exchange rate depreciation for the initiating country, which exerts a negative effect on exports to this country. Indeed, the trade spill-over now loses its significance after one year.

While the above variations on the baseline already address to some extent the potential importance of cross-country heterogeneity, we explore the issue further by estimating both the fiscal and the trade block for each country separately and combining the results into a country-specific impulse response of foreign exports to the country implementing the fiscal shock (i.e., a country-specific version of Figure 8). The estimation of each individual trade block is based on observations of bilateral trade between the country and each of its 13 partners over the sample period. Figure 9 depicts the median of the responses of foreign exports to the individual countries initiating the fiscal shock, as well as the boundaries on the ten individual responses closest to the median. The figure confirms a tendency towards a fiscal spill-over in the first periods after the shock. Indeed, with one exception, whenever the effect of the fiscal expansion is significant (in, respectively, 4 and 8 cases for government spending and net tax shocks), it is positive. The figure also suggests non-negligible differences in the individual responses. However, in this connection, it is important to realize that there is substantial inaccuracy in the estimates of the individual countries' fiscal block (see Appendix C.5), likely leading to an exaggeration of the heterogeneity suggested by Figure 9. To support this argument, Figure 10 shows the median over the individual impulse responses obtained by combining the fiscal and trade block estimates on the individual countries, as well as the medians of the upper- and lower-bounds of the 90% confidence intervals around the individual impulse responses. Clearly, 'on average' the width of the individual confidence band is substantial, thus motivating the use of panel data in order to enhance accuracy.[20]

---

[20] The summary responses of output to fiscal shocks reported in Appendix C show that it is the inaccuracy of the individual fiscal block estimates that causes the confidence bands to be so wide.

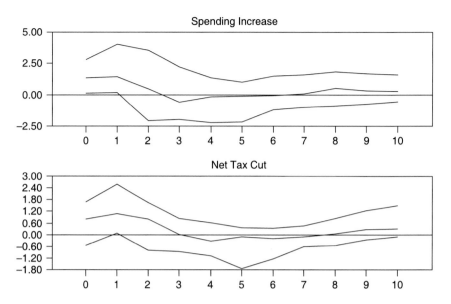

Figure 9. Impulse response of bilateral foreign exports to a domestic fiscal shock after combining the fiscal and trade blocks estimated for individual countries – boundaries of ten responses closest to median

Notes: In each case the size of the fiscal shock equals 1% of GDP. The figure is based on the combined responses for each individual country and takes the 10 responses closest to the median (the middle line, which is the average of the 7th and 8th response). The bottom line thus corresponds to the 3rd response, while the top line corresponds to the 12th response.

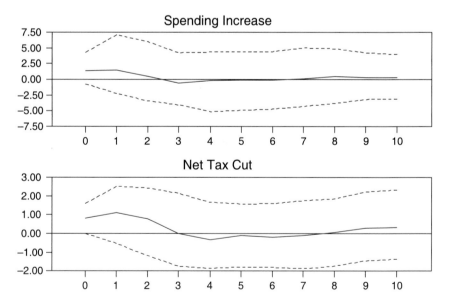

Figure 10. Impulse response of bilateral foreign exports to a domestic fiscal shock after combining the fiscal and trade blocks estimated for individual countries – medians of confidence intervals and central line

Notes: In each case the size of the fiscal shock equals 1% of GDP. The figure is based on the responses for each individual country and shows the median over the lower- and upper-bounds of the 90% confidence intervals for the 14 countries, as well as the median over the individual mean responses.

5.2. The effect of a domestic fiscal impulse on foreign output

By combining the cumulative and normalized responses of the bilateral foreign exports with the actual shares of bilateral foreign exports in foreign output, we can calculate the effects of domestic spending and net tax shocks on foreign output. We calculate only the *direct* contemporaneous contributions of higher exports to output and ignore contemporaneous multiplier effects of exports on foreign economic activity, future effects of current activity increases and further feedback effects among the economies. The numbers are only intended to give a rough sense of what could be the possible order of magnitude and, therefore, the economic significance of the fiscal spill-overs. Computation of the total effects on foreign output is complicated and beyond the scope of the present paper.

Obviously, there is a large variation in the size of the spill-over effects, depending on the country of origin of the fiscal shock and on the intensity of trade between the partner and origin country. Table 5 reports the normalized responses of EU countries' output to a spending increase or a net tax reduction in the two largest economies in the Euro area (Germany and France). The computation of these responses is analogous to those for the net exports responses in Table 4. A German fiscal expansion (especially a spending shock) has quite strong effects on its small neighbours. An increase in public spending (a decrease in net taxes) by 1% of GDP in Germany leads to a more than 0.4% (0.13%) normalized increase in GDP of Austria, Belgium-Luxemburg and the Netherlands after two years. In accordance with the gravity model, the effects on these countries are larger than the effects on other small countries that are further away and do not share a common border with Germany. For example, the corresponding number for Greece is only a 0.06% increase in GDP. Based on a GDP-weighted average across all partner countries, the normalized effect of a German fiscal stimulus is 0.15% (0.05%) of foreign GDP. Naturally, the spill-over effects of a French fiscal impulse are smaller (on average, roughly half of the size of the spill-overs from the German shock), but they are still non-negligible. Of course, fiscal shocks originating in the smaller economies tend to lead to smaller spill-over effects. The smallest effect is found for a fiscal stimulus in Greece, which raises normalized weighted-average foreign GDP after two years by only 0.01% in the case of a spending increase and 0.005% in the case of a net tax reduction.

The reported effect of a domestic fiscal impulse in Germany on foreign output seems rather large compared to what the limited empirical literature, in particular Marcellino (2002), finds. His model includes German and foreign (French, Italian or Spanish) variables in one VAR. A German output shock has a significant positive effect on partner countries, an effect that is consistent with our finding for the panel trade model. However, a German fiscal shock has no contemporaneous effect on German output (in contrast to what we find) and only small and insignificant effects on the other economies. A major difference with our work is that we have more observations because we use a panel VAR approach for our fiscal block, while Marcellino

Table 5. 'Normalized' foreign output multipliers of fiscal shocks in Germany and France

	Germany			France		
	Impact effect	After 2 years	After 5 years	Impact effect	After 2 years	After 5 years
Panel A: Spending increase (1% of GDP)						
Austria	0.353	0.401	0.377	0.038	0.043	0.040
Belgium-Lux	0.394	0.448	0.420	0.265	0.301	0.283
Denmark	0.196	0.223	0.209	0.041	0.047	0.044
Finland	0.113	0.129	0.121	0.027	0.031	0.029
France	0.094	0.107	0.100	–	–	–
Germany	–	–	–	0.067	0.076	0.072
Greece	0.050	0.057	0.054	0.013	0.015	0.014
Ireland	0.191	0.217	0.204	0.108	0.123	0.116
Italy	0.085	0.096	0.090	0.058	0.065	0.061
Netherlands	0.374	0.425	0.399	0.118	0.135	0.126
Portugal	0.126	0.144	0.135	0.081	0.092	0.086
Spain	0.081	0.092	0.087	0.100	0.114	0.107
Sweden	0.103	0.118	0.110	0.039	0.044	0.041
UK	0.063	0.072	0.067	0.044	0.050	0.047
W-Average	0.128	0.145	0.137	0.071	0.081	0.076
Panel B: Net tax cut (1% of GDP)						
Austria	0.100	0.137	0.133	0.013	0.018	0.017
Belgium-Lux	0.112	0.153	0.149	0.090	0.123	0.120
Denmark	0.056	0.076	0.074	0.014	0.019	0.018
Finland	0.032	0.044	0.043	0.009	0.013	0.012
France	0.027	0.037	0.036	–	–	–
Germany	–	–	–	0.023	0.031	0.030
Greece	0.014	0.020	0.019	0.005	0.006	0.006
Ireland	0.054	0.074	0.072	0.037	0.050	0.049
Italy	0.024	0.033	0.032	0.019	0.027	0.026
Netherlands	0.106	0.146	0.141	0.040	0.055	0.053
Portugal	0.036	0.049	0.048	0.027	0.037	0.036
Spain	0.023	0.032	0.031	0.034	0.046	0.045
Sweden	0.029	0.040	0.039	0.013	0.018	0.017
UK	0.018	0.025	0.024	0.015	0.020	0.020
W-Average	0.036	0.050	0.048	0.024	0.033	0.032

Notes: Numbers are in percentage of annual GDP. Panel A (Panel B) shows the normalized multipliers of foreign output as a result of an initial government spending increase (net tax cut) equal to 1% of GDP. In our computations we use the 2003 bilateral exports over GDP ratio for each country and the 2004 cyclically adjusted net tax and government spending over GDP ratios for each country. These are the latest-available ratios. Further 'W-Average' stands for 'weighted average', with weights based on GDP. For details on the computations, see Notes to Table 4.

Source: Authors' calculations.

estimates a VAR only for Germany. Moreover, owing to some specification differences and the fact that Marcellino's set-up does not distinguish spill-overs via trade from other spill-overs, a detailed direct comparison between his and our results is not possible.

6. POLICY EXPERIMENTS AND COUNTERFACTUALS

In this section, we illustrate some policy consequences of our results so far. First, we explore the domestic and foreign effects of a budget squeeze in Germany and France. Then, we investigate how an erroneous neglect of the fiscal trade spill-overs affects the fiscal instrument settings as well as output. We stress that the experiments are only intended to illustrate the consequences of our estimation results and the type and methodology of the policy experiments that one can conduct. The numerical outcomes of these stylized experiments should thus not be taken too literally.

6.1. A 'Portugal-style' budget squeeze

The deficit of Portugal, as reported by Eurostat (2006), was 2.8% of GDP in 2002, down from 4.2% in 2001. An interesting question is what would have been the economic consequences had Germany, say, brought its deficit back from its actual level of 3.8% to 2.8% in 2002. To 'simulate' such a budget squeeze, we compute the size of the discretionary fiscal shocks (public spending or cyclically adjusted net taxes) needed to produce a contemporaneous deficit reduction of 1% of GDP. We can then also compute the implications for domestic and foreign GDP and the foreign public deficit of such a budget squeeze.

In the case of a government spending reduction, the computation is complicated by the fact that both output and cyclically adjusted net taxes respond within the same period and, moreover, that we need to transform the change in cyclically adjusted net taxes into a change in actual net taxes. Appendix B.3 shows the details of the computation. While a 1% reduction of GDP in government spending is equivalent to a reduction of 4.2% in the variable itself, to produce an improvement in the deficit of 1% of GDP, government spending has to be contracted by 6.8%. The difference is mainly accounted for by the large fall in output by 1.8% and the substantial effect on the cyclical component of net taxes. The same deficit reduction is attained with an increase in cyclically adjusted net taxes by 5.5% and results in an output fall of 0.40%. Obviously, on the basis of our estimates, Germany would have had to implement substantial budgetary contractions with serious short-run output consequences for the deficit to stay below the limit set by the SGP.

For France, the consequences would be even larger. According to Eurostat (2006), the French deficit peaked at 4.2% of GDP in 2003. A 'Portugal-style' budget squeeze to bring down the French deficit to 2.8% of GDP would have required a spending contraction of 9.5% and led to an output fall of 2.5%, or, alternatively, it would have required a 7.7% net tax increase which, in turn, would have caused output to fall by 0.56%.

A deficit reduction in Germany also affects EU partners via the trade spill-over. In fact, the government spending shock needed to produce a 1% reduction in the German deficit to GDP ratio equals 6.8/4.2 = 1.62 times the shock on which the numbers in Table 5 are based and thus leads to a contemporaneous average fall in partners' GDP by 0.21%. For the net tax increase the corresponding number is a 0.043% fall in GDP.

Finally, with these numbers we can calculate the effects of the German fiscal contraction on partners' public finances. We do this by feeding the change in partners' GDP as an output shock into the approximation expression for the deficit change in Appendix B.3. On average, a German deficit reduction of 1% of GDP attained with a spending contraction raises partners' current deficit/GDP ratio by 0.10%, while the corresponding number for a net tax increase is 0.021%. Hence, forcing Germany (or another country) to remain within the deficit limit set by the SGP may make it more difficult in the short run for its partners to obey the SGP limits. Of course, one expects that tighter short-run enforcement of the Pact on all countries is beneficial for the longer-run credibility of the Pact.

6.2. The consequences of ignoring trade spill-overs

This subsection shows how the estimates of the two blocks can be used to assess the consequences of mistakenly ignoring the spill-overs from fiscal policy via trade. We emphasize that this experiment can at most give an impression of the potential order of magnitude of the effects of these policy failures.

To simplify the illustration, suppose that Europe only consists of France and Germany. We consider two scenarios, one where both countries want to stimulate output (for instance, in response to a common adverse shock) and the other where one country wants to raise output and the other country wants to reduce output (for example, as a result of an asymmetric shock). Under both scenarios, we compare the setting of the policy instruments (government spending and cyclically adjusted net taxes) and the realized output effects when governments take the spill-overs into account and when they ignore the spill-overs. However, irrespective of the behaviour of the governments, spill-overs are always assumed to exist.

If the governments use government spending (e_i^g) to affect their economies, then the (percentage) increase in output of country i ($i = F$(rance) or G(ermany)) is given by:

$$dy_i = (\alpha_{tg}\alpha_{yt} + \alpha_{yg})e_i^g + (X_{ij}/Y_i)\beta_{20}dy_j, \tag{3}$$

where the first term on the right-hand side is the policy effect (its coefficient follows from inverting the structural VAR in Equation (1)) and the last term is the spill-over from abroad, where X_{ij} is exports in levels from country i to country j and Y_i is GDP of country i. We are only interested in contemporaneous effects. As in the earlier computations, we only account for the direct effect of exports on output, implying that the latter rises one-for-one with an increase in exports. An expression similar to (3) holds also for cyclically adjusted net taxes as the instrument. In our computations below, we take for the α parameters the estimates in the first column of Table 1 and use β_{20} from column 1 in Table 2. For exports and GDP we take the 2003 figures. Hence, the only unknowns are the two output changes and the two instrument settings.

In scenario 1, France and Germany want to stimulate their economies by 1%. If they are aware of spill-overs and of each other's objective and instrument setting, the governments choose their fiscal policy stances such that each one of them reaches the goal. Taking spending as instrument, each government i chooses $e_i^g = (1 - (X_{ij}/Y_i)\beta_{20})/(\alpha_{tg}\alpha_{yt}+\alpha_{yg})$, which is 3.51% (3.53%) for France (Germany) and, obviously, $dy_i = 1\%$ (see Table 6) – details on the computations are found in Appendix B.4. If both governments ignore spill-overs, they erroneously ignore the final term in (3), so that $e_i^g = 1/(\alpha_{tg}\alpha_{yt} + \alpha_{yg}) = 3.79\%$ and the resulting output change is 1.08% (1.07%) for France (Germany). Therefore, ignoring spill-overs leads to excessive government spending and overshooting of the GDP target. However, the deviation from the goal is not large. Likewise, if governments use cyclically adjusted net taxes as their instruments, incorporating spill-overs in policy leads to a net tax cut of 12.87% (12.93%) in France (Germany) and both countries meet the 1% output stimulus. Ignoring the spill-over, however, leads to a larger tax cut (namely, 13.89% for both countries) and output is stimulated by too much.

The overall result is that in case of a symmetric stimulus, once governments are aware of trade spill-overs, the perceived need for expansionary fiscal policy is smaller and the output target is perceived to be achieved more easily. This suggests that in case of a European-wide recession, governments find it easier to fulfil the SGP. In addition, note that we have assumed throughout that spill-overs exist. If they did not exist, then a more expansionary fiscal policy would be needed to reach the 1% target. Hence, from this perspective, the mere existence of trade spill-overs makes the SGP less binding.

In scenario 2, France (Germany) wants to stimulate (contract) its economy by 1%. If the policymakers are aware of the spill-overs, then France increases spending by

Table 6. Instrument settings when accounting for or neglecting spill-overs

Instr./ Spill.	Scenario I				Scenario II			
	e_F^g	e_G^g	dy_F	dy_G	e_F^g	e_G^g	dy_F	dy_G
G/yes	3.51	3.53	1.00	1.00	4.07	−4.05	1.00	1.00
G/no	3.79	3.79	1.08	1.07	3.79	−3.79	0.93	−0.94
NT^{CA}/yes	−12.87	−12.93	1.00	1.00	−14.91	14.84	1.00	1.00
NT^{CA}/no	−13.89	−13.89	1.08	1.07	−13.89	13.89	0.93	−0.94

Notes: 'Instr.' stands for 'instrument' and 'Spill.' stands for 'spill-over'. When 'Spill.' is 'no', then this means that the spill-over is ignored, while when it is 'yes', the spill-over is taken into account. 'Scenario I' refers to both France and Germany implementing a fiscal expansion aimed at expanding national GDP by 1%. In 'Scenario II' France aims at expanding GDP by 1%, whereas Germany aims at contracting GDP by 1%.

Source: Authors' calculations.

4.07%, whereas Germany reduces it by 4.05%, with both countries meeting their target (see Table 6). However, if the spill-overs are ignored, France (Germany) increases (reduces) public spending by 3.79%. Therefore, France expands too little as it ignores the negative spill-over from the Germany contraction, whereas the German fiscal contraction is too small to hit the output target. For cyclically adjusted net taxes Table 6 reports similar results. Hence, if the French expansion was to offset a negative shock and the German contraction was to offset a positive shock, erroneously neglecting spill-overs leads to insufficient smoothing of the business cycle.

7. CONCLUSION

In this paper, we have explored the empirical relevance of trade spillovers from discretionary fiscal policy shocks in the EU. Our estimates indicate that these spill-overs may be economically important, although their size varies quite substantially with the distance between trading partners and the size of the country where a policy shock originates. The presence of such spill-overs may have a number of consequences for policymakers. First, stronger spill-overs imply that a larger share of a national fiscal stimulus leaks away, thus reducing its effectiveness. Second, they make clear that policies of individual countries are a matter of common concern, thereby underlining the need for informal and formal meetings of policymakers in the Euro-group and ECOFIN. Yet, given the variation in the size of the spill-overs, policymakers will differ in the importance they attach to reaching a consensus on a broad European policy stance. More accurate information on the distribution of the costs and benefits of fiscal impulses also promotes a better understanding among countries of each other's policy preferences. Finally, exploiting the estimates of the separate steps that lead to the spill-over effect (that is, the fiscal and trade blocks), one can assess some of the consequences of a tight enforcement of the SGP, both for the domestic economy and the trading partners.

Our baseline estimates suggest that, measured over a two-year horizon, a German fiscal expansion equal to 1% of GDP implies a gain of 2.2% of annual bilateral exports by EU trading partners for a public spending shock and 0.8% for a net tax shock. Averaged across EU partners, the corresponding direct output gain of a fiscal stimulus in Germany is 0.15% in case of a spending increase and 0.05% for a net tax cut. Of course, the spill-overs on output are (substantially) smaller when the fiscal shock originates in another country. The purpose of this first attempt at quantification is to provide an indication of the potential economic significance of the spill-overs via trade. An all-inclusive calculation of such spill-overs on foreign output would have to take into account many other effects, such as contemporaneous multiplier effects of exports, lagged effects on future foreign output, feedback effects between economies and, even beyond the scope of the current model, issues such as possible shifts in the activity of multinationals to the country that initiates the fiscal expansion. This might be especially relevant in the case of well-targeted tax reductions.

We have done a large number of robustness checks on our estimates for the fiscal block, the trade block and the combination of the responses. The checks involved a variety of extended specifications (including extensions of the fiscal block with measures of the interest rate) as well as estimations on sub-samples and individual countries to obtain some indication of the importance of heterogeneity. Our baseline estimates of the two blocks and their combination have generally proved to be quite robust.

We have explored the consequences of ignoring the spill-overs of discretionary fiscal policies. Suppose that a domestic fiscal expansion leads to a rise in foreign output via trade. Then, neglecting this spill-over, countries have a tendency to conduct too expansive (contractive) fiscal policies if their aim is too raise (reduce) output in response to a common negative (positive) shock to the demand side of the economy. As a result, the output targets are not reached and fiscal policy becomes less stable. With asymmetric shocks, ignoring spill-overs leads to insufficient use of the fiscal instruments when the objective is to smooth the business cycle. If, in contrast to what we conjectured in the Introduction, other spill-overs (for example, via the interest rate) dominate the trade spill-over in such a way that the total fiscal spill-over on output becomes negative, then the consequences of neglecting this total spill-over go in exactly the opposite direction. For example, fiscal policies will be insufficiently expansive if they aim at stabilizing output after a common negative demand shock. Of course, if a government wants to take appropriate account of the fiscal spill-overs, it needs to be informed about the other governments' policy intentions. This is one reason why regular formal and informal meetings of the European Finance ministers are useful.

While the paper detects potentially important fiscal spill-overs via trade, its analysis is subject to a substantial number of limitations. The scope for exploring how the model parameters and spill-overs have changed in response to all major institutional changes during the sample period (for example, reductions in trade barriers and changes in the scope and size of the public sector) was only limited. We were also limited in our investigation of the cross-country homogeneity restrictions in our panels. In future work, both issues might be addressed with a more sophisticated model of the sources of time and cross-sectional variation of the parameters and using data on variables that are at the source of this heterogeneity.

Obviously, there are also limitations regarding the conclusions that we can draw from our work. In particular, the scope of the analysis is too limited to take a stand on the potential desirability of more formal fiscal coordination.[21] The magnitude of the spill-overs is still too uncertain while other potentially relevant transmission channels have, on purpose, not been taken into account here. Indeed, as empirical analysis in Darvas *et al.* (2005) suggests, discretionary fiscal policy, possibly resulting in less fiscal discipline, may actually be a source of divergence in business cycles.

[21] The issue is studied, for example, in a report of the German Federal Ministry of Finance (2002), which advises negatively on such co-ordination. In contrast, Jacquet and Pisani-Ferry (2001) argue strongly in favour of enhanced fiscal coordination in Europe.

As the preceding discussion suggests, there are many directions for further extension of analysis. One extension would be to come to a more complete assessment of the overall spill-overs of fiscal policy, not only quantifying the trade channel, but also other channels (for example, via the foreign interest rate – see Faini, 2006), and comparing the sizes of these channels.

Discussion

Volker Wieland

J.W. Goethe Universität Frankfurt am Main and Center for Financial Studies

Empirical analysis of fiscal policy spill-overs in Europe

Beetsma, Giuliodori and Klaassen (BGK in the following) investigate an interesting empirical question that is clearly relevant for European macroeconomic policy. In fact, contributors to the political debate on the virtues and drawbacks of fiscal policy coordination in the Euro area may easily be tempted to draw unwarranted conclusions from the authors' empirical analysis. I will provide support for my concerns in this regard further below by comparing BGK's findings based on panel vector auto-regression (PVAR) analysis of fiscal shocks and reduced-form trade equations with alternative policy scenarios studied in a structural model of the G7 economies. Before turning to this comparison, however, I will shortly comment on the empirical approach chosen by the authors.

I find the two-block approach pursued by the authors innovative, useful and very competently executed. Modelling the fiscal block as a PVAR (see equation (1) in the article) they are able to identify quantitatively significant Keynesian-style effects of fiscal shocks using annual data of government spending, cyclically adjusted net taxes and total output for 14 EU countries from 1965 to 2004. Their findings suggest that an unanticipated increase in government spending of 1% of GDP would lead to an increase in total aggregate demand by about 1.5% of GDP within the first two years. The authors relate their analysis to other VAR-based studies of fiscal shocks and conduct extensive robustness exercises that provide further corroboration of their findings.

The trade-block (equation (2) in the article) provides a reduced-form link between domestic output and demand for exports from other EU countries. The country-pair equations also take into account the effect of the bilateral exchange rate. They are estimated via OLS with data from the same 14 EU countries from 1965 to 2004. The authors find that an increase in real GDP of the importing country exerts a strong positive effect on demand for the foreign country's exports. A real depreciation of the exporting country's currency also has a strong positive effect on exports.

Combining the fiscal and trade blocks, the authors estimate partial-equilibrium effects of domestic fiscal shocks on foreign output. For example, Panel A in Table 5 of the article indicates that a government spending increase in Germany by 1% of GDP would raise output in other EU countries between 0.057% (in Greece) and 0.448% (in Belgium) within two years via the foreign-export channel. Thus, the authors conclude that fiscal spillovers via trade in the EU are quantitatively important and will influence the ability of individual countries to meet the requirements of the Maastricht Treaty. They conduct policy experiments suggesting, for example, that the upcoming fiscal contraction in Germany (due to an increase in VAT) will make it more difficult for other countries to meet the Maastricht deficit criteria due to negative trade spill-overs.

A criticism: systematic changes in macroeconomic policy such as the introduction of the Euro will modify the spill-over effects of fiscal shocks

In my view, the empirical effects identified by BGK provide a good summary of the 'normal' effects of fiscal shocks over most of the sample period, 1965–2004. However, I would question their validity as predictions of the size (and possibly even the direction) of spill-overs in today's Euro area. My scepticism derives from the following changes in the systematic conduct of macroeconomic policy in the Euro area since 1999:

(i)   the change from fixed-but-adjustable exchange rates to permanently fixed exchange rates due to the introduction of the common currency;

(ii) the change from national monetary policies to a single European monetary policy aiming to stabilize European-wide macroeconomic aggregates, and

(iii) the Maastricht fiscal criteria.

As suggested by the original Lucas critique, changing the systematic component of macroeconomic policy will affect expectations formation and thus also the coefficients of the fiscal and trade block estimated by the authors. For example, changing systematic exchange rate and interest rate policy will modify the effect of unanticipated fiscal shocks as well as the trade-weighted impact of exchange rates on aggregate output.

To illustrate the consequences of fixing exchange rates in Europe and delegating monetary policy to a single European Central Bank for the spill-over effects of fiscal shocks, I will refer to simulation results derived from a structural model of the G7 economies developed by John B. Taylor and described in detail in Taylor (1993) as well as alternative policy scenarios for the European countries (Germany, France, Italy and the UK) studied by Wieland (1996) using that same model. First, I will compare the effect of fiscal impulses under historical monetary conditions as quantified by Taylor (1993) with the findings presented in the article under discussion. Then, I will draw on the results in Wieland (1996) to illustrate how the spill-over effect of a fiscal shock in Germany would change if European exchange rates are fixed and interest-rate-setting aims to stabilize European-wide aggregates.

Comparing fiscal spill-overs in Taylor (1993) and the article under discussion

The multi-country model used in Taylor (1993) is a precursor of the New-Keynesian micro-founded models of the macro-economy developed in recent years. The model was estimated using quarterly data from 1971 to 1986. While not explicitly derived from microeconomic foundations, Taylor's model embodies many implications of optimizing behaviour by households and firms in its behavioural equations and explicitly accounts for forward-looking behaviour by assuming rational expectations. Monetary policy has short-run real effects arising from staggered wage contracts just as in the more recent New-Keynesian models. Recent studies of interest rate rules by Levin, Wieland and Williams (1999, 2003) confirm that Taylor's model provides recommendations for the design of such rules that are much closer to those derived from micro-founded New-Keynesian models with rational expectations than to those from more traditional Keynesian-style macroeconomic models with backward-looking expectations formation.

In chapter 5 (pages 178 to 181, Figures 5.11A to 5.11H), Taylor reports on the effect of an unanticipated and permanent fiscal expansion in Germany by 1% of GDP. Monetary policies in all G7 countries are assumed to follow their historical paths while nominal exchanges are flexible. As a result of this fiscal shock German GDP rises by 0.8% within one year. Furthermore, the German price level rises, the DM appreciates vis-à-vis the US$ and German short-term interest rates rise on impact. The effect on German imports is positive and peaks at 1.2%. Figure 5.11G summarizes the effect of the German fiscal shock on output abroad. The effect is positive within the first two years and peaks at 0.15% for France, 0.25% for Italy and 0.3% for the UK.

In Table 7 I compare the spill-over effects simulated by Taylor (1993) to the effects identified by BGK. In both cases, spill-overs are positive and of roughly similar

Table 7. Spill-over effects of German government spending: BGK vs Taylor's model

German expansion	Effect on France		Effect on Italy		Effect on UK	
	Impact	2 Years	Impact	2 Years	Impact	2 Years
BGK: unanticipated spending shock of 1% of GDP (with high endogenous persistence)	0.094%	0.107%	0.085%	0.096%	0.063%	0.072%
Taylor (1993): unanticipated permanent spending increase of 1% of GDP	0.1%	0.12%	0.18%	0.22%	0.17%	0.25%

Source: Taylor (1993) and the article by BGK under discussion.

magnitude. The effects are somewhat larger in Taylor's model, perhaps due to the fact that he considers an unanticipated but permanent increase in German government spending while the effect of the spending shock considered by BGK eventually dies out again. Overall, I would take BGK's empirical findings as a surprisingly close confirmation of the spill-overs computed in Taylor (1993) but requiring far fewer structural identification assumptions. From BGK's perspective I would consider the results in Taylor's monograph as a welcome confirmation of the validity of the direction and magnitude of 'normal' spill-over effects over the earlier part of the sample.

Fiscal spill-overs may change in magnitude and direction with a common currency and single monetary policy

I now turn to the spill-over effects of a German fiscal expansion of 1% of GDP presented in Wieland (1996) using Taylor's model. In this paper I considered the following regime changes:

(1) Exchange rates between the European countries (i.e. Germany, France, Italy and the UK) are permanently fixed.

(2) Nominal interest rates in all G7 countries are set according to Taylor-style monetary policy rules of the following form:

(1) $RS - RS^* = (LP(t + 4) - LP) + k(LP - LP^*) + k(LY - LY^*)$

Here LP denotes the natural logarithm of the price level and LY the natural logarithm of real output. * refers to target and long-run equilibrium values. This rule implies that the short-term nominal interest rate RS responds to changes in expected inflation as well as deviations of the price level and real output from target and equilibrium values with a response coefficient k.

(3) Interest rates in the European countries follow the same path and respond to European-wide averages LP^{EUR} and LY^{EUR}.

These regime changes capture important consequences of European monetary union in 1999 except that the UK did not join this union.

Table 8 reports the spill-over effects in France, Italy and the UK following an unanticipated, permanent increase in German government spending of 1% of GDP, i.e. the same policy shocked considered by Taylor (1993) under historical monetary conditions and flexible exchange rates. Following the increase in government spending, German overall GDP rises by 1.22% in the course of 2 years. Similarly the German price level increases above target. Germany has a large weight in European averages and as a result European interest rates increase by about 60 basis points. At the same time the European currency appreciates substantially vis-à-vis non-European currencies such as the US$ and the Yen (2.5 percentage points vis-à-vis the US$). Due to higher interest rates and exchange rate appreciation the GDP in the other European countries

Table 8. Spill-over effects of German government spending in a monetary union

German expansion	Effect on France	Effect on Italy	Effect on UK
	2 Years	2 Years	2 Years
Wieland (1996): unanticipated permanent spending increase of 1% of GDP. Fixed exchange rates and Taylor-style interest rate rule for Europe in Taylor's 1993 model	−0.47%	−1.03%	−0.17%

Source: Wieland (1996).

declines. Thus, not only the magnitude but also the direction of the spill-over effect changes compared to the earlier historical policy regime.

Conclusions for providing policy advice

Given the important regime changes towards the end of BGK's sample period that are the result of European Monetary Union, I would question whether the fiscal spill-over effects identified as typical during the sample period will remain the same in the future. The simulation of Taylor's multi-country model in Wieland (1996) suggests that a German fiscal shock in the Euro area would lead to increased interest rates for all member economies as well as a real appreciation of the Euro vis-à-vis countries outside the monetary union. As a result real output may well decline. This would be the case if the positive trade effect identified by BGK – although still present – were to be completely offset by the interest rate and exchange rate effects. These potential effects are not well covered by BGK's empirical analysis. The interest rate effect due to ECB policy would only be present in the last five years of their sample and may be underestimated. The exchange rate effect vis-à-vis the US, Japan and other non-European countries is neglected by their empirical analysis based on European country pairs.

Consequently, I would recommend against the use of BGK's estimates of fiscal spill-overs to evaluate the effect of the impending tax increase in Germany on aggregate output in France, Italy or other member economies of the Euro area. First, the direction and magnitude of these spillover effects would need to be corroborated by analysis based on current multi-country models of the Euro area which can account for the general-equilibrium effects of regime change. Such models are being developed at central banks and other institutions. For a review of new structural models used at policy institutions, I would refer the reader to the recent conference of the International Research Forum on Monetary Policy (consisting of the Federal Reserve Board, the European Central Bank, the Georgetown Center for German and European Studies and the Center for Financial Studies) and the IMF in December 2005 at the Federal Reserve Board. (For a list of papers see the conference website at www.cfs-frankfurt.eu.)

Panel discussion

Wendy Carlin pointed out that the relevant theoretical interactions are clearly those of textbook models, and attention should be paid to issues of price flexibility as well as of exchange rate flexibility. Giancarlo Corsetti remarked that the notion of a 'spill-over' needs to be defined carefully: if it is meant to refer to unintended consequences, there are no spillovers when policy reaction functions take into account other policymakers' instruments. Reinhilde Veugelers also wondered about the exact meaning and practical relevance of spill-overs. These and other panel members thought that it would be important to assess spill-overs in terms of a welfare metric more precise than output. Lans Bovenburg noted that the welfare relevance of output fluctuations depends crucially on whether there is unemployment, so it would be important to control for the business cycle, and that issues of debt sustainability should also play a role. Hans-Werner Sinn agreed in principle but remarked that, in practice, short-term Keynesian effects are a relatively unimportant factor in the assessment of fiscal policy.

WEB APPENDIX

Available at http://www.economic-policy.org

REFERENCES

Alesina, A., S. Ardagna, R. Perotti and F. Schiantarelli (2002). 'Fiscal policy, profits, and investment', *American Economic Review*, 92, 571–89.

Ardagna, S., F. Caselli and T. Lane (2004). 'Fiscal discipline and the cost of public debt service', ECB Working Paper Series, No. 411, November.

Barrell, R. and D.W. te Velde (2002). 'European integration and manufactures import demand: an empirical investigation of ten European countries', *German Economic Review*, 3, 263–93.

Barrell, R. and S. Dées (2005). 'World trade and global integration in production processes: a re-assessment of import demand equations', ECB Working Paper, No. 503, July.

Barro, R.J. and S. Tenreyro (2004). 'Economic effects of currency unions', Mimeo, Harvard University/London School of Economics.

Baxter, M. and R.G. King (1993). 'Fiscal policy in general equilibrium', *American Economic Review*, 83, 315–34.

Bergstrand, J.H. (1989). 'The generalized gravity equation, monopolistic competition, and the factor-proportions theory in international trade', *Review of Economics and Statistics*, 71, 143–53.

Blanchard, O.J. and R. Perotti (2002). 'An empirical characterization of the dynamic effects of changes in government spending and taxes on output', *Quarterly Journal of Economics*, 117(4), 1329–68.

Bun, M.J.G. and F.J.G.M. Klaassen (2007). 'The euro effect on trade is not as large as commonly thought', *Oxford Bulletin of Economics and Statistics*, forthcoming.

Canova, F. and E. Pappa (2003). 'Price dispersions in monetary unions: the role of fiscal shocks', CEPR Discussion Paper, No. 3746.

Canzoneri, M.B., R.E. Cumby and B. Diba (2003). 'New views on the transatlantic transmission of fiscal policy and macroeconomic policy coordination', in M. Buti (ed.), *Monetary and Fiscal Policies in EMU: Interactions and Coordination*, Cambridge University Press, Cambridge.

Claeys, P. (2004). 'Monetary and Budgetary Policy Interaction: An SVAR Analysis of Stabilization Policies in Monetary Union', Working Paper, ECO No. 2004/22, European University Institute, Florence.

— (2006). 'Fiscal and monetary policy interaction: an empirical analysis', PhD thesis, European University Institute, Florence.

Corsetti, G. and G.J. Müller (2006). 'Twin deficits: squaring theory, evidence, and common sense,' *Economic Policy*, this volume.

Darvas, A., A.K. Rose and G. Szápary (2005). 'Fiscal divergence and business cycle synchronization: irresponsibility is idiosyncratic', NBER Working Paper, No. 11580.

Eurostat (2006). http://epp.eurostat.cec.eu.int/portal/page?_pageid=1090,1&_dad=portal&_schema=PORTAL.

Faini, R. (2006). 'Fiscal policy and interest rates in Europe', *Economic Policy*, 47, 435–80.

Fatás, A. and I. Mihov (2001). 'The effects of fiscal policy on consumption and employment: theory and evidence', mimeo, INSEAD.

Favero, C.A. (2003). 'How do European monetary and fiscal authorities behave?' in M. Buti (ed.), *Monetary and Fiscal Policies in EMU: Interactions and Coordination*, Cambridge University Press, Cambridge.

Frankel, J. and A. Rose (2002). 'An estimate of the effect of common currencies on trade and income', *Quarterly Journal of Economics*, 117, 437–66.

Galí, J., J.D. López-Salido and J. Vallés. (2003). 'Understanding the effects of government spending on consumption', mimeo, Universitat Pompeu Fabra and Bank of Spain.

Galí, J. and R. Perotti (2003). 'Fiscal policy and monetary integration in Europe', *Economic Policy*, 18, 533–72.

German Federal Ministry of Finance (2002). 'Increased coordination of anti-cyclical fiscal policy in Europe?', Statement by the Advisory Board to the Federal Ministry of Finance, Monthly Report, August.

Giavazzi, F. and M. Pagano (1990). 'Can severe fiscal contractions be expansionary? Tales of two small European countries', in O.J. Blanchard and S. Fischer (eds.), *NBER Macroeconomics Annual*, MIT Press, Cambridge, MA, 75–111.

Giuliodori, M. and R. Beetsma (2005). 'What are the trade spillovers from fiscal shocks in Europe? An empirical analysis', *De Economist*, 153, 167–97.

Glick, R. and A. Rose (2002). 'Does a currency union affect trade? The time series evidence', *European Economic Review*, 46, 1125–51.

Gros, D. and A. Hobza (2001). 'Fiscal Policy Spillovers in the Euro Area. Where Are They?', CEPS Working Document, No. 176, Brussels.

Hemming, R., M. Kell and S. Mahfouz (2002). 'The effectiveness of fiscal policy in stimulating economic activity: a review of the literature', IMF Working Paper, No. 02/208.

IMF (2004). 'The global implications of the U.S. fiscal deficit and of China's growth', *World Economic Outlook*, Chapter II, April.

In't Veld, J. (2004). 'The spillover effects of German budgetary consolidations within EMU: Simulations with the QUEST model', mimeo, European Commission.

Jacquet, P. and J. Pisani-Ferry (2001). 'Economic policy co-ordination in the Eurozone: What has been achieved? What should be done?', mimeo, Centre for European Reform, London.

Kim, S. and N. Roubini (2003). 'Twin deficit or twin divergence: Fiscal policy, current account, and real exchange rate in the US', mimeo, University of Illinois at Urbana-Champaign and New York University.

Lane, P.R. and R. Perotti (1998). 'The trade balance and fiscal policy in the OECD', *European Economic Review*, 42, 887–95.

Levin, A., V. Wieland and J.C. Williams (1999). 'Robustness of simple monetary policy rules under model uncertainty', in J.B. Taylor (ed.), *Monetary Policy Rules*, NBER and Chicago Press.

Levin, A., V. Wieland and J.C. Williams (2003). 'The performance of forecast-based monetary policy rules under model uncertainty', *American Economic Review*, 93(3), 622–45.

Marcellino, M. (2002). 'Some stylized facts on non-systematic fiscal policy in the Euro area', CEPR Discussion Paper, No. 3635.

McCrorie, J.R. and M. Chambers (2003). 'Granger causality and the sampling of economic processes', mimeo, University of Essex.

Micco, A., E. Stein and G. Ordoñez (2003). 'The currency union effect on trade: early evidence from EMU', *Economic Policy*, 37, 315–56.

McKibbin, W.J. (1997). 'Empirical evidence on international economic policy coordination', in M.U. Fratianni, D. Salvatore and J. von Hagen (eds.), *Macroeconomic Policy in Open Economies*, Chapter 6, Greenwood Publishing, Westport, CT, 148–76.

Mountford, A. and H. Uhlig (2002). 'What are the effects of fiscal policy shocks?', CEPR Discussion Paper, No. 3338.

Müller, G.J. (2004). 'Understanding the dynamic effects of government spending on foreign trade', mimeo, European University Institute, Florence.

Muscatelli, A., C. Trecroci and P. Tirelli (2004). 'Monetary and fiscal policy interactions over the cycle: some empirical evidence', in R. Beetsma, C. Favero, A. Missale, V.A. Muscatelli, P. Natale and P. Tirelli (eds.), *Fiscal Policies, Monetary Policies and Labour Markets. Key Aspects of European Macroeconomic Policies after Monetary Unification*. Cambridge University Press, Cambridge.

OECD (2005). *Economic Outlook*, June, Paris.

Panopoulou, E. and N. Pittis (2004). 'A comparison of autoregressive distributed lag and dynamic OLS cointegration estimators in the case of a serially correlated cointegration error', *Econometrics Journal*, 7, 585–617.

Perotti, R. (2005). 'Estimating the effects of fiscal policy in OECD countries', CEPR Discussion Paper, No. 4842.

Persson, T. (2001). 'Currency unions and trade: how large is the treatment effect?', *Economic Policy*, 16, 435–48.

Rose, A.K. (2000). 'One money, one market: the effect of common currencies on trade', *Economic Policy*, 30, 9–45.

—— (2001). 'Currency unions and trade: the effect is large', *Economic Policy*, 16, 449–61.

Rose, A.K. and E. van Wincoop (2001). 'National money as a barrier to international trade: the real case for currency union', *American Economic Review*, Papers and Proceedings, 91(2), 386–90.

Taylor, J.B. (1993). 'Macroeconomic policy in a world economy: from econometric design to practical operation', http://www.stanford.edu/~johntayl/MacroPolicyWorld.htm.

Taylor, J.B. (1993). *Macroeconomic Policy in a World Economy: From Econometric Design to Practical Operation*, W. W. Norton, New York.

Van Aarle, B., H. Garretsen and N. Gobbin (2003). 'Monetary and fiscal policy transmission in the Euro-area: evidence from a structural VAR analysis', *Journal of Economics and Business*, 55, 609–38.

Wieland, V. (1996). 'Monetary policy targets and the stabilization objective: a source of tension in the EMS', *Journal of International Money and Finance*, 15(1), 95–116.

Can budget institutions counteract political indiscipline?

SUMMARY

The budget is an expression of political rather than economic priorities. We confirm this proposition for a group of new and potential members of the European Union, finding that politics dominates. The contemporary practice of democracy can increase budget deficits through not only ideological preferences, but also more fragmented government coalitions and higher voter participation. Long-term structural forces, triggered by societal divisions and representative electoral rules, have more ambiguous implications but also appear to increase budget pressures, as others have also found. However, our most robust, and hopeful, finding is that budget institutions – mechanisms and rules of the budget process – that create checks and balances have significant value in curbing fiscal pressures even when the politics is representative but undisciplined, and when long-term structural forces are unfavourable.

— *Stefania Fabrizio and Ashoka Mody*

Economic Policy October 2006 Printed in Great Britain
© 2006 International Monetary Fund
Journal compilation © CEPR, CES, MSH, 2006.

Can budget institutions counteract political indiscipline?

Stefania Fabrizio and Ashoka Mody

European Department, International Monetary Fund

1. INTRODUCTION

Political economists have reached important, but pessimistic, conclusions about long-term influences on fiscal performance. They find, for example, that constitutional provisions shaping electoral rules play a key role in determining fiscal outcomes, both directly and indirectly through their impact on the form of government (Persson and Tabellini, 2003, 2004). In particular, more representative electoral rules achieve inclusiveness but at the cost of reduced political and fiscal discipline. Aghion *et al.* (2004) find that the electoral rules are themselves the consequence of deeper structures in society. Where societies are divided along ethnic or religious lines, electoral rules are likely to be chosen to accommodate those interests, leading, in turn, to coalitional governments and a competition for fiscal resources. Since societal characteristics evolve slowly, and constitutions are, rightly, not often changed, the political processes

The authors are grateful to Guido Tabellini for discussions that led to this paper, to the *Economic Policy* editors, Giuseppe Bertola and Philippe Martin, and to the paper's discussants, Giancarlo Corsetti and Jonathan Temple. They are also grateful for valuable comments from Mark de Broeck, Xavier Debrun, Mark Hallerberg, Robert Franzese, participants at the Political Economy of International Finance workshop held at Ann Arbor, Michigan in October 2005, and seminar participants at the European Central Bank, the International Monetary Fund, the Magyar Nemzeti Bank, and the Reserve Bank of India. Michael Laver and Ken Benoit generously shared their ideology data. The views expressed in this paper are those of the authors and not necessarily those of the International Monetary Fund, its Executive Board, or its management.

The Managing Editor in charge of this paper was Philippe Martin.

Economic Policy October 2006 pp. 689–739 Printed in Great Britain they set in motion develop strong inertia, and, by implication, so do budgetary outcomes.

In this context, then, does policy have a role? Are policies, merely 'veils' or 'epiphenomena', mapping directly from history and politics with no substantive consequence? Even if they do have an independent bearing on outcomes, do policy measures offer the possibility of changing course despite the strong influence of history and politics? And, if so, for countries seeking to improve their fiscal position, what measures are likely to work?

In parallel, another group of scholars has examined whether budget formation rules influence fiscal performance (Alt and Lowry, 1994; Poterba, 1994; von Hagen and Harden, 1995; Hallerberg and von Hagen, 1999; Alesina et al., 1999; Stein et al., 1999). They conclude that checks and balances in the formulation and implementation of the budget are epiphenomena, but have real effects on budgetary outcomes.

Our contribution is twofold. First, we isolate the role of the budgetary institutional structure, while controlling for a more comprehensive set of economic and political conditioning factors than has been possible in past studies. Thus, Persson and Tabellini (2003, 2004) examine the influence of electoral rules but not of budget institutions; Perotti and Kontopoulos (2002) analyse government fragmentation and ideologies, as well as fiscal institutions, but do not consider electoral rules. Where, in principle, all factors are considered, as in Alesina et al. (1999), the findings are based on a cross-section of about 20 countries.

Second, we focus the empirical analysis on an important context: the new and potential member states of the European Union between 1997 and 2003. In anticipation of their accession to the European Union on 1 May 2004, the new member states made a commitment to budgetary discipline. This ongoing process – culminating in their commitment to adopt the euro – represents an important historical experiment. However, despite the commonality of this commitment, there has been no uniform tendency toward convergence to specific quantitative budgetary benchmarks. Estonia, for example, has managed its public finances well, even running a primary surplus in some years. Poland improved its fiscal position in the late 1990s, running a surplus in 1999 and 2000, but drifted back to deficits thereafter. Hungary's budget balance has generally worsened over the time span covered in this paper. The countries also have different legacies. While the Baltic nations have small governments, Hungary and Poland and, to a lesser extent, the Czech Republic have large governments, with expenditure-to-GDP ratios that lie above the line showing the tendency for governments to increase in size with per capita incomes (Figure 1).

For all of these countries, the challenges ahead are significant, not least because they have adopted proportional electoral rules, which, though varying in degree across countries, increase the likelihood of coalitional governments and, hence, generate pressures on the budget.

The empirical focus on this small set of central and eastern European countries has its limitations, but also has benefits. The concern – and it is an important one –

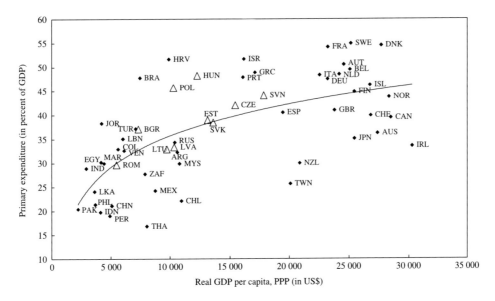

Figure 1. General government expenditure and per capita GDP, 2003

Source: Authors' calculations; fiscal notifications to the European Commission; IMF World Economic Outlook; and Penn World Tables.

is that the data do not contain enough information to draw the kinds of conclusions necessary for policy recommendations or to move this research agenda forward. We are encouraged, however, by the surprising robustness of the principal findings and their consistency with a broad range of studies that have had a narrower focus. The results strengthen the *prima facie* basis for specific institutional or rule-based measures to curb fiscal pressures. The advantage of this sample, making the results of potentially more general interest, is the time-series variation in the quality of fiscal institutions. As part of their reform agenda for transition to market economies, some countries improved their fiscal institutions, though the extent and pace of change varied considerably and at least one experienced significant slippages. Thus, while past studies have relied heavily on the cross-sectional relationship between budget institutions and fiscal performance, this sample allows us to relate their evolution to fiscal performance. At the same time, to guard against the risk of omitted variables, we also evaluate the role of time-invariant country characteristics in transmitting shocks to budgetary outcomes, using an approach developed by Blanchard and Wolfers (2000) and adapted to this context by, among others, Persson (2002, 2004), Persson and Tabellini (2003, 2004) and Milesi-Ferretti *et al.* (2002).

Also of broader methodological interest is the multidimensional characterization of the political determinants of fiscal performance. We find that the influences of these variables are more sharply discernible when they are considered as groups rather than as individual variables. This, we conjecture, reflects the fact that history and politics impact policy formulation through a variety of overlapping channels. While the choice

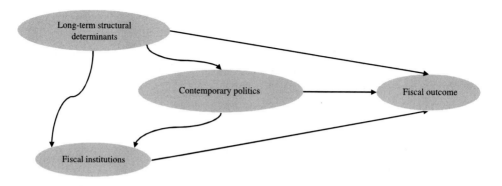

Figure 2. Determinants of fiscal performance

and grouping of variables used in this paper is ad hoc, we are struck, in particular, by the interactions between the degree of coalitional fragmentation and ideology, the latter itself best represented as a vector that included, in our case, the traditional left-right distinction along with the degree of nationalism and the attitude toward fiscal decentralization.

We reach three main conclusions. First, of greatest interest to policymakers, the quality of institutions continues to matter strongly in determining fiscal outcomes, even after including several conditioning variables and testing for a range of possible statistical biases. Second, contemporary politics is important and appears to trump the economic conditioning variables. In particular, more fragmented government coalitions, and those with an ideological disposition toward the 'left', toward a higher degree of nationalism, and toward greater fiscal decentralization, tend to be less fiscally conservative. Greater voter participation – a desirable attribute of a vibrant democracy – appears to loosen the budgetary purse strings, as discussed in Mueller and Stratmann (2003). Third, the 'deeper' the influence of historical and political factors – ethnic fractionalization and the district magnitude (the number of representatives elected per district) – supports the idea that more inclusiveness hurts budgetary outcomes; however, these results are unstable, possibly reflecting theoretical ambiguity in the relationships and, more likely, the absence of time variation in these variables in the small country sample. In sum, then, while contemporary democratic practice and long-standing political and societal characteristics have a significant bearing on fiscal outcomes, the more hopeful message of this paper is that policy initiatives that create checks in the competition for fiscal resources can materially help. These relationships are summarized in Figure 2.

The rest of this paper proceeds as follows. In line with Figure 2, Section 2 reports the conclusions of earlier research on the influence of structural features and contemporary politics on fiscal outcomes, followed by a closer look at the role of fiscal institutions in containing fiscal pressures in representative democracies. Section 3 describes the cross-country and over-time variation in fiscal institutions in our sample countries. The next three sections report the empirical results. Section 4 presents the benchmark findings relating the variations in the economic, political, and budgetary institutions variables to the evolution of the fiscal balance. Section 5 considers the possibility that factors that do not vary over time nevertheless have time-varying effects, because they condition the transmission of shocks to the fiscal balance. And Section 6 examines the influence of these same determinants separately on government revenues and expenditures. A final section concludes.

2. THE DETERMINANTS OF FISCAL PERFORMANCE: A SELECTIVE LITERATURE REVIEW

As Figure 2 depicts, a variety of factors operate – in direct and indirect ways – on budgetary outcomes, with the theory suggesting important non-linearities. To help guide a parsimonious empirical analysis, this section summarizes the theoretical propositions that have found empirical support. We begin with a description of 'structural' variables, those that change little over time and, moreover, condition the practice of the country's politics. Next, however, we note that democratic practice has its own short-term dynamics, with (possibly independent) implications for fiscal decisions. Finally, we discuss whether fiscal institutions are merely a veil or can contain politics in democratic societies.

2.1. Structural determinants

The principal tension arises from the balance a democracy must strike between achieving broad representation while maintaining fiscal accountability. This tension is seen in the context of population diversity and electoral system design. Population diversity creates pressures for greater representation but potentially weakens fiscal discipline (Aghion et al., 2004). The electoral system, by defining the rules of political engagement, influences the formation of parties contesting elections and the eventual fragmentation of ruling coalitions, thereby establishing the balance between representation and accountability.

The feature of electoral systems that has drawn most attention is the proportionality of the electoral rule, though electoral systems do differ in other important ways and, especially, Hallerberg and Marier (2004) caution that the relationships may be non-linear (see Lijphart, 1994 for a classic treatment). In a majoritarian system, voters in a district elect one candidate to the legislature. Increasing proportionality (district magnitude) implies an increasing number of candidates elected per district (in proportion to the votes received) and, hence, increasing voice for an individual voter. Thus, proportional elections foster 'representativeness', while majoritarian elections are thought to encourage 'accountability'.

Consistent with this view, Persson and Tabellini (2003, 2004) find, in a cross-country setting, that majoritarian systems are associated with greater fiscal discipline than are proportional systems. Persson et al. (2005) further conclude that electoral

Table 1. Averages of country characteristics treated as time-invariant

Country	Ethnic fractionalization	Average district magnitude	Voter turnout
Bulgaria	0.40	7.7	66.9
Czech Republic	0.32	25.0	69.4
Estonia	0.51	9.2	61.5
Hungary	0.15	12.2	66.4
Latvia	0.59	20.0	76.2
Lithuania	0.32	35.3	62.1
Poland	0.12	16.7	48.7
Romania	0.31	7.8	70.7
Slovak Republic	0.25	150.0	76.6
Slovenia	0.22	11.0	76.7

Notes: Ethnic fractionalization is computed as one minus the Herfindal index of ethnolinguistic group shares in the population. *District magnitude* is the number of elected representatives per district. *Voter turnout* is the share of voters in the voting age population.

Source: See Appendix B for data sources and definitions of variables.

systems do not have a direct effect on fiscal outcomes; rather, the influence is indirect: greater proportionality induces more parties into the electoral process and into the ruling coalition, with a tendency to higher public expenditures.

This is not good news for the countries we consider. Not one of them has a majoritarian system. The average district magnitude is 29, with a low of 8 in Bulgaria and Romania and a high of 150 in the Slovak Republic (Table 1). Note also that the correlation between ethnic fractionalization and district magnitude is weak in our sample of countries (Table 2), implying that the effects of diversity are not mediated predominantly through electoral systems.

2.2. Contemporary politics

As Persson *et al.* (2005, p. 26) point out: 'there is considerable time variation in the type of government, which cannot be easily explained by sluggish electoral rule variables'. This is true in our context, where electoral rules have not changed during the sample period but the 'within-country' variation in the degree of government fragmentation and government ideologies is significant (Table 3).

In an early contribution, Roubini and Sachs (1989) found a tendency for more fragmented government coalitions to run larger budget deficits, consistent with the proposition that more fragmentation allows greater scope for multiple constituencies to exercise claims on limited fiscal resources without their bearing the full cost of the taxation needed to cover the benefits received (see Box 1). Subsequent cross-country studies have validated this conclusion (Hahm *et al.*, 1996; Alesina *et al.*, 1999). Similarly, across states within the United States, greater political fragmentation has been associated with more intense public spending pressures (see Alt and Lowry, 1994; Poterba, 1994; and Besley and Case, 2003).

Table 2. Political correlations

	Government fragmentation	Government ideology			Fiscal institutions index	Ethnic fractionalization	Distinct magnitude	Voter turnout
		Nationalism	Fiscal centralization	Left/right				
Government fragmentation	1.00							
Government ideology (nationalism)	−0.04	1.00						
Government ideology (centralization)	−0.07	0.23	1.00					
Government ideology (left/right)	−0.37	0.44	0.03	1.00				
Budget institutions index	−0.03	−0.06	0.10	−0.32	1.00			
Ethnic fractionalization	0.01	0.34	0.04	0.53	0.16	1.00		
Electoral rule (average district magnitude)	−0.14	0.22	−0.07	0.13	−0.36	−0.12	1.00	
Voter turnout	−0.28	0.29	−0.09	0.32	−0.34	0.29	0.30	1.00

Source: Authors' calculations.

Table 3. Descriptive statistics

Variable		Mean	Std. dev.	Min	Max
Unemployment rate	Overall	11.29	4.23	4.30	20.00
	Between		4.06	6.16	18.11
	Within		1.98	6.05	15.65
Inflation	Overall	9.17	11.12	−1.20	59.10
	Between		10.20	1.22	37.15
	Within		5.75	−12.68	31.12
Openness index	Overall	0.90	0.25	0.46	1.36
	Between		0.25	0.51	1.24
	Within		0.09	0.70	1.10
Fiscal institutions index	Overall	2.12	0.45	1.37	2.72
	Between		0.45	1.46	2.63
	Within		0.13	1.37	2.47
Government fragmentation	Overall	0.63	0.20	0.27	1.00
	Between		0.14	0.42	0.81
	Within		0.15	0.29	0.96
Left/right	Overall	11.11	3.53	5.81	17.35
	Between		2.84	6.41	16.40
	Within		2.32	5.55	15.95
Nationalism	Overall	11.44	3.48	6.80	17.57
	Between		2.80	7.11	16.28
	Within		2.37	6.15	15.28
Fiscal centralization	Overall	10.46	2.00	7.09	13.46
	Between		1.28	8.41	12.92
	Within		1.63	7.30	13.62
Ethnic fractionalization	Overall	0.31	0.14	0.12	0.59
	Between		0.15	0.12	0.59
District magnitude (logarithms)	Overall	2.83	0.81	2.00	5.00
	Between		0.90	2.00	5.00
Voter turnover	Overall	67.00	8.39	48.70	76.70
	Between		8.67	48.70	76.70
Lagged debt-to-GDP	Overall	33.99	23.34	5.80	107.50
	Between		23.75	6.69	82.90
	Within		5.63	12.80	58.60

Source: Authors' calculations.

More so than with coalitions, ideological predispositions do not follow in any simple manner from structural conditions. Though several authors test the effect of the traditional left-right distinction, the results have been ambiguous. This is not surprising. As Cukierman and Tomassi (1998) argue, just as it took 'a Nixon to go to China', leftist governments may be more credible in persuading their constituents of the urgency and value of budgetary conservatism. Also, ideology need not be unidimensional. For example, there is no necessary relationship between the traditional left-right distinction and the degree to which governments favour fiscal decentralization or promote nationalism. Table 2 reports correlations along these ideological dimensions.

Finally, Mueller and Stratmann (2003) find that higher voter participation in elections has been associated with larger governments and slower growth. Greater

---

Box 1. Fragmentation and fiscal discipline

As with non-renewable resources, the budget is subject to a common-pool problem (Shepsle and Weingast, 1981 and Weingast *et al.*, 1981). When many can claim access to a valuable resource for which they pay only a part of the cost, the pressure will be to over-consume that resource. In the context of a budget, a tendency will arise for public spending in favour of interest groups who bear only a fraction of the taxes needed to finance the expenditures that benefit them. The larger the number of interest groups, the greater the spending that will be induced. In a dynamic model, Velasco (1999) concludes that the spending pressures will, in the short run, lead to a drawdown of the national wealth (or an accumulation of debt). A country will continue to run deficits even as debt is being accumulated and will respond to the eventual need to repay that debt only when it has crossed a certain threshold – when the 'writing is on the wall', at which point distortionary taxes will need to be raised.

Hallerberg and von Hagen (1999) note the parties of a governing coalition have incentives to shift taxes onto the constituents supporting other parties. Persson *et al.* (2005) focus on competition within coalitions. A coalition member has an incentive to provide public goods or subsidies directed narrowly at its constituents to ensure their continuing loyalty. The costs arising from this competition are borne, in part, by coalition partners (who suffer future electoral losses) and by the general taxpayer. Since all members of the coalition have the same spending incentives, a coalition government will end up spending more than a single-party government would.

---

participation increases the pressure on governments to deliver for their constituents. A more cynical view is that increased participation is associated with greater involvement of uninformed voters, leading to worse policies. Either way, wider representation once again appears to conflict with policy discipline. Though voter participation can, and does, change from one election to another, in practice, the variations in our sample of countries have been small. As such, we treat it as an unchanging variable, but one that differentiates countries.

2.3. Budget institutions and fiscal performance

If a politically desirable increase in representation is accompanied by undesirable fiscal outcomes, can this unpleasant trade-off be alleviated? Fiscal institutions – the rules and procedures of budget formation – offer a possibility. These institutions,

Poterba (1996, p. 47) suggests, are a form of 'self control' imposed by fiscal actors on themselves. The aim, Eichengreen *et al.* (1999, p. 425) note, is not to 'depoliticize' fiscal decision-making but rather to improve the quality of decisions. This leaves open the question whether fiscal institutions can have real effects. In other words, even if sensible rules and procedures are set up, will self-interested political actors work around them to nullify their effectiveness? The international evidence and that from the US states are that fiscal institutions do matter, as Alesina and Perotti (1999) report.

To overcome the common-pool problem (Box 1), two perspectives have received attention (see, among others, Hallerberg and von Hagen, 1999). Under the centralized, or delegation, approach, budgetary power is concentrated in the hands of key policymakers (e.g., the prime minister or finance minister), who have an incentive to internalize the costs and benefits of public activities.[1] Under a more decentralized approach, the solution is collective negotiation and commitment to detailed multian-nual fiscal targets. These two approaches, combined with structures and devices to transparently and efficiently monitor and enforce budget decisions, can promote fiscal discipline.

Hallerberg and von Hagen (1999) suggest that a strong finance minister will play a critical role in one-party governments, since factions within a party have fewer policy disagreements and the party can credibly delegate budgetary power to a central player. In coalition governments – and especially in minority-coalition governments – a particular coalition partner may be unwilling to delegate decision-making powers to a central player from another party, and the contract-based approach, backed by well-informed and transparent rules, is likely to be superior. A role remains for the finance minister, but mainly to monitor and enforce the contract. The new and potential EU member countries in our sample typically have multiparty coalition governments, and, therefore, the contract-based approach would appear to be the most appropriate for them. We find in our empirical analysis that contracts help. However, formalized under medium-term budgetary frameworks (MTBFs), these are still in their early stages. As such, effective delegation to finance ministers, who retain considerable discretionary authority, has also helped contain fiscal pressures.

3. BUDGET INSTITUTIONS IN NEW AND POTENTIAL EU MEMBER STATES

A quantitative index of the overall quality of budget institutions (or fiscal institutions) was constructed for ten countries: Estonia, Bulgaria, the Czech Republic, Hungary, Latvia, Lithuania, Poland, Romania, the Slovak Republic, and Slovenia (Appendix A). The three steps of the budget process are (1) the preparation stage, when the

[1] Franzese (1999) models an independent central bank as one that is able to shift the weight of decisions toward the common good and away from the disparate interests of politicians. Not surprisingly, the call has been made for national fiscal councils to mimic independent central banks (see Eichengreen *et al.*, 1999; Annett *et al.*, 2005; and Wyplosz, 2005).

budget is drafted; (2) the authorization stage, in which the draft budget is approved and formalized; and (3) the implementation phase, where the budget is executed and may be modified/amended.

3.1. Preparation stage

Principles of stronger hierarchy and cooperative bargaining are applied in this phase through (1) the introduction of fiscal rules that limit deficit spending; (2) the establishment of quantitative budgetary targets based on a macroeconomic framework from the onset of the budget formulation; and (3) the relative dominance of the finance minister/prime minister in the budget negotiation process. With respect to variable 1, which refers to fiscal rules, Estonia and Latvia have limits on spending, and the Polish constitution restricts the debt-to-GDP ratio to below 60%, through a provision introduced in the organic budget law of 1999. With respect to variable 2 of the index, only Slovenia uses multiannual targets under an MTBF. However, five out of the ten countries did substantially improve their sequence of budgetary decision making. Less variation exists in the degree to which budget negotiations are centralized (variable 3 of the budget institutions index). The Minister of Finance is typically responsible for compiling the draft budget and bilateral negotiations with the spending ministries. Greater diversity exists in the reconciliation of disputes (variable 4 of the budget institutions index).

3.2. Authorization stage

This phase focuses on (1) explicit limits on the scope of amendments; (2) the sequence of decision making in the legislative budget process; (3) the relative power of the executive and parliament; and (4) the role of the president. In Estonia, Lithuania and Slovenia, amendments to the budget for higher expenditure have to be offset by specific sources of financing, so as to leave the overall budget target unchanged (variable 5 of the index). Poland and Bulgaria introduced formal limits on the scope of the legislature to amend the government budget in 1998 and 2003, respectively. These constraints help reduce the common-pool problem by forcing the legislators to recognize the trade-offs between projects. Only in the Czech Republic does the budget committee initially review the draft budget to set limits to the total revenue, expenditure, and deficit, which cannot be changed in the subsequent readings (variable 6). Institutional arrangements that favour the executive in conflicts arising with the parliament (variable 7) are considered more conducive to fiscal discipline. Poland gives the executive the greatest leverage, including the possibility of dissolving the parliament if an agreement cannot be reached. In the Czech Republic, in 2001 the rules were diluted if a draft budget was not approved on time. The Estonian position improved in 2003, when the possibility of the government's calling for a vote of confidence was introduced. With the exception of Hungary, Slovenia, and,

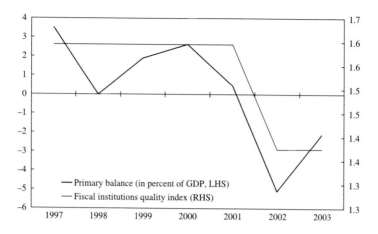

Figure 3. Hungary: Budget institutions and fiscal performance, 1997–2003

Source: Authors' estimates; Hungarian authorities; and fiscal notifications to the European Commission.

more recently, Poland, the president has had some power in the budget process (variable 8 of the budget institutions index). The index presumes that, when the president is permitted veto power, this authority will be exercised in pursuit of his/ her own policy agenda, creating a more fragmented process and one less conducive to fiscal discipline.

3.3. Implementation stage

In this stage, the degree of firmness in the execution of the budget is considered (variables 9, 10, and 11 of the budget institutions index), together with the procedures governing adjustments to unforeseen revenue shortfalls or unexpected overspending (variable 12 of the budget institutions index). The Hungarian position, already weak in this area, deteriorated in 2002 (Figure 3), as an amendment to the organic budget law was introduced that allowed considerable leeway in undertaking additional spending without supplementary appropriations and parliamentary approval. This change meant that the government could, to a certain extent, modify the budget parameters, and the agreements made in the budget planning and authorization phases could be undermined. The Czech Republic improved substantially in this dimension when it included in the 2000 budget law a formal rule that higher expenditure must be compensated for by decreasing other spending. However, the position worsened in 2001, when unused funds were allowed to be carried into the following year. Finally, in reaction to negative fiscal shocks, in four out of the ten countries (Bulgaria, Estonia, Latvia and Lithuania), the finance minister has been granted the authority to block expenditures if unforeseen revenue shortfalls or overspending occur. In the remaining countries, the cabinet, instead of the finance minister, can block expenditure without parliamentary approval.

These features of the budget formation and execution process are combined into a variety of sub-indices and an overall index of budget institution quality (Appendix A). By the overall index, Estonia and Slovenia stand out as countries that have done consistently well. Poland has considerably improved its position over this period. In contrast, the Hungarian position, already low, has deteriorated. Table 4 shows the ranking of the ten countries for 1997 and 2003. For comparison, we also constructed a partial index, using items 1–3, 5–6, and 9–12, for EU-15 countries, based on the coverage of rules and procedures in von Hagen *et al.* (2005). In general, the EU-15 countries have budget institutions superior to those in the new and potential EU member states. Sweden, France, the United Kingdom, and Spain stand out for advanced features.

4. BENCHMARK RESULTS

The goal in this section and the next is to explain the short-term dynamics of the primary budget balance, that is, the balance most under the control of the national authorities, thus the costs that arise on account of relatively inflexible debt repayment are excluded. We pool the observations from the ten countries over the seven years, 1997 through 2003. The following empirical specification is used:

$$y_{it} = \alpha + (v_i + \eta z_i) + \beta_t u_t + \delta x_{it} + \phi w_{it} + \gamma s_{it} + \varepsilon_{it}, \tag{1}$$

where y_{it} is the fiscal primary balance in country i and year t; v_i is a set of unchanging country-specific effects (proxied by country dummies); z_i are time-invariant institutional variables; and u_t are effects common to all countries in period t (time dummies). The three groups of time-varying explanatory variables are x_{it}, the economic control variables; w_{it}, the political control variables; and s_{it}, the fiscal institutions index.

To persuasively establish the relationships outlined in Equation (1), three econometric problems need to be addressed. First – and the most intractable of these – is the possibility that budget outcomes influence the evolution of fiscal institutions, rather than the other way around, as presumed. While the problem is widely recognized, it has not really been resolved, since identifying the exogenous component of fiscal institutions is hard. Alesina and Perotti (1999), Stein *et al.* (1999), Knight and Levinson (2000), and Perotti and Kontopoulos (2002) discuss the difficulties in dealing with this problem of reverse causality. Identifying an 'instrument', or a variable that influences the fiscal institutions but is not itself influenced by budgetary outcomes, is a hurdle that no one has yet crossed. Acemoglu (2005) is generally pessimistic about the possibility of identifying causal relationships in comparative political economy and argues that robust non-causal relationships nevertheless are of value to theoretical analysis and policymaking. The working assumption in the earlier papers, which we maintain, has been that budget performance cannot quickly feed back into alteration of budget institutions since these are costly to change. We do report results of Arellano-Bond and Keviet-bias procedures that statistically deal with the problem but are not conclusive in this regard.

Table 4. Fiscal institutions quality index

	1997 Rank[a]				2003 Rank[a]			
	Preparation	Authorization	Implementation	Overall	Preparation	Authorization	Implementation	Overall
Estonia	3	2	1	1	3	2	1	1
Poland	4	7	5	6	3	1	4	1
Slovenia	1	3	7	2	1	4	7	3
Latvia	2	8	1	3	2	9	1	4
Czech Republic	7	1	8	4	5	2	8	5
Lithuania	7	4	1	5	5	5	5	6
Romania	6	10	4	7	8	7	3	7
Bulgaria	7	9	6	9	5	10	5	8
Slovak Republic	10	5	9	10	10	6	9	9
Hungary	4	6	10	8	8	7	10	10

[a] Higher rank indicates better quality.

Source: Authors' calculations.

Second, and related, is the possibility of 'omitted variables'. These variables, although explaining the evolution of budget outcomes, because they are omitted, their effects are incorrectly attributed to the included variables, leading, in particular, to an overstatement of the fiscal institutions effect. A partial solution to this problem is disregarding variations across countries and analyzing only the variations within a country. Doing so, in effect, eliminates the unobserved v_i while also sweeping out the z_i, the observed but time-invariant effects that encompass a variety of influences on budget deficits. By thus focusing on variations within a country over time, the problem of omitted variables is alleviated but not eliminated. Most studies have not been able to pursue this 'within-country' or 'fixed-effects' approach, either because budget institutions do not move much over time or because these movements are difficult to measure. Where it is implemented, Knight and Levinson (2000) suggest, the results are typically different from those obtained in cross-sectional analysis, indicating that the problem of omitted variables is relevant. Since our data permit us to do so, the within-country analysis forms our benchmark.

Third, and paradoxically flowing from the solution to the second problem, because some of the unchanging country effects (the z_i) are of analytical interest, sweeping them away throws out important information. A partial solution to this problem has been proposed by Blanchard and Wolfers (2000). In effect, it allows the analyst to ask if the reactions to the time-varying variables are conditioned by the unchanging country characteristics of interest, as described below in Box 2.

Appendix B provides details of the explanatory variables used and their data sources. Table 3 reports the means and variations of the explanatory variables. These show that, even within this relatively homogenous group, considerable heterogeneity exists.

Since we are working with only ten countries, the cross-country regressions are only briefly presented (in Table 5) to contrast the findings with the subsequent results. Among the economic conditioning variables, a higher public debt-to-GDP ratio is associated with a larger primary surplus (or smaller deficit) and is significant in some specifications, suggesting greater fiscal effort when debt payments increase. Of the four variables representing democratic practice – fragmentation of the government coalition and the three ideology variables – only the nationalism variable is significant, albeit at the 10% level, in the cross section, with a more nationalistic ideology tending to reduce the budget surplus. Among the longer-term determinants of budgetary performance, the district magnitude shows the most action, as a larger district magnitude results in a smaller long-term surplus. Note that here, and in the rest of the paper, we use the log of the district magnitude as the explanatory variable to limit the influence of the Slovak Republic, which has an especially large district magnitude. Also, an IMF-supported programme tends to be associated with a larger primary surplus. And, once we control for an IMF-supported programme, there is some hint in the cross section that better budgetary institutions also help increase the primary surplus. These results are in line with the findings of Gleich (2003) and Yläoutinen (2004).

Box 2. Shocks and institutions

Blanchard and Wolfers (2000) sought to disentangle the influence of economic shocks (changes in oil prices and shifts in productivity trends) from that of sluggish labour market institutions on the evolution of unemployment. By examining the changes in the variables of interest within a country over time, they used the conventional approach to eliminate the unobserved, unchanging country influences, the so-called fixed effects (since the failure to do so creates the risk that the influence of those unobserved effects will be incorrectly attributed to the variable of interest to them). But since doing so also eliminates information on the unchanging labour market institutional variables of interest, they proposed estimating an equation of the following form:

$$y_{it} = \alpha + [1 + \lambda(z_i - \bar{z})](\beta u_t + \delta x_{it}) + \gamma s_{it} + \phi w_{it} + (v_i + \eta z_i) + \varepsilon_{it}. \quad (2)$$

In effect, this procedure (with coefficient estimates obtained by non-linear least squares) tests if time-invariant variables, such as labour market or political institutions, shape different responses to common and country-specific economic and political events (for recent applications, see Persson, 2002 and Milesi-Ferretti et al., 2002). Country-fixed effects (country dummies) control for the country-specific averages $(v_i + \eta z_i)$. The crucial new parameter is λ. The formulation postulates a common response, βu_t, to common shocks, u_t. In turn, however, the common response is shaped by the term $\lambda(z_i - z)$, reflecting the influence of country institutions z_i (e.g., the district magnitude). Because z_i is measured as a deviation from the mean across countries, βu_t is the measured response in the sample when the z_i is at the mean of the sample. In Tables 9–10, we allow also for z_i's to interact with country-specific events, the variables x_{it}, again following Blanchard and Wolfers (2000). In Table 10, the response to fiscal institutions, s_{it}, is also mediated through the unchanging political environment.

Notice that the specification implies that the same coefficient, λ, conditions all the shocks/events. In principle, it is possible to allow differential responses. However, the number of parameters quickly explodes. Blanchard (2005), in reviewing the evolution of recent research, recognizes the importance of exploring a variety of interactive effects but cautions that the differential effects may be difficult to identify. In the context of testing for the effect of central bank independence, Franzese (1999) allows for differential interactions but concludes, in that case, that the assumption of a common mediating effect is a justifiable approximation.

Table 5. Economics, politics and fiscal performance: evidence from cross-country regressions

	Primary balance-to-GDP ratio					
	(1)	(2)	(3)	(4)	(5)	(6)
Lagged debt-to-GDP ratio	0.06 (0.04)	0.05 (0.02)*	0.08 (0.02)**		0.06 (0.03)*	0.06 (0.02)**
Unemployment rate	−0.07 (0.23)					
Inflation	0.02 (0.08)					
Openness index	−1.72 (3.33)					
IMF program dummy		2.79 (1.33)*	3.09 (1.06)**			1.91 (1.06)
Government fragmentation				0.65 (6.04)		
Government ideology:						
Left/right				0.27 (0.32)		
Nationalism				−0.56 (0.34)		
Fiscal centralization				0.51 (0.61)		
Fiscal institutions index			2.74 (1.21)*			1.52 (1.18)
Ethnic fractionalization					3.37 (4.34)	
District magnitude					−1.50 (0.50)**	−1.03 (0.53)
Voter turnout					−0.04 (0.05)	
Number of countries	10	10	10	10	10	10

Note: This table displays estimates of the fiscal outcome:

$$\bar{y}_i = \alpha + v_i + \gamma \bar{s}_i + \delta \bar{x}_i + \phi \bar{w}_i + \eta z_i + \varepsilon_{it}$$

where an overbar denotes a time average of y_{it}, the primary balance in country i and year t, s_{it} the fiscal institutions index, x_{it} economic control variables, w_{it} other control variables, and z_i time-invariant institutional variables. The variable v_i is a country specific component. Standard errors in parentheses, * significant at 10%; ** significant at 5%; *** significant at 1%.

When we move from the cross-sectional to the within-country analysis in Table 6, we have, in principle, seven observations for each of the ten countries for a potential total of 70 observations. However, we lose five observations (1997 for Lithuania, 1997 and 1998 for Latvia, and 1997 and 1998 for the Slovak Republic) because the ideological orientation of some of the political parties in the early years could not be identified. Also, we drop two observations (Bulgaria and Romania in 1997, when they experienced very high inflation). Thus, we work throughout with 63 observations. Throughout, by including country fixed effects, we are, in effect, seeking to explain deviations from the country mean. We also include year dummies to control for common shocks.

Table 6. Economics, politics, and fiscal performance: evidence from panel data regressions (fixed effects)

	Primary balance-to-GDP ratio					
	(1)	(2)	(3)	(4)	(5)	(6)
Lagged debt-to-GDP ratio	0.05	0.03				
	(0.05)	(0.04)				
Unemployment rate	−0.34	−0.41				
	(0.17)*	(0.15)**				
Inflation	0.06	0.14				
	(0.06)	(0.06)**				
Openness index	4.78	7.89				
	(4.91)	(4.42)*				
Fiscal institutions index		7.52				4.27
		(2.08)***				(2.13)**
Government fragmentation			−0.82		6.23	4.27
			(1.81)		(2.74)**	(2.82)
Government ideology:						
Left/right				0.16	0.49	0.42
				(0.12)	(0.19)**	(0.18)**
Nationalism				−0.39	−0.66	−0.57
				(0.15)***	(0.18)***	(0.18)***
Fiscal centralization				0.30	0.48	0.40
				(0.20)	(0.20)**	(0.20)*
Time dummies	Y	Y	Y	Y	Y	Y
Observations	63	63	63	63	63	63
Number of countries	10	10	10	10	10	10

Note: This table displays estimates of the fiscal outcome:

$$y_{it} = \alpha + v_i + \gamma s_{it} + \delta x_{it} + \phi w_{it} + \varepsilon_{it}$$

where y_{it} is the primary balance in country i and year t; v_i is a country specific component; s_{it} is the fiscal institutions index; x_{it} comprises economic control variables; w_{it} are other control variables. Estimations of panel data regressions using random effects are reported. Standard errors in parentheses, * significant at 10%; ** significant at 5%; *** significant at 1%.

4.1. Economic and political influences

As in the previous section, we begin with standard economic influences on the budget deficit (Table 6). Briefly, a higher debt level apparently induces greater fiscal effort, increasing the primary balance. However, while the sign on this variable is always positive, it is not statistically significant at conventional levels. The unemployment rate, which is more often closer to statistical significance, has a negative sign, implying that an increase in the unemployment rate reduces the primary surplus (increases the deficit). A higher inflation rate is associated with a larger primary surplus, as if inflation reduces the real value of expenditures without compromising tax receipts. This result is consistent with that of Perotti and Kontopoulos (2002), although their finding is supported by a higher degree of statistical significance. Finally, country openness to external trade is sometimes significant, implying that countries that are more open also tend to greater fiscal conservatism. However, as we discuss below, and as is the case with the other economic variables, the significance tends to fall when pitted against the political variables, especially in the non-linear regressions.

With these controls in place, we add our overall index of the quality of budgetary institutions to the explanation of the primary balance. The results suggest that stronger budgetary institutions are associated with a larger primary surplus (or smaller deficit). The coefficient is significant at the 1% level of significance.

Turning to political influences, we consider in this section the time-varying variables of the 'practice of democracy' variety rather than structural or constitutional variables, which are considered via the non-linear estimation in the next section. In our taxonomy, voter participation also represents democratic practice, but because it displays only modest changes over time, we treat it in the next section as a time-invariant influence. When considered by themselves, the fragmentation and the three ideological variables, though appearing with plausible signs (Table 6, columns 3 and 4) do not have especially high statistical significance. The statistical significance of all variables increases sharply in column (5) when we place coalitional fragmentation alongside the three ideology variables. Since a larger coefficient on the fragmentation variable (the Herfindahl index derived from the shares of the coalitional partners) indicates less fragmentation, the positive sign on the coefficient indicates a larger surplus with reduced fragmentation.

Thus, the findings imply that fragmentation and ideology need to be examined together. Also ideology is multifaceted. Considering these as a package provides stronger results, consistent with priors that have long existed in the literature. The ideology variables indicate that a coalition that leans to the right, that is not highly nationalist, and that favours centralization of public finances is likely to deliver a conservative budget. In our sample, leftist coalitions have been less fragmented, and some rightist coalitions have had nationalistic tendencies. Only when these dimensions are simultaneously considered do the results show through. Again, when we add the budget institutions index, its coefficient maintains its strong statistical significance. However, the size of the coefficient is smaller, suggesting that the budget institutions are more correlated with political than with economic factors.

4.2. Economics versus politics

We bring together the findings in Table 7. As noted in the introduction, a concern with this exercise is the robustness of the findings. We address, first, the robustness issue through alternative estimation procedures and a search for outliers. This leads to a discussion of the substantive conclusions. Column 1 presents the results of the random-effects estimation, which uses the cross-country and within-country variations. The conditions required for the validity of these estimates are stringent; in particular, the possibility that the omitted variables, relegated to the error term, are correlated with the included variables raises the concern that the coefficient estimates may be

Table 7. Economics versus politics

| | Primary balance-to-GDP ratio | | | | | |
	(1)	(2)	(3)	(4)	(5)	(6)
	Random effects	Fixed effects	Fixed effects	Arellano–Bond	Kiviet-bias adjustment	Fixed effects
Lagged debt-to-GDP ratio	0.09	0.02	0.02	0.07	0.01	
	(0.02)***	(0.05)	(0.05)	(0.07)	(0.08)	
Unemployment rate	−0.08	−0.23	−0.31	−0.09	−0.03	−0.33
	(0.08)	(0.18)	(0.17)*	(0.26)	(0.19)	(0.16)*
Inflation	0.16	0.07	0.12	0.18	0.13	0.12
	(0.04)***	(0.08)	(0.08)	(0.12)	(0.13)	(0.08)
Openness index	3.62	7.39	8.80	12.66	13.78	8.96
	(1.57)**	(4.77)	(4.40)*	(5.25)**	(5.28)**	(4.35)**
Government fragmentation	1.78	6.78	4.39	6.13	6.86	4.66
	(1.72)	(2.96)**	(2.84)	(3.39)*	(3.12)**	(2.76)*
Government ideology:						
Left/right	0.38	0.49	0.37	0.29	0.40	0.39
	(0.12)***	(0.19)**	(0.18)**	(0.21)	(0.21)*	(0.17)**
Nationalism	−0.25	−0.63	−0.46	−0.60	−0.68	−0.48
	(0.16)	(0.20)***	(0.19)**	(0.24)**	(0.24)***	(0.19)**
Fiscal centralization	0.34	0.46	0.38	0.63	0.57	0.36
	(0.20)	(0.26)*	(0.24)	(0.32)*	(0.27)**	(0.24)
Fiscal institutions index	5.09		6.20	9.03	7.37	6.15
	(1.19)***		(2.13)***	(4.42)**	(4.47)*	(2.10)***
Lagged primary balance				0.11	0.24	
				(0.21)	(0.17)	
Time dummies	Y	Y	Y	Y	Y	Y
Observations	63	63	63	43	53	63
Number of countries	10	10	10	10	10	10

Note: This table displays estimates of the fiscal outcome:

$$y_{it} = \alpha + v_i + \beta_i u_t + \gamma s_{it} + \delta x_{it} + \phi w_{it} + \varepsilon_{it}$$

where y_{it} is the primary balance in country i and year t; u_t represents variables common to all countries; v_i is a country specific component; s_{it} is the fiscal institutions index; x_{it} comprises economic control variables; and w_{it} are political control variables. Column 1 reports results of a panel data regression using random effects. Columns 2, 3, and 6 are the results of panel data regression using fixed effects. In column 4, estimates of the coefficients using Arellano-bond method are shown (in this case, the Sargan test reject the hypothesis of over-identification, $(\Pr \geq \chi^2 = 0.27)$, and the hypothesis that average autocorrelation in residuals of order two is zero cannot be rejected $(\Pr \geq z = 0.93)$. Column 5 reports bias-corrected LSDV estimates for dynamics unbalanced panel data models (Bruno, 2005). Standard errors in parentheses, * significant at 10%; ** significant at 5%; *** significant at 1%.

biased. A comparison with the fixed-effects model (columns 2 and 3), which uses only the within-country variation, suggests that the correlation with omitted variables may not be serious.[2] One variable for which the coefficient changes significantly is lagged debt. The implication is that, across countries, higher debt induces greater fiscal conservatism (in line with Bohn, 1998); however, the same effect is not observed

---

[2] Formally, a Hausman test does not reject the random-effects estimates.

within a country over time. The statistical reason for this difference is that, as debt levels vary little within a country relative to the cross-country variation (see Table 3), the effects of the within-country movements are difficult to identify precisely – and hence we come back to examining the debt-to-GDP ratio as an unchanging variable in the next section.

While our basic approach to dealing with omitted variables is through the use of country-fixed effects, we also examine if the errors are serially correlated and the lagged dependent variable is picking up additional time-varying omitted effects. The Lagrange multiplier test for serial correlation in residuals, following Baltagi (2005), suggests no serial correlation. Recognizing that this test is only approximate for unbalanced panels, we examine the possibility of dynamics through two different estimation approaches.[3] The Arellano–Bond estimator, which, in principle, deals also with the possibility of reverse causality from budget outcomes to fiscal institutions, allows for the possibility of persistence in budget deficits (Table 7, column 4). However, because this estimator performs well for large samples, which is not exactly our case, we also use the Kiviet-bias adjustment, which works better for unbalanced panels with a small number of units (Table 7, column 5). Given the already small size of the sample, the drop in sample size when using lagged values cautions against a heavy reliance on these results. However, the consistency of the results is reassuring. In particular, the lagged dependent variable is not statistically significant. In the rest of this paper, therefore, we use as a benchmark the fixed-effects, or within-country, estimates without the lagged dependent and debt variables, as in column (6) of Table 7.

Another relevant concern is the robustness of the results to possible outliers. In particular, because of the large changes in fiscal institutions in Poland and Romania, and the small sample, the question arises whether the results are driven by these countries. We follow Milesi-Ferretti et al. (2002) and exclude one country at a time to test for the possibility of 'influential' countries. However, the relevance of the fiscal institutions index does not appear to be driven by any single country.[4]

Substantively, when we put the economic conditioning variables alongside the political variables, politics seems to win. In general, the strength of the economic variables declines, though their signs remain as before. Among the political variables, fragmentation becomes less significant, but it retains its expected positive sign. The

[3] There is also the possibility of an 'Ashenfelter dip'. If a country experiences a large deficit, budget institutions may improve in response to this dip and the subsequent reduction of that deficit may be overly attributed to budget institutions. Similarly, an improvement in the budget balance may reduce the incentive to improve fiscal institutions. We regress the fiscal balance residuals from Equation 1 (ε_{it}) on two indicator variables. The first takes a value of 1 if there was an improvement in the fiscal institutions' quality in the following year and a zero otherwise (the dip indicator) the second takes a value of 1 if there was a deterioration in the fiscal institutions' quality one year later (the rise indicator). The coefficients of the two indicator variables are not significant, suggesting the absence of an Ashenfelter dip or rise.

[4] The fiscal institutions index is significant at the 7% level when either Hungary and Poland is dropped and at the 5% level when one of the other countries or both Poland and Romania are dropped.

Table 8. External anchors

	Primary balance-to-GDP ratio			
	(1)	(2)	(3)	(4)
Unemployment rate	−0.33	−0.36	−0.33	−0.35
	(0.17)*	(0.17)**	(0.17)*	(0.18)*
Inflation	0.12	0.11	0.12	0.11
	(0.09)	(0.08)	(0.08)	(0.09)
Openness index	8.97	8.88	9.19	9.02
	(4.41)**	(4.38)**	(4.72)*	(4.85)*
Government fragmentation	4.60	4.19	4.71	4.26
	(2.91)	(2.87)	(2.82)	(3.05)
Government ideology:				
Left/right	0.38	0.35	0.39	0.36
	(0.19)*	(0.19)*	(0.18)**	(0.20)*
Nationalism	−0.48	−0.45	−0.49	−0.45
	(0.19)**	(0.19)**	(0.19)**	(0.20)**
Fiscal centralization	0.35	0.36	0.37	0.37
	(0.26)	(0.24)	(0.25)	(0.27)
Fiscal institutions index	6.16	6.52	6.21	6.55
	(2.13)***	(2.19)***	(2.17)***	(2.29)***
EU accession dummy		−0.85		−0.85
		(1.31)		(1.38)
IMF program dummy	−0.07			0.04
	(1.01)			(1.05)
Election year dummy			0.08	0.05
			(0.61)	(0.63)
Time dummies	Y	Y	Y	Y
Observations	63	63	63	63
Number of countries	10	10	10	10

Note: This table displays estimates of the same fiscal outcome as in Table 8. Standard errors in parentheses, * significant at 10%; ** significant at 5%; *** significant at 1%.

two political variables that remain most clearly significant are the measures of left-right and nationalist ideology. Once more, the overall index of budgetary institutions is highly significant in these specifications, which include the economic and political conditioning variables. Thus, while politics has a strong influence on the budget, discipline appears to be possible through the checks and balances of budgetary processes and institutions. This, then, is our principal finding, one that is confirmed in the more refined specifications discussed below.

For robustness as well as substantive reasons, we also examine two external anchors: membership in the European Union (EU) and an IMF-supported programme (Table 8). EU membership is, in fact, a misnomer since we time the EU dummy to take the value 1 from the year in which negotiations for EU entry were initiated. The premise is that the discipline required for entry into the EU and, subsequently, for euro adoption creates an anchor that reduces the fiscal deficit. The results indicate otherwise. The sign on the EU dummy is negative, showing, if anything, that the prospect of EU entry raises the deficit, though the effect is not statistically significant. We do not probe this issue in greater detail but presume that two opposing forces are working against each other: a disciplining effect counteracted by increased expenditures in response to new requirements for EU entry. Similarly, the IMF-supported programme dummy is also not significant. As noted above in the cross-section results, an IMF-supported programme was associated with smaller deficits. The fact that this is no longer the case in a 'within' regression suggests that unobserved country factors lead to both an IMF-supported programme and to smaller deficits. Once these unobserved factors are controlled for through country dummies, the direct influence of an IMF-supported programme disappears.

We finally analyse the effect of the timing of elections. Unlike in Brender and Drazen (2005), the 'political cycle' – a larger deficit in the election year – does not appear to be significant for the countries in our sample. Brender and Drazen analyse the effect of the election cycle just after these countries became democracies, while our study focuses on a somewhat later period (1997–2003). That we do not find a significant effect could be in line with Brender and Drazen findings, which show that, as countries become more developed and achieve stronger democracies, the cycle is weaker. Second, we focus on the legislative cycle since these countries have parliamentary regimes, while Brender and Drazen also consider the presidential cycle.

5. THE ROLE OF DEEPER DETERMINANTS: TIME-INVARIANT FACTORS

There remains the possibility that the political determinants of budgetary performance, as well as the restraints exercised through sound budgetary institutions, are mainly a reflection of deeper underlying variables. Because these deeper determinants typically change very little over time (and, in our sample, do not change at all), it has become customary to assess their influence through the reaction they induce to shocks. Blanchard and Wolfers (2000) have analysed two types of shocks: country-specific shocks (represented by time-varying country variables) and common shocks (represented by time dummies). The shocks are interacted with the time-invariant variables, and the influence of the latter is assessed by isolating their effects through a non-linear regression (Box 2). In essence, as Blanchard and Wolfers (2000) note, the methodology evaluates whether the shocks persist longer if the deeper determinants are more salient. In a short time span, a longer persistence implies a higher average realization.

As discussed above, the theory creates some expectations regarding the direction of influence of the time-invariant political institutions but cautions about possible ambiguities and non-linearities. Thus, Aghion *et al.* (2004) argue that greater fractionalization is divisive and leads to greater competition for resources and, hence, less fiscal discipline; however, these negative effects may be offset through the choice of political institutions.[5] As noted in the introduction, electoral rules have many dimensions, which cannot be captured in a single index. Here we use the simple measure of proportionality or district magnitude (the number of elected candidates per district). In principle, this index measures the extent to which voters' voices count – or the degree to which political parties court all voters. With reduced proportionality, parties can ignore 'safe' districts, focusing their electoral promises towards 'swing' constituencies.[6] Thus, greater proportionality in electoral rules is expected to lead to the formation of more diverse coalitions, which, in turn, can hurt fiscal discipline. Since we also control for the diversity of coalitions, the measured effect of a larger district magnitude may either be an additional influence, reflect non-linearities, or represent inadequacies in our measure of government fragmentation. Finally, as Mueller and Stratmann (2003) show, when voter participation is high, pressures to meet the demands of a variety of constituencies may lead to higher public expenditures and/or lower taxes and, hence, to larger deficits.

5.1. The main results

In general, as we have cautioned, the effects of the time-invariant variables are sensitive to the specifications. Though the direction of influence is typically plausible, both the strength and statistical significance of the influence tend to be unstable.[7] The results are presented in four steps, each step testing the robustness of the findings while also addressing issues of substantive interest. In the first step (columns 1–3 of Table 9), we allow the possibility that the time-invariant variables mediate domestic shocks (developments in inflation, employment, and the trade-to-GDP ratio) and the common shocks (represented by time dummies). Greater ethnic diversity appears to amplify adverse shocks, i.e., an adverse shock to the budget has a bigger impact under conditions of greater diversity. The sign of this coefficient, however, is not significant in this specification. A larger district magnitude and greater voter turnout also amplify adverse shocks, and, in these cases, the statistical significance varies between 5 and 10%.

In the second step (columns 4–6, Table 9), we add the lagged debt-to-GDP ratio as a time-invariant variable. The results above showed that the time variation in the

---

[5] As noted, the measure of language fractionalization is virtually the same as that of ethnic fractionalization. Though religious fractionalization is also highly correlated with ethnic fractionalization, it gives quite different results, often appearing with a positive sign, suggesting that more fractionalization is associated with greater budget discipline. Importantly, the variables of interest to us, the quality of budgetary institutions and the time-varying political variables, remain significant and important even when religious fractionalization is included.

[6] Milesi-Ferretti *et al.* (2002) propose a 'standardized' measure of district magnitude, which corrects for the threshold number of votes to gain representation. This measure attempts to predict the number of political parties, rather than voter voice, and gives, in our case, less precise results for the time-invariant variables. The main result on budget institutions, fragmentation and ideology hold strongly.

[7] The greater instability in the coefficient on the time-invariant variables, compared with the other political controls we have used so far, is to be expected since we have a sample of only ten countries and changes in specification are more likely to influence the time-invariant variables.

Table 9. Deeper determinants – interaction with common and country-specific events: non-linear least squares regressions

	Primary balance-to-GDP ratio					
	(1)	(2)	(3)	(4)	(5)	(6)
Constant	−0.05	−7.49	−11.82	4.07	−7.07	−12.13
	(12.28)	(6.24)	(6.13)	(13.85)	(6.43)	(6.26)
Inflation	0.06	0.06	0.06	0.11	0.10	0.09
	(0.05)	(0.04)	(0.05)	(0.07)	(0.07)	(0.07)
Unemployment rate	0.19	0.21	0.14	0.32	0.33	0.16
	(0.13)	(0.13)	(0.14)	(0.18)*	(0.18)*	(0.18)
Openness index	1.65			3.29		
	(2.30)			(3.60)		
Fiscal institutions index	5.47	5.38	5.86	6.28	6.08	6.17
	(2.45)**	(2.40)**	(2.33)**	(2.52)**	(2.47)**	(2.38)**
Government fragmentation	8.12	7.69	6.10	9.74	9.06	6.37
	(2.87)***	(2.83)**	(2.72)**	(2.99)***	(2.96)***	(2.79)*
Government ideology:						
Left/right	0.46	0.45	0.42	0.55	0.52	0.43
	(0.18)***	(0.18)**	(0.18)**	(0.18)***	(0.18)***	(0.18)***
Nationalism	−0.77	−0.75	−0.74	−0.88	−0.85	−0.78
	(0.21)***	(0.21)***	(0.21)***	(0.22)***	(0.22)***	(0.23)***
Fiscal centralization	0.95	1.01	0.98	1.05	1.10	1.02
	(0.30)***	(0.29)***	(0.31)***	(0.30)***	(0.30)***	(0.33)***
Time-invariant variables:						
Ethnic fractionalization	−4.34	−3.59		−3.75	−3.08	
	(3.02)	(2.73)		(1.73)**	(1.65)*	
District magnitude	−1.44	−1.34	−1.18	−0.96	−0.90	−0.92
	(0.85)*	(0.70)*	(0.64)*	(0.46)**	(0.41)**	(0.55)
Voter turnout	−0.13	−0.12	−0.09	−0.09	−0.08	−0.07
	(0.05)**	(0.05)**	(0.04)**	(0.03)***	(0.03)***	(0.04)*
Debt-to-GDP ratio				−0.12	−0.11	−0.01
				(0.01)**	(0.01)**	(0.01)
Time dummies	Y	Y	Y	Y	Y	Y
Country dummies	Y	Y	Y	Y	Y	Y
Observations	63	63	63	63	63	63
Adjusted R-squared	0.63	0.63	0.63	0.64	0.64	0.64

Note: This table displays non-linear least squares estimates of the fiscal outcome:

$$y_{it} = \alpha + [1 + \lambda(z_i - \bar{z})](\beta u_t + \delta x_{it}) + \gamma s_{it} + \phi w_{it} + (v_i + \eta z_i) + \varepsilon_{it}$$

where y_{it} is the primary-balance-to-GDP ratio in country i and year t; u_t represents variables common to all countries; v_i is a country specific component; s_{it} is the fiscal institutions index; w_{it} are country-specific control variables; and z_i are time-invariant institutional variables. Idiosyncratic economic variables x_{it} include inflation, unemployment rate, and openness index. Time-invariant terms interact with time dummies and idiosyncratic economic variables x_{it}. In columns 4–6 debt-to-GDP ratio is treated as a time-invariant variable. Standard errors in parentheses, * significant at 10%; ** significant at 5%; *** significant at 1%.

debt-to-GDP ratio did not have a material bearing on the movements in the primary surplus. This reflects, in part, the fact that much of the sample variation in the debt-to-GDP ratio is across countries rather than within countries over the short time period covered. Thus, for such short periods, we ask if the level of debt conditions the responses to shocks. The negative sign on the debt-to-GDP variable suggests that a country experiencing a positive shock – an improving budgetary position – will be less conservative if it has a heavier debt burden. While the intertemporal budget constraint would need to be satisfied eventually, the relatively low debt levels in some of the countries and the relative ease of market financing where debt levels are higher imply that the stock of debt need not constrain short-term budgetary priorities (as also implied by Velasco, 1999, Box 1). Notice that, with the introduction of the debt ratio as a conditioning variable, most results are strengthened.

Moreover, the role of contemporary politics remains salient. Indeed, if anything, with the inclusion of the time-invariant variables, the four contemporary political variables – coalitional fragmentation and the three ideological variables – are now all highly significant. The implication is that contemporary politics is not entirely driven by deeper determinants. Rather, short-term forces can generate political configurations that can move politics against the direction dictated by the longer-term forces, thereby aggravating or mitigating the role of divisive forces.

Finally, the budgetary institutions index remains strongly significant. Relative to earlier estimates, the point estimate is now somewhat lower, at about $5^1/_2$–6; this suggests that a move in institutional quality from the 25th to the 50th percentile leads to an improvement in the primary surplus of about 1.5% of GDP.

In the third and fourth steps (Table 10), we allow for the possibility that shocks to fiscal institutions are also conditioned by the time-invariant variables. In columns 1–3, we do not include the debt-to-GDP ratio, and in columns 4–6 we do. The coefficient on the fiscal institutions index should now be interpreted as the response of the primary budget to fiscal institutions at the mean value of the time-invariant influences (since those variables are entered into the regressions as deviations from their sample means). Thus, in this representation, each country has its own response to improvements in fiscal institutions, depending on the specific values of the time-invariant variables. Estimates show that, though varying in strength, stronger fiscal institutions help everywhere, except possibly in the Slovak Republic, with its large district magnitude and high voter participation. Clearly, these results reflect the imposition of a linear conditioning response, which forces a structure that may not be tenable. Since that was not the main purpose of this paper, we did not pursue non-linear possibilities in any depth, leaving it to be examined in the context of a larger sample.[8]

5.2. Model predictions

How well do these models perform? We present two examples. Figure 4 shows the actual and model-predicted values of the budget balance for Poland and Hungary. The predictions match the actual values rather well, both in absolute magnitudes and changes in direction. For Poland, the early improvement in budget balance reflects,

---

[8] Following a suggestion by Hallerberger and Marier (2004), we examined the possibility of piecewise linearity for district magnitude: the results suggest that an initial rise in district magnitude may help fiscal discipline before the influence turns negative at a district magnitude of about 20.

Table 10. Deeper determinants – interaction with fiscal institutions and common and country-specific events: non-linear least squares regressions

	Primary balance to-GDP ratio					
	(1)	(2)	(3)	(4)	(5)	(6)
Constant	18.50	8.93	6.51	28.59	12.35	6.71
	(14.75)	(8.14)	(8.34)	(17.48)	(8.84)	(8.56)
Inflation	0.06	0.06	0.07	0.12	0.10	0.07
	(0.04)	(0.04)	(0.05)	(0.07)	(0.07)	(0.06)
Unemployment rate	0.19	0.21	0.15	0.31	0.32	0.16
	(0.12)	(0.12)*	(0.13)	(0.15)**	(0.16)*	(0.15)
Openness index	2.10			4.24		
	(2.19)			(3.38)		
Fiscal institutions index	2.35	2.40	3.08	3.99	3.75	3.29
	(0.86)**	(0.87)***	(1.08)***	(1.52)**	(1.46)**	(1.57)**
Government fragmentation	8.34	7.82	6.09	10.07	9.23	6.16
	(2.72)***	(2.67)***	(2.65)**	(2.81)***	(2.80)***	(2.72)**
Government ideology:						
Left/right	0.49	0.47	0.41	0.59	0.55	0.42
	(0.17)***	(0.17)***	(0.17)**	(0.17)***	(0.17)***	(0.18)**
Nationalism	−0.78	−0.74	−0.75	−0.88	−0.84	−0.76
	(0.20)***	(0.17)***	(0.21)***	(0.20)***	(0.21)***	(0.23)***
Fiscal centralization	0.96	1.03	1.01	1.04	1.12	1.03
	(0.28)***	(0.28)***	(0.30)***	(0.27)***	(0.29)***	(0.32)***
Time-invariant variables:						
Ethnic fractionalization	−4.78	−3.95		−4.47	−3.67	
	(2.92)	(2.63)		(1.72)**	(1.68)**	
District magnitude	−1.32	−1.24	−1.05	−0.91	−0.87	−0.99
	(0.71)*	(0.59)**	(0.51)**	(0.40)**	(0.36)**	(0.58)**
Voter turnout	−0.15	−0.13	−0.10	−0.11	−0.10	−0.09
	(0.06)**	(0.05)***	(0.04)**	(0.03)***	(0.03)***	(0.05)**
Lagged debt to-GDP ratio				−0.01	−0.01	0.00
				(0.01)**	(0.01)**	(0.01)
Time dummies	Y	Y	Y	Y	Y	Y
Country dummies	Y	Y	Y	Y	Y	Y
Observations	63	63	63	63	63	63
Adjusted R-squared	0.66	0.63	0.64	0.67	0.67	0.63

Note: This table displays non-linear least squares estimates of the same fiscal outcome as in Table 10.

$$y_{it} = \alpha + [1 + \lambda(z_i - \bar{z})](\beta u_t + \delta x_{it}) + \gamma s_{it} + \phi w_{it} + (v_i + \eta z_i) + \varepsilon_{it}$$

The variables x_{it} include inflation, unemployment rate, openness index, and fiscal institutions index. Time-invariant terms interact with time dummies and idiosyncratic economic variables x_{it}. In columns 4–6 debt-to-GDP ratio is treated as a time-invariant variable. Standard errors in parentheses, * significant at 10%; ** significant at 5%; *** significant at 1%.

in part, the improvement in the domestic fiscal institutions. However, budget performance deteriorated thereafter. Mechanically, this reflects a decline in the inflation rate, which results in a drop in the fiscal balance. The interpretation is that some part of the apparent strength in the fiscal balance was achieved by higher inflation, and the underlying weaknesses were revealed once the inflation rate fell. Thus, while improved fiscal institutions helped, the endemic problems require stronger solutions.

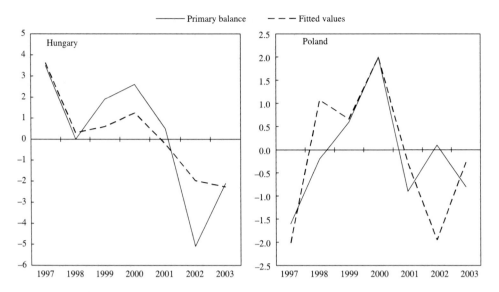

Figure 4. Primary balance and fitted values (non-linear least squares estimates, in percentage of GDP)

Source: Authors' estimates; and fiscal notifications to the European Commission.

In Hungary, the worsening prediction for the budget balance in the last two years of the sample period reflects the worsening institutions.

5.3. Components of the budget institutions index

Finally, we examine if the three components of the budget institutions index have a different impact on performance (Table 11). While each component appears to have a strong and independent force, the implementation stage appears to be the most relevant. The implication, therefore, is that, while the rules in the preparation phase and the bargaining that goes on during the authorization stage restrain fiscal irresponsibility, the greater danger arises from the budget implementation; this, in turn, implies that checks are needed to ensure that the efforts of the first two phases are not undone. The political fragmentation and ideological variables remain strong influences. While the three time-invariant variables are important, there is a difference across the stages of some interest. In the two earlier phases of preparation and legal authorization, voter participation has a strong influence; however, in the final implementation phase, when, presumably, the actions are less visible to voters, the degree of voter participation in the democratic process has a smaller influence.

Column (4) examines if the three different phases that we identify are substitutes for each other. In other words, if any one of the phases is weakly developed, is it possible to compensate another phase with stronger checks and balances? To examine this question, we created a new index that took the lowest of the three values from

Table 11. Budget process stages and the delegation/contract-based approaches: non-linear least squares regressions

	Primary balance-to-GDP ratio					
	Budget preparation phase	Budget authorization phase	Budget implementation phase	Lowest score	Delegation approach	Contract-based approach
Constant	2.96 (7.28)	0.29 (6.19)	19.63 (18.42)	1.12 (6.38)	14.99 (11.28)	6.02 (7.98)
Inflation	0.04 (0.05)	0.07 (0.05)	0.02 (0.03)	0.07 (0.05)	0.08 (0.05)	0.07 (0.05)
Unemployment rate	0.13 (0.14)	0.18 (0.14)	0.02 (0.12)	0.19 (0.14)	0.15 (0.13)	0.14 (0.13)
Fiscal institutions index	2.99 (1.41)**	1.33 (0.53)**	3.79 (1.36)***	1.92 (0.85)**	4.49 (1.47)***	2.95 (0.95)***
Government fragmentation	6.18 (2.80)**	6.31 (2.72)**	7.47 (2.60)***	6.30 (2.76)**	6.34 (2.58)**	6.26 (2.58)**
Government ideology:						
Left/right	0.47 (0.18)**	0.40 (0.18)**	0.49 (0.18)***	0.43 (0.18)**	0.41 (0.17)**	0.39 (0.17)**
Nationalism	−0.75 (0.21)***	−0.77 (0.21)***	−0.68 (0.20)***	−0.77 (0.21)***	−0.73 (0.20)***	−0.72 (0.20)***
Fiscal centralization	1.04 (0.32)***	1.04 (0.31)***	0.72 (0.29)**	1.06 (0.31)***	0.98 (0.30)***	0.97 (0.30)***
Time-invariant variables:						
District magnitude	−1.26 (0.79)	−0.92 (0.45)**	−1.80 (0.69)**	−1.00 (0.55)*	−1.17 (0.52)**	−1.13 (0.47)**
Voter turnover	−0.12 (0.05)**	−0.10 (0.04)**	−0.04 (0.06)	−0.11 (0.40)***	−0.11 (0.04)**	−0.09 (0.04)**
Time dummies	Y	Y	Y	Y	Y	Y
Country dummies	Y	Y	Y	Y	Y	Y
Observations	63	63	63	63	63	63
Adjusted R-squared	0.61	0.62	0.64	0.61	0.65	0.65

Note: This table displays non-linear least squares estimates of the same fiscal outcome as in Table 10. Time-invariant variables interact with time dummies and the idiosyncratic variables x_{it} unemployment rate, openness, and fiscal institutions index. The fiscal institutions index in the first column is the budget preparation index, in the second column the budget authorization index, and in the third column the budget implementation index. In the fourth column, the fiscal institutions index is built by taking the lowest score among the three indexes used in the first three columns for each year. In the fifth column, the fiscal institutions index is constructed by taking into account the features relevant for the delegation approach; in the last column the characteristics relevant in a contract-based setting are considered. Standard errors in parentheses. * significant at 10%; ** significant at 5%; *** significant at 1%.

the three phases for each country in each year. The goal was to assess if the weakest phase could undermine fiscal responsibility. The results suggest that the phases are not substitutes and that weak links in the budget preparation, authorization, and implementation phases can hurt fiscal discipline; therefore, policy attention to all phases is required.

Columns (5) and (6) test for the differences between the delegation and contract-based approaches. The indices for the delegation and contract-based approaches were obtained by summing up items of the fiscal institutions index that are relevant in those settings. The delegation-approach index was formed by items 2–7 and 9–12, while the contract-based index by items 1, 5–7, and 9–11 (Appendix A, Table A1). The results suggest that both are statistically important. This appears to go against the Hallerberg and von Hagen (1999) hypothesis, which states that the contract-based approach is most relevant for multiparty coalitions because the finance minister cannot be trusted fully by coalitional partners to act on their behalf and, hence, delegation may prove ineffective. However, these authors also find that when budgetary institutions are 'young', the delegation and contract-based indices are correlated and both aspects are salient. Their results for the EU-15 show that between 1981 and 1994 the delegation approach was statistically significant in countries where it was expected to work and in the 'contract-based' states where it was not. Only since 1998 has the divergence between the two approaches become evident, with the delegation approach significant only in the 'delegation' states; similarly, the contract-based approach is significant only in the 'contract' states (Hallerberg, Strauch, and von Hagen, 2004). It is possible, then, that such divergence will appear in central and eastern Europe. However, Poterba and von Hagen (1999, p. 4) offer the following caution: 'The empirical evidence suggesting that institutions matter is stronger than the evidence on the mechanisms by which these institutions matter.' Thus, moving from these results to specific policy advice will ultimately depend on a more careful consideration of individual country circumstances.

6. DIFFERENTIATING THE EFFECTS ON EXPENDITURES AND REVENUES

Finally, we examine if fiscal institutions operate through the expenditure or revenue side of the budget. We estimate expenditure and revenue equations, jointly using the seemingly unrelated regressions methodology to gain efficiency. These results should be interpreted with caution, because the data available for revenue and expenditure (from the World Economic Outlook database) are not always consistent with the primary balance data used in the previous analysis (European System of Accounts '95 data from the countries' fiscal notifications to the European Commission) and are affected by breaks in the series.

In Table 12, we report results obtained by jointly estimating the expenditure and revenue equations (see Box 3). Following Persson (2002), we use in this analysis a more direct measure of 'observable' shocks, as distinct from the time dummies used

Table 12. Expenditure and revenue developments

	EU15 growth shock		Oil price shock		France/Germany primary balance	
	Exp-to-GDP	Rev-to-GDP	Exp-to-GDP	Rev-to-GDP	Exp-to-GDP	Rev-to-GDP
Lagged expenditure	0.38 (0.08)***		0.38 (0.08)***		0.38 (0.08)***	
Lagged revenue		0.26 (0.08)***		0.26 (0.08)***		0.26 (0.08)***
Unemployment rate	0.41 (0.13)***	0.08 (0.08)	0.41 (0.13)***	0.08 (0.08)	0.41 (0.13)***	0.08 (0.08)
Inflation	-0.02 (0.06)	0.06 (0.04)	-0.02 (0.06)	0.06 (0.04)	-0.02 (0.06)	0.06 (0.04)
Openness index	-6.46 (3.33)*	0.77 (2.25)	-6.46 (3.33)*	0.77 (2.25)	-6.46 (3.33)	0.77 (2.25)
Government fragmentation	1.80 (2.08)	2.12 (1.42)	1.80 (2.08)	2.12 (1.42)	1.80 (2.08)	2.12 (1.42)
Government ideology:						
Left/right	-0.02 (0.13)	0.06 (0.09)	-0.02 (0.13)	0.06 (0.09)	-0.02 (0.13)	0.06 (0.09)
Nationalism	0.31 (0.14)**	0.02 (0.10)	0.31 (0.14)**	0.02 (0.10)	0.31 (0.14)**	0.02 (0.10)
Fiscal centralization	-0.11 (0.18)	0.10 (0.12)	-0.11 (0.18)	0.10 (0.12)	-0.11 (0.18)	0.10 (0.12)
Fiscal institutions index	-3.59 (1.64)**	-1.02 (1.11)	-3.59 (1.64)**	-1.02 (1.11)	-3.59 (1.64)**	-1.02 (1.11)
Shock	-0.56 (0.28)**	-0.27 (0.19)	0.96 (0.25)***	0.84 (0.18)***	-0.45 (0.20)**	-0.32 (0.14)**
Time dummies	Y	Y	Y	Y	Y	Y
Country dummies	Y	Y	Y	Y	Y	Y
Observations	63	63	63	63	63	63

Note: This table displays seemingly unrelated estimates of the fiscal outcome:

$$y_{it} = \alpha + \beta u_t + \gamma s_t + \delta x_{it} + \phi w_{it} + v_i + \varepsilon_{it}$$

where y_{it} is the primary expenditure/revenue-to-GDP ratio in country i and year t; v_i is a country specific component; s_{it} is the fiscal institutions index; w_{it} are political control variables; and x_{it} are economic variables. u_t represents variables common to all countries (EU15 GDP growth, oil prices, German/France primary balance). Standard errors in parentheses, * significant at 10%; ** significant at 5%; *** significant at 1%.

Box 3. Observable shocks, institutions, and the evolution of expenditures and revenues

The expenditure and revenue equations are estimated jointly through the seemingly unrelated regressions procedure (to allow for correlations in error terms of these equations), enhancing the efficiency of the estimates. For each equation, the following parametrization is used:

$$y_{it} = \alpha + (\beta + \phi z_i)u_t + \delta x_{it} + \phi w_{it} + \gamma s_{it} + (v_i + \eta z_i) + \varepsilon_{it}, \tag{3}$$

where y_{it} represents either expenditure or revenues at time t in country i. As above, country-fixed effects eliminate the unchanging country features, $(v_i + \eta z_i)$. The movement of observed variables proxies for common shocks, u_t. In addition to the oil prices used by Persson (2002), we also use growth in the EU-15 and the primary budget balance in France and Germany. The response to these shocks is shaped by the time-variant variables, z_i.

---

earlier to proxy 'unobservable' shocks. We use three alternative shocks: GDP growth in the EU-15, oil price movements, and the average of the lagged primary balances in Germany and France.

Three findings emerge from the expenditure equation.[9] First, stronger fiscal institutions are clearly associated with lower primary expenditures, validating the expectation that common-pool problems affect the expenditure side and, moreover, that checks and balances can contain the tendency to satisfy all interest groups. Second, although the political variables have the expected signs, only the nationalism variable is consistently significant. Third, the shocks matter. More rapid European growth is associated with a lower expenditure-to-GDP ratio, as if higher European growth stimulates higher growth in our sample of countries but expenditures do not rise commensurately. Higher oil prices are associated with higher expenditures, possibly reflecting subsidies and increased operational costs (though, as noted below, higher oil prices also bring in more revenues). More fiscal discipline in Germany and France apparently creates some pressure to be fiscally responsible.

Not surprisingly, it is not easy to explain movements in the tax-to-GDP ratio (Table 12).[10] Political economy models speak less to the determinants of taxation than they do to the common-pool problems relating to expenditures (see also Perotti and Kontopoulos,

---

[9] The error terms in the two equations are highly correlated, with a correlation coefficient of just under 0.5.

[10] Here, as elsewhere, we explored if the 'output gap', the difference between actual and potential output, influenced the tax-to-GDP ratio. Given the difficulties in constructing such a measure from the short time series available for countries that have emerged from transition only in the mid-1990s, it is not surprising that the measured output gap was not associated with taxes, or with expenditures or budget deficits.

2002). Inertia in tax receipts, reflected in the significant coefficient on the lagged tax variable, explains part of the movement. Interestingly, external shocks play a more salient role in the evolution of tax receipts. Of these, a rise in oil prices is most consistently related to higher tax receipts, possibly due to import and excise duties. As with expenditures, revenues do not keep pace with externally induced growth. Also, a large surplus in Germany and France is associated with a lower tax-to-GDP ratio; hence, if a discipline effect exists, it is mainly through the expenditure side and the gains are partially relinquished on the tax receipts.

Finally, do the external shocks interact with the time-invariant variables, and, if they do, is the role of fiscal institutions altered? The answer to the latter question is no: the role of fiscal institutions remains strong and robust on the expenditure side (Table 13). With respect to the role of the interactions, the results are mixed and suggest that the different shocks work through different time-invariant variables. A larger district magnitude is associated (weakly) with higher expenditures when EU growth increases, that is, countries with larger district magnitudes tend to raise their expenditures to a greater extent than those with smaller district magnitudes. Larger district magnitudes also are associated with lower tax receipts when oil prices rise. In contrast, a larger voter turnout appears to operate through higher expenditures when there is an oil price shock.

7. CONCLUSIONS

Politics has a crucial influence on budget outcomes – a widely accepted conclusion, which we confirm for a group of new and potential members of the European Union over the period 1997–2003. We find, moreover, that politics works not only through long-term determinants but more evidently through the operation of contemporary democratic practice. In other words, contemporary politics is not predetermined by the structural and historical features of an economy and, hence, exercises an independent influence on budgets. Also, contemporary politics itself is best represented by a vector of attributes. In the context of this paper, the combination of government fragmentation in the ruling coalition, the ideological predispositions along different dimensions (the traditional left-right divide, nationalism, and the emphasis on decentralization of government), and the degree of voter participation contribute to budgetary outcomes. We note, in particular, that government fragmentation will often not reveal itself to be important unless juxtaposed with ideological orientation. The results on voter participation, supporting earlier findings of Mueller and Stratmann (2003), are troubling and suggest that greater democratic participation is accommodated by increased budgetary indiscipline.

If politics is so influential – and, particularly if politics is set on an unrelenting long-term historical course – then is budget discipline a hopeless cause? The answer, apparently, is no – hope is not lost. Stronger checks and balances in the budgetary process, through hierarchical rules and collegiality, materially improve budgetary

Table 13. Expenditure and revenue developments: the role of time-invariant factors

	EU15 growth shock		Oil price shock		France/Germany primary balance	
	Exp-to-GDP	Rev-to-GDP	Exp-to-GDP	Rev-to-GDP	Exp-to-GDP	Rev-to-GDP
Lagged expenditure	0.33 (0.08)***		0.34 (0.08)***		0.38 (0.08)***	
Lagged revenue		0.26 (0.08)***		0.23 (0.08)***		0.26 (0.08)***
Unemployment rate	0.39 (0.15)***	0.02 (0.10)	0.60 (0.15)***	0.05 (0.10)	0.41 (0.13)***	0.08 (−0.08)
Inflation	−0.04 (0.06)	0.05 (0.04)	0.00 (0.06)	0.07 (0.04)*	−0.02 (0.06)	0.05 (0.04)
Openness index	−3.57 (3.67)	1.43 (2.56)	−7.40 (3.27)**	1.79 (2.20)	−6.46 (3.42)*	0.61 (2.30)
Government fragmentation	1.27 (2.08)	1.80 (1.45)	2.33 (1.99)	2.02 (1.36)	1.91 (2.20)	1.99 (1.51)
Government ideology:						
Left/right	0.00 (0.13)	0.06 (0.09)	−0.02 (0.12)	0.05 (0.09)	−0.02 (0.13)	0.06 (0.09)
Nationalism	0.32 (0.14)**	0.04 (0.10)	0.25 (0.14)*	0.04 (0.10)	0.31 (0.14)**	0.02 (0.10)
Fiscal centralization	−0.29 (0.21)	0.03 (0.15)	−0.02 (0.20)	−0.01 (0.13)	−0.10 (0.19)	0.09 (0.13)
Fiscal institutions index	−3.83 (1.62)**	−0.92 (1.11)	−3.42 (1.55)**	−0.84 (1.05)	−3.60 (1.69)**	−0.91 (1.14)
Shock	−2.06 (1.71)	−1.54 (1.19)	0.46 (0.53)	1.30 (0.36)***	−0.28 (1.43)	−0.64 (0.96)
Interacted with:						
District magnitude	0.47 (0.26)*	0.02 (0.18)	−0.07 (0.05)	−0.10 (0.03)***	−0.02 (0.20)	−0.02 (0.14)
Voter turnover	0.00 (0.02)	0.02 (0.02)	0.01 (0.00)**	0.00 (0.00)	0.00 (0.02)	0.01 (0.01)
Time dummies	Y	Y	Y	Y	Y	Y
Country dummies	Y	Y	Y	Y	Y	Y
Observations	63	63	63	63	63	63

Note: This table displays seemingly unrelated estimates of the fiscal outcome:

$$y_{it} = \alpha + (\beta + \phi z_i) u_i + \gamma x_{it} + \delta z_{it} + \phi w_{it} + (v_i + \eta z_i) + \varepsilon_{it}$$

where y_{it} is the primary expenditure/revenue-to-GDP ratio in country i and year t; v_i is a country specific component; s_{it} is the fiscal institutions index; w_{it} are political control variables; x_{it} are economic variables; and z_i are time-invariant institutional variables. u_t represents variables common to all countries (EU15 GDP growth, oil prices, German/France primary balance). Standard errors in parentheses). * significant at 10%; ** significant at 5%; *** significant at 1%.

discipline. This discipline, apparently, acts through constraints on expenditures, which is where the scope for indiscipline is greatest, because politicians, while benefiting themselves and their constituents from additional expenditures, do not fully bear the costs of those additional expenditures.

The question of policy interest then is: What are the determinants of good fiscal institutions? This is not a question that we tackle. Clearly, in the context of the countries we examine, there was a window of opportunity during the transition from centrally planned to market economies, when the old political constraints were (partially) broken down, that created the possibility of a wide-ranging set of reforms. Enhancing the quality of fiscal institutions was apparently part of the agenda of reformers during this period. However, as we document, progress was not uniform, and there were slippages.

This leads to the further question: Is the necessary institutional engineering feasible elsewhere or, indeed, even in these same countries as a new politics takes over? The answer, to the extent our paper hints at one, is yes, if the politics behaves. Fiscal institutions are somewhat correlated with both the practice of contemporary politics and long-term structural features. This is seen in our finding that the coefficient on budget institutions' quality, though remaining highly significant, is whittled down as we introduce these political determinants of budgetary outcomes. In part, then, the quality of budgetary institutions is a reflection of a fiscally conservative political system. To the extent that political forces turn away from fiscal conservatism, the likelihood of fiscal institutions reforms will decline. Thus, although our principal message is that of hope – because, empirically, long-term determinants do not exercise the tyranny that is sometimes feared – the tussle between the forces supporting sound institutions and the politics of claims on budgetary resources will continue.

Discussion

Giancarlo Corsetti
European University Institute, Rome III and CEPR

Recent literature has shown many ways in which the fiscal performance of a country depends on constitutional provisions/electoral rules; but these in turn are likely to be a function of deep structures of a society (division along ethnic or religious lines etc.). The paper by Fabrizio and Mody takes up the challenge to address an important question for policy design. Can budget institutions still make a difference for fiscal outcomes?

The authors address this question empirically. The analysis aims at disentangling the role of budget institutions from structural and political factors. For reason that will be discussed later, the sample includes new and potential EU members, observed over a limited time period (between 1997 and 2003). However, it will be misleading to think of the new EU members as the subject of the analysis. On the contrary, the ambition of the paper is to reach very general conclusions about policy design, and provide an empirical contribution to both the theoretical and policy debate. The extent to which they succeed is of course an open issue.

To pursue their goal the authors set up regression models where, after controlling for a number of economic variables, there is a horse race between three different sets of determinants of fiscal outcome: (a) structural determinants (such as diversity of population and electoral systems); (b) contemporary politics (political fragmentation, ideology, voter participation – which can be interpreted as an index of demand on government, but also as an index of quality of vote); (c) the quality of budget institutions (proxied by a synthetic multidimensional index).

Somewhat surprisingly, the results show that, when it comes to explain fiscal performance, budget institutions are significant, and robustly so. In addition, contemporary politics appears to trump economic conditioning variables, while inclusiveness (meaning representation of different interests in the budget process) seems to hurt budgetary outcomes.

The quality of budget institutions is proxied by an index aggregating different stages of the budget process: preparation, authorization and implementation. One section of the paper presents useful examples and institutional detail to illustrate the logic underlying the index.

Now, what matters for fiscal discipline is not only the overall average index score, but also the value of each one of its components. Clearly, there is no substitutability in the quality of institutions at different stages of the budget process – being loose in the preparation cannot be compensated by being rigorous in the implementation! Conversely, a low value of the index at any stage indicates that there are opportunities to breach the rules and loopholes that can easily undermine overall fiscal discipline.

In my comments, I will focus on three dimensions of the paper, theory, sample choice, welfare.

Theory

The theoretical underpinning of the exercise is the 'common pool problem'. Fragmentation of interests in the budget process compromise discipline because each group of actors fails to internalize the costs of public goods and/or redistribution going mainly to their benefits.

It is important to stress that these costs can be shifted not only onto other active tax-payers, but also intertemporally, to future generations. Hence, the lack of fiscal discipline can be mirrored by either a sub-optimally large government; or a large deficit.

Most of the paper focuses on the latter. However, the authors also add a section where the dependent variable in the regression model is government spending. The model proposed by the authors appears to work comparatively well in either case.

Yet, there is a tension between different implications of the common pool problem. For instance, consider the two approaches to the common pool problem in budgetary matters discussed in the text. One is centralization of budget decision (so as to internalize the costs and benefits of public activities); the other one is negotiation of multi-annual fiscal targets, making sure that there is full commitment to them. It is reasonable to expect these two approaches to have different merits/problems in addressing the intertemporal or redistributive implications of budget decisions.

Sample

Why only ten countries, observed for less than ten years? The authors motivate their choice by pointing to the fact that during the sample period their countries display time-series variation in the quality of their fiscal institutions.

This is an advantage in the following sense: to the extent that country dummies capture many time-invariant features, using fixed effects may alleviate the problem of omitted variable. This option is not available when focusing on countries with no within-sample variability in budget institutions.

Nonetheless, the small size of the sample raises two issues. First, is there enough time for a new budget institution to become effective/biting? New institutions may take some time before being fine-tuned. On defence of the author, it may well be possible that some of the teething problems of new institutions be captured by the quality index (which in principle could record improvements at each stage of the budget process).

Second, there is a danger for spurious correlation. The sample consists of potential members of the EU. It is plausible that the goal of participating in the EU is what ultimately motivates reforms and fiscal discipline. It may be possible that the political drive towards the EU simultaneously explains the adoption of strict budget institutions and fiscal retrenchment. How can one disentangle the role of institutions from the role of an 'external constraint'?

The experience of the euro area is relevant in this respect. As is well known, the deficit criterion has been binding before the creation of the euro, less so afterwards.

Welfare

In the paper and the theoretical literature in the background, a large primary deficit is positively correlated with a severe common pool problem. But the countries in the sample are emerging markets/transition countries. How can one draw a clear line between excessive deficits, and optimal deficits vis-à-vis the need for infrastructure and, say, pension reforms. Paradoxically, a government with more credibility in fiscal matters should be able to run larger deficits!

Note that this observation just mirrors the ongoing debate on the Stability and Growth Pact in Europe.

Concluding comments

Provided that one likes the methodology (being fully aware of problems of endogeneity, omitted variables, non-linearity, threshold effects and so on), there are a few things to learn from the authors' *tour de force* through the data. Examples are the results regarding the contribution of inflation to public finance, pointing to the revenue loss from convergence policies, but especially the treatment of political variables.

Multi-dimensionality is the point stressed by the authors. Looking at historical and political determinants of budget, regression results clearly improve when variables are grouped in indexes. Aggregation criteria are, however, ad hoc and arbitrary. In this respect, one should note that the main constraint to the analysis of multi-dimensionality is theoretical rather than empirical.

Overall, I find the paper informative. It provides empirical evidence corroborating the idea that good institutions make a difference – a welcome input to the current debate on budget policy in Europe and elsewhere. More in general, it is a contribution to the core debate about European political and institutional process, and, using a popular term, European governance. Is there a role for European institution and politics to foster institutional development among its members? The empirical results in this paper suggest that 'all hope is not lost'.

Jonathan R.W. Temple
University of Bristol

Using a small panel of countries, this paper asks whether changes in fiscal institutions over time are associated with changes in a government's primary surplus. There are ten countries, all in transition from central planning, and the data set runs from 1997 to 2003. One feature of the transition economies is that, given their recent history, they have been especially likely to see significant changes in their institutions. As a result, the authors not only ask an interesting question, but also have a data set that may be unusually informative.

A particular strength of the paper is that it is careful in defining and examining a specific set of institutions. Interpreting the concept of 'institutions' broadly has been a successful strategy in recent empirical work, but it is clear that the task of designing and building better institutions will soon require sharper definitions. The paper goes a long way in this direction, in relation to the budget-setting role of government. The authors identify a set of dimensions to the budget-setting process, and assess the ten countries in terms of these various dimensions. One consequence is that the paper embeds a clear view of the changes that might constitute a feasible and successful institutional reform. This attention to the 'detail' or 'fine structure' of institutions is all too rare in economics, where a liking for abstract reasoning sometimes leads to impatience with issues that may be critical in practice.

Moreover, the empirical results suggest that changes to budget-setting institutions can have significant effects on fiscal outcomes, notably the primary surplus. The paper finds that moving from the 25th percentile of institutional quality to the 50th percentile raises the primary surplus by at least 1.5 percentage points of GDP. Given the likely range of variation of the primary surplus, this is a powerful effect, and one that is worth investigating in more detail.

I have three main criticisms. First, the empirical analysis looks at year-to-year movements in fiscal outcomes over 1997–2003. But typically, one might think of the primary surplus as a realization. In other words, it is a stochastic outcome, rather than wholly under government control from one year to the next. After all, predicting tax revenues is not an exact science. With this in mind, I think the specifications in the paper would be more persuasive if they allowed for lags in the responses of the primary surplus to changes in budget-setting institutions. But in fairness to the authors, the short time dimension of the panel means that there is only limited scope for experiments along these lines.

My second criticism concerns the origin of the policy changes. The empirical results are mainly based on fixed effects estimators, using several different methods. The logic of the fixed-effects approach is similar to the difference-in-differences estimator used in the programme evaluation and 'treatment effect' literature. Here, the treatment corresponds to changes in budget-setting institutions. A central question is then, what determines the assignment of the treatment? The empirical methods and discussion in the paper generally treat the institutional reforms as randomly assigned, which may be a mistake. After all, these reforms are choices, rather than exogenously imposed by an outside party.

Why does this matter for the empirical work? One reason to be cautious is that, in practice, countries that choose to undertake reforms may differ in a number of ways from the implicit control group (non-reformers). As a result, the estimates are less likely to be recovering a causal effect. For example, reforms may be especially likely after the fiscal position has worsened significantly, and it may be the latter driving a fiscal 'rebound' rather than the reform itself. This could be seen as similar to the phenomenon of Ashenfelter's Dip in the evaluation of labour market programmes. If the likelihood of reforms depends on time-varying, country-specific factors, there will be systematic differences between the treatment and control groups at the time of the treatment, and this will tend to undermine the identification of a causal effect. The final version of the paper briefly addresses this possibility, but I would have liked to see it pursued in more detail.

A related and final criticism is a technical one, concerning the size of the sample. There are two countries in which the extent of reform is much greater than the others. The remaining countries could be seen as a control group, but it is clear that the estimates have to rely on contrasts between a small number of cases. It could even be argued that, given the small size of the panel, the standard errors attached to the key parameters are surprisingly low. One possibility is that the standard errors are exaggerating the amount of information in the sample, something that could occur if the errors are dependent over time. Tests and parametric corrections of the kind used in the paper cannot rule this out completely, but the small cross-section dimension of the panel largely precludes other solutions, such as clustering or bootstrapping.

In summary, I found this to be an unusually interesting paper. Above all, it gets to grips with a specific and well-defined set of institutions, and examines a set of countries where the experience of institutional reform may be especially illuminating. The paper presents some empirical results that are new and valuable although, as ever with observational data, some significant uncertainties and qualifications remain.

Panel discussion

Gilles Duranton stressed it was important to disentangle history from current events and therefore suggested a two-step approach to first look at the fixed effects and then analyse them, looking at long-term determinants. He also suggested that policy was not driven by long-run considerations and thought IMF interventions, potentially driven by bad institutions rather than history, could be an important factor. The authors replied that a dummy for IMF programmes was included, but it did not have an effect.

Allan Drazen pointed out that fiscal institutions are hard to measure, particularly on a yearly basis and was also concerned about the subjectivity of the measures. In the presence of a larger deficit, it is more likely that institutions get bad scores. The authors answered that data collection as described in Appendix A was not survey based.

Drazen also noted that, electoral variables contrarily to voter turnout, are not significant. Drazen suggested that deficits do matter for *new* democracies in very robust ways. In his own work, he found that new democracies are fragile and thus a deficit is used to convince voters of the benefits of democracy itself (and increase voter turnout) rather than to win particular votes. This mechanism would be consistent with voter turnout mattering in this paper. Drazen concluded that it was important to beware of extrapolating results from countries, formerly communist regimes that are very recent democracies.

Wendy Carlin felt that the most interesting information may come from reform *reversals* and whether budget institutions can explain them. Carlin suggested that as soon as the country is part of the EU, the pressures of populist institutions may return, defeating any incentive to reform. The authors replied that external influence was surely an issue, but noted that the accession negotiations do not involve budget process rules.

APPENDIX A: CONSTRUCTION OF THE BUDGET INSTITUTIONS INDEX

The index is a quantitative measure of budget institutions – the rules and mechanisms that govern the budget process (Table A1). The goal is to consolidate the objective

Table A1. Constructions of the index: fiscal institutions and their index parameters

	Weighting factors			Numerical coding
	Index	Sub-index	Item	
A. Preparation	0.33			
1. Existence of statutorily mandated fiscal rules		0.25		
a. Balanced budget rule.				4.00
b. Limits on public borrowing.				2.00
c. No legal limits on borrowing.				0.00
2. Sequence of budgetary decision making		0.25		
a. MF sets forth aggregate and specific budget targets in initial budget circular.				4.00
b. MF proposes, cabinet decides on targets for budget aggregates and spending limits are assigned to each ministry before spending ministries develop budget requests.				3.00
c. MF proposes, cabinet decides on targets for budget aggregates before spending ministries develop budget requests.				2.00
d. Budgetary targets are set on the basis of preliminary budget requests.				1.00
e. No budget targets are determined.				0.00
3. Compilation of the draft budget		0.25		
a. Finance ministry holds bilateral negotiations with each spending ministry.				4.00
b. Finance ministry holds bilateral negotiations, other parties included.				2.00
c. Finance ministry only collects budget requests and compiles summary for cabinet session.				0.00
4. Members of executive responsible for reconciling conflicts over budget bids		0.25		
a. MF or PM can veto or overrule cabinet decision.				4.00
b. Senior cabinet committee, then whole council of ministers or cabinet.				2.00
c. Executive collectively (e.g., council of ministers or cabinet).				0.00
B. Legislation				
5. Constraints on the legislature to amend the government's draft budget		0.25		
a. Deficit provided in the draft budget cannot be exceeded, or individual amendments have to indicate offsetting changes.				4.00
b. No restrictions.				0.00
6. Sequence of votes		0.25		
a. Initial vote on total budget revenues, expenditures, and the deficit.				4.00
b. Final vote on budget aggregates.				0.00
7. Relative power of the executive vis-à-vis the parliament		0.25		
a. Cabinet can combine a vote of confidence with a vote on the budget.			0.33	4.00
b. Draft budget is executed if parliament fails to adopt the budget before the start of the fiscal year.			0.33	4.00

	Weighting factors			Numerical coding
	Index	Sub-index	Item	
c. Parliament can be dissolved if it fails to adopt the budget in due time.			0.33	4.00
8. Authority of the national president in the budget procedure		0.25		
a. No special authority.				4.00
b. President has veto right (president elected by parliament).				2.67
c. President has veto right (president directly elected by citizens).				1.33
d. President has veto right (qualified majority required to override veto).				0.00
C. Implementation	0.33			
9. Flexibility to change budget aggregates during execution		0.25		
a. Any increase in total revenues, expenditures and the deficit needs to be approved by parliament in a supplementary budget.				4.00
b. Revenue windfalls can be used to increase expenditure without the approval of parliament as long as the deficit is not increased.				2.67
c. Simultaneous changes in revenue and expenditures allowed without approval of parliament if budget balance is not changed.				1.33
d. At total or large discretion of the government.				0.00
10. Transfers of expenditures between chapters (i.e. ministries' budgets)		0.25		
a. Require approval of parliament.				4.00
b. FM or cabinet can authorize transfers between chapters.				2.67
c. Limited.				1.33
d. Unrestricted.				
11. Carryover of unused funds to next fiscal year		0.25		
a. Not permitted.				4.00
b. Only if provided for in initial budget or with finance ministry approval.				2.67
c. Limited.				1.33
d. Unlimited.				0.00
12. Procedure to react to a deterioration of the budget deficit (due to unforeseen revenue shortfalls or expenditure increase)		0.25		
a. MF can block expenditures.				4.00
b. The cabinet can block expenditures.				2.67
c. Approval of the parliament necessary to block expenditures.				1.33
d. No action is taken.				0.00

Source: IMF staff; Gleich (2003).

features of the budget process such that a larger value implies greater checks and balances. Following Gleich (2003), values (ranging from 0 to 4) were assigned to the three phases of the budget process: preparation, authorization and implementation. Sources of information on these features include the countries' annual fiscal budget laws, Reports on the Observance of Standards and Codes (ROSC) Fiscal Transparency Module, produced by the International Monetary Fund, and direct contact with the countries' authorities. We also made use of the information on budget institutions collected by Gleich (2003) and Yläoutinen (2004).

Budget preparation stage

The institutional features considered are (1) fiscal rules that limit *a priori* the fiscal deficit; (2) the establishment of quantitative budget targets based on a macroeconomic framework; and (3) the relative power of the finance/prime minister in the budget negotiations. The following variables, shown in Table A1, are taken into consideration during this stage:

- Variable 1 refers to the strictness of permanent constraints on budgetary parameters, such as legal limits on the size of budget deficits or government borrowing.
- Variable 2 assesses control by the finance minister in setting fiscal targets and ceilings to guide the budget preparation.
- Variable 3 captures the power of the finance minister in compiling and negotiating the draft budget.
- Variable 4 reflects how remaining disputes from the bilateral negotiations are reconciled in the executive branch. Procedures in which the whole cabinet is involved are classified as more decentralized than procedures in which senior cabinet committees discussing the matter before it is presented to the whole cabinet.

Budget authorization stage

Given the common-pool dilemma, spending and deficit pressures can emerge if legislators are left unconstrained to amend the draft budget proposal. Therefore, institutional regulations that limit the scope of amendments to the budget proposal enhance discipline. The institutional characteristics considered are (1) explicit limits on the scope of amendments; (2) the sequence of decision making in the authorization process; (3) the relative power of the executive branch and the parliament; and the role of the president in this process. The four variables considered during the authorization stage follow (Table A1):

- Variable 5 regards formal constraints on the scope for the legislature to amend the government budget, and classifies processes as stricter if the amendments allowed are limited.

- Variable 6 refers to the sequence of decision making during the budget delibera-tion, and focuses on whether a decision is made on the size of major budget aggregates before details are worked out.
- Variable 7 summarizes three institutional devices that reflect the strength of the executive branch (the government) vis-à-vis the parliament during the budget deliberation.
- Variable 8 captures the power of the president in the budget process; the less the power, the stronger implicitly the ability of the government in achieving its budget priorities.

Budget implementation stage

The first focus at this stage is on how binding the approved budget is. If the govern-ment can easily modify budget parameters, the agreements made in the preparation and implementation stages could be undermined and the authorization function of parliament weakened. Also, a degree of flexibility to react to unforeseen revenue shortfalls or spending overruns is necessary at the implementation phase. The varia-bles considered during this stage are the following:

- Variable 9 gets a high score if parliament needs to approve a supplementary budget to institute changes. Similarly, Variable 10 gets a high score if transfers of allocations between ministries require parliamentary approval. Finally, in Vari-able 11, the inability to carry over of unused funds to the next year is regarded as conducive to discipline.
- With respect to the flexibility to react to unforeseen shocks, in Variable 12 the finance minister's ability to block expenditures is seen as the best option, with progressive weakening if expenditure blocking requires cabinet approval, parliamentary approval, or no approval at all.

On this basis, four indices were constructed for each country. Three refer to the quality of budget institutions in the three different stages of the budget process – preparation, authorization and implementation – and the fourth that represents the overall index. Table A1 reports the weights used in the aggregation to create the three component indices and the overall index. The variables are constructed as follows:

$$\text{Budget preparation index} = 1/4 \sum_{i=1}^{4} x_i$$

$$\text{Budget authorization index} = 1/4 \sum_{i=5}^{8} x_i$$

$$\text{Budget implementation index} = 1/4 \sum_{i=10}^{13} x_i$$

Table A2. Construction of the index: scores

	A. Preparation stage						B. Authorization stage						C. Implementation stage						Overall index	
	Variable				1997 Score	2003 Score	Variable				1997 Score	2003 Score	Variable				1997 Score	2003 Score	1997 Score	2003 Score
	1	2	3	4			5	6	7	8			9	10	11	12				
Bulgaria	0	0, 3[a]	4	0	1.00	1.75	0	0	1.33	1.33	0.67	0.67	1.33	2.67	4	4	3.00	3.00	1.54	1.79
Czech Republic	0	0, 3[a]	4	0	1.00	1.75	0	4	4, 2.67[b]	2.67	2.67	2.34	1.33, 4[c]	2.67	4, 1.33[b]	2.67	2.67	2.67	2.09	2.23
Estonia	2	3	4	0	2.25	2.25	4	0	1.33, 2.67[d]	2.67	2.00	2.34	4	4	2.67	4	3.67	3.67	2.61	2.72
Hungary	0	2	4	0	1.50	1.50	0	0	1.33	4	1.33	1.33	2.67, 0[c]	1.33	1.33	2.67	2.00	1.33	1.59	1.37
Latvia	2	2	2	4	2.50	2.50	0	0	0	2.67	0.67	0.67	4	4	2.67	4	3.67	3.67	2.26	2.26
Lithuania	0	0, 1[f]	4	0, 2[f]	1.00	1.75	4	0	1.33	1.33	1.67	1.67	4	2.67	4, 1.33[b]	4	3.67	3.00	2.09	2.12
Poland	0, 2[a]	0, 1[f]	4	2	1.50	2.25	0, 4[a]	0	4	0, 4[a]	1.00	3.00	4	2.67	2.67	2.67	3.00	3.00	1.82	2.72
Romania	0	1, 2[d]	4	0	1.25	1.50	0, 4[d]	0	0	1.33	0.33	1.33	4	2.67	4	2.67	3.34	3.34	1.62	2.04
Slovak Republic	0	1	2	0	0.75	0.75	0	0	2.67	2.67	1.34	1.34	2.67	2.67	1.33	2.67	2.34	2.34	1.46	1.46
Slovenia	0	3	4	4	2.75	2.75	4	0	1.33	4	2.33	2.33	2.67	2.67	2.67	2.67	2.67	2.67	2.56	2.56

[a] Changed in 1998.
[b] Changed in 2001.
[c] Changed in 2000.
[d] Changed in 2003.
[e] Changed in 2002.
[f] Changed in 1999.

Source: Authors' calculations.

The overall index is calculated as the simple average of the three indices above. Table A2 shows the underlying measures on each of the sub-measures, indicating also the year in which a change occurred.

Delegation and contract-based indices

The indices for the delegation and contract-based approaches were obtained by summing up items of Table A1 that are relevant in those settings. The delegation-approach index was formed by items 2–7 and 9–12, which emphasize the role of a centralized fiscal authority. The contract-based index was constructed using items 1, 5–7, and 9–11, which highlight the presence of well-informed and transparent rules (the role of the minister of finance remains in this approach but mainly to monitor and enforce pre-existing contracts rather taking a proactive role in the formation of the budget).

Lowest-score index

In order to analyse whether the lowest index is the crucial one (or in other words, if a high value on a particular component can substitute for a low value on another component), we have constructed an index using the lowest score of the three components for each year and country.

APPENDIX B: VARIABLES AND DATA SOURCES

Dependent variables

For the fiscal outcome, the general government primary balance is considered. Data from the fiscal notifications to the European Commission are used. Total revenue and grants and total expenditure and net lending minus interest payments are also considered in the analysis. Since these data are not available for all countries in the sample from the fiscal notifications, data from the IMF *World Economic Outlook* (WEO) database are used.

Time-varying economic conditioning variables

- Public debt as percentage of GDP (lagged); unemployment rate; openness index (imports plus exports normalized by GDP); output gap, applying the Hodrick-Prescott filter to GDP data. These are based on data from the IMF WEO.
- Dummy for an IMF programme, taking value 1 if the country had a programme with the Fund during that year, 0 otherwise.
- Dummy for the preparation to EU accession, taking a value of 1 from the year the country was invited to start the negotiations on *aquis communitaire* chapters.

- France/Germany primary balance is the average of the lagged primary balances in France and Germany. Data are from the EUROSTAT database.

Time-varying political variables

- *Government fragmentation.* This variable is constructed as the Herfindhal index. It is the sum of squares of the shares of each party in the government coalition. The index ranges in value from 0 (in the case of very fragmented coalitions to 1 (if one party forms the government). *Data sources: Database on Political Institutions, 2000* (updated in 2004); http://www.worldbank.org/research/bios/pkeefer.htm; *Parties and Elections in Europe,* www.parties-and-elections.de; and Economist Intelligence Unit reports.
- *Ideological orientation of governing coalitions.* Three dimensions are used to characterize the ideological orientation of the government coalition. These relate to: (a) left/right orientation, with a larger value indicating a greater leaning to the right; (b) nationalism (promotes a national rather than cosmopolitan consciousness, history, and culture); and (c) centralization (opposes any decentralization of administration and decision-making). For each dimension, the government coalition's ideological position is estimated as the sum of each party's position, weighted by the party's seats in parliament. *Data source: Database on Party Policy in Modern Democracies* by Benoit and Laver (2005) http://www.politics.tcd.ie/ppmd/, which quantifies the position with respect to these and other dimensions for all parties in 47 countries.
  Dummy assuming a value of 1 for the year of parliamentary elections, 0 otherwise.

Fiscal institutions indices

These variables are described in Appendix A.

Ethnic fractionalization

The variable is constructed as one minus the sum of squares of the shares of identified ethnic groups. If the country has only one ethnic group, the value of the index is zero; as the number of ethnic groups increases, the index of fractionalization increases to 1. *Source:* Alesina, Devleeshauwer, Easterly, Kurlat, and Wacziarg (2003) http://www.stanford.edu/~wacziarg/papersum.html

District magnitude

The number of representatives elected by a single district. *Data source: Database on Political Institutions, 2000* (updated in 2004) http://www.worldbank.org/research/bios/pkeefer.htm;

Voter turnout

Voter turnout as percent of voting age population (see Mueller and Stratmann, 2002). *Data source: Institute for Democracy and Electoral Assistance* http://www.idea.int/vt/index.cfm

REFERENCES

Acemoglu, D. (2005). 'Constitutions, politics, and economics', *Journal of Economic Literature*, 43(4), 1025–48.

Aghion, P., A. Alesina and F. Trebbi (2004). 'Endogenous political institutions', *Quarterly Journal of Economics*, 119 (May), 565–612.

Alesina, A., R. Hausmann, R. Hommes and E. Stein (1999). 'Budget institutions and fiscal performance in Latin America', *Journal of Development Economics*, 59(2), 253–73.

Alesina, A. and R. Perotti (1999). 'Budget deficits and budget institutions', in J. Poterba and J. von Hagen (eds.), *Fiscal Institutions and Fiscal Performance*, University of Chicago Press, Chicago.

Alesina, A., A. Devleeschauwer, W. Easterly, S. Kurlat and R. Wacziarg (2003). 'Fractionalization', *Journal of Economic Growth*, 8(2), 155–94.

Alt, J. and R. Lowry (1994). 'Divided government, fiscal institutions, and budget deficits: evidence from the States', *American Political Science Review*, 88, 811–28.

Annett, A., J. Decressin and M. Deppler (2005). 'Reforming the Stability and Growth Pact', IMF Policy Discussion Paper, PDP/05/2, Washington DC.

Baltagi, B.H. (2005). *Econometric Analysis of Panel Data*, J. Wiley and Sons, Chichester.

Benoit, K. and M. Laver (2006). *Party Policy in Modern Democracies*, Routledge, London.

Besley, T. and A. Case (2003). 'Political institutions and policy choices: evidence from the United States', *Journal of Economic Literature*, 41(1), 7–73.

Blanchard, O. (2005). 'European unemployment: the evolution of facts and ideas', Massachusetts Institute of Technology, Department of Economics, Working Paper 05/24, Cambridge, MA.

Blanchard, O. and J. Wolfers (2000). 'The role of shocks and institutions in the rise of European unemployment: the aggregate evidence', 1999 Harry Johnson Lecture, *Economic Journal*, 100 (March), C1–33.

Bohn, H. (1998). 'The behavior of U.S. public debt and deficits', *Quarterly Journal of Economics*, 113, 949–63.

Brender, A. and A. Drazen (2005). 'Political budget cycles in new versus established democracies', *Journal of Monetary Economics*, 52(7), 1271–95.

Cukierman, A. and M. Tomassi (1998). 'When does it take a Nixon to go to China?' *American Economic Review*, 88(1), 180–97.

Eichengreen, B., R. Hausmann and J. von Hagen (1999). 'Reforming budgetary institutions in Latin America: the case for a National Fiscal Council', *Open Economies Review*, 10, 415–42.

Franzese, R. (1999). 'Partially independent central banks, politically responsive governments, and inflation', *American Journal of Political Science*, 43(3), 681–706.

Gleich, H. (2003). 'Budget institutions and fiscal performance in Central and Eastern European Countries', European Central Bank, Working Paper No. 215, Frankfurt.

Hahm, S., M. Kamlet and D. Mowery (1996). 'The political economy of deficit spending in nine industrialized parliamentary democracies', *Comparative Political Studies*, 29(1), 52–77.

Hallerberg, M. and P. Marier (2004). 'Executive authority, the personal vote, and budget discipline in Latin American and Caribbean countries', *American Journal of Political Science*, 48(3), 571–87.

Hallerberg, M., R. Strauch and J. von Hagen (2004). 'Budgeting in Europe after Maastricht: patterns of reforms and their effectiveness', *Hacienda Pública Española*, 167, 201–25.

Hallerberg, M. and J. von Hagen (1999). 'Electoral institutions, cabinet negotiations, and budget deficits in the European Union', in J. Poterba and J. von Hagen (eds.), *Fiscal Institutions and Fiscal Performance*, University of Chicago Press, Chicago.

Knight, B. and A. Levinson (2000). 'Fiscal institutions in US States', in R. Strauch and J. von Hagen (eds.), *Institutions, Politics, and Fiscal Policy*, Kluwer Academic Publishers, Boston.

Lijphart, A. (1994). *Electoral Systems and Party Systems*, Oxford University Press, Oxford.

Milesi-Ferretti, G.M., R. Perotti and M. Rostagno (2002). 'Electoral systems and public spending', *Quarterly Journal of Economics*, (May), 609–57.

Mueller, D. and T. Stratmann (2003). 'The economic effects of democratic participation', *Journal of Public Economics*, 87(9–10), 2129–55.

Perotti, R. and Y. Kontopoulos (2002). 'Fragmented fiscal policy', *Journal of Public Economics*, 86, 191–222.

Persson, T. (2002). 'Do political institutions shape economic policy?' *Econometrica*, 70 (May), 883–905.

—— (2004). 'Consequences of constitutions', *Journal of the European Economic Association*, 2(2–3), 139–61.

Persson, T., G. Roland and G. Tabellini (2005). 'Electoral rules and government spending in parliamentary democracies', unpublished.

Persson, T. and G. Tabellini (2003). *The Economic Effects of Constitutions*, MIT Press, Cambridge, MA.

—— (2004). 'Constitutional rules and fiscal policy outcome', *American Economic Review*, 94 (March), 25–45.

Poterba, J. (1994). 'State responses to fiscal crises: the effects of budgetary institutions and politics', *Journal of Political Economy*, 102(4), 799–821.

—— (1996). 'Do budget rules work?' National Bureau of Economic Research Working Paper 5550, Cambridge, MA.

Poterba, J. and J. von Hagen (eds.) (1999). *Fiscal Institutions and Fiscal Performance*, University of Chicago Press, Chicago.

Roubini, N. and J. Sachs (1989). 'Government spending and budget deficits in the industrial democracies', *Economic Policy*, 8, 100–32.

Shepsle, K. and B. Weingast (1981). 'Political preferences for the pork barrel: a generalization', *American Journal of Political Science*, 25(1), 96–111.

Stein, E., E. Talvi and A. Grisanti (1999). 'Institutional arrangements and fiscal performance: the Latin American experience', in J. Poterba and J. von Hagen (eds.), *Fiscal Institutions and Fiscal Performance*, University of Chicago Press, Chicago.

Velasco, A. (1999). 'A model of endogenous fiscal deficits and delayed fiscal reforms', in J. Poterba and J. von Hagen (eds.), *Fiscal Institutions and Fiscal Performance*, University of Chicago Press, Chicago.

von Hagen, J. and I. Harden (1995). 'Budget processes and commitment to fiscal discipline', *European Economic Review*, 39 (April), 771–79.

von Hagen J. M. Hallerberg and R. Strauch (2005). 'The design of fiscal rules and forms of governance in European Union countries', mimeo.

Weingast, B., K. Shepsle and C. Johnson (1981). 'The political economy of benefits and costs: A neoclassical approach to distributive politics', *Journal of Political Economy*, 89, 642–64.

Wyplosz, C. (2005). 'Fiscal policy: institutions versus rules', *National Institute Economic Review*, 191(January), 64–78.

Yläoutinen, S. (2004). 'Fiscal frameworks in the Central and Eastern European countries', Finnish Ministry of Finance Discussion Paper No. 72, Ministry of Finance of Finland.

Competition economics and antitrust in Europe

SUMMARY

This paper aims to assess the influence that economic analysis has had on competition policy in the European Union over the last twenty years. Economists are increasingly used in antitrust cases; the annual turnover of the main economic consultancy firms has increased by a factor of 20 since the early 1990s and currently exceeds £20 million. This is about 15% of the aggregate fees earned on antitrust cases, a proportion close to that in the US. The economic resources mobilized by the EU Commission are, however, an order of magnitude smaller and this imbalance is a source of concern. The legal framework and the case decisions have also been influenced by economic analysis in important ways. For instance, the analysis of agreements between firms has increasingly focused on effects; the analysis of the factors that determine effective competition has become more sophisticated; the concept of collective dominance has been progressively developed in terms of the theory of collusion in repeated interactions, and quantitative methods have become more important. However, enforcement has sometimes appealed to economic reasoning in flawed or speculative ways; the paper discusses procedural reasons why this may have occurred. This paper assesses the system of evidence gathering implemented by the Commission in the light of the law and economics literature. It is concluded that while the reforms recently implemented by the Commission do address the main weaknesses of this system, they may still not allow for the most effective development of economic theory and evidence in actual cases.

— Damien J. Neven

Economic Policy October 2006 Printed in Great Britain

Competition economics and antitrust in Europe

Damien J. Neven

Graduate Institute of International Studies, Geneva and CEPR

1. INTRODUCTION

This paper aims to evaluate the influence that economic analysis has had on competition policy in Europe[1] over the last twenty years. It uses evidence from the involvement of economists in competition investigations, as well as from the evolving content of competition decisions, to argue that there has been a significant increase in the economic sophistication of competition enforcement. However, at a number of points enforcement has appealed to economic reasoning in flawed or speculative ways. The paper discusses procedural reasons why this may have occurred, and evaluates current and potential reforms with an eye to ensuring this occurs less often in the future.

Why does any of this matter? At the outset, it is worth emphasizing that the state of competition in a modern economy has an appreciable effect on economic efficiency – though, as I discuss below, the extent to which the state of competition

I would like to thank a number of lawyers and in particular D. Gerardin, P. Mavroidis, Nicolas Petit, A. Sykes and W. Wils for guidance on the legal framework, B. Bishop, C. Mayer and M. Williams for their insights on the market for economic consultants, K. Metha, L.-H. Röller, S. Evenett for useful comments and discussions, John Vickers and two anonymous referees for comments on a previous version of this paper and S. Baler and S. Boffa for excellent research assistance.

The Managing Editor in charge of this paper was Paul Seabright.

[1] I will focus on antitrust policy at the level of the European Union. Considering the antitrust policies of the member states is a book-length project which is beyond the scope of this paper.

Economic Policy October 2006 pp. 741–791 Printed in Great Britain
© CEPR, CES, MSH, 2006.

can be determined by conscious policy is a matter of some debate. There is also an important constitutional issue surrounding competition policy. It is one of the few areas in which competence was ceded very early to the European institutions from the member states, probably because it was considered (somewhat simplistically) to be a largely technocratic domain in which important political trade-offs were unlikely to be considered necessary. Yet in recent years there has been a tendency to delegate enforcement to the member states, largely because more and more member states have developed active and sophisticated enforcement regimes. There is no doubt that the evolution of economic reasoning in policy-making has played an important part in this interesting and unusual constitutional development.

Judge Learned Hand once observed that 'Possession of unchallenged economic power deadens initiative, discourages thrift and depresses energy. . . . Immunity from competition is a narcotic and rivalry a stimulant to industrial progress.'[2] Over the last twenty years, a significant body of evidence has accumulated which confirms his intuition, indicating that competition matters for economic efficiency and in particular for productive efficiency and incentives to innovate.[3] For instance, in one of the early papers in this literature, Nickell (1996) considered a sample of UK firms and evaluated whether their productivity growth was affected by competition. He measured the lack of competition by the importance of the profits accruing to firms. His estimates allow for a comparison of the productivity growth for firms at the 80th percentile and firms at the 20th percentile of the distribution of profits in the sample. The difference is a remarkable 4 percentage points, confirming that competition matters in providing adequate incentives to control cost and improve productivity over time. Very large effects have also been observed in transition economies that provide a natural laboratory to consider the effect of competition (see Djankov and Murrell, 2002, for a survey). Ahn (2002) considered a large sample of studies on the link between competition and innovation and concluded that competition encourages innovative activities and has a significant sorting effect between efficient and less efficient firms over time.

Whether competition policy, as currently practised, stimulates competition is another, possibly more controversial, matter. Much of the evidence on this issue relates to the US and relies on accounts of particular cases in which decisions have had effects on competition and others where it is has not (see, for instance, Baker, 2003 for a vigorous case in favour of antitrust enforcement, and Crandall and Winston, 2003 for a more sceptical view). Some insights can be gained from international cartels: the effects of the Vitamin cartel for instance appear to be stronger (in terms of price increases) in those countries without antitrust enforcement (relative to those with enforcement).[4] Exploiting cross-country differences, Connor (2003) also finds

[2] *United States v. Aluminum Co. of America*, 148 F.2d 416, 427 (2d Cir. 1945).

[3] See Evenett (2005), for a survey (from which Judge Learned Hand's statement is borrowed).

[4] Clarke and Evenett (2003).

that fines have a deterrent effect on cartels (but not one that will ever be sufficient to deter all of them) and that leniency programmes increase the probability that cartels will be uncovered. The record of the EU in terms of the prosecution of cartels certainly confirms that effective cartels can be harmful with long lasting and substantial increases in prices.[5] The record also suggests that leniency programmes may lead to prosecutions of cartels that may otherwise have remained secret and possibly in operation but of course, the very frequency of cartel prosecution also indicates that deterrence is currently far from sufficient. With respect to mergers, Duso *et al.* (2007) use stock market reactions for the merging firms and their competitors to construct a benchmark against which EU decisions can be assessed.[6] They find that the EU prohibits very few mergers that the stock market perceives as pro-competitive (it makes few Type I errors) but may still fail to prohibit quite a few mergers that the stock market perceives as anti-competitive (the frequency of Type II errors may be greater).[7]

The implementation of competition rules is a core European policy. Competences with respect to anti-competitive agreements and the abuse of dominance were explicitly allocated by the founding treaty (respectively Article 85 and Article 86 of the Treaty of Rome, later renumbered as Article 81 and Article 82). It was conceived as an essential component of the internal market and unusual powers of enforcement were granted to the Commission (by delegation from the Council). In one of its early decisions,[8] the European Court of Justice (ECJ) made this clear: 'The treaty, whose preamble and content aim at abolishing the barriers between states . . . could not allow undertakings to reconstruct such barriers. Article 81(1) is designed to pursue this aim'. In addition, the Council adopted procedures in which implementation was centralized; Regulation 17[9] established that in order to obtain the benefit from an exemption under Article 81(3), firms had to notify their agreements to the Commission, which accordingly became a 'Passage oblige'. Further competences for merger control were granted in 1989, through the EC Merger Regulation[10] (ECMR), again with a centralized mechanism of implementation.

Competition is also an area in which competences are shared with the member states, which have developed their own antitrust rules. Jurisdiction is allocated by formal rules and has not been an important source of conflict. Finally, a few years ago, the Council replaced Regulation 17 by a new set of rules that partly delegate the implementation of EU law to the competition authorities of the member states.[11]

---

[5] See Connor (2003) and the Annual Reports of the European Commission.

[6] The basic intuition behind this approach being that at least in some circumstances, mergers which harm consumers should benefit competitors (and vice versa).

[7] For the first few years of merger control, Neven *et al.* (1994) find some case of possibly anti-competitive mergers that have been allowed because of political pressure.

[8] *Consten and Grundig v. Commission*, case 56–58/64.

[9] EC Reg. 17/62 of 6 February 1962, OJ 21/02/62, pp. 204–11.

[10] Council Regulation No. 4064/89 of 21 December 1989.

[11] EC Reg. 1/2003 of 16 December 2002, OJ L/1/1 of 4 January 2003.

This delegation is not immune from incentives problems as member states have no clear interest in considering effects which take place outside their jurisdiction (see for instance, Neven and Mavroidis, 2001). Still, this architecture of enforcement is unusual among EU policies and as experience accumulates, its functioning may be a useful source of inspiration in other areas.

The fact that economics has become more important in EU antitrust policy and practice since this journal was first published is hardly controversial. One of the objectives of this essay will be to attempt some quantification of the relative importance of economic inputs in antitrust practice. Focusing on the fees earned by economic consultants, we will observe that the EU may be converging towards the US in terms of the relative importance of economics and law as inputs in cases. By comparison, economic resources at the level of the EU Commission remain meagre, and the asymmetry in resources between the authorities and the businesses they regulate is a cause for significant concern.

Evidence that economists have been hired increasingly to provide advice is merely an indication that parties and their legal advisers have found economists useful in order to prevail. It provides only limited evidence with respect to the role that economics, as a discipline, has played. The role that economic insights, in terms of theory and empirical evidence, have played can only be inferred from decisions and judgments and the reasoning that supports them, as well as the evolution of the legal framework (including soft laws like guidelines) and policy statements. This essay will thus evaluate whether economic insights have had an effect on policy and case law and whether some insights have been neglected.

We observe that economic analysis has had a strong impact in a number of areas:

- the analysis of agreements between firms, in particular vertical agreements under Article 81, has increasingly focused on effects;
- the assessment of competition has moved away from the formal notion of dominance towards effective competition;
- the analysis of the factors that determine effective competition has become more sophisticated, in particular regarding the definition of the relevant markets, bidding markets, the proximity of competitors' position and buyer power;
- the concept of collective dominance has been progressively developed in terms of the theory of collusion in repeated interactions;
- quantitative methods have become more important;
- enforcement procedures, like the leniency programmes, which find some foundation in economic analysis, have been implemented.

Both the Commission and the courts seem to have played a part in enhancing the role of economic analysis. There are, however, two areas of concern. The first is the implementation of Article 82, on the abuse of dominant positions, which has remained rather formalistic. The Commission, however, has launched a debate in this area and has published a discussion paper, which moves some way towards an effects based approach.[12] Hence, it may only be a matter of time for economic analysis to have a stronger impact on the implementation of Article 82. The second area is a matter of process and procedure. The process through which the concept of collective dominance has emerged has involved the annulment of a Commission decision, in which the Commission's treatment of economic theories and evidence has been criticized. Another two important merger prohibitions have been annulled[13] by the Court of First Instance (CFI) (*Tetra Laval/Sidel*[14] and *Schneider/Legrand*[15]), and another one largely annulled on similar grounds (*GE/Honeywell*[16]). We also observe more generally that the record of the Commission in court may not be all that impressive.

The way in which the Commission develops and uses economic analysis therefore deserves attention. We develop a framework to think about antitrust procedures and identify the factors that will influence how theories and evidence are handled. We identify the system of proof taking implemented by the Commission, which is mostly inquisitorial with a prosecutorial bias, and discuss this system of proof-taking at greater length in light of the literature. We observe that the reforms implemented by the Commission go in the right direction, suggest some additional reforms and discuss the implementation of an alternative, adversarial, regime of proof taking.

The paper is organized as follows. Section 2 attempts to provide some quantitative measure of the role that economists have played in European Antitrust. Section 3 discusses the economic insights that have had an effect on case law and policy. Section 4 provides a framework to analyse antitrust proceedings along five dimensions: namely, the scope of the decision (what has to be proven?), the system of proof taking (how is the proof gathered?), the standard of proof (what should be the degree of confidence in the proof?), the type of evidence which is deemed sufficient to meet the standard of proof (what elements of proofs should be considered as sufficiently telling to conclude that the required degree of confidence is reached?) and the standard of review (how is the proof assessed in case of appeal?[17]). Section 5 characterizes EU procedures in terms of these dimensions. Section 6 discusses in more detail the system of proof taking in light of the law and economics literature. Section 7 summarizes our findings and discusses the scope for further reforms. Section 8 concludes.[18]

---

[12] DG Comp Discussion Paper on the application of Article 82 or the Treaty to exclusionary abuses, December 2005, available from http://ec.euroPa.eu/comm/competition/antitrust/others/Art.icle_82_review.html#14062006

[13] In what follows, I will give references of the decisions and judgments only when they appear in the discussion for the first time.

[14] Case COMP/M2416 and judgments Case T-5/02 at the CFI and Case C-12/03 P at the Court of Justice.

[15] Case M 2283 and judgment C 380/01.

[16] Case COMP/M2220 and judgment Case T-210/01.

[17] Appeal is somewhat of an abuse of language as EU courts formally only exercise a judicial review. In what follows we will still use 'appeal' for ease of reference.

[18] I have been involved in a number of cases discussed in the paper and in particular Volvo/Scania, Airtours/First Choice, EMI/Time Warner, TotalFina/Elf and Tetra Laval/Sidel. My discussion of these cases relies on public information only.

2. ECONOMIC INPUTS

Economic advice was marginal in antitrust proceedings up until the late 1980s. It was undertaken mostly by individual academics (there are references to some of them in early decisions like *Soda/Ash*[19] or *Wood Pulp*[20]). With the implementation of the Merger Regulation in 1990, demand for economic advice seems to have risen. NERA opened an office in London in 1984 and London Economics was set up in 1986. Lexecon Ltd was set up in January 1991 and up until the mid 1990s, Lexecon, London Economics and NERA were the main suppliers with a total amount of fees around £2.5 million in 1995. This turnover corresponds to EU related competition work but also to competition work in national jurisdictions. UK related work accounts for the vast majority of the latter. The market for EU related advice grew rapidly in the late 1990s, as the number of merger notifications (as well as other types of cases) grew but also following the preparation and implementation of the notice on market definition. This notice,[21] inspired by the US practice, used economic concepts explicitly.[22] As indicated by Figure 1,[23] for the

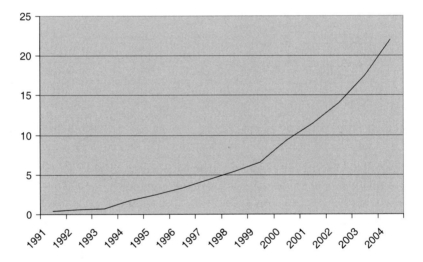

Figure 1. Turnover of economic consultancy firms (current £ million)

Source: See text.

[19] Case T-36/91.

[20] Joined cases C-89/85, C-104/85, C-114/85, C-116/85, C-117/85 and C-125/85 to C-129/85.

[21] Notice on the definition of the relevant market for the purposes of Community competition law. OJ C 372 on 9/12/1997.

[22] The fact that a quantitative analysis was used for market definition in the high profile acquisition of Perrier by Nestlé in 1992 may also have been significant in alerting legal advisers to the potential of economic analysis in this regard.

[23] The aggregate turnover has been obtained by adding the antitrust turnover of Lexecon, NERA, London Economics, Frontier, OXERA, RBB Economics, LBE, CRA and LECG. Figures for some individual firms are confidential and cannot be reported individually. Others have been estimated on the basis of the number of staff. Some of the figures have been interpolated on the basis of a constant growth. Independent consultancy firms on the continent, which have remained small over the period, have not been considered. The turnover of independent academics, which was probably significant in the earlier years relative to the turnover of commercial firms has not been considered. Traces of the role played by these academics (in particular B. Yamey, G. Yarrow and D. Morris) can be found in some UK cases.

following ten years, total turnover grew[24] at some 25–30% per year, reaching about £24 million in 2004.[25]

It is also interesting to consider the turnover of economic consultancy relative to the turnover for legal advice. Lexecon Ltd estimated that economic consultancy amounted to about 5% of the total amount of fees (legal and economic) in 1995.[26]

If one assumes that legal fees have increased at the same pace as the number of cases (the annual flow of cases has increased by a factor of about 2.5) in the last ten years, economic consultancy would now amount to about 15% of the total amount of fees. This is only a rough guess, which however seems in line with the perception of some key players in the market. Interestingly, it would mean that the European market has converged with the US in this respect as 15% appears to be a commonly accepted figure in the US.[27]

Some evidence on the relative importance of economic and legal fees can also be gathered from the records of the *Airtours* case.[28] Airtours, which attempted to acquire First Choice and was prevented from doing so by the Commission, succeeded in its appeal in front of the CFI[29] and the Commission was ordered to pay the cost that Airtours had incurred for the procedure. The Commission refused to pay the amounts that Airtours requested, claiming that they were exaggerated. Airtours asked the CFI to order the Commission to pay and the court had to rule on the amount that the Commission should repay. Accordingly legal and economic fees became public.[30] The amounts shown in Table 1 were spent by Airtours and claimed to the Commission (second column).[31]

Fees charged by economists thus amount to about 21% of the total. The court considered the various categories of fees. Economic fees account for about 10% of the fees eventually reimbursed by the Commission.

The amount of economic input into the *Airtours* case is probably unusual (as the case revolved around some conceptual economic issues). On the other hand, one would expect economic fees to be lower in a court case than in the initial administrative

---

[24] This rapid growth is to some extent a consequence of the fact that different parties in a competition case often have different interests – or, in other words, 'where a single economist starves, two will make a living'.

[25] This growth gives a biased estimate of the growth of competition work in Europe as some firms (like Lexecon) started to generate very substantial fees from work outside Europe (in particular South Africa).

[26] The turnover of legal advice was estimated as follows: at the time, law firms in the UK had to obtain insurance from a common industry scheme. They had to publish their turnover for this purpose. In order to obtain the fees related to antitrust, it was assumed that each partner would generate the same amount of fees (an assumption which was validated with law firms) and partners undertaking mostly antitrust work were identified). These fees relate mostly to UK and European work (which was performed mostly from London at the time). However, it does not consider the turnover of Brussels based law firms which were performing European work at the time (in particular the traditional Belgian law firms and the Belgian operations of US law firms). From this perspective, the figure of 5% for economic fees is probably an upper bound.

[27] Source: Lexecon, Inc.

[28] Case IV/M 1524.

[29] T-342/99.

[30] The amount that the Commission spent on external economic advice is not publicly available.

[31] See §32 of the decision – Case T-342/99 DEP.

Table 1. Legal and economic fees in *Airtours* (£)

	Claimed	Accepted
Barrister	279 375.00	170 000
Solicitors	850 000.00	250 000
(expenses)	(19 509.18)	
Economic consultancy	281 051.52	30 000
Academic economists	33 885.35	19 485
Legal fees in Luxemburg	620.00	
Total	1 464 441.55	

Source: Case T-342/99 DEP.

procedure (in which evidence is gathered). This particular case may thus confirm that a figure of 15% is not unrealistic.

A survey by PriceWaterhouseCoopers[32] for the International Bar Association lends some further support to this estimate. The study that focuses on the cost of mergers and acquisitions found that about 20% of the amount of legal fees was paid to other types of advisers. These presumably include lobbyists as well as economists but one can presume that the bulk of external fees went to economists.

The market structure has also changed over the last 15 years. Lexecon had a market share that could be referred to as 'dominant' at some point in the mid 1990s. Entry by US firms (LECG and CRAI), domestic entry and split-ups increased the number of significant players over time. Currently, the industry appears to be more fragmented with comparable markets shares (in the 20s) for CRA International (which took over Lexecon in the summer of 2005), LECG, RBB Economics, with Frontier and NERA being somewhat smaller.[33] This fragmentation has also been observed in the US market and from this perspective the two markets seem to have converged as well. The market structure is also characterized by the presence of three firms with global (or at least transatlantic) operations.[34] In this respect, economic consultancy seems to have followed the same path as legal advice, both moves being triggered by clients with operations and antitrust filings across jurisdictions.[35]

A more qualitative estimate of the importance of economics in antitrust can be obtained by considering the proportion of decisions in which explicit reference is made to economic advice. Table 2 shows the number of Phase II decisions taken every year since the implementation of the Merger Regulation and the number of

---

[32] http://archive.ibanet.org/news/Newsitem.asp?newsID=99

[33] RBB Economics was set up by former NERA consultants. LECG also grew markedly in 2004 as a number of consultants joined the firm from NERA.

[34] RBB Economics has a cooperation agreement with Competition Policy Associates (the consulting operation set up by Ordover and Willig) in the US so that Frontier Economics is the only firm with a domestic focus at the moment.

[35] Cross-border deals may not be numerous but they generate fees in excess of the average.

Table 2. References to economic reports in Phase II cases

Year	Phase II decisions (A)	Phase II decisions with econ. (B)	B/(A–D)	Unpublished phase II (D)
2005	4	0	0.00	3
2004	7	5	0.71	0
2003	7	2	0.29	0
2002	6	1	0.17	0
2001	20	10	0.50	0
2000	17	2	0.12	0
1999	9	2	0.22	0
1998	8	1	0.13	0
1997	9	1	0.11	0
1996	6	3	0.50	0
1995	7	2	0.18	4
1994	5	1	0.17	1
1993	3	1	0.25	1
1992	4	1	0.25	0
1991	5	1	0.20	0
TOTAL	118	34	0.27	9

Source: DG Comp and own calculations.

published decisions in which reference is made to economic advice.[36] There is a positive trend (five-year averages increase, for instance) but there are also some important variations around the trend. A closer look at the cases in which economic advice is referred to reveals that economists are involved in the more important cases (those involving new issues, delicate competitive situations and large transactions). As the frequency of such cases varies from year to year (even among Phase II cases), it may explain the variance of economic advice around the trend. It also suggests, however, that the nature of competition among economic consultants differs from that among legal advisers. By comparison with lawyers, economists tend to compete for bigger but less numerous cases. This should enhance rivalry.

The amount of resources that the Directorate-General Competition (DG Comp) mobilizes for economic analysis can also be roughly assessed. There are currently 83 professionals with a background in economics at DG Comp[37] and 184 with a background in law (hence roughly a ratio of 1 to 2). The ratio of economists to lawyer has increased greatly over time; according to Wilks and McGowan (1996), the ratio was 1 to 7 in the early 1990s. Still, as indicated by Röller (2005), most economists do not undertake technical economic analysis. Only 20 have a PhD in economics and about 10 have a PhD with a specialization in industrial organization. The position of Chief Competition Economist was only created in 2003 and his team consists of 10

[36] This evidence was gathered by searching for key words (generic words, such as economic advice, economic consultancy, economic studies as well as the names of the main economic consultancy firms).

[37] See www.euroPa.eu.int/comp/dgs/competition

economists. This can be compared with the (roughly) 150 professionals currently working in the economic consultancy firms considered above. Even if one assumes that only half of the time of those professionals is devoted to European work, the discrepancy between the resources invested by the parties and those invested by the EU is very large. The team of the Chief Competition Economist can also be compared with the economists working at comparable agencies in the US. The antitrust division of the US Department of Justice and the US Federal Trade Commission have together well over 100 professional economists.[38]

3. ECONOMIC INPUT IN THE CASE LAW AND POLICY

The fact that economists have been hired in procedures is only a signal that economics as a discipline may have had an impact on the case law. This section attempts to gather some further evidence that economics has affected the case law and EU policy. In order to do so, we have considered the main issues that antitrust authorities consider and tried to identify whether economic insights (in terms of theory, empirical evidence and methodologies) have been used and whether some of them may have been neglected.

In order to document the influence of economic analysis, we have considered the evolution of the legal framework including soft laws like guidelines and notices. The main developments are presented in Table 3. The economic insights that these new soft laws have taken on board will be discussed further below together with the evolution of the case law.

The evolution of the case law is harder to trace in a systematic manner. I have relied on two complementary sources. First, I have compiled a list of the cases that have been the subject of a specific commentary by the economic consultancy firms reviewed above (see Box 1). This source is certainly not free of biases; in particular, the decision whether to publish a comment is presumably dependent on whether the firm prevailed. This may not matter if two firms were involved on opposite sides but we have no control on the proportion of cases in which this occurred.[39]

Second, I have drawn up a list of important developments and significant cases from my experience and knowledge of the case law. This exercise involves a great deal of judgment (and my knowledge of the case law is not free of biases). In order to validate this exercise I sought comments form a number of prominent competition economists. I obtained substantial comments and suggestions from four of them.[40]

[38] See www.oecd.org/dataoecd/53/15/2406946.pdf

[39] The list of cases appearing in Box 1 has also been compared to the list of cases that have been subject to a focused article in the *European Competition Law Review* (since 1995). The second list is broader but includes many articles dealing with legal issues only. Considering only the articles with an economic focus, it does not appear that the list in Box 1 has significant omissions.

[40] I posted a survey on my website and sent an email to the 45 European competition economists that appear in the list of top 100 competition economists compiled by the Global Competition Review, asking them to fill in the survey. I obtained only four substantial contributions. Evans and Graves (2005) also provide an evaluation of important developments during the Monti years with respect to mergers and was also a useful source to validate the content of Box 2.

Table 3. Main developments in the legal framework

Article 81	Article 82	Merger control
Notice on the definition of the relevant market for the purposes of Community competition law. *OJ C 372 on 9/12/1997*		
Regulation (EC) No 2790/1999 on vertical agreements	Discussion Paper on the application of Art. 82 of the treaty to exclusionary abuses, December 2005	Merger Regulation Reg 4064/89
Guidelines on vertical restraints *OJl C 291, 13.10.2000*	Regulation 1/2003 (modernization) *OJ L 1, 04.01.2003*	Council Regulation (EC) No 139/2004
Guidelines on the application of Art 81(3) *OJ C 101, 27.04.2004*, Leniency notice I *OJ C 207, 18.07.1996* Leniency notice II *OJ C 45, 19.02.2003* Guidelines on technology licensing agreements *OJ C 101, 27.04.2004*	Regulation (EC) No 772/2004 on technology transfer agreements

Regulations 2658–9/2000 on the application of Art 81(3) to specialization and R&D agreements | Horizontal guidelines *OJ C 31, 05.02.2004* |
| Guidelines on the application of Art 81 to horizontal cooperation agreements *OJ C 3 of 06.01.2001* | Regulation 1/2003 *OJ L 1, 04.01.2003* | |

Source: DG Comp.

Box 2 presents my findings.[41] For each topic, I have considered the main developments of economic analysis in the legal framework (presented in Table 3) and the relevant case law (see Box 1). I also indicate when the analysis undertaken by the Commission has been criticized as being flawed or speculative. Hence, this box is meant to summarize both the development of economic analysis and its implementation by the Commission. Each item in this box could be discussed at length and all items are not equally important. The following elements could be highlighted.

First, there is a striking evolution over time with respect to the analysis of competitive positions. Early on in the period, a firm's competitive position was considered with a focus on dominance and dominance was often related to structural indicators like market shares; this prevailed in the implementation of Article 82 but also to a lesser extent in the implementation of the Merger Regulation. Relevant markets were sometimes defined excessively narrowly without much consideration for competitive constraints. Early commentaries (like Lexecon/CRA's competition memo of April 1995, citing decisions like *Boosey and Hawkes* or *Sealink/B&I* or the discussion in Neven

---

[41] The question marks that appear in the box identify some issues on which there is apparent disagreement among the five economists involved in gathering this evidence.

Box 1. Cases subject to a specific commentary by economic consultancy firms

Lexecon/CRAI	RBB
Air Liquide/BOC	Airtours/First Choice
Airtours	British Airways v Commission
Boeing/McDonnell Douglas	GE/Honeywell
Boosey & Hawkes	GE/Instrumentarium
British Airways	Michelin
British Plaster Board/Saint-Gobain	Microsoft
Carrefour/Promodes	P&O Princess (POPC), Carnival
	Corporation and Royal Caribbean Cruises.
Coca Cola/Carlsberg	Shell/DEA
Coca Cola/Amalgamated Beverages	Tetra Laval/Sidel
Ernst & Young/KPMG	
GE/Honeywell	
Gencor/Lonrho	NERA
Guinness/Grand Metropolitan	
Hoffman La Roche/Boehringer Mannheim	Airtours/First Choice
Kimberly Clark/Scott	BA/Virgin
Michelin	Boeing/Hughes
Microsoft/Liberty Media/Telewest	Coca Cola
New Holland/Case	Enso/Stora
Norske Skog/Parenco/Walsum	General electric/Honeywell
Oracle/PeopleSoft	Guiness/Grand Metropolitan
Price Waterhouse/Coopers & Lybrand	Kali und Salz AG and Mitteldeutsche Kali AG
Procter & Gamble/VP Schickedanz	Kimberly-Clark/Scott Paper
Scott Paper/Kimberly-Clark	Michelin
Sealink/B&I Holyhead	Oscar Bronner vs Mediaprint
Telepiù/NewsCorporation	Pirelli/BICC
Tetra Laval/Sidel	Sea containers vs Sealink
UPM-Kymmene/Haindl	
Vodafone Airtouch/Mannesmann	Others
	Ims Health
	Microsoft
	Visa I, II

et al., 1994) are quite telling in this respect. Over time, the definition of the relevant market has been clarified; it emphasizes economic principles and recommends the use of the SSNIP (Small but Significant Non-transitory Increase in Price by a hypothetical monopolist) test in line with the US practice. The analysis of the competitive constraints faced by firms has also become much more sophisticated, considering for instance the role of bidding markets, durability, strategic barriers to entry, potential competition or buyer power. More sophisticated quantitative techniques have been implemented (for market definition and simulations of unilateral effects in mergers). The prospect for the coordination of behaviour ('collective dominance') has been clarified and firmly rooted in the theory of repeated games. Interestingly however, the major shift in policy in this area came through a court judgment (*Airtours/First Choice*)

Box 2. Development of economic analysis in the legal framework and case law

1. Market power / effective competition
Market definition
The notice on relevant market focuses on competitive constraints and adopts the SSNIP test. The definition of the geographic market (which emphasizes the conditions of competition) market is however different from that of the products market (which emphasizes demand/supply substitution). This may lead to excessively narrow geographic markets.

Quantitative methods are increasingly used (first in *Nestlé/Perrier* in the early 1990s and then routinely).
Implementation: Captive sales (sales within firms) tend to be excluded from the relevant market. This approach may be overly mechanistic (*Shell/DEA*).

Unilateral effect in merger control
The horizontal merger guidelines (2004) provide a clear framework to analyse unilateral effects. The guidelines make a direct reference to economic models (Cournot and Bertrand). This may be misleading, however, to the extent that it may suggest that any market can be neatly characterized in terms of one or the other model.

Merger simulations techniques have used both by parties and the Commission (for instance in *Volvo/Scania*, Comp M 1672; *Philip Morris/Papastratos*, Comp M 3191; *Lagardère/Natexis/VUP*, Comp M 2978; *Oracle/People Soft*, Comp M 3216). *Implementation*: The procedure may not always have allowed for a proper validation of the simulation models when they were introduced (*Volvo/Scania*). A more balanced evaluation of the models (allowing for some cross-examination) has been organized in later proceedings (*Oracle/People Soft*).

Competitive analysis
The early case law relied on dominance and dominance was often assessed in terms of market shares. Over time, the analysis of effective competition has become much more sophisticated. In particular:

- The competition induced by tendering for contracts (bidding markets) has been introduced. It was neglected in *Boeing/McDonnell*, but soon after integrated in *Pirelli/BICC*, Comp M 1882 and widely used thereafter.
- The competitive pressure exercised by the stock of service embodied in durable goods on new products has been considered (*Boeing/McDonnell*, Commission decision 97/816/EC; and *New Holland/Case*, Comp M 1571).

- The pattern of substitution and the competitive relationship between products has been considered in details (*GE/Instrumentarium*, Commission decision 2004/322/EC; *Piaggio/Aprilia*, Comp M 3570).
- Dynamic aspects of competition have been increasingly considered (for instance in *Hoffman La Roche/Boehringer Mannheim*, Comp M 950).
- The analysis of entry includes potential competition (*Air Liquide/Boc*, *Tetra Laval/Sidel*). Developments of entry in new markets has been anticipated taking into account potential barriers (for instance network effects in *Microsoft/Liberty Media/Telewest* (Notification withdrawn – investigation discussed in Lexecon Competition Memo, September 2000)).
- Assessment of exit conditions and the failing firm defence has involved a careful examination of the competitive counterfactual (*News Corp/Telepiu*, Comp M 2876; and *Andersen/EY*, Comp M 2816).

Implementation: The fact that firms may have 'dominant' positions across several geographic markets (*Volvo/Scania*, Comp M 1672; *Schneider/Legrand*) has been emphasized without clear justification. The importance of the rivalry induced by bidding markets may have been exaggerated. For instance the significance of credible bidders may have been overplayed (*PW/Coopers*, Comp M 1016)? The competitive pressure from entry (in the absence of barriers) in new markets may have been underestimated in *Vodafone/Mannesman* (Comp M 1795). Impact of non-price issues of importance to consumers, i.e. quality, variety, and convenience (which may off-set or add to anti-competitive pricing effects) may have been neglected.

Buyer power

The analysis of buyer power has rightly focused on the mechanism that will allow buyers to inflict damages on suppliers (*Enso/Stora*, Comp M 1225).

Implementation: The Commission has appealed to a 'spiralling effect' in *Carrefour/Promodes* (Comp M 1684) such that buyer power is self-reinforcing which may not have been properly validated. (?)

2. Collusion

Article 81

The court has imposed a very high standard of proof with respect to the inference of collusion from firms' behaviour. This may be interpreted as stemming from excessive confidence on the identification of behaviour from economic models (*Wood Pulp*, Court decision, Joined cases C-89/85, C-104/85, C-114/85, C-116/85, C-117/85 and C-125/85 to C-129/85). This standard still prevails.

The Commission has introduced incentives for parties to act as whistleblower to undermine collusive agreements (leniency notices – see Table 3). These schemes are supported by economic analysis (even if in economic models, leniency mostly reduces the incentive to collude and should not be observed in equilibrium).

Quantitative methods have been largely neglected as tools to test for the presence of collusion effects and evaluate damages.

Co-ordinated effects in merger control

The early case law was not firmly grounded in the theory of co-ordination. Some emphasis was given to the presence of structural links among firms (*Kali/ Salz*, Case Comp M 308 and Court cases C-68/94 and C-30/95; *Gencor/ Lonrho*, Case Comp M 619 and judgment T 102/96). The CFI has clarified that structural links were not necessary.

The Commission introduced some confusion in *Airtours*, using language suggesting that joint dominance was not clearly associated with co-ordination but rather with general oligopolistic coordination.

The theory of collusion in repeated games was affirmed by the Court in *Airtours*.

The approach was refined in the horizontal merger guidelines. The guidelines may, however, put an excessive emphasis on the characteristics of the market, relative to the effect of the merger, for assessing the likelihood of co-ordination. The list of factors, discussed by the guidelines, which may favour co-ordination, may also not be very robust.

Implementation: The Commission has become sophisticated in its discussion of co-ordination. For instance, regarding the discussion of capacity coordination (*UPM-Kymmene/Haindl*, Comp M 2498 and *Norske/Skog/Parenco/Walsum*, Comp M 2499).

The link between collusion and the degree of asymmetry in market share or capacity has, however, been neglected (*Nestlé/Perrier*, Comp M 190; *EMI/Time Warner*, Comp M 1852).

There has been no development of empirical tools to consider the likelihood of co-ordinated effects arising post-merger.

3. Agreements

Horizontal

There has been a progressive (but slow) move away from a formalistic approach toward an economic effects-based assessment of Article 81(1) (*Wouters*, C-309/99, preliminary ruling by the CFI) and a recognition of the pro-competitive effects of agreements involving small firms.

The modernization regulation has introduced a direct effect for Article 81.

Vertical

The Commission has introduced a new block exemptions regulation (1999) and guidelines (2000), which emphasize effects rather than form. The guidelines emphasize market power as a necessary condition for anti-competitive effects but rely on arbitrary thresholds to clear some agreements or introduce strong presumptions of illegality. The guidelines may not recognize sufficiently the free-rider rationale for territorial protection and imposes a harsh treatment on restrictions to intra-brand competition when inter-brand competition is weak. If the guidelines recognize efficiency benefits stemming from vertical agreement, they fail to acknowledge that such agreements may also be pro-competitive. The residual reliance on form implies that different vertical restraints with similar effects are treated differently.

Two sided markets

Insights from theory have not had much influence (*Visa I* and *II*).

4. Efficiencies

Article 81(3)

The Commission has introduced a new block exemption for R&D agreements and a notice on the application of 81(3). The latter may not make sufficient distinctions between vertical and horizontal agreements and does not provide guidance on some issues (hold up/free rider problems).

Implementation: Too much credence may have been given to efficiency justifications (possibly in the early case law – see e.g. *Ford/VW*, Case IV/33.814; *Night Services*, Case IV/34.600).

Merger Regulation

Initially it was unclear whether there is an efficiency defence and there are even some cases of efficiency offences in the early case law (see e.g. *ATT/NCR*, Case IV/M0050) but also later (*Guinness/Grand Med*, Case COM M938).

The revision of the Merger Regulation (2004 – see Table 3) has however clarified that efficiencies can be taken into account.

Implementation: In imposing partial divestitures, the Commission may have failed to recognize their consequences for the realization of efficiencies. Efficiencies in non-horizontal mergers (pricing and contractual efficiencies) have sometimes been ignored – e.g. *Aol/Time Warner* (Case M 1845) especially in the earlier case law. They have been extensively considered in some recent cases like *PG/Gillette* (Case M 3732).

5. Exclusion

Article 82

With respect to tying, the early case law relied on form. In *Microsoft*, the Commission has developed more sophisticated dynamic theories (which emphasize network effects for instance).

More generally, until the discussion paper on the reform of Article 82 (2005 – see Table 3), there is an emphasis on form rather than effects and a failure to recognize genuine efficiency and competition benefits from practices that can have exclusionary effects.

For instance, both the Commission and the court have failed to recognize that discriminatory pricing and rebates in oligopoly may not be anti-competitive. (*Michelin II*, Case T-203/01; *BA/Virgin*, Commission Decision 2000/74/EC and Court judgment T 219/99).

With respect to predation, the literature on financial predation has been largely neglected.

Merger Regulation

Dynamic models of tying have been developed (*Aol/Time Warner*, Case COMP M 1845).

Implementation: According to CFI judgments, models of anticompetitive foreclosure through tying have been used out of context and without proper evidence – see also Ahlborn *et al.* (2004), Grant and Neven (2005), Neven (2006) – (*Tetra Laval/Sidel*, *GE/Honeywell*).

which annulled a Commission decision, on the grounds that the Commission theory of coordination was unclear and that the evidence presented by the Commission was insufficient and used in a manner which was sometimes contradictory.

Of course, commentators may sometimes have disagreed about particular applications (as reflected in the box) but overall the trend towards a more sophisticated analysis of effective horizontal competition is impressive. In the area of merger control, this has been accompanied by new soft law, in particular the merger guidelines and a change in the wording of the substantive criteria which gives less prominence to the concept of dominance.[42] Progress with respect to the analysis of competitive constraints under Article 82 has been much less clear, however. The recent discussion paper on the reform of Article 82, however, proposes to (re-) interpret the classical definition dominance (the 'power to behave to an appreciable extent independently of its

[42] The wording of the substantive criteria has changed from concentration which 'create or strengthen a dominant position as a result of which effective competition is impeded' to concentration which 'significantly impede effective competition, in particular as the result of the creation or strengthening of a dominant position' (Article 2, Council Regulation 139/2004).

competitors, its customers and ultimately of the consumers'[43]) in terms of market power.[44]

Second, the analysis of vertical agreements has shifted markedly at the turn of the century, from a focus on form towards a focus on effects, which explicitly recognizes the efficiency rationale of many vertical agreements. Arguably the shift could have been even more pronounced – for instance, with a recognition of the pro-competitive effects of some vertical agreements. But here again, the evolution is remarkable.

Third, the application of exclusionary theories (foreclosure) is an area in which less progress has been made. With respect to Article 82, the Commission and the courts have focused mostly on form instead of effects. The pro-competitive element of some practices as well as the efficiency benefits that may stem from them has been largely ignored. As mentioned earlier, the Commission has still recently launched a debate on the application of Article 82; the discussion paper that it has published goes some way toward an 'effects based' enforcement and recent cases like *Microsoft*[45] focus on effects and considers sophisticated theories of foreclosure. With respect to merger control, the court has annulled the Commission's analysis of foreclosure (in *Tetra Laval/Sidel* and *GE/Honeywell*). In both instances, the court failed to be convinced by the exclusionary theories and the elements of proofs that the Commission had put forward.

Fourth, the analysis of efficiencies is also an area in which less progress has been made. There has been some suspicion early in the period that Article 81(3) may have been used in some instances in order to promote industrial policies, so that arguments regarding efficiencies may have been taken at face value.[46] The Commission has recently published a notice on the application of Article 81(3) which still fails to make sufficient distinctions between horizontal and vertical agreements and does not provide a framework to consider the sources of efficiencies. With respect to merger control, the policy has evolved: early in the implementation of the Merger Regulation, it was not clear whether efficiencies could be taken into consideration, and even then, efficiencies were sometimes considered as an offence rather than as making a merger more acceptable. The revision of the Merger Regulation in 2004 has made it clear that efficiencies could be taken into account. The Commission has been considering them, even in the context of non-horizontal mergers.

Overall, two conclusions emerge. First, economic insights, theories and evidence are increasingly used by the Commission, even if progress is more impressive in some areas than others. The Commission has also been proactive in these developments, in terms of decisions, soft laws and reforms of the statute. Second, the court has exposed at least four instances (*Airtours*, *Tetra Laval/Sidel*, *GE/Honeywell* and *Schneider/Legrand*) in which the Commission has mishandled economic theory and evidence.

---

[43] From judgments on United Brands (case 27/76) and Hoffmann-La Roche (case 85/76).

[44] See Paragraph 23, DG Comp Discussion Paper on the application of Article 82 or the Treaty to exclusionary abuses, December 2005.

[45] Case 37/792.

[46] See, for instance, Neven *et al.* (1998).

This second observation reveals that anti-competitive theories and evidence had not been properly evaluated at the time of the decisions, which suggests that procedures to ensure this evaluation may not have been adequate at the time. This was indeed the reaction of many observers at the time of these decisions.[47] This observation should also be considered in a wider perspective. In the early 1980s, there was some concern that decisions, in particular merger control decisions, could be affected by outside pressures from the companies involved and the member states (possibly acting as agents for the companies). This is documented for instance in Neven *et al.* (1994) (see also Lexecon Competition Memo, April 1995). Procedures at the time were thus not immune to capture by corporate interests.

To avoid any bias arising from the consideration of just a few cases, it may be useful to consider a wider sample such as the record of the court's rulings on the Commission's decisions that have been appealed. Montag (1996) considered the 29 decisions imposing fines in excess of 3 million ECU since Regulation 17 came into force until 1996. He found that 24 decisions had been appealed, of which 18 had been judged at the time of his study. Out of those, 4 four were upheld, 12 were annulled or fines were reduced (sometimes annulled) for all companies. In two cases, fines were reduced for some companies only. He interpreted this finding as providing 'remarkable evidence of the Commission's poor record in reaching decisions imposing fines'. Neven *et al.* (1998) observe that the reduction in fines is very often associated with the imposition of a higher standard of proof (such that the CFI finds that the Commission's evidence is insufficient to justify the fines that it has imposed). Wils (2004) suggests that the high frequency of annulment in this period is also associated with the imposition of stricter procedural requirements (like rights of access to files).

In order to complement the evidence of Montag (1996), I considered all cases that have been appealed to the CFI since 1994 and computed the proportion of cases in which the Commission prevailed. In a number of cases, in particular regarding Article 81, the evaluation of whether the Commission prevailed involves a fair amount of judgment and the results should be considered as indicative.[48] Results are presented in Table 4.

The Commission's record with respect to Article 82 is striking in absolute terms but also relative to the other provisions. The difference can possibly be related to the nature of the evidence brought forward in these procedures: as discussed above, Article 82 has remained focused on form, whereas the Merger Regulation and increasingly Article 81 (at least with respect to vertical agreements) are focusing on effects, which involves the development of economic theories and evidence. Such

---

[47] See, for instance, Ahlborn (2002).

[48] The same applies to some extent with respect to the ECMR. For instance, GE/Honeywell was classified as a case where the Commission did not prevail, despite the fact that the prohibition was affirmed, because most of the Commission's analysis was annulled.

Table 4. The Commission's record at the CFI

	Success rate
Article 81	0.75
Article 82	0.98
Merger Regulation	0.58

Source: Court case law and own calculations.

differences in success rates are consistent with the view that the scope for disagreement is greater when economic theory and evidence are important. This is probably the most important insight from Table 3, as there is otherwise no clear benchmark to evaluate the absolute level of the success rate with respect to the Merger Regulation and Article 81; given the deference that the court gives to the Commission's analysis (as discussed below), one would expect the Commission to prevail in most 'marginal cases'.[49] Hence, the success rate of the Commission in (infra-marginal) cases in which the parties believe that the Commission's analysis was biased possibly as a result of a systemic problem is likely to be lower than those observed in Table 4. Seen in this light, a success rate around 60% may not impress, but this remains highly judgmental.

The next section thus attempts to provide a framework to think about the relevant characteristics of procedure from a law and economics perspective in order to investigate the potential weakness of EU procedures.

4. THE PROCEDURE: A PERSPECTIVE FROM LAW AND ECONOMICS

Five important features of the legal framework towards competition enforcement can be highlighted, namely the scope of the decision (what has to be proven?), the system of proof taking (how is the proof gathered?), the standard of proof (what should be degree of confidence in the proof?), the type of evidence which is deemed sufficient to meet the standard of proof (what elements of proofs should be considered as sufficiently telling to conclude that the required degree of confidence is reached?) and the standard of review (how is the proof assessed in case of appeal?).[50]

4.1. What has to be proven?

First, the legal framework will typically specify the scope of the decision that has to be made, in other words what needs to be proven. In particular, the legal framework

---

[49] Of course, the proportion of such marginal cases may not be all that high as the parties will anticipate this and may prefer not to appeal.

[50] To the best of my knowledge, there is no encompassing model of competition decisions in the law and economics literature. Even if most of the elements discussed here have been analysed separately, either in law or economics and sometimes in formal models, their interactions have not been extensively discussed.

will indicate whether decisions should take the form of prohibitions (negative decisions), authorizations (positive decisions) or both. The scope of decisions is related at least in part to the screening mechanism that is used to detect potentially illegal conduct. A notification system will naturally require both positive and negative decisions. By contrast, a legal system with direct effect may only require negative decisions. The choice of a screening mechanism and associated types of decisions also expresses some 'prior' regarding the likelihood that the conduct at stake is unlawful. A system of direct effect and negative decisions may, for instance, express the expectation that the conduct is less likely to be harmful than a system of notification involving both positive and negative decisions.

4.2. How is the evidence gathered?

Second, the procedures will specify how evidence is gathered. In this respect, the law and economics literature distinguishes between two alternative systems of proof taking, namely the inquisitorial and adversarial systems. In the inquisitorial system, the entity (whether a person or an institution), which takes the decision, is also responsible for gathering the evidence. This entity is meant to gather all relevant facts and analysis, in favour and against the decision that it is taking. In the adversarial system, proof taking is delegated to opposing parties (typically, a prosecutor and a defence lawyer). The entity making decisions does not take initiative with respect to evidence and takes a decision on the basis of the evidence presented by both parties.

The dichotomy between adversarial and inquisitorial systems may be excessively sharp. As suggested by Parisi (2002), one can think of procedures in a continuum from adversarial to inquisitorial in terms of the (decreasing) degree of control that the parties have over the procedure. This insight will be useful to characterize EU procedures.

More generally, one can wonder about the relevance of the distinction between inquisitorial and adversarial systems with respect to antitrust proceedings. The framework in which these polar models are discussed involves two parties that have opposing interest (a plaintiff and defendant) and sufficient incentives to defend these interests. In the field of antitrust, the party that would play the role of plaintiff may not be easy to identify; they may also be numerous (as in the case of final consumers) and they may face serious free-rider problems in engaging in collective action. Accordingly, a truly inquisitorial system in which the antitrust agency plays the role of an impartial but active judge seeking evidence is hardly feasible. It is thus probably inevitable that the antitrust agency as decision maker will make up for the relative absence of well-organized plaintiffs and act to some extent as a prosecutor. We will refer to this as the inquisitorial model with prosecutorial bias. By contrast, the opposite polar model of adversarial proceedings, in which the antitrust agency acts as a plaintiff in front of a passive judge, is entirely feasible. This is the model adopted in the US in the context of proceedings handled by the Department of Justice, which needs to acts as plaintiff in front of a federal court (which takes the enforcement decisions).[51]

4.3. What degree of confidence in the proof?

Third, the legal system will specify the standard of proof. This can be thought of as the degree of confidence that is required in order to make a finding. Various standards are used in legal proceedings. The standard of a 'balance of probability' (or 'preponderance of the evidence') is often used in civil proceedings. The requirement that a finding should be right 'beyond reasonable doubt' is associated with a much greater degree of confidence and is typical of criminal proceedings. In the antitrust field, however, the standard is typically not specified in the statutes but emerges from the case law.

The combination between the scope of decisions that have to be made and the standard of proof determines the weight that is given to both types of errors. For instance, a system of negative decisions with a standard of proof such that the probability that the decision is right is 0.7 allows Type I errors with a probability of 0.3. A system of authorization with the same standard allows Type II errors with the same probability.[52]

The alternative systems of evidence gathering (an economic construct) are closely associated with the allocation of the burden of proof (a legal concept); in a formal sense, a burden of proof only takes effects with respect to outside review and the entity taking the decision bears the burden of proof for its findings in case of appeal. In other words, the 'judge' is responsible for its findings in both systems (despite the fact that the evidence on which he will base its decision is gathered in different ways) and the institution in charge of appeal will consider whether the judge has met the standard of proof. More generally, the investigation of a case may be structured in terms of sequential findings (so that for instance, the investigation first considers the presence or absence of effective competition before considering the effect of particular practices). In the case of an adversarial system, each party bears the burden of proving the findings that it advances. The judge will then decide whether the parties have met the standard of proof with respect to the findings that they advance. Such 'burden of proof', however, is loose in the sense it is never formally evaluated. It is the evaluation, by the judge, of whether the parties have met the standard of proof that will be considered in the case of appeal. In a purely inquisitorial system,

---

[51] Procedures handled by the Federal Trade Commission are also adversarial but also involve a combination of prosecutorial and decision-making roles for the FTC (this is further discussed below).

[52] Instead of specifying the scope of decisions as well as a degree of confidence, the evaluation of any particular practice could be undertaken in terms of its expected value. For instance, the expected value of a merger could be seen as the probability that it is uncompetitive multiplied by the welfare that would obtain if it is, plus the probability that it is not multiplied by the welfare that is obtained it is not. This alternative framework (discussed in Heyer, 2005) has the advantage of considering the value of outcomes and not only the probability that is attached to them.

the parties involved merely respond to the request and bear no burden of proof. But as mentioned above, a purely inquisitorial system is a bit of an abstraction and parties often have some control over the procedure. To the extent that this involves making particular claims, parties will naturally bear the burden of proving their assertions.

4.4. What evidence will ensure the required degree of confidence?

The statement of a particular standard of proof, however important, begs the really difficult question, namely the question of what particular body of evidence can be considered to be sufficient to consider that it meets the required standard. Most legal systems in the field of antitrust further specify the type of evidence that can be considered sufficient to meet a particular standard of proof, at least in a restricted number of areas. This is the fourth characteristic. The (legal) concept of a *per se* rule can be considered in those terms. A *per se* rule is effectively a threshold on the amount of evidence that is required, such that the mere observation of a particular set of (easily identifiable) facts can be considered (*ex ante*) as sufficient evidence to meet the standard of proof that is required to make a finding. The alternative of a 'rule of reason' is effectively the recognition that there is *a priori* no set of easily identifiable observations that are sufficient to meet the required standard of proof. The truncated rule of reason that was recently developed by the Supreme Court in the US,[53] can be thought of as a contingent rule; according to this approach, facts that are normally considered to be sufficient to meet the required standard of proof (*per se*) can be considered are insufficient if another set of facts is observed. If those other facts are observed, a full rule of reason will apply.

A richer set of contingent decisions could also be considered in the form of structured rules of reasons and have sometimes been advocated (for instance, Evans and Padilla, 2004, or Neven, 2006). For instance, conglomerate effects could be considered as neutral unless effective competition is substantially reduced in one market. If effective competition is absent, a full rule of reasons may be dependent on other factors such as the extent to which additional markets can be foreclosed.

Of course, the amount and quality of evidence that needs to be adduced in order to make a finding will depend on priors that are informed by economic principles and accumulated evidence. As Lord Hoffman famously said in *Rehnam*, 'more convincing evidence is required to conclude that it was more likely than not that the sighting of an animal in a park was a lion than it would to satisfy the same standard of probability that the animal was a dog'. For instance, evidence to make a finding that unilateral effects are pro-competitive will have to be more convincing than the evidence necessary to make a finding that the conglomerate effects are pro-competitive.

[53] California Dentists Association, S. Ct. 1999.

4.5. How is the proof evaluated on appeal?

Fifth, the legal system will specify a standard of review, to be applied by the institution which will make a decision in case of appeal. This fifth dimension is of course essential in order to provide adequate incentives for the entity making the initial decision to meet the standard of proof that it is meant to observe, i.e. to take its decision with the required amount of confidence. The threat of a meaningful review is an important mechanism to ensure that the entity making the initial decision will not be easily captured.

In the next section, I will characterize the EU legal framework along the five dimensions just identified and discuss (in the light of the literature) whether particular features of this framework might help understand why the court has found that economic theories and evidence were inadequate in the Commission's decision. Some potential effects are easy to identify in principle, given the role of economic analysis; for instance a failure in the system of proof taking or a strengthening of the standard of proof or standard of review may lead to such outcomes. Particular features of economic analysis are also worth mentioning in this respect;[54] unlike the mere analysis of facts, economic analysis of effects involves the construction of a theory of the case and a validation of this theory. Many alternative theories can be constructed and may involve sophisticated and involved reasoning, so that their internal consistency can be hard to verify without a formal model. Besides their internal consistency, the validation of these theories involves the evaluation of their robustness to slight changes in assumption and most importantly an evaluation of whether they fit with the facts of the case and an evaluation of the magnitude of the effect that they predict. Both the construction and evaluation of the theory and the evidence may involve sophisticated techniques (mostly borrowed from the fields of applied game theory and econometrics). These methods impose a strong discipline on the professional economists using them but the scope for presenting misleading analysis, whether by neglect or design, should not be underestimated. That is also to say that whatever economic analysis is presented in a case should be closely checked and evaluated.

This section will also try to identify, more generally, some of the strengths and weaknesses of the EU framework.

5. AN ECONOMIC PERSPECTIVE ON THE EU LEGAL FRAMEWORK

In this section, I characterize the main EU instruments, namely Article 81, Article 82 and the Merger Regulation in terms of the five characteristics outlined above and discuss whether these characteristics are adequate from the perspective of handling economic evidence. Key characteristics are summarized in Table 5. The discussion focuses on the most important elements.

---

[54] See Röller (2005).

Table 5. Some key characteristics of EU procedures

	Article 81	Article 82	Merger control
Scope	Finding that an agreement restricts competition Finding that an agreement does or does not entail efficiency benefit	Finding that a firm has a dominant position and abuses it	Finding that a concentration does or does not restrict effective competition
Proof taking	Inquisitorial system with prosecutorial bias and a degree of political control Odd allocation of the burden of proof with respect to 81(3)	Inquisitorial system with prosecutorial bias and a degree of political control	Inquisitorial system with prosecutorial bias and a degree of political control Greater degree of control for the merging parties
Standard of proof	No less than for mergers	No less than for mergers	More than balance of probabilities
Set of sufficient facts (per se)	Horizontal price fixing, market sharing cartel	Dominant position with market share > 50? % Pricing below avoidable cost	No
Standard of review	Id?	Id?	Manifest error Facts, reasoning and inferences

5.1. Standard of proof and review

As discussed by Vesterdorf (2004), what standard should be applied in competition cases has not been considered at great length by the court until recent cases.[55]

In *Tetra Laval/Sidel*, the CFI held that the Commission should prove that the merger will have anti-competitive effects 'in all likelihood'. The CFI further insisted that the evidence brought forward by the Commission should be 'convincing'. These pronouncements suggest that the standard of proof may be stricter than a mere balance of probabilities (see Vesterdorf, 2004). The Commission appealed this judgment partly on the ground that the CFI had raised the standards. The court, however, confirmed the approach of the CFI suggesting that the economic developments should be 'plausible'.[56] One can wonder whether the standard established in this merger case can be applied in Article 81 or Article 82 cases. Given that the latter are

[55] See also Bailey (2003) for a discussion of the standard of proof with respect to mergers.

[56] At §45 of the judgment: 'The Court of First Instance did not err in law when it set out the tests to be applied in the exercise of its power of judicial review or when it specified the quality of the evidence which the Commission is required to produce in order to demonstrate that the requirements of Art 2(3) of the Regulation are satisfied.'

ex post and the former *ex ante*, it would seem that the standard of proof cannot be any lower.[57]

The standard of review has not been discussed much either, which is surprising given the importance that this standard has in order to provide adequate incentives to the Commission. The CFI and the ECJ have recently indicated that the scope of their review should not be restricted to mere factual issues but should also include an examination of the Commission's reasoning (including economic reasoning) and its inferences. This naturally raises the accountability that the Commission is subject to and enhances the credibility of the standard of proof that it is meant to respect.[58] Importantly, the Commission challenged the formulation of the standard of review adopted by the CFI and lost. This suggests that the Commission has been operating with an expectation about the standard of review, which was biased downwards.

This development may explain in part why economic evidence has sometimes been considered by the court as having been mishandled; the Commission seems to have misjudged both the standard of proof that it had to meet and the standard of review that would apply in case of appeal. Accordingly, it may have satisfied itself with unduly low standards of proof.

5.2. Scope of decisions and proof taking

5.2.1. Article 81.

Since the reform of the implementation measures,[59] the Commission takes only negative decisions with respect to Article 81(1). If the Commission does not observe that an agreement falls under the conditions laid out in §1, it will not take a decision[60] and the agreement will be lawful.[61]

With respect to Article 81(3), the matter is different. Its provisions are formulated as an exception of the prohibition expressed by Article 81(1), so that there is no 'presumption' that agreements entail efficiency benefits. The Commission also takes

[57] According to Legal (2005), §39 of the judgment is also drafted in such a way that the court's statement on the burden of proof applies to all competition cases.

[58] The court indicated at §39: 'Whilst the Court recognises that the Commission has a margin of discretion with regard to economic matters, that does not mean that the Community Courts must refrain from reviewing the Commission's interpretation of information of an economic nature. Not only must the Community Courts, inter alia, establish whether the evidence relied on is factually accurate, reliable and consistent but also whether that evidence contains all the information which must be taken into account in order to assess a complex situation and whether it is capable of substantiating the conclusions drawn from it. Such a review is all the more necessary in the case of a prospective analysis required when examining a planned merger with conglomerate effect.'

[59] Regulation 1/2003, which as discussed above replaced Regulation 17/1961.

[60] In addition, the decision not to open a case with respect to anti-competitive practices cannot be effectively challenged in court (Auto Mec, T-2490, ECR 92, p II-22501992, Bemin T-11492 ECR 95, p II-150). In other words, the Commission cannot be forced to show that a practice is not anti-competitive.

[61] Note that before the reform of the implementation regulation, matters were less clear. In order to obtain the benefit of Article 81(3), agreements had to be notified and the Commission did grant quasi positive decision with respect to Article 81(1), in the form of comfort letters.

positive as well as negative decisions with respect to the application of this provision but it does not have to take positive decisions (the exception applies directly).[62]

The system of proof taking with respect to Article 81 involves the following elements. The case team (supervised by its hierarchy within DG Comp) has a large degree of control over the investigation of the case. From that perspective, it would correspond to what has been described above as an inquisitorial system with a (inevitable) prosecutorial bias. There are at least two important qualifications, however. First, the system is also not purely inquisitorial to the extent that firms involved can exert some control over the procedure: for instance, they can request meetings with the case team and submit documents making particular claims. Second, the ultimate decision is not taken by the case team (supervised by its hierarchy). The ultimate decision is taken by the college of Commissioners, upon recommendation from the Commissioner in charge of competition. This body has no particular competence in competition matters; one would expect the Commissioners to refrain from interfering with the decisions proposed by their colleagues in specialized areas (as they would anticipate that they may be the subject of interference with respect to their own portfolios). This equilibrium of mutual deterrence ensures that Commissioners maintain control over their areas of competence. Interference is, however, a matter of degree (so that mild pressure could be exercised) and the equilibrium may also break down when particularly important issues are at stake. As discussed above, recommendations from the Commissioner in charge of competition have sometimes not been followed by the College. These instances may be rare and the threat of being overturned may not be sufficiently strong to affect the behaviour of the inquisitors significantly (at least in the field of antitrust, state aids being possibly different). Still, from that perspective, the system of proof taking is not formally inquisitorial; it is best characterized as inquisitorial with a degree of political control.

The system of proof taking with respect to Article 81(3) deserves particular attention. The new implementation regulation (which crystallizes past practice in this respect[63]) makes it clear that parties bear the burden of proof with respect to Article 81(3).[64] This is a bit surprising; it suggests that the Commission gives up the control of the procedure when it comes to the evaluation of Article 81(3) and acts as a 'passive' judge which merely examines whether the efficiency claims made by the parties deserve an exemption. The Commission thus plays the role, which is that of a 'judge' in an adversarial system in so far as it delegates proof taking and does not

[62] Interestingly, however, only the Commission (and courts) can take both positive and negative decisions. Relevant authorities in member states can only take negative decisions (see Article 5 of Regulation 1/2003).

[63] See Wils (2004).

[64] Article 2 of Regulation 1/2003 reads as follows: 'In any national or community proceedings for application of Article 81 or Article 82 of the Treaty, the burden of proving an infringement of Article 81(1) or of Article 82 of the Treaty shall rest on the party of the authority alleging the infringement. The undertaking or association of undertaking claiming the benefit of Article 81(3) of the Treaty shall bear the burden of proving that the conditions of that paragraph are fulfilled'.

seek to assemble evidence. However, it is not a truly adversarial system either, in the sense that only one side of the argument is formally represented. There is no delegation of proof taking to a party seeking to show that efficiency benefits are limited (there is no prosecutor).

This imbalance would suggest that there is a bias in the procedure in favour of a finding that efficiency benefits prevail (and justify an exemption of Article 81(1)). This conclusion resonates with the observation made above that unconvincing efficiency claims have been accepted under Article 81(3). The imbalance of this procedure in terms of proof taking may thus be one reason behind this apparent overextension.

5.2.2. Merger control. The implementation of the Merger Regulation involves a system of notification and the Commission has to take either a positive or a negative decision. That is, the Commission needs to find that the proposed concentration is compatible with the common market (possibly with amendments) and allow it, or to find that it is not compatible and prohibit it. By comparison with the legal framework of Article 81, there is less of a presumption that mergers will be lawful than in the case of agreements.

As discussed above, the standard of proof that applies probably goes beyond the mere balance of probabilities, so that a decision can only be taken if the probability that it is right is above some benchmark in excess of 50%. The combination of such a standard with the obligation to take either positive or negative decisions is a little odd and raises an issue of consistency.[65] Indeed, there may be instances where there is no decision that the Commission can take while abiding with the required standard. Assume for the sake of argument that the balance of probability is 70%. All mergers that impede effective competition with a probability that is higher than 70% should be prohibited and all mergers that impede effective competition with a probability that is less than 30% should be allowed. What about those for which the probability falls in between? The Commission can simply not take one of the decisions that it is supposed to take towards those cases while meeting the required standard of proof.[66]

The system of proof taking with respect to the merger regulation appears to be inquisitorial with a prosecutorial bias and a degree of political control (as in the case of Articles 81 and 82). However, parties may exert a greater degree of control over the procedure than in the context of Articles 81 and 82. They can submit documents but can also request 'state of play' meetings with the case team as well as 'triangular' meetings (with the case team and third parties).[67] Importantly, unlike what happens with Article 81(3), the system of proof taking and the allocation of the burden of proof

---

[65] See Vesterdorf (2004).

[66] This issue does also arise, to some extent, with respect to the implementation of Article 81(3), for which the Commission takes both positive and negative decisions (but in that case the Commission does not have to take a positive decision).

[67] See DG Competition best practices on the conduct of merger control proceedings, available at http://ec.euroPa.eu/comm/competition/mergers/legislation/bp1.htm

are not modified when an efficiency defence is considered. Even if it is often argued informally that the parties should bear the burden of proof with respect to efficiencies (see for instance, Röller *et al.*, 2006), there is no explicit shift in the burden of proof in the Merger Regulation.[68]

This feature is important and may be a factor which helps explaining why the efficiency defence has not been overextended in the same way in merger control as in Article 81(3). As discussed above, there is no perception that unconvincing efficiency claims have been accepted under the merger regulation (on the contrary, the Commission may have neglected important efficiency benefits). The fact that the burden of proof is not explicitly shifted to the parties under the merger regulation, so that the procedure remains consistent and balanced may help to explain this difference. Of course, the fact that the status of the efficiency defence was not entirely clear until 2004 has probably also played a role.

Given the unusual features of the system of evidence gathering in the EU and its importance for the processing of economic evidence, the following section will discuss it more fully in light of the existing literature.

6. THE SYSTEM OF EVIDENCE GATHERING

As discussed above the EU procedure can be seen as inquisitorial, with a prosecutorial bias and some degree of political control. The relative merits of the adversarial and inquisitorial systems have long been considered in the law and economics literature and we will discuss the main insights from this literature. The significance of a prosecutorial bias has also been discussed. I take both issues in turn and start with the latter.

6.1. Prosecutorial bias

The fact that the Commission is a decision maker which takes responsibility for uncovering the evidence that would normally be brought forward by plaintiffs may introduce some biases, which are discussed in Wils (2004). He observes that officials may be the victim of 'hindsight' bias, namely the 'tendency for people with the benefit of hindsight to falsely believe that they could have predicted the outcome of an event'. For instance, if it is found in the course of a Phase II investigation that there is no competition concern, officials will tend to believe that they should have known this at the time when they wrote the statement of objection which led to a Phase II. This hindsight will lead to a problem of cognitive dissonance, which might

---

[68] In the recent (21 September 2005) judgment on *EDP/Gaz Natural* (Case T-87/05), the CFI further discussed the allocation of the burden proof with respect to remedies. Despite the fact that the notice on remedies stipulates that it is for the parties to show that the proposed commitment meet the competition concern, the court held that the burden of proof rests with the Commission.

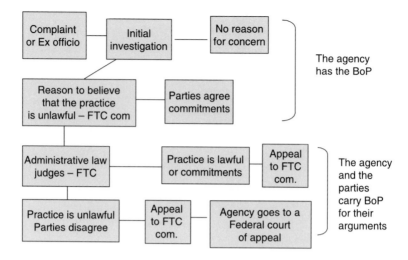

Figure 2. FTC procedure

call into question the confidence that officials have in their judgment, and they will naturally try to avoid this dissonance. The consequence would be that officials would tend to concentrate on evidence that confirms their own judgment.[69] The symptom is a 'self-confirming bias' which some commentators claim to observe in fact (see Kühn, 2002). Burnside (2001) for instance observes: 'The frequent opinion of industry is that a view, once entrenched in the Commission's thinking, cannot be dislodged: "I have made up my mind. Do not try to confuse me with the facts"'.

Some empirical evidence on the significance of such a bias can be obtained from the FTC procedures in the US. The FTC procedure is complex but its essential features are presented in Figure 2. The FTC Commission actually plays a mixed role to the extent that it acts both as a prosecutor and a judge on appeal: the FTC Commission acts as a prosecutor in the initial phase and brings the case to an administrative law court. However, if the administrative law court finds against the parties (or imposes commitments that the parties do not accept), the parties can appeal its decision to the FTC Commission, which therefore acts as judge on appeal.

This particular feature of the FTC procedure has been exploited by Coate and Kleit (1998). They test whether the result of the appeal is affected, other things being equal, by the composition of the FTC Commission and in particular the proportion of members which rule on appeal while having also taken the decision to initiate proceedings. They find that the effect is both statistically and economically significant; an overlap of three Commissioners (out of seven) easily doubles the probability

---

[69] According to Wils (2004), the significance of this hindsight bias is well documented in the psychology literature.

that the Commission will confirm the decision of the administrative law court (relative to the probability when there is no overlap).

By contrast, there is some experimental evidence suggesting that pre-mature judgment (which gets reinforced) is less likely to occur in adversarial systems (see Parisi, 2002 and references therein).

Overall, it would thus appear that the self-confirming biases that may be induced by the prosecutorial role that the Commission assumes cannot be dismissed as insignificant.

6.2. Adversarial versus inquisitorial

The analysis of adversarial versus inquisitorial procedures has a long tradition in the law and economics literature. In the context of an early debate, Posner (1988) argued that competition between parties in the adversarial system would ensure that every relevant piece of information would be produced. The adversarial model was also defended as it allows for a dialectics of assertion and refutation, which may be instrumental in revealing the true state of world. Tullock (1988), by contrast, emphasized the fact that parties would attempt to mislead the decision maker.

Various formal models have explored the merits of these arguments. One strand of the literature assumes that the underlying facts of the case strike a balance between the interests of the parties involved. In other words, the evidence is never inconclusive.

(1) Milgrom and Roberts (1986) examine the intuition of Posner according to which competition between interested parties will ensure that 'true' facts will be uncovered. They do not consider the cost of gathering information but allow agents to have different information. Information is verifiable but may be concealed. The decision maker is naive but knows whether the agents are well informed. They show that if there is always an interested party who is well informed, has an opportunity to report and prefers the full information decision, the full information outcome is the only equilibrium. This result suggests that a naive decision maker faced with evidence that is strategically reported will enforce the full information decision as long as the interests of the parties are sufficiently opposed.[70]

(2) Froeb and Kobayashi (1996) extend this line of work by assuming that the decision maker may be biased and evidence is costly to produce. In their model, the parties produce evidence by making random draws from the same distribution and only report favourable evidence (so that the parties know the true state and have the same technology in producing evidence). This distribution is however biased in favour of one party (the true facts are thus conclusive and favour one party). They show that

---

[70] They also show that agents' limited ability to communicate the information that they have may not matter if the decision maker is sophisticated; here again, as long as there is an agent that prefers the full information outcome over any alternative, the decision maker can enforce the full information outcome.

the decision maker will again take the full information decision. This arises because the party favoured by the underlying distribution will produce more evidence (because it is less costly to do so). In addition, parties take advantage of the bias of the jury to produce less (costly) evidence in the direction of the bias. These results, while sensitive to a number of assumptions including the modelling of the decisions maker's bias and the functional form of the underlying distribution, still suggest that the importance of the decision maker's lack of sophistication in the adversarial system should not be exaggerated.

(3) Froeb and Kobayashi (2001) compare the outcome of the inquisitorial and adversarial system in a similar model. Again, they assume that parties have the same technology in producing evidence and focus on the incentive to reveal information. In the adversarial system, evidence on either side is provided by making random draws from the same distribution, each litigant reports only the most favourable information, and uses an optimal stopping rule to determine the number of draws. The judge simply splits the outcome, whereas an arbitrator uses the average of his observations. The authors focus on the variance of the estimator for a given number of draws across all parties (i.e. a given total cost). They find that that the adversarial system may lead to a lower variance if the underlying distribution itself exhibits a large variance (for instance with a uniform distribution). This suggests that the average of strategic (extreme) reporting is not necessarily more variable than the average of truthful reports. In other words, the adversarial system is not necessarily worse even when it is assumed that the inquisitor has the same technology as the parties to uncover evidence.

(4) The assumption that the decision maker knows about the information that is available to the parties is considered by Shin (1998). He shows that competition between agents with sufficiently opposed interests will no longer suffice to ensure the full information outcome. The decision maker is then faced with a pooling between agents that are genuinely ignorant and agents that conceal information. He assumes that there is a signal that is observed with different probabilities by the two parties and observed with some probability by an inquisitor. One can then compare the outcome reached by the inquisitor with that of an arbitrator who knows the probabilities that the agent will have received the signal. He shows that the adversarial procedure still fares well in this set-up because the arbitrator can adjust the standard of proof across agents as a function of the probability that they have received the signal. In essence, the judge reasons that if one party who is thought to be better informed does not come up with evidence, he 'must' be wrong.

Hence, it appears that two pieces of biased information processed by a naïve judge may be at least as good as one (possibly two) piece(s) of unbiased information processed by an inquisitor, when the judge knows what the agents know and the interest of agents are opposed, when the agents have the same technology of producing evidence, and when differences in the quality of information that the agents have access to can be observed.

(5) Dewatripont and Tirole (1999)[71] consider an alternative set-up, in which there are three possible states of the world (and associated decisions); one party wins, the other party wins, and the status quo. This structure differs from that adopted in the models reviewed so far in which one party always wins. If there is information in favour of both parties, the status quo should prevail (from a social point of view). Agents invest in getting information and may obtain it with some probability. If there is no information in its favour, the agent will not get any. If there is favourable information the agent will get it with some probability. Hence, in this set up, there are some situations of genuine inconclusiveness as there may be no fact in favour of either party.

An inquisitor can look for reasons to support either side of the argument and incurs a fixed cost of searching for each side. He obtains evidence with some probability and he can make a finding in favour of either side or choose the status quo. His payoff is lowest in the case of the status quo (it is equal to the payoff that he gets if he does not search). In an adversarial system, both parties can incur a cost of searching.

Assuming that evidence cannot be manipulated, the adversarial system dominates. This arises because the inquisitor may not actually look for both sides of the argument. When the probability of finding evidence is high enough, he actually focuses on one side of the argument; indeed, he is afraid that by looking for evidence on both sides, his evidence will not be conclusive and that he will have to choose the status quo. By contrast, in the adversarial system, the parties will always search and there is full information collection.

In order to consider the manipulation of evidence, the authors assume that a party can either get a positive signal or conflicting evidence. He can suppress evidence, either by not reporting information that he has or suppressing information which is not helpful to his case, if he has conflicting information. The authors show that an inquisitor will choose not to reveal information, which would lead to the status quo. Errors in decision making take the form of 'extremism', such that one side of the argument is endorsed when the status quo would be appropriate. By contrast, in the adversarial system, an advocate might suppress conflicting evidence: if the opposite party has positive evidence, this will lead to the status quo when decisions in favour of the opposite case would be favourable. The error takes the form of inertia. However, when the opposite party has no evidence, it will lead to a decision in favour of the party suppressing evidence. The error takes the form of extremism.

Hence, an adversarial system generates inertia in addition to extremism and accordingly it will tend to dominate the inquisitorial system when the cost of inertia

---

[71] See also Palumbo (2001) who extends the work of Dewatripont and Tirole by assuming that the effort is continuous. She shows that an excessive amount of proof taking can take place (as agents invest in information partly because of the scope for additional manipulation that it allows for). She also shows that the adversarial system fares relatively less well than the inquisitorial system in this environment.

is 'much' less than the cost of extremism. The authors also show that the adversarial system is more attractive when the parties have a high probability of finding evidence in favour of their case, if it exists.

(6) Some experimental evidence on the relative performance of inquisitorial and adversarial systems is available. Block *et al.* (2000) consider an experimental design in which one party is right and the other is wrong (so that evidence, if it is available, is conclusive).[72] They consider two scenarios; one in which Mr Wrong has private information to the effect that he is wrong and one in which, in addition, Mr Right also has a hint that he is right. In the adversarial set up, the parties are free to debate whereas in the inquisitorial set up, the inquisitor controls the debate.

The results are striking: when Mr Wrong has private information, the inquisitorial system performs better. The private information is revealed in 28% of cases and only in 7% with an adversarial system. By contrast, when the information is correlated, the reverse obtains but the difference is more dramatic. The information is revealed in 71% of cases with the adversarial system and in 14% of cases with the inquisitorial system.

Block and Parker (2004) further exploit this experiment by characterizing the settlement imposed by the judge when the information was not revealed. They find that, relative to an adversarial regime, the inquisitorial regime will produce more extreme settlements, in favour of one party over the other. This finding is consistent with the predictions of Dewatripont and Tirole.

To sum up, the literature seems to provide the following insights:

- There is some validation of Posner's intuition that competition between interested parties leads to the revelation of information particularly in circumstances which may resemble those of antitrust proceedings (in which it is likely that the decision maker has reliable prior knowledge on the information available to the parties).
- The inquisitorial regime can be expected to produce more extreme decisions than the adversarial regime. This result may however be highly dependent on the assumption that it is made with respect to the objective of the inquisitor. The inquisitor's aversion to the status quo which is built into the model of Dewatripont – Tirole is not, however, obviously ill-founded, and seems to accord with intuition in light of inquisitors' career objectives.
- Experimental evidence provides some validation of this assumption and confirms that the adversarial regime fares better when information is not totally skewed. This would seem to fit with the circumstances of antitrust proceedings in which plaintiffs (or their proxies) can be expected to have some information regarding the merits of the case.
- Existing theoretical models do not consider explicitly what is potentially one of the main advantages of the adversarial regime, namely the dialectics of assertion and refutation in the evaluation of evidence produced by the parties.

---

[72] See also Block and Parker (2004).

6.3. EU procedures and reform

The prosecutorial bias and the intrinsic features of an inquisitorial procedure would appear to reinforce each other; in particular the conclusion that an inquisitor might not invest in seeking evidence towards both sides of the argument (when evidence is hard to manipulate) or might suppress conflicting evidence will be reinforced in the presence of a hindsight bias. The tendency towards extremism in the EU is also probably reinforced by the inconsistency between the standard of proof and the scope of the decisions mentioned above, at least with respect to the implementation of the merger regulation. Indeed, when evidence is not very conclusive, the Commission cannot meet the required standard of proof with either decision. In those circumstances, it will have a further incentive to shift towards extreme outcomes (by suppressing evidence or failing to fully consider some alternatives).

The tendency to focus on one side of the evidence would also appear to be consistent with the way in which the Commission has been found by the court to mishandle economic theories and evidence. The court decisions on *Airtours/First Choice*, *Tetra Laval/Sidel* and *Schneider/Legrand* illustrate this vividly. In those decisions, the court explicitly criticized the Commission for not pursuing arguments and for suppressing (or misinterpreting) evidence.

This interpretation is congruent with some of the criticism that has been formulated towards merger control in the EU from direct observations of the procedures. For instance, Kühn (2002) describes what he refers to as a 'self-confirming' bias in the Commission's analysis, namely that the Commission takes a view on cases early on and subsequently focuses on findings which support that view.

It is tempting to associate extreme decisions with high fines and clearance and the status quo with moderate fines (with respect to collusion under Article 81). From this perspective, it is interesting to note (as discussed above) that the court almost invariably reduces the fines imposed by the Commission. This is consistent with the view that the Commission suffers from the extremism that can be expected in inquisitorial procedures.

The absence of a proper validation of economic evidence in some procedures can also be observed; this is easy to illustrate with the proceedings of the *Volvo/Scania* case. Marc Ivaldi and Frank Verboven undertook a merger simulation for the EU. The parties and their econometrician (J. Hausman) criticized their analysis at the hearing. These authors, however, felt that some of the criticisms was misplaced, but had no way to defend themselves[73] as the procedure does not allow for a second round of discussion. One cannot help thinking that an adversarial regime, which allows for cross-examination and direct confrontation, would have been more effective in

---

[73] A non-confidential version of the study, as well as the criticism of Hausman, and a proper reply by the authors have now been published (see Ivaldi and Verboven, 2005a and 2005b; and Hausman and Leonard, 2005).

validating the evidence in this instance and more generally in other procedures.[74] Evidence that is not subject to rigorous scrutiny can be easily abused; key assumptions in theoretical reasoning can be disguised as innocuous and an empirical result that is not robust can be disguised as such.[75] Even if the presentation of evidence is not distorted, investigating its robustness is more effectively undertaken by several parties with different perspectives.

Of course, the EU procedure would also appear particularly weak in validating economic evidence in light of the current imbalance in resources observed above. Inquisitorial procedures may not be best suited to distil and improve economic evidence, but such a procedure without adequate resources for the inquisitor would seem particular prone to abuse.

Following the court decisions mentioned above, the EU has implemented a couple of significant reforms: the office of the Chief Competition Economist has been created (with a staff of about 10 professional economists). A review of the analysis of the case team at a late stage of the procedure by a set of different Commission officials has been introduced. This institution commonly referred to as the 'fresh pair of eyes' is arguably well targeted at the main weakness of an inquisitorial procedure with a procedural bias, namely its tendency to suppress information or to fail to look for it. Whether it intervenes at a sufficiently early stage in the procedure and whether the fresh pairs of eyes have the right incentives with respect to their colleagues (who may turn out to be the fresh pair of eyes on other cases) is unclear.[76]

7. REMEDIES?

From this discussion of procedures, the following conclusions emerge:

- The allocation of the burden of proof with respect to Article 81(3) is a bit odd and possible overextensions of the efficiency defence may be related to this feature. As a corollary, shifting the burden of proof towards the parties with respect to efficiencies in merger control, and with respect to Article 82 (as proposed by the discussion paper on Article 82) may be misplaced.

- The observations that the Commission may decide early on cases and search for selective evidence or that theories are neglected are consistent with the incentives

---

[74] In recent cases, however, the Commission has introduced some element of cross-examination within the existing procedure (by allowing the economic advisers to the parties to access data and evaluate the analysis performed by the Commission (or plaintiffs) on its premises).

[75] In the words of Posner (1999), referring to economic expert witnesses 'the expert witness can mislead judges and juries more readily than lay witnesses can because they are more difficult to pick apart in cross-examination, they can hide behind an impenetrable wall of esoteric knowledge'.

[76] The merger between EDP and Gaz Natural which presumably was subject to a fresh pair of eyes (and benefited from the input of the chief economist) was prohibited and challenged in court, partly on the basis that the Commission made an error of assessment. The Commission prevailed (Case T-87/05).

generated by the inquisitorial regime with a prosecutorial bias implemented by the EU.

- There is some inconsistency between the scope of the decisions enforced under the Merger Regulation and the standard of proof that the Commission is supposed to meet. This inconsistency reinforces the biases of the inquisitorial systems towards extremes.

- The nature of economic evidence, which needs to be validated, may be such that it is best handled by a process of assertion and refutation, which is typical of an adversarial system of proof taking.

- As the US experience suggests, validation of economic evidence is helped by a clear set of rules which forces the economic experts to state 'fully and in a timely manner' the economic reasoning and the facts on which they rely. This is enforced in a code of conduct (the Reference Manual on scientific evidence used by federal courts), which incorporates the standards set by the Supreme Court in the *Daubert* decision.[77] The EU could adopt a similar standard. Whatever the system of evidence gathering, a set of rules on handling of economic evidence would prove useful.

- The imbalance in resources between the Commission and the parties is an impediment to a proper validation of economic evidence.

- Both the standard of proof and the standard of review have remained surprisingly vague until recent cases. The Commission probably did not fully appreciate the standard of proof that it would be expected to meet and the standard of review that would be applied to its decisions. Recent decisions by the court should significantly reduce the scope for mismanagement of economic evidence.

- A strengthening of the standard of review cannot, by itself, fully correct the incentives provided by an inquisitorial procedure. The Commission can hardly be made accountable for the effort that it does not exert in pursuing some argument.

As discussed above, it is hard to tell whether the reforms implemented by the Commission will prove effective in redressing the biases induced by the inquisitorial procedure. In view of the intrinsic advantages of an adversarial procedure discussed above, it is still worth considering what the implementation of such a procedure would entail. There are at least two possible institutional arrangements. First, the case team could become a public prosecutor (as in the US system). The office of a 'judge' would have to be created. Presumably, the 'judge' and his office could belong to the Commission but it should be separated in a credible way from the institution to which the case team belongs. Such a separation between prosecutors and judge is enforced in many judicial (and administrative) systems and seems therefore feasible. This institutional arrangement would effectively involve the establishment of an administrative tribunal within the Commission (like that of the FTC).

---

[77] See Posner (1999), Werden (2005) and Breyer (2004).

Alternatively, the decisions could be taken by the CFI, with the 'Commission' acting a plaintiff. This would involve a broadening of the tasks entrusted to the court by the Council which according to Wils (2004) is feasible within the current EC treaty.[78]

Whether decision making is entrusted to an administrative law judge or the CFI, it will also be necessary to provide them with support in particular regarding economic analysis. As emphasized by Posner (1999), the ability to appoint experts is essential for the functioning of US courts. This option would seem to be open at least in the case of the CFI.[79]

Those changes would imply in any event that the College of Commissioners would no longer take the final decision. This may be attractive in itself. As mentioned above, the scope for capture by corporate interests and member states at the level of the College of Commissioners has been a concern in the past. Clearly, Commissioner Monti has established very high standards of independence towards corporate interests[80] and member states and the focus has sifted away from that sort of capture. However, since there is no clear benefit from granting decision-making power to the College of Commissioners and no guarantee that this form of capture may not surface again[81] in the future, a delegation of decision making would seem attractive.

8. CONCLUSION

According to Richard Posner (1999), 'there is a remarkable isomorphism between legal doctrine and economic theory. The isomorphism becomes an identity when, as in antitrust (but not only there), the law adopts an explicitly economic criterion of legality'. The isomorphism and possible identity is constructed as economics influences the interpretation of the law. The evidence reviewed in this paper confirms that important progress has been made in this respect in Europe in the last twenty years. Furthermore, the wording of the law itself has occasionally been changed to allow for more economics-friendly implementation. Some conditions are also in place to deepen the process. A number of national antitrust agencies are headed by economists and have accumulated economic expertise (including sometimes the creation of an office of chief economist). The proportion of antitrust lawyers with a sound understanding of economics and the proportion of competition economists with a good understanding of the law has increased. The CFI in recent judgments has not shied away from the review of economic analysis.

---

[78] There is, however, no consensus among lawyers on this issue. See Wils (2004) for a discussion.
[79] See Botteman (2006).
[80] The biography of J. Welch provides an amusing illustration of this (Welch and Byrne, 2001).
[81] See for instance Vives (2005) who highlights renewed risks of capture by member states.

What are the most significant impediments to further progress? First, the imbalance in economic resources between parties and the Commission is gross. The Commission needs to mobilize further resources, in particular by reinforcing the team of the Chief Competition Economist. What is required is a step and not a marginal increase. Second, as argued in the paper, the procedures used by the Commission, in particular its system of proof taking, may not allow for the most effective development of economic theory and evidence in actual cases.

Discussion

John Vickers
Oxford University

My first encounter with European competition law was long ago, before the dawn of *Economic Policy*. I spent the summer of 1979, and subsequently much of 1981, working as a neophyte economist for IBM on a case brought by the European Commission alleging abuse of dominance in the market for IBM-compatible mainframe computers. This may have been the largest EC case until the recent Microsoft matter. My task was to help to try to establish that IBM was not dominant – a proposition less than self-evident on the facts of the 1970s, but increasingly plausible, especially after the case was settled in 1984, as the PC revolution got under way. This job gave a wonderful opportunity to learn practical competition economics from distinguished economists such as Derek Morris, David Stout, Christian von Weizsäcker and, as the parallel US case neared conclusion, Frank Fisher. I learned just as much from the equally distinguished lawyers on the case – a number of whom went on to become very senior judges – and came to appreciate the subtle differences that exist between a barrister from Gray's Inn and a lawyer from Manhattan.

Indeed lawyers and judges will be central to these comments on Damien Neven's paper, since they are crucial to the transmission mechanism from competition economics to competition policy – a mechanism which he surveys with particular reference to the central role played by the European Commission. His general conclusion is fair – that recent reforms by the Commission have been in the right direction, but that there is considerably further to go if economics is to be deployed to best effect in EC competition cases and policy. I will seek to make two broader but complementary points. The first is to note some wider positive developments in European competition law and economics. Second, that future progress will depend in good part upon whether better mutual understanding between law and economics can be developed in Europe as it was long ago in the United States. Unless this happens the scope for economics to shape European competition law will be limited, not least because the ultimate decisions in this sphere lie in the hands of those former lawyers called judges.

Economics and the constitution of competition law

Most discussion about competition law concerns its interpretation – a matter ultimately for the judiciary to decide case by case but which competition authorities can
strongly influence. But first we need to consider three prior questions of a 'constitutional' kind:

- Are serious competition laws enacted?
- Are the laws squarely about competition, or do other – e.g. 'industrial policy'
  – considerations matter?
- Is application of the laws independent and free from political interference?

Answers to these questions primarily depend on governments and legislatures
nationally, and on ministerial councils at EC level. There is of course a powerful
economic case for three positive answers.

During the twenty-year lifespan of *Economic Policy* good progress has been made on
this front at national level, especially in recent years. The UK, despite its relatively
long tradition of competition policy, is a prime case in point. Prohibitions of anti-
competitive agreements and abuse of dominance with serious deterrent force came
into effect only in March 2000. Merger law explicitly based on competition, and with
no role for government ministers except in narrowly defined circumstances (national
security), started in June 2003. Far more remarkable transformations, given their
starting points, have been achieved in the formerly communist countries that joined
the EU on 1 May 2004. That date also saw the implementation of the 'Modernization' Regulation 1/2003 that devolved application of EC Articles 81 and 82 to
national authorities and courts, thereby underpinning positive answers to the three
basic questions above at least as far as matters where inter-state trade is affected.

At EC level, Articles 81 and 82 (previously 85 and 86) were themselves implemented in 1962, and besides modernization, their constitutional position has not
changed, though, as Neven's paper details, their application has.

Within the past twenty years the main fundamental development in the constitution
of EC competition law itself has been the Merger Regulation, which came into force
in 1990 and was revised in 2004. It was a great success of the original ECMR that,
despite the politically and nationally controversial nature of some merger policy, it
enshrined positive answers to the three basic questions above. The substantive merger
test – of whether a merger created or strengthened a dominant position – had the
great merit of excluding non-competition factors from consideration.

However, the original test had the awkwardness for policy that, on the face of it,
many mergers would seem to have the potential to lessen competition without creating or strengthening a dominant position (at least if 'dominance' is to carry the same
meaning as in the Article 82 prohibition on abuse of dominance). A partial remedy
was for the Commission to develop the notion of 'collective' or 'joint' dominance,
notably in the Nestlé/Perrier mineral water case of 1992. If a merger would tend to

lead to an oligopoly adopting a 'common policy' on the market – i.e. collude tacitly
– then it could still be caught. This approach was accepted by the courts, and indeed
the Court of First Instance in *Airtours* (2002), in the course of over-turning the
Commission's prohibition of the merger, gave an account, admirably in line with the
teachings of dynamic game theory, of necessary conditions for tacit collusion.

But that situation was second-best. More risk of tacit collusion is not the only, or
the most straightforward, way for a merger to lessen competition. Anti-competitive
non-coordinated effects are equally possible (e.g. think of the merger shifting a non-
cooperative oligopoly equilibrium). With a merger law concentrated on tacit collusion,
however, good economic arguments can fail to receive adequate consideration,[82] and
strained economic arguments might have to be relied on.

The problem with the unduly narrow wording of the Regulation was solved by
revising the test so that it now asks whether a merger would significantly impede
effective competition. (The creation or strengthening of dominance is now a specified
instance of SIEC, not the test itself.) Economic argument was decisive in securing this
revision in the law, which along with other developments – notably internal reform
in the Competition Directorate of the Commission – should facilitate better economics
in casework. The horizontal merger guidelines that accompanied the revised ECMR
are an encouraging signal in this direction.

Economics and the interpretation of competition law

Since the wording of competition law, once established, tends not to change, the
question of how the language of the law is interpreted becomes paramount. Economics
can have a powerful impact on the evolution of the interpretation of the law, and
related to that, on the enforcement priorities of the competition authorities.

Perhaps the most striking example of this impact – and the most rapid evolution
– is the treatment of non-price vertical restraints in US law. The Supreme Court in
its 1977 judgment in the Sylvania case, much influenced by Chicago School thinking,
overturned the per se condemnation of such restraints – i.e. illegality regardless of
likely competitive effects – a decade earlier and held that rule-of-reason analysis
should apply.[83]

Compared with the late 1970s, economics is now much better placed to influence
the interpretation of competition law. The game theory revolution in industrial
economics had not quite got going, still less settled down, at the start of the *IBM*
case mentioned above. For example, the economics of network externalities,
switching costs and compatibility – rather important issues for the case – were largely
undeveloped. There were Chicago School and contestability-oriented critics of the

---

[82] For example, Motta (2004, pp. 279–86) criticizes the Commission's analysis in *Nestlé/Perrier* for its lack of attention, given the
then test in the ECMR, to unilateral (i.e. non-cooperative) effects.

[83] See Kovacic and Shapiro (2000, p. 53).

structure-conduct-performance mainstream, but no synthesis in sight. (Parallels with macroeconomic disputes at that time come to mind.) But now, though arguments naturally continue, there has been movement in economics towards – perhaps to – what Kovacic and Shapiro (2000) call a post-Chicago synthesis.

How then, from an economic perspective, to assess the recent development of the interpretation of European competition law and the enforcement approach of the Commission? As to the three main substantive elements of competition law[84] – those to combat anti-competitive mergers, anti-competitive agreements and abuse of dominance – my answer is two cheers and a deep breath.

The first cheer is for the merger reforms of 2004, discussed above, where economics not only played a prominent role but was in turn boosted in the process. The second cheer is for economically sensible reforms of policy against anti-competitive agreements. Of particular note are

- the clearer and wider safe harbour for non-price vertical agreements in un-concentrated markets created by the reformed block exemption regulation of 1999;
- the greatly increased toughness and effectiveness of policy against cartels; and related to that
- the creation of economic incentives through leniency arrangements for whistle-blowing on cartels.

The deep breath is for policy to address abuse of dominance, which the Commission is actively reviewing now.[85] For the reasons set out in Vickers (2005) I believe that the path of economic effects-based evolution of the law must be taken – and form-based approaches rejected – in this area of European competition law as it has been in the other two. Only if the law on abuse of dominance becomes more firmly anchored in economic principles will it be aligned with its economic purpose in a clear and internally consistent manner. We shall see where the Commission, and the wider European Competition Network, takes the review of law and policy on abuse of dominance, and in due course what the courts make of it.

As Neven's paper emphasizes, the interpretation of the law matters for process as well as substance, and recent years have seen important developments from the courts in Luxembourg regarding the required quality of economic evidence and reasoning. Table 4 in the paper highlights the (curious) contrast between the significant reversals by the Court of First Instance of Commission merger decisions (where economic issues are invariably paramount), and its general acceptance of Commission prohibitions

---

[84] Arguably policy against anti-competitive state aids is a fourth element, but it is particular to the EU and not competition law, or antitrust, in the usual sense that applies to company behaviour, so I do not discuss it here.

[85] See http://europa.eu.int/comm/competition/antitrust/others/article_82_review.html, in particular the DG Competition *Discussion paper on the application of Article 82 of the Treaty to exclusionary abuses*, December 2005, which is broadly favourable to a more economic-effects based approach.

of abuse of dominance under Article 82 (where, until now, rather formalistic approaches have often been deemed adequate). Strictures from the court about the Commission's economic analysis of mergers have not only concerned prohibition decisions – such as those in the *Airtours* and *GE/Honeywell* cases – originally taken (c. 2000) before the recent reforms, but also the July 2004 clearance by the Commission of the merger of the recorded music businesses of Sony and BMG.[86] Whatever one thinks of particular judgments, overall it is probably welcome for economics and on general grounds that the courts have set higher standards for the conduct and exposition of economic analysis in EC merger cases. It will be interesting to see whether in due course comparable rigour will be judicially required in abuse of dominance cases.

Law and economics: European merger prospects?

Lest two cheers and a deep breath appears an unduly positive view of the recent development of European competition law, let me end on two cautionary notes. The first is that competition law, the topic here, is but part of competition policy in the broad sense that also addresses government-imposed restrictions on competitive freedoms. Despite successes of the single market programme, progress on this front both within Europe and in terms of wider trade relations[87] has been depressingly slow. As to intra-EU policy, however, the Commission does now have potentially important initiatives under way, including the sector inquiries concerning energy and financial services, and the review of state aid policy that aims to achieve less and better-targeted aid. With state aid as with competition law, less formalism and greater effectiveness should be the goals.

Second, the impact of economics on the future development of European competition law will be limited unless we get better at talking to lawyers. In their review of a century of US antitrust, Kovacic and Shapiro (2000, p. 58) conclude that, whereas economics had little direct impact in the early decades,

> 'Today, the links between economics and law have been institutionalized with increasing presence of an economic perspective in law schools, extensive and explicit judicial reliance on economic theory, and with the substantial presence of economists in government antitrust agencies.'

In Europe the last of these elements is in place, including among agency heads. Indeed meetings of Directors General in Brussels and of the Competition Committee of the OECD were in my experience largely economics-oriented. But the first two elements are not. The proportion of European competition lawyers with a sound

---

[86] Judgment of the Court of First Instance in Case T-464/04, 13 July 2006.

[87] A recent anti-competitive manifestation of which is the imposition of so-called 'anti-dumping' duties on imports of leather footwear from China and Vietnam.

understanding of economics is growing but nowhere near that in the US, and the same can be said for the relative ratios of competition economists with a sound understanding of the law. Unless this continues to change rapidly, the transmission mechanism from economics to competition law in Europe will be limited. Lawyers and judges are not generally resistant to good arguments that are put well, so the opportunities for economics are certainly there. Whether they are seized depends more than anything on how much robust sense economics can make in forums of law.

Diane Coyle
Enlightenment Economics

I am here as a practitioner of competition policy but I must make the disclaimer that I am speaking in a personal capacity, however, not for the Competition Commission (CC).

I am also not an expert on EU competition policy, so instead I would like to comment on two of the areas of economics which Damien has identified as having affected policy: application of static oligopoly theory to the relevant markets; and co-ordinated effects.

I would like to preface my comments with a brief explanation of how we operate in the UK.

Institutionally, the Office of Fair Trading (OFT) conducts a preliminary investigation and makes references to the CC. A new inquiry group and staff team is formed for each separate case. The decision of the CC group is determinative.

Conceptually, the question is: can we form an expectation of an SLC (substantial lessening of competition)? Expectation means 'more likely than not'. 'Substantial' is a matter of judgment.

In practice, in the eight inquiries in which I have been involved, one of the key areas of economic input is nothing to do with oligopoly theory, but the much more basic question of defining the relevant market.

Our Guidance sets out the way we use the SSNIP (small but significant non-transitory increase in price) test to define the market: could a hypothetical monopolist profitably impose a sustained 5% price rise? We start with a narrow definition of the product set and look at the scope for demand and supply side substitution.

This isn't always the natural definition, certainly in the eyes of the public, and it can therefore sometimes be difficult to communicate the rationale. For example the previous supermarket inquiries have found a distinction between markets for big one-stop (weekly) shopping trips and top-up shops, which seems artificial to many non-economists when the same company operates both big supermarkets and convenience stores.

But the economics in theory and practice is straightforward: the task is to look for econometric and other evidence on elasticities.

Or is it so straightforward? There are at least three reasons why not.

1. Customer inertia makes it difficult to interpret demand elasticities. Arguments about the scale of non-monetary switching costs are almost impossible to confront with either theory or evidence. At present, we tend to rely on consumer surveys to gather evidence. But we urgently need to understand better the insights from behavioural economics and integrate them here.
2. Static analysis is of limited use. Many, many inquiries now face the argument that technology is changing the relevant market definition. Examples include whether or not the Internet is replacing electronic data interchange over the relevant (2 year) timescale. Another example is how much online directories substitute for classified directories. These are obvious examples but the claim of substantial technological change relevant to market definition is raised in many inquiries now.
3. Finally, many markets overlap, and it isn't helpful to draw a sharp boundary before going on to analyse competition in the defined market. In fact, you need to include the overlapping markets in the competitive analysis.

I think for these reasons the panoply of economic tools such as SSNIP tests and HHI indices are decreasingly interesting. The analytical action is in the dynamic assessment of competitive effects, where the tools of economics are less well codified and more matters of judgment.

CC Guidance lists a number of factors groups must consider in this context:

- market shares/concentration ratios;
- structural changes, e.g. technology;
- other structural factors (asymmetric costs, network effects, switching costs, information asymmetries);
- behaviour of firms.

The list certainly shows the influence of economic theory, which supports Damien Neven's argument. The point I want to make is just that systematic application of the theory is harder.

In practice, one begins with an assessment of whether there are unilateral effects of merger. If so, there is no need to consider whether there are co-ordinated effects.

Co-ordinated effects make lawyers fretful precisely because of the difficulty of finding decisive evidence.

CC Guidance sets out three conditions for co-ordinated effects to be possible:

- sufficient concentration of market so pricing, if not transparent, is still known by all players;
- incentives for firms to co-ordinate – costly to deviate;
- competitive constraints are weak, e.g. b/c high barriers to entry, no competitive fringe, lack of spare capacity.

Under this umbrella, however, there are many possible types of evidence, some of them ambiguous. Recall, we are only even looking for co-ordinated effects where there is no strong evidence of unilateral effects. What types of evidence might prove most important?

One key type would be evidence of co-ordination pre-merger, and reason to believe the merger makes it easier to continue. One might look for:

- timing and size of price increases, and responsiveness if any to costs;
- spare capacity being held by large but not small companies;
- sustained high profits across the market;
- facilitating practices such as pre-announcement of price increases;
- signs of market sharing, for example in bidding decisions.

If there is no evidence of co-ordination pre-merger, when might it emerge as the result of a merger?

- if the merger brings about a change in market structure such as removal of a competitive maverick;
- if it raises strategic entry barriers;
- if it results in a significant increase in multi-market contacts between the remaining firms.

But this kind of understanding is work in progress. So while the paper rightly singles out theory of repeated games in co-ordination as an area where economic theory has had a policy impact, I think that here too there is an unfinished agenda for economists.

Finally, I'd like to comment on a different part of the paper, the discussion of the inquisitorial versus adversarial approaches. The theoretical models discussed find the inquisitorial approach inferior: the costs of search mean the inquisitor might not invest in finding evidence on both sides of the argument; or might be inclined to ignore a set of arguments. The inquisitorial approach also, for a given standard of proof, biases the decision towards the party with superior information where there are asymmetries. However, the paper is too swift to accept the superiority of the adversarial approach.

For the arguments presented overlook the importance of specific institutional structures and the group nature of decisions: within an inquisitorial group, you always get advocates for each side of the argument.

For one thing, people have different experiences and professional training – lawyers and economists, for example, differ very much in their methods of analysis and approach to making judgments about evidence.

There is also an important feature of the psychology of a group which has clear responsibility for attaining a clear goal. People do seem to accept a role in such circumstances, and take responsibility for one side of the argument. Individuals do also change their minds – mostly, our decisions at the CC reflect a consensus, and that almost always means some people have changed their initial view. However, there is almost always an initial difference of views which means all sides of the argument are assessed.

Making the group work effectively has an implication for the management of staff – the full-time staff on the team must feel at ease with arguing. Sometimes, in groups I've been involved in, members of staff have been 'given permission' to disagree by being asked to play the part of devil's advocate, to test an emerging consensus – one would try to choose the person who seemed most likely to disagree.

In addition at the CC we use part-time outsiders, with limited terms, as members of the group. Such people have no problems about vigorous debate. Maybe there are parallels with what the Monetary Policy Committee has learnt about group decision making. This would be an interesting area to explore.

Combining an inquisitorial system with an adversarial appeal procedure seems to give the best of both worlds, in the sense that the incentives it gives for seeking evidence and overcoming asymmetries of information are about as good as they could be.

REFERENCES

Ahlborn, C. (2002). 'Comment: Airtours/First choice: CFI clips MTF's wings', *In competition*, available at www.linklaters.com/incompetition/200206.htm.

Ahlborn, C., D. Evans and J. Padilla (2004). 'The antitrust economics of tying: a farewell to per se illegality', *Antitrust Bulletin*, 49(1–2), 287–341.

Ahn, S. (2002). 'Competition, innovation and productivity growth: a review of theory and evidence', Economics Department Working Papers No. 37, OECD. Document number ECO/WKP (2002) 3.

Bailey, D. (2003). 'Standard of proof in EC merger proceedings: a common law perspective', *Common Market Law Review*, 40, 845–88.

Baker, J. (2003). 'The case for antitrust enforcement', *The Journal of Economics Perspective*, 17(4), 27–50.

Block, M. and J. Parker (2004). 'Decision making in the absence of successful fact finding: theory and experimental evidence on adversarial versus inquisitorial systems of adjudication', *International Review of Law and Economics*, 24, 89–105.

Block, M., J. Parker, O. Vyborna and L. Dusek (2000). 'An experimental comparison of adversarial versus inquisitorial procedural regimes', *American Law and Economics Review*, 2(1), 170–94.

Botteman, Y. (2006). 'Mergers, standard of proof and expert economic evidence', *Journal of Competition Law and Economics*, 2, 71–100.

Breyer, S. (2004). 'Economic reasoning and judicial review', AEI-Brookings Joint Center 2003 Distinguished Lecture, Brookings, Washington DC.

Burnside, A. (2001). 'Comment: merger control green Paper: SLC', *In Competition*, December 2001, at www.linklaters.com/in_competition/200112.htm.

— (2002). 'Comments on "Reforming European merger review: targeting problem areas in policy outcomes"', *Journal of Industry, Competition and Trade*, 2(4), 365–78.

Clarke, J. and S. Evenett (2003). 'The deterrent effect of national anti-cartel laws: evidence from the international vitamins cartels', *Antitrust Bulletin*, 48(3), 689–726.

Coate, M. and A. Kleit (1998). 'Does it matter that the prosecutor is also the judge? The administrative complaint process at the Federal Trade Commission', *Managerial and Decision Economics*, 19(1), 1–11.

Connor, J. (2003). 'International price fixing, resurgence and deterrence', mimeo, Purdue.

Crandall, R. and C. Winston (2003). 'Does antitrust policy improve consumer welfare? Assessing the evidence', *Journal of Economic Perspectives*, 17(4), 3–26.

Dewatripont, M. and J. Tirole (1999). 'Advocates', *The Journal of Political Economy*, 107(1), 1–39.

Djankov, S. and P. Murrell (2002). 'Enterprise restructuring in transition: a quantitative survey', *Journal of Economic Literature*, 40(3), 739–92.

Duso, T., Neven D. and L.-H. Röller (2007). 'The political economy of European merger control: evidence using stock market data', *The Journal of Law and Economics*, forthcoming.

Evans, D. and J. Padilla (2004). 'Designing antitrust rules for unilateral practices: a neo-Chicago approach', CEPR Discussion Paper No. 4625, London.

Evans, D. and C. Grave (2005). 'The changing role of economics in competition policy decisions by the European Commission during the Monti years', *Competition Policy International*, 1(1), 133–54.

Evenett, S. (2005). 'What is the relationship between competition law and policy and economic development?', University of Oxford, mimeo.

Froeb, L. and B. Kobayashi (1996). 'Naïve, biased, yet Bayesian: can juries interpret selectively produced evidence?', *Journal of Law, Economics and Organization*, 12(1), 257–76.

— (2001). 'Evidence production in adversarial vs inquisitorial regimes', *Economics Letters*, 70(2), 267–72.

Grant J. and D. Neven (2005). 'The attempted merger between General Electrics and Honeywell. A case study of transatlantic conflict', *Journal of Competition Law and Economics*, 1, 595–633.

Hausman, J. and G. Leonard (2005). 'Using merger simulation models: testing the underlying assumptions', *International Journal of Industrial Organization*, 23(9–10), 693–98.

Heyer, K. (2005). 'A world of uncertainty: Economics and the Globalization of Antitrust', *Antitrust Law Journal*, 72, 375–422.

Ivaldi, M. and F. Verboven (2005a). 'Quantifying the effects from horizontal mergers in European competition policy', *International Journal of Industrial Organization*, 23(9–10), 669–91.

— (2005b). 'Using merger simulation models: comments on the underlying assumptions', *International Journal of Industrial Organization*, 23(9–10), 699–702.

Kovacic, W. and C. Shapiro (2000). 'Antitrust policy: a century of economic and legal thinking', *Journal of Economic Perspectives*, 43–60.

Kühn, K.-U (2002). 'Reforming European merger review: targeting problem areas in policy outcomes', *Journal of Industry, Competition and Trade*, 2(4), 311–64.

Legal, H. (2005). 'Standards of proofs and standards of judicial review in EU competition law', Fordham Annual conference on international antitrust law and policy.

Milgrom, P. and J. Roberts (1986). 'Relying on the information of interested parties', *Rand Journal of Economics*, 17, 18–32.

Montag, F. (1996). 'The case for a radical reform of the infringement procedure under regulation 17', *European Competition Law Review*, 8, 428.

Motta, M. (2004). *Competition Policy: Theory and Practice*, Cambridge University Press, Cambridge.

Neven, D. (2006). 'The analysis of conglomerate effects in merger control', in P. Buccirossi (ed.), *Advances in the Economics of Competition Law*, MIT Press, forthcoming.

Neven, D. and P. Mavroidis (2001). 'From the white paper to the proposal for a council regulation: how to treat the new kids around the block', *Legal Issues of Economic Integration*, 28, 151–71.

Neven, D., P. Papandropoulos and P. Seabright (1998). *Trawling for Minnows: Agreements in EC Competition Policy*, CEPR, London.

Nuttal, R., D. Neven and P. Seabright (1994). *Merger in Daylight: The Economics and Politics of EU Merger Control*, CEPR, London.

Nickell, S. (1996). 'Competition and corporate performance', *Journal of Political Economy*, 104, 724–46.

Palumbo, G. (2001). 'Trial procedures and optimal limits on proof-taking', *International Review of Law and Economics*, 21, 309–27.

Parisi, F. (2002). 'Rent-seeking through litigation: adversarial and inquisitorial systems compared', *International Review of Law and Economics*, 22(2), 193–216.

Posner, R. (1988). 'Comment: Responding to Gordon Tullock', *Research in Law and Policy Studies*, 2, 29.

Posner, R. (1999). 'The law and economics of the economic expert witness', *Journal of Economic Perspective*, 13(2), 91–99.

Röller, L-H. (2005). 'Economic analysis and competition policy enforcement in Europe', mimeo.

Röller, L.-H., J. Stennek and F. Verboven (2006). 'Efficiency gains from mergers', Chapter 3 in F. Ilzkovitz and R. Meiklejohn (eds.), *European Merger Control: Do We Need an Efficiency Defense?*, Edward Elgar, London.

Shin, H.-S. (1998). 'Adversarial and inquisitorial procedures in arbitration', *Rand Journal of Economics*, 29(2), 378–405.

Tullock, G. (1988). 'Defending the Napoleonic code over the common law', *Research in Law and Policy Studies*, 2, 3–27.

Vesterdorf, B. (2004). 'Standard of proof in merger cases: reflections in the light of recent case law of the Community Courts', Third Annual Merger Control Conference, BIICL, mimeo.

Vickers, J. (2005). 'Abuse of market power', *Economic Journal*, 115, F244–261.

Vives, X. (2005). 'Brussels has not gone far enough in its merger reforms', *Financial Times*, 15 December.

Welch, J. and J. Byrne (2001). *Jack: What I've Learned Leading a Great Company and Great People*, Headline Books, London.

Werden, G. (2005). 'Making economics more useful in competition cases: procedural rules governing expert opinions', Fordham Annual Conference on international antitrust law and policy.

Wilks, S. and L. McGowan (1996). 'Competition policy in the European Union: creating a federal agency?', in G. Doern and S. Wilks (eds.), *Comparative Competition Policy: National Institutions in a Global Market*, Oxford University Press, Oxford.

Wils, W. (2004). 'The combination of the investigative and prosecutorial function and the adjudicative function in EC antitrust enforcement: a legal and economic analysis', *World Competition*, 27(2), 201–24.

Author Services

Economic Notes

Blackwell Publishing
9600 Garsington Road
Oxford
OX4 2DQ
UK

Tel: +44 (0) 1865 776868
Fax: +44 (0) 1865 714591

The Review of Banking, Finance & Monetary Economics

Edited by: Antonio Roma, Alessandro Vercelli, Flavio Delbono, Ian Cooper, Walter Torous, Andrea Berardi, Alberto Dalmazzo and Giovanni Ferri

+ Publishing high-quality research by first-class economists and experts in the field for over 35 years.

+ Open, easily readable debate of contemporary issues in banking, finance and monetary economics.

+ Published on behalf of the Banca Monte Dei Paschi Di Siena SpA: the world's oldest banking institution.

For more information visit

www.blackwellpublishing.com/ecno

Or visit **www.blackwell-synergy.com/loi/ecno** for more information about accessing the journal online.

Blackwell Synergy

Register FREE at Blackwell Synergy and you can:

- Receive tables of contents e-mail alerts directly to your desktop with links to article abstracts
- Search across all full text articles for key words or phrases
- Access free sample issues from every online journal
- Browse all journal table of contents and abstracts, and save favourites on your own custom page.

Published three times a year, ISSN 0391-5026

beetsma Roel is Professor of Macroeconomics at the University of Amsterdam. His main research interests are fiscal and monetary policy and the macroeconomics of ageing.

giuliodori Massimo is Assistant Professor of Monetary Economics at the University of Amsterdam. His research interests are fiscal and monetary policy and housing economics.

klaassen Franc is Associate Professor of International Economics at the University of Amsterdam. His research mainly concerns empirical work on international economics and finance (exchange rates, trade, the euro), fiscal policy and sports (mainly tennis).

müller Gernot J. is a Post Doctorate student at the Department of Money and Macroeconomics at Goethe University Frankfurt. He works on monetary and fiscal policy and on international macroeconomics.

corsetti Giancarlo is Pierre Werner Chair at the Robert Schuman Centre of the Europe University Institute, and professor of Economics at the University of Rome III. He has written extensively on the international transmission of monetary policy, currency and financial crises, and European economic integration.

neven Damien J. is Professor at the Graduate Institute of International Studies in Geneva (on leave) and currently Chief Competition Economist at the Competition Directorate of the European Commission. His research focuses on competition economics and enforcement.

fabrizio Stefania is a Senior Economist in International Monetary Fund's European Department. Her research interests include fiscal policy, employment, exchange rate and competitiveness issues.

mody Ashoka is an Assistant Director in International Monetary Fund's European Department. He writes for scholarly journals as well as for policy audiences.

CES

ps
e

CE
PR

ISBN 1-4051-4512-9

0266-4658(200610)21:04;1-N

9 781405 145121

ECONOMIC POLICY

49

January
2007

fiscal decentralization
KESSING, KONRAD and KOTSOGIANNIS

wage inequality
KOENIG... ...EONARDI

seniority
...RI and MALIRANTA

ecosystems
GARTNER

ECONOMIC POLICY

Editorial address: Centre for Economic Policy Research, 90–98 Goswell Road, London EC1V 7RR, UK; Center for Economic Studies, University of Munich, Schackstr. 4, 80539 Munich, GERMANY; Paris-Jourdan Sciences Economiques, ENS, 48 Boulevard Jourdan, 75014 Paris, FRANCE. URL: http://www.economic-policy.org

Publisher: *Economic Policy* is published by Blackwell Publishing, 9600 Garsington Road, Oxford OX4 2DQ, UK and 350 Main Street, Malden, MA 02148, USA.

Information for subscribers: *Economic Policy* is published in four issues per year. Subscription prices for 2007 are:

	Europe	The Americas	ROW
Premium Institutional:	£330	US$501	£330
Personal:	€71	US$70	£47
Student:	€35	US$38	£23

Customers in the UK should add VAT at 6%; customers in the EU should also add VAT at 6%, or provide a VAT registration number or evidence of entitlement to exemption. Customers in Canada should add 6% GST or provide evidence of entitlement to exception. The Premium institutional price includes online access from current content and all online back files to January 1st 1997, where available. For other pricing options or more information about online access to Blackwell Publishing journals, including access information and terms and conditions, please visit www.blackwellpublishing.com/ecop.

Delivery Terms and Legal Title: Prices include delivery of print journals to the recipient's address. Delivery terms are Delivered Duty Unpaid (DDU); the recipient is responsible for paying any import duty or taxes. Legal title passes to the customer on dispatch by our distributors.

EEA members: Subscriptions are available now at 40 euro. Apply to the European Economic Association, Voie du Roman Pays, 34, B-1348 Louvain-la-Neuve, Belgium (tel: +32 10 472 012, fax: +32 10 474 021/474 301, email: eea@core.ucl.ac.be, URL: http://www.eeassoc.org).

Available online: This journal is available online at *Blackwell Synergy*. Visit www.blackwell-synergy.com to search the articles and register for table of contents e-mail alerts.

Journal Customer Services: For ordering information, claims and any enquiry concerning your journal subscription please contact your nearest office:

UK: Email: customerservices@blackwellpublishing.com; Tel: +44 (0) 1865 778315; Fax: +44 (0) 1865 471775

USA: Email: customerservices@blackwellpublishing.com; Tel: +1 781 388 8206 or 1 800 835 6770 (Toll free in the USA); Fax: +1 781 388 8232 or Fax: +44 (0) 1865 471775

Asia: Email: customerservices@blackwellpublishing.com; Tel: +65 6511 8000; Fax: +44 (0) 1865 471775

Production Editor: David Thresher (email: david.thresher@edn.blackwellpublishing.com).

Back issues: Single issues from current and recent volumes are available at the current single issue price from Blackwell Publishing Journals. Earlier issues may be obtained from Periodicals Service Company, 11 Main Street, Germantown, NY 12526, USA. Tel: +1 518 537 4700, Fax: +1 518 537 5899, Email: psc@periodicals.com.

Advertising: Andy Patterson (email: andy@patads.co.uk).

Abstracting and Indexing Services: ABI-INFORM; AgBiotech News and Information; Asian-Pacific Economic Literature; Bibliography of Asian Studies; Contents of Recent Economics Journals; Current Contents; Emeraid Management Reviews; Environmental Sciences and Pollution Management; GEOBASE; International Bibliography of the Social Sciences; International Political Science Abstracts; Journal of Economic Literature; Leisure, Recreation and Tourism Abstracts; PAIS International in Print; Periodicals Content Index; Plant Genetic Resources Abstracts; Risk Abstracts; Sage Public Administration Abstracts; Social Science Citation Index; World Agricultural Economics and Rural Sociology Abstracts.

Disclaimer: The Publisher, Centre for Economic Policy Research, Center for Economic Studies, Maison des Sciences de l'Homme and Editors cannot be held responsible for errors or any consequences arising from the use of information contained in this journal; the views and opinions expressed do not necessarily reflect those of the Publisher, Centre for Economic Policy Research, Center for Economic Studies, Maison des Sciences de l'Homme and Editors, neither does the publication of advertisements constitute any endorsement by the Publisher, Centre for Economic Policy Research, Center for Economic Studies, Maison des Sciences de l'Homme and Editors of the products advertised.

Paper: Blackwell Publishing's policy is to use permanent paper from mills that operate a sustainable forestry policy, and which has been manufactured from pulp that is processed using acid-free and elementary chlorine-free practices. Furthermore, Blackwell Publishing ensures that the text paper and cover board used in all our journals has met acceptable environmental accreditation standards.

CarbonNeutral: Blackwell Publishing is a CarbonNeutral company. For more information visit www.blackwellpublishing.com/carbonneutral

Printed in Great Britain by Page Brothers Ltd.

For submission instructions, subscription and all other information visit: www.blackwellpublishing.com/ecop

ISSN: 0266-4658 (print); ISSN: 1468-0327 (online)

ISBN-13: 978-1-4051-5544-1

49

January
2007

ECONOMIC POLICY

SENIOR EDITORS
GEORGES DE MÉNIL
RICHARD PORTES
HANS-WERNER SINN

MANAGING EDITORS
GIUSEPPE BERTOLA
PHILIPPE MARTIN
PAUL SEABRIGHT

Published in association with the European Economic Association

Blackwell Publishing Ltd for Centre for Economic Policy Research,
Center for Economic Studies of the University of Munich, and
Paris-Jourdan Sciences Economiques (PSE)
in collaboration with the Maison des Sciences de l'Homme.

STATEMENT OF PURPOSE

Economic Policy provides timely and authoritative analyses of the choices which confront policy-makers. The subject matter ranges from the study of how individual markets can and should work to the broadest interactions in the world economy.

Economic Policy is a joint activity of the Centre for Economic Policy Research (CEPR), the Munich-based Center for Economic Studies (CES) and the Paris-based Maison des Sciences de l'Homme (PSE). It offers an independent, non-partisan, European perspective on issues of worldwide concern. It emphasizes problems of international significance, either because they affect the world economy directly or because the experience of one country contains important lessons for policy-makers elsewhere.

All the articles are specifically commissioned from leading professional economists. Their brief is to demonstrate how live policy issues can be illuminated by the insights of modern economics and by the most recent evidence. The presentation is incisive and written in plain language accessible to the wide audience which participates in the policy debate.

Prior to publication, the contents of each volume are discussed by a Panel of distinguished economists from Europe and elsewhere. The Panel rotates annually. Inclusion in each volume of a summary of the highlights of the Economic Policy Panel discussion provides the reader with alternative interpretations of the evidence and a sense of the liveliness of the current debate.

Economic Policy is owned by the Maison des Sciences de l'Homme, CEPR and CES. The 43rd Panel meeting was held in Vienna and was hosted by the Österreichische Nationalbank. We gratefully acknowledge this support, without implicating any of these organizations in the views expressed here, which are the sole responsibility of the authors.

PANEL

49

January 2007

CONTENTS

Editors' introduction

The four papers published in this issue were among those presented in draft form at the panel meeting hosted in April 2006 by the Austrian National Bank in Vienna. In this introduction we place their contribution in the context of wider debates.

FISCAL DECENTRALIZATION

Poorly coordinated, time-inconsistent policy decisions can defeat their own purposes, and credible commitment devices are valuable in many contexts. In the monetary policy area, a credible commitment to low inflation avoids self-fulfilling inflation expectations. Similarly, tax policy can benefit from constraints preventing the kind of *ex post* exorbitant taxation that, eliminating *ex ante* incentives to invest and produce income, would lower revenue yields. Tax competition between independent fiscal constituencies is one such constraint. It has been argued that investors should expect taxes to be low in countries where tax-setting powers are decentralized, and that such countries should therefore be able to attract foreign direct investment (FDI) flows more easily than centralized countries. Sebastian G. Kessing, Kai A. Konrad and Christos Kotsogiannis make a forceful theoretical and empirical case against this line of reasoning. They point out that in exactly the same situations where *ex ante* tax expectations affect tax bases – that is, when taxable income results from forward-looking investment decisions – 'horizontal' tax competition between the regions or states of federal countries is ineffective in keeping *ex post* taxes low: once investors have allocated projects irreversibly to a specific location within a country, there is no competition between that and other constituencies, and fiscal decentralization cannot eliminate each region's temptation to exploit its tax power. A similarly simple mechanism may in fact deliver the opposite prediction. If income produced in a specific geographical location within a federal country is subject to taxation by more than one level of government, lack of 'vertical' coordination between numerous such layers of tax-setting decisions may lead investors to fear more intense *ex post* tax pressure in more decentralized countries. Kessing, Konrad and Kotsogiannis confront this insight with empirical evidence, and uncover strong evidence that more numerous layers of government are associated with smaller inward FDI flows. The panel was keenly interested in the panel draft's theoretical and, especially, empirical results, but voiced some doubts as to the latter's statistical strength. This encouraged the authors to clarify further the relationship between their theoretical reasoning and unavoidably imperfect and incomplete empirical information. A wide variety of specifications allows the published version of the paper to establish that the correlation between 'vertical' decentralization and FDI flows is an empirically robust fact that will need to be taken into account by the policy debate on the allocation of tax powers. The many countries that are considering or implementing fiscal decentralization should not do so in the hope of fostering FDI-friendly tax competition and, to prevent 'vertical' multiplication of tax pressure from discouraging investment, should carefully coordinate tax- and base-setting decisions at different levels of their government structure.

The next paper also explores institutional influences on cross-country investment evidence, albeit from a different, labour-market oriented perspective.

WAGE INEQUALITY

Everybody knows that involuntary unemployment can result from institutions that prevent wages from falling so low as to make it profitable for employers to hire workers, and it is widely thought that collective bargaining, minimum wages, and welfare benefits are the reason why low-skill workers are not employed in many European countries. Employment patterns, however, are not the only consequence of institutional constraints. Firms choose not only how many and which workers to hire, but also how much to invest, and how. While some types of equipment can substitute low-skill workers, others can make such workers more productive. In a 'frictional' labour market, where firms cannot easily replace their employees with unemployed workers, investing in ways that increase incumbent workers' productivity can be an attractive option, and all the more attractive if rigid wages prevent those workers from appropriating that investment's returns. Winfried Koeniger and Marco Leonardi assess the empirical relevance of this channel comparing employment and investment patterns across countries, over time and across industries. Their data come from Germany, where wage floors are binding, and from the US, where labour markets are flexible. Over time, their data span a period when manufacturing equipment became cheaper. The paper's regressions establish that industries employing unskilled workers tend to invest more in Germany than in the US in the available sample. Thus, the data support the view that firms react to institutions which imply high, rigid, compressed wage structures not only by reducing employment, but also by investing so as to boost the productivity of workers above binding minimum-wage floors. The paper's careful and extensive empirical work and findings make an important contribution to the broader and evolving literature that studies interactions between capital costs, capital accumulation, and the labour market opportunities of differently skilled workers. As the discussants' comments make clear, data limitations have so far prevented this literature from offering a coherent and robust picture to policy makers and public opinion, and the paper by Koeniger and Leonardi is also unable to offer conclusive evidence on the relevant issues. But the paper will remain a relevant reference for work on more detailed data as they become available, and usefully reminds policy-makers that investment patterns are one of the many consequences of institutions that interfere with labour market equilibria: while no way out of the standard 'equity vs efficiency' trade-off, investments that boost the productivity of low-skill workers are another way in which profits and competitiveness are reduced in countries where institutions aim at slicing the pie in favour or less advantaged individuals.

SENIORITY

The growing importance of information technology in modern economies has prompted fears that some groups of workers may be increasingly disadvantaged, because of inadequate skills. One group of workers about whom particular concern has been expressed is older workers. There is evidence of poor labour market performance of older workers, and evidence that an ageing workforce can become a burden for some kinds of firm. Francesco Daveri and Mika Maliranta investigate this question by providing evidence on the relation between age, seniority and experience, on the one hand, and the main components of labour costs, namely productivity and wages, on the other, for a sample of plants in three manufacturing industries (forestry, industrial machinery and electronics) in Finland during the IT revolution in the 1990s.

They uncover evidence of a significant divergence between the wage and productivity profiles of more senior workers – that is, those who have been a long time with the same employer. It is this group rather than older workers *per se* who are most at risk of becoming a burden on firms in IT-intensive sectors. In 'average' industries – those not undergoing major technological shocks – both productivity and wages keep rising with the accumulation of either seniority (in the forestry industry) or experience (in the industry producing industrial machinery). In electronics, however, the seniority–productivity profile shows a positive relation first and then becomes negative as one looks at plants with higher average seniority. This body of evidence is consistent with the idea that fast technical change brings about accelerated skill depreciation of senior workers. The authors cannot rule out, however, that their correlations are also simultaneously produced by worker movements across plants. The seniority–earnings profile in electronics is instead rather similar to that observed for the other industries – a likely symptom of the prevailing Finnish wage bargaining institutions which tend to make seniority one essential element of wage determination.

In the end, seniority matters for labour costs, not age as such. But only in high-tech industries, not in the economy at large. This is well tuned with previous research on gross flows of workers and jobs in the US and other OECD countries which unveiled the productivity-driving role of resource reallocation between plants. To improve the employability of the elderly at times of fast technical change, the authors argue that public policy should divert resources away from preserving existing jobs and lend more attention to the retraining of old workers to ease their reallocation away from less productive plants (or plants where they have become less productive) into new jobs.

Discussion at the panel focused on whether the undoubted statistical association between seniority and declining productivity was more likely to reflect a decline in productivity among older workers, or a sorting process by which less productive workers were less likely to leave their employers and join new firms. The existing data do not allow this question to be answered with any confidence, but it remains an important issue for future research.

ECOSYSTEMS

As public debate and public policy focus increasingly on the protection of environmental resources it is becoming important to find rigorous methods for valuing environmental assets such as ecosystems whose future may be threatened by economic change. The paper by Edward Barbier explores two methods for valuing such ecosystems by valuing the services that they yield to various categories of user and that are not directly valued in the market. It applies these methods by way of illustration to the valuation of mangrove ecosystems in Thailand. The first method is known as the production function approach and relies on the fact that ecosystems may be inputs into the production of other goods or services that are themselves marketed, such as fisheries. Barbier discusses issues that arise in measuring the input into fisheries, particularly those due to the fact that the fishery stock is changing over time, and the shadow value of the ecosystem consists in its contribution to the maintenance of the stock as well as its contribution to current output. The second method is known as the expected damage approach and is used to value the services of storm protection in terms of the reduction in expected future storm damage that the ecosystem can provide. These two methods are shown to yield very different valuations of ecosystems from those that would be derived by the methods typically used in cost–benefit analyses. The author argues that they represent a significant improvement on current practice.

The panel was somewhat divided on the appropriateness of the methods proposed, largely because current practice was widely felt to be highly unsatisfactory, and opinions differed as to how much improvement could reasonably be expected of methods that could be implemented in practice. Both the production function and the expected damage approach leave out many potential benefits from ecosystems, so the fact that they also correct for unsatisfactory assumptions made in existing valuation methodologies was not thought by all panellists to be enough reason to recommend their widespread adoption. However, most panellists agreed that important policy decisions might turn on issues of valuation of precisely this kind, and that urgent attention needs to be given to refining methods of measurement and valuation for use in the future.

Fiscal decentralization
VERTICAL, HORIZONTAL, AND FDI

SUMMARY

Both in the developed and developing world, decentralization of fiscal policy is frequently argued to foster investment, because allowing investors to choose between competing locations should make it difficult for each jurisdiction to tax the investment's returns. We point out that this 'horizontal' dimension of decentralization cannot eliminate ex post incentives to tax investments once they are irreversibly located in a jurisdiction, and that the negative ex ante investment effects of such 'hold up' problems are actually stronger when decentralization inevitably leads to multiple levels of taxation power in each location. Empirically, we detect significant negative effects on FDI of the 'vertical' dimension of decentralization, measured by the number of government layers, in a data set containing many countries and many suitable control variables. Indicators of overall fiscal decentralization do not appear to affect the investment climate negatively per se, but our theoretical arguments and empirical results suggest that policymakers should consider very carefully the form and degree of government decentralization if they aim at improving the investment climate.

— *Sebastian G. Kessing, Kai A. Konrad and Christos Kotsogiannis*

Economic Policy January 2007 Printed in Great Britain
© CEPR, CES, MSH, 2007.

Foreign direct investment and the dark side of decentralization

Sebastian G. Kessing, Kai A. Konrad and
Christos Kotsogiannis

Wissenschaftszentrum Berlin für Sozialforschung (WZB); Wissenschaftszentrum Berlin für Sozialforschung (WZB) and Freie Universität Berlin; University of Exeter and Athens University of Economics and Business

1. INTRODUCTION

Countries differ in their government architecture. Some countries are characterized by a high degree of concentration of fiscal, administrative, judicial, executive and lawmaking powers, whereas others have decentralized many functions and responsibilities of government to different jurisdictions and various levels of government. The cross-country differences in the organization of government are also not static but have been subject to substantial change in many countries. The co-existence of different organizational patterns of government has created an important debate regarding the determinants of particular government structures as well as questions regarding the optimality of different forms of organization.

We are grateful to Nils Herger and Steve McCorriston who have allowed us to make use of the data set they use in their work on cross-border mergers and acquisitions and institutional quality. We also thank them for many discussions, comments and advice during the preparation of the first draft of this paper. Likewise, we thank Daniel Treisman for providing us with his decentralization data. For very helpful comments we thank our discussants and the Panel as well as Johannes Becker, Thiess Büttner, Michael Devereux, Bruno Frey, Clemens Fuest, Achim Wambach, and seminar participants at research seminars and conferences in Berlin, Bonn, Copenhagen, Cyprus, Cologne, Frankfurt, Hanoi, Munich and Warwick. The usual caveat applies.

The Managing Editor in charge of this paper was Giuseppe Bertola.

Economic Policy January 2007 pp. 5–70 Printed in Great Britain
© CEPR, CES, MSH, 2007.

We aim at contributing to this debate by analysing the role of decentralized governance for attracting foreign direct investment (FDI). Decentralized governance, understood here as institutional rules which allocate some governmental decision rights in a country to independent regional governments of non-overlapping territories inside the country, has important effects on the potential of countries to attract FDI. We offer a number of theoretical considerations in this regard, and highlight various effects of the degree of decentralization on FDI that we believe have not been sufficiently recognized. Our main contribution, however, is empirical in nature as we empirically assess the effects of decentralization on FDI.

We point out that, in theory, decentralization of government operates along both a *horizontal* and a *vertical* dimension. Consider first the *horizontal* dimension. Decentralization comes along with the partitioning of the state territory into smaller districts or regions with some autonomy in governmental decision making. The local governments are 'closer' to their constituency, both physically and in terms of accountability. Also, potential competition and benchmarking between the regions becomes feasible whereas this is not feasible under a unified central government. In the policy debate, these aspects of horizontal segregation play an important role. In the traditional view it is argued that horizontal disintegration may also have some disadvantages, as it becomes more difficult for the disintegrated entities to cope with inter-regional spillovers and economies of scale in the public sector. But it is frequently maintained that the beneficial effects that stem from inter-regional competition dominate, in particular with respect to attracting FDI. Horizontal segregation 'permits a degree of institutional competition between centres of authority that can . . . reduce the risk that governments will expropriate wealth' (World Bank, 2004, p. 53). To a large extent, this reasoning is rooted in the view that bureaucrats and politicians are not purely benevolent but they may try to use their power to tax in order to extract revenues, and investment projects that are owned by foreigners may be welcome targets for extractive activities. Competition between jurisdictions for mobile factors of production makes opportunistic behaviour of bureaucrats and politicians more difficult (see Weingast, 1995; Qian and Weingast, 1997), a view that can be traced back to Hayek (1939) and Tiebout (1956). That inter-jurisdictional competition may serve as a welcome supplement to inadequate constitutional constraints and imperfect political institutions has also been emphasized by Brennan and Buchanan (1977, 1980). Also, it is argued that the competition between horizontally segregated regional governments may alleviate some time consistency problems of taxation that emerge even if politicians pursue the welfare of their citizens (Kehoe, 1989).

Complete horizontal disintegration and competitive governmental decision making on the regional level is the implication of decentralization, if decentralization is meant to be a complete break up of a nation into many small and fully independent nations. However, such a complete break up typically does not happen, and should not happen from an efficiency point of view: scale effects and difficulties with the internalization of inter-regional spill-over effects or global public goods suggest that only some, but not all decision rights should be allocated to local or regional governments. Some decisions will continue to be made on more aggregate levels, for example, by the district level government, by state level government, or by the federal government, depending on the architecture of government layers that is chosen. The creation of local governments and the process of horizontal segregation are typically accompanied by a process of *vertical* disintegration. A firm owner who is located in a particular city deals with the governmental decision making of governments of the city, the district in which this city is located, the state in which this district is located and the federal government. When choosing locations, investors should accordingly take into account that they will be subject to the jurisdiction of all such government tiers. An exclusive focus on the benchmarking, competition and accountability features of inter-regional competition that may result from horizontal segregation fails to acknowledge this other side of decentralization.

Our analysis identifies the vertical disintegration of governmental decision making as a major source of disadvantages of decentralization. If the private sector has dealings with several tiers of government, this will potentially create problems of rivalry between the different tiers, coordination failures, free-riding incentives between government decision makers from different government tiers, common pool problems between them when making independent tax and expenditure decisions, problems when it comes to the enforcement of implicit contracts between the government and private investors, and moral hazard problems from joint accountability of politicians from different vertical tiers. These problems affect a country's attraction as a location for FDI in several ways. Suppose governments are tempted to extract revenue from existing investment projects that are owned by foreigners. If governments from several tiers are able to extract revenue from the same investment project a common pool problem emerges that may increase the amount of extractive activity. Governments may also subsidize or make bids for attracting investment projects that are future targets for extractive policy or benefit the host-country in other ways. If local, regional and federal governments can make such bids, they may free ride on one another.

At the end of the day, only empirical evidence can tell whether decentralization, and its different dimensions, has positive or negative effects on the level of FDI inflows. Our econometric analysis provides novel evidence in this respect. Introducing measures of decentralization in a 'knowledge-capital' model and using firm data on cross-border acquisitions, our findings suggest, in line with our theoretical perspective, that a one-dimensional and positive view of decentralization is not appropriate. Employing various decentralization measures in our empirical work, we derive insights as to which aspects of decentralization are conducive to FDI and which turn out to be rather problematic.

The vertical dimension of decentralization, measured by the number of government tiers in a country, is found to affect FDI negatively. On the other hand, fiscal decentralization can have significant positive effects. Expenditure decentralization is found to be correlated with more FDI, while revenue decentralization appears to have a negative influence on FDI.

Our results are highly relevant for policy makers as policy reforms that change the degree of decentralization of governance have been high on the policy agenda both for the developed and the developing world. Poor economic performance of many developing countries is often attributed to the failure of centralized bureaucracy and centralized decision making, and many consultants advocate decentralization of policy-decision making as a way to sustain or increase growth and prosperity. Decentralization is also a frequent advice given by international organizations. Substantial resources have been geared towards programs that promote decentralization of policy decision making. Recently, for instance, the OECD, the World Bank, the Council of Europe, the Open Society Institute (Budapest), the UNDP and USAID have joined forces and introduced the Fiscal Decentralization Initiative to assist developing countries in carrying out intergovernmental reforms (OECD, 2002). The prime objectives of this initiative are to encourage local democracies to improve the capacity of local governments to plan and administer expenditures and raise revenues, and to support local governments in their efforts to become more responsive and accountable. This tendency is expected to continue well into the future.

Practitioners and academics have not been unaware of potential pitfalls of decentralization. For example, the World Bank states that 'sub-national governments are not immune from governance problems – and in some contexts may be more vulnerable to them than national authorities' (World Bank, 2004, p. 53). Similarly, Bardhan and Mookherjee (2000, 2005) discuss the incidence of corruption in centralized and decentralized systems. From our perspective, the question whether local or central governments are more corrupt, easier captured, better informed, etc. is only one aspect of the decentralization debate, albeit an important one. Still, our argument is that this view remains incomplete. It is not sufficient to consider just the incentives and capabilities of each *individual* government. We stress that the *distribution* of power, responsibilities and accountability across different government levels within a federal system has important effects. These effects interact and typically reinforce the governance problems that exist at each individual level of government. This paper is not the first to highlight problematic aspects of decentralization, and that tries to single out more precisely the specific conditions and institutional provisions that are necessary for federalism to unleash its potential for improving the countries' economic performance. For instance, an important feature of the usual efficiency argument for decentralization is that it is developed in a system within which there is a clear division of powers between the different government tiers, in which all spillovers, including vertical fiscal externalities are absent by assumption or are contracted away (Riker, 1964). Vertical fiscal externalities have recently been identified as a source of inefficiency in the context of tax competition (see, for instance, Wrede, 1997, 2000; and Keen and Kotsogiannis, 2002, 2003, 2004) and it has been argued that they are difficult to avoid, even if seemingly different tax bases are assigned to different tiers of government, and regardless whether politicians and bureaucrats are assumed to be benevolent or perfectly selfish.

Treisman (1999a, 1999b, 2000b, 2003) has put forward a number of further arguments why decentralization may lead to a less satisfactory performance, and Cai and Treisman (2005) show that the disciplinary effect of inter-regional competition, even where it could be at work in principle, may lead to adverse effects if regions are asymmetric, making some of them drive out all mobile capital and specialize on a high level of oppression. This and other consequences of a federal structure may also reduce FDI.

2. DECENTRALIZATION AND FOREIGN DIRECT INVESTMENT

The analysis of the benefits and costs of decentralization has generated a number of important general insights. We provide a brief overview in Box 1. While the conclusions from this work also have a bearing on countries' ability to attract FDI, we seek to go beyond these established results and to dwell deeper into the specific relationship between decentralization and the attractiveness of host countries for potential foreign investors. In particular, we focus on two questions. First, can the potentially beneficial effect of inter-regional fiscal competition really unfold its effectiveness on FDI? Second, are there potentially harmful effects of the vertical dimension of decentralization on FDI and how do they operate?

2.1. The nature of FDI and the hold-up problem

Consider the timing of decision making between the investor and the government that has jurisdiction in the location in which the FDI takes place, which creates what is called the *hold-up problem* in the context of FDI[1]: an investor can freely choose where to locate its FDI. Once the investment is made, some share of it is sunk and irreversible. The host government which has the jurisdiction in this location can now choose how much to demand from the investment returns, and may even choose to appropriate the investment completely. These incentives arise if the government is simply revenue maximizing, but also if the government is benevolent or acts in the interest of the citizens in the host country for political reasons, simply because the owners of the FDI that occurs in a host country are foreigners in that country by definition. If foreign investors anticipate this extractive behaviour, they will invest too little or not invest at all. Even investment projects that yield a very high gross return and would be highly profitable in the absence of the threat of confiscatory taxation do not take place. Unless the government can credibly commit not to make use of the opportunities to extract, or can compensate investors upfront, investors will not invest if they anticipate that the whole returns on their investments are confiscated.

---

[1] For a characterization and some essential aspects of this problem see Eaton and Gersovitz (1983), Janeba (2000), Konrad and Lommerud (2001) and Schnitzer (1999).

Box 1. Arguments for and against decentralization

Decentralization of fiscal responsibility to sub-central government is thought to change the public sector's *allocative efficiency*, and the policy makers' *accountability* to their constituencies.

Oates (1972, 1999) suggested that decentralization allows local preferences to be reflected more sensitively in the decentralized provision of local public goods. One of his arguments is rooted in the view that the central government is relatively poorly informed about local tastes for public goods and about the cost of producing them, pointing to the problem of discovering local preferences. Also, he suggests a tendency of the central government to choose local public goods uniformly across different regions. Mobility of labour across jurisdictions has been suggested as a solution to this information problem in a decentralized context. If citizens feel discontent with the pattern of local taxes and spending in their own locality, they may express this discontent by 'voting with their feet' and may move to other jurisdictions they find more suited to their preferences. In the limit one can conceive a situation in which citizens sort themselves across localities in such a way that the allocation of resources is entirely efficient: no reallocation is possible such that citizens' welfare increases. This view, that labour mobility alone is enough to secure efficiency in the pattern of local public expenditure, is known as the Tiebout hypothesis (see Tiebout, 1956).

Decentralization may change the accountability of government that stems from the existence of local elections in decentralized structures (see, e.g., Seabright, 1996). With decentralized policy decision making, and separate elections in each locality, politicians are elected on the basis of their performance on the local policies and not on 'an average' measure of performance as it would be under centralization (see, among others, Besley and Smart, 2003, and Kessler *et al.*, 2005). There is a variety of considerations pointing to centralized policy decision making. With the risk of over-simplification these considerations can be divided into two broad categories: *efficiency* and *administration*. As regards efficiency, the mobility of factors of production may generate inefficiencies in the allocation of resources due to fiscal externalities in the context of tax competition between localities for a mobile tax base. Possible remedies to this problem are multilateral reforms that coordinate taxes, or, inside a federation with a central government, Pigouvian subsidies for the localities, 'presumably administered by a higher level government' (Wildasin, 1989). As regards administration, decentralization entails duplication of certain fiscal activities. As Oates (1972, p. 201) notes, this may suggest that the optimal degree of centralization is a function of country size.

This picture alludes to an empirically important investment obstacle. Full expropriation may be less likely to be the outcome in reality, because the actual returns that accrue from an investment depend, to a considerable extent, on other factors of production (such as the amount of workers employed, or managerial effort) that are chosen by the investor at the point when the host government(s) made their choices on taxes and other extractive efforts.[2] This ability to adjust production activity *ex post* will generally lead to less than full confiscation. The relationship between the anticipated level of confiscatory taxation and overall revenue that accrues will typically follow a 'Laffer' curve. The overall tax burden in the equilibrium depends on the governance structure, and we may ask whether the hold up problem of FDI is mitigated or aggravated by (a) horizontal competition between independent regions, and (b) the vertical organization of governance. We turn, starting with the former question, to this next.

2.2. The benefits of horizontal competition

Federalism and decentralization of authority comes along with horizontal and vertical disintegration. Consider first the aspect of a horizontal split up of a unitary country into regions with independent governments. Kehoe (1989) highlighted an important aspect of inter-regional competition. He addressed a time consistency problem in capital income taxation that is related to the hold-up problem in FDI and had been discussed by Kydland and Prescott (1980). They considered the choice of savings of private households if they have to invest their savings within one country with a unitary government. The government chooses its future tax system time consistently. It minimizes the excess burden that is caused by the taxes at the point in time when the taxes are chosen. In such a single unitary country, households anticipate that their savings will constitute a fully immobile tax base in the future and that the government will try to make use of this non-distortionary source of taxes. But if the households anticipate that their savings will be taxed quite heavily, or even completely confiscated, they will not save. Kehoe (1989) suggested that this problem of time consistent capital income taxation can be solved if there are many countries or many regions with local governments who choose their tax policy independently, if the private households can choose in which country to locate their savings at a point in time when the countries have already chosen their capital income tax rates. Even though the total amount of savings is given when the countries or regions choose their tax policy, governments still have to consider that the owners of capital may relocate its existing stock from a country that chooses high tax rates to low tax countries, and in the equilibrium, this drives down the tax rates chosen by the different governments.

Formally, decentralization of single countries into many small regions is not needed to implement this type of competition. International capital mobility may be sufficient.

---

[2] Charlton (2003) argues that only a share in the total assets, that constitute an FDI project, consists of fully immobile property plant and equipment.

But this mechanism may function even better for the competition between regions, as the transaction cost of shifting capital from one region to another may be lower than for shifting capital across country borders.

Applied to FDI, the competition between the governments in different regions could be to the benefit of foreign investors who can choose their investment location, as they can choose the most attractive offer, and competition between the regions is likely to drive down the rents that can be appropriated by the regional government and its citizens. This competition aspect is emphasized by many writers on federalism and FDI. As a prominent example Weingast (1995, pp. 5–6) expresses this view in the following statement:

> [i]f a jurisdiction attempts to confiscate the wealth of an industry, the mobility of capital implies that firms will relocate. The mobility of resources thus raises the economic cost of those jurisdictions that might establish certain policies, and they will do so only if the political benefits are worth these and other costs. Federalism thus greatly diminishes the level of pervasiveness of economic rent-seeking and the formation of distributional coalitions.

This view is quite influential in the policy debate. However, it is important to note that inter-regional competition of the kind underlying Kehoe's (1989) argument addresses the problem of savings well, but it is not suitable to address and solve the hold-up problem in FDI. One of the implicit preconditions for Kehoe's mechanism to work in the FDI context is that the investors or capital owners are able to relocate their capital between regions or countries at a point of time when the politicians or bureaucrats have made their policy choices. To some extent, this may also be true for some FDI, and, but to a different degree, for different types of investment.[3] Also, if the existing stock of investment and future investment has to be treated equally and uniformly, competition for future flows of FDI may make the aggregate stock of FDI that accumulates over time more elastic with respect to how foreign investors are treated once the investment has been made and is sunk. Still, much of the investment in a specific FDI project, and most notably the physical capital is fixed and tied to the local region in which it is installed, and cannot react further to changes in taxes, regulation and bureaucratic demands.

For the beneficial effects of competition between localities for investors to unfold it is required that this competition opens up alternatives for investors at the point of time when a locality has chosen how investors are treated in terms of taxes and public services. Only if investors can easily adjust their activities by moving from one locality to another as a reaction to this treatment, the threat to do this will discipline the policy makers and give them incentives not to exploit investors. If, at some stage, the investors have irreversibly made investments in a locality that are sunk, moving these investments into another locality is no longer an option, and the investors are at the mercy of the decision makers who have jurisdiction over the particular locality in which they are locked.

---

[3] For instance, the share in property plant and equipment in total assets that is used in Charlton (2003) is a rough measure for how immobile a given foreign direct investment is.

2.3. Harmful effects of vertical disintegration

Consider now how the vertical dimension of decentralization bears on investment and taxation decisions. (For a formalization and extensions of the following reasoning, readers should refer to Kessing *et al.*, 2006a.)

Delegation of some governmental choices to lower tiers of government, without complete disintegration of the top level of government, leads to a situation in which an investor who made a decision to build a plant in, say, Munich has to deal with several governments: with the city government of Munich, with the district government in the district in which Munich is located, with the government of the State of Bavaria in which Munich is located, and with the federal government of Germany, as Munich also belongs to Germany. If one considers the European Union as another level of government, since Germany is a member of the European Union, and the Union's decisions affect most firms in important ways, there is even a fifth level.

To the extent that the investment is fixed and irreversible, the investor is subject to all these governments' policies, whereas the existence of other cities or states and their different jurisdiction becomes unimportant for the investor. This joint responsibility of several government tiers is an inevitable consequence of federal decentralization and can have a significant effect on the attractiveness of a locality for FDI. The argument put forward in this paper is that the various governance problems that exist between a host government and a foreign investor, and in particular the severity of the hold-up problem, may depend on whether an investor who has chosen a given investment location has to deal with few or many vertical layers of government.

2.3.1. The common pool problem. Suppose that an investor contemplates investing in one of two countries: a hierarchically organized one (federal), denoted by F, and one where there is only one level of government (unitary), denoted by U. Suppose also that in both countries governments cannot credibly commit to not making use of the opportunity to extract revenue from the investor's project, and that investment is irreversible: its cost cannot be recovered, and production activities cannot be relocated.

Consider first the choices open to an investor who is vulnerable to *ex post* expropriation. In both countries, governments' inability to commit not to expropriate (and the resulting weakness of private property rights) implies lower incentives to invest. Once investment has been made, and to the extent that production uses variable factors and effort as well as irreversible physical assets, it also bears on the amount of production and profits resulting from a given investment. More intense extractive efforts (higher tax rates) lead to lower production, so that the relationship between the overall rate and the overall tax revenues is an inverted-U 'Laffer curve'. Revenues are zero for a zero tax rate, and also zero if taxes approach a 100% confiscatory rate.

Consider next the choice of the tax rate by the two types of government. For simplicity assume that governments maximize tax revenue that can be extracted from the foreign direct investor. A unitary country will choose a confiscatory tax rate that generates the maximum overall tax revenue. It chooses the peak of the Laffer curve. In a decentralized country, several governments can try to appropriate from the same source of revenues, and typically do. They may also choose their appropriation activities non-cooperatively and extract from a common pool. Because of the presence of vertical fiscal externalities the resulting joint tax rate will be excessive. The country F therefore will end up with an overall tax on the wrong side (i.e., the right-hand side) of the Laffer curve. The actual tax revenue will not be larger than in a unitary country, but the marginal tax burden will be higher. When investors consider where to invest, they anticipate this behaviour and this makes the federal country with many government tiers a less attractive place as an investment destination.

Countries are typically decentralized to some degree in the sense that economic power and responsibility are shared between interdependent levels of government. This is likely to create fiscal interdependencies between the different levels of government. A clear-cut instance in which vertical interdependencies arise is when there is commonality of tax bases between the central government and lower-level governments (in the sense that several levels of government tax the same tax base).

Tax base commonality creates a common pool problem (with the fiscal decisions of each level of government inducing responses that affect the common tax base) that gives rise to negative vertical fiscal externalities. It generally leads to excessive taxation. Note that the common pool problem cannot be alleviated by an increase in horizontal competition between regions. Once the investment is sunk, and has taken place in a particular locality, say S, the existence or behaviour of other local governments which do not have jurisdiction over investors in locality S is not relevant for the resulting common pool problem. The common pool problem emerges because of the vertical dimension of decentralization, that is, because there are several government tiers who all have some independent jurisdiction over investments made in S, and which have independent policy objectives that are not perfectly aligned.

Of course, in a larger picture tax policy is not completely targeted towards a single investment project. Hence, some tax policy will affect a stock of projects that cannot be relocated in reaction to the tax policy, and the flow of new projects. The larger or more important is this latter share, the more important becomes the dimension of horizontal tax competition and the closer become the results to the standard results on the interaction between horizontal and vertical tax competition for a generally mobile tax base.[4]

The common pool problem could be avoided if the ability to expropriate revenues from the foreign direct investor could be attributed to one of the government tiers. This is often assumed to be the case in the literature on federalism, and sometimes

---

[4] There is a growing literature on vertical externalities. Johnson (1988), Dahlby (1996), Boadway *et al.* (1998), Wrede (2000), Keen and Kotsogiannis (2002, 2004) provide, among others, a treatment of vertical externalities when the policy makers are benevolent. For a treatment of the case in which policy makers are revenue-maximizing Leviathans see Wrede (1996), and Keen and Kotsogiannis (2003). For an early survey on vertical externalities see Keen (1998).

even included in the definition of what ideally constitutes federalism. However, it is extremely difficult or impossible in reality. Different tax bases are (implicitly) inter-dependent with similar incidence effect. The different levels of government might have formally different tax bases, but these may overlap in real terms through general equilibrium effects. Taxes on labour income and VAT taxes, or the corporate income tax and local business taxes may, for instance, be governed independently by different government tiers. As these pairs of taxes have very similar tax incidence, the common pool problem emerges, despite the nominal independence.

2.3.2. The free-rider problem in the subsidy game.

A further disadvantage that decentralized countries with disintegrated vertical government tiers face, vis-à-vis unitary countries, emerges when locations can compete for foreign direct investors by offering them economic favours in a process that has been described by the term 'bidding for firms'. Bidding for firms (and to pay a firm upfront what the firm will have to pay in terms of confiscatory taxation in later periods) is one way to cope with the hold-up problem. Central ('federal') and lower-level ('regional') governments may engage in either active or defensive incentive strategies aimed at attracting FDI in competition with other locations. Bids offered by governments to foreign investors may be direct cash payments or indirect in the form of offering cheap or subsidized investment ground, or of special deals when taking over existing plants and equipment or consumer relations in the context of foreign direct investment that takes place as a joint venture.

Turning to the difference between unitary and federal countries in the bidding process, the bid of a unitary government internalizes the country's full benefits of the foreign direct investment and in particular the full tax revenues that will emerge from this investment. If the bid is made by a government which belongs to a hierarchical system of governments then, in the absence of full cooperation between the govern-ments at all levels of hierarchy, it will only take into account the benefits that accrue to its own sphere of responsibility. This, as a consequence, results in the government bidding less aggressively for the foreign investor if the government belongs to a federation. In the bidding competition between various countries with various degrees of decentralization the investment is therefore more likely to be attracted by the country that has fewer government levels.

2.3.3. Interaction between common pool and free-riding problems.

The free-riding problem in bidding for firms reduces the equilibrium bids of a government that belongs to a federation, compared to a government in a unitary state for the same, given total benefits that accrue to the country as a whole from attracting the FDI project. The common pool problem suggests that the total gross benefits that accrue from attracting an FDI project are smaller in the federally structured country than if the country is governed by a unitary government. Reconsider, for instance, the Laffer curve analysis. If the federal country chooses an aggregate tax rate that exceeds the tax rate that maximizes total tax revenue, the total amount of taxes obtained by all government tiers is smaller than in the unitary country, and each tier receives only a share of this smaller amount, with all shares adding up to this smaller amount. Accordingly, the government of each tier has a smaller gain from attracting the FDI than the government in a unitary government, and even all governments in the federal country taken together have a smaller willingness to pay to attract the FDI project than the government in the unitary country. This shows that the two problems compound and mutually enforce each other. Not only is the government in a federation unwilling to bid according to the whole benefits that accrue to this country if it attracts the FDI project, in addition, this total amount would be smaller in the federally organized country.

2.3.4. Multiple tiers weaken implicit contracts.

The preceding analysis has emphasized the possibility that hold-up problems in FDI may be more severe in decentralized government structures with many government tiers. This then raises the question how 'likely' it is for these countries to develop institutions that credibly commit to pre-announced policies and, hence, do not resort to confiscatory taxation or to other extractive activities *ex post*. Given the interaction between the hold-up problem and the common pool problem, countries with more government tiers have more to gain from developing such 'credible' institutions. If such institutions are successfully implemented, foreign direct investors can more safely invest in these countries, and as a consequence the number of government tiers becomes less important as an impediment to FDI.

The term 'institutions' may, but need not be meant in a literal sense. An important 'institution' in the interaction between economic agents is the implicit contract that may be enforced and enforceable by repeated interaction. Previous work on the hold-up problem in FDI (see, for instance, Eaton and Gersovitz, 1983; Thomas and Worrall, 1994) has stressed that the main element that prevents governments from expropriation and confiscatory taxation is the prospect of future benefits from repeated investment. Kessing *et al.* (2006b) show that it may be more difficult to develop such implicit institutions and to sustain an equilibrium with 'tacit collusion' in a country with a federal structure with several tiers of governments than in a unitary country.

Consider an investor who invests in a decentralized host country infinitely repeatedly. The sequential nature of the relationship means that 'players' (the government levels and the investor) can adopt strategies that depend on behaviour in previous interactions. The returns to investment accrue in every period for which investment takes place, and the taxation of these returns is subject to the common pool problem identified earlier. Similar to the discussion of tacit collusion in oligopoly theory, governments may collude in the sense that they all abstain from excessive taxation and share in the continued flow of benefits of tacit collusion, because a deviation from the collusive outcome by any of the players would be 'punished' by all players by reversion to an equilibrium in which no investment takes place and, hence, no tax revenue at all occurs in all future periods. Each government may also decide in a given period to deviate and extract more than the share that it should receive according to the collusive outcome, and, in the period in which a government makes use of this opportunity, its payoff is higher. However, it will be punished for this in all future periods. Tacit collusion is feasible if a government's additional period benefit from deviating does not exceed its present value of the sacrifice in future periods. Both the gain and the loss from deviating depend on the number of governments. In particular, the potential to punish a deviating government is reduced with an increase in the number of governments. This provides the intuition for why vertical decentralization reduces the range of feasible implicit contracts with 'tacit collusion'. First, with a larger number of governments the spoils of cooperation for each government is lower than with a smaller number of governments and so is the punishment (loss of future tax revenues if punished). Hence, the future losses from deviating decrease in the number of governments. Second, it is also the case that it is more rewarding for each of the government players to defect from the agreed cooperation if the number of government layers is larger. Both identified effects make cooperation more difficult to be sustained in more decentralized government structures. The situation is largely analogous to the possibility of sustaining collusion between firms. The more firms are operating in a given market, the more difficult it becomes to sustain collusion.

2.3.5. Multiple tiers and joint accountability.

The issue of accountability in federal systems can be analysed in a political economy context in which politicians are elected and, among other things, care about re-election. These studies typically compare the politicians' and voters' choices for a case in which decentralization simply means that a given territory is governed by one government, or broken up into two completely separate countries with independent governments (see, for an example and further references, Hindriks and Lockwood, 2005). Due to the higher measurability of a politician's performance, and possibly due to benchmarking, accountability may increase by this break up. But as discussed, the horizontal separation of a country into regions is only one side of decentralization. Decentralization also leads to vertical disintegration. As a result of decentralization, many relevant economic performance measures for a region will depend not only on the decisions and the competence of the local politician, but also on the decisions of the politicians on the higher government tiers that join in the jurisdiction of a given local region. Compared to unitary government, this joint responsibility leads to joint accountability. In turn, this may generate problems similar to those that have been discussed in other contexts as the problems of moral hazard in teams, sabotage in team work production etc. An aspect that makes this reasoning less straightforward in the context of FDI is the fact that there may be a conflict of interests and an accountability problem not only between the government(s) and its citizens, but also between the citizens and the foreign direct investors, where citizens have the right to vote and foreign investors do not.

2.3.6. The importance of property rights and other institutions. The discussion of feasibility of tacit collusion as a function of the number of tiers already
shows that the ability of countries to attract FDI should depend on institutions. Of
course, vertical disintegration is a potentially important institutional aspect, but not
the only institutional aspect that matters. In addition, some other institutional
features may interact with the aspect of vertical disintegration, and may lighten up
or further darken this dark side of federalism.

Any government strong enough to protect property rights can also use this strength
to coerce (e.g., North and Weingast, 1989). When illustrating the dark aspects of vertical
decentralization, we focused on governments which do not have the appropriate
institutions to restrain themselves from using their strength to enforce high confiscatory taxes. More generally speaking, governments may use their power for extracting
rents, including the means of expropriation, and this caused the hold-up problem in
FDI. As discussed, even a benevolent government that acts on behalf of its citizens
or politicians who are motivated by prospects of re-election would like to attract FDI
first and then, once the investment has been made, would like to extract revenue from
the investor. Good institutions that endow the government with the power to commit
not to extract an excessively large share in the returns *ex post* are therefore very
desirable.

Countries differ both in the quality of institutions that restrain government from
using its power to coerce and in the degree of vertical disintegration. A natural
question to ask now is how the vertical dimension and the protection of property
rights interact. No clear answer, however, can be given from a theoretical point of
view. As a starting point it is useful to think about two extreme cases. First, if property
rights protection is perfect, that is, if governments do not resort to confiscatory taxation at all, there should be no effect of increasing the extent of vertical disintegration.
If government actors do not affect the investors' profits, increasing their number does
not have any effect. On the other hand, if property rights protection is completely
absent, that is, if any single government would completely appropriate the investors'
profits, there would also be no additional effect of further vertical disintegration.
Increasing the number of government actors does not have an additional effect, if the
entire investment is taken anyway. For levels of property rights protection in between
these two extreme cases there will be an additional effect of increased vertical disintegration, but it is not clear *a priori*, whether this effect will be stronger for high or low
levels of property rights protection. If property rights protection is low, there may be little
scope for further worsening the effect on FDI, but the interaction may compound the
effect sufficiently. On the other hand, for higher levels of property rights protection,
the interaction may not have such strong compounding effects, but there is more
scope for reducing the level of FDI. The bottom line of this reasoning is that we
expect a non-monotonic relationship regarding the interaction of the level of property
rights protection and the vertical dimension of decentralization. It should be zero at
the two extremes and positive in between, potentially displaying an inverted U-shape.

Before we turn to the empirical analysis, we should mention that there are potential further channels through which vertical decentralization can negatively affect FDI, and that those other channels are typically related to some other dimension of governance. While we have focused on the governments' incentives to extract revenue from the investment, similar arguments should hold for the regulatory framework an investor is facing, for example. The commonality problem will typically result in over-regulation, possible mismatch of regulatory activity and an excess of red tape the investor faces.

3. EMPIRICAL ANALYSIS

3.1. The main hypothesis

Our theoretical perspective suggests that vertical decentralization impinges negatively on the amount of FDI inflows. We can accordingly state our main hypothesis:

> **Hypothesis 1**: An increase in the amount of vertical decentralization of a host country has a negative effect on the amount of FDI that is attracted by this host country.

Our discussion has acknowledged that federalism affects a country's performance along several dimensions and also has beneficial effects. We would expect that the negative relationship between FDI and the measure of decentralization is strongest for measures of decentralization that are closest to measuring the aspect of vertical disintegration. We will be able to draw on a variable that is closely related to the vertical dimension of decentralization when we test hypothesis 1.

As discussed, other dimensions of decentralization may improve or worsen the climate for FDI. On *a priori* grounds, decentralization measures that quantify other aspects besides vertical decentralization may therefore have a positive or a negative impact on the size of FDI in the empirical analysis. Introducing such variables is interesting and important for at least two reasons. First, to some degree they allow to disentangle the effects of vertical decentralization (for which we have a fairly good measure) from these other effects. Second, the quantitative effects of these decentralization variables are of interest for policy making.

3.2. Empirical strategy

Our empirical strategy to test our hypothesis and to reveal the effects of decentralization on FDI is straightforward. We add decentralization variables to the 'knowledge-capital' model.

3.2.1. The 'knowledge-capital' model.   The 'knowledge-capital' model has solid theoretical foundations from the theory of the multinational firm and has emerged over recent years as the workhorse for analysing international FDI flows. Multinationals are typically distinguished in 'horizontal' firms which produce the same goods and services in multiple countries, and 'vertical' firms, which geographically fragment production by stages. The 'knowledge-capital' model, developed by Markusen *et al.* (1996), and Markusen (1997), is a framework that nests both horizontal and vertical motives for FDI into a unified framework. It assumes that 'knowledge' (or 'knowledge-based' assets) is (a) skilled labour intensive relative to production, (b) geographically mobile, and (c) a joint input to multiple production facilities and so has a public-goods character in that it can be supplied to additional facilities at very low cost. The latter assumption implies there is a market size motive if there are plant scale economies and so gives support to horizontal FDI. The first two assumptions relate to differences in relative factor endowments, and these consequently give rise to an incentive for vertical fragmentation of production. The proper treatment of relative factor endowments in the estimation of the model has spanned some considerable controversy, see Carr *et al.* (2001, 2003) and Blonigen *et al.* (2003). We avoid this debate and employ a variant that has become popular recently among scholars of international economics. It circumvents some of the problems involved in the earlier formulations and has been proposed by Markusen and Maskus (2002), and employed by Buch *et al.* (2005) and Herger *et al.* (2005). This version possesses the following structure. The amount of FDI from source country i to host country j is a function of

- the sum of source and host country's GDP, ΣGDP
- the square of the difference in source and host country GDP, $(\Delta GDP)^2$
- measures of proximity between source and host country
- measures of trade costs between source and host countries[5]
- measures of investment costs in the host country
- three interaction variables ($INT1$, $INT2$, $INT3$).

These interaction variables relate to the different incentives for vertical and horizontal fragmentation of production. They interact factor endowments with relative country size and market size. The first interaction we introduce, $INT1 = \Delta SKILL * \Delta GDP$, if $\Delta SKILL > 0$, 0 otherwise, captures vertical fragmentation. Horizontal motives are captured in the second and third interaction variables $INT2 = \Delta SKILL * \Sigma GDP$, if $\Delta SKILL > 0$, 0 otherwise, $INT3 = -\Delta SKILL * \Sigma GDP$, if $\Delta SKILL < 0$, 0 otherwise, where $\Delta SKILL$ captures the skill endowment difference between the source and the host countries. The theoretical foundation and the relationship of this specific formulation to its theoretical foundation are summarized in Markusen and Maskus (2002).

---

[5] The original formulation of the 'knowledge-capital' model asks for the specification of trade costs in the host and the source country separately. The availability of such measures for individual countries is limited, so that, because we are interested in having a large cross-section of countries, we use bilateral trade costs proxies instead.

3.3. Data

To measure international direct investment flows we use a recent data set on international cross-border mergers and acquisitions (CBAs) provided by the SDC platinum database of Thomson Financial. These data appear to be currently the only ones that allow us to (a) cover a large number of host countries that differ in their degree of decentralization, (b) embed our analysis in the 'knowledge-capital' model which requires bilateral FDI flows, and (c) increase the power of our analysis by using a large cross-section of source countries which substantially increases the number of country pairs. This database is increasingly employed in the analysis of international capital flows, see, for instance, Di Giovanni (2005), Rossi and Volpin (2004), and Herger *et al.* (2005). The former two contributions have focused on the values of CBAs whereas the latter also considers counts of CBAs constructed from the original dataset. These CBA counts are constructed by counting the number of firms acquired by buyers from a source country i, in a host country j in a given year t. Only deals in which the acquiring firm acquired a controlling share of at least 50% are counted.[6]

In our analysis we consider both types of aggregate measures, in terms of values and of counts, since arguments can be made in favour of both measures. Using counts of CBAs may be justified by three reasons. The first is the limited coverage of the value of the deals in the original data set. For the OECD countries, for instance, for less than 50% of all deals the value of the transaction paid by the acquiring firm is reported. For developing countries this number is lower and in some instances well below 15%.[7] Second, the focus on the value of acquisitions might introduce a particular bias in the analysis as some major deals, which were particularly observed in the stock market rally of the late 1990s, may dominate the aggregate values (see Herger *et al.*, 2005). Third, the literature on FDI, typically, refers to the decision of the mother company in the source country to invest (or not) in a host country rather than to the value of the investment. On the other hand, there are also good arguments in favour of considering the values of the investments. First, the values contain information on the size of the investments which obviously also depends on the investment conditions in the host country. Moreover, most factors that determine the profitability of an investment should determine the price actually paid for acquiring a given firm and therefore, we should be interested in the effect of decentralization on the value of the transactions. Using both measures gives justice to both sides of the argument and insures that the results do not hinge on the particular way of measuring FDI. It turns out that the results are very similar for the two measures, which is not surprising given that the number of CBAs for a particular year country pair and the aggregate value of these deals are closely correlated. Considering only the deals where the value is reported in the original data, the correlation coefficient between them is 0.79.

[6] The count data set has been assembled by Herger *et al.* (2005), from the original data, for the time period 1997–2003.

[7] For the total sample around 57% of completed CBAs have no reported deal value.

The coverage of the data is extensive. Our original sample reports yearly CBAs counts and yearly values in US$ millions for the period 1997–2003. It contains information on CBAs from 67 source countries to 147 host countries.[8] Table 1 gives an overview of the most important host countries for CBAs. Table 2 lists the host countries that are actually included in our study. Developed countries experience more CBAs, in total value and in numbers. There are, however, a large number of developing countries that are experiencing substantial amounts of CBAs, with, important for our purpose, substantial variation among these countries.

There are also some potential problems with using CBAs as a measure of FDI. They are only an imperfect measure of total FDI activity, since not all FDI takes the form of CBAs. However, CBAs comprise a substantial part of world FDI which makes them suitable for such an analysis. UNCTAD (2001) has recently reported that, by around 2000, CBAs' share of all FDI was around 80% in value of the investment. CBAs play an increasingly important role in developing countries too: with the share of CBAs being around 40% in the late 1990s, up from around 10% in the late 1980s. This tendency is most likely to continue in the future (UNCTAD, 2001).

One must notice that, because CBAs only comprise a part of all FDI, albeit an important one, there are potential composition effects caused by our variable(s) of interest, which could give rise to invalid inference. In particular, if an increase in vertical decentralization leads to an increase or decrease in the share of CBAs in total FDI, this will affect the estimations that consider only the number of CBAs. From our theoretical perspective, however, we expect green field investment to be more strongly negatively affected by the vertical dimension of decentralization. Thus, this will make it even harder to detect a negative effect of vertical disintegration using data on CBAs, and our estimations are likely to underestimate the negative effect of vertical decentralization on total FDI.[9]

3.3.1. Measurement of decentralization and intergovernmental overlap.

For the main variable of interest to test our hypothesis regarding the negative effects of the vertical dimension of decentralization, we consider the number of government tiers in the host country. This variable has been constructed by Daniel Treisman (see Treisman, 2000a). It measures particularly well the vertical dimension of decentralization. The theory aspects identified in Section 2 are conceptually directly related to the number of tiers of government. This is because what is decisive for the amount and the success of foreign direct investment is (a) the number of rival decision makers that potentially try to appropriate their share after an investor has irreversibly

---

[8] In the actual estimations the number of the source and host countries will reflect the availability of the control and the decentralization variables.

[9] A similar argument holds with respect to CBAs induced by bad governance and hold-up problems. To escape the bad governance, locals sometimes own their own firms through some foreign holdings, and that inflates the number of CBAs even if it is just disguised local investment. However, since we expect a negative correlation between vertical disintegration and local property rights security, such induced CBAs bias the results against our main hypothesis.

Table 1. CBA host countries

Rank	Host country	# CBA	Fraction of CBA in %	Value in US$ millions
1	United States	6939	14.9	1 178 252.8
3	Germany	3259	7.0	446 918.3
5	Canada	2447	5.2	189 863.8
6	China	1537	3.3	87 190.8
7	Australia	1512	3.2	92 411.2
8	Netherlands	1389	3.0	158 434.2
9	Italy	1229	2.6	152 145.5
10	Spain	1189	2.5	62 169.4
11	Sweden	1172	2.5	117 019.1
12	Switzerland	944	2.0	64 707.9
13	Brazil	888	1.9	66 594.9
14	India	876	1.9	8641.0
15	Hong Kong, China*	827	1.8	30 136.1
16	Belgium	780	1.7	71 391.7
17	Poland	725	1.6	15 186.6
18	Norway	652	1.4	52 621.7
19	Argentina	618	1.3	48 055.4
20	Denmark	613	1.3	29 090.7
21	Finland	597	1.3	32 931.9
22	Mexico	559	1.2	40 786.0
23	Singapore	559	1.2	18 605.1
24	Korea, Rep.	554	1.2	55 608.8
25	Czech Republic	535	1.1	16 355.0
26	Japan	529	1.1	40 492.2
27	Austria	509	1.1	20 333.3
28	New Zealand	451	1.0	17 585.8
29	Ireland	449	1.0	24 707.7
30	Thailand	432	0.9	9143.8
31	Malaysia	412	0.9	4292.6
32	South Africa	407	0.9	24 594.7
33	Indonesia	365	0.8	13 496.3
34	Hungary	354	0.8	6206.3
35	Russian Federation	311	0.7	4076.3
36	Portugal	309	0.7	9127.1
37	Israel	285	0.6	14 234.8
38	Chile	268	0.6	21 863.6
39	Romania	255	0.5	4360.2
40	Philippines	250	0.5	7333.5
41	Bulgaria	215	0.5	3362.7
42	Estonia	196	0.4	733.4
43	Lithuania	168	0.4	1644.3
44	Turkey	160	0.3	3372.3
45	Slovak Republic	158	0.3	4247.2
46	Ukraine	138	0.3	866.0
47	Luxembourg*	133	0.3	26 452.3
48	Colombia	129	0.3	6522.7
49	Peru	128	0.3	6543.9
50	Venezuela, RB	124	0.3	7424.1
51	Greece	119	0.3	4327.5
52	Croatia	113	0.2	2357.1
53	Latvia	103	0.2	846.6
54	Egypt, Arab Rep.	83	0.2	4514.2
55	Vietnam	77	0.2	620.2

Table 1. *Continued*

Rank	Host country	# CBA	Fraction of CBA in %	Value in US$ millions
56	Bermuda	76	0.2	21 573.9
57	Puerto Rico	70	0.1	5367.9
58	Kazakhstan	59	0.1	4204.8
59	Slovenia	53	0.1	1554.9
60	Uruguay	52	0.1	619.2
...	...	...	...	...
All		45 168	100	4 162 966

Note: Countries marked with * not included in the analysis for lack of available control variables.

Table 2. Decentralization variables

Country	Tiers	Exp.-decentralization	Rev.-decentralization
Angola	4		
Albania	3	0.20	0.02
United Arab Emirates	3		
Argentina	3	0.38	0.32
Armenia	3		
Australia	3	0.41	0.28
Austria	4	0.30	0.27
Azerbaijan	3		
Burundi	3		
Belgium	4	0.12	0.06
Burkina Faso	4	0.03	
Bangladesh	5		
Bulgaria	4	0.19	0.16
Belarus	4	0.30	0.28
Bolivia	4	0.18	0.18
Brazil	4	0.34	0.25
Botswana	3		
Canada	4	0.57	0.52
Switzerland	3	0.51	0.46
Chile	4	0.08	0.06
China	5		
Côte d'Ivoire	5		
Cameroon	6		
Colombia	3	0.29	0.19
Costa Rica	4	0.03	0.03
Czech Republic	3		
Germany	4	0.41	0.35
Denmark	3	0.44	0.31
Dominican Republic	3	0.03	0.01
Algeria	4		
Ecuador	4		
Egypt, Arab Rep.	4.5		

Table 2. *Continued*

Country	Tiers	Exp.-decentralization	Rev.-decentralization
Spain	4	0.24	0.15
Estonia	3	0.27	0.21
Ethiopia	5	0.02	0.02
Finland	3	0.39	0.32
France	4	0.19	0.12
United Kingdom	4	0.25	0.13
Georgia	4		
Ghana	6		
Guinea	4		
Greece	4.5	0.04	0.03
Guatemala	4	0.04	0.05
Guyana	3		
Honduras	3		
Croatia	3		
Haiti	5		
Hungary	3	0.21	0.12
Indonesia	5	0.11	0.03
India	5	0.46	0.33
Ireland	3	0.24	0.09
Iran, Islamic Rep.	4	0.03	0.04
Iceland	2	0.23	0.23
Israel	3	0.11	0.07
Italy	4	0.22	0.07
Jamaica	2		
Jordan	3		
Japan	3		
Kazakhstan	4		
Kenya	6		
Kyrgyz Republic	4		
Cambodia	4		
Korea, Rep.	4		
Kuwait	3		
Lebanon	4		
Sri Lanka	4	0.03	0.04
Lithuania	3	0.29	0.22
Latvia	3	0.23	0.19
Moldova	3		
Madagascar	5		0.05
Mexico	3	0.20	0.20
Macedonia, FYR	2		
Mali	4		
Mongolia		0.37	0.27
Mauritania	4		
Mauritius	3	0.04	0.01
Malawi	4		
Malaysia	3	0.19	0.16
Namibia	3		
Niger	4		
Nigeria	4		
Nicaragua	4	0.07	0.08
Netherlands	3	0.25	0.07
Norway	3	0.33	0.22
Nepal	3		

Table 2. *Continued*

Country	Tiers	Exp.-decentralization	Rev.-decentralization
New Zealand	3		
Oman	3		
Pakistan	4.5		
Panama	4	0.02	0.02
Peru	4	0.18	0.07
Philippines	4		
Poland	3	0.23	0.15
Korea, Dem. Rep.	4		
Portugal		0.10	0.07
Paraguay	3	0.04	0.03
Romania	3	0.13	0.09
Russian Federation	4	0.38	0.40
Rwanda	4		
Saudi Arabia	3		
Sudan	4		
Senegal	6		
Singapore	1		
Sierra Leone	4		
El Salvador	3		
Suriname	3		
Slovak Republic	4		
Slovenia	2		
Sweden	3	0.36	0.33
Swaziland	4		
Togo	4		
Thailand	5	0.08	0.05
Tajikistan	4		
Turkmenistan	4		
Trinidad and Tobago	2	0.04	0.03
Tunisia	4	0.05	0.02
Turkey	4		
Tanzania	6		
Uganda	6		
Ukraine	4		
Uruguay	2	0.09	0.10
United States	4	0.44	0.40
Uzbekistan	4		
Venezuela, RB	4	0.00	0.00
South Africa		0.24	
Congo, Dem. Rep.	5		
Zambia	3	0.04	0.05
Zimbabwe	5	0.19	0.17

Note: Baseline regressions without decentralization variables also include Benin, Bosnia-Herzegovina, Congo, Fiji, Morocco, Mozambique, Papua New Guinea, Syria, Chad, Vietnam, and Yemen as host countries. Expenditure and revenue decentralization are 1980–95 averages of the ratio of sub-national government expenditures to total government expenditures and the ratio of sub-national government revenues to total government revenues, respectively.

invested in the host country, and (b) the amount of implicit or explicit (tax) overlap between these government players. The tax overlap is difficult to assess in a unified measure that can be compared across countries. The number of decision makers, however, is approximated quite well by the number of government tiers.

One can argue that the number of government tiers should be corrected for some measure of country size, such as population or area. This would be in line with the insights of Oates (1972) in his classic study of federalism, where the optimal degree of decentralization is related to the size of the country in terms of population.[10] Of course, any normalization carries the danger of inducing spurious correlation, if FDI is correlated with the variable used for the normalization. We consider the unadjusted number of government tiers as our main variable of interest to avoid these potential problems, but also report some results for the number of government tiers adjusted by population.

We also consider the effects of fiscal decentralization in the host country. As empirical measures of fiscal decentralization we employ the ratio of sub-national tax revenues to total government revenues, and the ratio of sub-national government expenditures to total government expenditures. Of course, the ratio of sub-national tax revenues to total government revenues could be low because there is little fiscal autonomy at the sub-national level (and so minimum tax base overlap), or because there is a lot of fiscal autonomy (with tax base overlap effects) but tax competition between sub-national governments has resulted in low tax revenues at sub-national level. The same applies to the other fiscal decentralization measure, the ratio of sub-national government expenditures to total government expenditures. These share measures, however, do pick up some aspects of decentralization, such as the power distribution between the central government and lower levels of government within the host country. By the same token one may regard these measures as measuring 'closeness' of the government to its people and firms. Given their distinct focus on government revenues and expenditures, they also allow additional qualitative insights into the nature of decentralization and its effects on governments' behaviour and the consequences of these for firms.

To avoid potential endogeneity problems and to increase the cross-section of host countries, we use the 1980–95 average of the fiscal decentralization variables. An overview of the values of tiers, and the fiscal decentralization variables of the host countries present in our study, are presented in Table 2. Before we turn to our estimations, we have a first cursory look at the data. Figures 1–4 plot the decentralization

---

[10] Oates (1972, pp. 200–1) writes: 'one important factor influencing the extent of centralization should be the size of the nation in terms of population . . . In a relatively small country, for example, there are likely to be real cost-savings in centralizing a substantial portion of the activity in the public sector. As a nation becomes larger, however, it becomes efficient for decentralized jurisdictions, because of their own significant size, to provide their own outputs of a wide range of public services. Moreover, as a country grows in size, central administration becomes more difficult and is likely to result in a less effective use of resources within the public sector. For these reasons we would expect the degree of fiscal centralization to vary inversely with the size of a country.'

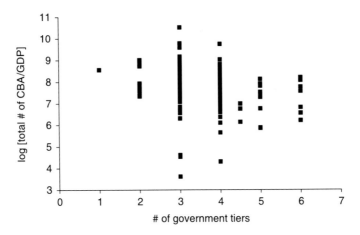

Figure 1. Number of government tiers and log of # of CBA over GDP

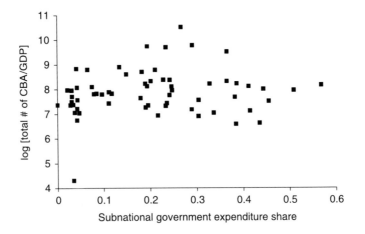

Figure 2. Average (1980–1995) expenditure decentralization and log of # of CBA over GDP

variables against the log of the number of acquired firms by foreigners over average host country GDP for the entire period 1997–2003. These figures are quite illustrative and partly foreshadow the results of our more formal analysis. Figure 1 suggests a negative relationship between the number of government tiers and FDI. On the other hand, average expenditure decentralization and average revenue decentralization appear to be somewhat positively correlated with incoming CBAs. Also, we see that the differential effect of average expenditure and average revenue decentralization is positively correlated with CBA inflows.

3.4. Estimation

We employ two different econometric techniques in our estimations depending on whether we consider the count or the value of CBA. To explain the number of firms

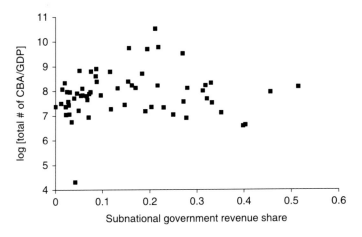

Figure 3. Average (1980–1995) revenue decentralization and log of # of CBA over GDP

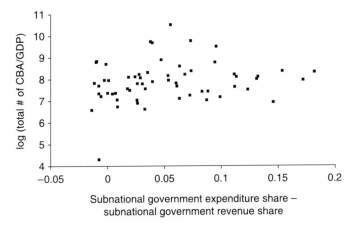

Figure 4. Average (1980–1995) differential fiscal decentralization and # of CBA over GDP

acquired by buyers from source country i in host country j in a given year t we use a negative binomial model for count data. The conditional expected number of CBAs from country i to country j in year t is specified as a non-linear function of the vector of control variables, the decentralization variable(s), and the parameter vectors to be estimated. The details of this model are spelled out in Appendix 1. To explain the aggregate value of all CBAs from source country i to host country j in a given year t we run Tobit regressions, thus accounting for the fact that the left-hand side variable is zero for many country pairs in many years.

Our basic control variables are the key factors for estimation of the 'knowledge-capital' model: the sum of source and host country GDP, the squared difference of source and host country GDP, and the three interaction variables (explained above) *INT*1, *INT*2, and *INT*3. Furthermore, we control for the costs of starting a business in the host country, taken from Djankov *et al.* (2002): the number of days it takes to start a business which we call duration, the number of procedures to complete, and the costs of setting up business as a percentage of per capita GDP. The variables measuring the proximity of source and host country and the ease of trade between them are dummy variables regarding the existence of a common language and the existence of a common border, respectively, and a dummy on the existence of an agreement on trade in services, a dummy that captures the existence of a free trade agreement, and a dummy that captures the existence of a customs union. We also use the distance between the capitals of source and host countries. Di Giovanni (2005) has emphasized that capital market deepening is an important determinant of FDI flows. To capture this, we include domestic stock market capitalization relative to GDP. Furthermore, we include the real exchange rate, since changes of the real exchange rate alter the price of CBAs. Finally, we include variables for the size of the host country, as a country's size may systematically influence capital inflows. In particular, decentralization ('tiers') is systematically correlated with these variables, so including them avoids that the tiers variable picks up the effects of country size. The host country size variables are the surface area of the host country and the population of the host country. We also use the inverse and the square of both of these variables to make sure that the decentralization variables do not pick up existing non-linear relationships between country size and FDI inflows. All estimations with yearly data also contain time dummies. A description and the sources of all variables used in our analysis can be found in Appendix 2.

Although the tiers variable and past average fiscal decentralization are constant over time, we use panel estimations including all observations from all 7 years from 1997–2003 to exploit the variance in the controls over time. Given that some of the controls are not available for all years the panel is unbalanced. We also report the estimation results using the pure cross-section of averages to make sure that the significance of our results regarding the number of tiers are not driven by the increased sample size or the unbalanced nature of the panel.

3.5. Results

3.5.1. Benchmark model with count data.
In Table 3 we report the results of estimating negative binomial models using the count data on cross-border acquisitions. We first estimate a benchmark 'knowledge-capital' model without any decentralization variables. The results are given in column (1) of Table 3. The signs of the estimated coefficients are by and large in accordance with the theoretical predictions. The theoretical foundations of the 'knowledge-capital' model predict a positive coefficient of the sum of host and source country GDP, and a negative coefficient of the squared difference of the two countries' GDPs. The negative signs of the first and the third

interaction variables are also perfectly in line with the 'capital-knowledge' model. The positive coefficient of the second interaction variable indicates evidence for vertical FDI. Several variables measure proximity between host and source countries, either physically, as in the case of distance and the existence of a common border, or culturally as in the case of a common language. Higher proximity implies larger FDI flows between host and source countries. In line with the findings of Di Giovanni (2005), domestic stock market capitalization in the source country plays a significant positive role, and also the real exchange rate affects CBAs significantly. The existence of a free trade agreement, a customs union, or an agreement on trade in services all affects bilateral investment flows positively. The costs of setting up a business, as measured directly by the setup costs, or indirectly by the number of procedures to be fulfilled, affects investment negatively. Thus, all control variables are significant with signs that can be theoretically justified, except for the duration to set up a business.[11] Not surprisingly, these results are broadly consistent with the results of Herger *et al.* (2005), who use a slightly different set of control variables. The control variables for the size of the host country are also found to be significant determinants of FDI flows.

To the benchmark model we subsequently add the decentralization variables we are interested in. Column (2) of Table 3 reports the results of individually adding tiers. The number of government tiers has a significant negative effect on inward CBAs. If the sub-national expenditure share and the sub-national revenue share are added individually, they both are found to have a significant positive impact on the number of CBAs (results not displayed). Column (3), which includes both fiscal decentralization measures, shows that this finding is spurious regarding the degree of revenue decentralization. The positive effects found for revenue share is due to the high correlation between expenditure decentralization and revenue decentralization.[12] Expenditure decentralization affects investment positively, whereas revenue decentralization affects it negatively. This is also confirmed by the estimation reported in column (4) of Table 3 which includes all three decentralization variables, and by column (5) which replaces 'tiers' with 'tiers normalized by population size'.

3.5.2. Benchmark with CBA values.
Table 4 shows the results for the specification with values. By and large, they are very similar to the analysis using CBA counts. We report the estimates of the baseline model without decentralization variables in column (1). The findings are mainly analogous to the count data model with the exception of two of the interaction variables. Interaction variable 1 is now positive, but insignificant, and interaction variable 2 is now negative and significant. The latter

---

[11] The positive sign of the coefficient may reflect better institutions in developing countries that are positively correlated with the duration of setting up a business. In fact, estimates we report below show that when we re-estimate the model using only OECD host countries, duration is found to have a negative coefficient. Alternatively, the costs of setting up a business may be more important for green field investment, and the positive sign may reflect a substitution effect from green field investment to mergers and acquisitions.

[12] The correlation coefficient between them is 0.92.

Table 3. Benchmark estimations counts

	(1)	(2)	(3)	(4)	(5)
ΣGDP	1.31 (0.07)***	1.27 (0.07)***	1.07 (0.07)***	1.06 (0.07)***	1.03 (0.07)***
$(\Delta GDP)^2$	−0.09 (0.01)***	−0.09 (0.007)***	−0.08 (0.01)***	−0.08 (0.01)***	−0.08 (0.01)***
$INT1$	−0.03 (0.01)***	−0.03 (0.01)***	−0.003 (0.01)	−0.001 (0.01)	−0.001 (0.01)
$INT2$	0.02 (0.01)**	0.02 (0.01)**	0.000 (0.007)	−0.001 (0.006)	−0.001 (0.01)
$INT3$	−0.01 (0.002)***	−0.01 (0.002)***	−0.01 (0.002)***	−0.01 (0.002)***	−0.005 (0.002)**
POP	0.003 (0.001)***	0.004 (0.001)***	0.004 (0.002)**	0.004 (0.002)***	0.002 (0.002)
POP^{-1}	−1.39 (0.31)***	−1.92 (0.49)***	−1.04 (0.32)***	−0.96 (0.26)***	1.65 (1.05)
POP^2	$-2.99 \ast 10^{-6}$ $(7.54 \ast 10^{-7})$***	$-3.63 \ast 10^{-6}$ $(8.2 \ast 10^{-7})$***	$-4.19 \ast 10^{-6}$ $(1.45 \ast 10^{-6})$***	$-5.03 \ast 10^{-6}$ $(1.47 \ast 10^{-6})$***	$-3.2 \ast 10^{-6}$ $(1.53 \ast 10^{-6})$**
$AREA$	$3 \ast 10^{-4}$ $(4 \ast 10^{-5})$***	$2 \ast 10^{-4}$ $(4 \ast 10^{-5})$***	$2 \ast 10^{-4}$ $(4 \ast 10^{-5})$***	$2 \ast 10^{-4}$ $(4 \ast 10^{-5})$***	$1.71 \ast 10^{-4}$ $(4.26 \ast 10^{-5})$***
$AREA^{-1}$	0.98 (0.17)***	0.38 (0.18)**	−3.14 (0.94)***	−3.69 (0.98)***	−2.1 (1.17)*
$AREA^2$	$-1.92 \ast 10^{-8}$ $(2.47 \ast 10^{-9})$***	$-1.74 \ast 10^{-8}$ $(2.4 \ast 10^{-9})$***	$-1.34 \ast 10^{-8}$ $(2.65 \ast 10^{-9})$***	$-1.39 \ast 10^{-8}$ $(2.63 \ast 10^{-9})$***	$-1.36 \ast 10^{-8}$ $(2.64 \ast 10^{-9})$***
$DISTANCE$	−0.13 (0.01)***	−0.13 (0.01)***	−0.12 (0.01)***	−0.12 (0.01)***	−0.12 (0.01)***
$COMMON\ BORDER$	1.26 (0.14)***	1.19 (0.14)***	0.88 (0.15)***	0.81 (0.15)***	0.8 (0.15)***
$COMMON\ LANGUAGE$	1.31 (0.1)***	1.31 (0.11)***	1.51 (0.13)***	1.5 (0.13)***	1.51 (0.13)***

Table 3. *Continued*

	(1)	(2)	(3)	(4)	(5)
DOM. MARKET CAPITALIZATION	0.77	0.78	0.83	0.84	0.83
	(0.04)***	(0.05)***	(0.06)***	(0.06)***	(0.06)***
REAL EXCHANGE RATE	−0.38	−0.38	−0.58	−0.6	−0.63
	(0.05)***	(0.05)***	(0.06)***	(0.07)***	(0.07)***
FREE TRADE AGREEMENT	0.45	0.42	0.43	0.41	0.42
	(0.12)***	(0.13)***	(0.16)***	(0.16)**	(0.16)**
SERVICE AGREEMENT	0.81	0.8	0.63	0.61	0.56
	(0.17)***	(0.17)***	(0.19)***	(0.18)***	(0.18)***
CUSTOMS UNION	0.38	0.36	0.44	0.4	0.4
	(0.19)**	(0.19)*	(0.2)**	(0.2)**	(0.2)**
SET UP COSTS	−0.01	−0.005	−0.002	−0.002	−0.002
	$(2*10^{-3})$***	$(2*10^{-3})$***	$(4*10^{-4})$***	$(4*10^{-4})$***	$(3.7*10^{-4})$***
DURATION	0.002	0.003	0.002	0.002	0.002
	(0.002)	(0.002)*	(0.002)	(0.002)	(0.002)
PROCEDURES	−0.11	−0.11	−0.07	−0.07	−0.07
	(0.01)***	(0.01)***	(0.02)***	(0.01)***	(0.01)***
TIERS		−0.39		−0.14	
		(0.06)***		(0.08)*	
TIERS/POPULATION					−1.16
					(0.54)**
SUBNAT. EXPENDITURE SHARE			5.28	5.46	5.61
			(0.82)***	(0.84)***	(0.82)***
SUBNAT. REVENUE SHARE			−3.38	−3.57	−3.45
			(0.88)***	(0.87)***	(0.86)***
Obs.	49 969	44 464	22 103	21 355	21 355

Notes: Panel estimates (1997–2003) including all countries as given in Table 2. Dependent variable is the count of yearly CBA for source-host country pairs. Standard errors are clustered by country pair. All estimations include year dummies.

Table 4. Benchmark estimations: Values

	(1)	(2)	(3)	(4)	(5)
ΣGDP	2683.21	2680.02	2818.87	2824.73	2775.78
	(68.96)***	(71.54)***	(101.19)***	(103.47)***	(102.61)***
$(\Delta GDP)^2$	−174.91	−174.04	−196.04	−200.09	−188.96
	(7.91)***	(8.27)***	(11.61)***	(11.92)***	(11.84)***
$INT1$	2.79	3.74	19.86	21.17	19.51
	(3.5)	(3.61)	(4.52)***	(4.57)***	(4.58)***
$INT2$	−23.72	−24	−36.56	−36.63	−35.89
	(3.68)***	(3.79)***	(4.61)***	(4.65)***	(4.66)***
$INT3$	−33.17	−34.42	−27.62	−27.29	−24.37
	(2.5)***	(2.57)***	(3.5)***	(3.54)***	(3.57)***
POP	8.13	10.43	15.78	17.86	9.37
	(1.52)***	(1.65)***	(3.11)***	(3.26)***	(3.36)***
POP^{-1}	−3287.46	−4465.09	−2958.07	−2706.5	9436.5
	(355.73)***	(426.2)***	(494.54)***	(480.1)***	(1878.05)***
POP^2	−0.007	−0.008	−0.02	−0.02	−0.01
	(0.001)***	(0.001)***	(0.003)***	(0.003)***	(0.003)***
$AREA$	0.81	0.8	0.7	0.74	0.7
	(0.06)***	(0.07)***	(0.09)***	(0.09)***	(0.09)***
$AREA^{-1}$	2875.63	1622.73	−6312.7	−7569.11	162.39
	(314.45)***	(356.01)***	(2750.35)**	(2835.11)***	(2949.99)
$AREA^2$	−50.6*10^{-6}	−49.8*10^{-6}	−51.1*10^{-6}	−54.2*10^{-6}	−51.7*10^{-6}
	(4.57*10^{-6})***	(4.71*10^{-6})***	(6.18*10^{-6})***	(6.29*10^{-6})***	(6.28*10^{-6})***
$DISTANCE$	−240.15	−254.5	−286.68	−297.75	−311.97
	(15.72)***	(16.69)***	(22.92)***	(23.34)***	(23.66)***
COMMON BORDER	1758.3	1662.41	922.16	841.73	797.27
	(238.8)***	(251.48)***	(322.69)***	(329.82)**	(330.81)**
COMMON LANGUAGE	3024.16	3141.96	4213.66	4253.85	4229.62
	(162.89)***	(176.5)***	(252.7)***	(255.71)***	(256.64)***
DOM. MARKET CAPITALIZATION	1477.41	1523.91	1875.11	1899.4	1884.63
	(75.06)***	(80.18)***	(110.87)***	(113.42)***	(113.93)***

Table 4. *Continued*

	(1)	(2)	(3)	(4)	(5)
REAL EXCHANGE RATE	-913.32	-936.2	-1578.58	-1656.73	-1762.96
	(85.24)***	(90.62)***	(125.88)***	(130.15)***	(131.89)***
FREE TRADE AGREEMENT	1618.99	1505.43	1296.09	1229.98	1206.81
	(253.02)***	(274.93)***	(357.62)***	(363.1)***	(360.91)***
SERVICE AGREEMENT	1611.84	1683.79	1580.78	1524.66	1374.28
	(316.71)***	(335.57)***	(411.26)***	(417.94)***	(415.16)***
CUSTOMS UNION	2318.9	2291.06	1642.69	1572.42	1550.55
	(368.18)***	(389.61)***	(472.49)***	(481.28)***	(478.86)***
SET UP COSTS	-9.99	-7.6	-3.16	-2.87	-2.87
	(0.87)***	(0.89)***	(0.85)***	(0.87)***	(0.85)***
DURATION	5.56	7.14	-0.98	-2.47	0.75
	(2.38)**	(2.57)***	(4.01)	(4.08)	(4.11)
PROCEDURES	-258.99	-259.17	-173.58	-166.13	-178.69
	(22.42)***	(23.75)***	(32.06)***	(32.39)***	(32.56)***
TIERS		-845.02		-310.19	
		(101.01)***		(176.67)*	
TIERS/ POPULATION					-5619.96
					(890.34)***
SUBNAT. EXPENDITURE SHARE			13410.68	14073.75	13685.89
			(1831.28)***	(1914.77)***	(1887.85)***
SUBNAT. REVENUE SHARE			-10441.19	-10884.59	-9952.08
			(1949.9)***	(1975.54)***	(1988.2)***
Obs.	48212	42901	21330	20608	20608
Uncensored obs.	3771	3584	2834	2786	2786
Pseudo R²	0.09	0.09	0.08	0.08	0.08

Notes: Panel estimates (1997–2003) including all countries as given in Table 2. Dependent variable is total yearly value of CBA for source-host country pairs. All estimations include year dummies.

findings would be in line with the horizontal model of FDI (Markusen and Maskus, 2002).[13]

Adding decentralization variables to the baseline model gives a set of results that entirely parallel the results of the count data specification. Adding tiers shows a significant negative effect. Again, both fiscal decentralization variables have a positive effect if added individually (not shown). However, if both enter the estimation simultaneously, as reported in column (3), only expenditure decentralization is found to influence investment positively, whereas revenue decentralization affects investment negatively. Analogously to the count specification, the positive coefficient of expenditure decentralization is larger in absolute value than the coefficient of revenue decentralization, suggesting that a simultaneous increase in expenditure and revenue decentralization has a net positive effect. If tiers and the fiscal decentralization variables are added at the same time the significance of tiers drops to the 10% level, analogously to the count data model. This drop in significance may be caused either directly by the fiscal decentralization variables, or it may be due to the reduction in the sample that is caused by lower availability of the fiscal decentralization variables. Re-estimating the model using only tiers for the reduced sample reveals that the main factor is the effect of the fiscal decentralization variables, since tiers are found to be significantly negative in that specification (not shown). However, we demonstrate in the next section that the low significance of tiers in the joint specification results from controlling insufficiently for the quality of governance in the host country.

3.5.3. Governance quality. We now extend our analysis to allow for additional measures of governance quality. This is interesting from a theoretical point of view, because we have highlighted potential relationships between several dimensions of governance quality, in particular in the form of property rights protection, and the vertical dimension of decentralization. Thus, we ask, whether the significance and the size of the effects of decentralization variables we have found in our benchmark estimation are changed by the inclusion of governance variables. This is also an important check of the robustness of our findings. In particular, in the raw data there are some countries from sub-Saharan Africa with a high number of government tiers. Therefore we need to inquire whether our findings regarding the number of government tiers are possibly spurious and only driven by a potential correlation with important governance variables.

Not only property rights protection, but also other dimensions of host country governance are likely to be important determinants of foreign investment flows, and likely to be linked to government architecture. Corruption, for example, has been

---

[13] It may be possible to explain these differences between the estimations using the counts and the values of the investment respectively by the average size of the investment. A plausible conjecture would be that horizontal investments are larger in size on average and therefore the horizontal investment motive dominates if we consider the value of the overall investments, whereas the pure count could be dominated by the vertical motive. We do not analyse these questions further, since they are beyond the scope of this analysis.

shown to negatively influence FDI (see, for example, Wei, 2000). Corruption has also been related to government structure, see Shleifer and Vishny (1993). Thus, the effect of tiers we find in the baseline specification without governance variables may be picking up the importance of corruption which deters foreign investors. Similar arguments are likely to hold for other dimensions of governance. Therefore, we employ a large set of governance variables. These are voice and accountability, regulatory quality, corruption, government effectiveness, rule of law, political stability, and property rights protection. The latter variable is measured by the Heritage Foundation property rights index. All other governance variables are taken from Kaufman *et al.* (2005).[14]

Table 5 presents our estimation results when the governance variables are included in the specification. We use CBA counts as well as their value as our dependent variable. Columns (1)–(3) present the count specification. Column (1) includes only tiers. Column (2) includes the fiscal decentralization variables and tiers, and column (3) includes both fiscal decentralization variables and tiers divided by population. Column (1) of Table 5 shows that all governance variables with the exception of the rule of law are found to be significantly important for the determination of foreign investment. Except for corruption, all have the expected positive sign, that is, better quality of governance in the host country increases the amount of foreign investment inflows. The effect on the tiers variable is a drop in its coefficient to around 0.3. In the specification with all decentralization variables, rule of law is found to be significant, but regulatory quality is insignificant in this case. The more important message of column (2), however, regards the tiers variable. The inclusion of the governance variables results in an increase in the significance level of tiers to 1%. Thus, tiers are a significant negative determinant of CBAs. This specification also returns a coefficient of 0.27, which is very close to the estimate without the fiscal decentralization variables. Columns (4)–(6) report the same specifications for the Tobit estimations using the values of yearly CBAs as the dependent variable. The evidence on the significance of the various governance variables mirrors the findings of the count specification. In both estimations, nearly all are significant, and only corruption has the wrong sign. Column (4) indicates that, including these variables, the coefficient of tiers is reduced in absolute magnitude, just as in the count specification, but in case of the joint specification shown in column (5), the effect of tiers is increased compared to the estimation that does not include the governance variables. However, the evidence on the tiers variable in column (4) shows again, that, controlling for governance quality raises dramatically the significance of tiers in the joint specification.[15]

Finally, we also consider interaction effects between the level of property rights protection and the number of government tiers. As argued above, our theoretical perspective

[14] The Heritage Foundation index is available on a yearly basis. It ranges from 1 to 5 (with integer values only) and we use it in inverse scale, so that higher values imply better property rights protection. The other governance variables range from −2.5 to 2.5. It is available on a bi-annual basis from 1997–2003, and we use linearly interpolated values for the three intermediate years.

[15] To achieve this effect it is already sufficient to include only property rights protection as an additional governance variable.

Table 5. Governance

	(1)	(2)	(3)	(4)	(5)	(6)
VOICE AND ACCOUNTABILITY	0.6	0.3	0.41	1295.38	610.85	910.2
	(0.07)***	(0.12)**	(0.12)***	(162.47)***	(318.24)*	(316.87)***
REGULATORY QUALITY	0.34	0.03	0.18	1222.76	530.21	1134.32
	(0.09)***	(0.1)	(0.09)**	(221.54)***	(299.8)*	(314.11)***
CORRUPTION	-0.92	-0.95	-0.94	-1987.69	-1745.26	-1934.17
	(0.14)***	(0.17)***	(0.17)***	(315.38)***	(464.95)***	(470.94)***
RULE OF LAW	-0.03	0.56	0.4	15.47	1104.47	1076
	(0.17)	(0.22)**	(0.22)*	(368.77)	(650.85)*	(643.93)*
GOVERNMENT EFFECTIVENESS	0.92	0.37	0.35	1912.9	376.92	142.36
	(0.13)***	(0.14)***	(0.14)**	(298.6)***	(441.56)	(443.84)
PROPERTY RIGHTS PROTECTION	0.18	0.35	0.28	238.22	881.97	572.91
	(0.06)***	(0.07)***	(0.08)***	(145.75)	(222.51)***	(225.8)**
TIERS	-0.3	-0.28		-648.1	-628.62	
	(0.05)***	(0.07)***		(106.07)***	(187.2)***	
TIERS/POPULATION			-1.48			-6748.28
			(0.51)***			(925.89)***
SUBNAT. EXPENDITURE SHARE		3.33	3.77		8339.83	8721.67
		(0.98)***	(0.95)***		(2276.86)***	(2262.66)***
SUBNAT. REVENUE SHARE		-2.28	-2.04		-7758.7	-6457.94
		(0.95)**	(0.95)**		(2163.79)***	(2192.63)***
Obs.	42 994	21 126	21 126	41 483	20 387	20 387
Uncensored obs.				3553	2782	2782
Pseudo R²				0.09	0.08	0.08

Notes: Panel estimations (1997–2003) including all controls as displayed in Table 3 and Table 4. Dependent variable in (1), (2), and (3) is the count of yearly CBA for source-host country pairs. Dependent variable in (4), (5), and (6) is total yearly value of CBA for source-host country pairs. Standard errors of (1), (2), and (3) clustered by country pair. All estimations include year dummies.

Table 6. Interaction between tiers and property rights protection

	(1)	(2)	(3)	(4)
. . .	.	.	.	.
VOICE AND	0.6	0.32	1269.32	641.08
ACCOUNTABILITY	(0.07)***	(0.12)***	(162.91)***	(319.3)**
REGULATORY QUALITY	0.35	0.07	1183.85	567.27
	(0.09)***	(0.1)	(222.46)***	(300.46)*
CORRUPTION	−0.94	−0.94	−1903.93	−1758.75
	(0.14)***	(0.17)***	(318.78)***	(464.78)***
RULE OF LAW	−0.1	0.51	−40.45	1065.28
	(0.17)	(0.22)**	(369.79)	(652.44)
GOVERNMENT	0.91	0.34	1934.72	338.78
EFFECTIVENESS	(0.13)***	(0.14)**	(298.74)***	(442.76)
PROPERTY RIGHTS	0.41	0.98	−381.38	1617.85
PROTECTION	(0.19)**	(0.25)***	(380.52)	(653.25)**
TIERS	−0.08	0.38	−1231.46	142.18
	(0.17)	(0.24)	(348.91)***	(668.72)
TIERS*PROPERTY	−0.06	−0.17	170.67	−200.53
RIGHTS PROTECTION	(0.05)	(0.06)***	(97.0)*	(167.08)
SUBNAT. EXPENDITURE		2.85		7864.05
SHARE		(0.99)***		(2316.78)***
SUBNAT. REVENUE		−1.83		−7266.2
SHARE		(0.96)*		(2207.28)***
Obs.	42 994	21 126	41 483	20 387
Uncensored obs.			3553	2782
Pseudo R^2			0.09	0.08

Notes: Panel estimations (1997–2003) including all controls as displayed in Table 3 and Table 4. Dependent variable in (1) and (2) is the count of yearly CBA for source-host country pairs. Dependent variable in (3) and (4) is total yearly value of CBA for source-host country pairs. Standard errors of (1) and (2) clustered by country pair. All estimations include year dummies.

does not exclude the possibility of interaction between the number of tiers and governance variables such as property right protection. However, theoretically, it is *a priori* not clear which way such interaction effects should point. Columns (1) and (2) of Table 6 report count estimations with only tiers and with tiers and the fiscal decentralization variables, respectively, where we have added an interaction variable between property rights protection and tiers in both specifications. Columns (3) and (4) report the same exercise for the Tobit model using the values. Here we encounter the rare instance of differences between the count and the value specification. The count specification finds no evidence of interaction if the fiscal decentralization variables are left out, and a significant negative interaction effect if they are included. The value specification, however, indicates a positive interaction effect without the fiscal decentralization and no interaction, if the fiscal decentralization variables are included. These conflicting results are in line with our perspective that has argued in favour of an ambiguous prediction for the direction of potential interaction effects.

3.5.4. Non-linear relationships.   Thus far we have included the number of tiers as such into our estimations. However, this may be insufficient for at least two reasons. First, the specification of the count estimation implies that a reduction or an increase in the number of government levels has the same proportional effect on the amount of FDI received by a particular host country regardless of its given number of government levels. Similarly, the value specification implies a constant marginal effect of a change in government tiers. Second, also from a theoretical perspective, it may be that there is something like an optimal amount of vertical decentralization and one should expect inverted U-shapes regarding the optimal amount of decentralization. Of course, such an optimal degree of decentralization will also depend on several other characteristics of countries, in particular their size in terms of population or area.

Since we found the governance variables to be important determinants of foreign investment, we use our benchmark specification enlarged with the set of governance variables as the baseline in all further specifications. We add quadratic and cubic terms of tiers to assess whether there are signs of such non-linear structures in the data. Similar to the analysis of the interaction terms, the results are somewhat different depending on whether all decentralization variables are included or whether the decentralization variables are being left out.

Columns (1) and (3), and (2) and (4), respectively, of Table 7 show the result of adding quadratic and cubic terms of tiers to the specification including only tiers and to the specification including all decentralization variables for the count specification. In both cases there is strong evidence of a non-linear relationship regarding tiers and FDI. However, the nature of this relationship appears quite different in the two specifications. Without the fiscal decentralization variables, tiers and its cubic term are found to have a significant negative coefficient and the quadratic tiers term has a positive significant coefficient (column (3) of Table 7). In the specification that includes expenditure and revenue decentralization shown in column (4), however, all the signs of these terms are reversed. This effect appears to be driven by the reduced sample of countries for which the fiscal decentralization variables are available, since estimating the same specification for this reduced sample, but without the fiscal decentralization variables, gives very similar results.

It is interesting to characterize the estimated third degree polynomials more closely. In the case of the estimation without the fiscal decentralization variables, column (3) in Table 7, FDI is decreasing in the number of tiers over the entire relevant range of the tiers variable between 1 and 6 tiers. With the fiscal decentralization variables, column (4), the polynomial has a more volatile shape over this range. FDI is decreasing in the range of 3 and 4 tiers only, where, however, most of the observations are located. The estimated parameters are more sensible in the former estimation as we discuss below when we consider the quantitative importance of our results. The Tobit estimates for the values show an analogous picture, again indicating that non-linearity is important, and that the form of the non-linearity is quite dependent on the controls added and sample that is being used. In summary, there is evidence of non-linear patterns regarding the effects of tiers on FDI, but its specific form depends on the

Table 7. Non-linearity in tiers

	(1)	(2)	(3)	(4)	(5)	(6)	(7)	(8)
⋮								
TIERS	0.23	-2.74	-2.39	19.07	993.28	-7167.85	-11388.39	27751.7
	(0.23)	(0.65)***	(1.1)**	(3.11)***	(622.16)	(1643.68)***	(2831.4)***	(8861.52)***
$TIERS^2$	-0.07	0.34	0.61	-5.77	-209.58	912.51	3021.56	-8921.87
	(0.03)**	(0.09)***	(0.29)**	(0.88)***	(78.63)***	(228.4)***	(727.21)***	(2445.09)***
$TIERS^3$			-0.06	0.56			-268.73	899.94
			(0.02)**	(0.08)***			(60.37)***	(221.55)***
SUBNAT. EXPENDITURE SHARE		3.67		1.42		9404.4		5357.98
		(1.0)***		(1.13)		(2277.4)***		(2477.2)**
SUBNAT. REVENUE SHARE		-2.48		-1-28		-8334.01		-5898.21
		(0.94)***		(0.99)		(2162.53)***		(2241.39)***
Obs.	42 994	21 126	42 994	21 126	41 483	20 387	41 483	20 387
Uncensored obs.					3553	2782	3553	2782
Pseudo R^2					0.09	0.08	0.09	0.08

Notes: Panel estimations (1997–2003) including all controls as displayed in Table 3 and Table 4, and including all governance controls as given in Table 5. Dependent variable in (1), (2), (3) and (4) is the count of yearly CBA for source-host country pairs. Dependent variable in (5), (6), (7), and (8) is total yearly value of CBA for source-host country pairs. Standard errors of (1), (2), (3) and (4) clustered by country pair. All estimations include year dummies.

specific sample of countries and the added control variables. Also the non-linear estimates suggest that there is a negative relationship between tiers and FDI, at least over the most relevant range.

3.5.5. Quantitative importance.

The estimated coefficients can be interpreted quantitatively. The estimated negative coefficient of tiers somewhere between −0.25 and −0.3 implies that reducing the number of government tiers will increase the number of CBAs per year by around 30%. This is a large number and should be treated with care. The estimations using also squared and cubic tiers, suggest different magnitudes. These estimations do not assume that the effects of reducing the number of tiers are independent of the number of existing levels. The estimated third degree polynomials suggest that moving from 4 to 3 levels of government increases the number of firms acquired by about 5% in the estimation without the fiscal decentral-ization variables, see column (3) in Table 7, whereas the estimation with the fiscal decentralization variables (see column (4) in Table 7), suggests an increase by 120%! However, the change from 5 to 4 levels or from 3 to 2 levels is found to reduce CBAs substantially in that latter specification.

The Tobit estimates also suggest substantial magnitudes of the effects of the number of tiers. The coefficient of the tiers variable imply that an increase in the number of tiers by 1 in all countries will result in a reduction of the average value of yearly CBA flows between any two countries in the sample by US$61 million.[16] This is again a high number in relation to the average yearly CBA flow of US$170 million, but is quite in line with the results from count data. The total marginal effect can be split up into the effect of increased investment for those country pairs that are already experiencing CBA inflows (−18 million) and in the effect of those country pairs that will seize to have positive flows, as the number of government tiers in the host country are reduced (−43 million). Again, these numbers should not be taken at face value. The significance of the non-linear specification as shown in Table 7 underlines that the simple linear specification using tiers is open to challenge, and that its estimated quantitative implications are subject to substantial qualifications.

We can also consider the quantitative effects of the estimated coefficients for fiscal decentralization. The estimated coefficients such as from the count specification given in Table 5, column (2), indicate that an increase in average expenditure decentrali-zation by one percentage point would have, on average, increased the number of CBAs by about 3%. An increase of revenue decentralization by one percentage point would have resulted in a reduction of CBAs by about 2%. This implies that a joint increase in expenditure and revenue decentralization would have increased CBAs by about 1%. The Tobit estimates, such as reported in column (5) of Table 5, imply that an increase in average expenditure decentralization by one percentage point would have resulted in an increase of the average value of CBA flows by about US$8

---

[16] These calculations assume that the errors are normally distributed.

million, compared to an average flow of US$170 million. An increase in average revenue decentralization by one percentage point would have resulted in a reduction by US$7.5 million. Thus, joint fiscal decentralization of expenditure and revenue would have resulted in an average net increase of about US$0.5 million. These magnitudes of the effects of fiscal decentralization appear plausible and give an indication of the size of the potential gains from fiscal decentralization on the investment climate, although it should be stressed that the actual magnitudes will vary largely for different host countries.

In summary, the effects of the vertical dimension of decentralization are found to be substantial. We find that the size of the effects for the number of government tiers can be quite large. However, different specifications leave us with a substantial range of the effects, which imply that the results should not be taken at face value but must be treated with care. With regards to fiscal decentralization, the results are also found to be substantial and quite plausible in size.

3.6. Extensions and robustness

We have seen that the magnitude of the effects of the decentralization variables and their significance are somewhat sensitive to the inclusion of appropriate control variables. To ensure that our findings are sufficiently robust, we carry out a number of robustness checks. These exercises also generate further qualitative insights and important qualifications regarding the validity of specific policy recommendations that can be derived from our analysis. Again, all robustness and sensitivity checks are carried out including the full set of all governance variables.

3.6.1. Poor countries, rich countries.   Rich countries are different from poor countries. It is, therefore, conceivable that the motivations of firms to invest are different for these groups of countries. Our approach of imposing one model with constant parameters may be too restrictive, and could be a source of potential bias. Furthermore, the effects of the different forms and the degree of decentralization on FDI could be different across these two groups of countries.

To investigate these possibilities, we split up the sample of our host countries into OECD and non-OECD countries. The latter group consists mainly of developing countries, although it also contains a few countries which have a relatively high level of per capita income. Table 8 reports results for the non-OECD countries, Table 9 the analogous estimations for the OECD host countries. For both groups of host countries we again use the evidence from the negative binomial model using count data, as well as the Tobit estimates using values. The conjecture that FDI in OECD countries may be structurally different from FDI in the developing world is reflected in the findings regarding the coefficients of the 'knowledge-capital' model. For instance, the estimations for the OECD countries (Table 9) show a negative coefficient for the second interaction variable, consistent with the theoretical implications of horizontal

Table 8. Non-OECD host countries

	(1)	(2)	(3)	(4)	(5)	(6)	(7)	(8)
INT1	−0.05	−0.05	−0.05	−0.05	−15.10	−17.62	−17.51	−17.55
	(0.01)***	(0.01)***	(0.01)***	(0.01)***	(1.63)***	(2.85)***	(2.86)***	(2.85)***
INT2	0.03	0.02	0.02	0.02	5.53	1.85	1.81	1.79
	(0.01)***	(0.01)***	(0.01)***	(0.01)***	(1.54)***	(2.65)	(2.65)	(2.65)
INT3	0.08	−0.16	0.17	−0.15	23.78	−81.86	−83.45	−80.36
	(0.03)**	(0.11)	(0.11)	(0.11)	(9.85)**	(39.27)**	(39.34)**	(39.25)**
TIERS	−0.27	−0.02	6.48		−119.04	−25.3	1416.57	
	(0.05)***	(0.09)	(4.53)		(19.92)***	(45.06)	(2097.84)	
TIERS²			−1.91				−420.66	
			(1.32)				(613.26)	
TIERS³			0.18				39.65	
			(0.12)				(58.55)	
TIERS/POPULATION				−0.62				−357.1
				(0.5)				(280.27)
SUBNAT. EXPENDITURE SHARE		2.18	1.07	1.99		1931.52	1690.44	1856.64
		(1.82)	(2.2)	(1.79)		(744.8)**	(827.7)**	(746.1)**
SUBNAT. REVENUE SHARE		3.78	4.6	3.88		−376.26	−192.69	−289.54
		(2.1)*	(2.3)**	(2.13)*		(941.21)	(995.86)	(938.75)
Obs.	32 498	12 970	12 970	12 970	31 357	12 517	12 517	12 517
Uncensored obs.					1483	989	989	989
Pseudo R²					0.12	0.1	0.1	0.1

Notes: Panel estimations (1997–2003) including all controls as displayed in Table 3 and Table 4, and including all governance controls as given in Table 5. Dependent variable in (1), (2), (3), and (4) is the count of yearly CBA for source-host country pairs. Dependent variable in (5), (6), (7) and (8) is total yearly value of CBA for source-host country pairs. Standard errors of (1), (2), (3) and (4) clustered by country pair. All estimations include year dummies.

Table 9. OECD host countries

	(1)	(2)	(3)	(4)	(5)	(6)	(7)	(8)
⋮								
INT1	0.01	0.00	0.00	0.00	26.07	19.20	18.46	21.20
	(0.00)	(0.00)	(0.00)	(0.00)	(6.12)***	(7.00)***	(6.99)***	(6.98)***
INT2	-0.00	-0.01	-0.01	-0.01	-37.67	-45.99	-48.80	-48.43
	(0.02)***	(0.00)***	(0.00)***	(0.00)***	(5.70)***	(6.41)***	(6.42)***	(6.43)***
INT3	-0.00	-0.00	-0.00	-0.00	-27.70	-23.14	-23.40	-24.73
	(0.00)***	(0.00)*	(0.00)**	(0.00)**	(4.14)***	(4.97)***	(4.96)***	(4.96)***
⋮								
TIERS	-0.31	-0.87	-481.67		-720.37	-3513.56	-16 03464	
	(0.1)***	(0.2)***	(65.0)***		(343.69)**	(731.26)***	(222 641)***	
$TIERS^2$			125.11				414 195.6	
			(16.90)***				(57 907.32)***	
$TIERS^3$			-10.69				-35 160.19	
			(1.44)***				(4952.38)***	
TIERS/POPULATION				-14.28				-45 880.33
				(1.88)***				(6746.13)***
SUBNAT. EXPENDITURE SHARE		-3.19	12.31	4.93		-24984.02	32454.57	6116.66
		(2.61)	(3.55)***	(2.27)**		(7531.24)***	(11151.14)***	(7650.78)
SUBNAT. REVENUE SHARE		1.5	-10.19	-3.9		13616.22	30110.81	-5966.92
		(1.98)	(2.73)***	(1.9)**		(6130.12)**	(8857.86)***	(6676.02)
Obs.	10 496	8156	8156	8156	10 126	7870	7870	7870
Uncensored obs.					2070	1793	1793	1793
Pseudo R²					0.07	0.06	0.07	0.06

Notes: Panel estimations (1997–2003) including all controls as displayed in Table 3 and Table 4, and including all governance controls as given in Table 5. Dependent variable in (1), (2), (3) and (4) is the count of yearly CBA for source-host country pairs. Dependent variable in (5), (6), (7) and (8) is total yearly value of CBA for source-host country pairs. Standard errors of (1), (2), (3) and (4) clustered by country pair. All estimations include year dummies.

FDI, whereas the estimations for the non-OECD hosts (Table 8) find a positive coefficient for that variable, consistent with vertical FDI (Markusen and Maskus, 2002). This implies the possibility that decentralization may impact differently on FDI in these countries for two reasons. The different nature of FDI may make certain investments more or less vulnerable to the problems originating from multiple layers of government. On the other hand, the lower level of socio-economic development and the development of the institutional framework in these countries may change the nature and the magnitude of the effects of decentralization on FDI.

The results for the non-OECD countries are mainly in line with the findings of the overall sample (see Table 8). Including tiers as the only decentralization variable shows a significant negative effect and the size of the coefficient is very similar to the results using the full sample. In the specification using tiers and the fiscal decentralization variables, however, the coefficient of tiers remains negative but is no longer significant, either in the specification using the values or using the counts. If tiers divided by population is used in this joint specification, we also find it not to be significant, although significance is substantially increased. Regarding the fiscal decentralization, we find that in the count estimation (see columns (2)–(4)), only the sub-national revenue share is found to be significant, and, contrary to the full sample, has a positive coefficient. However, the estimates using the values, columns (6)–(8), show results that are analogous to the full sample, with a significant positive effect of expenditure decentralization and a negative effect of revenue decentralization, although the latter is not significant.

For the OECD countries (see Table 9) we find that tiers have a significant negative effect on FDI inflows in all specifications. Without the fiscal decentralization variables, the estimated coefficient of 0.3 is slightly bigger than in the full sample. In the count specification, the fiscal decentralization variables are not significant, but they are in the specification using the values. However, if one considers also non-linear specifications, see columns (3) and (7), the results are highly significant and very similar to the results in the overall sample, with expenditure decentralization affecting FDI positively and revenue decentralization affecting it negatively.

In summary, decentralization appears to be important for OECD and non-OECD hosts. Tiers have a significant negative effect in both groups of countries. However, for the non-OECD hosts the effect is no longer significant, if fiscal decentralization variables are added. This finding indicates that for poorer countries the problem of government overlap may be less of a problem. One alternative explanation of this finding could be that in less developed countries the formal existence of a government level does not imply the existence of a government actor that can affect the profitability of a foreign investor's investment. In other words, the measurement error in tiers may be systematically correlated with the development level of a country. In developing countries, the number of government levels as counted from the constitutional rules of each country, may overstate the number of actual levels that hold effective power in reality.

3.6.2. Excluding countries with extreme values of tiers.   It may appear that our results on the negative effects of vertical decentralization are driven by the extreme values in our sample. For example, Singapore is the only country in our sample with only one government level and this country had a relatively strong record of attracting FDI. On the other hand, there are several countries from sub-Saharan Africa with 5 or 6 levels of government, and most of these countries did not receive sizable amounts of foreign investments. Therefore, we ran our regressions including only those countries which have either 3 or 4 level of government. This is also a necessary exercise to understand better the results of the estimations that include the fiscal decentralization variables. These estimations suffer from the reduction of the sample, which leave very few observations with less than 3 and more than 4 levels of governments. These outliers may then affect the results strongly. Columns (1)–(4) of Table 10 report the results of the count data as well as the Tobit specifications. We find that the negative effect of tiers is robust, but the fiscal decentralization variables lose their significance in both specifications.

3.6.3. Taxes.   Our theoretical perspective has stressed the fiscal externalities that arise between different levels of government in the hold-up problem. This makes it potentially interesting to consider whether our findings are robust to the inclusion of measures of tax burden on the investment. Columns (5)–(8) of Table 10 report results for specifications that use the statutory corporate tax rate of 2002 as reported by Ernst & Young (2002) as an additional control variable. The statutory tax rate is found to have a negative effect on FDI. This is in line with existing results in the literature (see De Mooij and Ederveen, 2003, for a survey and a meta-analysis). We also see that the results for the decentralization variables are hardly affected by the inclusion of this additional variable.[17]

3.6.4. Regions.   As a further robustness check, we consider estimates for particular regions only. Given that the regions need to comprise a certain minimum number of countries for cross-sectional analysis we focus on three regions, Europe, Asia and Africa. Only for Europe does it make sense to also consider estimations that include the fiscal decentralization variables. We report the results in Table 11. The results from the full sample are broadly confirmed by the estimates for Europe, columns (7)–(10), and Africa, columns (1) and (2), which shows significant negative effects for tiers on FDI. In the case of Asia, however, we either find an insignificant negative effect of tiers for the CBA counts, column (3) or even a significant positive effect for the values, column (4). This conflicting result appears to be driven by several large economies in Asia that have received large amounts of FDI over recent years. This is confirmed by results using tiers divided by population. In the count specification, column (5), we now find

---

[17] If one uses data for 2002 only, the significant negative results for tiers can still be found, but the reduction in the sample causes the significance of the fiscal decentralization to drop below common significance levels.

Table 10. Countries with 3–4 government tiers / Inclusion of corporate taxes

	(1)	(2)	(3)	(4)	(5)	(6)	(7)	(8)
CORP. TAX RATE	•	•	•	•	−0.03	−0.01	−45.05	−15.95
					(0.007)***	(0.01)	(12.33)***	(17.02)
TIERS	−0.37	−0.8	−668.53	−1742.58	−0.36	−0.31	−740.41	−740.9
	(0.08)***	(0.11)***	(172.19)***	(264.22)***	(0.05)***	(0.07)***	(112.55)***	(192.94)***
SUBNAT. EXPENDITURE SHARE		−0.77		641.32		2.36		6065.72
		(1.31)		(2909.81)		(1.01)**		(2402.58)**
SUBNAT. REVENUE SHARE		0.07		−2183.05		−1.48		−6595.74
		(1.05)		(2490.23)		(0.98)		(2273.64)***
Obs.	33 632	18 186	32 453	17 551	34 199	19 545	32 998	18 862
Uncensored obs.			3025	2512			3365	2693
Pseudo R²			0.09	0.08			0.09	0.08

Notes: Panel estimations (1997–2003) including all controls as displayed in Table 3 and Table 4, and including all governance controls as given in Table 5. Dependent variable in (1), (2), (5), and (6) is the count of yearly CBA for source-host country pairs. Dependent variable in (3), (4), (7) and (8) is total yearly value of CBA for source-host country pairs. Standard errors of (1), (2), (5) and (6) clustered by country pair. All estimations include year dummies.

Table 11. Regions

	(1)	(2)	(3)	(4)	(5)	(6)	(7)	(8)	(9)	(10)
	AFRICA	AFRICA	ASIA	ASIA	ASIA	ASIA	EUROPE	EUROPE	EUROPE	EUROPE
TIERS	-0.28	-55.49	-0.01	185.21			-0.3	-1102.67	-0.33	-1585.01
	(0.16)*	(33.71)	(0.2)	(65.77)***			(0.09)***	(305.6)***	(0.19)*	(593.99)***
TIERS/POPULATION					-0.67	-1168.84				
					(1.83)	(509.07)**				
SUBNAT. EXPENDITURE SHARE									-0.94	-6508.89
									(1.65)	(5285.28)
SUBNAT. REVENUE SHARE									2.33	7926.13
									(1.4)*	(4316.341)*
Obs.	10 141	9785	10 307	9943	10 307	9943	12 765	12 315	10 038	9686
Uncensored obs.		117		684		684		1721		1556
Pseudo R²		0.14		0.13		0.13		0.08		0.07

Notes: Panel estimations (1997–2003) including all controls as displayed in Table 3 and Table 4, and including all governance controls as given in Table 5. Dependent variable in (1), (3), (5), (7), and (9) is the count of yearly CBA for source-host country pairs. Dependent variable in (2), (4), (6), (8), and (10) is total yearly value of CBA for source-host country pairs. Standard errors of (1), (3), (5), (7) and (9) clustered by country pair. All estimations include year dummies.

a negative but insignificant effect, and the value specification, column (6), shows a negative and significant effect.

3.6.5. The role of country size.
Our analysis has shown that appropriately controlling for governance variables is important to detect the effects of decentralization on FDI. Controlling for country size is equally important, since large countries can be expected to feature higher decentralization. But country size itself may be an important determinant of FDI, so the specification of our regression's functional forms is very delicate and debatable.

We have included tiers unadjusted for country size in most of our regressions. However, since tiers is itself systematically correlated with country size, it is essential to include sufficient controls to ensure that our tiers variable does not pick up FDI effects that should be accounted for by the effects of country size. Columns (1)–(6) of Table 12 show what happens if a reduced number of country size controls are used. The estimations of columns (1) and (2) do not control for the squared terms of area and population, columns (3) and (4) display the results of using only area and population as controls, and, finally, (5) and (6) show what happens if there are no controls at all for country size. The size of the coefficient of tiers decreases, and the significance of tiers also drops as we take out the controls for country size. Without any country size controls tiers is found to have a significant positive impact on CBAs in the values specification. This demonstrates that appropriately controlling for country size is very important. We should stress, however, that all the country size controls we use are typically found to be significant in our estimations, at least when we use the full sample, as can be seen from Tables 3 and 4.

3.6.6. Estimates using averages.
As our final robustness check we consider estimating the model using averages. Since our variable of government tiers and our fiscal decentralization measures do not change over time, estimating a panel may be regarded as an unjustified inflation of the sample size. We therefore collapse all time varying variables to their 1997–2003 averages. For the count data model, we consider how these averages determine the total number of acquired firms of a given country pair. The Tobit specification also uses the average yearly value as the dependent variable. The results are displayed in Table 13. The coefficient of tiers is negative and significant in all specifications, and of a magnitude that is similar to the estimated coefficients in the panel model. The fiscal decentralization variables are, however, no longer found to be significant.

4. DISCUSSION

Our empirical analysis has detected a dark side of decentralization. Its vertical dimension, measured by the number of government tiers in the host country, has a negative effect on foreign FDI inflows into the host country. This finding is robust in the type of FDI data used as the dependent variable: count or aggregate values. It is also quite robust to the division of the sample into particular subsets of countries.

Table 12. Sensitivity with respect to country size variables

	(1)	(2)	(3)	(4)	(5)	(6)
POP	$91.16*10^{-5}$	2.56	$74.5*10^{-5}$	2.51		
	$(20.25*10^{-5})$***	(0.36)***	$(20.89*10^{-5})$***	(0.36)***		
POP^{-1}	-2.87	-6339.61				
	(0.56)***	(450.19)***				
POP^2						
$AREA$	$7.34*10^{-5}$	0.24	$9.39*10^{-5}$	0.29		
	$(1.2*10^{-5})$***	(0.02)***	$(1.25*10^{-5})$***	(0.02)***		
$AREA^{-1}$	0.58	1687.8				
	(0.21)***	(407.27)***				
$AREA^2$						
$TIERS$	-0.31	-603.59	-0.14	-204.4	-0.06	158.25
	(0.05)***	(104.34)***	(0.05)***	(87.53)**	(0.05)	(81.81)*
Obs.	42 994	41 483	42 994	41 483	42 994	41 483
Uncensored obs.	3553	3553	3553	3553	3553	3553
pseudo R^2	0.09	0.09	0.09	0.09	0.09	0.09

Notes: Panel estimations (1997–2003) including all controls as displayed in Table 3 and Table 4, and including all governance controls as given in Table 5. Dependent variable in (1), (3), and (5) is the count of yearly CBA for source-host country pairs. Dependent variable in (2), (4), and (6) is total yearly value of CBA for source-host country pairs. Standard errors of (1), (3), and (5) clustered by country pair. All estimations include year dummies.

54

SEBASTIAN G. KESSING, KAI A. KONRAD AND CHRISTOS KOTSOGIANNIS

Table 13. Averages

	(1)	(2)	(3)	(4)	(5)	(6)
TIERS	-0.34 (0.05)***	-0.25 (0.08)***				
TIERS/POPULATION			-1.83 (0.36)***	-289.68 (69.97)***	-335.24 (135.47)**	-2159.5 (669.52)***
SUBNAT. EXPENDITURE SHARE		1.71 (0.99)*	1.77 (0.98)*		423.14 (1742.54)	707.35 (1741.96)
SUBNAT. REVENUE SHARE		-0.48 (0.94)	0.21 (0.95)		-658.75 (1628.1)	-218.34 (1648.08)
Obs.	5923	3340	3340	5740	3237	3237
Uncensored obs.				1291	959	959
Pseudo R²				0.08	0.07	0.07

Notes: Cross-section of 1997–2003 averages. Dependent variable in (1), (2), and (3) is count of total 1997–2003 CBA for source-host country pairs. Dependent variable in (4), (5), and (6) is 1997–2003 average yearly value of CBA for source-host country pairs.

Finally, this finding is robust to the inclusion of variables that control for governance as well as for other variables. Interestingly, the inclusion of governance variables is found to increase the significance of the results. The results are quantitatively important, although the magnitudes of the effects are sensitive to the specification and set of control variables included in the estimation.

We have found robust evidence of the negative effects of the vertical dimension of decentralization, very much in line with our Hypothesis 1. The importance of the different channels through which these negative effects are working is difficult to be identified. We have suggested several of such channels in our conceptual analysis in Section 2, but, with our data, it is not feasible to evaluate which of these channels is most important. Further evidence for the operation of the various mechanisms identified could be obtained with better availability of comparable cross-country data, as well as from individual case studies. We have used a large set of governance variables as controls and still identified a significant negative effect of tiers, although the inclusion of governance variables reduced the size of the effects of tiers. This latter finding relates to the results of Dreher (2006), who considers the effects of decentralization on various indicators of the quality of governance. He finds a negative effect of the number of government tiers on various measures of governance. More specifically, he finds a negative effect of the number of tiers on the rule of law, as measured by the Kaufman *et al.* (2005) index. These interdependencies point at potential endogeneity of several important variables in our analysis, including not only the governance variables, but potentially, also the decentralization variables. This may call for a modification of our econometric approach. However, there appear to be many channels through which tiers affect CBA, and it is not clear how to select among these, and what an adequately specified multi-equation model should look like. As regards the potential endogeneity problems of our decentralization variables, these are likely to differ between them. Our main variable of interest, the number of government tiers, is typically determined at the constitutional level. Further, since the tiers variable is treated as constant and relates to the beginning of our sample period, it can be regarded as exogenously given for our period under consideration. For the case of fiscal decentralization the possibility of endogeneity is more important. If the foreign investment generates substantial tax revenue, and if this revenue accrues differently to the various levels of government compared to other tax revenues, then the amount of FDI clearly affects the revenue ratio. Again, we may argue that the tax revenues stemming from a CBA in a given year will only arise in later years, and this implies that contemporaneous fiscal decentralization is exogenous to the number and the value of CBA inflows. However, since we use past average fiscal decentralization, our estimates do not suffer from this potential endogeneity problem.

The empirical analysis also showed that unlike vertical disintegration, fiscal decentralization may have positive effects. First, it should be noted that they do not contradict our theoretical perspective, but highlight that decentralization policy has several dimensions. Where the tiers variable is most suitable for measuring the vertical dimension, fiscal decentralization measures may account for other effects. They may relate more closely to the horizontal dimension of federalism, and therefore can be seen, for instance, as measuring 'closeness' of the government to firms and individuals.

We have not provided an explicit theoretical perspective on the potential aspects captured by the fiscal decentralization variables, and an interpretation of the findings on the fiscal decentralization measures is of an exploratory nature. However, it is still feasible to link them to various theoretical arguments made in the literature and we can also square them with several empirical results that have been obtained by previous research. First, we can relate our findings on the research that has been carried out on the direct relationship between decentralization and governance. Fisman and Gatti (2002) and Treisman (2000b) have considered the effect of decentralization on corruption. Fisman and Gatti (2002) consider the fiscal decentralization variables only, and find that more fiscal decentralization reduces the level of corruption. Such potential positive effect of fiscal decentralization on governance in the host countries may be an additional channel that explains the positive findings of fiscal decentralization on FDI. Conversely, Treisman (2000b) considered federalism (proxied by a dummy variable) and did not find an effect on corruption. Dreher (2006) also finds a positive effect of revenue decentralization on governance variables. This is in line with reduction in the magnitude of our estimated effects when governance variables are included, but we should stress that fiscal decentralization still has significant effects when we control for the quality of governance.

Another explanation for the increased attractiveness to foreign investors caused by fiscal decentralization can be found in the argument of Keen and Marchand (1997). They suggested that competition between cities or regions will result in a distortion of the mix of public goods provided by the regions and cities. In particular they will over-invest in infrastructure. This effect is likely to be stronger, if regions and cities have larger fiscal autonomy, as measured by fiscal decentralization. Investors will profit from such overinvestment in infrastructure and increase their investment, potentially explaining the positive effect of fiscal decentralization. This argument is also in line with the findings on the differential effect of expenditure and revenue decentralization, since it essentially relies on expenditure decentralization. Given the nature of this infrastructure competition, it is less likely in this case that fiscal decentralization is to the benefit of the country.

Finally, we should also point out that our results regarding tiers are derived on a cross-sectional base only and are therefore sensitive to unobserved country differences that could be correlated with CBAs and tiers. This is a common problem of research addressing the effects of government architecture, as variation over time is negligible compared to cross-sectional differences, and we do not have any *a priori* evidence for why such a correlation should exist, but this caveat needs to be mentioned. This caveat also holds with respect to our findings for fiscal decentralization. Nevertheless, we see our results as a useful first step uncovering the effects of the various facets of decentralization on FDI and more detailed analysis should be very welcome. This is particularly true with respect to quantifying the potential effects, as our results showed them to be sensitive to the set of controls, the specification regarding the decentralization variables themselves, and the sample of countries included.

5. POLICY IMPLICATIONS

Important policy lessons can be learned from our results on the impact of decentralization on FDI. Both in the developed and developing world policy reforms towards decentralization are high on the policy agenda. Frequently, it is argued that decentralization is beneficial for improving the investment climate. In particular, the competition between regional governments could result in improved investment conditions for private investors and reduced possibilities for local governments to appropriate parts of the investment's return through taxation after an investor has invested in a particular location. This competition effect is caused by the *horizontal dimension* of decentralization, the breaking up of one state in many jurisdictions.

Policy makers who want to attract FDI, however, need to be aware of the pitfalls of decentralization. The horizontal dimension of decentralization need not resolve the hold-up problem in FDI, since this problem is rooted in the *ex post* irreversibility of investment. And the *vertical dimension* of decentralization, implied by the inevitable multiplicity of government levels that are created in the process of decentralization, has potentially negative effects for FDI. These theoretical arguments find strong support in the data, and suggest that decentralization programmes can be detrimental to growth and efficiency.

To avoid these negative consequences, policies and constitutional set-ups should be designed in a way as to minimize the negative potential arising from vertical disintegration. Our theoretical perspective leads to a number of important considerations. First, the number of government layers should not be overly expanded. In fact, the number of government levels should be reduced wherever possible. Second, as a certain amount of vertical disintegration will be unavoidable, policies and constitutional set-ups need to minimize the negative effects originating from this vertical dimension. The overlap regarding tax bases, regulatory authority, and other policies that impinge on investors should be reduced as far as possible. Thus a clear delineation of responsibilities is a pivotal aspect of the proper functioning of federal systems. But since some overlap will be unavoidable, coordination devices need to be installed that coordinate the actions of the different government levels. Such coordination has the potential to resolve the free-riding and common pool incentives outlined in Section 2.

There is also good news for proponents of decentralization. Fiscal decentralization may improve the investment climate, such that, from an investment policy perspective, expenditure and revenue decentralization can have positive effects for FDI. Further, the results on the differential effect of expenditure and revenue decentralization point at the importance of expenditure decentralization for improving the investment climate for foreign investors. As can be seen from Table 2, there is large variation in fiscal decentralization among countries, such that there is scope for many countries to engage in fiscal decentralization. Of course, the measures of fiscal decentralization are rather crude measures and do not say much about the actual autonomy, nor do they tell us something about the kind of taxes and expenditures that are more effective in improving the investment climate. As can be conjectured from the results regarding the differential effect of expenditure and revenue decentralization, interesting results are to be expected from more detailed analyses of the structure of fiscal decentralization if the appropriate data was available. Going deeper into the structure of actual fiscal powers regarding different taxing rights and expenditure responsibilities would also allow much better targeted policy advice than what can be offered currently.[18]

Decentralization is often proposed as a means to improve the governance within a country. While we have treated governance as exogenously given in our empirical analysis, our findings nevertheless shed some light on the potential of decentralization to improve governance. It appears that the vertical dimension impinges negatively on the quality of governance. Fiscal expenditure decentralization appears to have positive effects. Of course, this evidence is rather indirect, but seems to point towards the same direction as our above arguments. If the problems of the vertical dimension cannot be sufficiently controlled, decentralization might not appear very suitable to improve governance. But if the vertical dimension can be controlled, decentralization in the form of fiscal decentralization has potential to improve governance.

Our results may also provide a further argument in favour of special economic zones. Such zones with special conditions regarding taxes and tariffs have been set up in many developing countries for foreign investors. From our perspective, one of the main advantages of such zones may be that several local or regional government actors, which would play a role elsewhere in the country, are locked out in such zones and the investor will typically have to deal with one government authority only.

Finally, it should again be stressed that for a sound formulation of decentralization policies two considerations are central. On the one hand, one has to consider what level of decentralization is most appropriate for the government to perform its tasks in the most efficient way. On the other hand, it is also important to consider the interaction of various government players at various levels in the government hierarchy. Our results point towards the intrinsic tension between these objectives.

Discussion

Allan Drazen
University of Maryland

Any comprehensive discussion of the determinants of foreign direct investment (FDI) in a country needs to consider the effect of government policy choices on FDI.

---

[18] The recent contribution by Stegarescu (2006) can be regarded as a first important step in that direction.

This includes not only actual policy decisions, but also the decision-making mechanism itself, since this will be a key determinant of the investment environment. The decision of foreigners on whether or not to invest in a country will in turn depend on their expectations of the policy environment.

This paper by Kessing, Konrad and Kotsogiannis makes a crucial contribution to this question. It has long been realized that decentralization of government decision making across levels of government may have a significant effect on FDI. Along the horizontal dimension, that is, with competing jurisdictions at a given level of government with some autonomy in decision making, decentralization may have a positive effect on FDI. Local governments may be more able to tailor fiscal programmes to the needs of the local constituency, and this increases accountability. More importantly for FDI, potential competition and benchmarking between regions may help attract FDI, among other things because it is argued to reduce the risk that governments will expropriate wealth.

What has been less appreciated, and is the focus of this paper, is the potential *negative* effect along the vertical dimension, that is, at different levels of government, for example: local, regional, state (in a federal system), and national. More specifically, less than total vertical decentralization, so that there is overlapping authority on investment decisions may have a strong negative effect. This is the 'dark side' of decentralization. When investors are subject to jurisdiction of several tiers of government, there may be significant problems of coordination failures, free-riding, common pool problems, and 'enforcement' of implicit contracts between government and private investors.

The authors have done an extremely good job not only of highlighting this issue, but also of investigating it. Moreover, since many of my concerns about earlier drafts were admirably addressed, this discussion will be short.

Several types of arguments are presented on why less-than-complete vertical 'dis-integration' may have a negative effect on FDI. These problems are most easily understood by comparing, as the paper does, two hypothetical countries, identical in all respects, except that in country U there is a unitary government, while in country F there is a federal system with multiple tiers of government (for simplicity, say two tiers) that have overlapping fiscal authority. Kessing, Konrad and Kotsogiannis assume that in both countries 'property rights are weak' in the sense that government cannot credibly commit to not extracting revenue from the investors' projects *ex post*, that is once the investment is sunk and cannot be relocated. Moreover, investors are aware of government incentives to expropriate one investment is irreversibly in place. (I return to a discussion of the hold-up problem below, and, following the organization of the paper, begin by assuming both types of countries share equally weak property rights.)

First, there is the common pool problem. If government maximizes tax revenue that can be extracted from a foreign direct investor, U will choose the tax rate that maximizes overall tax revenue. In F if the two levels of government that can both tax the foreign investor choose tax rates non-cooperatively, the overall tax rate on the investor will be higher, and both investment (which is chosen anticipating this problem) and tax revenue will be lower. (Similar considerations apply when governments give subsidies to attract foreign investment – the free-rider problem is simply another inter-government externality.)

This is certainly true, but governments can foresee this common pool problem as well as investors. Hence, to the extent that the common pool problem has the potential to significantly lower investment, one might expect a federal system to try to alleviate it, for example, by defining property rights to tax bases. (In many US states, for example, certain types of taxes are constitutionally reserved for the state government, others reserved for local governments.) Kessing, Konrad and Kotsogiannis are aware of this when they write that 'the common pool problem could be avoided if the ability to expropriate revenues from the foreign direct investor could be attributed to one of the government tiers'. They argue, however, that in practice such effective assignment is hard to do. But, this is an empirical question: do we in fact see such mechanisms in place in some countries, but not others? It would not be easy, but nonetheless useful, to see empirical evidence on the success or failure of federal systems to assign such property rights to taxes across government tiers. Their tests suggest that countries don't fully solve the problem, but it would be nice to see more direct evidence.

It also seems that there is no reason to believe that all government tiers in a given country actually have fiscal jurisdiction over FDI and certainly not equal jurisdiction. Of course, any 'weighting' scheme for tiers would depend on country specifics and hence could not be applied across the sample, even if it could even be discovered. Hence, this is not a criticism of construction of the variable itself, but more a question of what are the limitations of this sort of cross-country empirical analysis.

The severity of the *ex post* 'hold-up' problem depends on the extent that governments try to commit themselves successfully not to expropriate sunk investment. An inability of government to make it convincing that *ex post* expropriation will not take place is listed by investors as a major disincentive to investment. However, country governments clearly differ significantly in the extent they can credibly commit not to expropriate. Hence, though in theory the hold-up problem certainly exists, its seriousness in practice is also an empirical question of effective government pre-commitment mechanisms.

A key question then becomes whether countries having a federal structure where different tiers have overlapping authority are less likely to develop institutions which address the hold-up problem than countries with a unitary government. As Kessing, Konrad and Kotsogiannis point out, since the hold-up problem in FDI may be more severe in a federal system due to the common pool problem, F countries have more to gain than U countries from developing mechanisms or institutions that address it, and hence, they may in fact have more incentive to do so.

To suggest why this may not happen, Kessing, Konrad and Kotsogiannis consider repeated interaction between governments and investors as an important mechanism in the case of FDI. Will reputational effects in the 'implicit contract' inherent in repeated interactions help constrain governments, and, more importantly, is the implicit contract weaker in federal systems? Based on oligopoly theory concerning collusion among firms, they argue that the enforcement of good behaviour in the 'implicit contract' will be weaker in F than in U countries. With repeated interaction, agents – government levels and an investor – can adopt strategies that depend on behavior in previous interactions. Good behaviour is enforced by the threat of punishing a 'player' that deviates from the collusive (that is, lower-tax) equilibrium. However, as with an increase in the number of firms in oligopoly, the ability to punish a deviating government may be reduced with an increase in the number of governments. The benefit from cooperation is lower as the number of governments increase, while the net benefit from deviating may be higher.

This argument makes sense, but governments are not exactly like firms in this analogy. Government is defined as having (or supposed to have) monopoly on the use of certain powers. Hence, higher levels may have far greater powers than firms in enforcing cooperation by lower tiers (and the number of tiers is often small). The analogy of governments colluding among themselves in this repeated interaction game (induced by the existence of a dominant player on the government side) may be more realistic.

To summarize, I think Kessing, Konrad and Kotsogiannis have pointed out a number of reasons why the problems of government interaction and overlap in a federal system may depress FDI when investment has an irreversible component and investors are forward-looking. By the same token, overlapping governments that care about attracting FDI should be forward-looking as well. Hence, their attempts to address these problems may mitigate the effects. More generally, simple stylized models of government behaviour focusing on institutional differences can be very misleading. Modelling is necessarily simple and stylized, but in fact, governments facing problems due to institutional features (multiple tiers, allocation of powers, etc.) have incentives to get around them. Predictions of what can happen due to these features may be in error if it fails to take this into account.

Hence, theory alone cannot answer the question of how strong an effect the problems of incomplete vertical decentralization will have on FDI. Moreover, since even in theory, horizontal decentralization may have strong positive effects, the overall empirical effect could certainly go in either direction. I think the authors are wise therefore to focus on investigating the empirical relation between government tiers and FDI.

At the same time, I think one should be careful about interpreting the results. My point is a standard one. When countries are so different in institutional features which we cannot easily measure or control for (such as institutions to address the dark side of decentralization or even comparability of government tiers across countries), cross-country studies like this are suggestive, but far from definitive. I think that in the final analysis, some sort of country studies may also be needed to shed more light on the effect of tiers on FDI. Not to replace the analysis here, but to supplement it. The question is too important and the paper too interesting not to take this next step.

Manuel Arellano
CEMFI and CEPR

This paper reports empirical evidence on the effects of various aspects of decentralization on FDI. This is an interesting question. The paper provides a detailed background discussion of the literature and potential effects according to theory. The central part of the paper develops an empirical strategy:

- The FDI annual flow from a source country to a host country is proxied by the number or the value of firms acquired by firms from the source country in the host country.
- In this way it is possible to use data from up to 74 source countries and 177 host countries for 7 years.
- The basic empirical equation is a knowledge-capital regression model to which decentralization variables are added as extra regressors.

The main decentralization variable is the number of government tiers. Its estimated effect on FDI is negative, and this is the 'dark side' of decentralization.

Assessment

This is a welcome contribution to the empirical assessment of decentralization. The paper contains much useful discussion and empirical results on an issue of policy relevance. It is nicely written and I enjoyed reading it.

The contribution of the paper is empirical: the finding of a negative association between the number of government layers and FDI after controlling for country differences. Since FDI itself is positively associated with growth, the policy implication is that the number of government levels should be reduced 'wherever possible'.

Most of the limitations of this exercise are related to problems with data that hamper credibility of the estimates as causal effects. Moreover, the causal effect of decentralization on FDI is likely to be heterogeneous across countries. Understanding this heterogeneity and being able to relate it to observables is important for policy. In the remainder, I review some data limitations and provide some suggestions for future work.

Data issues

Lack of data on FDI flows. As the authors note, the choice of dependent variable is problematic. One problem is that CBA is only a part of FDI (firm creation is excluded) and we do not know how the CBAs' share of FDI depends on decentralization and other variables. Thus, the reported estimates compound the effects of decentralization on FDI and the effects of decentralization on the CBA/FDI ratio.

The other problem is the focus on counts of CBAs due to severe under-reporting of the value of the investments. Aside from necessity, there are no good reasons for using counts of CBAs as a measure of FDI.

However, from the perspective of evaluating decentralization, CBA counts could be regarded as an outcome of interest in its own right. After all, it is also associated with growth. One can also take some comfort in the fact that count and value based estimates tend to be similar to each other, at least as far as the signs of effects and their significance is concerned.

Lack of variation in policy regimes.   Results are based on cross-sectional comparisons: differences in FDI associated with differences in number of tiers. So it is the effect of 'being in a situation with so many government levels' that we are looking at, as opposed to the before-after effect of undergoing decentralization. The latter is a closer notion to the policy effect of interest. The fact that results are cross-sectional (together with lack of instrumental variables) diminishes their causal credibility, because they are sensitive to unobserved country differences that cause both FDI and number of tiers.

The policy effect of decentralization

The number of tiers has a statistically significant negative effect on FDI, but how large is this effect? Is it economically plausible? Given the exponential specification of the model for counts of CBAs, an estimated coefficient on tiers of −0.4 implies that the average number of CBAs becomes 50% larger when one government tier is removed, which is a very large effect. Probably too large. The estimated effect is even larger in some of the specifications excluding countries with extreme values of tiers.

One explanation for such large effects would be the potential endogeneity of the number of tiers. Since this variable does not vary with time, we would expect a larger scope for endogeneity if the error term also contains a substantial component which does not vary with time. In this regard, it would be nice to do an analysis of variance of the residuals in order to ascertain the importance of time-invariant country-pair effects.

Heterogeneity

Large variations in the size of the estimated effect for different subsamples suggests that heterogeneity may be important. I consider some possible dimensions.

Different effects at different margins.   In the baseline model, the FDI effects of going from, say, 6 to 5 tiers or from 2 to 1 tier are constrained to be the same. The authors find evidence of non-linearities, but the lack of stability of the non-linear pattern across subsamples suggests that non-linear responses are not a major reason for heterogeneity in responses.

Cross-country dependence.   The theoretical predictions implicitly hold the amount of decentralization in other countries constant. Empirically, this creates the possibility that decentralization in one potential host country affects FDI in another. Also, spacial clustering in number of tiers suggests that the effects of *TIERS* may differ depending on the neighbours' situation. One way of addressing this issue would be to divide the world in broad regions and include an interaction of *TIERS* with average *TIERS* in the region.

Other interactions and optimal decentralization.   The effect of *TIERS* on FDI may vary with country size, political culture, diversity, or with the nature of decentralization. It may also vary with characteristics of the source country. Regarding country size, interaction terms are as theoretically plausible as additive controls.

   As for the nature of decentralization, the effect may be different, for example, depending on whether decentralization goes alongside with fiscal decentralization or not. In fact, the policy discussion in the paper suggests an interest in the effects of the nature of decentralization as much as in decentralization itself. Taken *prima facie*, the paper estimates suggest that the less decentralization the better. A different policy perspective is to presume an optimal degree of decentralization and seek its empirical characterization (searching for 'U shapes').

   The analysis of heterogeneity in the impact of *TIERS* is important because an estimated effect that is an average of very different country effects is not so useful for policy (i.e. what is good for some may be bad for others). Unfortunately, we do not seem to have enough data variability to capture well determined interaction effects.

Econometric remarks

There are nearly 7500 country pairs and more than 22 000 data points in the panel. The error terms of a given host country are likely to be correlated, and so are the errors for a given pair over time. Standard errors that treat these errors as independent may be overoptimistic. Standard errors reported in the paper are clustered by country-pair. So it is potentially important to allow for clustering in these dimensions, as done in the paper for country pairs.

   Over-dispersion may be a problem for Poisson probabilities but not for estimates of the conditional mean, which are robust to distributional misspecification. In fact, they are more robust than estimates from the negative binomial model.

   The Tobit model is a restrictive specification for values in that it presumes that the same equation that determines total values when investments are positive, also determines the probability of zeros.

Conclusion

This paper is an honest and thorough investigation of the relationship between FDI and government decentralization, which has uncovered an interestingly dark empirical regularity. It makes a policy relevant contribution and, no doubt, it will be a rich source for further research.

Panel discussion

Wendy Carlin wondered about the welfare implications of the paper's analysis: there may or may not be good reasons to focus on incentives to attract FDI, and the relevant institutions and policies certainly have other roles. Gilles Duranton noted that perhaps the same countries that can afford the high bureaucratic costs of multi-tiered governments are also inclined to let their local governments engage in wasteful policies meant to attract FDI. Several panellists wondered whether the paper's empirical results are robust to examination of subsamples and to correlation between the number of government tiers and other relevant factors, such as corruption and the availability of natural resources, and encouraged the authors to perform the robustness checks now reported in the published version of the paper. Pierre Pestiau noted that different mechanisms may be at work in very heterogeneous countries. Decentralization may be more or less democratically chosen, and while it is often motivated by concern for efficiency, it may also lead to inefficient conflicts between layers of government. Hans-Werner Sinn and Gilles Duranton emphasized the important role of hierarchical power in layered government structures. In federal countries, such as Germany and Canada, decentralization of fiscal powers is not as extensive as it may appear, as higher levels of government can react to the behaviour of lower levels by adjusting transfers of resources.

APPENDIX 1: ECONOMETRIC SPECIFICATION

For our study of the determinants of the number of CBA between source and host countries we use standard methods for the econometric analysis of count data. The theory of count data analysis is well summarized by Cameron and Trivedi (1998), see Cameron and Trivedi (1999) for a comprehensive introduction. The structure of the econometric model we estimate can be described by the expected number of cross-border acquisitions, conditional on the vector of controls, $CONTROLS$, the decentralization variables DEC, β, the parameter vector to be estimated and a shift variable d_{ij}:

$$E[CBA_{ijt} \,|\, x_{ijt}, d_{ijt}] = \exp(CONTROLS'_{ijt}\beta_1 + DEC'_{ijt}\beta_2 + d_{ijt}). \tag{1}$$

In their simplest form, count data models assume that the counts, that is in our case the number of CBA from source country i to host country j in year t, denoted by CBA_{ijt} follow a Poisson distribution with parameter λ_{ijt}. Thus,

$$f(CBA_{ijt} \,|\, x_{ijt}) = \frac{e^{-\lambda_{ijt}} \lambda_{ijt}}{CBA_{ijt}!}, \tag{2}$$

where

$$\lambda_{ijt} = \exp(x'_{ijt}\beta), \tag{3}$$

with x_{ijt} the vector of covariates, and β the parameter vector to be estimated. However, given the assumption of the Poisson distribution, this model assumes equality of mean and variance. This property is termed equi-dispersion. However, in most applications the analysed data displays over-dispersion, that is, a larger variance larger than the mean. Also in our case, standard tests clearly reject equi-dispersion. This problem can be resolved, if one assumes that the Poisson parameter λ_{ijt} is also affected by an additional shift parameter d_{ijt} that is:

$$\tilde{\lambda}_{ijt} = \exp(x'_{ijt}\beta + d_{ijt}) = \exp(x'_{ijt}\beta)\exp(d_{ijt}). \tag{4}$$

In this case, the Poisson parameter λ_{ijt} becomes itself a random variable with realization $\tilde{\lambda}_{ijt}$. Further, we assume that $\alpha_{ijt} = \ln d_{ijt}$ is gamma distributed with precision parameter θ, so that $E[\alpha_{ijt}] = 1$ and $V[\alpha_{ijt}] = 1/\theta$. In this case, the marginal distribution of CBA_{ijt}, given the covariates, can be shown to follow a negative binomial distribution, and the parameter vector β can be estimated via maximum likelihood estimation.

APPENDIX 2

Table A1. Description of covariates used in the analysis and their sources

Variable	Units	Description	Source
Number of cross border acquisitions	Count	Number of international merger and acquisition deals between source and host countries.	Compiled from Thomson Financial by Herger et al. (2005).
Value of cross border acquisitions	US$ millions	Value of international merger and acquisition deals between source and host countries.	Compiled from Thomson Financial by Herger et al. (2005).
ΣGDP	US$ billions	Real Gross Domestic Product in US$ with base year 1995 cumulated over source and host country.	Compiled from World Development Indicators (WDI).
ΔGDP	US$ billions	Real Gross Domestic Product in US$ with base year 1995 in terms of difference between source and host country.	Compiled from WDI.
POPULATION	Count (in millions)	Total population in host country.	Compiled from WDI.
AREA	Thousand square km	Area of host country.	Compiled from WDI.
$\Delta SKILL$	US$ thousands	Wage difference between source and host country measured by the corresponding difference in real GDP per capita with base year 1995.	Compiled from WDI.

Table A1. *Continued*

Variable	Units	Description	Source
DISTANCE	Thousand km	Great circular distance between capital cities of source and host country.	Compiled.
COMMON LANGUAGE	Indicator	Indicator variable identifying a common official language between host and source country.	Compiled from CIA World Factbook.
COMMON BORDER	Indicator	Indicator variable identifying a common border between host and source country.	Compiled from CEPII, available online at http://www.cepii.fr/anglaisgraph/bdd/distances.htm.
DOMESTIC MARKET CAPITALIZATION	Percent	Average market capitalization as a percentage of GDP in source country calculated by dividing the value of traded stocks in percent of GDP through the turnover ratio.	Compiled from WDI.
REAL EXCHANGE RATE	Ratio	Real exchange rate in terms of price conversion factor multiplied with the nominal exchange rate.	WDI.
CUSTOMS UNION	Indicator	Indicator variable identifying a customs union between source and host country.	Compiled from WTO.
FREE TRADE AGREEMENT	Indicator	Indicator variable identifying a free trade agreement between source and host country.	Compiled from WTO, provided by Herger *et al.* (2005).
SERVICE AGREEMENT	Indicator	Indicator variable identifying a service agreement between source and host country.	Compiled from WTO, provided by Herger *et al.* (2005).
DURATION	# of days	# of days it takes to start a business in host country.	Djankov *et al.* (2002).
PROCEDURES	Count	# of procedures to be completed before starting a business.	Djankov *et al.* (2002).
SET-UP COSTS	Percent	Cost of starting business expressed as % of host country GDP per capita.	Djankov *et al.* (2002).
TIERS	Count	Number of government tiers.	Provided by Daniel Treisman.
SUB-NATIONAL EXPENDITURE SHARE	Percent	Ratio of sub-national government expenditure to total government expenditures, 1980–1995 average.	Provided by Nils Herger, based on IMF government finance statistics.

Table A1. *Continued*

Variable	Units	Description	Source
SUB-NATIONAL REVENUE SHARE	Percent	Ratio of sub-national government tax revenues to total government tax revenues, 1980–1995 average.	Provided by Nils Herger, based on IMF government finance statistics.
PROPERTY RIGHTS PROTECTION	Index Score	Rating of property rights in host country. Original values have been reversed on a scale from 1 to 5 with higher values indicating more secure property rights.	Heritage Foundation.
VOICE AND ACCOUNTABILITY	Index Score	Rating of voice and accountability in host country. Ranges from −2.5 to 2.5 with higher values indicating higher accountability.	Kaufman *et al.* (2005).
CORRUPTION	Index Score	Rating of the control of corruption in host country. −2.5 to 2.5 with higher values indicating a better control of corruption.	Kaufman *et al.* (2005).
RULE OF LAW	Index Score	Rating of the rule of law in host country. −2.5 to 2.5 with higher values indicating a stronger rule of law.	Kaufman *et al.* (2005).
GOVERNMENT EFFECTIVENESS	Index Score	Rating of government effectiveness in host country. −2.5 to 2.5 with higher values indicating higher effectiveness.	Kaufman *et al.* (2005).
CORPORATE TAX RATE	Percent	Statutory corporate tax rate.	Provided by Margarita Kalamova, compiled from Ernst & Young (2002).

REFERENCES

Bardhan, P. and D. Mookherjee (2000). 'Capture and governance at local and national levels', *American Economic Review, Papers and Proceedings*, 90(2), 135–39.
— (2005). 'Decentralizing antipoverty program delivery in developing countries', *Journal of Public Economics*, Special Issue ISPE, 89(4), 675–704.
Besley, T. and M. Smart (2003). 'Fiscal restraints and voter welfare', London School of Economics, *mimeo*.
Blonigen, B.A., R.B. Davies and K. Head (2003). 'Estimating the knowledge-capital model of the multinational enterprise: Comment', *American Economic Review*, 93, 980–94.
Boadway, R., M. Marchand and M. Vigneault (1998). 'The consequences of overlapping tax bases for redistribution and public spending in a federation', *Journal of Public Economics*, 68, 453–78.
Brennan, G. and J.M. Buchanan (1977). 'Towards a tax constitution for Leviathan', *Journal of Public Economics*, 8, 255–73.

— (1980). *The Power to Tax: Analytical Foundations of a Fiscal Constitution*, Cambridge University Press, Cambridge.

Buch, C.M., J. Kleinert, A. Lipponer and F. Toubal (2005). 'Determinants and effects of foreign direct investment: Evidence from German firm-level data', *Economic Policy*, 20(41), 52–110.

Cai, H. and D. Treisman (2005). 'Does competition for capital discipline governments? Decentralization, globalization, and public policy', *American Economic Review*, 95(3), 817–30.

Cameron, A.C. and P.K. Trivedi (1998). *Regression Analysis of Count Data*, Cambridge University Press, Cambridge.

— (1999). 'Essentials of count data regression', *mimeo*.

Carr, D.L., J.R. Markusen and K.E. Maskus (2001). 'Estimating the knowledge-capital model of the multinational enterprise', *American Economic Review*, 91(3), 693–708.

— (2003). 'Estimating the knowledge-capital model of the multinational enterprise: Reply', *American Economic Review*, 93(3), 995–1001.

Charlton, A. (2003). *Incentives for Foreign Direct Investment*, MPhil thesis, St John's College, Oxford University.

Dahlby, B. (1996). 'Fiscal externalities and the design of intergovernmental grants', *International Tax and Public Finance*, 3, 397–412.

De Mooij, R.A. and S. Ederveen (2003). 'Taxation and foreign direct investment: A synthesis of empirical research', *International Tax and Public Finance*, 10(6), 673–93.

Di Giovanni, J. (2005). 'What drives capital flows? The case of cross-border M&A activity and financial deepening', *Journal of International Economics*, 65(1), 127–49.

Djankov, S., R. La Porta, F. López-de-Silanes and A. Shleifer (2002). 'The regulation of entry', *Quarterly Journal of Economics*, 117, 1–37.

Dreher, A. (2006). 'Power to the people? The impact of decentralization on governance', KOF Working Paper No. 121.

Eaton, J. and M. Gersovitz (1983). 'Country risk: Economic aspects', in R.J. Herring (ed.), *Managing International Risk*, Cambridge University Press, Cambridge, 75–108.

Ernst & Young (2002). 'Worldwide corporate tax guide', Ernst & Young.

Fisman, R., and R. Gatti (2002). 'Decentralization and corruption: Evidence across countries', *Journal of Public Economics*, 83, 325–45.

Hayek, F.A. (1939/1960). *The Constitution of Liberty*, University of Chicago Press, Chicago.

Herger, N., C. Kotsogiannis and S. McCorriston (2005). 'Cross border acquisitions and institutional quality', *mimeo*, University of Exeter.

Hindriks, J. and B. Lockwood (2005). 'Fiscal centralization and electoral accountability', University of Warwick, *mimeo*.

Janeba, E. (2000). 'Tax competition when governments lack commitment: Excess capacity as a countervailing threat', *American Economic Review*, 90(5), 1508–19.

Johnson, W.R. (1988). 'Income redistribution in a federal system', *American Economic Review*, 78(3), 570–73.

Kaufman, D., A. Kraay and M. Mastruzzi (2005). *Governance Matters IV: Governance Indicators for 1996–2004*, World Bank, Washington.

Keen, M.J. (1998). 'Vertical tax externalities in the theory of fiscal federalism', *IMF Staff Papers*, 45, 454–85.

Keen, M.J. and C. Kotsogiannis (2002). 'Does federalism lead to excessively high taxes?', *American Economic Review*, 92(1), 363–70.

— (2003). 'Leviathan and capital tax competition in federations', *Journal of Public Economic Theory*, 5, 177–99.

— (2004). 'Tax competition in federations and the welfare consequences of decentralization', *Journal of Urban Economics*, 56, 397–407.

Keen, M.J. and M. Marchand (1997). 'Fiscal competition and the pattern of public spending', *Journal of Public Economics*, 66(1), 33–53.

Kehoe, P.J. (1989). 'Policy cooperation among benevolent governments may be undesirable', *Review of Economic Studies*, 56, 289–96.

Kessing, S.G., K.A. Konrad and C. Kotsogiannis (2006a). 'Federalism, weak institutions and the competition for foreign direct investment', Social Science Research Centre, Berlin, *mimeo*.

— (2006b). 'Federal tax autonomy and the limit of cooperation', *Journal of Urban Economics*, 59, 317–29.

Kessler, A., C. Lülfesmann and G. Myers (2005). 'Federations, constitutions and bargaining', *mimeo*.

Konrad, K.A. and K.E. Lommerud (2001). 'Foreign direct investment, intra-firm trade and ownership structure', *European Economic Review*, 45(3), 475–94.

Kydland, F.E. and E.C. Prescott (1980). 'Dynamic optimal taxation, rational expectations and optimal control', *Journal of Economic Dynamics and Control*, 2(1), 79–91.

Markusen, J.R. (1997). 'Trade versus investment liberalization', National Bureau of Economic Research Working Paper 6231, Cambridge, MA.

Markusen, J.R., A.J. Venables, D.E. Kohan and K.H. Zhang (1996). 'A unified treatment of horizontal direct investment, vertical direct investment, and the pattern of trade in goods and services', National Bureau of Economic Research Working Paper 5696, Cambridge, MA.

Markusen, J.R. and K.E. Maskus (2002). 'Discriminating among alternative theories of the multinational enterprise', *Review of International Economics*, 10, 694–707.

North, D.C. and B.R. Weingast (1989). 'Constitutions and commitment: The evolution of institutional governing public choice in seventeenths-century England', *Journal of Economic History*, 49, 803–32.

Oates, W.E. (1972). *Fiscal Federalism*, Harcourt-Brace, New York.

— (1999). 'An essay on fiscal federalism', *Journal of Economic Literature*, 37, 1120–49.

OECD (2002). *Fiscal Decentralization in EU Applicant States and Selected EU Member States*, Paris.

Qian, Y. and B.R. Weingast (1997). 'Federalism as a commitment to preserving market incentives', *Journal of Economic Perspectives*, 11, 83–92.

Riker, W.H. (1964). *Federalism: Origin, Operation and Significance*, Little, Brown and Company, Boston.

Rossi, S. and P. Volpin (2004). 'Cross-country determinants of mergers and acquisitions', *Journal of Financial Economics*, 74(2), 277–304.

Schnitzer, M. (1999). 'Expropriation and control rights: A dynamic model of foreign direct investment', *International Journal of Industrial Organization*, 17, 1113–37.

Seabright, P. (1996). 'Accountability and decentralisation in government: An incomplete contracts model', *European Economic Review*, 40, 61–89.

Shleifer, A. and R. Vishny (1993). 'Corruption', *Quarterly Journal of Economics*, 108(3), 599–617.

Stegarescu, D. (2006). *Decentralised Government in an Integrating World*, Physica-Verlag, Heidelberg.

Thomas, J. and T. Worrall (1994). 'Foreign direct investment and the risk of expropriation', *Review of Economic Studies*, 61, 81–108.

Tiebout, C.M. (1956). 'A pure theory of local expenditures', *Journal of Political Economy*, 64, 416–24.

Treisman, D. (1999a). 'Russia's tax crisis: explaining falling revenues in a transitional economy', *Economics and Politics*, 11, 145–69.

— (1999b). 'Political decentralization and economic reform: A game-theoretic analysis', *American Journal of Political Science*, 43, 488–517.

— (2000a). 'Decentralization and the quality of government', UCLA *mimeo*.

— (2000b). 'The causes of corruption: a cross-national study', *Journal of Public Economics*, 76, 399–457.

— (2003). 'Rotten boroughs', UCLA, *mimeo*.

UNCTAD (2001) *World Investment Report 2000*. United Nations Conference on Trade and Development, Geneva.

Wei, S.-J. (2000). 'How taxing is corruption on international investors?', *Review of Economics and Statistics*, 82(1), 1–11.

Weingast, B.R. (1995). 'The economic role of political institutions: Market-preserving federalism and economic development', *Journal of Law, Economics and Organization*, 11, 1–31.

Wildasin, D.E. (1989). 'Interjurisdictional capital mobility: Fiscal externality and a corrective subsidy', *Journal of Urban Economics*, 25, 193–212.

World Bank (2004). 'A better investment climate for everyone', *World Development Report 2005*, World Bank and Oxford University Press.

Wrede, M. (1996). 'Vertical and horizontal tax competition: Will uncoordinated *Leviathans* end up on the wrong side of the Laffer curve?', *FinanzArchiv*, 53, 461–79.

— (1997). 'Tax competition and federalism: The underprovision of local public goods', *FinanzArchiv*, 54, 494–515.

— (2000). 'Shared tax sources and public expenditures', *International Tax and Public Finance*, 7, 163–75.

Wage inequality, investment and skills

SUMMARY

In flexible labour markets, capital increases the productivity of skilled workers more than that of unskilled workers, and in the US faster investment is associated with wider wage inequality. But labour market institutions that keep unskilled workers' wages high also imply that firms may find it profitable to invest so as to boost those workers' productivity. Our empirical analysis based on industry-level data confirms that a higher capital intensity in Germany is associated with smaller wage differentials and with a larger share of unskilled workers in the labour costs. Changes in capital–labour ratios during the 1980s reduced wage differentials by 5–8% in German industries, while in the US capital deepening in such industries as machinery and retail was accompanied by an increase of wage differentials larger than 7%.

— *Winfried Koeniger and Marco Leonardi*

Economic Policy January 2007 Printed in Great Britain
© CEPR, CES, MSH, 2007.

Capital deepening and wage differentials: Germany versus US

Winfried Koeniger and Marco Leonardi

IZA and University of Bonn; University of Milan and IZA

1. INTRODUCTION

European labour markets are different not only in terms of unemployment (see Blanchard, 2006), but also in terms of wage inequality. The two aspects are related, in that distributional concerns may make it difficult to employ low-skilled people at low wages. In Germany, for example, a generous welfare system and powerful unions induce wage floors which prevent wages of unskilled workers from falling, and while unemployment is very much a problem there is substantial political support for such statements as 'A person who does a good job must earn enough to support a family' or 'It is shameful for a civilized society if human beings are put off with 3.50 euro per hour for decent work.'[1] In the US, where unemployment is much less of a problem, low wages are only mildly

For very helpful comments we thank Lans Bovenberg, Gilles Duranton, Omer Moav, Hans-Werner Sinn, Gianluca Violante, anonymous referees, participants of the *Economic Policy* panel in Vienna and the IZA workshop on 'Structural Change and Labor Markets'. Bertrand Koebel, Plutarchos Sakellaris, Focco Vijselaar, Gianluca Violante and Daniel Wilson kindly provided some of the data we use in our analysis. Financial support of DAAD-Vigoni is gratefully acknowledged.

The Managing Editor in charge of this paper was Giuseppe Bertola.

[1] The citations are from the recent German debate on minimum wages, published in the magazine *Stern*. Franz Müntefering (Minister for Labor and Social Affairs): 'Wer seinen Job richtig macht, muss auch so viel Geld bekommen, dass er seine Familie davon ernähren kann.' Michael Sommer (head of the German unions, DGB): 'Dass Menschen für anständige Arbeit mit 3.50 Euro pro Stunde abgespeist werden, ist beschämend für eine zivilisierte Gesellschaft' (*Stern*, 9.2.2006).

Economic Policy January 2007 pp. 71–116 Printed in Great Britain
© CEPR, CES, MSH, 2007.

constrained by the federal minimum wage ($5.15 per hour), unemployment benefits are short-lived, and union membership rates average half the German ones over the 1970–90 period, and have declined much more sharply.

1.1. Two theories and the facts

These institutional differences are related to the differences in the evolution of unemployment and wage inequality in these and other countries (see for example, Blau and Kahn, 1996; Abraham and Houseman, 1995; and further references in Koeniger *et al.*, 2006). The wage differential between skilled and unskilled workers has remained remarkably stable in Germany but has increased substantially in the US in the last decades (see Tables A1 and A2 in the Appendix, which we will discuss further below). Krugman (1994, p. 37) argued that 'the growth of earnings inequality in the United States – and quite possibly therefore much of the rise in structural unemployment in Europe – has been the result of technological changes that just happen to work against unskilled workers'. Indeed, different labour market institutions may have implied different responses in the European and US labour markets in the aftermath of a common positive shock to the relative demand for skilled labour. In countries like the US where wages are flexible, the positive relative demand shock for skills increases the skill-wage differential. In countries like Germany with wage floors, the relative unemployment among the unskilled increases.

This 'Krugman hypothesis' of a well-defined trade-off between wage inequality and employment is at the core of the debate on labour market policy. But is the choice facing developed countries so simple? In this paper, we bring to bear on the relevant issues another interesting and less well-known cross-country difference: the capital–labour ratio has increased more in Germany than in the US in the period 1975–91, especially in the unskilled labour intensive sectors.

A larger increase of the capital–labour ratio in Germany than in the US may appear consistent with the standard 'Krugman hypothesis': after an adverse relative demand shift, institutions that prevent unskilled wages from falling might well induce substitution not only between unskilled and skilled workers, but also between labour and capital (Blanchard, 1997; Caballero and Hammour, 1998). As we discuss below, however, this cannot explain the fact that unskilled employment and value added have behaved very similarly in both countries and across sectors with different skill intensities. It is also difficult for the 'Krugman hypothesis' to explain other aspects of the evidence, such as the fact that the stronger German increase of the capital/labour ratio in unskilled labour intensive sectors was driven by faster capital accumulation rather than by a decline of (unskilled) employment levels.[2]

---

[2] Some empirical features related to those we document have already been noted in the literature. Krueger and Pischke (1998) show that employment trends are similar across skill groups in Germany (and not worse for the unskilled as the 'Krugman hypothesis' implies). Nickell and Bell (1996) have argued that the evolution of the relative unemployment of unskilled workers in Germany is much the same as in the US in the 1980s and early 1990s while wage inequality is stable in Germany but rising in the US.

Since it is difficult for the 'Krugman hypothesis' to explain the different joint evolution of capital, employment, and wage inequality in Germany and the US, what alternative mechanisms might have been at work? We confront the evidence with an alternative hypothesis, according to which wage floors reduce the skill premium by encouraging more investment in capital equipment complementary to unskilled workers (in Germany). This perspective blends institutions and skill-biased investment as an explanation for the different evolution of wage differentials in the US and Germany, and views changes in the relative price of capital equipment as a key common driving process. Cheaper capital implies higher capital intensity and, as in Krusell *et al.* (2000), can explain some of the increase in the skill-wage differential in the US since the 1970s (see also Caselli, 1999; Moaz and Moav, 2004; Hornstein *et al.*, 2005; and Leonardi, 2006). We point out that the same change in the relative price of capital has very different implications if investment is also influenced by institutional wage floors, and labour market frictions do not allow firms to easily substitute expensive unskilled workers with cheaper capital. When replacing a worker would require costly 'search and matching' activities, workers can appropriate, through higher wages, a portion of their employers' investments in their job's productivity, and this 'hold-up' problem reduces employers' incentives to invest. This is mitigated when wages are rigid, and unresponsive to productivity. Hence, wage rigidity increases employers' incentives to train their workers or invest in capital complementary to their skills (Acemoglu and Pischke, 1999). To the extent that wage floors lead to increases in the productivity of low-wage workers, rather than to their substitution with other factors, smaller skill-wage differentials are accompanied by more intense investment directed to unskilled workers.

1.2. Empirical evidence

Some previous literature has looked into the relationship between minimum wages and training finding inconclusive or quantitatively small effects (see Neumark and Wascher, 2001; Acemoglu and Pischke, 2003, for evidence within US states and Pischke, 2005, for a comparison across OECD countries).[3] We focus on capital investment and we investigate whether firms invest in different types of capital goods in Germany compared with the US because of institutional constraints on wages of unskilled workers. For example, firms might invest in a conveyor belt which is complementary to unskilled labour due to wage floors in Germany whereas in the US with flexible wages firms invest more in high-tech machines for a chemical laboratory which are complementary to skilled labour. Since we do not have data which allow

---

[3] Nickell and Bell (1996), in a model without capital, argue that unskilled workers have enjoyed higher wages and low unemployment rates in Germany (relatively to the US at least until 1991) because the German schooling system induces a stronger performance of the bottom half of the ability range thanks to the comprehensive system of vocational training. We investigate this hypothesis further below when we check the robustness of our results defining the skill premium according to different skill groups.

us to link explicitly workers by skill type to capital equipment, our empirical strategy is to use information on factor prices and quantities to test whether capital equipment is more complementary to unskilled workers in Germany than in the US.

We provide descriptive evidence at the industry level on the association between capital–labour ratios and wage differentials in the US and Germany. Following Acemoglu and Pischke (1999) and Acemoglu (2003), we investigate how institutions affect wage differentials and also firm investment. We find evidence consistent with the view that German institutions distort investment towards unskilled workers and thus compress wage differentials relative to the US. Our estimates imply that capital deepening in Germany in the 1980s is associated with a reduction in the skill-wage differential of about 5–8% in most industries. In the US instead, capital deepening is associated with an increase of the wage differential between 7 and 8% in important industries like machinery and retail. Similarly, capital deepening in the 1980s is associated with a 3–5% lower share of unskilled labour in the wage bill in the US in sectors like machinery and retail whereas there is no significant association in Germany. This suggests that differences in firm investment are an important part of the overall effect of institutions on wage inequality and on the unskilled labour share.[4]

1.3. Policy relevance

Our empirical results indicate that the implications of institutions for equality and efficiency interact with investment patterns, as well as with structural shocks, in important and policy relevant ways. Through their influence on productivity-enhancing investments, the effect of labour market institutions on inequality may well be stronger than would be implied by their commonly considered direct effects on wages and employment. But of course investments that foster unskilled workers' productivity are no free lunch. The investment that is induced by wage rigidities in equilibrium reduces employers' profits and job-creation incentives. Thus, our theoretical perspective and empirical findings can explain patterns of industry development. As industries with low skill intensity invest relatively more, and in low-skill-complementary capital, there will be slower growth of high-skill intensive sectors like banking and insurance, and business, personal or health services. This may explain the slow pace of structural change in Germany, where manufacturing industries are still strong, and its negative implications for employment growth (which in other countries mostly takes place in the service sector), as well as for efficiency and income growth. While our results may tempt governments to subsidize investment complementary to unskilled labour, in

---

[4] These results relate to previous work of Beaudry and Green (2003) who show that the wage differential between skilled and unskilled workers would have been smaller in the US if the capital accumulation in the US had matched the German pattern. Whereas they analyse interactions between different accumulation patterns and changes in technology, this paper proposes institutions as one possible explanation for why countries use different capital intensities (see also Pischke, 2005).

order to alleviate the employment and profit impacts of institutions that constrain wages of unskilled workers, that goal is addressed more directly and efficiently by policies that improve the human capital of workers at the bottom of the skill distribution.

2. THEORETICAL BACKGROUND AND EMPIRICAL PREDICTIONS

In this section we first present the predictions of a simple neoclassical model and confront these predictions with some facts. These facts then motivate an alternative explanation based on costly locating and hiring of workers.

2.1. A neoclassical view

Neoclassical theory predicts that a binding minimum wage for unskilled workers induces substitution by either capital, skilled labour or both where the quantitative importance of this cost-induced substitution depends on the chosen production function. We focus on substitution between capital and unskilled labour since the facts we present below show striking differences in capital investment between the US and Germany in the *unskilled labour intensive* sectors.

Consider a sector in which capital is combined with unskilled labour and the rental price of capital is determined in the global capital market (see Web Appendix I.A for formal derivations). Capital and unskilled labour are imperfectly substitutable and each factor has decreasing returns to scale (but both of them together have constant returns to scale). With such a standard production function, a binding wage floor induces substitution of unskilled labour by capital as unskilled labour becomes more costly. This is illustrated in Figure 1 which plots the marginal product of capital as a function of the capital–labour ratio. In a flexible economy like the US, the equilibrium ratio $(K/L)_{flex}$ equates the marginal product to the global rental price of capital. In a rigid economy like Germany instead the employment level of unskilled labour will be lower so that that the marginal product of *unskilled labour* equals the binding minimum wage. Lower employment also implies a higher capital–labour ratio $(K/L)_{rigid}$, which is not sustainable, however, since the marginal product of capital is below the rental price of capital on global capital markets. The only way that the unskilled labour intensive sector can remain in business in Germany is that production falls and unskilled workers become unemployed until the final good is sufficiently scarce and its price increases (Krugman, 1995). The final-good price goes up until the marginal product of both capital and unskilled labour are high enough to equal the global rental price of capital and the minimum wage, respectively. In the figure, the increase of the final-good price shifts the marginal-product of capital up and the capital–labour ratio $(K/L)_{rigid}$ to the left (the dashed lines in the figure). The new capital–labour ratio is $(K/L)^*$.

Thus, this simple neo-classical framework predicts that in the unskilled labour intensive sector of a rigid economy like Germany,

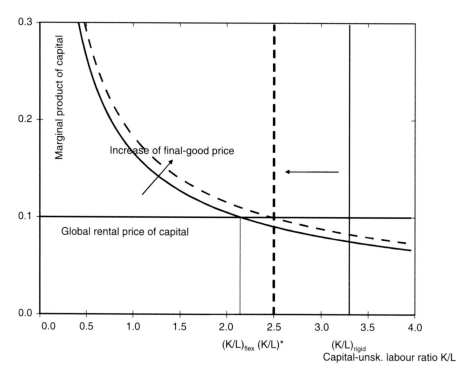

Figure 1. The minimum wage and capital–labour substitution in the neoclassical model

Source: Authors' calculation.

- the capital–labour ratio is higher because unskilled employment is lower,
- the output of the unskilled labour intensive sector is lower than in the flexible economy.

An adverse shock to the relative demand of unskilled labour (as analysed by Krugman, 1995) increases the bite of the minimum wage and also the difference between the rigid and flexible economy in terms of these two predictions.

2.2. Some facts

In order to assess the relevance of this theoretical perspective, let us first consider the evolution of the capital–labour ratio and the skill-wage differential in the US and Germany for two important industries in our sample period: the machinery industry as a representative industry for the manufacturing sector and the retail industry for the service sector. To facilitate comparisons, we normalize all variables to one in 1975.

Figure 2 displays three-year averages on the evolution of wage differentials by education (which we also call skill premium, that is, the logarithm of the ratio of wages of workers with some college education over the wages of workers with no

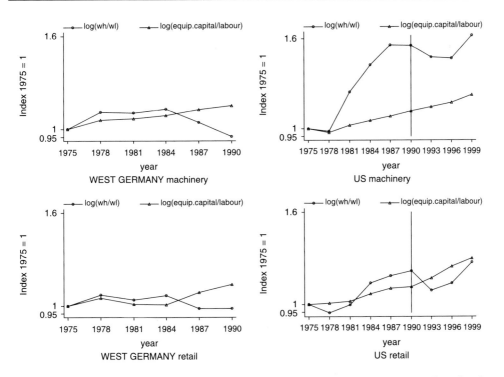

Figure 2. Wage differentials by skill and capital equipment per worker in the machinery and retail industry in the US and West Germany, 1970s–1990s, three-year averages

Source: Authors' calculations based on CPS, IAB, and national accounts data.

college education) and the capital-equipment per worker in the US and Germany. Wage differentials increased substantially in the US especially in the 1980s whereas they remained relatively stable in West Germany. On the contrary, the capital–labour ratio increased more in West Germany than in the US. In Germany, the capital–labour ratio increased by 15% in the machinery sector and by 13% in the retail sector from 1975 to 1990. In the same sectors and in the same period in the US, the increase was only 11% until 1990 (the vertical line in the right panels of Figure 2).

The descriptive graphs could be explained by simple capital–labour substitution. We now provide further evidence, however, which casts doubt on the simple explanation of factor substitution. In Table 1 we take a closer look at the predictions of the neoclassical framework in the previous subsection concerning value added, capital equipment and *employment*. Capital–labour substitution, due to wage floors induced by generous unemployment insurance, of course also implies *unemployment*. This might be considered a more problematic measure, however, since it depends on the generosity of benefit payments as well as on other policy details which matter for labour market participation, for example whether these benefits are paid conditional on active job search.

Table 1. Average three-year percentage changes of production factors and value added in the 1980s

	Capital equipment/ Value added		Low-skilled employment/ Value added		Capital equipment/ Low-skilled employment		Skilled/Low-skilled employment		Value added	
	US (1)	Germany (2)	US (3)	Germany (4)	US (5)	Germany (6)	US (7)	Germany (8)	US (9)	Germany (10)
Low-skill-intensive industries	-0.029 (0.082)	0.043 (0.048)	-0.037 (0.077)	-0.054 (0.035)	0.008 (0.098)	0.098 (0.051)	0.072 (0.038)	0.115 (0.039)	0.037 (0.051)	0.046 (0.046)
Skill-intensive industries	0.101 (0.085)	0.076 (0.065)	-0.026 (0.046)	-0.049 (0.037)	0.127 (0.084)	0.125 (0.077)	0.098 (0.022)	0.158 (0.052)	0.085 (0.035)	0.099 (0.040)

Notes: The averages for the low-skill and skill-intensive industries are weighted by real value added. The ten low-skill-intensive industries (in increasing order in the US in year 1975) are Textiles, Plastic and Leather, Wood, Stone and Clay, Food and Tobacco, Construction, Primary Metals, Transport Equipment, Agriculture and Mining, Electrical Machinery. The ten skill-intensive industries are Transport and Communication, Machinery, Utilities, Paper and Printing, Professional Goods, Wholesale and Retail, Business and Personal Services, Chemicals and Petroleum, Health Services, Banking and Insurance. The correlation with the skill intensity ranking in Germany is 0.76. Standard deviations are in parentheses. See the Web Data Appendix for further details.

Source: Authors' calculations.

In Table 1 we display average three-year percentage changes of factor inputs and value added for the ten sectors with the highest skill ratios in the US in 1975, and compare them with changes in the ten sectors that, on the same basis, appear least skill-intensive. We find the following patterns:

- Capital equipment (columns (1) and (2)): changes in capital equipment per unit of value added are quite evenly spread across all industries in Germany. In the US instead, they are concentrated in the skill intensive industries.
- Unskilled employment (columns (3) and (4)): unskilled employment per value added falls more in Germany than in the US. The difference, however, is larger in the skill-intensive industries.
- Capital-unskilled labour ratio (columns (5) and (6)): consequently, the capital–labour ratio increases in Germany across all industries, but only in the skill-intensive industries in the US.
- Skill intensity (columns (7) and (8)): the skill intensity increases in all industries both in the US and Germany.
- Value added (columns (9) and (10)): value added grows at similar rates in the US and Germany but more in the skill-intensive industries in both countries.

These patterns are robust to using the different capital or skill measures which we introduce in our robustness checks below. The most striking fact of Table 1 is the larger increase of the capital–unskilled labour ratio in the low-skill-intensive sectors in Germany compared with the US which is accompanied by faster labour productivity growth in Germany (the inverse of the statistics reported in Table 1, columns (3) and (4)).[5]

The patterns documented in Table 1 are not in line with the two predictions of the simple neoclassical framework in the previous subsection. The stronger increase of the capital–unskilled labour ratio in the low-skill intensive sectors is due to a larger increase in capital equipment (the numerator) rather than a stronger decrease of unskilled employment (the denominator). Moreover, the difference in the employment trend of unskilled workers between Germany and the US is larger, if anything, in the skill-intensive industries. In a neoclassical model with some factor complementarity, one would expect more capital–unskilled labour substitution in the low-skill intensive sector and a relative decrease in the output of that sector. Furthermore, this fall in output should be larger in Germany. Empirically, however, value added grows at a similar rate in the low-skilled industries in the US and Germany.

2.3. A search-and-matching view

Confronting comparative evidence with the neoclassical model's predictions, we have found that simple cost-induced substitution mechanisms do not suffice to explain the

[5] The differences in capital investment across developed countries have been already noted by Pischke (2005). He finds that investment growth is more positively correlated with the skill intensity across sectors in Anglo-Saxon countries than in continental European countries where labour market institutions compress wages.

differences in capital investment in the unskilled labour intensive sectors. Substituting expensive unskilled workers with capital, in fact, need not be as easy in reality as in that model. If workers and employers meet in a random, costly process, some investment decisions have to be taken *after* a worker (of a given skill level) has been located and hired: and since replacing that worker would be costly, the worker can in general try and bargain for higher wages if investment increases the job's productivity. The employer is 'held up' by the worker which lowers the employer's incentive to invest.

In models with such frictions in the labour market, rent sharing and binding minimum-wage constraints, different mechanics are at work (see Web Appendix I.B for formal derivations) and can explain some key aspects of the evidence in Table 1. To see how the interaction between investment and wage floors may be very different from that outlined in Section 2.1, imagine a US firm that produces shirts. The firm posts a vacancy for a worker who produces such shirts where we suppose that the wage of the worker is half of his output. There are two ways to produce the shirt, either by using a sewing machine or by hand. The firm decides whether to buy a sewing machine only after the vacancy is matched with a worker. Once the vacancy has been matched, it is costly to search for another worker to perform the same task so that the firm employs either an unskilled or a skilled worker depending on whom it meets first. After the match, the firm decides whether to increase the productivity of the worker by purchasing a sewing machine. Here it is important to note that the firm only appropriates half of the output increase if the sewing machine is bought since the worker's bargained wage increases in output. Thus, if workers have low skills and are not productive enough, firms do not find it optimal to invest. Firms only purchase the sewing machine if the vacancy is matched with a more productive skilled worker: this worker knows better how to operate the sewing machine so that the output increase, which is shared between the worker and firm, is larger to begin with. In this case, the hold-up problem implies purchases of the sewing machine only for matches with skilled workers.

Imagine the same firm in Germany where wage floors are binding for low-skilled workers. It is now easy to see how the presence of wage floors will change the purchase decision for German firms that employ low-skilled workers (these workers are still hired when located since it is costly to search for a more skilled worker). Although a binding minimum wage implies a higher wage *level*, it also implies no *change* of the wage if the firm buys the sewing machine. Hence, the minimum wage mitigates the hold-up problem and results in firms buying the sewing machine also for unskilled workers. In general, this is true also if investment in the sewing machine increases the worker productivity above the minimum wage. In this case unskilled workers appropriate part of the productivity increase in the form of a higher wage and the skill premium is reduced further. Given that the minimum wage is binding *before* the firm's investment, the change of the wage after the investment is still smaller compared with a US firm so that the hold-up problem continues to be mitigated.

Now consider how a fall in the price of the sewing machine affects the investment incentives in Germany and the US. As a starting point, consider a price of the sewing machine that is so high that neither German nor US firms purchase sewing machines. The interesting case is now if the price of the sewing machine falls so that US firms buy a sewing machine for the skilled but not for the unskilled workers (if the price is very low, US firms also invest in unskilled workers). German firms buy a machine for both skilled *and* unskilled workers even if the price falls to a level at which US firms do not find it optimal to invest in unskilled workers. The reason is, as explained above, that firms in Germany appropriate more of the job's productivity increase since binding minimum wages make wages of unskilled workers less responsive to output changes. Because investment of firms is less skill-biased in Germany, the skill premium remains more compressed than in the US.

This simple example is meant to illustrate the important differences in investment incentives in the US and Germany. The interaction of the well-documented fall in the price of capital (Krusell *et al.*, 2000) with labour market institutions in this modelling environment can explain the stronger investment in the unskilled labour intensive sector in Germany than in the US which we observed in Table 1. Notice that a fall in the price of capital does not help to fully reconcile the qualitative predictions of the neoclassical model with the empirical evidence. Cheaper capital helps neoclassical firms to sustain the minimum wage so that output of the final good needs to fall less and fewer unskilled workers become unemployed. In terms of Figure 1, the loci of the marginal product of capital and $(K/L)_{\text{rigid}}$ would shift less so that the new capital–labour ratio $(K/L)^*$ is higher at the new *lower* global rental price of capital. The problem remains, however, that in contrast to the facts in Table 1 the higher capital–labour ratio in the unskilled labour intensive sector in Germany compared with the US should be borne out in differences in employment rather than investment. Finally, if the price of capital falls so much that the minimum wage is no longer binding, there should be no differences in employment and the use of capital equipment between the US and Germany. In Figure 1, the minimum wage stops to bind if the global rental price is below the intersection point of $(K/L)_{\text{rigid}}$ and the schedule of the marginal product of capital.

Let us briefly discuss the main differences between the neoclassical framework and the search-and-matching environment which is used for the argument in this subsection. Costly search for vacancies by workers and costly filling of these vacancies by employers imply that each job match earns rents after such a match is formed between a worker and employer. These rents are split so that, compared with the neoclassical framework, employers can afford to pay a minimum wage above the neoclassical flexible market wage. Employers anticipate this higher labour cost and will post fewer vacancies so that job creation is lower. As a consequence equilibrium unemployment is higher, like in the neoclassical model, unless the minimum wage helps to alleviate the search congestion externality: firms do not take into account that their posting of vacancies congests the market and in the aggregate reduces the probability of filling a vacancy for each individual employer.

The fact that workers and firms split rents is especially important since wages are bargained after the firm sinks the full cost of the investment and the worker appropriates part of the gains of that investment. Knowing this, firms invest less. The key in this subsection is that labour market institutions may alleviate this hold-up problem and increase investment (Acemoglu, 2003). In the example given above, unskilled workers receive the binding minimum wage before and after the investment so that they do not appropriate part of the rents of the *additional* investment and firms are more willing to invest in them. We have chosen minimum wages as a simple way to explain this mechanism. In reality, in countries like Germany, other institutions like benefit replacement ratios or unions do not only matter for the wage floor but also for the share of rents which the worker appropriates in the bargain. Hence, the hold-up problem is not necessarily fully solved by these institutions as in the simple example presented in this subsection. Such complications are less important, however, if the level of bargaining is not at the level of the individual worker-firm pair but at the level of a centralized union. In this case, the union sets wages at the aggregate level and individual employers take them as exogenous when deciding about investment. Therefore, the hold-up problem does not arise.

It is important to emphasize that investment in unskilled workers in Germany is a second-best response by firms to distorted wages. Firms would not boost low-skilled workers' productivity in the absence of the minimum wage floor, and their costly investments in the presence of the distortion reduce job creation so that overall efficiency is lower than in the flexible economy.

We have assumed for our argument that matches are found at random. If firms could 'direct' their search more towards a specific pool of workers, it would be towards the more productive skilled workers, especially if the minimum wage is binding. A fall in the price of capital then would imply a different employment trend for skilled and unskilled workers in Germany compared with the US which is not supported empirically in our sample period 1975–91.

Importantly for the empirical application, costly search and matching implies inter-industry wage differentials. The same worker can earn a different wage depending on the firm and industry. Search frictions imply imperfect labour mobility and impede factor-price equalization across industries. These more realistic implications of the model come at the cost of simplifications concerning the missing distinction between jobs and firms or an explicit modelling of sector-specific labour supply.

3. EMPIRICAL SPECIFICATION AND DATA

The theory and simple evidence reviewed in the previous section indicate that, in frictional labour markets, cheaper capital prices can induce a smaller increase of the wage differential in Germany than in the US if institutions (which induce wage floors) encourage employers to invest in equipment that is complementary to unskilled labour.

In this section, we proceed to seek more formal and detailed support for this prediction using industry-level data on skill-wage differentials and capital–labour ratios for the US and Germany. We estimate the different degree of complementarity between capital and unskilled labour in the two *countries*, exploiting data variation across *industries* and *time*. Variation across time is essential since our hypothesis is that the interaction of a time change (the fall of the price in capital) and country differences (labour market institutions that induce a wage floor) cause the different degree of complementarity between capital equipment and worker skill types. Industry variation is useful because the effect of labour market institutions and the fall of the price of capital can be expected to differ across them.

The ideal data would allow us to combine information on the skills and type of equipment capital of a worker. Unfortunately it is impossible to tell which (skilled or unskilled) workers use each piece of equipment in each industry. Under the maintained hypothesis, however, that technology is the same (for each industry) in the two countries, and to the extent that wages contain information on workers' productivity, standard production-function relationships between factor quantities and prices allow to infer whether changes in capital intensity influence the productivity of skilled and unskilled workers differently in the two countries.

In our specifications, we control for unobserved time-invariant differences across industries and countries as well as industry-specific linear time trends. These trends control for time changes of omitted variables like biased changes in technology within industries (as is suggested by the more formal expressions for the specifications in Box 1). Since these trends may pick up a lot more than technology, such as changes in demand conditions or price and cost shocks, we will report results using R&D as an alternative observable measure of technology (see Table 4 in Section 4 below).

Box 1. Econometric specifications

Specification 1. The first specification approximates the relationship between the skill premium, skill intensity and capital equipment which is implied by a nested CES production function (Acemoglu, 2002, and Krusell *et al.*, 2000). Assume that the production function uses capital K, skilled labour H and unskilled labour L so that:

$$F(K, H, L) = \left[\lambda \left[\mu (A_k K)^\rho + (1 - \mu)(A_h H)^\rho \right]^{\frac{\sigma}{\rho}} + (1 - \lambda)(A_l L)^\sigma \right]^{\frac{1}{\sigma}}$$

The skill premium is then:

$$\frac{w_h}{w_l} = \frac{\lambda (1 - \mu)(A_h H)^{\rho - 1} \left[\mu (A_k K)^\rho + (1 - \mu)(A_h H)^\rho \right]^{\frac{\sigma - \rho}{\rho}}}{(1 - \lambda)(A_l L)^{\sigma - 1}}$$

Since the elasticity between unskilled labour and capital is $1/(1 - \sigma)$ and the elasticity between skilled labour and capital is $1/(1 - \rho)$, capital is more complementary to skilled than unskilled labour if $\sigma > \rho$. In this case, the skill premium increases if firms employ more capital as:

$$\partial \left(\frac{w_h}{w_l} \right) / \partial K > 0 \text{ if } \sigma > \rho$$

If we assume that the same production function applies in each industry i in country c, we can approximate the skill premium at time t as a function of capital and the skill intensity:

$$\ln \left(\frac{w_h}{w_l} \right)^c_{it} = a^c_i + \gamma^c_1 \ln \left(\frac{H}{L} \right)^c_{it} + \gamma^c_2 \ln(K)^c_{it} + \gamma^c_3 \ln \left(\frac{A_h}{A_l} \right)^c_{it}$$

The coefficient of interest is γ^c_2, which indicates the degree of complementarity between capital and skilled labour. Under the assumption that the US and Germany have the same technology for each industry, our hypothesis that capital is more complementary to unskilled labour in Germany than in the US corresponds to $\gamma^{US}_2 > \gamma^{GER}_2$.

This specification implies permanent differences a^c_i across industries. This assumption is difficult to defend in a neoclassical model but can be more easily motivated by a search and matching framework in which costly search frictions prevent factor-price equalization across industries (see Section 2.3).

Several concerns arise in estimating the specification above, which we discuss further in the paper. The first concern is the measurement of the technology changes $(A_h / A_l)^c_{it}$. We proxy these by using industry-specific linear trends in all specifications and in Table 4 we report results using R&D as an alternative observable measure of technology. The second concern is the measurement of skills and capital so that we provide robustness checks using different measures in Section 4. See also the description of the measures in the data section, Section 3.1. The third concern is the endogeneity of the skill intensity and capital–labour ratio which we discuss further in Section 4 when we present the results.

Specification 2. The second specification is based on a trans-log cost function C with two variable factors, skilled labour H and unskilled labour L for industry i in country c and year t:

$$C \left[\log(w_h)^c_{it}, \log(w_l)^c_{it}, \log(K)^c_{it}, \log(y)^c_{it}, A^c_{it} \right]$$

where w_h, w_l are the wages of the skilled and unskilled, and y denotes value added. Capital intensity K and technology A are quasi-fixed factors. From Sheppard's lemma it follows that the cost share of unskilled labour in the wage bill is:

$$\left(\frac{w_l L}{w_h H + w_l L} \right)^c_{it} = \alpha^c_i + \beta^c_1 \ln \left(\frac{w_h}{w_l} \right)^c_{it} + \beta^c_2 \ln(K)^c_{it} + \beta^c_3 \ln(y)^c_{it} + \beta^c_4 A^c_{it}$$

The equation for the share of H is redundant because the cost shares sum to unity. If $\beta_2^c > 0$, capital and unskilled labour are complementary. The hypothesis that wage-compressing labour market institutions in Germany induce investment in capital equipment which is more complementary to unskilled labour than in the US is a test of $\beta_2^{GER} > \beta_2^{US}$.

As in specification 1 we include industry fixed effects to control for time-invariant unobserved differences across industries and countries, and industry-specific linear trends to proxy changes in technology. The same estimation issues of endogeneity and measurement arise (as for specification 1) which will be discussed further in Section 4 and in the data section, Section 3.1.

The differences in the degree of capital–skill complementarity in the US and Germany are thus estimated by using time variation that remains after controlling for linear time trends within industries. We argue that the different estimates of capital–skill complementarity for the US and Germany are due to interactions between (rather persistent) differences in labour market institutions and cheaper capital. As we discuss further in Section 5, however, we will not be able to rule out completely that the estimates are affected by changes of other country-specific factors. As an attempt to check the importance of labour market institutions for our results, we use available measures of institutions that vary over time (but not across industries) in each country. If the differences in the estimates of capital–skill complementarity are due to changes in labour market institutions in the US and Germany, we expect that the difference in the estimates becomes less significant if we include measures for institutions in our specifications. We have also tried to add interactions of these measures with the (price of) capital equipment to gauge the importance of the interaction directly. The limited sample size and variation, however, prevented us from estimating these interactions with enough precision.

We estimate two specifications that relate employment, capital, and wages (see also Box 1). The first specification can be derived from standard profit-maximizing behaviour of neoclassical firms, as in Section 2.1, and focuses on the relationship between skill premia and capital equipment (for US evidence based on aggregate data see Krusell *et al.*, 2000; Acemoglu, 2002). Estimating this specification with industry-level data is consistent with a search-and-matching model in which skill premia may differ across industries because of costly frictions. The second specification is based on cost minimization and relates labour shares (compounding wages and employment) to capital equipment (for example, Machin and van Reenen, 1998). In both specifications, the coefficient estimate of capital equipment allows us to infer the degree of capital–skill complementarity in each of the two countries.

In the first specification, a positive coefficient of the capital–labour ratio indicates complementarity between capital equipment and skilled labour. The prediction that capital is more complementary to unskilled labour in Germany than in the US corresponds to the test that the coefficient of the capital–labour ratio is *smaller* in Germany than in the US.

The second specification links the share in labour costs of *unskilled* workers to the capital–labour ratio. In this case a positive coefficient of the capital–labour ratio indicates complementarity between capital equipment and *unskilled* labour. The prediction that capital is more complementary to unskilled labour in Germany than in the US corresponds to the test that the coefficient of the capital–labour ratio is *larger* in Germany than in the US.

3.1. Data

In this subsection we mention how we construct the data used for the analysis and briefly describe some of the variables before we provide the results of the estimations in the next section.

3.1.1. Equipment capital. We use data on capital equipment from the national accounts (Bureau of Economic Analysis and Statistisches Bundesamt, respectively). We construct the stock of capital equipment for Germany using the series on gross capital equipment formation and applying the perpetual inventory method. Capital equipment in both countries is deflated with the chain-price indices provided by the respective statistical office. Since these price deflators have been criticized for their accuracy, we check the robustness of our results below using an alternative deflator provided by Cummins and Violante (2002). As adjustment of capital equipment takes time and we are interested in the medium and low-frequency variation of the data, we use three-year averages and check robustness of the results for five-year averages. This also helps us to reduce problems of measurement error in the data for higher frequencies.

3.1.2. Wages and employment by skill type. Wages and employment by skill and industry are constructed using CPS data (May surveys and Outgoing Rotation Group) for the US and the dataset on the social-security records from the Institut für Arbeits- und Berufsforschung (IAB) for Germany. For both countries our sample includes employees in full-time employment, age 20–60 with potential labour market experience up to 39 years. In the German IAB dataset we only use the information on West Germany and drop all East German observations after 1990. We prefer to omit later years in our estimations since disentangling East and West German data is not straightforward for all variables. Thus, in the estimations the sample period is 1975–91. Note further that the CPS is a representative sample of all employees whereas the IAB dataset is a 1% random sample of employees with a social-security record.

We define skilled workers as those with at least some college in the US and at least *Abitur* (high-school degree) in Germany. This educational skill measure achieves some comparability (if imperfect) across the two countries because 13 years of schooling imply a high-school degree in Germany and some college in the US. All those with less education in the respective country are classified as unskilled. Although Fitzenberger *et al.* (2005) find evidence of under-reporting for higher education degrees in the IAB data, they show that these measurement issues are not important when they estimate the college premium, controlling for other worker characteristics like gender and experience in Mincer-type wage regressions. We find that our results are robust when we use the college premium obtained from such regressions which control for some observable worker heterogeneity (see Table 3 in Section 4 below).

One major issue is to compare skills across countries. Our skill measure implies that the skill *ratio* (H/L) is much smaller in Germany, with an average of 0.05 across industries, than in the US, with an average of 0.5 (see also the industry averages in Tables A1 and A2). The main reason is that the education system in the US and Germany is very different. The German education system is a two-tier system in which vocational training is important to enter many occupations. Only those who intend to go to college obtain a formal high school degree (*Abitur*). Thus, a high school degree is not as prevalent in Germany as in the US and approximately 60% of the working population in Germany between 1975 and 1991 had only a vocational degree. Hence, we also construct two alternative skill measures for Germany. One can be considered an upper bound and includes all employees with a vocational degree in the skilled group. In this case the sample average of the skill ratio is 2.43 (see Table A2, third column). Since this skill ratio is substantially higher than in the US, we also construct an alternative measure where we only include in the skilled group those workers with a vocational degree who are in a white-collar position (*Angestellter*). These vocational degrees should be most comparable to college education in the US. With this skill measure the resulting average skill-ratio for Germany is 0.68 and more similar to the US (see Table A2, fourth column). However, the skill ratio is still quite high in Germany in some industries. For example, the skill ratio is 3.91 in the banking and insurance sector which has a lot of white-collar workers. Because of these measurement problems we will check the robustness of our results for all of the three measures.

We prefer the education-based measure of skills since it measures the level of general human capital. The other measures contain more firm-specific skills acquired through vocational training, and are more likely to be endogenous in our application: a firm can make a worker more productive with equipment capital or firm-specific training. Of course, as Acemoglu and Pischke (1999) point out, the same applies to general training if minimum wages are binding but we suspect the endogeneity problem to be less severe for a measure of general skills. We suspect that few (if any) workers are classified as having a high-school degree or some college in Germany just because firms have subsidized their general education due to wage compression.

3.1.3. R&D intensity. We proxy changes in technology by industry-specific linear trends in our econometric specification. As an alternative observable measure for technology we also use the R&D intensity in Section 4. The R&D intensity is defined as R&D expenditure divided by value added. Value added is taken from the 60-Industry Database available online at the Groningen Growth and Development Centre. The data on R&D expenditure are from the Stan-Anberd database provided by the OECD. An obvious criticism of the OECD measure is that it need not be related to technology improvements in the same industry and country. As an alternative, we construct a measure of technology change embodied in one important input, capital equipment. This variable is based on data by Wilson (2002) who combines data on R&D expenditure for capital equipment goods with data on capital equipment inputs by industry.

3.1.4. Descriptive statistics.   Tables A1 and A2 display the averages of the main variables of interest: the wage differential, skill intensity and capital equipment per worker. Besides reporting the averages for each industry in the 1970s, we compute the three-year average percentage changes in the sample period. Tables A1 and A2 show that while the skill intensity has increased in all industries in both countries, the skill premium has increased in the US but has remained stable in Germany. Equipment capital per worker has increased in all industries but one in Germany and eight in the US. In most industries capital equipment per worker has increased at a higher rate in Germany than in the US.

4. RESULTS

Table 2, panel A, presents the results of the first specification that relates the skill premium to the capital–labour ratio. Panel B presents the results of the regression of the share of unskilled labour in the wage bill on the capital–labour ratio. The coefficients are estimated on the full sample of 20 industries in the US and West Germany in the period 1975–91. All specifications include industry fixed effects to control for unobservable heterogeneity and industry-specific trends to proxy for changes in technology. All observations in the regressions are weighted by industry employment.

   The robust finding in panel A is that capital equipment and the skill premium are less positively associated in West Germany than in the US. Consistently with our hypothesis we find that capital is more complementary to unskilled labour in Germany, that is, the point estimate of capital equipment for Germany is smaller.

   One concern in our estimations is the endogeneity of the skill intensity. This endogeneity could arise if the supply of skills responds to the skill premium. Endogeneity is a concern for us only if it biases the coefficient estimate of capital equipment which is our main interest. To assess the sensitivity of our results we estimate specifications with and without skill intensity. We exclude the skill intensity in columns (1a) and (2a). The results show that a 1% increase in capital equipment per worker is associated with an increase of the skill premium of 9 basis points in the US and with a statistically insignificant decrease of the skill premium in Germany. These results

Table 2. Estimation results for the skill premium and unskilled-labour share as a function of capital equipment per worker

Panel A: Dependent variable is the log-skill premium

Independent variables	Benchmark specification without skill intensity		Benchmark specification		Benchmark specification with institutions	
	US (1a)	Germany (2a)	US (3a)	Germany (4a)	US (5a)	Germany (6a)
log(equipment capital per worker)	0.087 (0.039)**	−0.039 (0.025)	0.091 (0.042)**	−0.032 (0.025)	0.046 (0.044)	−0.028 (0.023)
log(skill intensity)			−0.019 (0.070)	−0.108 (0.063)*	0.026 (0.065)	−0.101 (0.058)*
union density					0.313 (0.589)	1.814 (0.454)***
minimum wage					−0.474 (0.152)***	
Adjusted R-squared	0.9614	0.9341	0.9610	0.9956	0.9676	0.9460

Panel B: Dependent variable is the share of unskilled labour in the wage bill

Independent variables	Benchmark specification without skill premium		Benchmark specification		Benchmark specification with institutions	
	US (1b)	Germany (2b)	US (3b)	Germany (4b)	US (5b)	Germany (6b)
log(equipment capital per worker)	−0.073 (0.019)***	−0.001 (0.005)	−0.057 (0.017)***	−0.004 (0.005)	−0.058 (0.019)***	−0.002 (0.005)
log(value added)	−0.005 (0.018)	−0.003 (0.013)	−0.009 (0.016)	0.002 (0.013)	−0.020 (0.018)	−0.014 (0.013)
log(skill premium)			−0.204 (0.044)***	−0.057 (0.019)***	−0.233 (0.050)***	−0.081 (0.020)***
union density					−0.129 (0.267)	0.291 (0.098)***
minimum wage					−0.037 (0.068)	
Adjusted R-squared	0.9929	0.9957	0.9944	0.9961	0.9944	0.9965

Notes: Estimated with ordinary least squares using 120 observations for 20 industries based on three-year averages 1970–91 in both countries. All regressions include industry dummies and industry-specific time trends for each country. Observations are weighted by employment in each industry. Standard errors in parentheses. See the notes of Table 1 and the Web Data Appendix for further details. * 10%; ** 5%; *** 1% significance level.

Source: Authors' calculations.

are confirmed in our benchmark specification which includes the skill intensity in columns (3a) and (4a), suggesting that the possible endogeneity of the skill intensity does not bias the coefficient estimate of capital. Consistently with a downward sloping relative demand for skilled labour, the coefficient of the skill intensity is negative in both countries.

The theory we want to test implies that the differences in the degree of capital–skill complementarity across countries are due to labour market institutions. When laying out the econometric specification in Section 3, we have discussed one imperfect but informative way to assess the importance of changes in labour market institutions. Controlling directly for measures of labour market institutions which vary across time (but not across industries), we assess the importance of institutions for our results by checking whether the differences in the coefficient estimates of capital become less significant for both countries when we insert these measures in our specifications.

In columns (5a) and (6a) we include the OECD measures of the federal minimum wage and union density for the US and union density for Germany (Germany has no economy-wide minimum wage, minimum wages have only been introduced in some industries in the 1990s). The coefficient of the minimum wage in the US is negative and significant as expected. The coefficient of the union density in Germany, however, is positive and significant. This result is not necessarily opposite to the expected wage-compressing effect of more powerful unions across industries since the positive coefficient is estimated using only aggregate time variation in union density. More interestingly, the results show that the coefficient of capital becomes insignificant in the US once we control for institutions. This suggests that the coefficient in the benchmark specification (which excludes institutional measures) reflects the effect of time-varying institutions on the skill premium through capital investment. Getting more directly at the effect of the interaction of *persistent* differences of labour market institutions across countries and the change in the price of capital is more challenging and the limited variation in our data has not allowed us to estimate interaction terms with enough precision.

Although the coefficient estimates are not estimated precisely enough in some specifications to allow us to formally reject the hypothesis that the coefficients are the same in the US and Germany at standard significance levels, our evidence suggests that capital equipment is more complementary to unskilled workers in Germany than in the US. This result remains robust if we use capital equipment per worker *hour* to control for differences in hours worked across countries, time and industries.

The insignificance of the coefficient of capital in Germany may pose a concern about our interpretation of the coefficient on capital as a measure of complementarity between capital and skills. It could be that we find an insignificant coefficient because relative wages in Germany do not reflect relative productivities (for example because of institutional constraints) rather than because capital is more complementary to unskilled labour. This cannot explain, however, the *significantly* negative coefficient of capital equipment for Germany when we use alternative measures for skills (Table 3 below). Moreover, this concern should apply less to our specification with the unskilled labour share which we discuss next because this dependent variable combines wage and employment effects.

One remaining concern is that the capital–labour ratio is endogenous. Even after controlling for unobserved time-invariant differences across industries and linear industry-specific time trends, firms within an industry may change their capital in response to a change in the skill premium. Without a suitable source of exogenous variation that would allow us to instrument the capital–labour ratio, we cannot interpret the coefficients as causal. Endogeneity is more of a problem in this specification than in the next specification which *assumes* that capital is a quasi-fixed factor so that it is predetermined when firms decide about employment of skilled and unskilled labour. Obviously this assumption may be violated and the estimates below also have to be interpreted with care.

Panel B reports the results of the regression of the unskilled labour share on the capital intensity. These results provide even stronger evidence that equipment capital is more complementary to unskilled labour in Germany than in the US. Consistently with our hypothesis we find that the point estimate of capital equipment for Germany is larger in this specification. This is good news if one believes the assumption that capital is a quasi-fixed factor so that endogeneity is less of a concern.

Similar to Panel A we approach the issue of the possible endogeneity of the skill premium comparing the results including or excluding the skill premium from the estimated equation. The issue of endogeneity arises because changes in wages affect both the skill premium (the regressor) and the share of workers in the wage bill (the dependent variable). If we exclude the skill premium from the regression, the coefficients on capital intensity in columns (1b) and (2b) show that a 1% increase in capital intensity is associated with a reduction of the share of the unskilled in the wage bill of 7 basis points in the US. The association is insignificantly different from zero in Germany. These results indicate that unskilled labour and capital are substitutes in the US but much less so in Germany. The implied elasticity of substitution evaluated at the mean of the unskilled labour share is −0.104 in the US and −0.005 in Germany. These results are qualitatively robust to the inclusion of the skill premium (columns (3b) and (4b)) and suggest that endogeneity of the skill premium is not a serious issue for the estimation of the coefficient of capital.

Compared with the results of panel A, adding the measures of labour market institutions to the specification leaves the difference between the coefficients for the US and Germany nearly unchanged (columns (5b) and (6b)). In this case, time-variation of institutions does not matter for the different degree of capital–skill complementarity in the two countries. This does not exclude that interactions between (persistent differences in) labour market institutions and exogenous shocks (like the fall in the price of capital) matter for the different degree of capital–skill complementarity.

Concerning the control variables, value added is never significant in any of the regressions whereas the skill premium has the expected negative sign. The institutional variables are not significant for the US but the union density in Germany is positively related to the unskilled workers' share in the wage bill. This is more in line with the expected effect of more powerful unions compared with the results of panel A.

As a further robustness check for the results of both specifications in panels A and B, we dropped one industry at a time from our sample. We found that for both specifications the difference in the coefficients of capital equipment does not depend on a specific industry. Moreover, the results are robust to restricting the sample to the manufacturing sector and to using five-year averages (not reported). Finally, the adjusted R-squared statistic shows that our specifications explain most of the variation in the data.

Quantitative implications   To gauge the quantitative size of the association between capital equipment and the skill premium in West Germany, we use the predicted skill premium obtained from the benchmark regression specification in Table 2, column (4a). We compare these values with the predicted values obtained holding capital equipment per worker constant at the initial level in 1975. Taking the difference of these two measures of predicted skill premia at the end of the sample (1991), we find that the skill premium would have been about 5–8% higher in most industries in Germany had capital per worker remained unchanged at its value in 1975.

The industries where the accumulation of capital equipment per worker had the smallest effect on the wage differential are primary metals, utilities, business and personal services, and health services. The biggest effect of capital equipment per worker is in the banking sector where the wage differential would have been 33% higher had the capital–labour ratio stayed at the same level as of 1975.

Doing the same exercise for the US (on the basis of the coefficients in Table 2, column (3a)), we find that, had the capital–labour ratio not grown beyond its 1975 level, the skill premium would have been between 7 and 8% lower in important industries like machinery and retail than what was observed in 1991. Weighting the industry-specific results by valued added, we find an aggregate average change of 3%. This number is below the estimates presented in Krusell *et al.* (2000) who, in a similar exercise, use aggregate time-series data for the US and a different estimation method. One of the main differences is that we control for (industry-specific) time trends in our specification. Time trends are likely to be correlated with capital deepening at the industry level so that their inclusion in the regression changes the estimate of the capital coefficient. A linear time trend, for example, wipes out the significant effect of capital on the skill premium for aggregate data in the US (Acemoglu, 2002).[6] Hence, it is not surprising to find a smaller association of capital deepening and skill premia than Krusell *et al.* (2000) in our regressions which include linear industry-specific trends. Moreover, the differences in the degree of capital–skill complementarity between Germany and the US are robust to the inclusion of trends in our estimations.

---

[6] Acemoglu (2002), Table 2, finds that a 1% fall of the relative price of capital equipment is associated with a 0.323% increase of the college premium in a regression without a time trend. With a time trend this number falls to 0.051%.

Doing the same counterfactual exercise for the share of unskilled labour in the wage bill (on the basis of the coefficients in Table 2, columns (3b) and (4b)), we find that changes in capital equipment per worker have a negligible effect on the share of unskilled labour in Germany. In the US instead, the unskilled labour share would have been between 3 and 5% higher in the machinery and retail industries had capital equipment stayed at its level in 1975.

4.1. Robustness

We probe the robustness of the results across two dimensions. Regarding the definition of the skill premium and the unskilled labour share, we check robustness using two alternative measures for skills for Germany. Concerning the measurement of capital and technology, we construct two alternative measures for the capital stock and a measure for embodied R&D as proxy for process innovations.

4.1.1. Robustness of wage measures.   The first two columns of Table 3, panels A and B, display the results for two alternative skill measures in Germany. As mentioned in the data section, Section 3.1.2, skill intensities are much lower in Germany than in the US if we define skilled workers as those workers with some college education. A common concern is that this is because workers without a high-school degree are of higher quality in Germany than in the US due to the important vocational training system (Nickell and Bell, 1996). Hence, we construct a first measure (columns (1a) and (1b)) which includes all employees with a vocational degree in the skilled group and can be considered an upper bound. The second skill measure (columns (2a) and (2b)) only includes those workers with a vocational degree in the skilled group who are in a white-collar position.

We find that in both specifications these alternative skill measures deliver even stronger support for the hypothesis of more complementarity of capital and unskilled labour in Germany. Equipment capital in Germany is negatively associated with the skill premium and positively associated with the share of the unskilled in the wage bill. In both specifications the coefficients are significant at least at the 5% level. These two alternative education-based skill measures have the drawback that the extent of vocational training may be itself endogenous to the institutional environment. Hence, we prefer the skill measure which we use in our benchmark specification.

Worker heterogeneity   As a further robustness check, we improve our measure of the wage differential exploiting the information in the CPS and IAB micro data sets to control for differences in worker characteristics such as gender and experience across industries. The wage differential is obtained by regressing log wages on a dummy for education (at least some college in the US and *Abitur* or more in Germany) controlling for experience, experience squared, gender and their interactions. The regression is run for each industry and year in the CPS and IAB data, respectively. We then keep the

Table 3. Robustness for different measures of the wage differential

Panel A: Dependent variable is the log-skill premium

Independent variables	Include vocationally trained in skilled group for Germany (two alternative measures)		College premium of Mincer-type wage regression	
	Germany (1a)	Germany (2a)	US (3a)	Germany (4a)
log(equipment capital per worker)	−0.022	−0.030	0.079	−0.037
	(0.009)**	(0.013)**	(0.035)**	(0.023)
log(skill intensity)	−0.113	−0.096	0.018	−0.060
	(0.027)***	(0.034)***	(0.059)	(0.057)
Adjusted R-squared	0.9898	0.9857	0.9344	0.9148

Panel B: Dependent variable is the share of unskilled labour in the wage bill

Independent variables	Include vocationally trained in skilled group for Germany (two alternative measures)		College premium of Mincer-type wage regression	
	Germany (1b)	Germany (2b)	US (3b)	Germany (4b)
log(equipment capital per worker)	0.018	0.030	−0.053	−0.001
	(0.007)**	(0.009)***	(0.012)***	(0.002)
log(value added)	−0.006	−0.044	−0.001	−0.002
	(0.018)	(0.023)*	(0.011)	(0.005)
log(skill premium)	0.067	−0.079	−0.428	−0.063
	(0.074)	(0.067)	(0.035)***	(0.008)***
Adjusted R-squared	0.9960	0.9990	0.9955	0.9951

Notes: Standard errors in parentheses. * 10%; ** 5%; *** 1% significance level. The Mincer-type wage regressions in columns (3) and (4) are run for each industry and year in the CPS and IAB, respectively. The regressors are education and experience, experience squared, gender and their interactions. The coefficients of the education dummy are a measure of the education wage differential after controlling for the other variables. We use the inverse of the standard errors to weigh each obtained estimate. See the notes to Table 1 and the Web Data Appendix for further details.

Source: Authors' calculations.

coefficients of the education dummy as a measure of the college premium. We use the inverse of the standard errors to weigh each obtained estimate.

The results of both specifications in columns (3) and (4) in Table 3 indicate that controlling for observed worker heterogeneity leaves the results nearly unchanged with respect to the benchmark specification in Table 2, columns (3) and (4).

Overall the difference in the coefficients of capital equipment in Germany compared with the US is robust across regressions which are based on quite different skill measures. This gives us some confidence that the difficulties in comparing education-based skill measures between the US and Germany are not driving the results. We now investigate whether measurement of capital is important for our results.

4.1.2. Robustness of capital measures and embodied R&D. Table 4 displays the results for different measures of capital and embodied R&D. Since an appropriate deflator of capital is notoriously hard to build, we first check the robustness of the benchmark specification in Table 2, columns (3) and (4), by applying the capital–price deflator provided by Cummins and Violante (2002). This deflator controls better for quality adjustments and updates the price deflator for capital equipment in the US constructed by Gordon (1990). Compared with the deflator of Cummins and Violante, the deflator of the Bureau of Economic Analysis underestimates quality improvements and thus results in a slower decline of relative prices for capital equipment. We apply the deflator of Cummins and Violante, available for 1975–99, to our measure of capital in the US and Germany. The estimation results in Table 4, columns (1a) and (2a), show that the capital equipment is no longer significantly positively associated with the skill premium in the US[7] but is still larger than the coefficient for Germany which remains negative and is now significant at the 10% level. The results for the share of unskilled labour in the wage bill are more robust for the US (see columns (1b) and (2b)): capital equipment is negatively associated with the share of unskilled labour in the wage bill in the US but not in Germany.

The RAS procedure The construction of internationally comparable capital stocks requires particular attention with respect to the use of comparable price deflators when constructing capital from investment series and comparable depreciation rates and lifetime periods for different equipment types.

We further investigate whether the different results for Germany are driven by compositional effects in terms of different equipment types. We use information from the German statistical office on capital formation for different equipment types to construct a time series for capital equipment by investment good and industry, applying the so-called RAS procedure (see the Web Data Appendix for a detailed description). This procedure allows us to apply separate depreciation rates and price deflators for five different categories of equipment goods, before we aggregate the series at the industry level. This way of constructing the stock of capital equipment implies a growth rate in the stock of capital equipment that is more than twice as high (see Sakellaris and Vijselaar, 2005, for similar results).

Using the new measure, the coefficient of capital equipment per worker turns positive for Germany (see Table 4, column (3a)). The result is not robust, however, if we use the capital equipment for communication technology in Germany (see column (4a) where we lose some observations due to data availability). In this case the coefficient returns to be negative and is significant at the 5% level.[8] Moreover,

---

[7] The lack of positive significance is not inconsistent with Krusell *et al.* (2000) since we have time trends in our specifications which are correlated with capital deepening.

[8] Using the series for the other types of equipment, we do not find significant results. We also used the series on office machinery and computers for Germany constructed by Falk and Koebel (2004): the coefficient of capital equipment per worker and the corresponding standard error changes to −0.0254 (0.013) which is significant at the 10% level. This coefficient is less negative than the coefficient of capital equipment in the benchmark specification of Table 2, column (4a).

Table 4. Robustness for different measures of capital and embodied R&D

Panel A: Dependent variable is the log-skill premium

Independent variables	Capital deflated with Violante and Cummins deflator		Capital calculated with RAS	Software capital calculated with RAS	Benchmark with embodied R&D instead of trends	
	US (1a)	Germany (2a)	Germany (3a)	Germany (4a)	US (5a)	Germany (6a)
log(equipment capital per worker)	−0.002	−0.040	0.045	−0.017	0.032	−0.012
	(0.044)	(0.023)*	(0.013)***	(0.008)**	(0.029)	(0.030)
log(skill intensity)	0.037	−0.110	−0.136	−0.085	0.076	−0.024
	(0.071)	(0.062)*	(0.059)**	(0.063)	(0.045)	(0.027)
log(embodied R&D)					0.058	−0.002
					(0.016)***	(0.009)
Number of observations	120	120	120	106	72	72
Adjusted R-squared	0.9586	0.9368	0.9429	0.9581	0.9126	0.8782

Panel B: Dependent variable is the share of unskilled labour in the wage bill

Independent variables	Capital deflated with Violante and Cummins deflator		Capital calculated with RAS	Software capital calculated with RAS	Benchmark with embodied R&D instead of trends	
	US (1b)	Germany (2b)	Germany (3b)	Germany (4b)	US (5b)	Germany (6b)
log(equipment capital per worker)	−0.050	−0.004	0.006	0.0003	−0.042	−0.0004
	(0.017)***	(0.004)	(0.003)*	(0.002)	(0.015)***	(0.011)
log(value added)	−0.005	−0.0004	−0.018	−0.007	−0.061	−0.076
	(0.016)	(0.012)	(0.013)	(0.012)	(0.010)***	(0.010)***
log(skill premium)	−0.239	−0.057	−0.069	−0.069	−0.331	0.062
	(0.044)***	(0.019)***	(0.020)***	(0.025)***	(0.068)***	(0.052)
log(embodied R&D)					−0.029	0.008
					(0.008)***	(0.004)**
Number of observations	120	120	120	106	72	72
Adjusted R-squared	0.9942	0.9961	0.9963	0.9965	0.9786	0.9691

Notes: Standard errors in parentheses. * 10%; ** 5%; *** 1% significance level. Regressions in columns (1)–(4) include industry dummies and industry-specific trends. Regressions in columns (5) and (6) only include industry dummies. See the notes of Table 1 and the Web Data Appendix for further details.

Source: Authors' calculations.

the new measure is positively associated with the share of unskilled labour in the wage bill in Germany at a significance level of 10% (see column (3b)). If we use only capital equipment for communication technology, the coefficient remains positive but is no longer significant. Thus, whereas the association of the new measure with the skill premium gives mixed results, the coefficients on the association with the share of unskilled labour in the wage bill are more supportive for the hypothesis that capital equipment is more complementary to unskilled labour in Germany than in the US.

Embodied R&D   As mentioned when we discussed the econometric issues, approximating technology change with (industry-specific) time trends leaves much to be desired since it is unclear what the time trends really capture. In this section we use R&D as a more direct measure for technology change instead of the industry-specific time trends. The measure of R&D expenditure provided in the OECD STAN database captures expenses for all inputs (such as capital and labour) used for product as well as process innovations. These measures turn out not to be significant if added to the specifications (not reported). An obvious criticism of the OECD measure is that this R&D expenditure need not be related to technology improvements in the same industry and country. As an alternative measure we construct technology change embodied in one important input, capital equipment, for the manufacturing industries.

   Wilson (2002) combines data on R&D expenditure for capital equipment goods provided by the National Science Foundation with data on capital equipment inputs by industry from the Bureau of Economic Analysis for the years 1973–97. This allows us to compute a measure of R&D embodied in the capital equipment per value added in each industry which is more likely to capture process innovations. Assuming that the R&D contained in capital goods is the same in the US and Germany, we use the different investment into capital equipment by good type and industry to construct the corresponding series for Germany. Columns (5a) and (6a) show that the coefficient for R&D embodied in capital equipment is positively and highly significantly associated with the skill premium for the US, reducing the size of the coefficient of capital equipment so that it is no longer significant. The coefficient of embodied R&D for Germany is negative but not significant. Moreover, R&D intensity embodied in capital equipment is negatively and significantly associated with the share of unskilled labour in the wage bill in the US but positively in Germany (see columns (5b) and (6b)).

   Overall the results for alternative measures of capital equipment and embodied R&D in capital equipment suggest that the difference in the association with the skill premium and unskilled labour share in the US and Germany is very robust. The differences seem to stem from different types of capital investment in the US and Germany and thus also different technology improvements embodied in capital goods.

5. DISCUSSION

The empirical evidence presented above is consistent with our hypothesis that wage-compressing labour market institutions might have induced changes in capital equipment or embodied R&D which in turn have reduced the skill premium and increased the share of unskilled labour in Germany compared with the US in the period 1975–91.

Of course, the available data do not allow us to interpret the different coefficient estimates as causal. Since the US and Germany differ across many dimensions, one main concern is that the correlations reflect changes of other omitted variables which might cause both changes in the skill premium and capital equipment or R&D. For example, governments that regulate the labour market do also tend to regulate the product market or financial market. Then the estimated results could capture the effects of product or financial market institutions rather than of labour market institutions. In this case controlling for time-invariant differences across countries and industries would help little to distinguish the effect of different types of institutions. Institutions in product markets and financial markets, however, have become more similar in Germany and the US as both markets have been deregulated since the 1970s (see, for example, Alesina *et al.*, 2005). Labour markets instead have remained much more regulated in Germany. This is why we consider it more likely that the differences in the estimated coefficients on capital in the two countries (which remain after controlling for industry dummies and industry-specific time trends) capture the persistent differences of labour market institutions rather than the withering differences in product and financial market institutions (which are more likely to be accounted for by industry trends).

5.1. Employment trends versus investment patterns

We have argued that the different association between the skill premium and the capital–labour ratio in the US and Germany is due to different investment patterns in these countries (that is, we stress differences in the numerator rather than the denominator of the capital–labour ratio). We now try to distinguish the quantitative importance of changes in capital from changes in employment. While there is no strong evidence for different trends in the *composition* of employment across skills in the US and Germany in our sample period (see Table 1 and Beaudry and Green, 2003), *total* employment growth has been higher in the US than in Germany.

As a first rough assessment of whether these different employment trends are important, we do a simple statistical decomposition exercise. We apply the US employment growth rates to the German employment levels in 1975 for each industry. We then use this employment series to compute the counterfactual capital–labour ratio had Germany experienced the same employment performance as the US. Since the US has had a stronger employment performance than Germany, the counterfactual capital–labour ratio is smaller. Recall that the predicted values for the skill premium with the actual German capital–labour ratios imply a decrease of the wage differential of about 5–8% in most manufacturing industries (see Section 4 above). The predicted values for the skill premium using the *counterfactual* capital–labour ratio (holding the estimated coefficient constant), still imply a fall in the skill premium in Germany for 15 industries out of 20. The negative association between the capital–labour ratio and the skill premium does not vanish if we correct for the worse employment performance in Germany, suggesting that the differences in capital investment between the US and Germany are important. This relates to results of Beaudry and Green (2003) who find in a similar exercise that wages of the low educated workers would have been 17% lower had Germany experienced the US employment miracle, and 40% lower if Germany had also had the US capital accumulation.

5.2. Alternative explanations

In principle, all changes of omitted variables, which are correlated with capital investment and factor prices and are not captured by the linear trends, challenge our interpretation of the results. For example, differences in technology change that are not captured by the linear trends might explain our findings. Such differences across countries could arise, for example, because skills of workers in Germany are more specific than in the US. Krueger and Kumar (2004) have argued that growth differences between the US and Europe are explained by the higher degree of skill specificity in Europe.[9] In their model, more vocational training hampers technology adoption and, if technology change is skill-biased, this implies that the skill premium increases less in Europe than in the US. Slower technology adoption *per se*, however, cannot explain a negative correlation between the skill premium and capital equipment or embodied R&D in Germany which we find in most specifications. Moreover, the amount of vocational training might be related to wage compressing institutions, as firms can make workers more productive by giving them equipment and/or training them. To distinguish these two hypotheses further, one would need detailed data with a time series dimension and information on capital equipment and worker training.

Another view is that wage differentials in Germany are compressed because labour market institutions imply not only wage floors but also wage ceilings. In the latter case, however, the skilled would be paid below their marginal product and firms would appropriate all productivity increases. Therefore capital investment and technology change should be directed more towards skilled workers in Germany. As we have seen in Table 1, however, the striking difference in capital investment patterns between Germany and the US occurs in the unskilled labour intensive sectors. Moreover, wages of the very unskilled workers have fallen in the US since the 1970s (Acemoglu, 2002) whereas this has not been the case in Germany. Since both economies

---

[9] See also Gould *et al.* (2001) for a model with endogenous specific versus general skill accumulation to explain changes in wage inequality in the US.

are exposed to similar exogenous changes, this suggests that wage floors have prevented the wages of German unskilled workers from falling to levels that are as low
as in the US.

Instead of the fall in the price of capital, an alternative exogenous driving force is
more openness to trade, which occurred both in Germany and the US since the 1970s.
Interactions of more openness with different labour market institutions can also
explain the observed differences in the evolution of skill premia or labour shares and
capital equipment. The consensus is that the direct effect of trade on skill premia, in
flexible economies like the US, and employment, in more rigid countries like Germany, has been quantitatively small in our sample period 1975–91, although this
debate is not completely settled. Interactions of openness and labour market institutions, however, are a plausible alternative explanation. A fall of the relative price of
the unskilled labour intensive good caused by more openness to trade (especially with
less developed countries) makes the minimum wage binding for firms producing that
good, generating similar results as the fall in the price of capital discussed in this
paper (Koeniger, 2006). Distinguishing these alternative explanations is challenging
and requires much better data than we currently have, especially if one takes seriously
the interactions between exogenous changes in prices (due to changes in technology
or market structure), institutions and investment.

Finally, the larger increase of the capital–labour ratio in Germany compared with
the US documented in Figure 2 could be explained by Germany converging towards
the same balanced growth path as the US. This cannot easily explain, however, why
at the same time the skill premia diverge in both countries and the larger increase of
the capital–labour ratio occurs mostly in the (unskilled labour intensive) manufacturing
industries which are already strong in Germany compared with the US.

6. CONCLUSIONS AND POLICY IMPLICATIONS

We have argued that capital deepening affects the evolution of the wage differential
between skilled and unskilled workers differently in countries with different labour
market institutions. If labour market institutions raise the wage of unskilled workers
in Germany and frictions in the labour market make locating and hiring of workers
costly, a fall in the price of capital can induce investment of firms into capital equipment that is more complementary to unskilled workers. Instead in the US, where
wage floors are lower, firms invest more in high-skilled workers.

We have provided evidence consistent with this view based on an industry panel
for West Germany and the US between the 1970s and 1990s. We have shown that
capital equipment per worker is less positively associated with the skill premium in
West Germany than in the US. Furthermore, capital investment tends to increase the
share of unskilled labour in the labour cost in Germany but decreases it in the US.
This descriptive evidence is robust to using alternative measures of capital and skills.
Our descriptive evidence is not conclusive: more detailed firm-level data is needed to

shed further light on the mechanism of how and why firms invest in unskilled workers in countries with stronger wage-compressing institutions. This would also allow to control further for changes in the composition of firms and workers over time.

Moreover, it would be interesting to extend the analysis to later years. Germany experienced a large increase in unemployment of unskilled workers in the 1990s which suggests that unskilled labour substitution has become more important. It would be interesting to investigate whether one can still detect more complementarity of capital and unskilled labour in Germany than in the US notwithstanding the big increase in unskilled unemployment after German reunification.

Our evidence has important policy implications. The debate on the role of institutions needs to consider the indirect effect of institutions on wage inequality due to distorted investment incentives. Our estimates imply that capital deepening in Germany in the 1980s is associated with a reduction in the skill premium of about 5–8% in most industries. In the US instead, capital deepening is associated with an increase of the wage differential between 7 and 8% in important industries like machinery and retail. Similarly, capital deepening in the 1980s is associated with a 3–5% lower share of unskilled labour in the wage bill in the US in the same sectors but there is no significant association in Germany. If we consider that at least some of this effect of capital is due to institutions, we have to reconsider the importance of institutions in the classic efficiency-equality trade-off. Institutions might have stronger effects on wage inequality than commonly perceived (if both the standard direct effect *and* the indirect effect through investment matter) and they distort investment decisions in favour of the unskilled. The investment distortions which boost the productivity of unskilled workers are no free lunch, however, and also imply lower employment. Hence, our findings also bear on the observed differences in the speed of structural change across developed countries (Rogerson, 2005). Since industries with low skill intensity in Germany invest relatively more and some of the service sectors like banking and insurance, business, personal or health services are skill intensive, the distorted incentives for capital investment in Germany may slow down the structural change from manufacturing industries towards services. Since most of the employment growth occurs in the service sector, these distortions may reduce employment growth, efficiency and income growth.

Since our results suggest that institutions induce higher investment complementary to unskilled labour in Germany, governments may be tempted to subsidize this investment in order to reduce the fall of firms' profits and the implied lower job creation. Policies that directly try to improve human capital at the bottom of the skill distribution, however, are more promising to reduce inequality in economic outcomes since they avoid the allocation and incentive distortions implied by subsidies in a second-best environment. An alternative would be to deregulate markets to reduce rents and mitigate the hold-up problem. More efficient financial markets would also allow workers to improve their productivity by paying for training out of their own pockets. However, more competitive markets at the same time make it more difficult to achieve distributional goals by institutional wage floors as labour and product demand become more elastic.

Discussion

Lans Bovenberg
Tilburg University, CentER, Netspar and CEPR

This paper combines two views on what lies behind the development of the skill premium. The literature has debated extensively whether institutional or technological factors are responsible for changes in wage inequality over time. This paper argues that institutions and technologies interact in determining the wage premium. The institutional setting affects the direction of technology and the nature of the capital–skill complementarity. In particular, institutions that compress wages result in less complementarity between capital investment and skill so that capital investment decreases rather than increases the skill premium. One thus cannot look at technology and institutions in isolation, but should explore the interaction between them.

This research also sheds a different light on the wage-compressing institutions in Europe. It is often argued that these institutions create more low-skilled unemployment and inactivity by pricing the low skilled out of the labour market. This paper argues instead that these institutions also encourage societies to invest more in low-skilled workers, thereby raising their productivity. Hence, wage-compressing institutions do not price low-skilled labour out of the labour market, but rather encourage employers to invest more in low-skilled workers. This is an important hypothesis, and if true, would have major consequences for how we should appreciate various European labour-market institutions that keep the wages of unskilled labour at high levels.

While I find the hypothesis intriguing, I am not yet convinced by the evidence in this paper that wage-compressing institutions would indeed invest low-skilled workers into the labour market rather than pricing these workers out of the labour market.

Do unskilled workers appropriate returns in the presence of wage floors?

Let me explain why, beginning with the analytical framework. The paper argues that minimum wages alleviate the hold-up problem associated with investments in physical capital. In the absence of minimum wages, workers tax away part of the benefits from investment. They do so by raising wage demands after firms have sunk their investments, thereby raising quasi rents from the employer-employee relationship. In the presence of binding minimum wages, in contrast, the model in the paper assumes that the benefits from investments accrue mainly to shareholders. The reason is that the wage remains at the binding wage and is thus not increased after investment has been sunk.

The presumption that employers enjoy all the benefits of investment in the presence of minimum wages relies on the strong assumption that the minimum wages do not affect the wage negotiations themselves. An alternative, more natural, assumption would be that the minimum wages affect the outside option of the workers. Indeed, wage floors in Germany are not the result of a legal minimum wage, which in fact does not exist, but rather of welfare benefits, which provide an outside option for workers. With welfare benefits determining the outside option for German workers, employers and employees negotiate over the quasi rents over and above the outside option of workers. Hence, workers are able to appropriate a share of the benefits of an investment – also in the presence of minimum wages. In fact, the empirical results show that investment in Germany does indeed raise unskilled wages. This shows that unskilled workers do indeed appropriate part of the benefits from investment. In fact, the empirical results suggest that German unskilled workers are more successful than US unskilled workers in appropriating the benefits from investment. Hence, the empirical results falsify the theoretical presumption that German labour-market institutions (including minimum wages) induce unskilled workers to expropriate a smaller part of the benefits of capital investments.

Substitution or complementarity?

The key policy question is whether higher wages for unskilled labour result in less low-skilled employment (as employers get rid of unskilled workers) or whether high labour costs induce firms to invest more in unskilled labour. The paper argues that German investment does not substitute for unskilled labour but rather augments the productivity of the unskilled.

In order to resolve the important issue whether high prices for unskilled labour cause less unskilled employment or upgrading of the productivity of the low skilled, I would encourage the authors to examine in their future work the volume of sectoral employment and output over time. Looking only at sectoral investment and wages is not enough to resolve whether capital investment is a substitute or complement to unskilled employment. For example, one would want to know whether the volume of employment of workers with little initial schooling is rising in sectors with high levels of capital investment. Indeed, it may well be that capital investments correlate with higher low-skilled wages because both investment and low-skilled wages are increased by early retirement schemes and active labour-market programmes that reduce the supply of low-skilled labour to a particular sector.

Indeed, in many European countries the unskilled workers in certain sectors were taken out of the labour market through disability or early retirement schemes in the period considered; many unskilled workers who were the victims of industrial restructuring were simply put in soft-landing schemes such as social insurance or early retirement schemes (i.e. hidden unemployment). In Germany, unemployment schemes have in fact acted as early retirement schemes, especially after the surge in unskilled unemployment following unification. Unfortunately, the study does not include the period since 1991, during which unskilled unemployment in Germany increased and the nature of capital investment changed as a result of the ICT revolution. This reduces the relevance of the study for modern economies in which ICT has not only fundamentally changed the nature of capital investment but has also weakened the position of older, low-skilled workers.

Another way through which governments try to depress the supply of unskilled labour is through training schemes and active labour-market policies. Indeed, an interesting hypothesis is whether wage-compressing institutions induce governments to invest more in education. Thus, whereas the paper argues that wage-compressing institutions induce firms to invest more in unskilled workers, I would expect that such institutions induce governments to do so. In this connection, it is of interest to note that the aggregate skill intensity of production rises more quickly in Germany than in the US (see the seventh and eighth column of Table 1 in the paper). Germany seems to be more successful in increasing the skill-intensity of production, both by training its workforce better and by taking unskilled workers out of the workforce through early retirement schemes and other soft-landing schemes.

Hold-up: labour-market institutions ...

The theoretical model underlying the paper implies that minimum wages are the key determinant of the seriousness of the hold-up problem. Other labour-market institutions, however, are much more relevant in this context. For example, corporatist institutions that allow workers to delegate wage negotiations to unions alleviate the hold-up problem (see, e.g., Teulings and Hartog, 1998). Indeed, negotiations between long-lived unions and firms can help address contract incompleteness by making reputation considerations more important. This may explain why union density has in fact the wrong sign in the estimated equations for the skill premium.

Various other contractual arrangements (e.g. the length of employment and wage contracts) can also help address the hold-up problem. Whereas European economies rely on long-term implicit contracts to address the hold-up problem, the US relies more on competition and labour market mobility and flexibility to contain the search and transaction costs that give rise to hold up. By pointing mostly to binding minimum wages as the solution for the hold-up problem, the authors overstate the differences in efficacy in which Europe and the US address hold-up problems.

... and empirical proxies for them ...

One of the basic problems of the empirical analysis in the paper is that it argues that labour-market institutions drive the different correlations between investment and wage inequality in Germany and the US, but that these labour-market institutions remain largely implicit in the paper. Put differently, the paper lacks institutional instruments for the endogenous capital–labour ratio at the right-hand side of regression. Indeed, one would need much more variation in labour-market institutions to test the hypothesis put forward in the paper. To illustrate, one would like to look at the variation of unionization, the nature of collective bargaining, employment protection and especially the replacement rates across sectors and time and explore whether capital–skill complementarity varies with these institutional variables. Also the nature of human capital is relevant in this context – particularly whether it is general or specific (i.e. whether labour is mobile across sectors or not).

If data on variation in sectoral institutions are not available, one might alternatively want to rely more on cross-country variation in institutions. The current paper does not exploit data on intersectoral variations in institutions and thus, in effect, relies on only two observations on institutions: Germany and the US. Indeed, in the current study, sectoral variation does not seem to help to identify the separate effects of capital–skill complementarity and skill-biased technological change: the difference in the coefficients for investment in the wage equations between the two countries is never statistically significant. The paper thus does not contain enough information to test its main hypothesis. What is needed in order to identify the effects the paper is after is either more detailed information on sectoral institutions or more cross-country variation.

. . . and capital-market institutions

Another important variable one would like to control for is the nature of capital and goods markets. Whereas the authors argue that product markets and financial markets have become similar during the period 1973–91, major differences remain during this period. In Germany, capital markets operate less efficiently, so that firms must rely mainly on internal and bank finance. Moreover, goods markets are less competitive in Germany, especially in non-traded sectors. Hence, high sectoral investment in Germany is likely to be correlated with high sectoral rents in less competitive sectors. These rents not only boost sectoral investment but also unskilled wages. In the US, in contrast, capital markets are likely to operate better, while goods market are more competitive. Hence, more investment occurs in new, innovative sectors employing more skilled labour. In this context, some more information on the types of investment in the two countries would be welcome. In any case, also here, one would like the authors to explore not only sectoral wages and investment but also other things such as the financial structure of the firms, the competitiveness of the markets these sectors operate on, and output in the various sectors. Indeed, one would like to have institutional variables as instruments for endogenous capital investment. These institutional instruments may work better than instruments for the labour market because exclusion restrictions are more likely to be met.

Empirical exercise: how to compare skills internationally?

One of the challenges facing the authors is to compare skills across countries. The authors employ initial education as a measure for skills. However, a possible response of employers to wage-compressing institutions is that they invest in training and raise the skills of workers, because wage costs do not rise much with skill.

Indeed, when workers with low skills are overpaid and workers with substantial skills are underpaid, employers face incentives to raise the skills of their workers. At the same time, they select those workers who can be trained. In view of these incentives to train and select employees, German unskilled workers who are employed are likely to be more skilled than the workers in the US who are classified as unskilled. It also suggests that initial training may not be a good indicator for skill, but that skill is endogenous. In any case, more attention to investment in human capital rather than physical investment is called for, although the separate impacts of these two types of investment may be difficult to identify if human capital and physical capital are complementary.

Another problem with the skill classification is that for the classification the authors prefer, only a very small portion of the German workforce of less than 10% is skilled, while in the US this percentage is 50%. This suggests that the unskilled in Germany are in fact on average more skilled than the American unskilled. Thus, the unskilled in the US seem to be a rather different category than the unskilled in Germany. Moreover, for the very large group of German unskilled, minimum wages seem to be relevant only for a small subgroup. When exploring the impact of minimum wages on unskilled employment, it would seem better to define the unskilled more narrowly, for example by confining attention to the lowest 20% of the skill distribution in both countries. My presumption would be that many of these individuals are in soft-landing schemes in Germany (disability, welfare, early retirement, unemployment without an obligation to apply for jobs), but in marginal employment in the US.

Conclusion

I like the idea that high minimum wages encourage societies to invest more in the unskilled so that their productivity matches at least the minimum wage. Whereas I believe there is certainly something in this hypothesis on a society-wide level, I am more sceptical about whether high minimum wages induce profit-seeking firms to invest more in low-skilled labour.

In any case, the empirical exercise in this paper does not have enough power to distinguish between the two main competing hypotheses about the impact of wage-compressing institutions – the one hypothesis being that these institutions price low-skilled workers out of the labour market and the alternative hypothesis being that these institutions induce employers to invest low-skilled workers into the labour market (by training workers, investing in complementary capital equipment or directing technological change so as to make low-skilled workers more productive). We need more information on sectoral and especially cross-country employment and training performances and labour-market institutions to identify the causal relationship between, on the one hand, labour-market institutions and, on the other hand, the complementarity between capital and skill and the labour-market position of the unskilled.

Gilles Duranton
University of Toronto

Over the last 15 years, very few topics in the economic literature have received more attention than the rise in wage inequalities. Despite this, we are still very far from a consensus about what has really happened. This fine paper by Koeniger and Leonardi gives us some clues about why. It is also part of a new generation of work in the literature indicating what the road ahead for research on this topic may be made of.

To be more precise about wage inequalities, think of the following production function for 'aggregation unit' (sector, country, or both) i and year t:

$$y_{i,t} = Q_{i,t}F_{i,t}\left(A_{i,t}^{k}k_{i,t}, A_{i,t}^{l}l_{i,t}, A_{i,t}^{h}h_{i,t}\right) \tag{1}$$

where Q is the price of the final output, k is capital, l is unskilled labour, h is skilled labour and the As are technology shifters.

The first generation of work about wage inequalities in the early 1990s (e.g., Katz and Murphy, 1992) mainly provided a careful descriptive account of what happened during the 1970s and 1980s. Following this, the second generation of work during most of the 1990s carefully scrutinized four major possible explanations. At a time of increased trade openness with developing countries (and particularly China), factor price equalization was a strong candidate driver behind the widening wage gap. Unfortunately, the action on Q turned out to be too small to be more than an accessory part in the main plot. Changes on the supply side were also problematic. It is true that the supply of unskilled labour may have increased more in the US than in Continental Europe. However, the supply of skills probably increased together with their price in many developed countries. No simple theory about changes in the supply of k, l and h is able to replicate convincingly the evolution of wage inequalities in the US, let alone the diverging evolution between English-speaking countries and Continental Europe.

The last two contenders, institutions and technology, seemed more promising. The 1980s was a decade of considerable institutional turmoil particularly in the labour markets of the US and the UK (two countries were wage inequalities rose markedly). However, changes in the way the price of skilled and unskilled labour form also turned out to be a problematic explanation. Most of the action on the institutional front seems to be associated with the minimum wage. This raises two issues. First, the minimum wage is possibly only a channel through which some deeper forces percolate rather than a true driver of wage inequalities. Depending on the institutional setting, these deeper forces may lead to rising wage inequalities or rising unemployment. This was captured by Krugman's famous aphorism: 'Europe jobless, America penniless'. Second, institutional change could be endogenous. After all, these changes were accepted by the electorate in many countries.

In the era of massive computerization of the economy, skill-biased technological change (i.e., changes in the shifters A^{k}, A^{l} and A^{l}) quickly became the favourite explanation of many. Intuitively, changes at the workplace seemed big enough to explain the profound divergence between skilled and unskilled wages. Again, although there was some support in the data for skill-biased technological change, it was far from overwhelming. Since technology is not observable directly, skill-biased technological change might be invoked to explain *any* evolution. If the differential evolution of the technology shifters is not enough, one can always add changes in the degree of substitutability or complementarity between factors (i.e., changes in the coefficients of $F(.)$ or even a change of specification). One way to circumvent this last criticism is to argue that technology itself evolves endogenously. Making technology endogenous puts some bounds on its possible evolutions and limits the scope for *ad-hoc* explanations. Following the lead of Daron Acemoglu, an abundant theoretical literature was developed to look at how technology could evolve endogenously (Acemoglu, 2002).

The empirical consensus at the turn of the century was that all four families of explanations probably mattered. The strategy then became to try to quantify the relative importance of these explanations by pitching them against each other in the same empirical framework. Unfortunately, this type of exercise does not seem to lead to any consensus about the relative importance of the four main explanations. At the same time, the theoretical literature about endogenous technological evolutions started to make the case that technology could interact with the supply of factors, for instance, through the development of innovations that benefit particular factors depending on their relative supply. Technology may also interact with trade or institutions. Hence, the rising wage gap may not be about technology *versus* institutions but instead technology *and* institutions.

The paper by Koeniger and Leonardi is at the forefront of the empirical work that takes this suggestion seriously. Since no simple mono-causal approach appears to explain the bulk of the rising wage gap, it is only natural to consider more complex explanations relying instead on two factors. Koeniger and Leonardi consider what might be the simplest relevant model of institutions and biased technological change. For a worker of skill level h, the general production function (1) is simplified into

$$y_{i,t} = A(1 + g(k_{i,t}))h_{i,t}$$

where $g(k_{i,t}) = \alpha$ if $k_{i,t} \geq 1$ and zero otherwise. In this framework investment is obviously skill-biased because it multiplies the skills of the workers (by α). The maintained assumption is that the price of investment, P^k, declines over time – an empirically plausible case. Imagine now that this production function is embedded into a standard random search framework in which successful labour market matches lead to a split of the production surplus between the worker and the firm. In an economy like the US, a firm wants to invest when its share of the surplus exceeds the cost of investment, that is, when: $(1 - \beta)\alpha Ah \geq P^k$ where β is the share of the surplus that accrues to the worker. In this case, there is a time when firms in that country start investing to increase the productivity of their skilled workers but not that of their unskilled workers. This implies that the wage ratio (the wage of skilled workers divided by that of unskilled workers) increases by a factor of $1 + \alpha$. Consider now an economy like Germany with a minimum wage. When the minimum wage is not binding, the decision rule of firms is the same as in the US. When the minimum is binding, firms act as residual claimants for the entire surplus and invest when $\alpha Ah \geq P^k$. A straightforward comparison between the two investment rules shows that the skill threshold above which firms invest is lower when the minimum wage is binding.

This simple framework is consistent with a number of the facts presented by the authors about the relative evolutions of the wage gap in Germany and the US. Unfortunately, the framework also delivers some predictions for which the *prima facie* evidence is much weaker. First, with the continuing decline of the price of investment all workers should eventually benefit and the prediction is thus of a decline in wage inequalities in the US. Nobody really expects this any time soon. Furthermore, the possibility of making profitable investment to improve low skill productivity in Germany should imply that low-skill jobs should become relatively more profitable for firms. In turn, with the matching framework used here, this should have led to more unskilled job openings. Thus, the rate of unskilled unemployment in Germany should have declined relative to the US. Is it really the case? Finally, more investment in Germany should also imply a higher productivity growth than in the US. Did we really observe this?

It would be harsh to blame the authors for these counterfactual predictions. The reason is that several ingredients are required to replicate the facts. In turn, having more ingredients generates more predictions than the more economical models of the previous generation. Then, with a large number of predictions, it is always easy to find some that fail. Put differently, with rising wage inequalities, no simple explanation will do and more sophisticated stories inevitably runs into counterfactual predictions. It is unclear to me how this major problem will be solved.

Turning to the empirics of the paper, a strict reading of the model indicates that a lower cost of investing and institutions determine both investments and wages. Hence, full consistency with theory requires regressing wages and investment on the price of investment, the institutional setting, and some interactions between the two. This is not what the authors do. There are very good reasons for that. Regressing wages and investment on the price of investment and institutions looks like a hopeless task. Investment per worker is impossible to get in the data. Besides, the two explanatory variables are extremely hard to measure and may be simultaneously determined with the outcomes.

In their empirical work, the authors use a slightly different framework which relates the shares of skilled and unskilled labour in the wage bill, the wage ratio, productivity, output, and the capital stock. This type of specification raises insurmountable simultaneity problems so that the authors finally end up regressing wages on the capital per worker, the skill intensity, and some measures of institutions across sectors for both Germany and the US. Put differently, they look for differences in the coefficient on capital across Germany and the US. This is arguably rather far from the initial theoretical specification (which assumes that technology is the same everywhere). Again, it would be harsh to hold this too much against the authors. The general issue behind this is that looking at institutions or technology was already hard enough when each was considered in isolation. Looking at the interactions between institutions and technology raises very serious empirical difficulties that we may not be able to solve.

The findings of Koeniger and Leonardi are suggestive that something may be happening at the interface between technology and institutions. This is an important conclusion. The case that institutions and technology matter 'together' is very useful to rationalize crucial stylized facts relating to the evolution of the wage gap across countries. On the other hand, the analysis of Koeniger and Leonardi is also suggestive that the technology–institutions interaction may not be the main driving force behind the evolution of US wage inequalities. This may be due to the specification chosen by the authors and measurement problems in the data. Better specification and better data may give better results. Alternatively, the technology and institution nexus may only be yet another small part of the overall story. The complete version of the wage inequality evolution may also require thinking about trade and supply changes as well. Allowing for all those things to interact with one another is a nice suggestion. Nonetheless, the interaction between technology and institutions is already at the limit of what we can deal with (or even beyond this limit). Allowing for more sophisticated frameworks may not be manageable. This suggests a very though road ahead. Some creative ideas will be needed to make progress.

Panel discussion

The panel had mixed views on the general idea that binding minimum wages would induce training and investment. Rudolf Winter-Ebmer mentioned that microeconomic evidence does support the notion that binding minimum wages induce more training and more careful selection of workers, but Hans Werner-Sinn pointed out that in standard models higher wages decrease demand for complementary equipment, and that in Germany expensive unskilled labour does appear to be rather frequently unemployed at the same time as investment lags behind other OECD countries. The authors replied that while capital–labour substitution does play a role, empirically it may be outweighed by the non-standard mechanisms put forward by recent theoretical contributions. In the Germany–US empirical comparison, employment trends are rather similar across skill, at least in the available sample, and Germany does feature strong investment trends.

Several panelists thought that other data, if available, could be usefully analysed from the paper's perspective. Wendy Carlin suggested that the results of numeracy and literacy tests could provide alternative benchmarks to define skilled and unskilled labour. In particular, she cited a large difference in the ratios of the 95th and 5th percentile of test scores in Germany (1.7 : 1) than in the USA (2.7 : 1). Francesco Daveri mentioned that he would be interested to see analysis for Germany including the post-reunification period, which would cover changes in capital intensity associated with the IT revolution, and Hélène Rey wondered whether differential outsourcing of jobs could play a role over the more recent period.

APPENDIX

Table A1. Summary statistics for the US 1975–1991

Sector name	H/L in 1975–1991	3-year average %-change in (H/L)	wh/wl in 1975–1991	3-year average %-change in (wh/wl)	Equipment capital per worker in 1975–1991	3-year average percentage change in (equipment per worker)
Agriculture and Mining	0.505	0.063	1.329	0.026	191.421	−0.001
Construction	0.334	0.062	1.165	0.022	60.740	−0.142
Wood	0.234	0.052	1.425	0.009	15.056	−0.068
Stone, Clay etc.	0.263	0.094	1.453	0.007	22.474	−0.040
Primary Metals	0.350	0.052	1.253	0.030	76.185	0.009
Machinery	0.536	0.115	1.365	0.034	35.801	0.076
Electrical Machinery	0.515	0.125	1.553	0.036	24.623	0.126
Transport Equipment	0.459	0.121	1.289	0.032	43.186	0.005
Professional Goods	0.558	0.130	1.778	−0.006	8.217	0.237
Food and Tobacco	0.333	0.053	1.331	0.031	41.134	0.046
Textiles	0.138	0.119	1.811	0.0003	24.181	−0.018
Paper and Printing	0.549	0.086	1.326	0.009	52.057	0.021
Chemicals and Petroleum	0.818	0.089	1.505	0.013	86.439	0.002
Plastic and Leather	0.221	0.123	1.467	0.030	26.959	−0.060
Transport and Communication	0.523	0.113	1.147	0.018	326.717	−0.077
Utilities	0.538	0.118	1.226	0.016	132.994	0.014
Wholesale and Retail	0.570	0.052	1.377	0.014	109.663	0.062
Banking and Insurance	1.143	0.073	1.628	0.004	110.845	0.109
Business and Personal Services	0.581	0.091	1.515	0.019	168.297	−0.080
Health Services	0.913	0.118	1.708	0.013	21.380	0.076
Total	0.504	0.092	1.433	0.018	78.918	0.015

Notes: Authors' calculations based on the data described in the Web Data Appendix. The total is the arithmetic mean across industries.

Table A2. Summary statistics for West Germany 1975–1991

Sector name	H/L in 1975–1991	3-year average %-change in (H/L)	H/L (vocational) in 1975–1991	H/L (vocational, white-collar) in 1975–1991	wh/wl in the 1975–1991	3-year average %-change in (wh/wl)	Equipment capital per worker in 1975–1991	3-year average percentage change in (equipment per worker)
Agriculture and Mining	0.027	0.114	1.268	0.145	1.413	−0.017	124.211	0.075
Construction	0.024	0.082	3.526	0.141	1.372	−0.005	61.504	0.068
Wood	0.014	0.153	1.683	0.176	1.341	−0.007	8.817	0.079
Stone, Clay etc.	0.030	0.105	1.095	0.210	1.366	−0.006	25.666	0.143
Primary Metals	0.040	0.077	1.366	0.262	1.361	0.001	102.068	0.014
Machinery	0.054	0.128	3.597	0.411	1.287	−0.002	51.917	0.114
Electrical Machinery	0.092	0.153	1.478	0.444	1.439	−0.003	72.145	0.119
Transport Equipment	0.044	0.127	2.516	0.294	1.294	0.005	56.596	0.159
Professional Goods	0.039	0.177	1.658	0.320	1.424	−0.001	13.013	0.099
Food and Tobacco	0.018	0.135	2.010	0.431	1.458	0.002	65.275	0.083
Textiles	0.017	0.142	0.924	0.204	1.572	−0.014	21.314	0.137
Paper and Printing	0.027	0.165	1.547	0.256	1.310	−0.006	38.192	0.142
Chemicals and Petroleum	0.082	0.127	1.604	0.486	1.316	−0.006	101.087	0.045
Plastic and Leather	0.018	0.225	0.838	0.218	1.576	−0.018	17.607	0.154
Transport and Communication	0.027	0.157	2.166	0.346	1.223	0.002	169.799	0.068
Utilities	0.081	0.096	5.058	0.595	1.229	−0.006	126.320	−0.042
Wholesale and Retail	0.038	0.123	4.309	1.575	1.350	−0.001	104.728	0.091
Banking and Insurance	0.087	0.219	5.264	3.906	1.205	−0.022	131.310	0.182
Business and Personal Services	0.164	0.092	3.570	1.210	1.509	0.001	60.920	0.037
Health Services	0.090	0.107	3.185	1.939	1.444	0.004	68.748	0.025
Total	0.051	0.135	2.433	0.678	1.374	−0.005	71.062	0.090

Notes: Authors' calculations based on the data described in the Web Data Appendix. The total is the arithmetic mean across industries.

WEB APPENDIX

Available at http://www.economic-policy.org

REFERENCES

Abraham, K. and S. Houseman (1995). 'Earnings inequality in Germany', in R.B. Freeman and L.F. Katz (eds.), *Differences and Changes in Wage Structures*, University of Chicago Press, Chicago.
Acemoglu, D. (2002). 'Technical change, inequality, and the labor market', *Journal of Economic Literature*, 40, 7–72.
— (2003). 'Cross-country inequality trends', *Economic Journal*, 113, F121–49.
Acemoglu, D. and J.-S. Pischke (1999). 'The structure of wages and investment in general training', *Journal of Political Economy*, 107, 539–72.
Acemoglu, D. and J.-S. Pischke (2003). 'Minimum wages and on-the-job training', in S.W. Polachek (ed.), *Research in Labor Economics*, 22, 159–202.
Alesina, A., S. Ardagna, G. Nicoletti and F. Schiantarelli (2005). 'Regulation and investment', *Journal of the European Economic Association*, 3, 791–825.
Beaudry, P. and D.A. Green (2003). 'Wages and employment in the United States and Germany: What explains the difference', *American Economic Review*, 93, 573–602.
Blanchard, O. (1997). 'The medium run', *Brookings Papers of Economic Activity*, 2, 89–157.
— (2006). 'European unemployment: the evolution of facts and ideas', *Economic Policy*, 21, 5–59.
Blau, F.D. and L.M. Kahn (1996). 'International differences in male wage inequality: Institutions versus market forces', *Journal of Political Economy*, 104, 791–837.
Caballero, R.J. and M.L. Hammour (1998). 'The macroeconomics of specificity', *Journal of Political Economy*, 106, 724–67.
Caselli, F. (1999): 'Technological revolutions', *American Economic Review*, 89, 78–102.
Cummins, J. and G.L. Violante (2002). 'Investment-specific technical change in the United States (1947–2000): Measurement and macroeconomic consequences', *Review of Economic Dynamics*, 5, 243–84.
Falk, M. and B. Koebel (2004). 'The impact of office machinery, and computer capital on the demand for heterogeneous labour', *Labour Economics*, 11, 99–117.
Fitzenberger, B., A. Osikominu and R. Völter (2005). 'Imputation rules to improve the education variable in the IAB employment subsample', ZEW Discussion Paper. No. 05-10.
Gordon, R. (1990). *The Measurement of Durable Good Prices*, University of Chicago Press, Chicago.
Gould, E., O. Moav and B.A. Weinberg (2001). 'Precautionary demand for education, inequality, and technological progress', *Journal of Economic Growth*, 6, 285–315.
Hornstein, A., P. Krusell and G.L. Violante (2005): 'The effects of technical change on labor market inequalities', in P. Aghion and S.N. Durlauf (eds.), *Handbook of Economic Growth*. Vol. 2, ch. 20, North-Holland, Amsterdam.
Katz, L.F. and K.M. Murphy (1992). 'Changes in relative wages, 1963–87: Supply and demand factors', *Quarterly Journal of Economics*, 107 (February), 35–78.
Koeniger, W. (2006). 'Openness, wage floors and technology change', *Berkeley Electronic Press, Contributions to Macroeconomics*, forthcoming.
Koeniger, W., M. Leonardi and L. Nunziata (2006). 'Labor market institutions and wage inequality', *Industrial and Labor Relations Review*, forthcoming.
Krugman, P. (1994). 'Past and prospective causes of high unemployment', *Economic Review*, Federal Reserve Bank of Kansas City, 4, 23–43.
— (1995). 'Growing world trade: Causes and consequences', *Brookings Papers on Economic Activity*, 1, 327–77.
Krueger, A.B. and J.-S. Pischke (1998). 'Observations and conjectures on the U.S. employment miracle', in *Public GAAC Symposium: Labor Markets in the USA and Germany*, German-American Academic Council, Bonn, 99–126.
Krueger, D. and K.B. Kumar (2004). 'Skill-specific rather than general education: A reason for US-Europe growth differences', *Journal of Economic Growth*, 9, 167–207.

Krusell, P., L.E. Ohanian, J.-V. Rios-Rull and G.L. Violante (2000). 'Capital-skill complementarity and inequality: A macroeconomic analysis', *Econometrica*, 68, 1029–53.

Leonardi, M. (2006). 'Firm heterogeneity in capital-labor ratios and wage inequality', *Economic Journal*, forthcoming.

Machin, S. and J. van Reenen (1998). 'Technology and changes in skill structure: Evidence from seven OECD countries', *Quarterly Journal of Economics*, 113, 1215–44.

Moaz, Y.D. and O. Moav (2004). 'Social stratification, capital-skill complementarity, and the non-monotonic evolution of the education premium', *Macroeconomic Dynamics*, 8, 295–309.

Neumark, D. and W. Wascher (2001). 'Minimum wages and training revisited', *Journal of Labor Economics*, 19, 563–95.

Nickell, S. and B. Bell (1996). 'Changes in the distribution of wages and unemployment in OECD countries', *American Economic Review, Papers and Proceedings*, 86, 302–308.

Pischke, J.-S. (2005). 'Labor market institutions, wages and investment: Review and implications', *CESifo Economic Studies*, 51, 47–75.

Rogerson, R. (2005). 'Structural transformation and the deterioration of European labor market outcomes', Arizona State University, *mimeo*.

Sakellaris, P. and F. Vijselaar (2005). 'Capital quality improvement and the sources of economic growth in the Euro area', *Economic Policy*, 20, 267–306.

Teulings, C.N. and J. Hartog (1998) *Corporatism or Competition? Labour Contracts, Institutions and Wage Structures in International Comparison*, Cambridge University Press, Cambridge.

Wilson, D.J. (2002). 'Is embodied technology the result of upstream R&D? Industry-level evidence', *Review of Economic Dynamics*, 5, 285–317.

Age, seniority and labour costs

SUMMARY

The bad labour market performance of the workforce over 50 indicates that an aged workforce is often a burden for firms. Our paper seeks to investigate whether and why this is the case by providing evidence on the relation between age, seniority and experience, on the one hand, and the main components of labour costs, namely productivity and wages, on the other, for a sample of plants in three manufacturing industries ('forest', 'industrial machinery' and 'electronics') in Finland during the IT revolution in the 1990s. In 'average' industries – those not undergoing major technological shocks – productivity and wages keep rising almost indefinitely with the accumulation of either seniority (in the forest industry) or experience (in the industry producing industrial machinery). In these industries, the skill depreciation often associated with higher seniority beyond a certain threshold does not seemingly raise labour costs. In electronics, instead, the seniority-productivity profile shows a positive relation first and then becomes negative as one looks at plants with higher average seniority. This body of evidence is consistent with the idea that fast technical change brings about accelerated skill depreciation of senior workers. We cannot rule out, however, that our correlations are also simultaneously produced by worker movements across plants. The seniority-earnings profile in electronics is instead rather similar to that observed for the other industries – a likely symptom of the prevailing Finnish wage bargaining institutions which tend to make seniority one essential element of wage determination. In the end, seniority matters for labour costs, not age as such. But only in high-tech industries, not in the economy at large. This is well tuned with previous research on gross flows of workers and jobs in the US and other OECD countries which unveiled the productivity-driving role of resource reallocation (or lack thereof) between plants. To improve the employability of the elderly at times of fast technical change, public policy should thus divert resources away from preserving existing jobs and lend more attention to the retraining of old workers to ease their reallocation away from less productive plants (or plants where they have become less productive) into new jobs.

— *Francesco Daveri and Mika Maliranta*

Economic Policy January 2007 Printed in Great Britain

Age, seniority and labour costs: lessons from the Finnish IT revolution

Francesco Daveri and Mika Maliranta

Università di Parma and IGIER; ETLA, Helsinki

1. INTRODUCTION

Workers over 50 participate less in the labour market than their younger counterparts and, when unemployed, they remain longer on the dole.[1] These are clear symptoms that companies are more reluctant to hire the elderly and that, ultimately, an aged workforce is a burden for most firms. Whether and why this is the case is not obvious, however.

We are very grateful to our discussants Wendy Carlin and Rudolf Winter-Ebmer, two referees and other panel participants for their comments on a previous draft. Previous drafts of this paper previously circulated as IGIER Working Paper 309 and ETLA Discussion Paper 1010 under the title 'Age, Technology and Labour Costs' and benefited from the comments of seminar participants at the Government Institute of Economic Research (Helsinki), Bocconi (Milan), Humboldt (Berlin), Parma, the 5th 'Economics of ICT Conference' in Mannheim, the 2005 ONS Conference on the 'Analysis of Enterprise Micro-Data' in Cardiff. Gilbert Cette, Pekka Ilmakunnas, Olmo Silva and Alexandra Spitz provided useful comments on previous drafts. Maliranta gratefully acknowledges financial support provided by Tekes within the Research Programme for Advanced Technology Policy (ProAct). We are grateful to the Research Laboratory of Statistics Finland for providing access to these data and especially to Satu Nurmi, the Head of the Laboratory, for constructing these data.

The Managing Editor in charge of this paper was Paul Seabright.

[1] While labour market participation (the ratio between the labour force and the total population in working age) ranges between 90% and 95% in all OECD countries, the same ratio was instead substantially lower for older workers (from a high of some 80% in Sweden to a low of about 45% in Italy). The OECD data on labour market transitions (see OECD, 2006) document that the hiring rate of older workers is much lower (between one-third and one-half) than for younger workers; very few of the older unemployed find a job and very few of those who left the labour force come back to work; older workers are more likely to quit their jobs than younger workers; finally, the old no longer working rarely move into unemployment, while more than half retire early and a significant proportion does not work because of reported disability.

Economic Policy January 2007 pp. 117–175 Printed in Great Britain
© CEPR, CES, MSH, 2007.

1.1. The controversy

Workforce ageing is known to entail skill deterioration and lessened ability to adapt and learn new things. The studies of psychologists and medical scientists have in fact often shown that cognitive abilities tend to deteriorate with age. Although this decline is not uniform across abilities, after a certain age threshold, further advancements in age are seemingly associated with lower productivity at work. Beyond that threshold, further increases of experience add little or nothing to the working ability of a given worker.[2]

This skill depreciation effect is possibly more pronounced, though, for a worker who stays within the same company for a long time. A senior worker is more likely to have exhausted her learning potential on the particular job or work environment she is attached to, while a worker of the same age but new to the firm and to the job may have not. This begs the question of whether seniority, rather than age, is behind the bad labour market performance of the elderly that we see in the data.

The importance of distinguishing the effects of age from those of seniority manifests itself in a related aspect too. Declining productivity is in fact not enough to make an old (or senior) worker a burden for her firm, as long as the additional year of age (or seniority) goes hand in hand with a parallel flattening of the individual earnings profile. Unfortunately, this is rarely the case. In many OECD countries, labour market institutions associated with the presence of collective agreements make the seniority-related part of the wage a particularly large fraction of workers' wages, thereby preventing companies from keeping wages aligned to the declining productivity of senior workers. And a seniority wage may also be the result of the internal dynamics of the firm. Workers with a high degree of seniority have usually reached top positions in their company, which often enable them to extract a rent over and above their productivity contribution to the company. Or employees and employers may have entered an implicit contract implying a deferred compensation scheme, so that the young are underpaid and the old overpaid with respect to their productivity. In all these cases, the stop or outright reversal in the process of skill accumulation becomes more pronounced right at a time when firms find it particularly hard to detach seniority from earnings. Note, however, that it is seniority, not age as such, that is the most likely cause of rising labour costs.

The productivity-wage race during the individual career paths and its counterpart for company costs is in turn crucially affected by the pace of technical change. Fast technical change, usually embodied in new machines and methods of work, accelerates

---

[2] It should not be forgotten that workforce ageing is not necessarily a burden, and may actually be a blessing for the firm. An older labour force is more experienced, and therefore potentially more productive. Moreover, having had more time to hang around and search the labour market, an old worker has potentially good chances of finding herself in a better job. Finally, thanks to the secular improvements in healthcare, ageing has the potential to raise workers' productivity by enhancing ability and attitude to work, also increasing and lengthening labour force participation. The balance between the good and the bad sides of ageing is duly discussed in the paper.

the depreciation of existing skills naturally occurring with age or seniority and thus makes it more likely that senior workers become a burden for the firm. As a result, the adverse effects of seniority on labour costs may be particularly striking in high-tech industries and, more generally, in firms where incessant changes in the methods of production and the set of goods and services offered to the public are crucial ingredients of the maintained competitive ability of the company.

1.2. Policy relevance

Policy-makers are increasingly worried about the labour market consequences of workforce ageing. In the last few years, the rapid diffusion of outright new and 'globalized' methods of production and work in those countries and industries most heavily affected by the IT revolution have possibly made the skill deterioration of older workers faster and hence contributed to the worsening of their labour market position. The shape of the relation between seniority and labour costs is seemingly well known to Wal-Mart managers, as exemplified by the following quote:

> 'Over the past 4 years, the average Associate tenure [at Wal-Mart] has increased by 0.2 months per calendar year. As a result, more Associates qualify for participation in benefits programs . . . and for more paid time off. An even more important factor is wages, which increase in lock-step with tenure and directly drive the cost of many benefits. Given the impact of tenure on wages and benefits, the cost of an Associate with 7 years of tenure is almost 55 per cent more than the cost of an Associate with 1 year of tenure, yet there is no difference in his or her productivity'. (Internal memorandum to the Board of Directors, Wal-Mart, March 2006)

But not too dissimilar preoccupations also probably underlie the recent move by Ericsson, the Swedish telecoms equipment maker, which, in April 2006, offered a voluntary redundancy package to up to 1000 of its Sweden-based employees between the ages of 35 and 50. Interviewed by the *Financial Times*, Carl-Henric Svanberg, Ericsson's CEO, justified his move as follows: 'the company's age structure and low staff turnover – about 1 per cent in a year – is storing up problems for the future and has to be addressed'. Accordingly, Mr Svanberg has set the minimum target for staff turnover at 3% per year.

The anecdotes on such almost quintessentially global companies as Wal-Mart and Ericsson may be representative of the problems that an enlarging set of companies will have to deal with in the future. If companies take action to stop the rise in labour costs due to declining or stagnating ability above a certain age or seniority threshold and higher wages than ever in career, this may further worsen the labour market position of the elderly. Yet the seniority of their employees seems to be the problem for Wal-Mart and Ericsson managers, not their age as such.

Whether the envisaged mechanism of wage-productivity misalignments potentially at the roots of the weak labour market position of the elderly is due to age or seniority also has far-reaching implications for the type of policy correction to undertake. If ageing as such is behind the worse labour market outcomes of the elderly, this calls for age-specific active labour market and educational policies to counteract depreciating skills, improve the employability and eventually facilitate the re-entry of old workers into the labour force. If instead seniority is really the problem, then no age-biased active labour market policy is warranted. Labour market policy should instead be mainly aimed at easing worker reallocation across jobs and firms, for instance by reducing firing and hiring costs.

1.3. Our contribution

Our paper seeks to illuminate the debate on the implications of workforce ageing for companies by contrasting age, seniority and general experience profiles with productivity and earnings for a sample of plants in three manufacturing industries ('forest', 'industrial machinery' and 'electronics') in Finland.

Finland is an appropriate laboratory to study our issues of interest in two respects. First, it was hit by the IT revolution in the 1990s, which affected firms in the various industries in different ways. Second, it has good data to study the problem. So not only does Finland provide the scope, but also the means for properly analysing the relation between seniority, experience, productivity and wages at the plant level.

To evaluate whether such relations differ across industries, we pick a subset of three industries that include the most traditional Finnish industry one can think of (the forest industry) and two industries producing capital goods, one (production of electronics equipment) playing a crucial role and another one (production of machinery and equipment) less involved in the IT revolution. We can thus study the relation between age, seniority and experience on the one hand and labour cost variables (productivity and earnings) in 'treated' industries (electronics) and 'control' industries (the other two industries), one of which is technologically dissimilar but representative of the average Finnish industry and another not too dissimilar from electronics. Altogether, our statistical analysis provides a reasonably coherent picture of the empirical relation between age-related variables, plant productivity and wages in Finland in the years of the IT revolution.

Our empirical exercise is implemented in two steps. First, we compute an overall productivity index for each plant from labour productivity data. Then, we analyse the statistical relation between the plant productivity index and age-related variables (age first but also, and crucially, seniority and potential experience) in each of the three industries separately. Clearly, within each industry, plant productivity may vary for many reasons in addition to changes in seniority or experience of workers. Some of these determinants – workers' education, vintage, foreign ownership, size of the plant – are observed. Some others (such as managerial ability) are not, but there are statistical methods to implicitly account for their effect. We investigate the significance of the same set of variables for earnings as well.

At first sight, our results seem to support the view that workforce ageing as such has adverse effects on labour costs. Age is essentially unrelated with productivity while it is positively correlated with wages. Upon a closer scrutiny, though, when we duly distinguish the effects of seniority on productivity and wages from those of general experience, we find that the picture sharply differs across industries.

In 'average' industries – those not undergoing major technological shocks – productivity and wages keep rising almost indefinitely with the accumulation of either seniority (in the forest industry) or experience (in the industry producing industrial machinery). In these industries, skill depreciation does not seemingly raise labour costs. Instead, the responses of plant productivity and wages to seniority are very different from each other in electronics – the industry where people are exposed to rapid technological and managerial changes. In electronics, the seniority-productivity profile shows a positive relation first and then becomes negative as one looks at plants with higher average seniority. This holds for plants with similar education, plant age and size and other conditions and is thus not related to plant differences in these other respects. The inverted-U-shaped correlation between plant seniority and productivity in electronics is most precisely measured when data are averaged over time, that is, when purged of the potential noise arising from year-to-year fluctuations, but a weaker correlation is still there when the time series variation of the data is considered.

This body of evidence is consistent with the idea that fast technical change brings about accelerated skill depreciation of senior workers. We cannot rule out, however, that our correlations are also simultaneously produced by worker movements across plants. The negative correlation between seniority and productivity may in fact also reflect the reallocation away of younger (and more productive) workers who leave behind older plants attracted by the career prospects offered in newly born high-productivity firms and plants. While we cannot precisely quantify the relative importance of the two effects in our statistical analysis, we conclude that both skill depreciation and worker reallocation affect the relation between seniority and productivity in the Finnish high-tech industry.

The change of sign (first positive, then negative) in the seniority-productivity profiles is not there for plant wages. The seniority-earnings profile in electronics is rather similar to that observed for the other industries – a likely symptom of the prevailing Finnish wage bargaining institutions which tend to make seniority one essential element of wage determination.

These latter findings indicate that the looming rise in labour costs coming about from seniority-based wages is particularly significant in high-tech industries (the most dynamic industries of the economy). This is well tuned with previous research on gross flows of workers and jobs in the US and other OECD countries which unveiled the productivity-driving role of resource reallocation (or lack thereof) between plants. The adverse link between seniority and productivity and the discrepancy between productivity and earnings profiles are instead less apparent for firms in other industries. In the end, seniority matters mostly for labour costs, not age as such. But in high-tech industries only, and not in the economy at large.

1.4. Organization of the paper

The structure of this paper is as follows. In Section 2 we discuss the main ideas that economists bring to bear when thinking about the relation between ageing, seniority, experience, productivity and wages. In Section 3 we present data explaining why Finland is an interesting case in point and how our variables of interest correlate to each other in the data set employed in our statistical analysis. In Section 4 we present and discuss our empirical strategy and main results. Section 5 concludes. This paper also includes an appendix, where we give a more detailed description of our data.

2. AGE, SENIORITY, EXPERIENCE, PRODUCTIVITY AND WAGES: THEORIES AND EMPIRICAL PREDICTIONS

Various theories of the functioning of the labour market bear distinct empirical predictions and help think about the relation between age, seniority, experience and the main components of labour costs, productivity and earnings. We briefly survey the various theories below before contrasting them with the data.

2.1. Age, productivity and wages: theories

The most straightforward way of tackling the question whether ageing is associated to higher labour costs for the firm is to look at whether workforce ageing drives a negative wedge between the worker's productivity and its wage.

But answering this question is not enough. Ageing usually manifests itself in two main guises: seniority and overall experience. Plainly, an older worker has very often spent more time in the labour market – and has thus a bigger general experience – than a younger worker. Instead, an old worker need not be a senior worker in a particular firm. Distinguishing the two facets of ageing in the labour market – as the various theories do – is particularly important for policy purposes, as ageing is essentially exogenous to the individual worker, while potential experience and, to an even greater extent, seniority are not.

2.1.1. The human capital hypothesis.   The most obvious benchmark for our discussion on ageing and labour costs is Becker's human capital hypothesis (1962, p. 119), according to which an older labour force is more experienced and therefore more productive.

First of all, ageing often – not always – comes about with higher seniority of the worker within a given firm. As long as some learning and training is undertaken on the job early on in a career, higher seniority should be associated to higher worker's productivity. Moreover, the human capital hypothesis posits that ageing should be associated with the acquisition of generic experience in the labour market over and above the increased seniority within a given firm. If generic experience buys enhanced flexibility and adaptability to the worker, this is again likely associated to higher productivity and market wages. Yet such productivity and wage enhancements are not the counterpart of higher seniority.

In turn, the extent to which higher productivity results in higher wages depends on whether training is general or firm-specific as well as on incentive considerations. If training is general, the worker fully appropriates the productivity increase enabled by training at a later stage in his/her career. If instead training is firm-specific, worker and firm will share the quasi-rents generated by training. In other words, with at least partially firm-specific human capital, one should expect the seniority-productivity profile to be steeper than the seniority-wage profile so that the productivity of senior workers eventually exceeds their earnings, while the opposite applies at early career stages.

Altogether, ageing affects productivity and wages both through seniority and general experience. Their effects, however, need not coincide empirically.

Finally, the theory of human capital also suggests that the returns from seniority and experience alone (i.e. without further educational or training inputs) do not stay constant over the worker's lifetime. As emphasized in the psychometric studies undertaken by medical scientists (see Skirbekk, 2003), cognitive abilities tend to deteriorate with age, so that, after a certain age threshold, growing older is seemingly associated to lower, not higher, productivity. (See Box 1 for a discussion of the main issues.)

Box 1. Age and individual productivity

The productivity of individual workers depends on a host of characteristics, such as education and skills, experience, motivation, intellectual and physical abilities. Some of these worker characteristics – notably the productive value of skills – may deteriorate with age.

Verhaegen and Salthouse (1997) present a meta-analysis of 91 studies on how mental abilities develop over the individual life span. Based on these studies, they conclude that the cognitive abilities (reasoning, speed and episodic memory) decline significantly before 50 years of age and more thereafter. Maximum levels are instead achieved in the 20s and the 30s. This is a universal phenomenon, independent of country and sex (this same phenomenon appears to hold even among non-human species – from fruit flies to primates). Kanazawa (2003) shows that age-genius curve of scientists bends down around between 20 and 30 years. Similar curves are also found for jazz musicians and painters. Given that the decline seems to apply mainly to married men, Kanazawa ventures the idea that changed levels of testosterone provide the psychological micro-foundation for this productivity decline.

In putting together our pieces of evidence, we will leave aside a few important aspects, which are likely to make the picture more complicated than this. First, a distinction must be drawn between fluid abilities and crystallized abilities. Fluid abilities concern the performance and speed of solving tasks related to new material, and they include perceptual speed and reasoning. They are strongly reduced at older ages. Crystallized abilities, such as verbal meaning and word fluency, even improve with accumulated knowledge and remain at a high functional level until a late age in life. The distinction between fluid and crystallized abilities is supported by empirical findings, where the psychometric test results of young and old men are analysed. It is found that verbal abilities remain virtually unchanged, while reasoning and speed abilities decline with age. Hence, one should not expect to see the declining part of the age-productivity profile to set in equally for all tasks and jobs.

Second, the relative demand for work tasks that involve certain cognitive abilities may have shifted asymmetrically over recent decades. As argued and empirically documented by Autor *et al.* (2003), the demand for interactive skills (hence for abilities that stay relatively stable over the life cycle) has likely increased more than the demand for mathematical aptitude (which instead declines substantially with age). This suggests that older workers may become relatively more productive in value terms over time. Whether such countervailing factors are relevant for Finland remains to be seen, being presumably particularly important for IT users rather than for the workers involved in the production of IT goods. The micro data employed by Maliranta and Rouvinen (2004) indicate that the use of ICT has had a particularly significant effect on productivity in ICT producing and using manufacturing industries. That study also provided evidence that the use of ICT has a stronger positive effect on productivity in younger organizations.

Our plant-level data set does not give us much leeway to exploit such additional interesting implications, and we leave them aside.

Particularly relevant for the topic of this paper, the deterioration of individual ability may be a more serious shortcoming at times of – and in companies and industries subject to – fast technological change. The misalignment of plant productivity and earnings was apparent in the Wal-Mart and Ericsson examples in Section 1. This has also possibly been the case in the Finnish economy since the early 1990s, when information technology started radically changing modes of production and work over a relatively short period of time. If these rapid changes had an impact, one would expect to observe an age-productivity (or seniority-productivity) profile with an earlier turnaround point and/or a steeper decline in high-tech industries (such as those today producing electronic equipment) than in traditional, technologically mature, industries (such as forest) as well as relatively less IT-intensive but still capital-good-producing industries (such as machinery and equipment).

To sum up, based on the human capital hypothesis, accumulation of skills, within and outside the firm, is an important, but not unceasing, productivity driver. Individual productivity profiles are expected to have an upward sloping part possibly changing its slope into negative beyond a certain threshold. Under the same hypothesis, wages are instead supposed to follow a flatter time profile than productivity.

A major problem for the research on the connections between age and productivity at the micro level has been the difficulty of measuring the marginal productivity of individuals, although their earnings can be measured with a reasonable degree of precision (see Box 2).

Box 2. Measures of individual productivity

To gauge indirect information about individual productivity, three main approaches have been followed: supervisors' ratings, piece-rate samples and the study of age-earnings data within matched employer-employee data sets.

Studies based on supervisors' ratings tend not to find any clear systematic relation between the employee's age and his/her productivity. At most, a slightly negative relation is found, albeit small. A problem with these studies is that managers often wish to reward loyalty rather than productivity. Hence supervisory evaluations may be inflated and results biased. Bosses are often senior workers and many older workers have been familiar to them for a long time. This may be positively reflected in the wage levels of older workers.

Work-samples provide evidence from task-quality/speed tests. Here, a negative relation between age and productivity is typically found. The slope of the decline is not steep for blue-collar workers and leads to cumulative declines of around 15–20% compared to peak levels, while the productivity decline of older workers in creative jobs is probably more pronounced.

Employer-employee linked data sets, such as the one we are using in this paper, are less prone to subjectivity issues than the studies based on supervisors' ratings and to selectivity issues than work-samples. The problem here is to isolate the genuine contribution of the age of the marginal worker to the company's value added from other intervening factors. How to deal with these issues is discussed in the main text.

One way out is to use data on wages. If wages were directly related to productivity, the age-earnings profile would also measure the productivity profile. Indeed, as reported by the OECD (2006, p. 66), earnings profiles are often hump-shaped, especially for men, which may reflect results from the decline of individual productivity.

2.1.2. The deferred compensation hypothesis. The human capital hypothesis offers one explanation and a few testable predictions on the relation between age, seniority, experience, productivity and earnings. It is not the only game in town, however. Its predictions on the wage-productivity race throughout the working career have been challenged by Lazear's deferred compensation hypothesis.

Seniority-based wages are indeed commonplace in many countries. This often comes in parallel with mandatory retirement.[3] In general, earnings appear to continue to grow well beyond the moment when the age-productivity profile would be predicted to flatten or change its sign into negative according to the human capital approach.

These pieces of evidence are at odds with one of the main implications of the human capital hypothesis, namely that the wage profile is flatter than the productivity profile. But they also raise the question of why firms should accept to grant workers pay raises in excess of their productivity performance. One possibility (see Lazear, 1981) is that firms are willing to pay high wages to motivate workers whose performance is hard to monitor to exert their work effort until late in career. Deferred compensation schemes would, however, distort workers' decisions to retire. Hence, deferred compensation schemes come together with mandatory retirement – an effective way to eventually put old workers out of the labour force and resolve the eventual unsustainability of the underlying pay systems.

The seniority-based wage systems observed in Korea and Japan are broadly consistent with the deferred compensation hypothesis. A complementary possibility – plausibly relevant for European countries – is the presence of collective agreements or social norms that often make seniority a firmly embedded feature of the wage setting process.

2.1.3. Sorting and matching models. Another problem with the human capital approach is its assumption that worker seniority and experience are essentially exogenous to the firm. Instead, the relation between firm seniority and productivity is not necessarily one-way only. Other theories draw on the widespread diffusion of sorting and matching in actual labour markets to emphasize that seniority and experience should not (only) be regarded as the causes of the observed productivity developments but also as their consequences.

The positive link between seniority and productivity may in fact be there for sorting reasons. Given that a worker stays with the firm only if the firm-worker match is good, senior workers presumably belong to the pool of the most productive (e.g. Teulings and Hartog, 1998). Hence, even in the absence of the relation implied by the human capital hypothesis, productivity and seniority may still be correlated in the

---

[3] The available OECD evidence indicates that explicit or implicit seniority-based rules lead earnings to rise even more steeply with age than early on in a career in Austria, France, Japan, South Korea, Luxembourg, and Switzerland. In Finland and the US, the non-wage components of labour costs (for health insurance purposes) rise steeply with age.

data. Moreover, feed-back effects may also be at work, as emphasized by Manning (2000) when the link between experience and productivity is examined. Labour market search, by raising the chance of finding a good job-worker match, may also imply upward sloping experience-earnings profiles in parallel with flat or declining productivity and absent seniority effects. Notice that this search argument would imply a pure effect of experience such that, when age is controlled for, firm-specific seniority would have no impact on wage. Clearly, the feed-back effects implied by sorting and matching models should be taken into account in the empirical analysis.

2.2. Empirically testable questions

To be able to discriminate between the different theories of the functioning of the labour market briefly summarized above, we use our Finnish data set to investigate four main questions on the relation between workforce ageing, seniority, experience, and labour costs:

1. Is age as such related to productivity and wages at all?
2. Is the effect of seniority on productivity and earnings different from the effect of age through the general experience channel?
3. Are the effects of age (and seniority in particular) on productivity and wages significantly different from each other and across industries (in particular, between industries subject to fast technical change and the other industries)?
4. Is the correlation between age and age-related variables, on the one hand, and productivity and wages on the other really the result of causation?

3. WORKFORCE AGEING, SENIORITY AND LABOUR COSTS IN FINLAND: BASIC FACTS

In this section, we present some basic pieces of information on the variables of interest in the statistical analysis below.

In Section 3.1 we argue that Finland shares some common demographic and labour market trends with other European countries, such as the difficult labour market position of old workers. Hence the Finnish case discussed here may be seen as paradigmatic of issues faced by many countries. At the same time, though, the Finnish case also presents some specificity, namely the intensity of the technological and managerial shock in the late 1990s. As discussed above, rapid technological change may accelerate skill depreciation, thereby making the cost-increasing effect of ageing and seniority a more serious concern for firms.

In Section 3.2, directly related to our main object of concern (i.e. investigating how workforce ageing may be a burden for firms), we briefly describe how plant age, seniority and potential experience pair-wise correlate with productivity and wages in our data set of manufacturing plants.

Table 1. The exceptional increase in the share of IT manufacturing goods in total manufacturing in Finland in the second half of the 1990s (1995–2001, percentage points)

Swe	Nor	Den	Jap	USA	UK	Fin	Ger	Net	Ire	Fra	Spa	Ita
−1.4	+0.4	+0.1	+2.0	+2.0	+0.6	+13.4	+1.0	−0.3	+2.3	+0.8	−0.4	−0.8

Source: OECD (2003).

3.1. Workforce ageing and the Finnish IT revolution in the 1990s

Finland is no exception in the OECD as far as the weak labour market situation of older workers is concerned. Old workers in Finland tend to achieve lower labour market participation and employment rates, and suffer from higher unemployment rates than workers in the same age group in other Nordic countries. At the same time, if one compares Finland to countries in Continental Europe, one finds that the old Finns enjoy relatively higher participation and employment and lower unemployment. So Finland is about half-way down the OECD ranking.

These labour market outcomes come with a twist of originality compared to the rest of the OECD, though: throughout the 1990s, the skills of older workers in Finland have also been challenged by the unusually fast pace of the IT revolution in that country.

In the 1990s, the world demand for cellular phones boomed under the push of declining semi-conductor prices. Thanks to Nokia's managerial ability and leadership in the cellular phone industry, the share of electronics (SITC 32–33) in the Finnish GDP markedly rose from about 3.5% of nominal GDP in 1995 to 8.2% in 2000.[4] Throughout the same period of time, the value added of the forest industry (and notably of the industry named 'Pulp, paper and wood products', SITC 20–21) fell from 7.5% in 1995 to 6% in 2000. In parallel – an example of how not all of the so called high-tech industries have gained throughout this period of time – the value added share of 'Industrial machinery and equipment' (SITC 29–31) slightly fell from 5.7% to 5.4% in 2000.

The Nokia-driven technological and managerial shock has been unique in an international landscape. As reported in Table 1, the share of IT goods production over total manufacturing went up by 13.4 percentage points in Finland between 1995 and 2001. This is also remarkable because the beneficial effects of declining semiconductor prices were potentially out there for every country. As shown in Table 2, however, the other OECD countries have seemingly not taken this opportunity or

---

[4] This increase was also the result of the rapid development of a myriad of ancillary manufacturing and high-tech consultancy activities around Nokia. Some of them are first-tier suppliers to Nokia. Some others provide such electronic manufacturing services as component sourcing, equipment renting, production design and testing, and thus bridge the gap between equipment manufacturers and component suppliers. See Ali-Yrkkö *et al.* (2000) and Daveri and Silva (2004) for more detailed renditions.

Table 2. Correlations between averages in 1995–2002

	Age	Experience	Seniority	log of TFP	log of wage
Forest industry					
Age	1				
Experience	0.9939*	1			
Seniority	0.7824*	0.7679*	1		
log of TFP	−0.1747*	−0.1766*	−0.1815*	1	
log of wage	0.4736*	0.4271*	0.6069*		1
Number of observations: 365					
Industrial machinery					
Age	1				
Experience	0.9790*	1			
Seniority	0.6792*	0.6605*	1		
log of TFP		−0.117	−0.1565*	1	
log of wage	0.2317*	0.1127	0.1635*	0.3495*	1
Number of observations: 567					
Electronics					
Age	1				
Experience	0.9528*	1			
Seniority	0.7085*	0.6971*	1		
log of TFP			−0.2118	1	
log of wage	0.2697*			0.2556*	1
Number of observations: 172					

have exploited it differently (perhaps on the IT services side). No doubt, the intensity of the IT technological and managerial shock in the 1990s was of much bigger magnitude in Finland than in any other OECD country.

3.2. Age, seniority, experience, productivity and earnings in Finnish manufacturing plants

To tackle the questions we are interested in before delving into the deeper statistical analysis enabled by multivariate techniques, we describe the main features of our plant-level data set as well as the sample statistics and correlation between age, seniority and potential experience, on the one hand, and the two main components of labour costs, productivity and wages, on the other.

3.2.1. Data set. Similar to the other Nordic countries, Finland is endowed with a rich register data of companies, plants and individuals. The unique identification codes for persons, companies and plants used in the different registers form the backbone of the Finnish administrative register network and the Finnish statistical system, whereby different sources of information can be integrated conveniently for various statistical purposes.[5]

---

[5] Data sources and linking of them are described in the Appendix of this paper and, in greater detail, in Ilmakunnas *et al.* (2001) and Maliranta (2003).

This paper employs linked plant-level information for plants and workforce from the Census of Manufacturing and Employment Statistics between 1990 and 2002 (1995 and 2002, in the main part of our statistical analysis).[6] Thanks to this link, we have valuable information on the characteristics of the labour input for the plants. This includes the average potential experience (the number of years after the last completed degree), seniority (the number of years spent working in the current company) and education (the number of schooling years needed for the degree). On the side of the plant labour costs, we have information about gross wage, value added per hour worked ('labour productivity'), capital stock per hour worked (the 'capital-labour ratio') and the value added shares of capital. These pieces of information, put together as detailed in Box 3, allow us to compute a total factor productivity (TFP) index, a measure of sheer efficiency of each plant.

Box 3. How we computed plant productivity

We numerically compute a TFP (total factor productivity) index – an index of disembodied technical knowledge under constant returns to scale and perfect competition in factor markets, from the standard growth accounting formula in natural logarithms:

$$\ln(TFP)_{pit} = \ln(Y/L)_{pit} - (1 - \bar{a}_i) * \ln(K/L)_{pit}$$

with $\bar{a}_i$ denoting the average industry specific labour share during the period. The average is calculated from the annual industry labour shares preliminarily smoothed by a non-linear filter. Thus we allow the output elasticity of capital and labour to vary between different industries, but not between plants within the same industry. Our TFP index is thus suitable both for analysing both the cross-sectional and time series variation of our data.

In the second step of our empirical analysis, we relate the computed TFP index to the plant characteristics, including average workers characteristics, indicated in the main text.

3.2.2. Summary statistics for Finnish industries and plants.
Tables 2 and 3 show data on the pattern of correlation in our data set, separately for each industry, both for period-averaged plant data (hence along the cross-sectional dimension; see Table 2) and along the time series dimension (see Table 3).

---

[6] The observations between 1990 and 1994 are employed as instruments for data concerning the 1995–2002 period in our statistical analysis.

Table 3. Correlation over time (between variable changes; from 1995 to 2002)

	Age	Experience	Seniority	log of TFP	log of wage
Forest industry					
Age	1				
Experience	0.9784*	1			
Seniority	0.7029*	0.7566*	1		
log of TFP				1	
log of wage					1
Number of observations: 199					
Industrial machinery					
Age	1				
Experience	0.9812*	1			
Seniority	0.7989*	0.7591	1		
log of TFP				1	
log of wage					1
Number of observations: 197					
Electronics					
Age	1				
Experience	0.9922	1			
Seniority			1		
log of TFP				1	
log of wage					1
Number of observations: 49					

Notes: We only report correlation significant at least at the 10% level. * indicates significance at the 1% level. Bonferroni adjustments have been made to significance levels.

As implied by how we measure potential experience, there is a very strong correlation between age and potential experience in all three industries, along both cross-sectional and time dimensions. Not surprisingly either, age and potentially experience have very similar correlations with other variables. The correlation between age and seniority is instead somewhat lower (it ranges between 0.7 and 0.8) but is still clearly statistically significant. The correlation regarding other variables is often statistically insignificant, particularly over time; if this is the case, we omit reporting correlation coefficients.

In the cross-sectional data age and wages are positively correlated, while age is negatively correlated (in the forest industry) or uncorrelated (in Industrial Machinery and Electronics) with TFP. Seniority instead has a negative correlation with TFP in all the three industries but has a positive correlation with the wage level except in Electronics where the correlation is not statistically significant. A positive correlation between the wage level and TFP is there instead for Industrial Machinery and Electronics. We have also computed these correlations separately for declining and expanding plants. Some of the earlier significant correlations turn out to be insignificant but the problem is the small number of observations in some cases (especially in Electronics) which makes it hard to draw further conclusions from these calculations.

4. WORKFORCE AGEING AND THE FIRM: THE EVIDENCE FROM FINNISH MANUFACTURING PLANTS

4.1. Empirical strategy

The aim of our statistical analysis is to identify the plant-wide relation between age and age-related variables (seniority, potential experience) on the one hand and labour costs (productivity and wages) on the other.

The logic of our empirical exercise is straightforward. To evaluate the relation between ageing and plant productivity, we first relate the plant productivity index (computed as in Box 3) to our main variables of interest: age, potential experience and seniority of the plant workforce, and (as indicated in Box 4) to a number of other relevant variables whose statistical significance is of secondary importance for our main purpose in this paper. Then we repeat the same type of exercise with earnings – instead of productivity – as a dependent variable.

Box 4. Two methods for calculating age-productivity profiles at the plant level

Hellerstein and Neumark (1995), Hellerstein *et al.* (1999), Haegeland and Klette (1999) and Ilmakunnas and Maliranta (2005) have used information on the shares of workers in different groups (such as to education, age and the like) to model the quality of the labour input of a plant in a production function estimated from plant level data. By directly estimating this production function jointly with an equation for average wage, they were able to quantify and compare the productivity and wage profiles.

At least with our Finnish data set (but this is known to be a more general problem), this method often tends to produce implausibly low estimates for the capital input coefficients, which may bias the estimated coefficients for age-productivity profiles. Thus, following Griliches and Rinstad (1971) and, more recently, Ilmakunnas *et al.* (2004), we employ a two-step procedure.

First, we numerically compute a TFP (total factor productivity) index (as described in Box 4). Then, in the second step of our empirical analysis, we relate the computed TFP index to the plant characteristics, including average workers characteristics, indicated in the main text. Our variables of interest are seniority (the number of years spent working in the current company), average potential experience (the number of years after the last completed degree) and the number of schooling years (usually needed for the degree). Other included variables are plant age, foreign ownership, and a dummy variable for disappearing plants.

> In the end, our two-step specification, partly based on growth accounting techniques, comes at the cost of accepting the – possibly plausible but essentially untested – constant returns to scale and perfect competition assumptions mentioned above. Maliranta (1997) found that the assumption of constant returns to scale in the Finnish manufacturing sector is approximately correct.

In our empirical analysis we exploit three industry panels along the cross-plant and time series dimensions. The three industries have been selected for being representative, respectively, of an 'average' pre-boom manufacturing industry ('forest'), a non-booming capital-intensive industry ('industrial machinery') and a booming high-tech industry ('electronics'). As reported in the summary statistics in Table A1 of the appendix, we have data for 365 plants for the forest industry, 567 plants for 'industrial machinery and equipment' and 172 plants for 'electronics'. For each of these plants, we have a maximum of eight observations over the years between 1995 and 2002. The unbalanced nature of our panel is such that, when using the variation of the data over time, we are able to employ at most respectively 1523, 1717 and 496 observations (hence about 52%, 38% and 36% of the total potential observations). A fraction of the missing observations is due to plant 'death' in 1996–2002, which represents about 12% of the forest industry, 20% of machinery and 22% of electronics. The share of disappearing plants is therefore one-fourth of the total missing for forest and about one-third for the other industries.

4.1.1. What we hope to learn.   The statistical significance and the size of the estimated coefficients of the variables of interest give us important information as to whether and how workforce ageing raises labour costs for the firm or not. Moreover, we want to learn whether age as such is important or if instead, as predicted by the theories discussed in the previous section, the productivity-wage implications of seniority ('ageing within the firm') are different from those of potential experience ('ageing outside the firm'), as predicted by some of the models discussed in the previous section. Moreover, to understand whether the intuition underlying human capital theories is borne by the data, we will also check whether ageing has a declining effect on productivity and wages for older people. Third, to learn whether human capital theories must be supplemented by the other explanations based on the institutions and incentive considerations discussed above as the deferred compensation hypothesis, we will check whether the effects of age, seniority and experience are different for productivity and wages.

In addition to that, the cross-industry variation in our data gives us the possibility of testing whether the industry (more ambitiously, the technological content of industrial production) makes a difference for age-productivity profiles. If new technologies significantly affect the wage-productivity race, we expect to find industry-specific patterns of partial correlation, with differences showing up in particular between electronics and the other industries.

Finally, productivity and wages do not depend on variables such as age, seniority or experience only, but also on education (measured as the number of years of schooling) as well as a few additional other observed and unobserved factors varying across plants but more or less constant over time (such as plant size, foreign ownership and outright time-invariant plant vintage, discussed right below), as well as those factors varying over time but equally for all plants (such as unobserved year-specific effects).[7] Hence, the influence of all these variables together with the effects of ageing is jointly tested in our statistical analysis. In each table, explanatory notes will report the list of the variables employed in the various specifications.

4.2. Implementation difficulties

Our undertaking confronts five main difficulties of implementation: attenuation, reverse causation, unobserved heterogeneity, selectivity and measurement error. We discuss each of them separately, also indicating how we tackle such problems in our empirical analysis.

4.2.1. Attenuation. A very common problem with panels such as the one at hand is that the variation over time of the panel data may be very noisy and subtract precision from the statistical analysis of the underlying phenomenon, giving rise to the so-called attenuation bias. In practice, if this problem is present, the estimated coefficient of age or seniority in the empirical analysis of the determinants of productivity would be artificially biased towards zero. Using plant data averaged over all available years allows one to get rid of this unnecessary noise and, hopefully, concentrate on the underlying long-run relation. This is why, in each table, we present one set of results where standard statistical techniques (such as ordinary least squares) are employed with the cross-section of plants estimated separately for each industry.

4.2.2. Reverse causation. Cross-sectional statistical analysis based on averaged data is not problem-free either, unfortunately. A big problem is potential reverse causation. The statistical relations we intend to analyse posit that age or age-related variables are the independent variables and productivity the dependent variable. But cross-sectional data as such (be they observed at a given point in time or averaged over time) only indicate correlation, not causation. Therefore, if the estimated coefficient linking seniority and productivity is negative (say, after a certain age threshold), this may not indicate that the plants where aged workers are employed are less productive. Rather, the negative correlation may simply signal that senior workers tend to be hired in less productive and older plants, probably featuring outdated machines and methods of production, while new, innovative and high-productivity plants may be

---

[7] Such period effects are appended to the list of the explanatory variables when the time variation of the data is considered, and not when cross-sectional plant data are used.

more often matched to young workers. If this is the case, we would be wrongly interpreting what causes what, attributing to seniority the effect of plant age on plant productivity.

We deal with this problem in two ways. First, in our cross-sectional analysis, we always include an additional explanatory variable: plant age, namely a categorical variable indicating the period of establishment of the plant. If the correlation between seniority or experience and productivity hides a causal correlation from low-productivity old machines onto old (potentially high-productivity) workers, the statistical effect of workers' seniority and experience on plant productivity should disappear once the effect of plant age is accounted for. Second, in another empirical specification (Instrumental Variables, or IV), we supplement the contemporaneous values of the explanatory variables with their lagged values (measured in 1990–94) as additional explanatory variables. If today's plant productivity (say, in 1995–2002) may have a contemporaneous feedback effect onto today's plant seniority, this feedback is less likely to be present when another explanatory variable such as seniority measured yesterday (i.e. in 1990–94) is appended to the list of the productivity determinants.

4.2.3. Unobserved heterogeneity.
Surely, a lot of unobserved heterogeneity in plant productivity is still there in the data even once we have augmented the list of productivity determinants with plant vintage and other lagged variables. Yet the problem of interpreting the statistical results from cross-sectional estimates arises if and only if the unobserved (therefore unmeasured) plant variables are correlated with the included explanatory variables. For example, if managerial ability – a typically unobserved plant variable – were unrelated to hiring decisions, then leaving it out of the empirical analysis would not be a major problem. Unfortunately, instead, an able plant manager may be particularly inclined to hire young productive workers (as Juuti, 2001 pointed out). Then if managerial ability is not observed and therefore omitted from the analysis, its effect may be picked up by the negative estimated relation between senior workers and productivity. We would be misperceiving the effect of managerial ability on hiring decisions as if it were the causal effect of age on productivity. To tackle this problem, we use fixed-effects estimation by appending to the list of explanatory variables terms summarizing the joint effect of the unobserved determinants of plant productivity as long as they are not variable over time (as managerial efficiency is). In this way, the estimated coefficient linking age and productivity is purged of the unwanted influence of unobserved variables constant over time.

By analysing the time variation of our data as well, we can significantly extend sample size, usually associated with enhanced statistical precision.[8] When adopting

---

[8] Clearly, however, the additional observations, being repeated for the same plants, cannot be taken as independent observations. Thus in our statistical analysis, we allow for the error term (the residual unobserved components not captured by the explanatory variable included in our statistical analysis) to be auto-correlated, i.e. to be time-dependent. This serves the purpose of not being misled by the potentially increased gain of precision achieved in capturing the phenomena at hand, thanks to the increased sample size. Accounting for auto-correlation is instead important to correctly appreciate the explanatory power of our model along the time dimension.

the fixed-effects statistical model, however, one effectively relinquishes information contained in the cross-sectional framework and concentrate on the so-called 'within-plant' variation in the panel data set. This may be a good thing if the goal is to answer some questions which – by construction – could not be addressed in the cross-sectional framework, the main of which is whether the relation between the age-related variables, education, productivity and wages is a simultaneous one or whether it operates with some delay.

4.2.4. Selectivity.   Our panel data set also presents selectivity problems, which manifest themselves in two fashions. The first problem is typical of any panel of plants or individuals. Longitudinal studies typically suffer from non-random attrition, that is, the loss of respondents over time tends to generate an upward bias in the age-productivity estimate, given that the plants remaining in the sample are usually positively selected, being very often the best ones. A remedy for this type of selectivity would entail splitting the statistical analysis into two steps. The first step is to estimate the probability that plants (and workers) will disappear from our sample. The second step entails correcting the estimated coefficients, taking into account the bias induced by the omission of the disappeared plants. We do not go that far. Plainly, in evaluating our cross-sectional evidence we check the statistical significance of a variable taking value equal to zero for the plants continuing throughout the period and one for the plants exiting the sample between 1996 and 2002 (as Griliches and Regev, 1995, did in their Israeli study). This variable is not significantly related to productivity or wages in our sample and therefore does not affect our results.

Within continuing plants, though, the between-plant movement of workers may add another bias, whose sign is not clear *a priori*. Those workers who choose to stay and continue to work in a given plant instead of engaging in job shopping to improve their existing match may be the least entrepreneurial (and possibly the least productive) workers. The most able and youngest workers, with a greater scope for job-to-job mobility, may instead be eager to leave the most inefficient firms. Hence, plant productivity may appear to decline as a result of the process of job turnover that leaves behind senior workers rather than being the sheer consequence of declining ability. Therefore a negative statistical correlation in a cross-section of plants may not be the result of skill depreciation of the workforce in each given plant and instead originate from the reallocation effects due to the movement of workers between plants.

By the same token, the rising part of the seniority-productivity profile may not be the result of the higher average productivity of expert workers. Experienced workers may well end up in more productive plants as a result of positive sorting: senior workers may have had the time to sort out plants and choose the best places for work.

Our statistical techniques allow us to evaluate the influence of the host of factors that may be causing attenuation, reverse causation and unobserved heterogeneity. But we are unable to precisely decompose how much of our results are due to reallocation and how much to skill depreciation. Hence, we cannot fully deal with this second type of selectivity issues due to workers' reallocation and sorting. Yet if one simply appends hiring and separation rates (lagged by one period to lessen reverse causation) in our empirical exercises to be discussed below, plant productivity is unrelated to hiring rates and negatively related to separation rates, while the statistical significance of the age-related variables does not change.

This is good news for us, for it implies that our results are not merely the figment of specification mistakes. Yet, given that hiring and separation rates are presumably jointly determined with productivity and wages, we hesitate to interpret our results as definite evidence that our correlations are only due to skill depreciation and not worker reallocation.

4.2.5. Measurement error in value added shares. As explained above, our empirical analysis goes in two steps. First, we numerically calculate productivity from value added data, imputing constant industry-specific value added shares of labour and capital and then we relate our productivity index to its likely determinants. The resulting residual is legitimately interpreted as 'plant productivity' as long as the assumptions of constant returns to scale and perfect competition are accepted. This may be hard-to-swallow assumptions that may bias our results in a direction hard to trace *a priori*. As a shortcut, we simply re-computed our productivity index with somewhat higher and somewhat lower value added shares (by plus and minus 10%). For brevity, we do not report the results of this experiment here. Their thrust, though, is that our findings carry over unchanged, irrespective of the imputed values of the value added shares.

Another way of tackling this issue is by directly estimating production or value added functions. We cannot estimate production functions for our data set does not include data on intermediate products. We did look, however, at the partial correlation between capital per hour worked and our variables of interest on the one hand and value added per hour worked on the other in simple value added regressions that are based on an idea of two inputs in production, labour and capital. The estimated coefficients for capital per hour worked are statistically significant for plants in the forest industry and industrial machinery but much lower than the imputed value for the share of capital in value added (usually about one-third), while they are instead not significantly different from zero for electronics.[9] In any case, the statistical significance of our variables of interest (age, seniority, experience) and education does not change.

4.3. Main results

The main results of this paper revolve around the questions listed at the end of Section 2. Is age related to productivity and wages at all? Is the seniority effect of age

---

[9] The unavailability of data for the intermediate inputs prevents from carrying out the Levinsohn-Petrin correction for the endogeneity of capital in production function and value added regressions.

on productivity and wages different from the effect of age through the general experience channel? Are the effects of age on productivity and wages significantly different from each other and across industries, in particular between 'average' and high-tech industries? And finally, are we capturing causal relations?

Our answers to these questions are presented in industry tables: Table 4 presents the results for the Forest industry, Table 5 for Industrial Machinery and Table 6 for Electronics. Each table is organized in two sub-tables, with the results on the determinants of productivity in the upper panel (panel a) and results for wages in the lower panel (panel b). In turn, each sub-table includes the estimated coefficients for the variables of interest (age, seniority, potential experience and education) computed in various ways, for there is no best statistical method to compute them. The reported results are obtained both averaging data over time (and using Ordinary Least Squares (OLS) and Instrumental Variables (IV) methods of estimation) and also simultaneously exploiting the cross-section and time series variation in the data, with the time-invariant plant-specific unobserved determinants of productivity and wages captured by fixed effects (FE). But, as discussed above, cross-section estimates minimize loss of precision (attenuation bias) at the cost of enhancing reverse causation, unobserved heterogeneity and selectivity biases. IV estimates reduce reverse causation and FE estimates tackle unobserved heterogeneity, but both (IV and FE) methods often entail substantial loss of precision of the estimated coefficients.

In any case, each table is structured so as to make the results from the various twists of our statistical exercises easily comparable. The list of the additionally included variables (potentially important determinants of productivity and wages which are not the main focus of this paper) is also provided at the bottom of each table.

4.3.1. Age as such is not related to productivity but is positively correlated to wages.
The statistical results in columns [1] and [2] in each table account for at least 50% (with a maximum of 60%) of the total variability of plant productivity and wages in the three industries. Most of the explanatory power of the estimated statistical relations comes, however, from two groups of variables which do not represent the main focus of this paper but are anyway possibly important determinants of productivity and earnings: education and plant age (more comments below in the next section).

The main result from columns [1] and [2] is that workforce age *per se* is unrelated to plant productivity. Age is instead positively related to wages in all of the three industries, with some evidence of declining effects of age on wages in industrial machinery. So, as payroll increases but productivity stays constant it means that a firm's profitability declines with ageing of the firm's labour force.

The different pattern of correlation between age, productivity and wages brings about another related point: if wages do not reflect the productivity contribution of older workers, approximating individually unobserved productivity by wages – as sometimes is done – may drive one to misleading conclusions.

Table 4. Statistical analysis of the determinants of plant productivity and wages: forest industry

| | OLS | | | | IV | Fixed effects |
| | Cross-section | | | | Cross-section | Panel |
	[1]	[2]	[3]	[4]	[5]	[6]
Panel a. Productivity						
Age	0.015 (0.154)	0.000 (0.011)				-0.198 (0.122)
Age²	-0.002 (0.019)					
log of tenure			0.181 (0.305)	0.240* (0.099)	0.373+ (0.221)	0.019 (0.012)
[log of tenure]²			0.017 (0.076)			0.082 (0.057)
Potential experience			-0.023 (0.016)	-0.022 (0.015)	-0.031 (0.025)	-0.014 (0.056)
Schooling years	-0.048 (0.082)	-0.048 (0.083)	-0.067 (0.090)	-0.063 (0.086)	0.052 (0.080)	0.046 (0.051)
Schooling y. (t-1)						
Schooling y. (t-2)						
R-squared	0.409	0.409	0.422	0.422	0.191	0.132
Adj. R-squared	0.385	0.387	0.398	0.399	0.157	0.089
R-squared, within						
Observations	365	365	365	365	279	1523
Overident. test					0.813	
Relevance test					0.000	
Panel b. Wages						
Age	-0.025 (0.046)	0.025*** (0.003)				
Age²	0.006 (0.006)	0.006 (0.006)				

Table 4. *Continued*

| | OLS | | | | IV | Fixed effects |
| | Cross-section | | | | Cross-section | Panel |
	[1]	[2]	[3]	[4]	[5]	[6]
log of tenure			−0.173*	0.112***	0.425***	0.136***
			(0.085)	(0.027)	(0.081)	(0.030)
[log of tenure]^2			0.081***			
			(0.023)			
Potential experience			0.009*	0.015***	−0.013	0.009**
			(0.005)	(0.004)	(0.009)	(0.003)
Schooling years	0.159***	0.157***	0.158***	0.174***	0.150***	0.245***
	(0.024)	(0.024)	(0.025)	(0.025)	(0.033)	(0.014)
Schooling y. (*t*−1)						0.179***
						(0.014)
Schooling y. (*t*−2)						0.096***
						(0.013)
R-squared	0.520	0.517	0.565	0.546	0.532	
Adj. R-squared	0.500	0.500	0.547	0.528	0.513	
R-squared, within						0.590
Observations	365	365	365	365	279	1523
Overident. test					0.467	0.670
Relevance test					0.000	

Notes: Dependent variable: is logarithm of plant productivity in panel a and log of wages in panel b. Other control variables (results not reported) for models reported in columns [1]–[4] include a dummy variable for foreign-owned plant, one for plants that disappear in 1996–2002 and other dummies for plant vintage groups (6 groups) and size groups (5 groups). In column [5], seniority is instrumented with a set of lagged variables (the average in the period 1990–94). They include schooling years, potential experience, potential experience squared, seniority and seniority squared. In column [5], high *p*-values (> 10%) for the over-identification test (Hansen *J* statistics) indicate that the validity of the instruments cannot be rejected and low *p*-values (< 0.1%) of relevance test (Anderson canonical correspondence LR statistic) gives indication that the employed instruments are relevant both in productivity and wage estimations.
+ *p* < 0.1, * *p* < 0.05, ** *p* < 0.01, *** *p* < 0.001.

Table 5. Statistical analysis of the determinants of plant productivity and wages: Industrial machinery

| | OLS | | | | IV | Fixed effects |
| | Cross-section | | | | Cross-section | Panel |
	[1]	[2]	[3]	[4]	[5]	[6]
Panel a. Productivity						
Age	0.103	0.005				0.077
	(0.079)	(0.005)				(0.087)
Age^2	−0.013					
	(0.010)					
log of tenure			0.135	−0.081	−0.035	−0.014
			(0.191)	(0.050)	(0.114)	(0.009)
[log of tenure]^2			−0.062			
			(0.051)			
Potential experience			0.014*	0.012+	−0.003	
			(0.007)	(0.007)	(0.011)	
Schooling years	0.124***	0.125***	0.138***	0.137***	0.086**	0.035
	(0.026)	(0.026)	(0.028)	(0.028)	(0.028)	(0.034)
Schooling y: (t−1)						0.001
						(0.037)
Schooling y: (t−2)						0.102**
						(0.036)
R-squared	0.394	0.392	0.397	0.395	0.219	0.212
Adj. R-squared	0.378	0.377	0.380	0.380	0.193	
R-squared, within						0.049
Observations	567	567	567	567	348	1717
Overident. test					0.351	
Relevance test					0.000	
Panel b. Wages						
Age	0.105***	0.015***				
	(0.024)	(0.002)				

Table 5. *Continued*

| | OLS | | | | IV | Fixed effects |
| | Cross-section | | | | Cross-section | Panel |
	[1]	[2]	[3]	[4]	[5]	[6]
Age²	-0.012*** (0.003)					
log of tenure			0.074 (0.073)	-0.012 (0.017)	0.097+ (0.055)	0.056* (0.024)
[log of tenure]²			-0.025 (0.019)			
Potential experience			0.017*** (0.002)	0.016*** (0.002)	0.008 (0.005)	0.003 (0.002)
Schooling years	0.117*** (0.008)	0.117*** (0.008)	0.133*** (0.008)	0.133*** (0.008)	0.124*** (0.011)	0.065*** (0.010)
Schooling y: (t-1)						0.005 (0.010)
Schooling y: (t-2)						0.019+ (0.010)
R-squared	0.470	0.454	0.457	0.455	0.437	0.836
Adj. R-squared	0.457	0.441	0.442	0.441	0.419	0.871
R-squared, within						
Observations	567	567	567	567	348	1717
Overident. test					0.024	
Relevance test					0.000	

Notes: Dependent variable: is logarithm of plant productivity in panel a and log of wages in panel b. Other control variables (results not reported) for models reported in columns [1]–[4] include a dummy variable for foreign-owned plant, one for plants that disappear in 1996–2002 and other dummies for plant vintage groups (6 groups) and size groups (5 groups). In column [5], seniority is instrumented with a set of lagged variables (the average in the period 1990–94). They include schooling years, potential experience, potential experience squared, seniority and seniority squared. In column [5], high p-values (> 10%) for the over-identification test (Hansen J statistics) indicate that the validity of the instruments cannot be rejected and low p-values (< 0.1%) of relevance test (Anderson canonical correspondence LR statistic) gives indication that the employed instruments are relevant in productivity but not in wage estimation.

+ $p < 0.1$, * $p < 0.05$, ** $p < 0.01$, *** $p < 0.001$.

Table 6. Statistical analysis of the determinants of plant productivity and wages: Electronics

| | OLS | | | | IV | Fixed effects |
| | Cross-section | | | | Cross-section | Panel |
	[1]	[2]	[3]	[4]	[5]	[6]
Panel a. Productivity						
Age	-0.408	0.024				0.937
	(0.377)	(0.026)				(0.599)
Age²	0.061					-0.356+
	(0.053)					(0.184)
log of tenure			1.741*	-0.062	2.380+	
			(0.749)	(0.232)	(1.443)	
[log of tenure]²			-0.549*		-0.639+	
			(0.230)		(0.349)	
Potential experience			0.028	0.030	-0.013	-0.010
			(0.035)	(0.036)	(0.045)	(0.032)
Schooling years	0.180**	0.178**	0.182*	0.207**	0.191***	-0.043
	(0.064)	(0.064)	(0.071)	(0.070)	(0.055)	(0.082)
Schooling y. (t-1)						-0.007
						(0.090)
Schooling y. (t-2)						0.182*
						(0.081)
R-squared	0.301	0.290	0.320	0.291	0.308	-0.203
Adj. R-squared	0.239	0.232	0.254	0.228	0.211	
R-squared, within						0.086
Observations	172	172	172	172	98	496
Overident. test					0.258	
Relevance test					0.000	
Panel b. Wages						
Age	-0.046	0.019***				
	(0.061)	(0.004)				
Age²	0.009					
	(0.009)					

Table 6. *Continued*

| | OLS | | | | IV | Fixed effects |
| | Cross-section | | | | Cross-section | Panel |
	[1]	[2]	[3]	[4]	[5]	[6]
log of tenure			0.192+	0.031	0.528	0.250+
			(0.112)	(0.044)	(0.420)	(0.146)
[log of tenure]^2			−0.049		−0.107	−0.068
			(0.033)		(0.105)	(0.045)
Potential experience			0.016*	0.016*	0.008	0.020*
			(0.006)	(0.006)	(0.012)	(0.008)
Schooling years	0.123***	0.123***	0.137***	0.140***	0.145***	0.160***
	(0.010)	(0.009)	(0.011)	(0.011)	(0.015)	(0.020)
Schooling y. (t−1)						0.120***
						(0.022)
Schooling y. (t−2)						0.134***
						(0.020)
R-squared	0.536	0.530	0.537	0.532	0.617	0.493
Adj. R-squared	0.494	0.492	0.492	0.491	0.563	
R-squared, within						0.615
Observations	172	172	172	172	98	496
Overident. test					0.001	
Relevance test					0.000	

Notes: Dependent variable: is logarithm of plant productivity in panel a and log of wages in panel b. Other control variables (results not reported) for models reported in columns [1]–[4] include a dummy variable for foreign-owned plant, one for plants that disappear in 1996–2002 and other dummies for plant vintage groups (6 groups) and size groups (5 groups). In column [5], seniority is instrumented with a set of lagged variables (the average in the period 1990–94). They include schooling years, potential experience, potential experience squared, seniority and seniority squared. In column [5], high p-values (> 10%) for the over-identification test (Hansen J statistics) indicate that the validity of the instruments cannot be rejected and low p-values (< 0.1%) of relevance test (Anderson canonical correspondence LR statistic) gives indication that the employed instruments are relevant in productivity but not in wage estimation.

+ $p < 0.1$, * $p < 0.05$, ** $p < 0.01$, *** $p < 0.001$.

4.3.2. Seniority matters for productivity more often than experience, but differently in traditional and high-tech industries.
The discussion in Section 2 invites thinking of why age may (or may not) be associated with productivity. It does so suggesting that the process of human capital accumulation takes place within the firm and outside the firm. Lumping together the two effects (as implicitly done in the empirical formulations underlying the results in columns [1] and [2], where age as such is related to productivity) may obscure that the two forms of human capital accumulation need not bear the same returns. The importance of distinguishing these two sources of skills in the analysis of productivity effects is emphasized for instance by Ilmakunnas *et al.* (2004) and Dygalo and Abowd (2005). For example, the accumulation of knowledge that occurs through seniority may be productivity-enhancing while the accumulation of human capital that occurs through the acquisition of overall labour market experience may not contribute positively. In the statistical analysis underlying the results in columns [3]–[6], we dropped this restriction. We find that the statistical significance of seniority and potential experience is indeed different from each other. This also holds across industries and across estimation methods. The overall goodness of fit of IV and FE-based specifications drops significantly.

In the forest industry as well as in electronics, we find that seniority, not potential experience, is positively related to productivity. Our formulation (in logs and logs squared, so as to obtain the best fit of the data) also implies that the effect of seniority on productivity depends on its starting level.

One additional year of seniority for a freshly hired worker adds to productivity less than it adds for a senior worker who has spent a considerable number of years within the same firm. In other words, there are positive but diminishing returns to seniority. In the electronics industry, the returns to seniority decline so much to become negative beyond a certain threshold. These results are well determined when using the period-averaged cross-section of plants and are still there – though less precisely measured – even when seniority is instrumented to allow for possible feedback effects from the lagged values. In the forest industry, the correlation disappears when the time variation of the data is considered through fixed-effects estimation, while a weaker correlation survives for plants in electronics.

In the industrial machinery plants, instead, potential experience positively correlates, though at the usual declining rates, with productivity. Seniority is instead not significantly related to productivity in a statistical sense in this industry. The pattern of partial correlations in this industry is, however, somewhat statistically weaker than for the other industries, for they do not survive when other methods of estimation than the cross-section OLS are employed. This is a symptom that our statistical model that links plant productivity to human capital variables is not equally effective in capturing the determinants of plant productivity in all industries.

4.3.3. Wage and productivity profiles are dissimilar from each other in electronics and similar in the other industries.
In our data set, searching for wage determinants is a more successful undertaking than searching for productivity

determinants. The line interpolating the data explains more than 50% of the total variability of plant wages in the forest industry and in electronics and more than 40% of the total in industrial machinery, even when the time dimension of the data set is considered. Among the age-related variables, seniority drives wages in forest and experience drives wages in the industrial machinery industry. Notably, the seniority-wage profile in the lower panel is not too far apart from the seniority-productivity profile estimated in the upper panel for the forest industry. The same applies to experience-wage and experience-productivity profiles for industrial machinery, although it should be kept in mind that, as emphasized above, the statistical relation is much less precisely measured for the plants in this industry.

When it comes to electronics, the picture instead changes substantially. Wages depend positively but to a declining extent on both tenure and experience in the cross-section of plants. This result is still there when the time variation of the panel data set is considered through fixed-effects estimation. This correlation is instead not there when variables are instrumented by their lagged values.

We interpret these results as showing that the profiles of wages and productivity with respect to age-related variables are significantly different from each other in electronics. Wages keep going up, though at declining rates, with both seniority and experience, while the seniority-productivity profile follows a very different path made of definite increases when seniority is low and a flattening out which also involves sheer productivity declines as seniority goes beyond a given threshold.

4.4. More results

The statistical analysis underlying Tables 4, 5 and 6 also includes some ancillary results on the determinants of plant productivity and wages, concerning education and plant age. The important implication of these additional results is that the correlations between age-related variables, productivity and wages (discussed above) do not hinge on the omission of other important determinants of plant productivity and wages. Reassuringly, education and plant age affect productivity and wages as expected, but consideration of these additional elements does not cancel our main results.

4.4.1. Education is positively related to productivity and wages. The earnings equations estimated by labour economists routinely include education as an explanatory variable and make inference as to the rate of return on additional years of education. And even the importance of workers' educational levels in determining plant productivity can hardly be overstated.

In our statistical analysis, education turns out always positively related to wages in the three industries, with estimated coefficients ranging between 0.12 and 0.15. Yet the estimated coefficient is bigger in forest than in more technologically advanced industries. As to its effects on productivity, they seem to be instead ranked in decreasing order of the technological level of the industry at hand. Education is positively and sizably related to plant productivity in electronics with a bigger coefficient than in industrial machinery. No relation is there for the forest industry.

When the time series dimension is considered, these effects are present only when the delayed values of the explanatory variables are considered instead of the current ones. Education is indeed positively associated with productivity with a delay of about two years (the lagged value of education is almost significantly related to productivity, though with a small coefficient, even for the forest industry).

Altogether, these effects indicate that high-education workers in more advanced industries are in some way 'exploited', while high-education people in forestry enjoy a rent. The idea that high-education people accept lower wages possibly in exchange for a bright future to buy the lottery of working in dynamic plants and industries is consistent with anecdotal evidence from Finnish newspapers.[10]

4.4.2. Newer plants are more productive.

Another ancillary result underlying Tables 4, 5 and 6 is that older plants tend to be less productive than newer plants. This effect is consistently present for the three industries. These results are not reported in the tables for brevity but are anyway singled out and pictured in Figure 1.

Figure 1 shows a graphical illustration of productivity and wage effects of plant vintage, whereas the horizontal bars indicate the average effects of plant vintage on productivity (printed light grey) and wages (printed dark grey), with 95% confidence intervals appended. The evidence in the graph points to the marked quantitative relevance of such effects. Younger plants are indeed definitely more productive in all industries. This also holds for wages, though the effect is much less marked. These results are consistent with the literature briefly surveyed in Box 5.[11]

4.5. Implications of our main results: a numerical illustration

If theory and the related empirical findings were to imply that the effect of age-related variables on productivity is always the same irrespective of age, seniority or experience, one might easily compute the numerical effect of ageing on productivity. The estimated coefficient would tell us by how many percentage points productivity varies as a result of a unit change in the age or seniority of a given person (or the average age of a typical worker in a given plant).

Unfortunately, psychometric studies and the economics of human capital teach us that the world is more complicated and the effect of age on productivity may change its sign from positive into negative starting from some threshold age onwards. This raises the empirical questions of *where* (*at which year of age, seniority or experience*) this

---

[10] A more academic argument following more or less the same lines is in Moen (2005).

[11] Maliranta (1999) experimented with alternative capital stock measures (perpetual inventory method vs. fire insurance value of capital stock). They yielded quite similar results for the plant vintage effects. More recent Finnish evidence of the plant vintage effects include Ilmakunnas *et al.* (2004) and Ilmakunnas and Maliranta (2005).

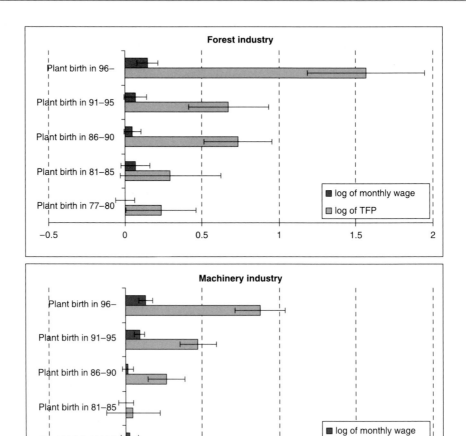

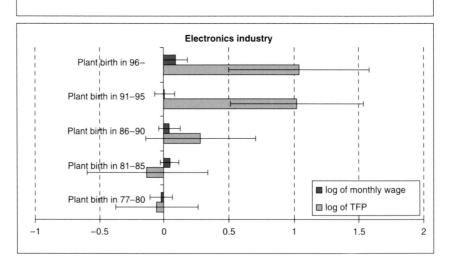

Figure 1. An illustration of productivity and wage effects of plant vintage

Notes: Bars indicate the log difference of total factor productivity and monthly wage with respect to the reference group (plants established in 1976 or earlier). Error bars around the mean bars indicate 95% confidence intervals. The estimates are from the models presented in column [3] of Tables 4–6.

threshold is. Moreover, having found that the returns to seniority decline with seniority or, as in electronics, actually become negative, it remains unclear *by how much* they decline.

Box 5. Old plants, old workers, productivity and wages

Old-aged firms may be less productive and disproportionately hire old-age workers. The evidence on the relation between firm age and productivity is not abundant, though. Dunne *et al.* (1989) report that manufacturing plants that have been in business longer are less likely to close, and Brock and Evans (1986) show that older firms are less likely to fail (controlling for plant and firm size, respectively). This may partly explain why older workers tend to stick with these probably less productive but more financially sound firms.

On the other hand, it has often been found that older firms pay higher wages, after controlling for other relevant firm characteristics. This is often taken to reflect the quality (and thus the higher productivity) of the workers they hire, as well as the working conditions they offer. Yet, as discussed in the main text, this need not be the case. Older firms may pay higher wages to extend fringe benefits, such as pensions or health insurance, to their most faithful workers or, more subtly, because they cannot deny pay raises to people who have developed a good knowledge of the company's ability to pay throughout the years.

Davis and Haltiwanger (1991) find that older manufacturing plants indeed pay higher wages, and age remains a significant determinant of wages once industry, region and size differences are accounted for, with and without controlling for the probability that the plant will close (usually lower for older firms). Troske (1999, Table 11.11) reports similar results: controlling for employer size and location, workers in plants that are less than 5 years old earn nearly 20% less than workers in plants that have been in business 15 years or more. Blanchflower and Oswald (1988) find no significant relationship between wages and years in operation in British data, while Winter-Ebmer (2001) found a positive relation with Austrian data. The very careful study by Kölling *et al.* (2005) shows that, in Germany, older firms pay on average higher wages for workers with the same broadly defined degree of formal qualification. More recently, Brown and Medoff (2003) have analysed the relationship between how long an employer has been in business (firm age) and wages. According to their analysis, firms that have been in business longer pay higher wages (as previous studies have found), but pay if anything lower wages after controlling for worker characteristics. There is some evidence that the relationship is not monotonic, with wages falling and then rising with the number of years in business.

Finally, regarding evidence with Finnish data, Nurmi (2004) finds that old and large firms are less likely to fail and less sensitive to exogenous shocks than young and small firms.

In this section, we employ statistical simulation – a quantitative technique that allows one to describe complicated phenomena in a flexible way (how is described in the top part of Box 5) – to illustrate these issues.

The simulation results are then translated out of the jargon using CLARIFY, the user-friendly software developed by Harvard political scientists Gary King, Michael Tomz and Jason Wittenberg (King *et al.*, 2000; Tomz *et al.*, 2003) expressly for delivering the results of the application of even complicated quantitative techniques to a wider audience not necessarily trained in statistics but still interested in achieving a rather precise knowledge of the quantitative aspects of economic and social issues (see more details in the bottom part of Box 6).

Box 6. Numerical simulations through CLARIFY

a. The issue

The starting point may be a standard multivariate regression exercise where the statistical relation between a dependent variable (say, productivity) and a host of potential explanatory variables (say: age, education and so on) is investigated. The result of a regression exercise usually consists of quantitative information ('estimated coefficients') on the sensitivity of the dependent variable to each of the explanatory variables, while holding the other explanatory variables constant. This piece of information is, however, subject to various sources of uncertainty (the statistical model may be wrong or incomplete; the available information on the explanatory variables may be incomplete as well; some variables of interest may be outright unobserved). Hence, this 'partial correlation' may thus be more or less precisely estimated. If the researcher obtains a precise estimate, the quantitative implication of his-her research may be trusted; otherwise not.

b. Simulation-based approach to interpreting statistical results

Among other things, numerical (so called 'Montecarlo') simulation essentially applies survey sampling techniques to proxy complicated (but presumably more realistic) mathematical relations and eventually determines how trust-worthy the results of a given regression are. In surveys, random sampling from the population of interest is commonly used to estimate key features (such as mean and variance) of such population, with the precision of the estimate increasing in sample size. Simulation essentially follows the same logic to learn about probability distributions of estimated coefficients, not populations. In the same fashion as with real samples, approximations can be computed to any desired level of precision by varying the number of simulations.

c. How statistical simulation works in practice through the software CLARIFY

Start from a set of point-wise estimated coefficients of age, education and the other variables set out to explain productivity. Each of these coefficients has a sampling distribution. The central limit theorem guarantees that, for a large enough sample, one can randomly draw ('simulate') coefficient ('parameter') values from a multivariate normal distribution, with mean equal to the point estimates of the coefficients and variances equal to the estimated variance and covariance matrix of the point-wise estimates. By random drawing, one can obtain a realization of the estimated coefficients on average consistent with their point-wise estimates. This is the result of one simulation round. This experiment can be repeated many times at will (clearly, if the coefficient were precisely known, each draw would be identical) and many values for the estimated coefficient of interest computed. Each coefficient can then be multiplied by the value of its corresponding explanatory variable (age). The variability in the values of the simulated coefficients translates in variability (randomness) of the expected value of productivity (the dependent variable), while the effects of the other variables on productivity are held constant at their means.

As a result, we can compute (and graph) the average partial effect of age on productivity and also confidence intervals that delimit the degree of trustworthiness of such an average. To sum up, in our case, the true relation between age and productivity is likely complicated, for the effect of age on productivity may be positive or negative depending on age. If this is the case, describing the results of statistical analysis becomes rapidly cumbersome and only imperfectly related to the question at hand. King *et al.* (2000) have developed a software program (CLARIFY) that, without changing any underlying data or statistical assumption, provides interpretation-friendly and graphical answers to the questions of interest.

Figures 2 and 3 are the outputs of CLARIFY and concern, respectively, the seniority and experience profiles of productivity and wages estimated *through Ordinary Least Squares from the period-averaged cross-section of plants.*[12] Being OLS cross-sectional OLS estimates, they suffer from many of the biases whose shortcomings have been extensively discussed above. Although precisely tracking the overall direction of the biases is not easy, the reported results likely represent upper bound estimates, and they include both skill depreciation and worker reallocation effects.

The statistical simulations underlying Figures 2 and 3 and Table 7 (based on those figures) revolve around the multivariate statistical analysis whose point-wise results and significance are reported in Table A2 in the appendix. To maximize the goodness

---

[12] To compute the necessary confidence intervals, CLARIFY requires relatively precisely estimated coefficients be imputed. This is why we use OLS cross-sectional estimates, with the caveats in the main text.

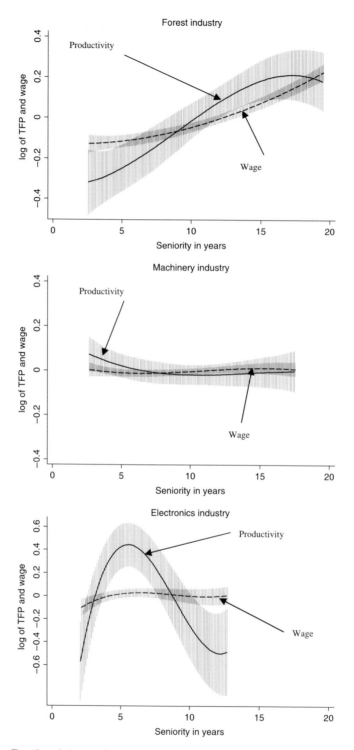

Figure 2. Productivity and wage responses to seniority: simulation analysis from estimates in Table A2

Notes: See Box 6 for a detailed explanation of how such profiles are constructed.

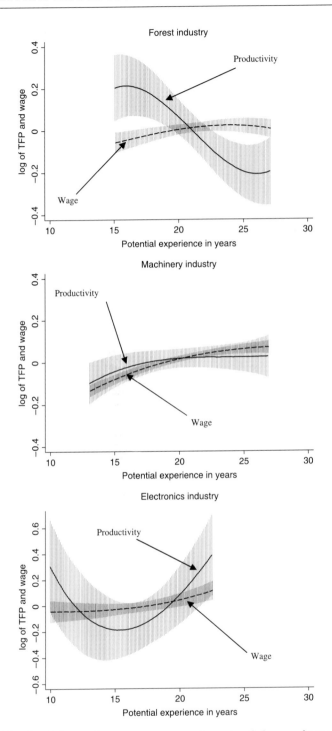

Figure 3. Productivity and wage responses to potential experience: simulation analysis from estimates in Table A2

Notes: See Box 6 for a detailed explanation of how such profiles are constructed.

Table 7. Simulations of cumulated productivity and wage responses under various settings

	Difference . . .		. . . in log of TFP			. . . in log of monthly wage		
	from . . .	to . . .	Mean	Std. err.	t-value	Mean	Std. err.	t-value
Seniority								
Forest								
Seniority in years and other variables	7 at their means	17 at their means	0.38	0.15	2.60	0.23	0.04	5.81
Machinery								
Seniority in years and other variables	7 at their means	17 at their means	0.00	0.08	0.01	0.02	0.03	0.73
Electronics								
Seniority in years and other variables	2 at their means	6 at their means	1.07	0.32	3.31	0.13	0.07	1.83
Seniority in years and other variables	6 at their means	10 at their means	−0.68	0.20	−3.34	−0.03	0.05	−0.61
Potential Experience								
Forest								
Experience in years and other variables	15 at their means	25 at their means	−0.40	0.17	−2.33	0.08	0.05	1.69
Machinery								
Experience in years and other variables	13 at their means	20 at their means	0.12	0.07	1.77	0.15	0.02	7.76
Electronics								
Experience in years and other variables	10 at their means	16 at their means	−0.48	0.22	−2.22	0.02	0.05	0.46
Experience in years Other variables	16 at their means	22 at their means	0.49	0.25	1.95	0.12	0.06	2.13

Table 7. *Continued*

	Difference . . .		. . . in log of TFP			. . . in log of monthly wage		
	from . . .	to . . .	Mean	Std. err.	t-value	Mean	Std. err.	t-value
Seniority and experience combined								
Forest								
Seniority in years	7	17	−0.02	0.12	−0.16	0.31	0.04	8.22
and experience in years	15	25						
and other variables	at their means	at their means						
Machinery								
Seniority in years	3	10	0.04	0.07	0.53	0.15	0.02	6.62
and experience in years	13	20						
and other variables	at their means	at their means						
Electronics								
Seniority in years	2	6	0.61	0.29	2.11	0.14	0.05	2.71
and experience in years	10	14						
and other variables	at their means	at their means						
Seniority in years	6	12	−0.69	0.25	−2.77	0.05	0.05	1.06
and experience in years	14	20						
and other variables	at their means	at their means						

Notes: Simulations are based on the same regression models (results in Table A2) used for drawing Figures 2–3. 'Mean' indicates the log difference of productivity (or wage) levels. Multiplying the number by 100 provides an approximation of percentage difference in productivity (or wage) levels in the different hypothetical situations. For more details on how these figures are computed, see Box 6.

of fit of the interpolating line, the empirical specification underlying the graphs is more flexible than those in Tables 4, 5 and 6. This boils down to appending more polynomial terms of the same variables to the list of the productivity and wage determinants, in addition to the linear and squared terms present in the tables seen above.

In each figure, along the vertical axis, one reads the marginal response of the dependent variables (logarithms of TFP and wages) to changes in seniority, experience and education years, measured along the horizontal axis. Such responses are defined over the interval of values taken by each explanatory variable in the industry at hand. The thick and dotted lines indicate, respectively, the average marginal response of TFP and wages (with the average taken over the very many potential values of the coefficients of interest). The dot-shaded and line-shaded intervals around such estimated average responses represent confidence intervals, which provide an indication of the degree of precision of the simulated estimates.

4.5.1. Seniority profiles (Figure 2). Productivity and wage responses to the cross-section variability in the number of seniority years are very similar to each other in the forest industry (both growing fast) and in industrial machinery (both essentially flat, once confidence intervals are taken into account). From the figures reported in the upper part of Table 7, one learns that, moving from a plant with a seniority of 7 years for the average worker to a plant with seniority equal to 17, having set the other determinants of productivity to their means results in a productivity increase of 38% in the forest industry. In electronics, the seniority-productivity profile follows a well-defined inverted-U shape, while the wage is mildly increasing. These trends correspond to a swift positive productivity response of cumulated 107% as one shift from plants with an average worker seniority of two years to plants with worker seniority equal to six years (with wages going up more moderately). If one moves further by another four years from plants with seniority equal to six to plants with seniority equal to ten, productivity undergoes a (relative) shortfall of cumulative 68%, with roughly unchanged wages. These are huge numbers. As mentioned in the caveat above, however, they are upper bound estimates also inclusive of worker reallocation effects. It should be noted, though, that very drastic declines in relative productivity levels with age have been documented for other countries such as France in the literature (see e.g. Figure 4.4 in Productivity Commission, 2005).

4.5.2. Experience profiles (Figure 3). Productivity and wage responses to the cross-section variability in the years of potential experience are much less precisely estimated, particularly for productivity. This may be the result of multi-collinearity between experience and seniority, which may be at the origin of the initially downward sloping response of productivity to experience in the forest industry and in electronics. In industrial machinery, one finds instead plausible results with positive wage and productivity responses to experience (with wages and productivity by 15% and 12% respectively over 7 years; see Table 7). A possible way out is to compute the implied productivity response of both higher experience and seniority (after all, if a worker stays with the same plant, he/she acquires both experience and seniority at once). When this is done (see the results in the lower panel of Table 7, 'Seniority and experience combined'), one finds an essentially flat productivity response to the combination of seniority and experience and a moderately positive wage response for a cumulated 15% over 7 years of time. The combination of seniority and experience leaves the results for electronics qualitatively unchanged, instead. When the number of seniority and experience years is relatively low, moving from low-seniority and low-experience plants to high-seniority and high-experience plants corresponds to a cumulated productivity increase of about 60%. When this is done moving from intermediate to high levels of seniority and experience, the productivity shortfall is of about 70%. Wages do not follow suit, instead, but keep going up.

4.6. Summing up and discussion

Our statistical analysis provides a reasonably coherent picture of the empirical relation between age, seniority and experience, on the one hand, and plant productivity and wages, on the other, in Finland in the years of the IT revolution.

At first sight, our results seem to support the view that workforce ageing as such has adverse effects on labour costs. Age is essentially unrelated to productivity while it is positively correlated with wages. As we distinguish the effects of seniority on productivity and wages from those of general experience, though, we find that the picture is more complicated and sharply differs across industries (see Box 7 for a survey of other studies emphasizing industry differences in productivity and wage profiles).

Box 7. Previous statistical evidence on age, seniority, experience, productivity and wages

About 25 years ago, Medoff and Abraham (1980, 1981) used performance evaluation to gauge separate information about individual productivity and wage profiles. They found that wages do not necessarily reflect productivity. Bishop (1987) and Flabbi and Ichino (2001) also put together measures of individual productivity, following the Medoff and Abraham methodology and confirming their results with other data sets.

Hellerstein *et al.* (1999), using US data, find that productivity and wages increase with age, except for the oldest age group in some specifications, and their patterns are fairly similar. Crépon *et al.* (2002) use French data and conclude that the relationship of productivity and age follows an inverted U-shape, but wage is increasing in age. In manufacturing, wage increases with skill level, but productivity increases even more. In non-manufacturing, wage

---

increases more than productivity as skill levels go up. Haegeland and Klette (1999) use Norwegian data and find that productivity and wage increase with education and the highly educated go hand in hand by productivity. Medium-level potential experience (age minus education years) gave higher productivity than short experience, but with long experience productivity declined although still stayed higher than with short experience. Medium-level experience was underpaid, but the wage premium for long experience corresponded to the productivity premium. They concluded that the wage-experience profile only partly reflected the productivity profile.

Only a few scholars have looked at cross-industry heterogeneity of productivity and wage responses. Aubert and Crépon (2004) estimated average earnings relations for France and found evidence of declining productivity after the age of 55, but they found that the age-productivity profile (as captured by such earnings functions) does not differ much across industries. In contrast, Aubert et al. (2004) estimated labour demand curves by using wage bill shares conditioned on value added as well as old and new economy capital; they did find significant evidence that innovative firms and work-practices present lower wage bill shares.

The same result seemingly applies within occupational groups for other countries. Similarly to our findings here, Neuman and Weiss (1995) found that earnings peaks are located earlier in age in the high-tech sector. Hellerstein and Neumark (1995), using Israeli data, find that earnings and productivity profiles are fairly similar for the relatively less skilled workers (the group that covers most of the workforce).

Other studies have in turn found that the relation has changed over time. The seniority-wage profile has seemingly become steeper and its peak moved forwards in Denmark as a result of the decentralization of wage determination (Bingley and Westergaard-Nielsen, 2003). Eriksson and Jäntti (1997) found that in 1971 the peak of the wage profile was at the age group 35–39 years but has then moved forward, being at the age group 45–49 years in 1990 in Finland.

Finally, a host of previous studies indeed highlights the productivity-enhancing role of worker mobility between plants. The mobility of workers has an additional important productivity effect that goes beyond the 'within firm' effect discussed above and examined in this paper. 'Churning' of plants/firms (i.e. simultaneous entries and exits) has been found to have a dominant role in industry productivity growth. Thanks to this mechanism, a worker's productivity may improve greatly when she moves from a low productivity plant/firm to a high productivity plant/firm (Foster et al., 2001; Disney et al., 2003). With the data from the Finnish manufacturing sector, Maliranta (2003) finds that the average productivity growth rate of the plants is typically 50–70% of the industry productivity growth rate, which is due to the fact that entries, but especially exits and the reallocation of labour and capital between the continuing plants have an important role to play as well. This gap between industry and plant productivity growth has been particularly pronounced in the Finnish electronics industry since the latter part of the 1980s, but has also been substantial for instance in the textile and wearing industry during the latter half of the 1980s and in the basic metal industry during the latter half of the 1980s and the first half of the 1990s.

Returns to seniority are usually positive but declining with the level of seniority in the forest industry plants; about the same applies to earnings profiles. Similar considerations hold for the productivity and wage effects of general experience in industrial machinery, although the estimated relation is statistically less solid. The similarity of the productivity and wages responses to the accumulation of human capital indicates that, in 'average' industries, skill depreciation does not seemingly lead to higher labour costs. And given that these industries are still quantitatively important in the Finnish economy, wage-productivity misalignments cannot be the main explanation for the bad labour market performance of the elderly in Finland.

The picture is quite different for the high-tech plants. In electronics – the industry where people are exposed to rapid technological and managerial changes – the responses of plant productivity and wages to seniority are very different from each other. The seniority-productivity profile shows a positive relation first and then negative as one looks at plants with higher average seniority, while wages instead keep going up with seniority.[13] This holds for plants with similar education, plant age and size and other conditions and is thus not related to plant differences in these other respects. How negative the productivity returns to seniority may become cannot be said with certainty. Numerical simulations based on our OLS cross-sectional results indicate that the change of sign in the seniority-productivity profile may be pronounced.

Altogether, our results are consistent with the idea that fast technical change brings about accelerated skill depreciation of senior workers. We cannot honestly rule out, however, that our correlations may also be the result of worker movements across plants. The negative correlation between seniority and productivity may in fact also reflect the reallocation away of younger (and more productive) workers who leave behind older plants attracted by the career prospects offered in newly born high-productivity firms and plants.[14] We cannot precisely quantify the relative importance

[13] This is not too surprising: as recently discussed at length by Uusitalo and Vartiainen (2005), the combination of highly centralized collective agreements with relatively autonomous but still highly unionized industry wage setting has resulted in a very low weight (4.4%, on average) given to performance-related firm-level corrections of wages.

[14] Evidence on the importance of reallocation for productivity purposes was indeed provided by Ilmakunnas *et al.* (2005) for the Finnish manufacturing sector, where it was shown that the churning of workers (i.e. simultaneous hiring and separation of workers within a plant) speeds up plant productivity growth, while holding back seniority.

of the two effects in our statistical analysis. Both skill depreciation and worker reallocation appear to affect the relation between seniority and productivity in the Finnish
high-tech industry.

It looks as though the deferred compensation hypothesis, perhaps amended with
the insights from sorting and matching theories, fits better the labour market facts in
high-tech industries than the human capital hypothesis. Yet the evidence for the
'average' industries is not consistent with this hypothesis. This is an open issue that
we briefly discuss further in the concluding section.

5. CONCLUSIONS

We started this paper asking ourselves whether we could explain the weak labour
market position of older workers. The simultaneous presence of a relatively aged –
and still rapidly ageing – workforce and a major external shock (such as the IT
revolution of the late 1990s) makes Finland a nice experiment to address this question
investigating the diverse responses of wages and productivity to age, seniority and
experience patterns across industries.

Our results do not indicate that age as such is responsible for the bad labour
market outcomes of the elderly. The differential effect of seniority and experience
on productivity and earnings is minor for two of the three Finnish manufacturing industries (the 'average' ones) we chose to analyse. These productivity and
wage patterns probably reflect the relatively more valuable role of tacit knowledge
in traditional industries. Productivity and wage profiles differ just in electronics,
not in the other industries. We interpret this as implying that exposure to
rapid technological and managerial changes seems to make a difference for plant
productivity, less so for wages for the high-tech plants. Yet this productivity-
wage discrepancy is not associated with age but rather with seniority, hence with a
variable which can be affected by individual and policy decisions to a greater extent
than age, that is largely exogenous for the individual (though not for the plant
manager).

In the end, our results give support to at least two important policy implications.
First, the similar shapes of productivity and wage profiles in 'average industries'
indicate that the weak labour market performance of older workers in Finland is not
because they are a burden for the average firm in the economy. Leaving high-tech
plants aside, the bad labour market outcomes of the elderly in the rest of the economy
are presumably driven by two other causes, such as discriminatory attitudes on the
employer side and public incentives schemes easing the way towards early retirement.
To ameliorate the labour market performance of the elderly, policy should address
these issues. Second, higher seniority is instead associated with higher labour costs in
high-tech plants. This is consistent with the anecdotal evidence from Wal-Mart and
Ericsson that we have reported. It is also consistent with the beliefs – entertained by
many Finnish employers – that older people could not adapt as easily as younger ones

to the arrival of the new technology.[15] And indeed a survey conducted by the Ministry of Labour in 2002 indicates that as much as 10% of prime-aged workers (and 15% of workers above 50) agree that 'workplace discriminates against old workers'.[16] In spite of government-mandated media campaigns to counteract such attitudes, the possibility that a negative employer bias against old workers has affected hiring and firing practices in the late 1990s cannot thus be easily ruled out. Our results suggest that this effect is not present in the Finnish economy at large but mainly in high-tech plants.

To improve the employability of older workers in these industries, public policy should divert resources away from preserving existing jobs and lend more attention on the retraining of old workers to ease their reallocation away from less productive plants (or plants where they have become less productive) into new jobs. Some governments are more worried and more interventionist than others in this respect. In the last few years, for instance, the Finnish Government has already embarked on a programme ('The National Programme on Ageing Workers'; see OECD, 2004, p. 119) aimed at deferring retirement and, in parallel, improving the so called 'employability' of older workers. It is unclear, however, to what extent grand plans may be effective to bring about a solution to these problems. Policies aimed at easing reallocation across plants even within the same industry would probably be a useful complementary tool in this respect.

Finally, our results are also somehow puzzling in at least one respect. They are not fully consistent with any of the existing theories that we know. The results for the high-tech plants are consistent with the deferred compensation hypothesis and not with the human capital hypothesis. As surveyed in the theoretical section of the paper, the human capital hypothesis would predict a negative discrepancy in plants with an older labour force where we instead find the opposite results. But even the Lazear hypothesis is not fully consistent with our Finnish data because the results found for electronics are not there for the other industries.

This begs the question of why the Lazear model is more relevant in high-tech plants than in the other plants. One possibility is that productivity is less easily observable in high-tech industries. This would make the asymmetric information mechanism envisaged by Lazear more sensible in those industries. This explanation would probably do if our results were there for plants producing immaterial 'weightless' services whose output is typically hard to measure. Our discussion here instead concerns plants producing 'concrete' manufacturing goods for which productivity mis-measurement is presumably a less serious concern. An alternative possibility is

---

[15] Juuti (2001) reports that young line managers with a good educational background often harboured prejudice against the ability of older workers to cope with new things. This is potentially important for hiring and firing practices. Although discriminating attitudes are rarely shared by top-level managers, recruitment decisions happen to be taken by the mid-management level.

[16] Kouvonen (1999) reports somewhat lower figures, with a 5% share of people above 45 having experienced age at discrimination at work for the average firm.

that seniority, being the other side of impeded resource reallocation, is particularly damaging in industries where changes – requiring flexibility and ability to quickly adapt – come about all the time. Hence, the adverse consequences of seniority manifest themselves in these industries and less so in other industries where changes are smoother. Under these circumstances, a less mobile ageing workforce might constitute an impediment to productivity growth of firms and their plants. To the extent that low productivity (and low immobility) is a consequence of declining ability to incessantly adopt new technologies due to weak basic education, public policy should focus on efforts to increase the quantity and improve the quality of the adult education. If, however, the main reason for staying still too long is not the inability of older workers to adopt new technologies, policy-makers should seek ways to encourage the mobility of the ageing workforce to maintain the scope for continued productivity enabled by learning-by-doing. Greater mobility of workers might also facilitate the diffusion of technologies and thereby speed up productivity growth of the firms – and stimulating 'creative destruction' (i.e. productivity-enhancing churning of plants and firms within industry) to boot.

Finally, how special are our results? Insofar as the use of ICT will spread to other industries in the years to come, it can be expected that the productivity patterns observed in electronics will emerge in other industries in the future. The findings for electronics may be foretelling more general developments in the other industries of the Finnish economy – and possibly other economies. For sure, in a world where innovation forces, as opposed to catching up forces, have become the key engine of growth (see Acemoglu *et al.*, 2003, and the Sapir Report, 2004), companies and governments will be more and more involved in such problems as the ones discussed in this paper.

Discussion

Wendy Carlin
University College London and CEPR

Four facts about the advanced economies provide the motivation for this paper: the poor labour market performance of older workers (unemployment and employment rates); the ageing of the labour force; evidence measured in surveys of a decline in physical and mental performance at higher ages; and finally, the change in industry structure toward 'high tech' industries. This raises the question of whether the employability of older workers declines because they become too costly (diminishing productivity is not compensated by lower wages) and whether this is especially marked in high-tech sectors of the economy. The authors of this paper do not find evidence supporting either of these hypotheses in their data from three Finnish manufacturing industries. However, their findings suggest that there is a hump-shaped relationship between a measure of productivity and the seniority (not age) of workers in plants in the high-tech industry in their sample: electronics. There is no corresponding pattern for wages. This is interpreted as signalling a potential problem in the matching of workers to jobs in industries with rapid technological progress in the context of constraints on worker mobility (e.g. costs of firing).

Channels through which ageing can affect economic performance are the average quality of the direct labour input, the effect on capital deepening because of the implications of ageing for private and public saving and its impact on technological progress (new ideas and diffusion). Older people may be less creative, entrepreneurial and risk-taking and the depreciation of their skill set may imply less adaptation and diffusion of new knowledge. On the other hand, an ageing population may create bigger incentives for labour and memory saving innovation.

In order to evaluate the economic impact of age-related variables, it is essential to specify whose perspective we are taking. From the perspective of workers, the decision is whether to remain in their job, to search for a new one, to leave the labour force or to invest in (re)training. And the key question is how age and or seniority affect wage and employment prospects, as well as training opportunities within and outside the firm. For firms, the question is how age or seniority affects the profitability of existing production and the firm's investment in human and physical capital and in innovation. What are the constraints on the wage structure they can deploy and on firing? From the perspective of a policy-maker concerned with welfare, the question is the impact of age-related variables on total factor productivity and the role of policy-related barriers to the reallocation of workers, training and early retirement programmes.

In this paper, Daveri and Maliranta take one slice of this question, focusing on the impact of age-related variables on the quality of direct labour input:

- How are productivity and wages related to age structure and seniority at the plant level in manufacturing?
- Does this relationship vary according to the innovativeness or technology intensiveness of the industry?

To answer these questions, it is necessary to have matched employer-employee data and a clear contrast in industry characteristics. This makes the use of data from Finland an appropriate choice: there is high-quality matched data and looking at the period of the late 1990s to the early 2000s provides a nice contrast among the traditional industry of 'forest products', a neutral one of industrial machinery and a high-tech industry, electronics.

The method is to use plant-level data to estimate an index of total factor productivity and to calculate the average wage. Each of these is then used as the dependent variable in a separate regression for each industry with various combinations of the age-related variables on the right-hand side along with a set of plant-level control variables (including years of schooling, a dummy for a foreign-owned plant and dummies for different vintages of plants including those that exit during the observation period). The age-related variables are worker age, seniority (i.e. years in the current firm) and labour market potential experience (age minus age when completed last qualification/degree) averaged for workers in each plant. It is somewhat odd that TFP is the productivity variable of choice when an initial motivation was the impact of age-related variables on firm profitability via labour costs, which suggests that it is labour productivity that is relevant, not TFP.[17]

Neither age nor age squared is ever significant in a productivity regression. In electronics but in neither of the other industries, there is a positive coefficient on seniority and a negative coefficient on the squared term in seniority. This says that when looking across plants, TFP initially rises as the average tenure of workers in the plant goes up but then falls in plants with higher levels of average seniority. The effects of age-related variables on wages are mainly (but not always) positive in forest products, hump-shaped for age (but with no robust tenure effects) in machinery and positive for age and weakly positive for tenure and experience in electronics.

The authors conclude that it is not age *per se* but seniority that affects TFP and that this effect is found only in the high-tech sector, electronics. In order to make their results more easily interpretable, they estimate modified versions of their equations and produce graphs showing the average partial effect of the variable of interest. From these equations they calculate the effect on TFP of a change in, for example, seniority. As acknowledged by the authors, the estimate that plant productivity doubles when average seniority of the workforce goes from 2 to 6 years and then falls by two-thirds as average seniority goes from 6 to 10 years is very large. My main concern with this central result in the paper is that it may reflect the dynamics of a rapidly growing industry rather than the inherent characteristics of long-tenure workers in electronics.

In electronics, a plant where the average tenure is six years is estimated to be at the 'turning point' from rising to falling TFP. As Table A1 shows, the mean tenure in the sample for electronics plants is six years, which reflects the rapid growth of the industry: it is 11 years and 9 years respectively in the forest products and machinery industries. The likely role of industry dynamics in generating tenure/productivity profiles of the kind shown in the paper can be illustrated by a simple example. If we assume that initially there are three industries, F, M and W with identical plants in terms of TFP, age and seniority structure. In particular, we assume there is no causal link from the average age or seniority of workers in a plant to the plant's TFP. We now introduce a different demand shock for each industry: a negative demand shock for industry F, no change for M and a positive shock for E. We assume that there is unobserved heterogeneity in managerial ability across plants. As a consequence of the

---

[17] TFP is calculated using a simple growth accounting framework with the assumption of a constant labour share (WL/Y). If the aim is to test whether seniority or ageing affects labour costs, which are measured by the ratio of wages to labour productivity, then this is perhaps not an ideal choice.

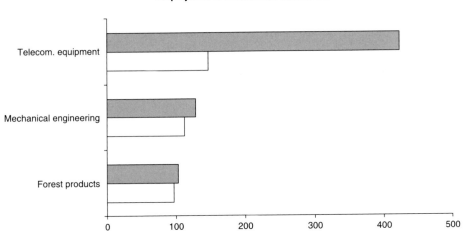

Employment & VA in 2002, 3 Finnish industries 1995=100

□ Employment ▪ VA current prices

Figure 4. Contrasting industry dynamics in Finland, 1995–2002

Note: Telecommunications equipment = ISIC322; Mechanical engineering = ISIC29; Forest products = ISIC20+21.

Source: Groningen Growth and Development Centre, 60-Industry Database, October 2005, http://www.ggdc.net/, updated from O'Mahony and van Ark (2003).

differential demand shocks and assuming there are costs of entry and exit, we will observe disequilibrium in the F and E industries. Good managers in E will expand output, increase hiring and raise TFP relative to other plants in E. Since hires have zero seniority, average seniority in these expanding, higher TFP plants will fall: lower seniority is associated with higher TFP but by assumption, this is independent of any relationship between individual human capital (and TFP) and tenure. Similarly, good managers in F identify the decline in their industry earlier and cease hiring sooner, with the result that higher TFP firms end up with on average longer tenure workers. This produces a positive relationship between seniority and TFP in the 'declining' industry and a negative relationship in the 'expanding' industry. In the industry where there is no shock, there is no relationship. This pattern is consistent with the contrast between the three industries shown in Figure 2 of the paper.[18]

Figure 4 provides some illustrative data showing that employment grew in telecommunications equipment and shrank in forest products over the time period considered in the paper.

---

[18] A similar story could be told to account for the within firm pattern that is shown in column [6] of Table 6. Using fixed effects estimation, the relationship between changes in TFP over time and in the age-related variables is uncovered, controlling for time invariant characteristics of plants such as managerial quality. A similar although a much weaker hump-shaped relationship between TFP and seniority is reported. If we now assume that a new higher TFP technology emerges in electronics during the period of observation but not in forest products, production in electronics becomes more profitable and each firm expands. The increase in hiring reduces seniority and we associate a within-firm rise in TFP with a fall in seniority.

The authors undertake a number of tests to check the robustness of their results but they are not able to separate out the possible impact of industry dynamics driven by exogenous demand or technology shocks from the causality of seniority producing a change in efficiency that they seek to identify. Another approach to identifying such an effect would be to focus on those who switch jobs. The Daveri–Maliranta story implies that in electronics longer tenure workers are worse substitutes for otherwise equivalent workers than is the case in the other two industries. This suggests that they should get a bigger wage cut if they switch jobs as compared with similar workers in one of the other industries.[19]

Hence although the results in the paper are suggestive, I think further investigation is required before we can be confident that there really is a causal link of policy-relevant magnitude in a high-tech industry from seniority (longer tenure in a given firm) to lower TFP.

Rudolf Winter-Ebmer
University of Linz, Institute for Advanced Studies (IHS), Vienna and CEPR

Daveri and Maliranta have produced a very interesting paper on the impact of age and seniority on wages and productivity in Finland. The main idea is that the effects of ageing on firm productivity are very different in traditional industries as compared to high-tech or information technology industries (electronics in their empirical analysis). Psychometric studies have shown that physical, cognitive and verbal abilities have different age gradients: whereas physical and cognitive skills, such as mathematical and logical skills decay pretty fast, organizational and verbal skills show no particular ageing pattern at all (Skirbekk, 2003). Daveri and Maliranta argue that ageing of the workforce is more problematic in high-tech industries because of a faster technical change, faster changes in production technologies and faster product development. While most psychometric and other studies relate to age as such, Daveri and Maliranta concentrate their argument on the impact of job tenure within a particular firm: while there is no difference between the productivity-experience and wage-experience paths in the electronics industry – nor in the machinery industry by the way – there is a significant divergence in the development of productivity and wages as seniority in a firm increases. This pattern cannot be seen in more traditional industries like forestry and machinery.

While the general pattern of a higher interdependence between firm seniority, technology adaptation and learning – and in turn productivity – in high-tech firms is sensible, the main empirical results seem to be out of line. Productivity in electronics firms increases by 61 log points in the first 4 years of tenure (in fact from year 2 to

---

[19] Using Finnish data, Uusitalo and Vartiainen (2005) report that firm exits and promotions increase earnings up to age 50, after which such events do not on average improve a person's relative position. Whether this is true of tenure and whether it differs across industries would be relevant evidence for the Daveri–Maliranta hypothesis.

year 6) but decreases in the following 6 years again by 69 log points (see Table 7). A literal interpretation of these results would be that workers who stay with their firms for more than 6 years lose more than half of their productivity; they become such a burden to the firm, that everybody would have to be fired otherwise the managers would be acting completely irresponsibly. This is probably not what we are seeing in these firms.

Moreover, the measured effect is basically a product of a simple OLS cross-section regression; it is much reduced and less well statistically determined if other methods or data are used. Some other possible explanations come to my mind which could have produced such an outcome. The data relate to mean characteristics of the workforce, such as mean age and mean tenure of workers. As the IT boom in Finland did not start before the mid 1990s, I suspect that there are not many firms with mean tenure of its workforce of more than 7 years – and if they exist, they might be fairly different firms with a different technology and firm organization. As Daveri and Maliranta correctly state, the causal impact of mean tenure on productivity cannot be properly distinguished from matching and selection problems: it is by no means a coincidence that some workers stay with the firm longer, others don't; it is no coincidence why some firms stick to their complete workforce longer or to phrase it differently, why workers want to stay longer with a particular firm. Good workers stay with good firms and vice versa. All these matching arguments make the strong point that a simple correlation between job seniority and productivity will be an upward biased estimate of the real causal effect of job seniority on productivity. Related labour economics studies on the causal effect of seniority on wages come to the conclusion that OLS estimates overestimate the true causal effect by a factor between two and four (Topel, 1991; Altonji and Shakotko, 1987).

It has to be said, though, that finding convincing estimates of the relation between firm employment structure and productivity is very difficult: simple fixed effects models using variation in the composition of the workforce over time to determine the variation of productivity fall again prey to the criticism of reverse causality: why do, and how can, firms change the composition of their workforce? Only by changing recruitment and lay-off policies, policies which are obviously related to past and expected productivity. While the causal impact is very difficult to establish in such studies, any work in this direction using new data sets is very interesting. Further important questions come to my mind, for instance concerning inter-firm mobility within the industry which seems to contribute to productivity growth throughout the industry (Parent, 2000). It seems that inter-firm mobility is higher in the high-tech sector which could contribute to explain the diverging pattern between seniority-productivity and experience-productivity profiles. Another important issue concerns wage-setting schemes: If indeed high-tech sectors have a higher prevalence of deferred payment schemes like stock options or profit sharing in some sort or the other, the relation between age or tenure and wages would be steeper and the divergence between wage and productivity development would shrink.

The personnel economics and firm organization literature has also stressed complementarities in the composition of the workforce: a good mix of old and young workers might be better for firm productivity than employing only young or only old workers (Lazear, 1998; Grund and Westergård-Nielsen, 2005). It might be interesting to see whether these results hold also in the high-tech industry. Such an analysis would require looking at the age and tenure composition of the workforce in more detail by using the underlying micro data.

In my view, policy conclusions are still difficult to draw from this paper. Maybe Finland was not such a good experiment in this respect, because its high-tech sector had an explosive growth after 1995, which is too short and too turbulent a period to draw firm conclusions about the effects of firm seniority and the like. Replicating the study for another country with a more smooth development of its high-tech sector might be a welcome complement.

APPENDIX: DATA SET AND VARIABLE DESCRIPTION

Similarly to the other Nordic countries, Finland is endowed with a rich register data of companies, plants and individuals (see Statistics Denmark *et al.*, 2003). The unique identification codes for persons, companies and plants used in the different registers form the backbone of the Finnish administrative register network and the Finnish statistical system, whereby different sources of information can be integrated conveniently for various statistical purposes.[20] By using this system, Statistics Finland has constructed the Finnish Longitudinal Employer-Employee Database (FLEED), which is tailored for various needs of economic research. Its most comprehensive and detailed version is maintained at Statistics Finland. It contains information of companies, plants and individuals. Plants are linked to their companies, and individuals to their employer plants and companies. Data are collected from Business Register (plants and companies in the business sector), Census of Manufacturing (manufacturing plants), Financial Statements Statistics (companies in the business sector), R&D survey and ICT survey (companies in the business sector), and Employment Statistics (individuals aged between 16 and 69 years). These data include a wide variety of detailed information on these units. A large proportion of variables are available from 1990 to 2002. These data cover essentially the whole target population of companies, plants and individuals. Due to confidentiality concerns, outside researchers do not have direct access to it. For the outside researchers, Statistics Finland has constructed a separate version of it. The variable set is more limited and some of the categorical variables are broader (many industries are combined, for example).

This paper employs plant level information for plants and workforce. Productivity measures, plant age, plant size originate from the Census of Manufacturing. We do not have information of the levels of value added, hours worked or capital stock as

---

[20] Data sources and linking of them is described in greater detail in Ilmakunnas *et al.* (2001) and Maliranta (2003).

Table A1. Descriptive statistics of data on plants by industry, plant averages in 1995–2002

Variables	Forest industry					Machinery industry					Electronics industry				
	Mean	Sd	p5	Median	95p	Mean	Sd	p5	Median	95p	Mean	Sd	p5	Median	95p
Log of TFP index	1.80	0.74	0.88	1.66	3.28	2.83	0.59	2.08	2.72	4.00	2.27	1.04	0.99	2.05	4.58
Log of monthly wage (in euros)	7.61	0.24	7.23	7.59	8.02	7.69	0.19	7.36	7.69	8.00	7.65	0.23	7.27	7.67	8.03
Schooling years	11.0	0.4	10.3	11.0	11.7	11.6	0.9	10.6	11.4	13.6	12.2	1.2	10.6	11.9	14.5
Age in years	39.6	3.8	33.3	40.1	45.0	39.3	4.0	31.8	39.8	45.0	35.6	3.8	29.4	35.8	41.6
Potential experience in years	21.6	3.9	15.1	22.1	27.1	20.7	4.2	13.1	21.1	26.9	16.4	4.0	9.3	16.6	22.5
Seniority in years	10.9	5.6	2.6	10.8	19.5	9.2	4.8	2.7	8.9	17.5	6.3	3.3	2.1	5.3	12.69
	Proportion (%)					Proportion (%)					Proportion (%)				
Plant birth before 1977	57.0					34.57					27.91				
Plant birth 1977–1980	6.3					8.47					7.56				
Plant birth 1981–1985	5.5					6.88					4.07				
Plant birth 1986–1990	10.7					16.58					23.26				
Plant birth 1991–1995	9.9					18.87					19.77				
Plant birth 1996–	10.7					14.64					17.44				
Plant size 5–9 persons	1.8					3.14					3.17				
Plant size 10–19 persons	9.0					10.20					6.85				
Plant size 20–49 persons	30.9					41.08					33.51				
Plant size 50–99 persons	21.7					20.56					20.65				
Plant size 100– persons	36.7					25.02					35.81				
Foreign-owned plant	6.2					19.86					12.95				
Plant death during 1996–2002	11.8					19.22					22.09				
Number of plants	365					567					172				

Notes: The data are constructed in the Research Laboratory of Statistics Finland by linking the plants in the Finnish Manufacturing Census and individuals in the Employment Statistics with plant codes.

Source: Authors' own calculations.

Table A2. Statistical analysis behind the simulation graphs, between plants estimation

	Forest TFP	Forest wage	Machinery TFP	Machinery wage	Elect. TFP	Elect. wage
Schooling years	-3.386	-0.073	0.826+	0.182	1.481	0.310
	(2.491)	(0.815)	(0.470)	(0.140)	(1.294)	(0.210)
[Schooling years]²	1.503	0.095	-0.285	-0.020	-0.511	-0.070
	(1.113)	(0.368)	(0.194)	(0.057)	(0.524)	(0.084)
Potential experience	1.017**	-0.014	0.171	0.082+	-0.785	0.007
	(0.371)	(0.118)	(0.151)	(0.044)	(0.616)	(0.110)
[Potential experience]²	-0.513**	0.021	-0.072	-0.024	0.364	-0.012
	(0.187)	(0.057)	(0.081)	(0.022)	(0.390)	(0.071)
[Potential experience]³	0.081**	-0.005	0.010	0.002	-0.047	0.005
	(0.030)	(0.009)	(0.014)	(0.004)	(0.078)	(0.015)
Seniority in years	-0.013	-0.003	-0.045	-0.020	1.276***	0.131*
	(0.086)	(0.027)	(0.054)	(0.018)	(0.272)	(0.062)
[Seniority in years]²	0.070	0.012	0.033	0.022	-1.665***	-0.161+
	(0.081)	(0.026)	(0.056)	(0.017)	(0.365)	(0.083)
[Seniority in years]³	-0.025	-0.000	-0.008	-0.007	0.622***	0.061+
	(0.022)	(0.007)	(0.017)	(0.005)	(0.153)	(0.034)
Plant birth in 77–80	0.237*	0.003	-0.051	0.019	-0.088	-0.027
	(0.119)	(0.032)	(0.066)	(0.029)	(0.154)	(0.044)
Plant birth in 81–85	0.247*	0.059	0.057	0.014	-0.210	0.032
	(0.117)	(0.041)	(0.079)	(0.021)	(0.257)	(0.043)
Plant birth in 86–90	0.658***	0.040	0.255***	0.013	0.094	0.019
	(0.104)	(0.027)	(0.057)	(0.018)	(0.209)	(0.046)
Plant birth in 91–95	0.575***	0.026	0.432***	0.083***	0.680**	-0.012
	(0.144)	(0.037)	(0.060)	(0.017)	(0.232)	(0.042)
Plant birth in 96–	0.969***	0.052	0.629***	0.077**	0.677*	0.029
	(0.196)	(0.037)	(0.088)	(0.025)	(0.286)	(0.052)
R-squared	0.545	0.647	0.486	0.516	0.527	0.581
Adj. R-squared	0.510	0.620	0.461	0.493	0.442	0.505
Number of plants	365	365	567	567	172	172

Notes: Other control variables include dummies for plant size (5 groups), foreign-ownership and death during 1996–2002. Robust standard errors are shown in parentheses.
+ $p < 0.1$, * $p < 0.05$, ** $p < 0.01$, *** $p < 0.001$.

such, but we do have the ratio of value added to the number of hours worked (by which we identify labour productivity) and the capital stock per hour worked (a measure of the capital-labour ratio). The capital stock measure is calculated through the perpetual inventory method (for more details, see Maliranta, 2003).

Since 1995 (our main period of analysis), all plants owned by firms that employ no less than 20 persons are included. Therefore, since 1995 the data also include the very small plants of multi-unit firms, but, on the other hand, the plants of small single-unit firms are left outside. Some plants are dropped from the sample because of failure of linking some plants in the Manufacture Census to other sources of information. Thanks to the link between Census of Manufacturing and Employment Statistics, we have information about plant workforce. This includes the average potential experience (the number of years after the last completed degree), seniority (the number of years spent working in the current company) and the number of schooling years (usually needed for the degree). The labour characteristics of the plants are computed in Statistics Finland by using the comprehensive version of the database. About 80–90% of individuals can be linked to their plants so that our variables should be measured with a reasonable accuracy. In the analysis, we have also dropped some outliers.[21]

REFERENCES

Acemoglu, D., P. Aghion and F. Zilibotti (2003). 'Vertical integration and distance to frontier', *Journal of the European Economic Association*, 1(2/3), 630–38.

Ali-Yrkkö, J., L. Paija, C. Reilly and P. Ylä-Anttila (2000). *Nokia: A Big Company in a Small Country*. ETLA, The Research Institute of the Finnish Economy, Series B162, Helsinki.

Altonji, J.G. and R.A. Shakotko (1987). 'Do wages rise with job seniority?', *Review of Economic Studies*, 54, 437–39.

Aubert, P. and B. Crépon (2004). *Age Salaire Et Productivité: La Productivité Des Salariés Décline-T-Elle En Fin De Carrière*. Technical report. Mimeo, Economie et Statistiques.

Aubert, P., E. Caroli and M. Roger (2004). *New Technologies, Workplace Organisation and the Age Structure of the Workforce: Firm-Level Evidence*. INSEE, Paris.

Autor, D.H., F. Levy and R.J. Murnane (2003). 'The skill content of recent technological change: An empirical exploration', *Quarterly Journal of Economics*, 118(4), 1279–333.

Becker, G.S. (1962). 'Investment in human capital: A theoretical analysis', *Journal of Political Economy*, 70(5, Part 2: Investment in Human Beings), 9–49.

Bingley, P. and N. Westergaard-Nielsen (2003). 'Returns to tenure, firm-specific human capital and worker heterogeneity', *International Journal of Manpower*, 24(7), 774–88.

Bishop, J. (1987). 'The recognition and reward of employee performance', *Journal of Labor Economics*, 5(4), s36–s56.

Blanchflower, D.G. and A.J. Oswald (1988). 'Internal and external influences upon pay settlements', *British Journal of Industrial Relations*, 26(3), 363–70.

Brock, W.A. and D.S. Evans (1986). *The Economics of Small Business*. Holmes & Meier, New York.

Brown, C. and J.L. Medoff (2003). 'Firm age and wages', *Journal of Labor Economics*, 21(3), 677–97.

---

[21] In the estimation, some extreme outliers are removed from the regression analysis. Identification has been carried out by using the method of Hadi (1992; 1994). The variables used in this procedure are the log of labour productivity, the log of monthly wage, the log of capital intensity, schooling years and potential experience. Overall, a couple of percentages of plants were dropped for being deemed outliers.

Crépon, B., N. Deniau and S. Pérez-Duarte (2002). *Wages, Productivity, and Worker Characteristics: A French Perspective*, January, INSEE. http://www.crest.fr/pageperso/crepon/CreponDeniauPerezDuarte2002.pdf

Daveri, F. and O. Silva (2004). 'Not only Nokia: What Finland tells us about new economy growth', *Economic Policy*, 19(38), 117–63.

Davis, S.J. and J. Haltiwanger (1991). 'Wage dispersion between and within U.S. manufacturing plants, 1963–86', *Brookings Papers on Economic Activity, Microeconomics 1991*, 115–80.

Disney, R., J. Haskel and Y. Heden (2003). 'Restructuring and productivity growth in UK manufacturing', *Economic Journal*, 113(489), 666–94.

Dunne, T., M.J. Roberts and L. Samuelson (1989). 'The growth and failure of U.S. manufacturing plants', *Quarterly Journal of Economics*, 104(4), 671–98.

Dygalo, N.N. and J.M. Abowd (2005). 'Estimating experience-productivity profiles from earnings over employment spells', unpublished manuscript, 27 November.

Eriksson, T. and M. Jäntti (1997). 'The distribution of earnings in Finland 1971–1990', *European Economic Review*, 41(9), 1763–79.

Flabbi, L. and A. Ichino (2001). 'Productivity, seniority and wages: New evidence from personnel data', *Labour Economics*, 8(3), 359–87.

Foster, L., J. Haltiwanger and C.J. Krizan (2001). 'Aggregate productivity growth: Lessons from microeconomic evidence', in C.R. Hulten, E.R. Dean & M.J. Harper (eds.), *New Developments in Productivity Analysis* (pp. 303–63). University of Chicago Press, Chicago.

Griliches, Z. (1995). 'R&D and productivity: Econometric results and measurement issues', in P. Stoneman (Ed.), *Handbook of the Economics of Innovation and Technological Change* (pp. 52–89). Blackwell Publishers Ltd, Oxford.

Griliches, Z. and V. Ringstad (1971). *Economics of Scale and the Form of the Production Function*. North Holland, Amsterdam, 1971.

Griliches, Z. and H. Regev (1995). 'Productivity and firm turnover in Israeli industry: 1979–1988', *Journal of Econometrics*, 65, 175–203.

Grund, C. and N. Westergård-Nielsen (2005). 'Age structure of the workforce and firm performance', IZA Working Paper No. 1816, Bonn.

Hadi, A.S. (1992). 'Identifying multiple outliers in multivariate data', *Journal of the Royal Statistical Society, Series (B)*, 54, 761–71.

—— (1994). 'A modification of a method for the detection of outliers in multivariate samples', *Journal of the Royal Statistical Society, Series (B)*, 56, 393–96.

Haegeland, T. and T.J. Klette (1999). 'Do higher wages reflect higher productivity? Education, gender and experience premiums in a matched plant-worker data set', in *The Creation and Analysis of Employer-Employee Matched Data* (pp. 231–59). Elsevier Science, North-Holland, Amsterdam.

Hellerstein, J.K. and D. Neumark (1995). 'Are earnings profiles steeper than productivity profiles?' *Journal of Human Resources*, 30(1), 89.

Hellerstein, J.K., D. Neumark and K.R. Troske (1999). 'Wages, productivity, and worker characteristics: Evidence from plant-level production functions and wage equations', *Journal of Labor Economics*, 17(3), 409–46.

Ilmakunnas, P. and M. Maliranta (2005). 'Technology, labour characteristics and wage-productivity gaps', *Oxford Bulletin of Economics and Statistics*, 67(5), 623–44.

Ilmakunnas, P., M. Maliranta and J. Vainiomäki (2001). 'Linked employer-employee data on Finnish plants for the analysis of productivity, wages and turnover', in T. Jensen and A. Holm (eds.), *Nordic Labour Market Research on Register Data* (pp. 205–46). TemaDord, Nordic Council of Ministers, Coperhagen.

—— (2004). 'The roles of employer and employee characteristics for plant productivity', *Journal of Productivity Analysis*, 21, 249–76.

—— (2005). 'Worker turnover and productivity growth', *Applied Economics Letters*, 12(7), 395–98.

Juuti, P. (2001). *Ikäjohtaminen*. Kansallinen ikäohjelma, Työministeriö, JTO-tutkimuksia No. 13. Helsinki.

Kanazawa, S. (2003). 'Why productivity fades with age: The crime-genius connection', *Journal of Research in Personality*, 37, 257–72.

King, G., M. Tomz and J. Wittenberg (2000). 'Making the most of statistical analyses: Improving interpretation and presentation', *American Journal of Political Science*, 44(2), 347–61.

Kouvonen, A. (1999). *Ikäsyrjintäkokemukset Työssä Ja Työhönotossa*. Työpoliittinen tutkimus No. 203.

Kölling, A., C. Schnabel and J. Wagner (2005). 'Establishment age and wages: Evidence from German linked employer-employee data', in L. Bellmann, O. Hübler, W. Meyer and

G. Stephan (eds.), *Institutionen, Löhne Und Beschäftigung* (pp. 81–99). Nürnberg. http://www.wiso.uni-erlangen.de/forschung/forschungsberichte/forschungsbericht2005.pdf

Lazear, E.P. (1981). 'Agency, earnings profiles, productivity, and hours restrictions', *American Economic Review*, 71(4), 606–20.

— (1998). *Personnel Economics for Managers*, John Wiley and Sons, New York.

Maliranta, M. (1997). 'Plant Productivity in Finnish Manufacturing – Characteristics of High Productivity Plants', The Research Institute of the Finnish Economy (ETLA), Discussion Paper No. 612, Helsinki.

— (1999). 'Factors of performance by plant generation: Some findings from Finland', in S. Biffignandi (ed.), *Micro- and Macrodata of Firms: Statistical Analysis and International Comparison* (pp. 391–424). Physica, Heidelberg.

— (2003). *Micro Level Dynamics of Productivity Growth. An Empirical Analysis of the Great Leap in Finnish Manufacturing Productivity in 1975–2000*. The Research Institute of the Finnish Economy (ETLA), Series A 38 (available at http://www.etla.fi/files/1075_micro_level_dynamics.pdf), Helsinki.

Maliranta, M. and P. Rouvinen (2004). 'ICT and business productivity: Finnish micro-level evidence', in *The Economic Impact of ICT; Measurement, Evidence and Implications* (pp. 213–40). OECD, Paris.

Manning, A. (2000). 'Movin on up: Interpreting the earnings-experience profile', *Bulletin of Economic Research*, 52, 261–95.

Medoff, J.L. and K.G. Abraham (1980). 'Experience, performance, and earnings', *Quarterly Journal of Economics*, 95(4), 703–36.

— (1981). 'Are those paid more really more productive? The case of experience', *Journal of Human Resources*, 16(2), 186–216.

Moen, J. (2005). 'Is mobility of technical personnel a source of R&D spillovers?', *Journal of Labor Economics*, 23(1), 81–114.

Neuman, S. and A. Weiss, (1995). 'On the effects of schooling vintage on experience-earnings profiles: Theory and evidence', *European Economic Review*, 39(5), 943–55.

Nurmi, S. (2004). *Essays on Plant Size, Employment Dynamics and Survival*. Helsinki School of Economics, A-230, Helsinki.

OECD (2003). *OECD Science, Technology and Industry Scoreboard*. OECD, Paris.

— (2004). *Ageing and Employment Policies: Finland*. OECD, Paris.

— (2006). *Live Longer, Work Longer*. OECD, Paris.

O'Mahony, M. and B. Van Ark (eds.) (2003). *EU Productivity and Competitiveness: An Industry Perspective: Can Europe Resume the Catching-Up Process*. European Commission, Enterprise Publications.

Parent, D. (2000). 'Industry-specific capital and the wage profile: Evidence from the NLSY and the PSID', *Journal of Labor Economics*, 18(2), 306–23.

Productivity Commission (2005). *Economic Implications of an Ageing Australia*. Research Report, Canberra (http://www.pc.gov.au/study/ageing/finalreport/).

Sapir Report (2004). *An Agenda for a Growing Europe*: Oxford University Press, Oxford.

Skirbekk, V. (2003). *Age and Individual Productivity: A Literature Survey*. MPIDR, Working Paper No. 2003-028.

Statistics Denmark, Statistics Finland, Statistics Iceland, Statistics Norway and Statistics Sweden (2003). *Access to Microdata in the Nordic Countries*. Statistics Sweden, Örebro.

Teulings, C. and J. Hartog (1998). *Corporatism or Competition?* Cambridge University Press, Cambridge.

Tomz, M., J. Wittenberg and G. King (2003). *Clarify: Software for Interpreting and Presenting Statistical Results* (Version 2.1), Stanford University, University of Wisconsin, and Harvard University, 5 January. Available at http://gking.harvard.edu/.

Topel, R.H. (1991). 'Specific capital, mobility and wages: Wages rise with job seniority', *Journal of Political Economy*, 99, 145–76.

Troske, K.R. (1999). 'Evidence on the employer size-wage premium from worker-establishment matched data', *Review of Economics and Statistics*, 81(February), 15–26.

Uusitalo, R. and J. Vartiainen (2005). 'Finland: Firm factors in wages and wage changes', unpublished manuscript, 9 June.

Verhaegen, P. and T.A. Salthouse (1997). 'Meta-analyses of age-cognition relations in adulthood. Estimates of linear and nonlinear age effects and structural models'. *Psychological Bulletin*, 122(3), 231–49.

Winter-Ebmer, R. (2001). 'Firm size, earnings, and displacement risk', *Economic Inquiry*, 39(3), 474–86.

Valuing ecosystem services

SUMMARY

This paper explores two methods for valuing ecosystems by valuing the services that they yield to various categories of user and that are not directly valued in the market, and illustrates the usefulness of these methods with an application to the valuation of mangrove ecosystems in Thailand. The first method is known as the production function approach and relies on the fact that ecosystems may be inputs into the production of other goods or services that are themselves marketed, such as fisheries. I discuss issues that arise in measuring the input into fisheries, particularly those due to the fact that the fishery stock is changing over time, and the shadow value of the ecosystem consists in its contribution to the maintenance of the stock as well as its contribution to current output. The second method is known as the expected damage approach and is used to value the services of storm protection in terms of the reduction in expected future storm damage that the ecosystem can provide. These two methods are shown to yield very different valuations of ecosystems from those that would be derived by the methods typically used in cost-benefit analyses. I argue that they represent a significant improvement on current practice.

— *Edward B. Barbier*

Valuing ecosystem services as productive inputs

Edward B. Barbier

University of Wyoming

1. INTRODUCTION

Global concern over the disappearance of natural ecosystems and habitats has prompted policymakers to consider the 'value of ecosystem services' in environmental management decisions. These 'services' are broadly defined as 'the benefits people obtain from ecosystems' (Millennium Ecosystem Assessment, 2003, p. 53).

However, our current understanding of key ecological and economic relationships is sufficient to value only a handful of ecological services. An important objective of this paper is to explain and illustrate through numerical examples the difficulties faced in valuing natural ecosystems and their services, compared to ordinary economic or financial assets. Specifically, the paper addresses the following three questions:

1. What progress has been made in valuing ecological services for policy analysis?
2. What are the unique measurement issues that need to be overcome?
3. How can future progress improve upon the shortcomings in existing methods?

I am grateful to David Aadland, Carlo Favero, Geoff Heal, Omer Moav and three anonymous referees for helpful comments. The Managing Editor in charge of this paper was Paul Seabright.

Economic Policy January 2007 pp. 177–229 Printed in Great Britain
© CEPR, CES, MSH, 2007.

1.1. Key challenges and policy context

As a report from the US National Academy of Science has emphasized, 'the fundamental challenge of valuing ecosystem services lies in providing an explicit description and adequate assessment of the links between the structure and functions of natural systems, the benefits (i.e., goods and services) derived by humanity, and their subsequent values' (Heal *et al.*, 2005, p. 2). Moreover, it has been increasingly recognized by economists and ecologists that the greatest 'challenge' they face is in valuing the ecosystem services provided by a certain class of key ecosystem functions – regulatory and habitat functions. The diverse benefits of these functions include climate stability, maintenance of biodiversity and beneficial species, erosion control, flood mitigation, storm protection, groundwater recharge and pollution control (see Table 1 below).

One of the natural ecosystems that has seen extensive development and application of methods to value ecosystem services has been coastal wetlands. This paper focuses mainly on valuation approaches applied to these systems, and in particular their role as a nursery and breeding habitat for near-shore fisheries and in providing storm protection for coastal communities.

The paper employs a case study of mangrove ecosystems in Thailand to compare and contrast approaches to valuing habitat and storm protection services. Global mangrove area has been declining rapidly, with around 35% of the total area lost in the past two decades (Valiela *et al.*, 2001). Mangrove deforestation has been particularly prevalent in Thailand and other Asian countries. The main cause of global mangrove loss has been coastal economic development, especially aquaculture expansion (Barbier and Cox, 2003). Yet ecologists maintain that global mangrove loss is contributing to the decline of marine fisheries and leaving many coastal areas vulnerable to natural disasters. Concern about the deteriorating 'storm protection' service of mangroves reached new significance with the 26 December 2004 Asian tsunami that caused widespread devastation and loss of life in Thailand and other Indian Ocean countries.

The Thailand case study also illustrates the importance of valuing ecosystem services to policy choices. Because these services are 'non-marketed', their benefits are not considered in commercial development decisions. For example, the excessive mangrove deforestation occurring in Thailand and other countries is clearly related to the failure to measure explicitly the values of habitat and storm protection services of mangroves. Consequently, these benefits have been largely ignored in national land use policy decisions, and calls to improve protection of remaining mangrove forests and to enlist the support of local coastal communities through legal recognition of their *de facto* property rights over mangroves are unlikely to succeed in the face of coastal development pressures on these resources (Barbier and Sathirathai, 2004). Unless the value to local coastal communities of the ecosystem services provided by protected mangroves is estimated, it is difficult to convince policymakers in Thailand and other countries to consider alternative land use policies.

Thus, as the Thailand case study reveals, the challenge of valuing ecosystem services is also a policy challenge. Because the benefits of these services are important and should be taken into account in any future policy to manage coastal wetlands in Thailand and other countries, it is equally essential that economics continues to develop and improve existing methodologies to value ecological services.

1.2. Outline and main results

The paper makes three contributions. The first is to demonstrate that valuing ecological services as productive inputs is a viable methodology for policy analysis, and to illustrate the key steps through a detailed case study of mangroves in Thailand. The second contribution is to identify the measurement issues that make valuation of non-marketed ecosystem services a unique challenge, yet one that is important for many important policy decisions concerning the management of natural ecosystems. The third contribution of the paper is to show, using the examples of habitat and storm protection services, that improvements in methods for valuing these services can correct for some shortcomings and measurement errors, thus yielding more accurate valuation estimates. But even the preferred approaches display measurement weaknesses that need to be addressed in future developments of ecosystem valuation methodologies.

Section 2 discusses in more detail the importance of valuing ecosystem services, especially those arising from the regulatory and habitat functions to environmental decision-making. Section 3 reviews various methods for valuing these services. Because the benefits arising from ecological regulatory and habitat functions mainly support or protect valuable economic activities, the production function (PF) approach of valuing these benefits as environmental inputs is a promising methodology. However, the latter approach faces its own unique measurement issues. To illustrate the PF approach as well as its shortcomings, the section discusses recent advances using the examples of the habitat and storm protection services of coastal wetland ecosystems. Section 4 compares the application of the different methods to valuing mangroves in Thailand. The case study indicates the importance of considering the key ecological-economic linkages underlying each service in choosing the appropriate valuation approach, and how each approach influences the final valuation estimates. In the case of valuing the mangroves' habitat-fishery linkage, modelling the contribution of this linkage to growth in fish stocks over time appears to be a key consideration. The case study also demonstrates the advantages of the expected damage function approach as an alternative to the replacement cost method of valuing the storm protection service of coastal wetlands. Section 5 concludes the paper by discussing the key areas for further development in ecosystem valuation methodologies, such as incorporating the effects of irreversibilities, uncertainties and thresholds, and the application of integrated ecological-economic modelling to reflect multiple ecological services and their benefits. Although substantial progress has been made in valuing some ecosystem services, many difficulties still remain. Future progress in ecosystem valuation for policy analysis requires understanding the key flaws in existing methods that need correcting.

2. BACKGROUND: VALUATION OF ECOSYSTEM SERVICES

The rapid disappearance of many ecosystems has raised concerns about the loss of beneficial 'services'. This raises two important questions. What are ecosystem services, and why is it important to value these environmental flows?

2.1. Ecosystem services

Although in the current literature the term 'ecosystem services' lumps together a variety of 'benefits', economics normally classifies these benefits into three different categories: (i) 'goods' (e.g. products obtained from ecosystems, such as resource harvests, water and genetic material); (ii) 'services' (e.g. recreational and tourism benefits or certain ecological regulatory functions, such as water purification, climate regulation, erosion control, etc.); and (iii) cultural benefits (e.g., spiritual and religious, heritage, etc.).[1] This paper focuses on methods to value a sub-set of the second category of ecosystem 'benefits' – the services arising from regulatory and habitat functions. Table 1 provides some examples of the links between regulatory and habitat functions and the resulting ecosystem benefits.

2.2. Valuing environmental assets

The literature on ecological services implies that natural ecosystems are assets that produce a flow of beneficial goods and services over time. In this regard, they are no different from any other asset in an economy, and in principle, ecosystem services should be valued in a similar manner. That is, regardless of whether or not there exists a market for the goods and services produced by ecosystems, their social value must equal the discounted net present value (NPV) of these flows.

However, what makes environmental assets special is that they give rise to particular measurement problems that are different for conventional economic or financial assets. This is especially the case for the benefits derived from the regulatory and habitat functions of natural ecosystems.

For one, these assets and services fall in the special category of 'nonrenewable resources with renewable service flows' (Just et al., 2004, p. 603). Although a natural ecosystem providing such beneficial services is unlikely to increase, it can be depleted, for example through habitat destruction, land conversion, pollution impacts and so

---

[1] See Daily (1997), De Groot et al. (2002) and Millennium Ecosystem Assessment (2003) for the various definitions of ecosystem services that are prevalent in the ecological literature.

Table 1. Some services provided by ecosystem regulatory and habitat functions

Ecosystem functions	Ecosystem processes and components	Ecosystem services (benefits)
Regulatory functions		
Gas regulation	Role of ecosystems in biogeochemical processes	Ultraviolet-B protection Maintenance of air quality Influence of climate
Climate regulation	Influence of land cover and biologically mediated processes	Maintenance of temperature, precipitation
Disturbance prevention	Influence of system structure on dampening environmental disturbance	Storm protection Flood mitigation
Water regulation	Role of land cover in regulating run-off, river discharge and infiltration	Drainage and natural irrigation Flood mitigation Groundwater recharge
Soil retention	Role of vegetation root matrix and soil biota in soil structure	Maintenance of arable land Prevention of damage from erosion and siltation
Soil formation	Weathering of rock and organic matter accumulation	Maintenance of productivity on arable land
Nutrient regulation	Role of biota in storage and recycling of nutrients	Maintenance of productive ecosystems
Waste treatment	Removal or breakdown of nutrients and compounds	Pollution control and detoxification
Habitat functions		
Niche and refuge	Suitable living space for wild plants and animals	Maintenance of biodiversity Maintenance of beneficial species
Nursery and breeding	Suitable reproductive habitat andnursery grounds	Maintenance of biodiversity Maintenance of beneficial species

Sources: Adapted from Heal *et al.* (2005, Table 3-3) and De Groot *et al.* (2002).

forth. Nevertheless, if the ecosystem is left intact, then the flow services from the ecosystem's regulatory and habitat functions are available in quantities that are not affected by the rate at which they are used.

In addition, whereas the services from most assets in an economy are marketed, the benefits arising from the regulatory and habitat functions of natural ecosystems generally are not. If the aggregate willingness to pay for these benefits is not revealed through market outcomes, then efficient management of such ecosystem services requires explicit methods to measure this social value (e.g., see Freeman, 2003; Just *et al.*, 2004). A further concern over ecosystem services is that their beneficial flows are threatened by the widespread disappearance of natural ecosystems and habitats across the globe. The major cause of this disappearance is conversion of the land to other uses, degradation of the functioning and integrity of natural ecosystems through resource exploitation, pollution, and biodiversity loss, and habitat fragmentation (Millennium Ecosystem Assessment, 2003). The failure to measure explicitly the aggregate willingness to pay for otherwise non-marketed ecological services exacerbates these problems, as the benefits of these services are 'underpriced' in development decisions as a consequence. Population and development pressures in many areas of the world result in increased land demand by economic activities, which mean that the opportunity cost of maintaining the land for natural ecosystems is rarely zero. Unless the benefits arising from ecosystem services are explicitly measured, or 'valued', then these non-marketed flows are likely to be ignored in land use decisions. Only the benefits of the 'marketed' outputs from economic activities, such as agricultural crops, urban housing and other commercial uses of land, will be taken into account, and as a consequence, excessive conversion of natural ecosystem areas for development will occur.

A further problem is the uncertainty over their future values of environmental assets. It is possible, for example, that the benefits of natural ecosystem services may increase in the future as more scientific information becomes available over time. In addition, if environmental assets are depleted irreversibly through economic development, their value will rise relative to the value of other economic assets (Krutilla and Fisher, 1985). Because ecosystems are in fixed supply, lack close substitutes and are difficult to restore, their beneficial services will decline as they are converted or degraded. As a result, the value of ecosystem services is likely to rise relative to other goods and services in the economy. This rising, but unknown, future scarcity value of ecosystem benefits implies an additional 'user cost' to any decision that leads to irreversible conversion today.

Valuation of environmental assets under conditions of uncertainty and irreversibility clearly poses additional measurement problems. There is now a considerable literature advocating various methods for estimating environmental values by measuring the additional 'premium' that individuals are willing to pay to avoid the uncertainty surrounding such values (see Ready, 1995 for a review). Similar methods are also advocated for estimating the user costs associated with irreversible development, as this also amounts to valuing the 'option' of avoiding reduced future choices for individuals (Just et al., 2004). However, it is difficult to implement such methods empirically, given the uncertainty over the future state of environmental assets and about the future preferences and income of individuals. The general conclusion from studies that attempt to allow for such uncertainties in valuing environmental assets is that 'more empirical research is needed to determine under what conditions we can ignore uncertainty in benefit estimation ...where uncertainty is over economic parameters such as prices or preferences, the issues surrounding uncertainty may be empirically unimportant' (Ready, 1995, p. 590).

3. VALUING THE ENVIRONMENT AS INPUT

Uncertainty and irreversible loss are important issues to consider in valuing ecosystem services. However, as emphasized by Heal et al. (2005), a more 'fundamental challenge' in valuing these flows is that ecosystem services are largely not marketed, and unless some attempt is made to value the aggregate willingness to pay for these services, then management of natural ecosystems and their services will not be efficient. The following section describes advances in developing the 'production function' approach, compared to other valuation methods, as a means to measuring the aggregate willingness to pay for the largely non-marketed benefits of ecosystem services.

3.1. Methods of valuing ecosystem services

Table 2 indicates various methods that can be used for valuing ecological services.[2] However, some approaches are limited to specific benefits. For example, the travel cost method is used principally for environmental values that enhance individuals' enjoyment of recreation and tourism, averting behaviour models are best applied to the health effects arising from pollution, and hedonic wage and property models are used primarily for assessing work-related hazards and environmental impacts on property values, respectively.

In contrast, stated preference methods, which include contingent valuation methods, conjoint analysis and choice experiments, have the potential to be used widely in valuing ecosystem goods and services. These valuation methods involve surveying individuals who benefit from an ecological service or range of services, and analysing the responses to measure individuals' willingness to pay for the service or services.

For example, choice experiments of wetland restoration in southern Sweden revealed that individuals' willingness to pay for the restoration increased if the result enhanced overall biodiversity but decreased if the restored wetlands were used mainly for the introduction of Swedish crayfish for recreational fishing (Carlsson et al., 2003). In some cases, stated preference methods are used to elicit 'non-use values', that is, the additional 'existence' and 'bequest' values that individuals attach to ensuring that a well-functioning system will be preserved for future generations to enjoy. A contingent valuation study of mangrove-dependent coastal communities in Micronesia demonstrated that the communities 'place some value on the existence and ecosystem functions of mangroves over and above the value of mangroves' marketable products' (Naylor and Drew, 1998, p. 488).

However, to implement a stated-preference study two key conditions are necessary: (1) the information must be available to describe the change in a natural ecosystem in terms of service that people care about, in order to place a value on those services; and (2) the change in the natural ecosystem must be explained in the survey instrument in a manner that people will understand and not reject the valuation scenario (Heal et al., 2005). For many of the services arising from ecological regulatory and habitat

---

[2] It is beyond the scope of this paper to discuss all the valuation methods listed in Table 2. See Freeman (2003), Heal et al. (2005) and Pagiola et al. (2004) for more discussion of these various valuation methods and their application to valuing ecosystem goods and services.

Table 2. Various valuation methods applied to ecosystem services

Valuation method[a]	Types of value estimated[b]	Common types of applications	Ecosystem services valued
Travel cost	Direct use	Recreation	Maintenance of beneficial species, productive ecosystems and biodiversity
Averting behaviour	Direct use	Environmental impacts on human health	Pollution control and detoxification
Hedonic price	Direct and indirect use	Environmental impacts on residential property and human morbidity and mortality	Storm protection; flood mitigation; maintenance of air quality
Production function	Indirect use	Commercial and recreational fishing; agricultural systems; control of invasive species; watershed protection; damage costs avoided	Maintenance of beneficial species; maintenance of arable land and agricultural productivity; prevention of damage from erosion and siltation; groundwater recharge; drainage and natural irrigation; storm protection; flood mitigation
Replacement cost	Indirect use	Damage costs avoided; freshwater supply	Drainage and natural irrigation; storm protection; flood mitigation
Stated preference	Use and non-use	Recreation; environmental impacts on human health and residential property; damage costs avoided; existence and bequest values of preserving ecosystems	All of the above

[a] See Freeman (2003), Heal *et al.* (2005) and Pagiola *et al.* (2004) for more discussion of these various valuation methods and their application to valuing ecosystem goods and services.
[b] Typically, use values involve some human 'interaction' with the environment whereas non-use values do not, as they represent an individual valuing the pure 'existence' of a natural habitat or ecosystem or wanting to 'bequest' it to future generations. Direct use values refer to both consumptive and non-consumptive uses that involve some form of direct physical interaction with environmental goods and services, such as recreational activities, resource harvesting, drinking clean water, breathing unpolluted air and so forth. Indirect use values refer to those ecosystem services whose values can only be measured indirectly, since they are derived from supporting and protecting activities that have directly measurable values, such as many of the services listed in Table 1.
Source: Adapted from Heal *et al.* (2005, Table 4-2) and Table 1.

functions, one or both of these conditions may not hold. For instance, it has proven very difficult to describe accurately through the hypothetical scenarios required by stated-preference surveys how changes in ecosystem processes and components affect ecosystem regulatory and habitat functions and thus the specific benefits arising from these functions that individuals value. If there is considerable scientific uncertainty surrounding these linkages, then not only is it difficult to construct such hypothetical scenarios but also any responses elicited from individuals from stated-preference surveys are likely to yield inaccurate measures of their willingness to pay for ecological services.

In contrast to stated-preference methods, the advantage of PF approaches is that they depend on only the first condition, and not both conditions, holding. That is, for those regulatory and habitat functions where there is sufficient scientific knowledge of how these functions link to specific ecological services that support or protect economic activities, then it may be possible to employ the PF approach to value these services. However, PF methods have their own measurement issues and limitations. These are also discussed further in the rest of this section, and illustrated using examples of key ecological services from coastal and estuarine wetlands.

3.2. The production function approach

Many of the beneficial services derived from regulatory and habitat functions are commonly classified by economists as indirect use values (Barbier, 1994). The benefits attributed to these services arise through their support or protection of activities that have directly measurable values (see Table 2). For example, coastal and estuarine wetlands, such as tropical mangroves and temperate marshlands, act as 'natural barriers' by preventing or mitigating storms and floods that could affect property and land values, agriculture, fishing and drinking supplies, as well as cause sickness and death. Similarly, coastal and estuarine wetlands may also provide a nursery and breeding habitat that supports the productivity of near-shore fisheries, which in turn may be valued for their commercial or recreational catch.

Because the benefits of these ecosystem services appear to enhance the productivity of economic activities, or protect them from possible damages, one possible method of measuring the aggregate willingness to pay for such services is to estimate their value as if they were a factor input in these productive activities. This is the essence of the PF valuation approaches, also called 'valuing the environment as input' (Barbier, 1994 and 2000; Freeman, 2003, ch. 9).[3]

The basic modelling approach underlying PF methods is similar to determining the additional value of a change in the supply of any factor input. If changes in the regulatory and habitat functions of ecosystems affect the marketed production activities of an economy, then the effects of these changes will be transmitted to individuals through the price system via changes in the costs and prices of final goods and services. This means that any resulting 'improvements in the resource base or environmental quality' as a result of enhanced ecosystem services, 'lower costs and prices and increase the quantities of marketed goods, leading to increases in consumers' and perhaps producers' surpluses' (Freeman, 2003, p. 259). The sum of consumer and producer surpluses in turn provides a measure of the willingness to pay for the improved ecosystem services.

[3] The concept of 'valuing' the environment as input is not new. Dose-response and change-in-productivity models, which have been used for some time, can be considered special cases of the PF approach in which the production responses to environmental quality changes are greatly simplified (Freeman, 1982).

An adaptation of the PF methodology is required in the case where ecological regulatory and habitat functions have a protective value, such as the storm protection and flood mitigation services provided by coastal wetlands. In such cases, the environment may be thought of producing a non-marketed service, such as 'protection' of economic activity, property and even human lives, which benefits individuals through limiting damages. Applying PF approaches requires modelling the 'production' of this protection service and estimating its value as an environmental input in terms of the expected damages avoided.

Although this paper focuses mainly on applications of the PF approach to coastal wetland ecosystems, as Table 2 indicates PF approaches are being increasingly employed for a diverse range of environmental quality impacts and ecosystem services. Some examples include maintenance of biodiversity and carbon sequestration in tropical forests (Boscolo and Vincent, 2003); nutrient reduction in the Baltic Sea (Gren et al., 1997); pollination service of tropical forests for coffee production in Costa Rica (Ricketts et al., 2004); tropical watershed protection services (Kaiser and Roumasset, 2002); groundwater recharge supporting irrigation farming in Nigeria (Acharya and Barbier, 2000); coral reef habitat support of marine fisheries in Kenya (Rodwell et al., 2002); marine reserves acting to enhance the 'insurance value' of protecting commercial fish species in Sicily (Mardle et al., 2004) and in the northeast cod fishery (Sumaila, 2002); and nutrient enrichment in the Black Sea affecting the balance between invasive and beneficial species (Knowler et al., 2001).

3.3. Measurement issues for modelling habitat-fishery linkages

Applying PF methods to valuing ecosystem services has its own demands in terms of ecological and economic data. To highlight these additional measurement issues, this section draws on the example of valuing coastal wetlands as a nursery and breeding habitat for commercial near-shore fisheries.

First, application of the PF approach requires properly specifying the habitat-fishery PF model that links the physical effects of the change in this service to changes in market prices and quantities and ultimately to consumer and producer surpluses. As with many ecological services, it is difficult to measure directly changes in the habitat and nursery function of coastal wetlands. Instead, the standard approach adopted in coastal habitat-fishery PF models is to allow the wetland area to serve as a proxy for the productivity contribution of the nursery and habitat function (see Barbier, 2000 for further discussion). It is then relatively straightforward to estimate the impacts of the change in the coastal wetland area input on fishery catch, in terms of the marginal costs of fishery harvests and thus changes in consumer and producer surpluses.

Second, market conditions and regulatory policies for the marketed output will influence the values imputed to the environmental input (Freeman, 1991). For instance, the offshore fishery supported by coastal wetlands may be subject to open access. Under these conditions, profits in the fishery would be dissipated, and equilibrium prices would be equated to average and not marginal costs. As a consequence, there is no producer surplus, and the welfare impact of a change in wetland habitat is measured by the resulting change in consumer surplus only.

Third, if the ecological service supports a harvested natural resource system, such as a fishery, forestry or a wildlife population, then it may be necessary to model how changes in the stock or biological population may affect the future flow of benefits. If the natural resource stock effects are not considered significant, then the environmental changes can be modelled as impacting only current harvest, prices and consumer and producer surpluses. If the stock effects are significant, then a change in an ecological service will impact not only current but also future harvest and market outcomes. In the PF valuation literature, the first approach is referred to as a 'static model' of environmental change on a natural resource production system, whereas the second approach is referred to as a 'dynamic model' because it takes into account the intertemporal stock effects of the environmental change (Barbier, 2000; Freeman, 2003, ch. 9).

Finally, most natural ecosystems provide more than one beneficial service, and it may be important to model any trade-offs among these services as an ecosystem is altered or disturbed. Integrated economic-ecological modelling could capture more fully the ecosystem functioning and dynamics underlying the provision of key services, and can be used to value multiple services arising from natural ecosystems. For instance, integrated modelling of an entire wetland-coral reef-sea grass system could measure simultaneously the benefits of both the habitat-fishery linkage and the storm protection service provided by the system. Examples of such multi-service ecosystem modelling include analysis of salmon habitat restoration (Wu *et al.*, 2003); eutrophication of small shallow lakes (Carpenter *et al.*, 1999); changes in species diversity in a marine ecosystem (Finnoff and Tschirhart, 2003); and introduction of exotic trout species (Settle and Shogren, 2002).

To illustrate the first three of the above issues, I next explore two ways of measuring the welfare effects of an environmental change on a productive natural resource system with the example of the coastal habitat-fishery linkage. I will return to the issue of integrated ecological-economic modelling of multiple ecological services in Section 5.

3.3.1. Habitat-fishery linkages: static approaches.   This section illustrates the use of a static model to value how a change in coastal wetland habitat area affects the market for commercially harvested fish. Many initial PF methods to value habitat-fishery linkages have relied on this static approach. For example, using data from the Lynne *et al.* (1981), Ellis and Fisher (1987) constructed such a model to value the support by Florida marshlands for Gulf Coast crab fisheries in terms of the resulting changes in consumer and producer surpluses from the marketed catch. Freeman (1991) then extended Ellis and Fisher's approach to show how the values imputed to the wetlands in the static model is influenced by whether or not the fishery is open access or optimally managed. Sathirathai and Barbier (2001) also used a static model of habitat-fishery linkages to value the role of mangroves in Thailand in supporting near-shore fisheries under both open access and optimally managed conditions.

As most near-shore fisheries are not optimally managed but open access, the following illustration of the static model of habitat-fishery linkages assumes that the fishery is open access. Any profits in the fishery will attract new entrants until all the profits disappear, and in equilibrium, the welfare change in coastal wetland is in terms of its impact on consumer surplus only.

As noted above, the general PF approach treats an ecological service, such as coastal wetland habitat, as an 'input' into the economic activity, and like any other input, its value can be equated with its impact on the productivity of any marketed output. More formally, if h is the marketed harvest of the fishery, then its production function can be denoted as:

$$h = h(E_i \ldots E_k, S) \tag{1}$$

The area of coastal wetlands, S, may therefore have a direct influence on the marketed fish catch, h, which is independent from the standard inputs of a commercial fishery, $E_i \ldots E_k$.

A standard assumption in most static habitat-fishery models is that the production function (1) takes the Cobb–Douglas form, $h = AE^a S^b$, where E is some aggregate measure of total effort in the off-shore fishery and S is coastal wetland habitat area. It follows that the optimal cost function of a cost-minimizing fishery is:

$$C^* = C(h, w, S) = wA^{-1/a}h^{1/a}S^{-b/a} \tag{2}$$

where w is the unit cost of effort. Assuming an iso-elastic market demand function, $P = p(h) = kh^\eta$, $\eta = 1/\varepsilon < 0$, then the market equilibrium for catch of the open access fishery occurs where the total revenues of the fishery just equals cost, or price equals average cost, i.e. $P = C^*/h$, which in this model becomes:

$$kh^\eta = wA^{-1/a}h^{1-a/a}S^{-b/a} \tag{3}$$

which can be rearranged to yield the equilibrium level of fish harvest:

$$h = \left[\frac{w}{k}\right]^{a/\beta} A^{-1/\beta}S^{-b/\beta}, \; \beta = (1 + \eta)a - 1 \tag{4}$$

It follows from (4) that the marginal impact of a change in wetland habitat is:

$$\frac{dh}{dS} = -\frac{b}{\beta}\left[\frac{w}{k}\right]^{a/\beta} A^{-1/\beta}S^{-(b+\beta)/\beta} \tag{5}$$

The change in consumer surplus, CS, resulting from a change in equilibrium harvest levels (from h^0 to h^1) is:

$$\Delta CS = \int_{h^0}^{h^1} p(h)dh - [p^1h^1 - p^0h^0] = \frac{k[(h^1)^{\eta+1} - (h^0)^{\eta+1}]}{\eta + 1} - k[(h^1)^{\eta+1} - (h^0)^{\eta+1}] \tag{6}$$

$$= -\frac{\eta[p^1h^1 - p^0h^0]}{\eta + 1}.$$

By utilizing (5) and (6) it is possible to estimate the new equilibrium harvest and price levels and thus the corresponding changes in consumer surplus associated with a change in coastal wetland area, for a given demand elasticity, γ.

Figure 1 is the diagrammatic representation of the welfare measure of a change in wetland area on an open access fishery corresponding to Equation (6). As shown in the figure, a change in wetland area that serves as a breeding ground and nursery for an open access fishery results in a shift in the average cost curve, AC, of the fishery. The welfare impact is the change in consumer surplus (area P*ABC).

3.3.2. Habitat-fishery linkages: dynamic approaches. If the stock effects of a change in coastal wetlands are significant, then valuing such changes in terms of the impacts on current harvest and market outcomes is a flawed approach. To overcome this shortcoming, a dynamic model of coastal habitat-fishery linkage incorporates the change in wetland area within a multi-period harvesting model of the fishery. The standard approach is to model the change in coastal wetland habitat as affecting the biological growth function of the fishery (Barbier, 2003). As a result, any value impacts of a change in this habitat-support function can be determined in terms of changes in the long-run equilibrium conditions of the fishery. Alternatively, the welfare analysis could be conducted in terms of the harvesting path that approaches this equilibrium or the path that is moving away from initial conditions in the fishery.

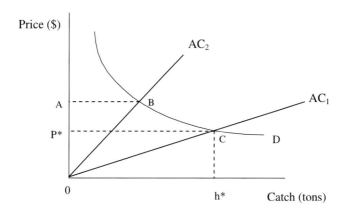

Figure 1. The economic value effects of increased wetland area on an open access fishery

Notes: AC: average cost; D: demand curve; P*: price per tonne; h*: fish catch in tonnes after change; P*ABC: change in consumer and producer surplus.

Source: Adapted from Freeman (1991).

Most attempts to value habitat-fishery linkages via a dynamic model that incorporates stock effects have assumed that the fishery affected by the habitat change is in a long-run equilibrium. Such a model has been applied, for example, in case studies of valuing habitat fishery linkages in Mexico (Barbier and Strand, 1998), Thailand (Barbier *et al.*, 2002; Barbier, 2003) and the United States (Swallow, 1994). Similar 'equilibrium' dynamic approaches have been used to model other coastal environmental changes, including the impacts of water quality on fisheries in the Chesapeake Bay (Kahn and Kemp, 1985; McConnell and Strand, 1989) and the effects of mangrove deforestation and shrimp larvae availability on aquaculture in Ecuador (Parks and Bonifaz, 1997).

However, valuing the change in coastal wetland habitat in terms of its impact on the long-run equilibrium of the fishery raises additional methodological issues. First, the assumption of prevailing steady state conditions is strong, and may not be a realistic representation of harvesting and biological growth conditions in the near-shore fisheries. Second, such an approach ignores both the convergence of stock and harvest to the steady state and the short-run dynamics associated with the impacts of the change in coastal habitat on the long-run equilibrium. The usual assumption is that this change will lead to an instantaneous adjustment of the system to a new steady state, but this in turn requires local stability conditions that may not be supported by the parameters of the model.

There are examples of pure fisheries models that assume that the dynamic system is not in equilibrium but is either on the approach to a steady state or is moving away from initial fixed conditions. The latter approach has proven particularly useful in the case of open access or regulated access fisheries (Bjørndal and Conrad, 1987; Homans and Wilen, 1997). The following model shows how this approach can be adopted here to the case of valuing a change in wetland habitat in terms of the dynamic path of an open access fishery.

Defining X_t as the stock of fish measured in biomass units, any net change in growth of this stock over time can be represented as:

$$X_t - X_{t-1} = F(X_{t-1}, S_{t-1}) - h(X_{t-1}, E_{t-1}), \frac{\partial^2 F}{\partial X_{t-1}^2} > 0, \frac{\partial F}{\partial S_{t-1}} > 0. \tag{7}$$

Thus, net expansion in the fish stock occurs as a result of biological growth in the current period, $F(X_{t-1}, S_{t-1})$, net of any harvesting, $h(X_{t-1}, E_{t-1})$, which is a function of the stock as well as fishing effort, E_{t-1}. The influence of the wetland habitat area, S_{t-1}, as a breeding ground and nursery habitat on growth of the fish stock is assumed to be positive, $\partial F/\partial S_{t-1} > 0$, as an increase in wetland area will mean more carrying capacity for the fishery and thus greater biological growth.

As before, it is assumed that the near-shore fishery is open access. The standard assumption for an open access fishery is that effort next period will adjust in response to the real profits made in the past period (Clark, 1976; Bjørndal and Conrad, 1987). Letting $p(h)$ represent landed fish price per unit harvested, w the unit cost of effort and $\phi > 0$ the adjustment coefficient, then the fishing effort adjustment equation is:

$$E_t - E_{t-1} = \phi[\, p(h_{t-1}) \, h(X_{t-1}, E_{t-1}) - wE_{t-1}], \quad \frac{\partial p(h_{t-1})}{\partial h_{t-1}} < 0. \tag{8}$$

Assume a conventional bioeconomic fishery model with biological growth characterized by a logistic function, $F(X_{t-1}, S_{t-1}) = rX_{t-1}[1 - X_{t-1}/K(S_{t-1})]$, and harvesting by a Schaefer production process, $h_t = qX_tE_t$, where q is a 'catchability' coefficient, r is the intrinsic growth rate and $K(S_t) = \alpha \ln S_t$, is the impact of coastal wetland area on carrying capacity, K, of the fishery. The market demand function for harvested fish is again assumed to be iso-elastic, i.e. $p(h) = kh^\eta$, $\eta = 1/\varepsilon < 0$. Substituting these expressions into (7) and (8) yields:

$$X_t = rX_{t-1}\left[1 - \frac{X_{t-1}}{\alpha \ln S_{t-1}}\right] - h_{t-1} + X_{t-1} \tag{9}$$

$$E_t = \phi R_{t-1} + (1 - \phi w)E_{t-1}, \quad R_{t-1} = kh_{t-1}^{1+\eta}. \tag{10}$$

Both X_t and E_t are predetermined, and so (9) and (10) can be estimated independently (see Homans and Wilen, 1997). Following Schnute (1977), define the catch per unit effort as $c_t = h_t/E_t = qX_t$. If X_t is predetermined so is c_t. Substituting the expression for catch per unit effort in (9) produces:

$$\frac{c_t - c_{t-1}}{c_{t-1}} = r - \frac{r}{q\alpha} \frac{c_{t-1}}{\ln S_{t-1}} - qE_{t-1}. \tag{11}$$

Thus Equations (10) and (11) can also be estimated independently to determine the biological and economic parameters of the model. For given initial effort, harvest and wetland data, both the effort and stock paths of the fishery can be determined for subsequent periods, and the consumer plus producer surplus can be estimated for each period. Alternative effort and stock paths can then be determined as wetland area changes in each period, and thus the resulting changes in consumer plus producer surplus in each period are the corresponding estimates of the welfare impacts of the coastal habitat change.[4]

3.4. Replacement cost and cost of treatment

In circumstances where an ecological service is unique to a specific ecosystem and is difficult to value, then economists have sometimes resorted to using the cost of replacing the service as a valuation approach.[5] This method is usually invoked because of the lack of data for many services arising from natural ecosystems.

For example, the presence of a wetland may reduce the cost of municipal water treatment because the wetland system filters and removes pollutants. It is therefore

---

[4] As along its dynamic path the open access fishery is not in equilibrium, producer surpluses, or losses, are relevant for the welfare estimate of a change in coastal wetland habitat.

[5] Such an approach to approximating the benefits of a service by the cost of providing an alternative is not used exclusively in environmental valuation. For example, in the health economics literature this approach is referred to as 'cost of illness' (Dickie, 2003). This involves adding up the costs of treating a patient for an illness as the measure of the benefit to the patient of staying disease-free.

tempting to use the cost of an alternative treatment method, such as the building and operation of an industrial water treatment plant, to represent the value of the wetland's natural water treatment service. Such an approach does not measure directly the benefit derived from the wetland's waste treatment service; instead, the approach is estimating this benefit with the cost of providing the ecosystem service that people value. Herein lies the main problem with the replacement cost method: it is using 'costs' as a measure of economic 'benefit'. In economic terms, the implication is that the ratio of costs to benefit of an ecological service is always equal to one.

The problems posed by the replacement cost method are illustrated in Figure 2, in the case of waste water treatment service provided by an existing wetland ecosystem. The cost of the waste water treatment service provided by the wetlands is 'free' and thus corresponds to the horizontal axis, MC_S. Given the demand curve for water, Q_1 amount of water is consumed. However, if the wetland is destroyed the marginal cost of an alternative, human-built waste treatment facility is MC_H. Thus, the 'replacement cost' of using the treatment facility to provide Q_1 amount of water in the absence of the wetlands is the difference between the two supply curves, or area $0BDQ_1$. However, this overestimates the benefit of having the wetlands provide the waste treatment service. The true benefit of this ecosystem service is the demand curve, or total willingness to pay, for Q_1 amount of water less the costs of providing it, or area $0ACQ_1$.

For these reasons, economists consider that the replacement cost approach should be used with caution. Shabman and Batie (1978) suggested that this method can provide a reliable valuation estimation for an ecological service if the following conditions are met: (1) the alternative considered provides the same services; (2) the alternative compared for cost comparison should be the least-cost alternative; and (3) there should be substantial evidence that the service would be demanded by society if it were provided by that least-cost alternative. In the absence of any information on benefits, and a decision has to be made to take some action, then treatment costs become a way of looking for a cost-effective action.

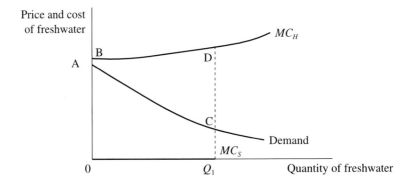

Figure 2. Replacement cost estimation of an ecosystem service

Source: Adapted from Ellis and Fisher (1987).

One of the best-known examples of a policy decision based on using the 'replacement cost' method to assess the value of an ecosystem service is the provision of clean drinking water by the Catskills Mountains for New York City (Heal *et al.*, 2005). In 1996, New York City faced a choice: either it could build water filtration systems to clean its water supply or the city could restore and protect the Catskill watersheds to ensure high-quality drinking water. Because estimates indicated that building and operating the filtration system would cost $6–8 billion whereas protecting and restoring the watersheds would cost $1–1.5 billion, New York chose to protect the Catskills. In this case, it was sufficient for the policy decision simply to demonstrate the cost-effectiveness of restoring and protecting the ecological integrity of the Catskills watersheds compared to the alternative of the human-constructed water filtration system. Thus, clearly this is an example where the criteria established by Shabman and Batie (1978) apply.

The main reason why economists have resorted to replacement cost approaches to valuing an ecosystem service, however, is that there is often a lack of data on the linkage between the initial ecological function, the processes and components of ecosystems that facilitate this function, and the eventual ecological service that benefits humans. The lack of such data makes it extremely difficult to construct reliable hypothetical scenarios through stated preference surveys and similar methods to elicit accurate responses from individuals about their willingness to pay for ecological services. As an illustration, in the Catskills case study, a stated preference survey may have elicited an estimate of the total willingness-to-pay by New York City residents for the amount of freshwater provided – for example, the total demand for freshwater Q_1 in Figure 2 – but it would have been very difficult to obtain a measure of the willingness-to-pay to avoid losses in the water treatment service that occur through *changes* in the land use in Catskills watershed that affect the free provision of this ecological service.

Similarly, as pointed out by Chong (2005), it is very difficult to use stated preference methods in tropical developing areas to assess the benefits to local communities of the storm protection service of mangrove systems. Although there is sufficient scientific evidence suggesting that such a service occurs, there is a lack of ecological data on how loss of mangroves in specific locations will affect their ability to provide storm protection to neighbouring communities. To date, the few studies that have attempted to value the storm prevention and flood mitigation services of the 'natural' storm barrier function of mangrove systems have employed the replacement cost method by simply estimating the costs of replacing mangroves with constructed barriers that perform the same services (Chong, 2005). Unfortunately, such estimates not only make the classic error of estimating a 'benefit' by a 'cost' but also may yield unrealistically high estimates, given that removing all the mangroves and replacing them with constructed barriers is unlikely to be the least-cost alternative to providing storm prevention and flood mitigation services in coastal areas.

3.5. Expected damage function approach

For some ecological services, an alternative to employing replacement cost methods might be the *expected damage function* (EDF) approach.[6]

The EDF approach, which is a special category of 'valuing' the environment as 'input', is nominally straightforward; it assumes that the value of an asset that yields a benefit in terms of reducing the probability and severity of some economic damage is measured by the reduction in the expected damage. The essential step to implementing this approach, which is to estimate how changes in the asset affect the probability of the damaging event occurring, has been used routinely in risk analysis and health economics, for example, as in the case of airline safety performance (Rose, 1990); highway fatalities (Michener and Tighe, 1992); drug safety (Olson, 2004); and studies of the incidence of diseases and accident rates (Cameron and Trivedi, 1998; Winkelmann, 2003). Here we show that the EDF approach can also be applied, under certain circumstances, to value ecological services that also reduce the probability and severity of economic damages.

Recall that one of the special features of many regulatory and habitat services of ecosystems is that they may protect nearby economic activities, property and even human lives from possible damages. As indicated in Table 1, such services include storm protection, flood mitigation, prevention of erosion and siltation, pollution control and maintenance of beneficial species. The EDF approach essentially 'values' these services through estimating how they mitigate damage costs.

The following example illustrates how the expected damage function (EDF) methodology can be applied to value the storm protection service provided by a coastal wetland, such as a marshland or mangrove ecosystem. The starting point is the standard 'compensating surplus' approach to valuing a quantity or quality change in a non-market environmental good or service (Freeman, 2003).

Assume that in a coastal region the local community owns all economic activity and property, which may be threatened by damage from periodic natural storm events. Assume also that the preferences of all households in the community are sufficiently identical so that it can be represented by a single household. Let $m(p^x, z, u^0)$ be the expenditure function of the representative household, that is, the minimum expenditure required by the household to reach utility level, u^0, given the vector of prices, p^x, for all market-purchased commodities consumed by the household, the expected number or incidence of storm events, z^0.

Suppose the expected incidence of storms rises from z^0 to z^1. The resulting expected damages to the property and economic livelihood of the household, $E[D(z)]$, translates into an exact measure of welfare loss through changes in the minimum expenditure function:

---

[6] The expected damage function approach predates many of the PF methods discussed so far, and has been used extensively to estimate the risk of health impacts from pollution (Freeman, 1982, chs. 5 and 9).

$$E[D(z)] = m(p^x, z^1, u^0) - m(p^x, z^0, u^0) = c(z) \qquad (12)$$

where $c(z)$ is the compensating surplus. It is the minimum income compensation that the household requires to maintain it at the utility level u^0, despite the expected increase in damaging storm events. Alternatively, $c(z)$ can be viewed as the minimum income that the household needs to avoid the increase in expected storm damages.

However, the presence of coastal wetlands could mitigate the expected incidence of damaging storm events. Because of this storm protection service, the area of coastal wetlands, S, may have a direct effect on reducing the 'production' of natural disasters, in terms of their ability to inflict damages locally. Thus the 'production function' for the incidence of potentially damaging natural disasters can be represented as:

$$z = z(S), \ z' < 0, \ z'' > 0. \qquad (13)$$

It follows from (12) and (13) that $\partial c(z)/\partial S = \partial E[D(z)]/\partial S < 0$. An increase in wetland area reduces expected storm damages and therefore also reduces the minimum income compensation needed to maintain the household at its original utility level. Alternatively, a loss in wetland area would increase expected storm damages and raises the minimum compensation required by the household to maintain its welfare. Thus, we can define the marginal willingness to pay, $W(S)$, for the protection services of the wetland in terms of the marginal impact of a change in wetland area on expected storm damages:

$$W(S) = -\frac{\partial E[D(z(S))]}{\partial S} = -E\left[\frac{\partial D}{\partial z}z'\right], \ W' < 0. \qquad (14)$$

The 'marginal valuation function', $W(S)$, is analogous to the Hicksian compensated demand function for marketed goods. The minus sign on the right-hand sign of (14) allows this 'demand' function to be represented in the usual quadrant, and it has the normal downward-sloping property (see Figure 3). Although an increase in S reduces z and thus enables the household to avoid expected damages from storms, the additional value of this storm protection service to the household will fall as wetland area increases in size. This relationship should hold across all households in the coastal community. Consequently, as indicated in Figure 3, the marginal willingness to pay by the community for more storm protection declines with S.

The value of a non-marginal change in wetland area, from S_0 to S_1, can be measured as:

$$-\int_{S_0}^{S_1} W(S)dS = E[D(z(S))] = c(S). \qquad (15)$$

If there is an increase in wetland area, then the value of this change is the total amount of expected damage costs avoided. If there is a reduction in wetland area, as shown in Figure 3, then the welfare loss is the total expected damages resulting from the increased incidence of storm events. As indicated in (15), in both instances the

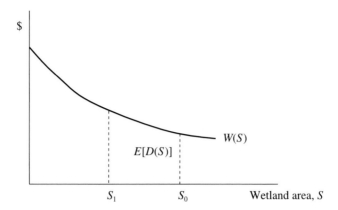

Figure 3. Expected damage costs from a loss of wetland area

valuation would be a compensation surplus measure of a change in the area of wetlands and the storm protection service that they provide.

As indicated in (14), an estimate of the marginal impact of a change in wetland area on expected storm damages has two components: the influence of wetland area on the expected incidence of economically damaging natural disaster events, z', and some measure of the additional economic damage incurred per event. Thus the right-hand expression in (14) can be estimated, provided that there are sufficient data on past storm events, and preferably across different coastal areas, and some estimate of the economic damages inflicted by each event. The most important step in the analysis is the first one, using the data on the incidence of past natural disasters and changes in wetland area in coastal areas to estimate $z(S)$. One way this analysis can be done is through employing *count data models*.

Count data models explain the number of times a particular event occurs over a given period. In economics, count data models have been used to explain a variety of phenomenon, such as explaining successful patents derived from firm R&D expenditures, accident rates, disease incidence, crime rates and recreational visits (Cameron and Trivedi, 1998; Greene, 2003, ch. 21; Winkelmann, 2003). Count data models could be used to estimate whether a change in the area of coastal wetlands, S, reduces the expected incidence of economically damaging storm events. The basic methodology for such an application of count data models is described further in the appendix.

However, applying the EDF method to estimating the storm protection value of coastal wetlands raises two additional measurement issues.

First, as the 2004 Asian tsunami and recent hurricanes in the United States have demonstrated, the risks to vulnerable populations living in coastal areas from the economic damages of storm events can be very large. This suggests that coastal populations will display a degree of risk aversion to such events, in the sense that they would like to see the least possible variance in expected storm damages. Applying standard techniques, such as the capital-asset pricing model, this implies in turn that there should be a 'risk premium' attached to the storm protection value of coastal wetlands that reduces the variance in expected economic damages from storm events (Hirshleifer and Riley, 1992).

Second, estimating how coastal wetlands affect the expected number of economic damaging events from the count data model and then multiplying the effect by the average economic damages across events could be misleading under some extreme circumstances. For instance, suppose a loss in wetland area is associated with a situation in which there is a change in the incidence of storms from one devastating storm to two relatively minor storms per year. The count data model would then be interpreted as not providing evidence against the null that the change in the wetland area increases expected storm damages. Clearly, there needs to be a robustness check on the count data model to ensure that such situations do not dominate the application of the EDF approach.

4. CASE STUDY OF MANGROVE ECOSYSTEMS IN THAILAND

This section illustrates the application of the PF approach and the EDF approach to valuation of ecological services with a case study of mangrove ecosystems in Thailand. The two services of interest are the provision of a breeding and nursery habitat for fisheries and the storm protection service of mangroves.

Both the dynamic and static PF approaches are used to estimate the value of the mangrove-fishery habitat service. The EDF approach to estimating the storm protection service of mangroves is contrasted with the replacement cost method.

4.1. Case study background

Many mangrove ecosystems, especially those in Asia, are threatened by rapid deforestation. At least 35% of global mangrove area has been lost in the past two decades; in Asia, 36% of mangrove area has been deforested, at the rate of 1.52% per year (Valiela *et al.*, 2001). Although many factors are behind global mangrove deforestation, a major cause is aquaculture expansion in coastal areas, especially the establishment of shrimp farms (Barbier and Cox, 2003). Aquaculture accounts for 52% of mangrove loss globally, with shrimp farming alone accounting for 38% of mangrove deforestation; in Asia, aquaculture contributes 58% to mangrove loss with shrimp farming accounting for 41% of total deforestation (Valiela *et al.*, 2001).

Mangrove deforestation has been particularly prevalent in Thailand. Some estimates suggest that over 1961–96 Thailand lost around 2050 km^2 of mangrove forests, or about 56% of the original area, mainly due to shrimp aquaculture and other coastal developments (Charuppat and Charuppat, 1997). Since 1975, 50–65% of Thailand's mangroves have been converted to shrimp farms (Aksornkoae and Tokrisna, 2004).

Figure 4 shows two long-run trend estimates of mangrove area in Thailand. In 1961, there were approximately 3700 km^2 of mangroves, which declined steadily to

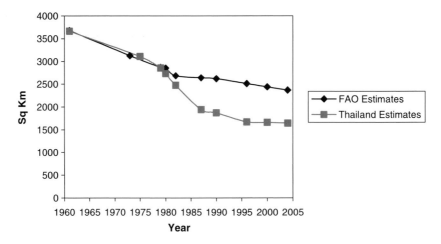

Figure 4. Mangrove area (km²) in Thailand, 1961–2004

Notes: FAO estimates from FAO (2003). 2000 and 2004 data are estimated from 1990–2000 annual average mangrove loss of 18.0 km². Thailand estimates from various Royal Thailand Forestry Department sources reported in Aksornkoae and Tokrisna (2004). 2000 and 2004 data are estimated from 1993–96 annual average mangrove loss of 3.44 km².

Sources: Based on FAO (2003), Aksornkoae and Tokrisna (2004) and author's estimates.

around 2700 to 2900 km² by 1980. Since then, mangrove deforestation has continued, although there are disagreements over the rate of deforestation. For example, FAO estimates based on long-run trend rates suggest a slower rate of decline, and indicate that there may be almost 2400 km² of mangroves still remaining. However, estimates based on Thailand's Royal Forestry Department studies suggest that rapid shrimp farm expansion during the 1980s and early 1990s accelerated mangrove deforestation, and as a consequence, the area of mangroves in 2004 may be much lower, closer to 1,645 km².

   Mangrove deforestation in Thailand has focused attention on the two principal services provided by mangrove ecosystems, their role as nursery and breeding habitats for offshore fisheries and as natural 'storm barriers' to periodic coastal storm events, such as wind storms, tsunamis, storm surges and typhoons. In addition, many coastal communities exploit mangroves directly for a variety of products, such as fuelwood, timber, raw materials, honey and resins, and crabs and shellfish. One study estimated that the annual value to local villagers of collecting these products was $88 per hectare (ha), or approximately $823/ha in net present value terms over a 20-year period and with a 10% discount rate (Sathirathai and Barbier, 2001).

4.1.1. Breeding and nursery habitat for fisheries. An extensive literature in ecology has emphasized the role of coastal wetland habitats in supporting neighbouring marine fisheries (for a review, see Mitsch and Gosselink, 1993; World Conservation Monitoring Center; World Resources Institute 1996). Mangroves in Thailand also provide this important habitat service (Aksornkoae *et al.*, 2004).

Thailand's coastline is vast, stretching for 2815 km, of which 1878 km is on the Gulf of Thailand and 937 km on the Andaman Sea (Indian Ocean) (Kaosa-ard and Pednekar, 1998). Since 1972, the 3 km offshore coastal zone in southern Thailand has been reserved for small-scale, artisanal marine fisheries. The Gulf of Thailand is divided into four such major zones, and the Andaman Sea comprises a fifth zone.[7] The mangroves along these coastal zones are thought to provide breeding grounds and nurseries in support of several species of demersal fish and shellfish (mainly crab and shrimp) in Thailand's coastal waters.[8] The artisanal marine fisheries of the five major coastal zones of Thailand depend largely on shellfish but also some demersal fish. For example, in 1994 shrimp, crab, squid and cuttlefish alone accounted for 67% of all catch in the artisanal marine fisheries, and demersal fish accounted for 5.3% (Kaosa-ard and Pednekar, 1998).

The coastal artisanal fisheries of Thailand are characterized by classic open access conditions (Kaosa-ard and Pedneker, 1998; Wattana, 1998). Since the 1970s, there have been approximately 36 000–38 000 households engaged in small-scale fishing activities. Although there are 2500 fishing communities scattered over the 24 coastal provinces of Thailand, 90% of the artisanal fishing households are concentrated in communities spread along the Southern Gulf of Thailand and Andaman Sea coasts. While the number of households engaged in small-scale fishing has remained fairly stable since 1985, the use of motorized boats has increased by more than 30% (Wattana, 1998). Gill nets still remain the most common form of fishing gear used by artisanal fishers. Although a licence fee and permit are required for fishing in coastal waters, officials do not strictly enforce the law and users do not pay. Currently, there is no legislation for supporting community-based fishery management (Kaosa-ard and Pednekar, 1998).

4.1.2. Storm protection.   The 26 December 2004 Indian Ocean tsunami disaster has focused attention on the role of natural barriers, such as mangroves, in protecting vulnerable coastlines and populations in the region from such storm events (UNEP, 2005; Wetlands International, 2005). Mangrove wetlands, which are found along sheltered tropical and subtropical shores and estuaries, are particularly valuable in minimizing damage to property and loss of human life by acting as a barrier against tropical storms, such as typhoons, cyclones, hurricanes and tsunamis (Chong, 2005; Massel *et al.*, 1999; Mazda *et al.*, 1997). Evidence from the 12 Indian Ocean countries affected by the tsunami disaster, including Thailand, suggests that those coastal areas

[7] The four Gulf of Thailand zones consist of the following coastal provinces: Trat, Chantaburi and Rayong (Zone 1); Chon Buri, Chachoengsao, Samut Parkakan, Samut Sakhon, Samut Songkhram, Phetchaburi, Prachaup Khiri Khan (Zone 2); Chumphon, Surat Thani, Nakhon Si Thammarat (Zone 3); and Songkhla, Patthani, Narathiwart (Zone 4). The fifth zone on the Indian Ocean (Andaman Sea) consists of the following coastal provinces: Ranong, Phangnga, Phuket, Krabi, Trang and Satun (Zone 5).

[8] Mangrove-dependent demersal fish include those belonging to the *Clupeidae, Chanidae, Ariidae, Pltosidae, Mugilidae, Lujanidae* and *Latidae* families. The shellfish include those belonging to the families of *Panaeidae* for shrimp and *Grapsidae, Ocypodidae* and *Portnidae* for crab.

that had dense and healthy mangrove forests suffered fewer losses and less damage to property than those areas in which mangroves had been degraded or converted to other land uses (Dahdouh-Guebas *et al.*, 2005; Harakunarak and Aksornkoae, 2005; Kathiresan and Rajendran, 2005; UNEP, 2005; Wetlands International, 2005).

In Thailand, the Asian tsunami affected all six coastal provinces along the Indian Ocean (Andaman Sea) coast: Krabi, Phang Nga, Phuket, Ranong, Satun and Trang. In Phang Nga, the most affected province, post-tsunami assessments suggest that large mangrove forests in the north and south of the province significantly mitigated the impact of the Tsunami. They suffered damage on their seaside fringe, but reduced the tidal wave energy, providing protection to the inland population (UNEP, 2005; Harakunarak and Aksornkoae, 2005). Similar results were reported for those shorelines in Ranong Province protected by dense and thriving mangrove forests. In contrast, damages were relatively extensive along the Indian Ocean coast where mangroves and other natural coastal barriers were removed or severely degraded (Harakunarak and Aksornkoae, 2005).

With the overwhelming evidence of the storm protection service provided by intact and healthy mangrove systems, since the tsunami disaster increased emphasis has been placed on replanting degraded and deforested mangrove areas in Asia as a means to bolstering coastal protection. For example, the Indonesian Minister for Forestry has announced plans to reforest 600 000 hectares of depleted mangrove forest throughout the nation over the next 5 years. The governments of Sri Lanka and Thailand have also stated publicly intentions to rehabilitate and replant mangrove areas (UNEP, 2005; Harakunarak and Aksornkoae, 2005).

Although the Asian tsunami has called attention to the storm protection service provided by mangroves, the benefits of this service extends to protection against many types of periodic coastal natural disaster events. As one post-tsunami assessment noted: 'It is important to recognize that any compromising of mangrove "protection function" is relevant to a wide variety of storm events, and not just tsunamis. Whereas the Indian Ocean area counted "only" 63 tsunamis between 1750 and 2004, there were more than three tropical cyclones per year in roughly the same area' (Dahdouh-Guebas *et al.*, 2005, pp. 445–6).

The EM-DAT International Disaster Database shows that the number of coastal natural disasters in Thailand has increased in both the frequency of occurrence and in the number of events per year (see Figure 5). Over 1975–87, Thailand experienced on average 0.54 coastal natural disasters per year, whereas between 1987–2004 the incidence increased to 1.83 disasters per year. Thus, a recent World Bank report identified the coastal and delta areas of Thailand as potentially high fatality (more than 1000 deaths per event) and other damage 'hotspots' at risk from storm surge events (Dilley *et al.*, 2005, pp. 101–3).

The EM-DAT database also calculates the economic damage incurred per event. Figure 6 plots the damages per coastal natural disaster in Thailand for 1975–2004. The 2004 Asian tsunami with estimated damages of US$240 million (1996 prices)

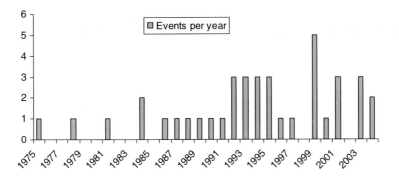

Figure 5. Coastal natural disasters in Thailand, 1975–2004

Notes: Over 1975–2004, coastal natural disasters included wave/surge (tsunami and tidal wave), wind storm (cyclone/typhoon and tropical storm) and flood (significant rise of water level in coastal region. In order for EM-DAT (2005) to record an event as a disaster, at least one or more of the following criteria must be fulfilled: 10 or more people reported killed; 100 people reported affected; declaration of a state of emergency; call for international assistance.

Source: EM-DAT (2005). EM-DAT: The OFDA/CRED International Disaster Database. www.em-dat.net – Université Catholique de Louvain, Brussels, Belgium.

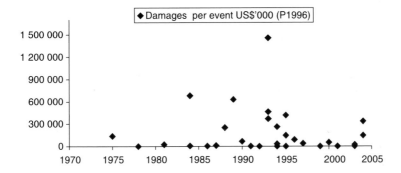

Figure 6. Real damages per coastal natural disaster in Thailand, 1975–2004

Notes: The EM-DAT (2005) estimate of the economic impact of a disaster usually consists of direct (e.g. damage to infrastructure, crops, housing) and indirect (e.g. loss of revenues, unemployment, market destabilization) consequences on the local economy. However, the estimate of 'zero' economic damages may indicate that no economic damages were recorded for an event. The estimates of economic damages are in thousands of US$ and converted to 1996 prices using Thailand's GDP deflator.

Source: EM-DAT (2005). EM-DAT: The OFDA/CRED International Disaster Database. www.em-dat.net – Université Catholique de Louvain, Brussels, Belgium.

was not the most damaging event to occur in Thailand. In fact, although the incidence of coastal damages has increased since 1987, in recent years the real damages per event has actually declined. For example, from 1979 to 1996, the economic damages per event were around US$190 million whereas from 1996 to 2004, real damages per event averaged US$61 million.

In sum, over the past two decades the rise in the number and frequency of coastal natural disasters in Thailand (Figure 5) and the simultaneous rapid decline in coastal mangrove systems over the same period (Figure 4) is likely to be more than a coincidence. Natural disasters occur when large numbers of economic assets are damaged or destroyed during a natural hazard event. Thus an increase in the incidence of coastal disasters is likely to have two sets of causes: the first is the natural hazards themselves – tsunamis and other storm surges, tidal waves, typhoons or cyclones, tropical storms and floods – but the second set is the increasing vulnerability of coastal populations, infrastructure and economic activities to being harmed or damaged by a hazard event.[9] The widespread loss of mangroves in coastal areas of Thailand may therefore have increased the vulnerability of these areas to more incidences of natural disasters.

4.2. Valuation of habitat-fishery linkage service

This subsection compares and contrasts the static and dynamic approaches outlined in Section 3.3 to valuing the habitat-fishery support service of mangroves in Thailand. As discussed above, in Thailand the near-shore artisanal fisheries supported by this ecological service are not optimally managed but largely open access.

To conduct the static production function analysis of the mangrove-fishery linkage, the methodology of Section 3.3.1 is applied to the same shellfish, demersal fishery and mangrove data over 1983–96 as in Barbier (2003). These comprise pooled time-series and cross-sectional data over the 1983–96 period for Thailand's artisanal and shellfish fisheries, as well as the extent of mangrove area, corresponding to the five coastal zones along the Gulf and Thailand and Indian Océan (Andaman Sea). Evidence from domestic fish markets in Thailand suggest that the demand for fish is fairly inelastic, and an elasticity of -0.5 was assumed for the iso-elastic market demand function. Thus the static analysis calculation of the marginal impact of a change in wetland area in Equation (5) requires specifying the unknown parameters of the Cobb–Douglas production function for the fishery, $h = AE^a S^b$. Section A1 in the appendix explains the approach used to estimate the unknown parameters (A, a, b) of the log-linear version of the Cobb–Douglas production function and reports the resulting preferred estimations (see Table A1). Using these results in Equations (5) and (6) allows calculation of the welfare impacts of mangrove deforestation on Thailand's two artisanal fisheries. The results are depicted in Table 3, which displays both the point estimates and the 95% confidence bounds on these estimates through use of the standard errors. All price and cost data for the fisheries used in the welfare analysis are in 1996 real terms.

[9] This view that natural disasters should not be viewed solely as 'acts of God' but clearly have an important anthropogenic component to their cause is reflected in much of the current expert opinion on natural disaster management. This is summarized succinctly by Dilley *et al.* (2005, p. 115): 'Hazards are not the cause of disasters. By definition, disasters involve large human or economic losses. Hazard events that occur in unpopulated areas and are not associated with losses do not constitute disasters. Losses are created not only by hazards, therefore, but also by the intrinsic characteristics of the exposed infrastructure, land uses, and economic activities that cause them to be damaged or destroyed when a hazard strikes. The socioeconomic contribution to disaster causality is potentially a source of disaster reduction. Disaster losses can be reduced by reducing exposure or vulnerability to the hazards present in a given area.'

Table 3. Valuation of mangrove-fishery linkage service, Thailand, 1996–2004 (US$)

Production function approach	Average annual mangrove loss	
	FAO (18.0 km²)[a]	Thailand (3.44 km²)[b]
Static analysis:		
Annual welfare loss	99 004 (12 704–814 504)	18 884 (2425–154 307)
Net present value	570 167	108 756
(10% discount rate)	(55 331–4 690 750)	(10 563–888 657)
Net present value	527 519	100 621
(12% discount rate)	(52 233–4 339 883)	(9972–822 186)
Net present value	472 407	90 108
(15% discount rate)	(48 080–3 886 476)	(9179–736 288)
Dynamic analysis:		
Net present value	1 980 128	373 404
(10% discount rate)	(403 899–2 390,728)	(164 506–691 573)
Net present value	1 760 374	331 995
(12% discount rate)	(357 462–2 104 176)	(147 571–614 058)
Net present value	1 484 461	279 999
(15% discount rate)	(299 411–1 747 117)	(126 178–516 691)

Notes: All valuations are based on mangrove-fishery linkage impacts on artisanal shellfish and demersal fisheries in Thailand at 1996 prices. The demand elasticity for fish is assumed to be −0.5. Figures in parentheses represent upper and lower bound welfare estimates based on the standard errors of the estimated parameters in each model (see Section A1 in the appendix).
[a] FAO estimates from FAO (2003). 2000 and 2004 data are estimated from 1990–2000 annul average mangrove loss of 18.0 km².
[b] Thailand estimates from various Royal Thailand Forestry Department sources reported in Aksornkoae and Tokrisna (2004). 2000 and 2004 data are estimated from 1993–96 annual average mangrove loss of 3.44 km².
Sources: Author's calculations.

As Figure 4 shows, there are two different estimates of the 1996–2004 annual mangrove deforestation rates in Thailand, namely the FAO estimate of 18.0 km² and the Royal Thai Forestry Department estimate of 3.44 km². For the welfare impacts arising from the FAO estimates of annual average mangrove deforestation rates in Thailand over 1996–2004, the static analysis suggests that the annual loss in the habitat-fishery support service is around US$99 000 ($13 000 to 815 000 with 95% confidence). The net present value of these losses over the entire period is between US$0.47 and 0.57 million ($48 000 to 4.7 million with 95% confidence). For the much lower Thailand deforestation estimates, the annual welfare loss is just under $19 000 ($2400 to 154 000 with 95% confidence) and the net present value of these losses over the 1996–2004 period is US$90 000 to 108 000 ($9000 to 0.9 million with 95% confidence).

Following the methodology of Section 3.3.2, we can also apply a dynamic production function model to mangrove-fishery linkages in Thailand. As explained in the section, this approach involves estimating the parameters of the dynamic mangrove-fishery model, and then using these parameters to simulate the dynamic path of the fishery and the corresponding consumer and surplus changes resulting from mangrove deforestation. Because there are no data on the biomass stock, X_t, for

Thailand's near-shore fisheries, the appropriate dynamic model is the version indicating the change over time in fishing effort, E_t, and catch per unit effort, c_t, i.e. Equations (10) and (11). To compare with the static analysis, we use the same shellfish, demersal fisheries and mangrove data, as well as assume the same iso-elastic demand, from Barbier (2003) to estimate Equations (10) and (11) (see Section A2 in the appendix). For example, the estimated parameters in the appendix correspond to the following parameters of the dynamic production function model: $b_0 = r$, $b_1 = -r/q\alpha$, $b_2 = -q$, $b_0/(b_1*b_2) = \alpha$, $a_1 = \phi$, $a_2 = 1-\phi w$ and $-(a_2 - 1)/a_1 = w$. These estimated parameters are then employed to simulate the dynamic effort and stock paths (9) and (10) of each fishery, starting from an initial level of effort, catch per unit effort and mangrove area, and assuming a constant elasticity of demand of -0.5.[10] By using 1996 data as the initial starting point in the simulation, i.e. for X_0, E_0, S_0 and h_0, the dynamic paths yield effort, stock and harvest for each subsequent year from 1996–2004.

In the base case dynamic simulation, mangrove area is held constant at 1996 levels. Two alternative paths for stock, effort and thus harvest are then also simulated, corresponding to the two different estimates of the 1996–2004 annual mangrove deforestation rates in Thailand, namely the FAO estimate of 18.0 km^2 and the Royal Thai Forestry Department estimate of 3.44 km^2 respectively. The resulting changes in consumer plus producer surpluses in each year over 1996–2004, between each deforestation simulation and the base case, provide the estimates of the welfare impacts of the decline in the mangrove-fishery support service. That is, the changes in consumer and producer surplus resulting from mangrove deforestation in each subsequent year of the simulation are discounted to obtain a net present value estimate of the resulting welfare loss. As in the static analysis, the discount rate is varied from 10% to 15% (see Table 3). The standard errors for the parameters of the model estimated from Equations (10) and (11) were also used to construct both lower and upper confidence bounds on the simulation paths, and thus also on the welfare estimates of the impacts of deforestation on the mangrove-fishery linkage.

The results for the dynamic mangrove-fishery linkage analysis are also depicted in Table 3, which indicates the welfare calculations associated with both the FAO and Thailand deforestation estimates over 1996–2004. The table reports calculations arising from the simulations based on the point estimates of the parameters of the dynamic mangrove-fishery model. The ranges of values indicated in parentheses for the dynamic analysis represent the lower and upper bound confidence intervals

---

[10] Although there are no reliable stock data for Thailand's near-shore fisheries, the Schaefer harvesting function, $h_t = qE_tX_t$, assumed in the model allows stock to be determined from catch per unit effort for a given estimated parameter q. That is, $X_t = c_t/q$, where $c_t = h_t/E_t$. See Schnute (1977) for further details. The procedure employed here is to use the known harvest and effort levels, as well as the estimated parameter q, for each fishery in the initial year 1996 to estimate the initial unknown stock level, X_0. Equations (9) and (10) were then used to simulate the dynamic path for X_t and E_t in the subsequent years (1997–2004), as well as the subsequent harvest, $h_t = qE_t X_t$. The dynamic simulation approach employed here is standard for an open access fishery model (see Bjørndal and Conrad, 1987; Clark, 1976; Homans and Wilen, 1997).

derived from the standard errors of the estimated model parameters (see Section A2 in the appendix). If the FAO estimate of mangrove deforestation over 1996–2004 is used, then the net present value of the welfare loss ranges from around US$1.5 to 2.0 million ($0.3 to 2.4 million in the upper and lower bound simulation estimates). In contrast, the lower Thailand deforestation estimation for 1996–2004 suggests that the net present value welfare loss from reduced mangrove support for fisheries is around US$0.28 to 0.37 million ($0.13 to 0.69 million in the upper and lower bound simulation estimates).

The welfare estimates in Table 3 indicate that the losses in the habitat-fishery support service caused by mangrove deforestation in Thailand over 1996–2004 are around three times greater for the dynamic production function approach compared to the static analysis. In addition, the confidence bounds on the welfare estimates produced with the static analysis are significantly larger, suggesting that the static approach yields much more variable estimates of the welfare losses. Given the disparity in estimates between the two approaches, a legitimate question to ask is whether or not one approach should be preferred to the other in valuing habitat-fishery linkages.

It has been argued in the literature that, on the methodological grounds, the 'dynamic' PF approach is more appropriate for valuing how coastal wetland habitats support offshore fisheries because this service implies that fish populations are more likely to be affected over time (Barbier, 2000). If this is the case, then the environmental 'input' of mangroves serving as breeding and nursery habitat for near-shore fisheries should be modelled as part of the growth function of the fish stock. In contrast, the static analysis, by definition, ignores stock effects and focuses exclusively on the impact of changes in mangrove area on fishing effort and costs in the same period in which the habitat service changes. The comparison of the dynamic and static analysis in the Thailand case study of mangrove-fishery linkages confirms that, by incorporating explicitly the multi-period stock effects resulting from mangrove loss, the dynamic model produces much larger estimates for the value of changes in the habitat-fishery support service. Since in this case study at least these stock effects appear to be considerable, then they are clearly an important component of the impacts of mangrove deforestation on the habitat-fishery service in Thailand.

In sum, the Thailand case study suggest caution in using the static analysis in preference to the dynamic production function approach in valuing the ecological service of coastal wetlands as breeding and nursery habitat for offshore fisheries. As Table 3 indicates, the static approach could underestimate the value of this service as well as yield more variable estimates. This may prove misleading for policy analysis, particularly when considering options to preserve as opposed to convert coastal wetlands. Certainly, the perception among coastal fishing communities throughout Thailand is that the habitat-fishery service of mangroves is vital, and local fishers in these communities have reported substantial losses in coastal fish stocks and yields, which they attribute to recent deforestation (Aksornkoae et al., 2004; Sathirathai and Barbier, 2001).

4.3. Valuation of storm protection service

To date, the most prevalent method of valuing the storm protection service provided by coastal wetlands is the replacement cost approach (Chong, 2005). This paper has suggested the use of an alternative methodology, the EDF approach. The purpose of the following subsection is to compare and contrast both approaches, using the Thailand case study.

Sathirathai and Barbier (2001) employed the replacement cost method to estimate the value of coastal protection and stabilization provided by mangroves in southern Thailand. The same approach and data will be employed here. According to the Harbor Department of the Royal Thai Ministry of Communications and Transport, the unit cost of constructing artificial breakwaters to prevent coastal erosion and damages from storm surges is estimated to be US$1011 (in 1996 prices) per metre of coastline. Based on this estimate, the authors calculate the equivalent cost of protecting the shoreline with a 75-metre width stand of mangrove is approximately US$13.48 per m^2, or US$134 801 per ha (1996 prices). Over a 20-year period and assuming a 10% discount rate, the annualized value of this cost amounts to $14 169 per ha. This is the 'replacement cost' value of the storm protection function per ha of mangrove.

The analysis for this paper uses this replacement cost value to calculate the annual and net present value welfare losses associated with the two mangrove deforestation estimates for Thailand over 1996–2004. The results are depicted in Table 4.

For the FAO mangrove deforestation estimate of 18.0 km^2 per year over 1996–2004, the annual welfare loss in storm protection service is around US$25.5 million, and the net present value of this loss over the entire period ranges from US$121.7 to 146.9 million. For the Thailand deforestation estimation of 3.4 km^2 per year, the annual welfare loss in storm protection is about US$4.9 million, and the net present value of this loss over the entire period ranges from US$23.2 to 28 million.

Section 3.5 describes the methodology for the EDF approach to estimating the value of the storm protection service of coastal wetlands such as mangroves. As emphasized in the appendix, the key step to this approach is to estimate the influence of changes in coastal wetland area on the expected incidence of economically damaging natural disaster events. The application of the EDF approach here employs a count data model for this purpose. The details of the estimation are contained in Section A3 of the appendix.

The analysis for Thailand over 1979–96 shows that loss of mangrove area in Thailand increases the expected number of economically damaging natural disasters affecting coastal provinces. Using this estimated 'marginal effect' (−0.00308), it is possible to estimate the resulting impact on expected damages of natural coastal disasters. For example, EM-DAT (2005) data show that over 1979–96 the estimated real economic damages per coastal event per year in Thailand averaged around US$189.9 million (1996 prices). This suggests that the marginal effect of a one-km^2

Table 4. Valuation of storm protection service, Thailand, 1996–2004 (US$)

Valuation approach	Average annual mangrove loss	
	FAO (18.0 km^2)[a]	Thailand (3.44 km^2)[b]
Replacement cost method:[c]		
Annual welfare loss	25 504 821	4 869 720
Net present value (10% discount rate)	146 882 870	28 044 836
Net present value (12% discount rate)	135 896 056	25 947 087
Net present value (15% discount rate)	121 698 392	23 236 280
Expected damage function approach:		
Annual welfare loss	3 382 169	645 769
	(2 341 686–5 797 339)	(447 106–1 106 905)
Net present value	19 477 994	3 718 998
(10% discount rate)	(13 485 827–33 387 014)	(2 574 894–6 374 694)
Net present value	18 021 043	3 440 818
(12% discount rate)	(12 477 089–30 889 671)	(2 382 292–5 897 868)
Net present value	16 138 305	3 081 340
(15% discount rate)	(11 173 553–27 662 490)	(2 133 404–5 281 692)

Notes: Figures in parentheses represent upper and lower bound welfare estimates based on the 95% confidence interval for the estimated coefficients in the model (see Section A3 in the appendix).
[a] FAO estimates from FAO (2003). 2000 and 2004 data are estimated from 1990–2000 annual average mangrove loss of 18.0 km^2.
[b] Thailand estimates from various Royal Thailand Forestry Department sources reported in Aksornkoae and Tokrisna (2004). 2000 and 2004 data are estimated from 1993–96 annual average mangrove loss of 3.44 km^2
[c] Re-calculated based on Sathirathai and Barbier (2001).

Sources: Author's calculations.

loss of mangrove area is an increase in expected storm damages of about US$585 000 per km^2. In Table 4, this latter calculation is combined with the FAO and Thailand estimates of the average annual rates of deforestation to compute the welfare losses in storm protection service for Thailand over 1996–2004. The table shows the welfare calculations based both on the point estimates of the count data regression and on using the standard errors to construct 95% confidence bounds on these estimates.

Table 4 shows that, for the FAO mangrove deforestation estimate of 18.0 km^2 per year over 1996–2004, the EDF approach estimates the annual welfare loss in storm protection service to be around US$3.4 million ($2.3 to 5.8 million with 95% confidence), and the net present value of this loss over the entire period ranges from US$16.1 to 19.5 million ($11.2 to 33.4 million with 95% confidence). For the Thailand deforestation estimation of 3.4 km^2 per year, the annual welfare loss in storm protection is over US$0.65 million ($0.45 to 1.1 million with 95% confidence), and the net present value of this loss over the entire period ranges from US$3.1 to 3.7 million ($2.1 to 6.4 million with 95% confidence).

Comparing the EDF approach and the replacement cost method of estimating the welfare impacts of a loss of the storm protection service due to mangrove deforestation confirms that the replacement cost method tends to produce extremely high estimates – almost 4 times greater than even the largest upper-bound estimate calculated using the EDF approach. This suggests that the replacement cost method should be used with caution, and when data are available, the EDF approach may provide more reliable values of the storm protection service of coastal wetlands.

4.4. Land use policy implications

Valuation of the ecosystem services provided by mangroves are important for two land use policy decisions in Thailand. First, although declining in recent years, conversion of remaining mangroves to shrimp farm ponds and other commercial coastal developments continues to be a major threat to Thailand's remaining mangrove areas. Second, since the December 2004 tsunami disaster, there is now considerable interest in rehabilitating and restoring mangrove ecosystems as 'natural barriers' to future coastal storm events.

To illustrate how improved and more accurate valuation of ecosystems can help inform these two policy decisions, Table 5 compares the per hectare net returns to shrimp farming, the costs of mangrove rehabilitation and the value of mangrove services. All land uses are assumed to be instigated over 1996–2004 and are valued in 1996 US dollars. The net economic returns to shrimp farming are based on non-declining yields over a 5-year period of investment, with the pond abandoned in subsequent years (Sathirathai and Barbier, 2001). These returns to shrimp aquaculture are estimated to be $1078 to $1220 per ha. In comparison, the costs rehabilitating mangrove ecosystems on land that has been converted to shrimp farms and then abandoned are $8812 to $9318 per ha. Thus valuing the goods and services of mangrove ecosystems can help to address two important policy questions: Do the net economic returns to shrimp farming justify further mangrove conversion to this economic activity, and is it worth investing in mangrove replanting and ecosystem rehabilitation in abandoned shrimp farm areas?

As indicated in Table 5, if the older methods of valuing habitat-fishery linkages with the static approach and storm protection with the replacement cost method are employed, then mangrove ecosystem benefits are considerably higher than the net economic returns to shrimp farming and the costs of replanting and rehabilitating mangroves in abandoned farm areas. However, the static analysis undervalues the habitat-fishery linkage of mangroves whereas the replacement cost method over-inflates storm protection. The replacement cost method estimates storm protection at $67 610 to 81 602 per ha, which is 99% of the value of all mangrove ecosystem benefits. In contrast, the net income to local coastal communities from collected forest products and the value of habitat-fishery linkages total to only $730 to $881 per ha, which suggests that these two benefits of mangroves are insufficient on their own to justify either halting conversion to shrimp farms or replanting and rehabilitating these ecosystems on abandoned pond land.

If improved methods of valuing habitat-fishery linkages by the dynamic approach and storm protection by the expected damage function method are employed, then

Table 5. Comparison of land use values per hectare, Thailand, 1996–2004 (US$)

Land use	Net present value per hectare (10–15% discount rate)	
Shrimp farming:[a]		
Net economic returns	1078–1220	
Mangrove ecosystem rehabilitation:[b]		
Total cost	8812–9318	
Ecosystem goods and services	*Older methods*	*Improved methods*
Net income from collected forest products[c]	484–584	484–584
Habitat-fishery linkage	246–297[d]	708–987[e]
Storm protection service	67 610–81 602[f]	8966–10 821[g]
Total	68 341–82 484	10 158–12 392

[a] Based on Sathirathai and Barbier (2001), updated to 1996 US$.
[b] Based on costs of rehabilitating abandoned shrimp farms, replanting mangrove forests and maintaining and protecting mangrove seedlings. From Sathirathai and Barbier (2001), updated to 1996 US$.
[c] Based on Sathirathai and Barbier (2001), updated to 1996 US$.
[d] Based on marginal value per ha based on the static analysis of this study (see Section 4.2).
[e] Based on average value per hectare over 1996–2004 based on the dynamic analysis of this study and assuming the estimated Thailand deforestation rate of 3.44 sq km per year (see Section 4.2).
[f] Based on average value per hectare of replacement cost method of this study (see Section 4.3).
[g] Based on marginal value per hectare of expected damage function approach of this study (see Section 4.3).

Sources: Author's calculations.

the outcome is somewhat different. Although the total value of mangrove ecosystem services is lowered to $10 158 to $12 392 per ha, it still exceeds the net economic returns to shrimp farming. Storm protection service is still the largest benefit of mangroves, but it no longer dominates the land use value comparison. The net income to local coastal communities from collected forest products and the value of habitat-fishery linkages total to $1192 to $1571 per ha, which now are greater than the net economic returns to shrimp farming. The value of the storm protection, however, is critical to the decision as to whether or not to replant and rehabilitate mangrove ecosystems in abandoned pond areas. As shown in Table 5, storm protection benefits make mangrove rehabilitation an economically feasible land use option.

5. CONCLUSIONS

The case study of valuing mangroves in Thailand illustrates the potential use of the PF approach to modelling key ecological regulatory and habitat services. The study also indicates the importance of choosing the appropriate PF method for modelling the key ecological-economic linkages underlying each service.

For example, the case study confirms that, if coastal wetlands such as mangroves serve as a breeding and nursery habitat for a variety of near-shore fisheries, then it seems more appropriate to model this environmental input as part of the growth function of the fish stock. In comparison, not accounting for the stock effects of a change in coastal nursery and breeding grounds may lead to an underestimation of the value of this habitat-fishery linkage. The case study also illustrates how the EDF approach can be applied to valuing the storm protection service provided by mangroves, and demonstrates why this method should be preferred to the less-reliable replacement cost method, which has been used extensively in the literature to date (Chong, 2005).

The case study also points to some important policy implications for Thailand. In recent decades, considerable mangrove deforestation has taken place in Thailand, mainly as a result of shrimp farm expansion and other coastal economic developments (see Figure 4). Over this period, mangrove conversion for these development activities was systematically encouraged by government land use policies (Aksornkoac and Tokrisna, 2004; Barbier, 2003; Sathirathai and Barbier, 2001). Such policies were designed without consideration of the value of the ecological services provided by mangroves, such as their habitat support for coastal fisheries and storm protection. The case study of valuing these ecological services for Thailand illustrates that their benefits are significant, and should certainly not be ignored in future mangrove land management decisions.

The case study applications in this paper of valuing coastal storm protection and habitat services have policy implications beyond Thailand as well. Even before Hurricanes Katrina and Rita devastated the central Gulf Coast of the United States in 2005, the US Army Corps of Engineers had proposed a $1.1 billion multi-year programme to slow the rate of wetland loss and restore some wetlands in coastal Louisiana. In the aftermath of these hurricanes, the US Congress is now considering expanding the programme substantially to a $14 billion restoration effort (Zinn, 2005). As noted in Section 4, in the wake of the 2004 Asian tsunami, mangrove restoration projects for enhanced coastal protection are underway in many countries throughout the region. International donor groups are also supporting mangrove restoration projects in Asia, especially in countries and regions devastated by the tsunami (Check, 2005). In addition, there is mounting scientific evidence that near-shore fisheries throughout the world are undergoing rapid decline, with loss of coastal habitat and nursery grounds for these fisheries a contributory cause (Jackson et al., 2001; Myers and Worm, 2003). Valuing the storm protection and habitat services of coastal wetlands, as illustrated by the Thailand case study in this paper, can therefore play a vital role in current and future debates about the state of coastal ecosystems worldwide and the assessment of the costs and benefits of restoring these vital ecosystems.

Thus, valuing the non-market benefits of ecological regulatory and habitat services is becoming increasingly important in assisting policymakers to manage critical environmental assets. However, further progress applying production function approaches and other methods to value ecological services faces two challenges.

First, for these methods to be applied effectively to valuing ecosystem services, it is important that the key ecological and economic relationships are well understood. Unfortunately, our knowledge of the ecological functions, let alone the ecosystem processes and components, underlying many of the services listed in Table 1 is still incomplete.

Second, natural ecosystems are subject to stresses, rapid change and irreversible losses, they tend to display threshold effects and other non-linearities that are difficult to predict, let alone model in terms of their economic impacts. These uncertainties can affect the estimation of values from an *ex ante* ('beforehand') perspective. The economic valuation literature recognizes that such uncertainties create the conditions for *option values*, which arise from the difference between valuation under conditions of certainty and uncertainty (e.g., see Freeman, 2003 and Just *et al.*, 2004). The standard approach recommended in the literature is to estimate this additional value separately, through various techniques to measure an *option price*, that is, the amount of money that an individual will pay or must be compensated to be indifferent from the status quo condition of the ecosystem and the new, proposed condition. However, in practice, estimating separate option prices for unknown ecological effects is very difficult. Determining the appropriate risk premium for vulnerable populations exposed to the irreversible ecological losses is also proving elusive. These are problems currently affecting all economic valuation methods of ecosystem services, and not just the production function approach. As one review of these studies concludes: 'Given the imperfect knowledge of the way people value natural ecosystems and their goods and services, and our limited understanding of the underlying ecology and biogeochemistry of aquatic ecosystems, calculations of the value of the changes resulting from a policy intervention will always be approximate' (Heal *et al.*, 2005, p. 218).

Finally, Section 3 noted recent attempts to extend the production function approach to the ecosystem level through integrated ecological-economic modelling. This allows the ecosystem functioning and dynamics underlying the provision of ecological services to be modelled and can be used to value multiple rather than single services. For example, returning to the Thailand case study, it is well known that both coral reefs and sea grasses complement the role of mangroves in providing both the habitat-fishery and storm protection services. Thus full modelling of the integrated mangrove–coral reef–sea grass system could improve measurement of the benefits of both services. As we learn more about the important ecological and economic role played by such services, it may be relevant to develop multi-service ecosystem modelling to understand more fully what values are lost when such integrated coastal and marine systems are disturbed or destroyed.

Discussion

Carlo A. Favero
IGIER, Bocconi University and CEPR

The objective of the paper is to apply a production function (and expected damage) approach to 'valuing the environment as input', with an application to a mangrove ecosystem in Thailand. I shall concentrate my discussion only on the production function approach, but the main methodological points raised are naturally extended to the expected damage function approach.

An environmental good or service essentially serves as a factor input into production that yields utility. The fundamental problem of the empirical application is the evaluation of the following value function:

$$V_t = E_t \sum_{j=0}^{T} \frac{B_{t+j}}{(1 + r)^j}$$

where B is the social benefits in any time period of the mangrove ecosystem, and r is the discount rate.

There are two fundamental questions:

1. What is the appropriate discount rate?
2. How to evaluate B?

The first question is not explicitly addressed and different scenarios on the discount rate are adopted; the production function approach is the answer to the second question.

In theory the production function approach can be described as follows:

- Specification of a dynamic intertemporal optimization problem, where one of the constraints is the production function relating the input of interest to the measurable output.
- Solution of the model.
- Identification and estimation (or, whenever estimation is not possible, calibration) of the technology and preference parameters of the model and of the auxiliary parameters.
- Dynamic stochastic simulation of the model to derive $E_t B_{t+j}$ and the associated confidence intervals.

In practice two alternative approaches are considered: a static one and a dynamic one. I shall not comment on the static approach because I find this inappropriate to the very nature of the problem at hand, which is, by definition, dynamic.

In the dynamic approach a model is postulated to determine the dynamics of the stock of fish measured in biomass units, X_t, the fishing effort, E_t, the landed fish price per unit harvested, p, and the harvest, h. The adopted model is described as follows:

$$X_{t+1} - X_t = F(X_t, S_t) - h(X_t, E_t)$$

$$E_{t+1} - E_t = \phi[\, p_t h_t - w_t E_t \,]$$

$$F(X_t, S_t) = rX_t \left[1 - \frac{X_t}{\alpha \ln S_t} \right]$$

$$h_t = qX_t E_t$$

$$p_t = kh_t^\eta$$

where $F(X_t, S_t)$ is biological growth in the current period, which is a function of S_t, the mangrove area, $h(X_t, E_t)$, harvesting is a function of the stock as well as fishing effort, E_t. Fishing effort is modelled as a partial adjustment model in which the equilibrium value is determined by fish price per unit harvested and the unit cost of effort, w.

The model is estimated and then simulated keeping w exogenous and taking alternative scenarios for S, that by consequence is taken as exogenous. Using some assumption for the discount rate the present value of a reduction in the mangrove area is then computed.

The results are interesting but there are a number of important questions that the modelling strategy leaves open:

- In the dynamic model S is exogenous and no law of motion for S is specified. The model is not capable of explaining the reduction in S that we observe in the data. In fact, if agents were acting following this model we would have never observed a reduction in S, because a reduction in S has only costs and no benefits. Macroeconometricians might see the applicability of the Lucas critique to this model as an immediate consequence of the assumption of exogeneity of S.
- Expectations do not explicitly enter the model.
- What are the costs incurred in omitting from the model the dynamics of w?
- What is the performance of this model when evaluated in sample by dynamic simulation?
- How is uncertainty added for estimation and more importantly for dynamic simulation? The result reported in Table 4 seems to take account of only coefficient uncertainty while, given the modelling choices, the fluctuations in the relevant variables not explained by the adopted model are likely to be the main source of uncertainty.

I think that the answer to this set of open questions could further enhance the potential of the interesting methods for valuing ecosystem services very well discussed in this paper.

Omer Moav
Hebrew University, University of London Royal Holloway, Shalem Center, and CEPR

Edward Barbier demonstrates how basic micro theory can be implemented to estimate the value of ecological services for human welfare. In particular, two methods are developed: the production function approach and the expected damage function approach. Both methods utilize exogenous variation in the size of the ecosystem service, such as the size of a mangrove forest, on a beneficial outcome. According to the former the outcome is welfare gained from the decline in the price of a consumption good, such as fish, that utilizes the ecosystem as an input in its production process. In the latter it is the economic value of the reduction in damage, arising, for instance, from storms, that is reduced by a larger ecosystem.

The theory is rather straightforward. It is the availability of the data that the estimation depends on, and it is not clear that for most practical problems there exists sufficient exogenous variation in the ecosystem, allowing for a reliable assessment. Nevertheless, Barbier convincingly illustrates that despite the difficulties, these methods have the potential to provide important information about the value of the ecosystem and thereby the value of preventing its disappearance. This information can become critical for policymakers, and might, even if only in marginal cases, generate the crucial political force to reverse processes of natural habitat destruction.

The value of the functions of the ecosystem include, as stated by Barbier, 'climate stability, maintenance of biodiversity and beneficial species, erosion control, flood mitigation, storm protection, groundwater recharge and pollution control'. This statement reveals another limitation of the estimation methods. It focuses on a limited set of benefits, implying a potentially huge underestimation of the value of the ecosystem. First, due to information problems regarding most functions, it is difficult to identify the size of the impact and/or its welfare value. For instance, most likely exogenous variety in the ecosystem is not sufficient to estimate its effect on climate stability, and the welfare value of biodiversity is a question hard to answer.

Second, the cost of preserving the ecosystem – giving up the benefits of its alternative use – is paid by the local population, while many of its services extend beyond that. As is well known, preserving natural ecosystems is a problem with large externalities that go beyond borders. In other words, who cares? Do we expect the poor fisherman in Thailand, or their government, to allocate a significant weight in its welfare function to biodiversity? In fact, it is the population of the developed world that cares, and this population's willingness to pay a compensating price, could be above and beyond the benefit of the ecosystem to the local population.

A more technical comment on the estimation process regards the open access assumption and, in particular, the implicit assumption that changes in the habitat are sufficiently small, relative to the economy, such that the producer's surplus is unchanged. Welfare gains from a larger ecosystem emerge only from the reduction in consumer goods prices. This assumption adds to the bias in the estimation, reducing the value of the ecosystem. To see this point, suppose that prices of the consumption good are also given (traded good in an open economy). In this case there is zero welfare gain from preserving the environment.

A final comment about the estimation method regards the implicit assumption of stability of the steady-state equilibrium. However, non-monotonic convergence to the steady state might characterize the dynamics of the ecosystem. For instance, the population of a species might converge to its steady state in oscillations, implying that a negative shock to the ecosystem might, once it is sufficiently fragile, result in extinction of a species rather than a proportional reduction in the size of the natural population.

Beyond the problems of estimating the direct value of the ecological services for human welfare, lies a somewhat deeper question regarding the long-run effects of the utilization of natural resources for the benefit of mankind in the production process. Maintaining natural habitats and benefiting their production services, or destroying them and benefiting from their alternative land use for agriculture, might have different long-run consequences on demographic variables, institutional development, and, in particular, human capital promoting institutions (e.g., public schools, loans, and child labour regulation), and the resulting accumulation of human capital.

Natural resources, according to many studies, are a hurdle for the process of development, in particular the accumulation of human capital. (e.g. Gylfason, 2001). But to the best of my knowledge, we do not know yet how to make a distinction in that regard between an open-access preserved ecosystem and agricultural land. Therefore, depleting resources or increasing the size of agricultural land on the account of the ecosystem, could have a significant impact on the economy.

Moreover, the transition from an open access ecosystem into private owned farmland might have an impact on wealth inequality, in particular inequality in the ownership of such land. Deninger and Squire (1998) show that inequality in land ownership has a negative impact on economic growth. Engerman and Sokoloff (2000) provide evidence that wealth inequality, brought about oppressive institutions (e.g., restricted access to the democratic process and to education). They argue that these institutions were designed to maintain the political power of the elite and to preserve the existing inequality. Galor *et al.* (2005) provide evidence that inequality in the ownership of agricultural land has a negative effect on public expenditure on education, and argue that the elite of landowners might prevent public schooling, despite the support of the owners of capital and the working class.

On the other hand, if the destruction of the ecosystem increases farmland and thereby possibly promoting industrial development, and if the process does not generate large wealth inequality, the return to human capital will most likely rise. This could trigger a process of development stemming from reduced fertility and increased investment in education. This brings us back to the main problem of preventing the distractions of an ecosystem: the externality. Each small economy might be better-off destroying the ecosystem, giving rise to an inefficient equilibrium. The analysis suggested by Barbier, could, at least, highlight the benefits of preserving natural habitats for the local economy.

APPENDIX: APPLICATION TO THAILAND CASE STUDY

This appendix outlines the econometric estimations for valuing habitat-fishery linkages and the storm protection service of mangroves in the Thailand case study of Section 4.

A1. Static valuation of habitat-fishery linkage

To apply the static analysis of habitat-fishery linkages of Section 3.3.1 to the Thailand case study, it is necessary to estimate the unknown parameters (A, a, b) of the log-linear version of the Cobb–Douglas production function:

$$\ln h_{it} = A_0 + a \ln E_{it} + b \ln M_{it} + \mu_{it} \tag{A1}$$

where $i = 1, \ldots, 5$ zones, $t = 1, \ldots, 14$ years (1983–96) and $A_0 = \ln A$.

Equation (A1) was estimated using the pooled data on demersal fisheries, shellfish and mangrove area from Barbier (2003). These were the data on harvest, h_{it}, and effort, E_{it}, for Thailand's shellfish and demersal fisheries, as well as mangrove area, M_{it} across the five coastal zones of Thailand and over the years 1983–96. Various regression procedures for a pooled data set were utilized and compared, including: (i) ordinary least squares (OLS); (ii) one- and two-way panel analysis of fixed and random effects; and (iii) a maximum likelihood estimation by an iterated generalized least squares (GLS) procedure for a pooled time series and cross-sectional regression, which allows for correction of any groupwise heteroscedasticity, cross-group correlation and common or within-group autocorrelation. Table A1 indicates the best regression model for the shellfish and demersal fisheries respectively, and the relevant test statistics.

For demersal fisheries, the preferred model shown in Table A1 is the GLS estimation allowing for groupwise heteroscedasticity and correcting for both cross-group and common autocorrelation. For the panel analysis of the demersal fisheries, the likelihood ratio tests of the null hypothesis of zero individual and time effects across all five zones and fourteen time periods were significant, thus rejecting the null hypothesis. In addition, the Breusch–Pagan Lagrange multiplier (LM) statistic was also significant at the 95% confidence level for both the one-way and two-models, which suggests rejection of the null hypothesis of zero random disturbances. The Hausman test statistic was also significant at the 99% confidence level, suggesting that the fixed effects specification is preferred to the random effects. However, in both the one- and two-way fixed effects model the t-test on the estimated parameter for a in Equation (A1) was insignificant, suggesting the null hypothesis that $a = 0$ cannot be rejected. As indicated in Table A1, from the pooled time series cross-sectional GLS regression for demersal fisheries, the likelihood ratio (LR) test statistic of the null hypothesis for homoscedasticity based on the least squares regression was computed to be 24.64, which is statistically significant. Although not shown in the table, the alternative Wald test for homoscedasticity is also statistically significant and confirms rejection of the null hypothesis. Thus the GLS model with correction of groupwise heteroscedasticity is preferred to the OLS regression. The LM statistic of 14.43 also reported in Table A1 for demersal fisheries is a test of the null hypothesis of zero cross-sectional correlation, which proves to be statistically significant. Although not indicated in the table, the LR test statistic for groupwise heteroscedasticity as a restriction on cross-group correlation was estimated to be 23.26, which is also statistically significant. Thus the null hypothesis of zero cross-group correlation in the demersal fisheries regression can be rejected. The common autocorrelation coefficient across all five zones was estimated to be 0.484, and as shown in Table A1, once the GLS model for demersal fish was corrected for this common autocorrelation, the null hypothesis that the coefficient $a = 0$ is now rejected.

For shellfish, as indicated in Table A1 the preferred estimation of Equation (A1) is the GLS estimation allowing for groupwise heteroscedasticity and correcting for cross-group correlation, with A_0 restricted to zero. For the panel analysis of shellfish, the likelihood ratio tests and Breusch–Pagan LM tests of the null hypothesis of no individual and time effects were significant, thus rejecting the null hypothesis. The

Table A1. Estimates of Equation (A1) for Thailand's shellfish and demersal fisheries

Coefficient	Demersal fishery[a]	Shellfish fishery[b]
A_0	11.213 (24.568)**	–
A	0.341 (4.992)**	1.688 (38.254)**
B	0.100 (2.763)**	0.196 (3.693)**
Log-likelihood[c]	5.401	−71.517
Likelihood ratio statistic[d]	24.643**	35.076**
Lagrange multiplier statistic[e]	14.426*	21.304**

Notes: *t*-statistics are shown in parentheses.
[a] Preferred model is groupwise heteroscedastic and correlated GLS, corrected for common autocorrelation.
[b] Preferred model is groupwise heteroscedastic and correlated GLS, with A_0 restricted to zero.
[c] In the demersal fishery regression, correction of cross-group correlation $Cov[e_{it}, e_{jt}] = \sigma_{ij}$ leads to a positive log-likelihood.
[d] Tests the null hypothesis of homoscedasticity based on OLS.
[e] Tests the null hypothesis of zero cross-group correlation based on OLS.
* Significant at 95% confidence level.
** Significant at 99% confidence level.

Sources: Author's estimations.

Hausman test statistic was significant, suggesting that the fixed effects specification is preferred to the random effects. However, in both the one- and two-way fixed effects model the *t*-test on the estimated parameters for *a* and *b* in Equation (A1) was insignificant, suggesting the null hypothesis $a = b = 0$ cannot be rejected. As indicated in Table A1, from the pooled time series cross-sectional GLS regression of shellfish, the LR test statistic of the null hypothesis for homoscedasticity based on the least squares regression is 35.08, which is statistically significant. Although not shown in the table, the alternative Wald test for homoscedasticity is also statistically significant and confirms rejection of the null hypothesis. Thus the GLS model with correction of groupwise heteroscedasticity is preferred to the OLS regression. The LM statistic of 21.30 also reported in Table A1 for the shellfish regression is a test of the null hypothesis of zero cross-sectional correlation, which proves to be statistically significant. Although not indicated in the table, the LR test statistic for groupwise heteroscedasticity as a restriction on cross-group correlation was estimated to be 43.90, which is also statistically significant. Thus the null hypothesis of zero cross-group correlation in the shellfish regression can be rejected. As shown in Table A1, once the GLS model of shellfish was corrected for groupwise heteroscedasticity and correlation, the null hypotheses that $a = 0$ and $b = 0$ are now rejected.

The estimations of Equation (A1) for Thailand's shellfish and demersal fisheries were used in conditions (5) and (6) to calculate the welfare impacts of mangrove deforestation over 1996–2004 on Thailand's artisanal fisheries. The analysis uses the same iso-elastic demand function as in Barbier (2003), with a demand elasticity, ε, of −0.5. The results are reported in Table 3, which shows welfare calculations for both the point estimates and upper and lower bounds on these estimates based on the standard errors of the regression coefficients reported in Table A1.

A2. Dynamic valuation of habitat-fishery linkage

The dynamic habitat-fishery modelling approach to valuing the habitat-fishery linkage is outlined in Section 3.3.2. The main difficulty in applying this approach to valuing mangrove-fishery linkages in Thailand is that data do not exist for the biomass stock, X_t, of near-shore fisheries. Thus the appropriate system of equations to estimate comprises (10) and (11). Because E_t and c_t are predetermined, both of these equations can be estimated independently (Homans and Wilen, 1997). For both the shellfish and demersal fisheries, the estimated equations are:

$$E_{it} = a_0 + a_1 R_{it-1} + a_2 E_{it-1} + \mu_{it-1} \tag{A2}$$

$$\frac{c_{it} - c_{it-1}}{c_{it-1}} = b_0 + b_1 \frac{c_{it-1}}{\ln M_{it-1}} + b_2 E_{it-1} + \mu_{it-1}, \tag{A3}$$

where $i = 1, \ldots, 5$ zones, $t - 1 = 1, \ldots, 13$ years (1983–95), $R_{it-1} = kh_{it-1}^{1+\eta}$, $a_1 = \phi$, $a_2 = (1 - \phi w)$, $b_0 = r$, $b_1 = -r/\alpha q$ and $b_2 = -q$. Both equations were estimated using the pooled data on demersal fisheries, shellfish and mangrove area from Barbier (2003). These were the data on harvest, h_{it-1}, and effort, E_{it-1}, for Thailand's shellfish and demersal fisheries, as well as mangrove area, M_{it-1} across the five coastal zones of Thailand and over the years 1983–96. In addition, to calculate R_{it-1} from h_{it-1} the elasticity $\eta = 1/\varepsilon = -2$ was assumed as in the static analysis. Various regression procedures for a pooled data set were utilized and compared, including: (i) OLS; (ii) one- and two-way panel analysis of fixed and random effects; and (iii) a maximum likelihood estimation by an iterated GLS procedure for a pooled time series and cross-sectional regression, which allows for correction of any groupwise heteroscedasticity, cross-group correlation and common or within-group autocorrelation. Tables A2 and A3 indicate the best regression models of Equations (A2) and (A3) for the shellfish and demersal fisheries respectively, and the relevant test statistics.

For demersal fisheries, the preferred model for the effort equation (A2) is the GLS estimation allowing for groupwise heteroscedasticity and corrected for common autocorrelation. For the panel analysis, the likelihood ratio and Breusch–Pagan LM tests of the null hypothesis of no individual and time effects were not significant; thus, the null hypothesis cannot be rejected. However, as indicated in Table A2, from the pooled time series cross-sectional regression of Equation (A2) for demersal fisheries, the LR test statistic of the null hypothesis of homoscedasticity based on the OLS regression is computed to be 93.22, which is statistically significant. Although not shown in the table, the alternative Wald test for homoscedasticity is also statistically significant and confirms rejection of the null hypothesis. Thus the GLS model with correction of groupwise heteroscedasticity is preferred to the OLS regression. The test statistics for the null hypothesis of zero cross-group correlation are mixed. The LM statistic of 12.24 indicated in Table A2 is significant, whereas the LR test statistic of 12.56 is not. When the GLS regression is corrected for groupwise correlation, however, the constant term a_0 is no longer significant. The common autocorrelation coefficient across all five zones is estimated to be 0.242, and although slight, correction of this autocorrelation improved the overall robustness of the GLS estimation.

As shown in Table A2, the preferred model for the effort equation (A2) for shellfish is the one-way random effects estimation corrected for heteroscedasticity. The LR and Wald tests of the pooled time series cross-sectional regressions of Equation (A2) for shellfish indicated that the null hypothesis of homoscedasticity can be rejected. Thus the GLS model with correction of groupwise heteroscedasticity is preferred to the OLS regression. However, in all versions of the GLS regression the coefficient a_1 was negative and statistically insignificant. The LR test for the presence of individual effects is statistically significant, thus rejecting the null hypothesis of no such effects, and although not shown, the equivalent F-test of the null hypothesis is also statistically significant. Neither the Breusch–Pagan LM test of the null hypothesis of random provincial-level disturbances nor the Hausman test of the random versus the fixed effects specification is statistically significant. Although these results are somewhat contradictory, they suggest that, if individual effects are present, they are likely to be random. The LR test and F-test of the presence of time effects is not significant, suggesting that the one-way is preferred to the two-way specification. Correction of heteroscedasticity improves the robustness of the one-way random effects estimation

Table A2. Estimates of Equation (A2) for Thailand's shellfish and demersal fisheries

Coefficient	Demersal fishery[a]	Shellfish fishery[b]
a_0	22.365 (2.254)*	808.720 (2.661)**
a_1	0.00004 (4.375)**	0.000003 (0.233)
a_2	0.84855 (21.703)**	0.70470 (8.183)**
Log-likelihood	−380.903	−520.513
Likelihood ratio statistic for homoscedasticity[c]	93.223**	—
Likelihood ratio statistic for correlation[d]	12.552	—
Lagrange multiplier statistic[e]	12.241*	—
Likelihood ratio statistic for individual effects[f]	—	16.285**
Breusch–Pagan Lagrange multiplier statistic[g]	—	0.04
Hausman test statistic[h]	—	1.88

Notes: t-statistics are shown in parentheses.
[a] Preferred model is groupwise heteroscedastic GLS, corrected for common autocorrelation.
[b] Preferred model is one-way random effects corrected for heteroscedasticity.
[c] Tests the null hypothesis of homoscedasticity based on OLS.
[d] Tests the null hypothesis of zero cross-group correlation based on OLS.
[e] Tests the null hypothesis of zero cross-group correlation based on OLS.
[f] Tests the null hypothesis of zero individual effects.
[g] Tests the null hypothesis of zero random disturbances based on OLS.
[h] Tests the null hypothesis of correlation between the individual effects and the error (i.e. random effects is preferred to fixed effects estimation).
* Significant at 95% confidence level.
** Significant at 99% confidence level.

Sources: Author's estimations.

without affecting the parameter estimates. Although not shown in the table, the preferred model displayed a very low estimated autocorrelation of 0.022.

As indicated in Table A3, the preferred model for the growth in catch per unit effort equation (A3) for demersal fisheries is the GLS estimation allowing for group-wise heteroscedasticity. For the panel analysis, the LR and Breusch–Pagan LM tests of the null hypothesis of no individual and time effects were not significant; thus, the null hypothesis cannot be rejected. However, from the pooled time series cross-sectional regression, both the LR and Wald test statistics of the null hypothesis of homoscedasticity are also statistically significant. Thus the GLS model with correction of groupwise heteroscedasticity is preferred to the OLS regression. The test statistics for the null hypothesis of zero cross-group correlation are mixed. The LM statistic of 11.03 indicated in Table A3 is significant, whereas the LR test statistic of 18.56 is not. However, correcting the GLS regression for groupwise correlation does not affect the estimation significantly. Although not shown in the table, the preferred model displayed a very low estimated autocorrelation of −0.006.

Table A3 displays the preferred model for the growth in CPE equation (A3) for shellfish, which is the GLS estimation allowing for groupwise and correlated hetero-scedasticity and corrected for common autocorrelation. For the panel analysis, the LR and Breusch–Pagan LM tests of the null hypothesis of no individual and time effects were not significant; thus, the null hypothesis cannot be rejected. However, from the pooled time series cross-sectional regression, both the LR and Wald test statistics of the null hypothesis of homoscedasticity are also statistically significant. Thus the GLS model with correction of groupwise heteroscedasticity is preferred to the OLS regression. Although the LR and LM test statistics for the null hypothesis

Table A3. Estimates of Equation (A3) for Thailand's shellfish and demersal fisheries

Coefficient	Demersal fishery[a]	Shellfish fishery[b]
b_0	0.4896 (2.908)**	0.2997 (2.371)*
b_1	−0.000187 (−2.368)*	−0.000201 (−2.354)*
b_2	−0.000204 (−2.637)**	−0.000060 (−2.007)*
Log-likelihood	−22.337	−30.350
Likelihood ratio statistic for homoscedasticity[c]	24.627**	109.342**
Likelihood ratio statistic for correlation[d]	18.235	11.434
Lagrange multiplier statistic[e]	11.026*	8.491

Notes: t-statistics are shown in parentheses.
[a] Preferred model is groupwise heteroscedastic GLS.
[b] Preferred model is groupwise heteroscedastic and correlated GLS, corrected for common autocorrelation.
[c] Tests the null hypothesis of homoscedasticity based on OLS.
[d] Tests the null hypothesis of zero cross-group correlation based on OLS.
[e] Tests the null hypothesis of zero cross-group correlation based on OLS.
* Significant at 95% confidence level.
** Significant at 99% confidence level.

Sources: Author's estimations.

of zero cross-group correlation are not significant, correcting the GLS regression for groupwise correlation improves the significance confidence level of the estimated parameter b_2 from 90 to 95%. The common autocorrelation coefficient across all five zones is estimated to be 0.147, and although slight, correction of this autocorrelation improved the overall robustness of the GLS estimation.

Using the estimated parameters for Equations (A2) and (A3) for Thailand's shellfish and demersal fisheries allows simulation of the welfare impacts of mangrove deforestation over 1996–2004 on Thailand's artisanal fisheries. Again, the same demand function with elasticity of −0.5 as in Barbier (2003) is employed. The results are reported in Table 3, which shows welfare calculations for both the point estimates and upper and lower bounds on these estimates based on the standard errors of the regression coefficients reported in Tables A2 and A3.

A3. Expected damage function valuation of storm protection service

As discussed in Section 3.5, the key step in applying the expected damage function approach to valuing the storm protection service of a coastal wetland such as mangroves is to estimate how a change in mangrove area influences the expected incidence of economically damaging natural disaster events.

Suppose that for a number of coastal regions, $i = 1, \ldots, N$, and over a given period of time, $t = 1, \ldots, T$ the ith coastal region could experience in any period t any number of $z_{it} = 0, 1, 2, 3 \ldots$ economically damaging storm event incidents. A common assumption in count data models is that the count variable z_{it} has a Poisson distribution, in which case the expected number of storm events in each region per period is given by:

$$E[z_{it}|s_{it}, x_{it}] = \lambda_{it} = e^{\alpha_i + \beta_S S_{it} + \beta' x_{it}}, \quad \frac{\partial E[z_{it}|S_{it}, x_{it}]}{\partial S_{it}} = \lambda_{it}\beta_S \tag{A4}$$

where as before, S_{it} is the area of wetlands, x_{it}, are other factors, and α_i accounts for other possible 'unobserved' effects on the incidence of disasters specific to each coastal region. Estimation of β_S, along with an estimate of the conditional mean λ_{it}, allows $\partial Z/\partial S$ in Equation (13) to be determined. One drawback of the Poisson distribution (Equation (A4)) is that it automatically implies 'equidispersion', that is, the conditional variance of z_{it} is also equal to λ_{it}. To test whether this is the case, the Poisson method of estimating (A4) should be compared to other techniques, such as the Negative Binomial model, which do not assume equidispersion in the variance of z_{it}.

For the Thailand case study, the estimation of (A4) is:

$$\ln E[z_{it}|M_{it}, x_{it}] = \ln \lambda_{it} = \alpha_i + \beta_S M_{it} + \beta' x_{it} + \mu_{it}, \tag{A5}$$

where $i = 1, \ldots, 21$ coastal provinces, $t = 1, \ldots, 18$ years (1979–96). The EM-DAT (2005) International Disaster Database contains data on the number of coastal disasters occurring in Thailand since 1975 and the approximate location and date of its impacts. From these data it is possible to determine z_{it}, the number of economically damaging coastal natural disasters that occurred per province per year over 1979–96. Mangrove area, M_{it}, is measured in terms of the annual mangrove area in square kilometres for each of the 21 coastal provinces of Thailand over 1979–96. Two control variables were included as the additional factors, x_{it}, which may explain the incidence of economically damaging coastal disasters, the population density of a province and a yearly time trend variable. The inclusion of the population density variable reflects the prevailing view in the natural disaster management literature that 'hazard events that occur in unpopulated areas and are not associated with losses do not constitute disasters' (Dilley et al., 2005, p. 115).[11] The yearly time trend was included as a control because the number of coastal natural disasters seems to have increased over time in Thailand (see Figure 5).[12]

Various regression procedures for a panel data set for count data models were utilized and compared, including: (1) Poisson models assuming equidispersion, i.e. equality of the conditional mean and the variance; (2) maximum likelihood estimation of Negative Binomial models allowing for unequal dispersion; and (3) comparing provincial to zonal fixed effects. Table A4 reports the best count data model for estimating Equation (A5) and the relevant test statistics.

As shown in Table A4, the preferred specification of the count data model is the Negative Binomial model with zonal fixed effects. In both the Poisson and Negative Binomial panel models, the zonal fixed effects specification (with coastal zone 5 as the default) is preferred to individual province effects, which is verified by LR tests of the two specifications. Although the parameter estimates for the zonal fixed effects are not shown, these estimated effects were significant at the 95% or 99% confidence levels. As indicated in Table A4, two standard tests were employed for the null hypothesis of equidispersion of the conditional mean and variance of the Poisson specification of the count data model (Cameron and Trivedi, 1998; Greene, 2003). Both the LM statistic and the t-test for equidispersion based on the residuals of the Poisson regression are significant, indicating that the null hypothesis can be rejected, and the Negative Binomial model that does not assume equidispersion is preferred to the Poisson specification. The LR statistic reported in the table tests the null hypothesis that the coefficients of the regressors are zero; as the statistic is significant, the hypothesis is rejected.

The results displayed in Table A4 for the preferred model show that a change in mangrove area has a significant influence on the incidence of coastal natural disasters in Thailand, and with the predicted sign. The point estimate for β_S indicates that a 1 km^2 decline in mangrove area increases the expected number of disasters by 0.36%.

---

[11] This view is also reflected in the criteria used in the International Disaster Database to decide which hazard events should be recorded as 'natural disasters'. In order for EM-DAT (2005) to record an event as a disaster, at least one or more of the following criteria must be fulfilled: 10 or more people reported killed; 100 people reported affected; declaration of a state of emergency; call for international assistance. The simple correlation between population density and mangrove area for the sample is relatively low (−0.389).

[12] This is a procedure recommended by Rose (1990), when such a trend effect is suspected.

Table A4. Negative binomial estimation of Equation (A5) with zonal fixed effects

Variable	Parameter estimate[a]	Marginal effect[b]
Mangrove area (M_{it})	−0.0036 (−4.448)**	−0.0031 (−2.745)**
Population density ($POPDEN_{it}$)	−0.0005 (−1.079)	−0.0004 (−0.894)
Annual time trend ($YRTRN_{it}$)	0.0781 (5.558)**	0.0669 (2.615)**
Dispersion parameter (α_{it})	0.0001	
Estimated conditional mean (λ)	0.8559	
Log-likelihood	−373.66	
Lagrange multiplier statistic[c]	39.967**	
Regression t-test[d]	−5.385**	
Likelihood ratio statistic[e]	74.919**	

Notes: t-statistics shown in parentheses.
[a] Parameter estimates for the zonal fixed effects are not shown. Zone 5 is the default and the fixed effects for zones 1 to 4 were negative and significant at the 95% or 99% confidence levels.
[b] Estimate of $\lambda_{it}\beta_3$ (see Equation (A4)).
[c] Tests the null hypothesis of equidispersion in the Poisson model.
[d] A regression-based test of the null hypothesis of equidispersion in the Poisson model.
[e] Tests the null hypothesis that the restricted regression without the explanatory variables M_{it}, $POPDEN_{it}$ and $YRTRN_{it}$ is the preferred Negative Binomial model with zonal fixed effects.
* Significant at 95% confidence level.
** Significant at 99% confidence level.

Sources: Author's estimations.

It is likely that the mangrove loss in Thailand, especially since the mid-1970s (see Figure 4), has increased the expected number of economically damaging coastal natural disasters per year. The estimated marginal effect corresponding to β_S of a change in mangrove area on coastal natural disasters (−0.0031) can be employed to estimate the resulting impact of mangrove deforestation over 1979–96 in Thailand on expected damages of natural coastal disasters. This is described further in Section 4.3 and shown in Table 4.

As discussed in Section 3.5, an underlying hypothesis of the expected damage function methodology is that, if coastal wetland loss increases the incidence of natural disaster per year, then wetland loss is also associated with increasing storm damages. However, under certain circumstances the results of a count data model could provide a misleading test of this null hypothesis. For instance, suppose a loss in wetland area is associated with a change in the incidence of storms from one devastating storm to two relatively minor storms per year. The count data model would then be interpreted as not providing evidence against the null that the change in the wetland area increases expected storm damages, when what has actually happened is that total storm damages have declined over time with wetland loss. This suggests the need for a robustness check on the count data model, such as Equation (A5) in the Thailand case study, to ensure that such situations do not dominate the application of the EDF approach.

One possible robustness check is to test the null hypothesis directly; that is, are total damages from storm events increasing with coastal wetland loss? In the Thailand case study, the relevant estimation is

$$D_{it} = \alpha_i + \beta_S M_{it} + \beta' x_{it} + \mu_{it} \tag{A6}$$

where the dependent variable, D_{it}, is total real damages from all storm events per province per year over 1979–96. The EM-DAT (2005) database provides data on the total economic damages per province per year in Thailand, and these data were deflated using the 1996 GDP deflator. The standard regression procedures for the panel analysis of Equation (A6) were performed, including comparing OLS with fixed and random effects. Table A5 reports the OLS and random effects specifications for the preferred version of Equation (A6).

The preferred model in Table A5 is the pooled weighted least squares estimation with correction for heteroscedasticity. The LR test of the null hypothesis of zero individual effects across all 21 provinces is not statistically significant. Although not shown in the table, an alternative F-test of the null hypothesis is also not significant. Neither the Breusch–Pagan LM test of the null hypothesis of random provincial-level disturbances nor the Hausman test of the random versus the fixed effects specification is statistically significant. These tests confirm that in the panel analysis of Equation (A5) of the weighted OLS regression is more efficient than either the random or fixed effects models.

The weighted least squares regression in Table A5 indicates that, over 1979–96 and across the 21 coastal provinces of Thailand, total real storm damages increased with mangrove loss. The point estimate suggests that a 1 km² decline in mangrove area increases real storm damages by around \$52 per province per year. The regression also confirms that, for the Thailand case study, the null hypothesis that storm damages increase with mangrove loss cannot be rejected.

Table A5. Panel estimation of Equation (A6) for total storm damages, Thailand

Variable[a]	Pooled OLS[b]	Random effects[b]
Mangrove area (M_{it})	−51.527 (−1.976)*	−52.378 (−1.563)
Population density ($POPDEN_{it}$)	−12.896 (−0.343)	−18.723 (−0.395)
Annual time trend ($YRTRN_{it}$)	965.325 (2.058)*	983.653 (2.100)*
Constant	1 3748.820 (1.275)	1 4728.707 (1.153)
Log-likelihood	−4598.425	
Likelihood ratio statistic[c]	14.173	
Lagrange multiplier statistic[d]		2.24
Hausman test[e]		1.04

Notes: t-statistics shown in parentheses.
[a] Parameter estimates for the zonal fixed effects for Zone 1 and Zone 4 are not shown. Although neither parameter was statistically significant, their inclusion improved the robustness of the overall regression.
[b] Weighted least squares with robust covariance matrix to correct for heteroscedasticity.
[c] Tests the null hypothesis of no fixed provincial effects.
[d] Tests the null hypothesis of no random provincial effects.
[e] Tests the null hypothesis that the random effects specification is preferred to the fixed effects. Test was performed excluding the zonal fixed effect for Zone 4.
* Significant at 95% confidence level.

Sources: Author's estimations.

REFERENCES

Acharya, G. and E.B. Barbier (2000). 'Valuing groundwater recharge through agricultural production in the Hadejia-Jama'are wetlands in northern Nigeria', *Agricultural Economics*, 22, 247–59.

Aksornkoae, S. and R. Tokrisna (2004). 'Overview of shrimp farming and mangrove loss in Thailand', in E.B. Barbier and S. Sathirathai (eds.), *Shrimp Farming and Mangrove Loss in Thailand*, Edward Elgar, London.

Aksornkoae, S., R. Tokrisna, W. Sugunnasil and S. Sathirathai (2004). 'The importance of mangroves: Ecological perspectives and socio-economic values', in E.B. Barbier and S. Sathirathai (eds.), *Shrimp Farming and Mangrove Loss in Thailand*, Edward Elgar, London.

Barbier, E.B. (1994). 'Valuing environmental functions: Tropical wetlands', *Land Economics*, 70(2), 155–73.

— (2000). 'Valuing the environment as input: Applications to mangrove-fishery linkages', *Ecological Economics*, 35, 47–61.

— (2003). 'Habitat-fishery linkages and mangrove loss in Thailand', *Contemporary Economic Policy*, 21(1), 59–77.

Barbier, E.B. and M. Cox (2003). 'Does economic development lead to mangrove loss? A cross-country analysis', *Contemporary Economic Policy*, 21(4), 418–32.

Barbier, E.B. and S. Sathirathai (eds.) (2004). *Shrimp Farming and Mangrove Loss in Thailand*. Edward Elgar, London.

Barbier, E.B. and I. Strand (1998). 'Valuing mangrove-fishery linkages: A case study of Campeche, Mexico', *Environmental and Resource Economics*, 12, 151–66.

Barbier, E.B., I. Strand and S. Sathirathai (2002). 'Do open access conditions affect the valuation of an externality? Estimating the welfare effects of mangrove-fishery linkages', *Environmental and Resource Economics*, 21(4), 343–67.

Bjørndal, T. and J.M. Conrad (1987). 'The dynamics of an open access fishery', *Canadian Journal of Economics*, 20, 74–85.

Boscolo, M. and J.R. Vincent (2003). 'Nonconvexities in the production of timber, biodiversity, and carbon sequestration', *Journal of Environmental Economics and Management*, 46, 251–68.

Cameron, C.A. and P. Trivedi (1998). *Regression Analysis of Count Data*, Cambridge University Press, Cambridge.

Carlsson, F., P. Frykblom and C. Lijenstolpe (2003). 'Valuing wetland attributes: An application of choice experiments', *Ecological Economics*, 47, 95–103.

Carpenter, S.R., D. Ludwig and W.A. Brock (1999). 'Management of eutrophication for lakes subject to potentially irreversible change', *Ecological Applications*, 9(3), 751–71.

Charuppat, T. and J. Charuppat (1997). *The Use of Landsat-5 (TM) Satellite Images for Tracing the Changes of Mangrove Forest Areas of Thailand*, Royal Forestry Department, Bangkok.

Check, E. (2005). 'Roots of recovery', *Nature*, 438, 910–11.

Chong, J. (2005). *Protective Values of Mangrove and Coral Ecosystems: A Review of Methods and Evidence*, IUCN, Gland, Switzerland.

Clark, C. (1976). *Mathematical Bioeconomics*, John Wiley and Sons, New York.

Dahdouh-Guebas, F., L.P. Jayatissa, D. Di Nitto, J.O. Bosire, D. Lo Seen and N. Koedam (2005). 'How effective were mangroves as a defence against the recent tsunami?' *Current Biology*, 15(12), 443–47.

Daily, G. (ed.) (1997). *Nature's Services: Societal Dependence on Natural Ecosystems*, Island Press, Washington DC.

De Groot, R.S., M.A. Wilson and R.M.J. Boumans (2002). 'A typology for the classification, description and valuation of ecosystem functions, goods and services', *Ecological Economics*, 41, 393–408.

Deninger, K. and L. Squire (1998). 'New ways of looking at old issues: Inequality and growth', *Journal of Development Economics*, 57, 259–87.

Dickie, M. (2003). 'Defensive behavior and damage cost methods', in P. Champ, K.J. Boyle and T.C. Brown (eds.), *A Primer on Nonmarket Valuation*, Kluwer, Boston, MA.

Dilley, M., R.S. Chen, U. Deichmann, A.L. Lerner-Lam and M. Arnold (2005). *Natural Disaster Hotspots: A Global Risk Analysis*. Disaster Risk Management Series, Hazard Management Unit, The World Bank, Washington, DC.

Ellis, G.M. and A.C. Fisher (1987). 'Valuing the environment as input', *Journal of Environmental Management*, 25, 149–56.

EM-DAT (2005). *EM-DAT: The OFDA/CRED International Disaster Database*. www.em-dat.net, Université Catholique de Louvain, Brussels, Belgium.

Engerman, S. and Sokoloff, K.L. (2000). 'Factor endowment, inequality, and paths of development among new world economies', UCLA.

FAO (2003). 'Status and trends in mangrove area extent worldwide' (by M.L. Wilkie and S. Fortuna) Forest Resources Assessment Working Paper No. 63, Forest Resources Division, Food and Agricultural Organization of the United Nations, Rome.

Finnoff, D. and J. Tschirhart (2003). 'Harvesting in an eight-species ecosystem', *Journal of Environmental Economics and Management*, 45, 589–611.

Freeman, A.M. III. (1982). *Air and Water Pollution Control: A Benefit-Cost Assessment*, John Wiley, New York.

— (1991). 'Valuing environmental resources under alternative management regimes', *Ecological Economics*, 3, 247–56.

— (2003). *The Measurement of Environmental and Resource Values: Theory and Methods*, 2nd edn, Resources for the Future, Washington DC.

Galor, O., O. Moav and D. Vollrath (2005). 'Inequality in land ownership, the emergence of human capital promoting institutions, and the great divergence', Brown University.

Greene, W.H. (2003). *Econometric Analysis*, 5th edn, Prentice-Hall, Englewood Cliffs, NJ.

Gren, I-M., K. Elofsson and P. Jannke (1997). 'Cost-effective nutrient reductions to the Baltic Sea', *Environmental and Resource Economics*, 10, 341–62.

Gylfason, T. (2001). 'Natural resources, education, and economic development', *European Economic Review*, 45, 847–59.

Harakunarak, A. and S. Aksornkoae (2005). 'Life-saving belts: Post-tsunami reassessment of mangrove ecosystem values and management in Thailand', *Tropical Coasts*, July, 48–55.

Heal, G.M., E.B. Barbier, K.J. Boyle, A.P. Covich, S.P. Gloss, C.H. Hershner, J.P. Hoehn, C.M. Pringle, S. Polasky, K. Segerson and K. Shrader-Frechette (2005). *Valuing Ecosystem Services: Toward Better Environmental Decision Making*, The National Academies Press, Washington DC.

Hirshleifer, J. and J.G. Riley (1992). *The Analytics of Uncertainty and Information*, Cambridge University Press, Cambridge.

Homans, F.R. and J.E. Wilen (1997). 'A model of regulated open access resource use', *Journal of Environmental Economics and Management*, 32, 1–21.

Jackson, J.B.C., M.X. Kirby, W.H. Berger, *et al.* (2001). 'Historical overfishing and the recent collapse of coastal ecosystems', *Science*, 293, 629–38.

Just, R.E., D.L. Hueth and A. Schmitz (2004). *The Welfare Economics of Public Policy: A Practical Approach to Project and Policy Evaluation*, Edward Elgar, Cheltenham, UK.

Kahn, J.R., and W.M. Kemp (1985). 'Economic losses associated with the degradation of an ecosystem: The case of submerged aquatic vegetation in Chesapeake Bay', *Journal of Environmental Economics and Management*, 12, 246–63.

Kaiser, B. and J. Roumasset (2002). 'Valuing indirect ecosystem services: The case of tropical watersheds', *Environment and Development Economics*, 7, 701–14.

Kaosa-ard, M. and S. Pednekar (1998). 'Background Report for the Thai Marine Rehabilitation Plan 1997–2001', Report submitted to the Joint Research Centre of the Commission of the European Communities and the Department of Fisheries, Ministry of Agriculture and Cooperatives, Thailand, Thailand Development Research Institute, Bangkok.

Kathiresan, K. and N. Rajendran (2005). 'Coastal mangrove forests mitigated tsunami', *Estuarine Coastal and Shelf Science*, 65, 601–606.

Knowler, D., E.B. Barbier, and I. Strand (2001). 'An open-access model of fisheries and nutrient enrichment in the Black Sea', *Marine Resource Economics*, 16, 195–217.

Krutilla, J.V. and A.C. Fisher (1985). *The Economics of Natural Environments: Studies in the Valuation of Commodity and Amenity Resources*, Resources for the Future, Washington, DC.

Lynne, G.D., P. Conroy and F.J. Prochaska (1981). 'Economic value of marsh areas for marine production processes', *Journal of Environmental Economics and Management*, 8, 175–86.

Mardle, S., C. James, C. Pipitone and M. Kienzle (2004). 'Bioeconomic interactions in an established fishing exclusion zone: The Gulf of Castellammare, NW Sicily', *Natural Resource Modeling*, 17(4), 393–447.

Massel, S.R., K. Furukawa and R.M. Brinkman (1999). 'Surface wave propagation data in mangrove forests', *Fluid Dynamics Research*, 24, 219–49.

Mazda, Y., E. Wolanski, B. King, A. Sase, D. Ohtsuka and M. Magi (1997). 'Drag force due to vegetation in mangrove swamps', *Mangroves and Salt Marshes*, 1, 193–99.

McConnell, K.E. and I.E. Strand (1989). 'Benefits from commercial fisheries when demand and supply depend on water quality', *Journal of Environmental Economics and Management*, 17, 284–92.

Michener, R. and C. Tighe (1992). 'A Poisson regression model of highway fatalities', *American Economic Review*, 82(2), 452–56.

Millennium Ecosystem Assessment (2003). *Ecosystems and Human Well-being: A Framework for Assessment*, Island Press, Washington DC.

Mitsch, W.J. and J.G. Gosselink (1993). *Wetlands*, 2nd edn, Van Norstrand Reinhold, New York.

Myers, R.A. and B. Worm (2003). 'Rapid worldwide depletion of predatory fish communities', *Nature*, 423, 280–83.

Naylor, R. and M. Drew (1998). 'Valuing mangrove resources in Kosrae, Micronesia', *Environment and Development Economics*, 3, 471–90.

Olson, M.K. (2004). 'Are novel drugs more risky for patients than less novel drugs?' *Journal of Health Economics*, 23, 1135–58.

Pagiola, S., K. von Ritter and J. Bishop (2004). *How Much is an Ecosystem Worth? Assessing the Economic Value of Conservation*, The World Bank, Washington DC.

Parks, P. and M. Bonfaz (1997). 'Nonsustainable use of renewable resources: Mangrove deforestation and mariculture in Ecuador', *Marine Resource Economics*, 9, 1–18.

Ready, R.C. (1995). 'Environmental valuation under uncertainty', in D.W. Bromley (ed.), *The Handbook of Environmental Economics*, Blackwell Publishers, Cambridge, MA, pp. 568–93.

Ricketts, T.H., G.C. Daily, P.R. Ehrlich and C.D. Michener (2004). 'Economic value of tropical forest to coffee production', *Proceedings of the National Academy of Science*, 101(304), 12579–82.

Rodwell, L.D., E.B. Barbier, C.M. Roberts and T.R. McClanahan (2002). 'A model of tropical marine reserve-fishery linkages', *Natural Resource Modeling*, 15(4), 453–86.

Rose, N.L. (1990). 'Profitability and product quality: Economic determinants of airline safety performance', *Journal of Political Economy*, 98(5), 944–64.

Sathirathai, S. and E.B. Barbier (2001). 'Valuing mangrove conservation in Southern Thailand', *Contemporary Economic Policy*, 19, 109–22.

Schnute, J. (1977). 'Improved estimates of the Schaefer Production Model: Theoretical considerations', *Journal of the Fisheries Research Board of Canada*, 34, 583–603.

Settle, C. and J.F. Shogren (2002). 'Modeling native-exotic species within Yellowstone Lake', *American Journal of Agricultural Economics*, 84(5), 1323–28.

Shabman, L.A. and S.S. Batie (1978). 'Economic value of natural coastal wetlands: A critique', *Coastal Zone Management Journal*, 4(3), 231–47.

Sugunnasil, W. (1998). 'Fishing communities and coastal resource management in Southern Thailand', mimeo, Department of Social Sciences, Prince of Songkla University, Pattani, Thailand.

Sumaila, U.R. (2002). 'Marine protected area performance in a model of a fishery', *Natural Resource Modeling*, 15(4), 439–51.

Swallow, S.K. (1994). 'Renewable and nonrenewable resource theory applied to coastal agriculture, forest, wetland and fishery linkages', *Marine Resource Economics*, 9, 291–310.

UNEP (United Nations Environment Program) (2005). *After the Tsunami: Rapid Environmental Assessment Report*, UNEP, Nairobi, 22 February; www.unep.org/tsunami/reports.

Valiela, I., J.L. Bowen and J.K. York (2001). 'Mangrove forests: One of the world's threatened major tropical environments', *BioScience*, 51(10), 807–15.

Wattana, S. (1998). 'Fishing Communities and Coastal Resource Management in Southern Thailand'. Mimeo. Department of Social Sciences, Prince of Songkla University, Pattani, Thailand.

Wetlands International (2005). *Natural Mitigation of Natural Disasters*. Assessment Report to Ramsar STRP12, Wetlands International, Jakarta, 2 February.

Winkelmann, R. (2003). *Econometric Analysis of Count Data*, 4th edn, Springer-Verlag, Berlin.

World Conservation Monitoring Centre (WCMC) (1992). 'Wetlands', in WCMC (ed.), *Global Biodiversity: Status of the Earth's Living Resources*, IUCN, Gland, Switzerland.

World Resources Institute (WRI) (1996). *World Resources 1996–7*, World Resources Institute, Washington DC.

— (2001). *World Resources 2000–2001. People and Ecosystems: The Fraying Web of Life*, World Resources Institute, Washington DC.

Wu, J., K. Skelton-Groth, W.G. Boggess and R.M. Adams (2003). 'Pacific salmon restoration: Trade-offs between economic efficiency and political acceptance', *Contemporary Economic Policy*, 21(1), 78–89.

Zinn, J. (2005). *Hurricanes Katrina and Rita and the Coastal Louisiana Ecosystem Restoration*. CRS Report for Congress, The Congressional Research Service, The Library of Congress, Washington DC, 26 September.

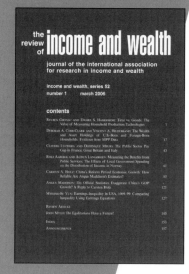

Sebastian G. **kessing** is Senior Research Fellow at Wissenschaftszentrum Berlin (WZB). His research deals with the international dimension of tax and labour market policies in an integrating world.

Kai A. **konrad** is Professor of Economics at the Free University of Berlin and Director of the unit "Market Processes and Governance" at the Social Science Research Center Berlin (WZB). His research interests are in the economics of the public sector and political economy.

Christos **kotsogiannis** is Senior Lecturer in Economics at the University of Exeter. His research interests are in the areas of Public Economics, International Trade and Political Economy.

Winfried **koeniger** is a Senior Research Associate at IZA and postdoctoral researcher at the University of Bonn. His research focuses on macroeconomic issues in labour and credit markets.

Marco **leonardi** is a Researcher at the University of Milan and research fellow at IZA. His research concentrates on labor economics with a particular focus on wage inequality and earnings mobility.

Francesco **daveri** is Professor of Economics at the University of Parma, and a Research Fellow at Igier. His research deals with the causes of productivity growth in Europe and its labour market counterparts.

Mika **maliranta** is the Head of Research at the Research Institute of the Finnish Economy (ETLA) in Helsinki. He has published widely on job and worker flows, firm dynamics and the determinants of firm productivity, such as ICT and labour skills.

Edward B. **barbier** is the John S Bugas Professor of Economics, Department of Economics and Finance, University of Wyoming. Professor Barbier is an environmental and resource economist, working on natural resource and development issues and the interface between economics and ecology.

ISBN 978-1-4051-5544-1

0266-4658(200701)22:01;1-O

9 781405 155441

ECONOMIC POLICY

50

April
2007

gender wage gaps
WEICHSELBAUMER & WINTER-EBMER

WTO agriculture reforms
HERTEL, IVANIC, KEENEY & WINTERS

international migration
HATTON

tax competition
BÉNASSY-QUÉRÉ, GOBALRAJA & TRANNOY

ECONOMIC POLICY

Editorial address: Centre for Economic Policy Research, 90–98 Goswell Road, London EC1V 7RR, UK; Center for Economic Studies, University of Munich, Schackstr. 4, 80539 Munich, GERMANY; Paris-Jourdan Sciences Economiques, ENS, 48 Boulevard Jourdan, 75014 Paris, FRANCE. URL: http://www.economic-policy.org

Publisher: *Economic Policy* is published by Blackwell Publishing, 9600 Garsington Road, Oxford OX4 2DQ, UK and 350 Main Street, Malden, MA 02148, USA.

Information for subscribers: *Economic Policy* is published in four issues per year. Subscription prices for 2007 are:

	Europe	The Americas	ROW
Premium Institutional:	£330	US$501	£330
Personal:	€71	US$70	£47
Student:	€35	US$38	£23

Customers in the UK should add VAT at 6%; customers in the EU should also add VAT at 6%, or provide a VAT registration number or evidence of entitlement to exemption. Customers in Canada should add 6% GST or provide evidence of entitlement to exception. The Premium institutional price includes online access from current content and all online back files to January 1st 1997, where available. For other pricing options or more information about online access to Blackwell Publishing journals, including access information and terms and conditions, please visit www.blackwellpublishing.com/ecop.

Delivery Terms and Legal Title: Prices include delivery of print journals to the recipient's address. Delivery terms are Delivered Duty Unpaid (DDU); the recipient is responsible for paying any import duty or taxes. Legal title passes to the customer on dispatch by our distributors.

EEA members: Subscriptions are available now at 40 euro. Apply to the European Economic Association, Voie du Roman Pays, 34, B-1348 Louvain-la-Neuve, Belgium (tel: +32 10 472 012, fax: +32 10 474 021/474 301, email: eea@core.ucl.ac.be, URL: http://www.eeassoc.org).

Available online: This journal is available online at *Blackwell Synergy*. Visit www.blackwell-synergy.com to search the articles and register for table of contents e-mail alerts.

Journal Customer Services: For ordering information, claims and any enquiry concerning your journal subscription please contact your nearest office:

UK: Email: customerservices@blackwellpublishing.com; Tel: +44 (0) 1865 778315; Fax: +44 (0) 1865 471775

USA: Email: customerservices@blackwellpublishing.com; Tel: +1 781 388 8206 or 1 800 835 6770 (Toll free in the USA); Fax: +1 781 388 8232 or Fax: +44 (0) 1865 471775

Asia: Email: customerservices@blackwellpublishing.com; Tel: +65 6511 8000; Fax: +44 (0) 1865 471775

Production Editor: David Thresher (email: david.thresher@edn.blackwellpublishing.com).

Back issues: Single issues from current and recent volumes are available at the current single issue price from Blackwell Publishing Journals. Earlier issues may be obtained from Periodicals Service Company, 11 Main Street, Germantown, NY 12526, USA. Tel: +1 518 537 4700, Fax: +1 518 537 5899, Email: psc@periodicals.com.

Advertising: Andy Patterson (email: andy@patads.co.uk).

Abstracting and Indexing Services: ABI-INFORM; AgBiotech News and Information; Asian-Pacific Economic Literature; Bibliography of Asian Studies; Contents of Recent Economics Journals; Current Contents; Emerald Management Reviews; Environmental Sciences and Pollution Management; GEOBASE; International Bibliography of the Social Sciences; International Political Science Abstracts; Journal of Economic Literature; Leisure, Recreation and Tourism Abstracts; PAIS International in Print; Periodicals Content Index; Plant Genetic Resources Abstracts; Risk Abstracts; Sage Public Administration Abstracts; Social Science Citation Index; World Agricultural Economics and Rural Sociology Abstracts.

Disclaimer: The Publisher, Centre for Economic Policy Research, Center for Economic Studies, Maison des Sciences de l'Homme and Editors cannot be held responsible for errors or any consequences arising from the use of information contained in this journal; the views and opinions expressed do not necessarily reflect those of the Publisher, Centre for Economic Policy Research, Center for Economic Studies, Maison des Sciences de l'Homme and Editors, neither does the publication of advertisements constitute any endorsement by the Publisher, Centre for Economic Policy Research, Center for Economic Studies, Maison des Sciences de l'Homme and Editors of the products advertised.

Paper: Blackwell Publishing's policy is to use permanent paper from mills that operate a sustainable forestry policy, and which has been manufactured from pulp that is processed using acid-free and elementary chlorine-free practices. Furthermore, Blackwell Publishing ensures that the text paper and cover board used in all our journals has met acceptable environmental accreditation standards.

CarbonNeutral: Blackwell Publishing is a CarbonNeutral company. For more information visit www.blackwellpublishing.com/carbonneutral

Printed in Great Britain by Page Brothers Ltd.

For submission instructions, subscription and all other information visit: www.blackwellpublishing.com/ecop

ISSN: 0266-4658 (print); ISSN: 1468-0327 (online)

ISBN-13: 978-1-4051-5545-8

50

April
2007

ECONOMIC POLICY

SENIOR EDITORS
GEORGES DE MÉNIL
RICHARD PORTES
HANS-WERNER SINN

MANAGING EDITORS
GIUSEPPE BERTOLA
PHILIPPE MARTIN
PAUL SEABRIGHT

Published in association with the European Economic Association

Blackwell Publishing Ltd for Centre for Economic Policy Research,
Center for Economic Studies of the University of Munich, and
Paris-Jourdan Sciences Economiques (PSE)
in collaboration with the Maison des Sciences de l'Homme.

STATEMENT OF PURPOSE

Economic Policy provides timely and authoritative analyses of the choices which confront policy-makers. The subject matter ranges from the study of how individual markets can and should work to the broadest interactions in the world economy.

Economic Policy is a joint activity of the Centre for Economic Policy Research (CEPR), the Munich-based Center for Economic Studies (CES) and the Paris-based Maison des Sciences de l'Homme (PSE). It offers an independent, non-partisan, European perspective on issues of worldwide concern. It emphasizes problems of international significance, either because they affect the world economy directly or because the experience of one country contains important lessons for policy-makers elsewhere.

All the articles are specifically commissioned from leading professional economists. Their brief is to demonstrate how live policy issues can be illuminated by the insights of modern economics and by the most recent evidence. The presentation is incisive and written in plain language accessible to the wide audience which participates in the policy debate.

Prior to publication, the contents of each volume are discussed by a Panel of distinguished economists from Europe and elsewhere. The Panel rotates annually. Inclusion in each volume of a summary of the highlights of the Economic Policy Panel discussion provides the reader with alternative interpretations of the evidence and a sense of the liveliness of the current debate.

Economic Policy is owned by the Maison des Sciences de l'Homme, CEPR and CES. The 43rd Panel meeting was held in Vienna and was hosted by the Österreichische Nationalbank. The 44th Panel meeting was held in Helsinki and was hosted by the Bank of Finland. We gratefully acknowledge this support, without implicating any of these organizations in the views expressed here, which are the sole responsibility of the authors.

PANEL

MANUEL ARELLANO
Centre for Monetary and Financial Studies

LANS BOVENBERG
CentER, Tilburg University

PIERRE CAHUC
CREST-INSEE

WENDY CARLIN
University College London

GIANCARLO CORSETTI
European University Institute

ALLAN DRAZEN
University of Maryland

GILLES DURANTON
University of Toronto

CARLO FAVERO
IGIER, Università Bocconi

NEIL GANDAL
Tel Aviv University

CHRISTIAN GOLLIER
University of Toulouse I

OMAR MOAV
Hebrew University of Jerusalem

PIERRE PESTIEAU
Université de Liège

STEPHEN J REDDING
London School of Economics

HELENE REY
Princeton University

ANNE SIBERT
Birkbeck College

JONATHAN TEMPLE
University of Bristol

REINHILDE VEUGELERS
Katholieke Universiteit Leuven

ERNST-LUDWIG VON THADDEN
Universität Mannheim

VOLKER WIELAND
Goethe Universität Frankfurt

50
April 2007

CONTENTS

Editors' introduction

Three of the papers published in this issue were presented in draft form at the panel meeting hosted in October 2006 by the Bank of Finland in Helsinki. We conclude the issue with a paper presented at the panel hosted by the Austrian National Bank in Vienna in April 2006.

INTERNATIONAL GENDER WAGE GAPS

Women are usually paid less than men, but the extent to which this is the case varies very much across individuals (many women's wages are higher than many men's wages), across countries, and over time. The paper by Doris Weichselbaumer and Rudolf Winter-Ebmer uses an impressive data set and very insightful meta-analysis techniques to analyse the extent to which wage differentials across individuals are due to their gender, rather than to observable productivity determinants such as education and work experience, and the extent to which the variation of gender wage gaps across countries and over time is determined by adoption of anti-discrimination legislation and/or by the strength of competitive pressures, which should tend to eliminate such inefficient practices as that of paying workers according to their gender (or race, or religion) rather than according to their productivity.

The panel was impressed by the paper's thorough analysis and by its results. Sensibly, the data indicate that 'equal pay' laws are associated with smaller gender wage gaps. Interestingly, they indicate that indicators of free-market conditions are roughly as important. The paper and its discussion pay special attention to the intuitive, but not obvious and highly policy relevant, finding that legal prohibition of dangerous or night-time work for women is associated with larger wage gaps. The direction of causality is unavoidably difficult to ascertain in this as in other aspects of the paper's analysis. It is possible that some societies are more inclined than others to treat men and women equally for unexplained cultural reasons, which result both in smaller wage differentials and lower inclination to outlaw women's employment in

Economic Policy April 2007 pp. 231–234 Printed in Great Britain
© CEPR, CES, MSH, 2007.

men's jobs. But the paper deserves the highest praise for its careful and appropriately qualified exposition of plausible and purely economic mechanisms that may explain its remarkable findings: when women are forbidden from engaging in certain activities, the market will pay higher wages for the (fewer, and male) workers who supply their labour in those sectors. Future work on wage and employment implications of legal provisions, in this and other areas, will certainly need to refer to this paper's approach and findings.

WTO AGRICULTURE REFORMS

Reforms in agriculture are the main reason for the present difficulties in the negotiations of the Doha Development Agenda of the World Trade Organization. They are also recognized as the source of potentially very large global welfare gains. The paper by Thomas Hertel, Roman Keeney, Maros Ivanic and Alan Winters analyses this issue by concentrating on the distributional effects of these reforms in both poor and rich countries. Using a global computable general equilibrium (CGE) model, the authors show that only a tiny fraction of the farmers in rich countries would lose a lot from Doha agriculture reforms. However, these rich farmers hold considerable political power. A second key result of the paper is that, contrary to what is often heard, Doha would have reduced poverty even in the poor agriculture-importing countries. The reason is that the poorest of the poor tend to be farmers and they would be the ones who would gain from higher agricultural prices that would follow trade liberalization. The panel was impressed by the amount of work that is involved in the exercise: it requires amending a CGE model to take into account the specificities of trade in agriculture, imperfect mobility of factors across sectors and household survey data in 15 developing countries. This allows analysing in detail the effects of agriculture reforms on income distribution and poverty. The clarity of the message and the importance of its political implications were also stressed by the panel. The main concern echoed some of the discomfort that economists have with CGE modelling that often resembles a black box with ad hoc assumptions. However, despite these caveats, the panel recognized that the unique analytical framework created for this study was the best tool available to analyse the distributional impact of agriculture reforms. The panel focused on the political-economy implications of the paper which should be at the heart of any strategy aimed at 'selling' agriculture liberalization to the public.

INTERNATIONAL MIGRATION

Globalization in the last decades of the twentieth century involved a very rapid increase in the international movement of goods and an even more rapid increase in the international movement of capital. But the movement of labour remains much more restricted than movement of goods or capital, and has substantially diminished in comparison with the great migrations of the second half of the nineteenth century.

Yet most estimates suggest that the worldwide economic gains to liberalizing migration are potentially very large. The paper by Timothy Hatton asks why migration policy remains so restrictive in the face of such large potential gains, and whether this is due to the presence of obstacles to international cooperation that could be alleviated through institutions analogous to the WTO in the field of trade. Hatton's paper shows that hostile public opinion does not appear to be the root of the problem: if anything public opinion is marginally more negative towards the liberalization of trade than of migration. The key obstacle, he suggests, lies elsewhere: it is the lack of a basis for reciprocity in negotiations over migration. Neither migrants to rich countries, nor the poor countries from which they come, can realistically offer any bargaining chips to the rich countries that can be used to win over the interest groups that perceive themselves as threatened by migration (unlike in trade where reciprocal market access can be an incentive). And this is because migration is largely driven by absolute advantage, rather than by comparative advantage as in the case of trade. Consequently, argues Hatton, there is no basis for WTO-style negotiations over migration and therefore no grounds for reforming the international architecture in the hope of fostering liberalization.

The paper provoked a lively debate at the panel, with a number of panellists doubting whether the political economy of trade and of migration could be compared as straightforwardly as is done in the paper. Jobs taken by immigrants may be much more conspicuous to voters than jobs lost to imports, and the fear that some immigrants free ride on public services, which is undoubtedly a source of political hostility to migration, has no obvious counterpart in the field of trade. The author's broadly pessimistic conclusion about the prospects for a World Migration Organization did not, however, provoke a great deal of dissent. But it was widely felt that the political economy of migration is a subject on which a great deal of research remains to be done.

TAX AND PUBLIC INPUT COMPETITION

Tax competition is a hot debate in Europe in the political arena and among policy-makers. For this debate to be useful, it needs informed theoretical and empirical work. This is the objective of the paper of Agnès Bénassy-Quéré, Nicolas Gobalraja and Alain Trannoy who make the important point that governments do not only compete in taxes but also in terms of the public goods they provide to mobile firms. The theoretical point dates back to Tiebout (1956) but this paper is a first attempt to disentangle both theoretically and empirically the effect of taxes and public inputs on the attractiveness of a country as a location for firms. The main finding of the paper is that even if public inputs that raise private productivity indeed attract firms, this does not compensate for the negative impact of corporate taxation used to finance these public inputs. This result is based on data for US foreign direct investment in 18 EU countries between 1994 and 2003. The finding has consequences for the debate on tax coordination that has so far concentrated too much on the setting of taxes. It also suggests that tax competition which is taking place in Europe is richer than a simple 'race to the bottom'. The importance of the policy question was recognized by the panel and the authors should be commended for addressing the complex empirical relations between foreign direct investment, taxation and the provision of public capital. Questions were raised during the panel on the identification of this relation as both taxation and public capital are themselves endogenous. Country specific factors such as productivity or endowments could, for example, affect foreign direct investment but also optimal choices of taxation and public capital. The paper also raises interesting questions on what optimal taxation and public investment should be in a context of dual competition when the menu of tax rates is richer than the one analysed by the authors. The panel also interpreted the paper as showing that, even if public infrastructure is appealing to firms, the net effect remains the possibility of a 'race to the bottom'.

REFERENCE

Tiebout, C. (1956). 'A pure theory of local expenditures', *Journal of Political Economy*, 64, 416–24.

International gender wage gaps

SUMMARY

Discrimination, if it is inefficient, can be eliminated by competition. In most countries, it is also forbidden by law. This paper evaluates the influence of economic and legal factors on the portion of male-female wage differentials that is not explained by other worker characteristics and may be due to discrimination. We use a new international data set of suitable gender wage gap measures, constructed from the results of existing studies. Meta-analysis of the data shows that increased competition and adoption of international conventions concerning equal treatment laws both reduce gender wage gaps, while legislation that prevents women from performing strenuous or dangerous jobs tends to increase it.

— *Doris Weichselbaumer and Rudolf Winter-Ebmer*

Economic Policy April 2007 Printed in Great Britain
© CEPR, CES, MSH, 2007.

The effects of competition and equal treatment laws on gender wage differentials

Doris Weichselbaumer and Rudolf Winter-Ebmer

University of Linz, Austria; University of Linz, Austria and Institute for Advanced Studies, Vienna

1. INTRODUCTION

Some of the observed unfavourable labour market outcomes of women, ethnic minorities, immigrants, disabled workers, religious and sexual minorities are arguably due to economic discrimination: individuals with identical productive characteristics are treated differently because of their demographic characteristics (sex, ethnical background, etc.). In this paper we examine wage evidence for the largest demographic group subject to discrimination: women.

The wage gap between men and women has strongly decreased within the last forty years, at least in industrialized countries. On the one hand, this may be

The authors wish to thank Lans Bovenberg and Wendy Carlin and other participants at the 44th Panel Meeting of Economic Policy in Helsinki for valuable comments. Rudolf Winter-Ebmer is also associated with CEPR, London and IZA, Bonn. This research was supported by the Austrian Theodor-Körner-Fonds and the Ludwig Boltzmann-Institut for Growth Research. Josef Fersterer, David Haardt, Sandra Leitner, Martin Mauhart and Andrea Kollman provided invaluable assistance with the data collection. Thanks to Erling Barth, Francine Blau, Peter Gottschalk, Stefan Klasen, Wilhelm Kohler, Steve Machin, Ronald Oaxaca, Solomon Polachek, Ken Troske, Rainer Winkelmann as well as seminar participants at the AEA meeting, in Bonn, Berlin, Mannheim, St Gallen, Bilbao, Oslo, Paris, Vienna and in Linz for helpful discussions.

The Managing Editor in charge of this paper was Giuseppe Bertola.

Economic Policy April 2007 pp. 235–287 Printed in Great Britain
© CEPR, CES, MSH, 2007.

explained by a number of productivity-relevant developments. Women accumulate more experience and do so with fewer labour market interruptions, their education is increasingly labour-market oriented, and technological change and industrial restructuring have led to a relative devaluation of physical strength and an increased demand for white-collar workers. On the other hand, developments such as increased global competition and the introduction of anti-discrimination laws may also be responsible for decreasing gender wage gaps.

An international analysis by Weichselbaumer and Winter-Ebmer (2005) indicates that the gender wage differential has dropped from about 65% in the 1960s to 30% in the 1990s in international data, and that the decline mostly reflects the first set of factors: women's increasing education and job experience endows them with relatively more advantageous 'productive characteristics' than in earlier times. The data also indicate that men earn 25% more than women with the same measurable characteristics, and this residual wage gap has remained roughly constant over the entire period of the last forty years in the Weichselbaumer and Winter-Ebmer (2005) data. For the United States, Blau and Kahn (1997) have instead found a substantial decline in the unexplained part of the gender wage gap during the 1980s, while for the 1990s a slower narrowing of the unexplained part is the main determinant of persistence in the overall male-female wage differential (Blau and Kahn, 2004).

The wage difference between men and women that is not explained by differences in productivity is large; it can at least partially be attributed to discrimination, and motivates policy efforts to eliminate it in most countries. But attempts to fight sex discrimination are not confined to national borders. International organizations like the United Nations and its agency the International Labour Organization (ILO) have set international conventions with the objective to combat discrimination. States that ratify these conventions legally commit themselves to the goal of eliminating discrimination. Economic conditions also play a role in shaping the extent to which discrimination can affect wage differentials. Following the work of Becker (1957), economists have argued that discrimination should take place under imperfect competition only. Employers who prefer to work with men instead of women may be prepared to pay members of their preferred group higher wages. However, employers who do not have such discriminatory preferences can produce at lower cost, for example they can hire only women if their wage is lower but their productivity is the same. Thus competition can solve the problem of discrimination, as more expensive, discriminatory firms cannot survive in the long run.

If we take the estimated discriminatory wage premium of on average 25% at face value, we may conclude that either some market imperfections remain also in today's relatively competitive markets or that some discrimination may persist even under competitive pressure. Other possible explanations may be, for example, that due to high transaction costs firms adapt only very slowly to the cost-advantage of non-discriminating firms or that markets are virtually free of non-discriminatory employers that could put pressure on discriminating firms. In either case policy interventions to combat discrimination become crucial.

In this paper we examine the effect of international conventions as well as of competition on the wage gap between men and women. One reason why these highly important issues have not been examined earlier is the lack of international data. While data on workers and their characteristics exist for most countries and allow national investigations, which have been conducted in vast numbers, international data is sparse. However, the effects of the ratification of international conventions or the competitive climate in a country on sex discrimination are best investigated using international data on gender wage differentials. This study takes advantage of the fact that a large number of national studies already has been done in the past and constructs its data via the method of meta-analysis. We collect all accessible published values for gender wage gaps for different countries and make them comparable by the use of meta-regression analysis. This rich data set is subsequently supplemented with information on competition and equal treatment laws, which allows us to investigate how big the often-proclaimed impact of these two factors really is.

This paper is structured as follows. In Section 2 we discuss the degree of competition and the ratification of international labour conventions as potential sources for gender wage gaps. Section 3 explains how we constructed our data by the use of meta-analysis and describes our methodological approach. Section 4 presents the results for the impact of competition and equal treatment laws on the development of gender wage gaps – along with a battery of robustness checks considering econometric methods and data reliability. Section 5 concludes.

2. INTERNATIONAL GENDER WAGE GAPS, COMPETITION AND LAWS

A number of factors may be responsible for differences in the gender wage gap between different countries. Most obviously, differences in education as well as occupational segregation may not allow women to be equally productive on the job. But also social norms with respect to childrearing and insufficient public support that prohibit women to combine family and work-life well may force women into occupations that do not allow them to achieve the same earnings as men. Another reason for differences in the gender wage gap may be due to differences in the selection of women into the labour market. For example, Mulligan and Rubinstein (2005) argue that in the United States over the last thirty years the correlation between women's employment and their cognitive skills as well as their family background has changed from negative to positive. According to them, since the early 1980s women who had better schooling, cognitive test scores and parental education increasingly selected themselves into the labour market. After controlling for this selection bias (as well as for investment decisions, since greater labour market attachment also increases women's willingness to invest in their human capital), they find that the apparently declining wage gap becomes roughly constant. Blau and Kahn (2004) also find a role, albeit a smaller one, for selection in the US labour market. Their results indicate that female entry into the labour market was positively selected in the 1980s; however, the smaller growth of the female labour supply in the 1990s appears to be slightly negatively selected. Olivetti and Petrongolo (2006) point out that there may be different patterns in different countries with respect to selection. In their international comparison, looking at 13 European countries and the United States, they find that women are indeed more positively selected into the labour market than men – with the exception of the Scandinavian countries and the Netherlands. For countries like Ireland, France and southern Europe, however, their results show that neglecting the effect of selection considerably underestimates the gender wage gap.

As Blau and Kahn (1992, 1996 and 2003) have pointed out, another determinant of differences in the gender wage gap may be the extent of overall wage inequality. In their work they analyze how general wage inequality and wage-setting institutions affect the observed gender wage gap in a country. In their 1992 and 1996 papers they use micro data from the International Social Survey Program (ISSP) and decompose international differences in the gender wage gap into a part due to gender specific factors and a part due to differences in the pay structure. They demonstrate that the general wage inequality in a country has a quantitatively big effect on the gender wage gap, since women are typically on the lower end of the wage distribution. Therefore, the higher the inequality of wages in a country, the higher will typically be the gender wage gap. In their 2003 paper they regress various gender gaps on wage inequality and female labour supply and find that a more compressed male wage structure as well as a lower female labour supply lead to lower gender pay gaps. Moreover, they find that collective bargaining reduces the wage differential.

While we are concentrating here on the impact of competition and equal treatment legislation on gender wage inequality, we will also take institutional and selection issues into account.[1]

2.1. Competition and discrimination

There is wide consensus in economic theory that market competition should tend to reduce discrimination by employers. Already Edgeworth argued with respect to gender wage differentials that: '[t]he best results will presumably be obtained by leaving employers free to compete for male or female labour. Thus equal pay for equal work would be secured in our sense of the term' (1922, p. 438).

---

[1] Equal treatment laws as well as institutions like unionization can have an impact on the wage setting, but also on the female labour supply, see e.g. Azmat et al. (2006) for gender gaps in unemployment and Bertola et al. (2005) for effects of institutions on gender differentials in employment.

Becker, in his seminal work (1957), developed the following insight in the context of race discrimination. Suppose employers can have a 'taste for discrimination': interactions with minority individuals are unpleasant for discriminatory employers. As a result, a utility maximizing employer hires fewer minority workers than a profit maximizing one. Indulging his tastes, and employing more expensive majority workers, he thereby forgoes profits. Non-discriminatory employers then can gain a cost advantage by hiring the cheaper minority workers. Given freedom of entry, non-discriminators will enter the market or expand given non-decreasing returns to scale. Hence they should be able to push discriminators out of the market in the long run and an equalization of wages between the different demographic groups should take place.

The implications of Becker's analysis are that if there is market power – in contrast to perfect competition – employers earn higher profits, which may allow them to continue 'consuming' discrimination more easily. Particularly if managers and owners are not the same person, monitoring of managers by capital owners will increase with competition and give managers less opportunity to forgo profits for discrimination. If market power is high, however, discriminating managers are more likely to go un-noticed. Likewise, in a regulated industry, firms are often not allowed to make excessive profits; in such a case, managers can hide part of these excessive profits from the regulatory body by consuming them in the form of discrimination. However, market power does not necessarily preserve discrimination. As Becker (1957) notes, if a monopoly is 'transferable' a discriminatory employer should be willing to sell it to a non-discriminating entrepreneur because he could receive an income higher than what he would make when keeping the firm. In that way, discriminatory behaviour should be reduced in 'transferable monopolies' just like in competitive markets.

While most authors adhere to the idea that in Becker's model, discrimination in competitive markets should disappear in the long run, it has to be noted that this is not necessarily the case. Different arguments have been brought forward that suggest that discrimination could persist also under competition (see Box 1). For example, it has been argued that if there is a positive entrepreneurial income this may be (partly) spent on discrimination also in competitive markets. Furthermore, models that assume nepotism instead of discrimination find the elimination of unequal treatment as a result of competition to be less likely. Recent search cost models receive similar results. Additional doubts have been raised by experimental economics, although here the focus is typically on labour market competition instead of product market competition. Already Becker argued that if discrimination results from co-workers, it can persist in the long run. Box 1 gives a short overview over this literature.

These different theories on discrimination have shown that more competition may or may not lead to a reduction in gender wage gaps. A number of studies have indeed found a negative relation between competition and the gender wage gap at the industry or firm level (see Box 2). However, no international investigation of the effect of competition on the gender wage differential has been conducted so far.

Box 1. Further theoretical arguments with respect to competition and discrimination

Even under perfect competition employers can use their income from their entrepreneurial activity in any way they please as, for example, Arrow (1980) and Heckman (1998) point out. Whether employers decide to spend their income on discrimination or consumption goods simply depends on their preferences. Discrimination will only be unambiguously driven out in its entirety by competitive pressure if the long-run supply of entrepreneurship is perfectly elastic at a prize of zero so that employers have no income to spend on discrimination. If there are enough non-discriminatory employers to hire all the minority workers, discrimination will not be observable, but discriminatory employers may still exist. Since it is the marginal firm hiring minority labour that determines the wage-rate, there may be many firms that have discriminatory tastes, which, however, never manifest themselves. The fact that individual employers can always simply avoid the negative utilities associated with minority workers and still achieve a competitive rate of return, leads Arrow (1980) finally to conclude – despite the previously mentioned caveat – that competition will go into the direction of eliminating employer's discrimination. The situation is different with respect to nepotism – when employers gain positive utility from working with majority workers. Already Becker (1957) has noted that given nepotistic tastes, long-term elimination of discrimination is not necessarily taking place. Goldberg (1982) has shown in more detail that nepotistic firms are expected to survive under competition in the long run.

More recently, a strand of models has developed that focuses on the effect of search costs on labour market discrimination (e.g. Black, 1995; Bowlus and Eckstein, 2002; Rosén, 2003). Typically, there are two types of employers, some with discriminatory preferences, the others without, and two types of workers, majority and minority workers. Due to search costs, these models find it unlikely that discrimination is eliminated in the long run. In Black's (1995) model, minority workers only receive wage offers from non-discriminatory employers and therefore have higher search costs. This allows non-discriminatory employers to offer them lower wages. In Bowlus and Eckstein's model (2002) it is the employers who are searching for currently employed or unemployed workers. Those employers with discriminatory tastes search less intensively for minority workers. If firms follow their optimal search strategies, minority workers receive lower wage offers from both discriminatory and non-discriminatory firms and are confronted with higher unemployment. In contrast to the previous two studies where employers set the wages, Rosén (2003) develops a model with wage bargaining. There is no wage equalization, and profits – but not utility – are highest for firms with a taste for discrimination. However, if management and ownership are separated then firms with discriminatory tastes can indeed achieve both the highest profits and the highest utility. Obviously, under such conditions, there is no mechanism that ensures that discrimination disappears.

As has been emphasized, in Becker's original model discrimination should be eliminated by competitive pressure in the long run if it is employers who hold discriminatory tastes. The situation is different, however, if it is co-workers or customers who have a distaste against minority workers. Majority co-workers may demand higher wages in order to be compensated for their distaste to work with minority workers. The result may be a sorting equilibrium with an entirely segregated workforce. However, such a segregated solution may not be possible for organizational reasons. For example, in the case of an increase in the number of women entering the labour market, employers may not be able to entirely exchange their workforce from one day to the next due to hiring and firing costs. This may lead to a reduced demand for female workers as well as to lower wages of women.

Also discriminatory tastes of customers can sustain in the long run. If customers simply prefer to interact with majority workers and are prepared to pay for their preferences then these discriminatory tastes will remain also in competitive markets, preserving the wage differentials between demographic groups.

Recent studies in experimental economics have also cast some doubts whether competition on the labour market is necessarily beneficial for women's relative labour market status. Gneezy *et al.* (2003) as well as Gneezy and Rustichini (2004) have documented that in a competitive setting women do not increase their performance as systematically as men. Niederle and Vesterlund (2005) show that men also choose to engage in competition more often than women. These gender differences with respect to competitive behaviour may explain part of the male-female wage differential and, in fact, should lead to higher wage differentials given higher competitive pressure. However, these experimental results are actually not in contrast to Becker's model in the strict sense: whereas Becker's theory relates to competitive pressure on product markets, these experiments have focused on labour market competition.

Schwieren (2003) has also used a laboratory experiment to investigate gender wage differentials; however, her study is located within an efficiency wage framework. She argues that two reasons may be responsible for employers paying women lower efficiency wages – stereotypes may cause employers to believe that women are in general less likely to shirk and therefore no efficiency wages are needed, but they may also assume that due to a lack of career orientation, women do not increase their effort in response to higher wages as much as males do; therefore paying them efficiency wages does not have the desired effect. Schwieren finds that in her experimental setting women are offered significantly lower wages than men which causes the female workers to exhibit such low effort that firms actually make losses. Under such conditions, the author argues, an elimination of discrimination in the long run as envisioned by Becker cannot take place, since hiring women for low wages is not profitable.

Box 2. Studies investigating the effect of competition on the industry or firm-level

Becker (1957) himself compared monopolistic and competitive industries in the US South of 1940 and found that in all but one of nine occupational categories, the number of non-white workers was higher in the competitive industries. However, more detailed analyses on the relation between competition and discrimination, in particular with respect to wages, have been conducted only later.

Ashenfelter and Hannan (1986) analysed the effect of market concentration in the banking industry. The advantage of this sector is the geographically limited nature of competition, which allows for variability in the degree of concentration within one industry. They found a negative and significant impact of market concentration on the share of female employees in a firm. Black and Strahan (2001) recently investigated the banking sector further and tested the effect of deregulation in this industry. Their results show that deregulation caused male wages to fall much stronger than female wages which indicates that in the previously protected market rents were mainly shared with men. Another study by Black and Brainerd (2004) looks at the effect of increased competition on women's relative wages where they compare the effect of trade in concentrated and unconcentrated sectors. They demonstrate that an increase in product market competition due to international trade reduces the gender wage gap. Hellerstein *et al.* (2002) examine profitability and sex composition of a firm's workforce and find that among firms with high market power, those with a large share of female employees obtain higher profits. This implies a discriminatory gender wage gap. However, no evidence was found that discriminatory firms were punished through lower growth nor are ownership changes related to the gender composition of the workforce.

All of these studies relate to US industry sectors and are in accordance with Becker's theory – at least to a certain degree. In our study we seek to examine whether the relation between competition and the gender wage gap holds internationally. For example, Berik *et al.* (2004) examine whether increased competition from international trade reduces the gender wage gap in Taiwan and South Korea, but their results are not consistent with Becker's theory – indeed they find that competition is positively associated with gender wage discrimination. Jolliffe and Campos (2005), on the other hand, find for Hungary that discrimination has indeed substantially declined during Hungary's transition to a competitive market economy. This paper looks at international data to investigate whether increased competition reduces discrimination more generally.

2.2. International conventions combating discrimination

Historically, labour standards have been developed to protect individuals that were seen as too weak to receive proper treatment in the market and who lack the political voice to influence legislation. As Engerman (2003) points out, initial concerns were often directed towards children and women, while adult males were considered to have sufficient rights and abilities to be able to care for themselves. This initial orientation is also reflected in the first international labour conventions of the International Labour Organization (ILO) in Geneva. In the foundational year of the ILO in 1919, five ILO conventions were set up. After two general conventions regulating hours of work and preventing or providing against unemployment, convention number three (C3) addressed maternity protection and C4 was designed to protect women from night work (C4 has been later replaced by other conventions). The following three conventions (C5–C7) addressed issues of young workers and the minimum working age.

Conventions to prevent discrimination, on which we want to focus in this study, have been adopted only considerably later, however. Two ILO conventions are directed at prescribing equal treatment: the Equal Remuneration Convention (C100) was adopted in 1951 and demands equal pay for work of equal value. It directly aims at combating discrimination against women in wages. The Discrimination (Employment and Occupation) Convention (C111) is slightly more general and was adopted in 1958. It prohibits different forms of discrimination (access to training, employment, conditions of employment etc.) on grounds of sex, race, ethnic background, religion, political opinion or social origin. So that international labour conventions set by the ILO become legally binding, states have to ratify them. Subsequently, states must adopt their national labour laws to fulfil the conventions; however, in some countries, the conventions are directly binding on employers and workers.

Besides ILO C100 and C111, which explicitly aim at combating discrimination, in our study we included also two conventions which reflect the view that women need protection in the labour market. As Chang (2000) notes, these labour standards aim at 'protecting women generally because of their sex, based on attitudes toward their capabilities and appropriate role in society' (p. 1672). In particular, we focus on convention 45, which prohibits women's underground work, and C89, the current convention prohibiting women's night work. Contrary to ILO C100 and C111, which combat discrimination, these regulations in fact restrict women's occupational choices and represent a work ban against women in certain jobs. Consequently, it is expected that these regulations, contrary to the others, *increase* the observed gender wage differential. Our variable 'work ban index' counts how many of the two conventions a state had signed at a certain point in time.

But not only the ILO has set international conventions to combat discrimination. In fact the UN itself has installed the 'Convention on the Elimination of All Forms of Discrimination against Women' (CEDAW) which has been adopted by the UN

General Assembly in 1979. This convention makes headway over earlier human rights conventions by addressing the specific nature of discrimination against women and aiming at 'all forms' of disadvantages women suffer. With ratification, states commit themselves to undertake a number of measures to combat discrimination, such as adopting the principle of equality of men and women in their legal system and establishing institutions to guarantee the protection of women against discrimination by persons, organizations or enterprises. Furthermore, state parties have to submit reports (in the first year after ratification and then every four years) to the United Nations Committee on the Elimination of Discrimination against Women that monitors to what degree nations adopt measures to realize the goals formulated by CEDAW. The committee meets annually to discuss state reports, examines states' compliance with the convention and makes non-binding recommendations on which measures to combat discrimination a state still has to take.[2] As Kevane (2003) has pointed out, if legislatures and executives are not changing the gender policy of a country to conform with the treaty, it may also be the judiciary of a country that brings about change. In certain legal traditions, courts can use and, in fact, have successfully used the very signing of the CEDAW convention as a decisive argument in domestic gender discrimination cases; successful examples concern law suits in India, Tanzania and Zambia.

Similarly to the supervisory system of the CEDAW, the supervisory system of the ILO demands regular reporting of governments (every two years for fundamental conventions like C100 and C111) and includes general complaints procedures as well as dialogues with member nations. The Committee of Experts examines the application of international labour standards in member states and points out areas where they could still be better applied.

Given that the supervisory systems rely on dialogue and the organizations setting the standards have no means to actually enforce them, the CEDAW and the ILO conventions have sometimes been criticized as having no substantial meaning ('no teeth'). Chau and Kanbur (2001), however, demonstrate that the ratification of an ILO convention is not random. The authors conclude that costs of ratification actually do exist and that ratification leads to higher domestic standards.[3] Boockmann (2001) argues that the threat of a loss of international reputation may be sufficient to provide governments with an incentive to comply with conventions or seek agreements with the supervisory organs of the ILO in case of previous non-compliance. To illustrate the effects due to ratification of ILO conventions he refers to Rodrik (1996) and Strang and Chang (1993) who have found significant increases of labour costs and social spending, respectively. Boockmann (2004), however, does not find any evidence that the ratification of ILO child labour standard would influence labour force participation and enrolment in schooling.

---

[2] Despite the achievements of CEDAW (for an overview see Schöpp-Schilling, 1998), the convention has some obvious limitations to its efficiency. For example, it can be ratified with a large number of reservations, which in part are substantial, and there are no sanctions. With the optional protocol, however, the previous handicap that no individual complaints to the committee were allowed, was eliminated in the year 2000.

[3] The ILO labour standards have become prominent in discussions on international trade and trade policies of the World Trade Organization (see Brown, 2001, for a survey). Singh (2001) gives a survey over the vast theoretical literature in the field.

For Anglo-Saxon countries there is an established literature looking at the impact, fairness and adequateness of national equal treatment laws. Neumark and Stock (2001) review and extend the US literature on the impact of equal pay laws by taking state-level anti-discrimination laws into account. They conclude that these laws boosted relative earnings of female workers, but led to a decline of relative employment rates. Gunderson (1994) gives an overview over the effects of national equal treatment laws for Canada, the United Kingdom, Australia and the United States. Obviously, the fundamental differences in national institutions and legislation make an international comparison of national regulations protecting women from discrimination difficult. However, the existence of international conventions, such as the CEDAW and the ILO conventions, which we make use of in this study, allows a comparison of the anti-discriminatory legal stance of a country nevertheless.

3. DATA AND RESEARCH METHOD

The goal of this study now is to test the hypothesis that increased competition as well as the ratification of international conventions designed to combat discrimination reduces the gender wage differential of a country. 'Protective' international conventions, however, that prohibit female employment in certain sectors are expected to increase the gender wage gap. The data for this study comes from our meta-analysis on the gender wage gap (Weichselbaumer and Winter-Ebmer, 2005). Meta-analysis is a helpful tool to cumulate, review and evaluate empirical research. Papers investigating one particular topic are collected and analysed concerning their data and method. Meta-analysis then allows evaluating the effect of different data characteristics and methodologies on the result reported – for example, a regression parameter (Stanley, 2001). Instead of the usual practice of analysing observations of individual workers, in meta-analysis each previously conducted study represents one data point. Meta-regression analysis uses regression techniques to explain these collected parameters by characteristics of the individual study. Meta-analysis is particularly suitable for the examination of gender wage differentials because the literature in this area is very standardized in the way the parameter of interest is usually estimated. As a result, the outcome variable is highly comparable across studies. Furthermore, there is a vast amount of literature available to be included in such a meta-analysis, which gives a large number of data points.

For our meta-analysis on gender wage differentials we collected all accessible published estimates for sex-discrimination. In November 2000 we searched the Economic Literature Index for any reference to: '(wage* or salar* or earning*) and (discrimination or differen*) and (sex or gender)'. This search strategy led to 1541 references; in a first step we excluded theoretical papers. As we were only interested in wage differences that may be due to discrimination between men and women, rather than to productivity differences between specific individuals, among the remaining studies we only retained in our meta-data estimates from papers where authors controlled for differences in productive characteristics of men and women. Such an estimate could simply be a

Box 3. Estimates for wage differentials

The most common way to analyse sex discrimination is to compare male and female earnings holding productivity constant. One method is to simply include a sex dummy in the wage regression model:

$$W_i = \beta X_i + \gamma sex_i + \epsilon_i, \tag{1}$$

where W_i represents the log wage and X_i the control characteristics (e.g. education, job experience, marital status, job characteristics) of an individual i: β and γ are parameters.

However, the standard procedure to investigate differences in wages is the one developed by Blinder (1973) and Oaxaca (1973) which allows for productivity characteristics of men and women to be rewarded differently. Wages are estimated separately for individuals i of the different groups g, males and females:

$$W_{gi} = \beta_g X_{gi} + \epsilon_{gi}, \tag{2}$$

where $g = (m, f)$ represents the two sexes; W_{gi} is the log wage and X_{gi} are the control characteristics of an individual i of group g.

The total wage differential between men and women can then be decomposed into an explained part due to differences in characteristics and an unexplained residual.

The difference in mean wages can be written as:

$$\bar{W}_m - \bar{W}_f = (\bar{X}_m - \bar{X}_f)\hat{\beta}_m + (\hat{\beta}_m - \hat{\beta}_f)\bar{X}_f \equiv E + U, \tag{3}$$

where $\bar{W}_g$ and $\bar{X}_g$ denote the mean log wages and control characteristics of group g and $\hat{\beta}_g$ represents the estimated parameter from Equation (2). While the first term stands for the effect of different productive characteristics (the endowment effect E), the second term represents the unexplained residual U which is due to differences in the estimated coefficients for both groups and is often referred to as 'discrimination effect'. Since the first use in the early 1970s, hundreds of authors have adopted and also extended the Blinder–Oaxaca approach. For our meta-study we included all estimates for log wage differentials, dummies as well as the unexplained gender wage residual U and its derivatives. (For derivatives of the B–O decomposition see e.g. Brown et al., 1980; Reimers, 1983; Cotton, 1988; and Neumark, 1988.) These estimates are taken as the dependent variable in our meta-regression-analysis which we try to explain by the respective papers' data and method characteristics.

sex dummy from a wage regression, which controlled for productive characteristics like education, job-experience etc., or – as in most cases – be the calculated 'discrimination-effect' from a Blinder–Oaxaca wage decomposition (see Box 3). The latter regresses wages of men and women separately and then (in its typical application) calculates the difference between male earnings and the earnings of women with identical characteristics to men.

Since it is never possible to include all potentially relevant productive characteristics when examining gender wage differentials, most authors abstain from the term 'discrimination' when evaluating their empirical results. An employer who has exact knowledge of *all* the relevant productive characteristics of an employee can compare wages to productivity on the basis of such exhaustive information. Conversely, the researcher only has data for a restricted number of productivity indicators. If the omitted variables correlate with sex, then the estimate might capture not only discrimination, but unobserved group differences in productivity as well. In particular, it has been argued that less investment in on-the-job training, less experience, greater time spent on housework and lower occupational attainments of women may be voluntary choices made by women that are not adequately captured in the data and may be responsible for estimated differences in wages that remain after controlling for available productive characteristics. To do justice to this concern,[4] in the following we will not speak of 'estimates for sex-discrimination' but rather *'gender wage residuals'* that remain after controlling for all available productive characteristics. In other words we examine that part of (log) gender wage differentials that is unexplained.

For our meta-data set, in total, 263 papers provided us with the respective estimates for differences in wages of men and women with identical characteristics in 62 countries. The meta-data cover a time span from 1963 to 1997, measured according to the time of the original data set not the publication of the paper.

Many articles included in our meta-data examine different countries and different time periods in one paper. All the estimates for these different units of observation have been included in our data set. Typically authors also present a number of estimates for each country and time unit based on different specifications of the regression model which also have been incorporated as we have no prior of which estimate to pick. Picking one particular estimate from a paper as 'the' right one would be arbitrary; such a procedure would also hamper replication efforts, which are very important for meta-studies. For each estimate all the corresponding data characteristics, econometric specifications and methods were collected and coded. This procedure yields one observation in our meta-data set per reported estimate. In total 1530 estimates for all countries and time units could be included in our study. To deal with the fact that we have several observations per country and period we will later weigh the data appropriately and use a clustering approach in our analysis.

Obviously, the collected estimates are based on different data sets with their specific characteristics; also different methods and specifications have been used to gain the results. However, meta-regression analysis allows evaluating the effect of different data characteristics and econometric methods on the result reported by the use of a

---

[4] See Weichselbaumer and Winter-Ebmer (2006) for a discussion of how authors assess such gender wage differentials and how their rhetoric in the respective papers can be used to analyse underlying attitudes.

simple regression, where the gender wage residual is explained by the characteristics of the concerned study (Stanley, 2001). (See Box 4 for a description of variables used in the meta-regression analysis.) Using this method, we could estimate what each paper would have reported if a standard method and data set had been used and make the results comparable. Figure 1 illustrates our data using country means. The

---

Box 4. A meta-analysis on the gender wage gap

Our meta-regression model takes the form:

$$R_j = \Sigma a_k Z_{kj} + bt + \Sigma d_l c_{lj} + \epsilon_j, \ (j = 1, 2, \ldots J) \ (k = 1, 2, \ldots M) \ (l = 1, 2, \ldots L) \tag{4}$$

where R_j represents the 'gender wage residual', i.e. the unexplained log wage differential, of study j, which can either be the Blinder–Oaxaca unexplained residual U_j from Equation (3) or the coefficient of the gender dummy γ_j in Equation (1), Z_{kj} are the k meta-independent variables, t is a time trend and c_{lj} are a set of country dummies; a_k, b and d_l are parameters to be estimated.

   To extract all the relevant characteristics of a paper and include them in our meta-dataset, we analysed each article just as a typical (qualitative) reviewer would, who reads the papers and makes an assessment based on the reported characteristics of the papers. But unlike a qualitative reviewer, we had to code these characteristics and quantify them. To quantify the characteristics of a study is time-consuming but not conceptually difficult, because any particular feature can be taken up as a dummy variable, at least. As a result, meta-regression analysis allows a more systematic review of a paper than a qualitative review, because it can take all aspects of a published paper simultaneously into account. An important aspect and problem of meta-regression analysis is the reliability of a particular study; an issue to which we will come back later.

   The included meta-independent variables can be grouped into three categories: variables concerning the data selection, variables capturing the applied econometric method and variables that specify the type of control variables which were (not) included in the original wage regressions. Data selection, in our case, refers to the source of the data used (administrative/survey data) and, in particular, which particular fraction of the population (categorized e.g. by age, marital status, place of residence) has been examined. Such data restrictions have a big impact on the measured wage differential, because, in general, wage differentials are much lower for persons in their first job or persons never married. The inclusion of variables concerning the econometric method in the meta-analysis is a first step towards verification and comparison of the sophistication of a study. The control variables used in a particular study again give an indication of how precisely factors such as the human capital of male and female workers have been measured and how dependent, in turn, the calculated gender wage differentials could be on such control variables: e.g. if a study missed to include real job experience, the resulting reported wage differential may be too high.

The meta-independent variables employed in our meta-analysis are: 14 variables for data set selection (e.g. data source (administrative statistics or survey data), data set restrictions to never-married individuals, minorities, etc.), 9 variables for econometric methods (like Blinder–Oaxaca, dummy variable approach, use of instrumental variables, Heckman sample selection or panel data methods), 21 variables for inclusion of specific human capital control variables (e.g. experience, training, tenure, occupation) in the underlying log wage regressions plus a variable for the sex of the researcher, since Stanley and Jarrell (1998) find systematically lower gender wage residuals for female authors.

The strongest and most significant impact on the gender wage gap results from the type of data set used. In comparison to a random sample of the population, the gender wage gap is lower by 8.7 log points if only a sample of new entries in the labour market is investigated. Likewise, the wage gap is lower in the public sector (−6.7 log points) and if only a narrow occupation is studied (−5.0), because in the latter case holding productivity equal is much easier. The wage gap is higher in the sample with only low-prestige occupations (+4.9) and lower for only high-prestige jobs (−12.1) as compared to a sample including all occupations. The wage gap is highest for married employees (+7.6) and significantly lower for singles (−13.3). Among minority workers, the gender wage gap is somewhat smaller (−7.3).

The impact of variables concerning method and inclusion of particular control variables is smaller and less systematic. If a study does not control for marital status this reduces the gender wage gap by 3.8 log points. If the variable tenure is missing the gender wage gap is higher by 4.7 and if the share of females in an occupation is not controlled for, this increases the wage gap by 7.4 log points. All the reported results are significant at the 1% level. Moreover, in our meta-analysis we do not find an effect of the sex of the researcher on the gender wage gap.

See Weichselbaumer and Winter-Ebmer (2005) for a more detailed description and for specification and robustness checks of the same general model that we use here.

left panel gives the relation between the reported total wage gap (i.e. the average wage gap in the original micro data that the researcher used, without any correction for human capital differences) and the reported wage residual (in general, the Blinder–Oaxaca decomposition residual which was calculated in the original research paper). These data show that in most studies the reported wage residual (the discrimination

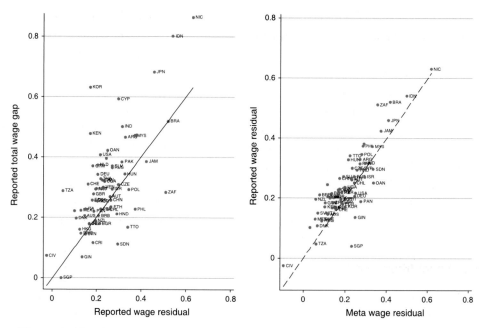

Figure 1. Total wage gap, reported wage residual and meta-wage residual

component) is smaller than the total wage gap between males and females, but there are some countries where women have better human capital endowments than men and therefore the discrimination component is larger than the total gender wage gap. Moreover, we can see that the standard deviation in reported wage residuals, at 0.12, is somewhat lower than that of the total wage gaps, 0.16.

The right panel of Figure 1 shows the relation between the reported gender wage residual and our calculated meta-wage residual which takes into account that all these studies have used different data sets and econometric models. For countries above the 45° line, the applied procedures and/or data of the original studies have led to a comparably high gender wage residual: a 'naïve' reader of these studies would have erroneously assumed that gender wage discrimination in South Africa, Brazil, Hungary or New Zealand was overly large; whereas the opposite applies to countries like Singapore, Guinea or Taiwan. Our meta-analysis does not change the variance in the estimates by country, though. The two parts of the figure illustrate that the biggest step in deriving comparable estimates for wage residuals across space and time is the first one: the decomposition of wage differentials into human capital components and the rest by the original study; harmonizing these estimates by the use of meta-analysis changes the ranking of countries less.

3.1. Competition

Typically in industry studies, four-firm concentration ratios or Herfindahls are used as indicators for competition in an industry. For an economy at large, such measures are not available. Therefore, we use the Index of Economic Freedom assembled by the Fraser Institute, Vancouver (Gwartney *et al.*, various years) to test whether competition does indeed reduce the gender wage gap. This index has the explicit aim to measure economic freedom, which is characterized by a lack of regulation, the lack of government intervention in markets and, generally, a high degree of competition. The index comprises several sub-components: size of government, structure of the economy and the use of markets, price stability, freedom to use alternative currencies, property rights, freedom in international exchange and freedom in financial markets. It also includes the mean tariff rates as a part of the international exchange section. The index has been designed to capture the degree of economic freedom in a society and has been used in many studies to explain development and growth. The index is available for 1970 up to 1999 for every 5 years; we use interpolated values to match our data.[5]

3.2. Equal treatment law

As has been said before, we use the ratification of CEDAW as well as of ILO conventions to test for the effect of equal treatment law on the gender wage gap. Data for the ratification of CEDAW were obtained from Wistat, Women's Indicators and Statistics Database, Version 4, by the United Nations. Since some reservations substantially devalue ratification, these were taken into account in the coding of the corresponding variable. While Article 2 is fundamental to the convention, reservations to other articles are less crucial (see Data appendix for respective coding). Data on ratification of ILO conventions were taken from the ILOLEX web-page.

Data on the ratification of these international conventions as well as mean values of the economic freedom index are presented in Table A1 of the Appendix. We can see here a lot of variation in the ratification time of the respective conventions across countries. Nonetheless, for some countries there is virtually no variation over time which makes a very detailed regional analysis impossible. We will therefore concentrate on the international comparisons – using OLS and fixed effects estimates – and will present some disaggregate estimations in Section 4.4.4.

4. RESULTS

Figure 2 shows that in the raw data, in fact, the hypothesized negative correlation exists between the degree of economic freedom in a country at a point in time and

---

[5] In a previous version we have also applied tariff rates (trade taxes as a percentage of revenues) as a measure for protection from foreign competition using data from Frankel and Rose (2001). This indicator has the disadvantage that its importance and relevance varies by country size, because larger countries typically have a lower share of foreign trade. Moreover, the amount of intra-country competition is totally ignored. Berik *et al.* (2004) use import penetration as a competition indicator in the analysis of gender wage gaps in Korea and Taiwan and fail to find the expected effect which might be due to their flawed competition indicator. Oostendorp (2004) examines the effect of globalization on the occupational gender wage gap by using FDI net inflows and trade (percentage of GDP) in his regression analysis and finds a narrowing impact of globalization on the occupational gender wage gap for low-skill occupations in poorer and richer countries, but for high-skill occupations only in richer countries.

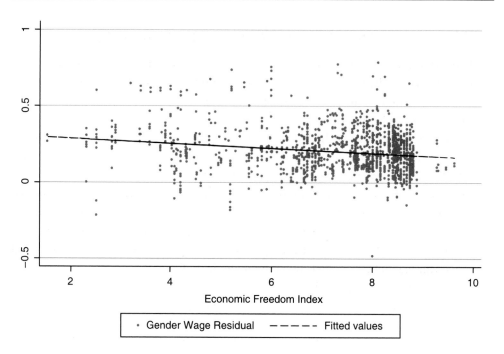

Figure 2. Economic freedom and the gender wage residual

the calculated gender wage residual. To explore this relation more formally, we use the technique of meta-regression analysis. In a first step, we estimate a meta-regression model following Stanley and Jarrell (1998) including a list of variables which characterize the data and econometric technique the authors used as well as a time trend.

To examine whether competition and equal treatment laws can explain gender wage residuals internationally, we extend this simple meta-regression by including variables for competition, equal treatment laws and other country-specific socio-economic factors. As we have several observations per country and period, we weigh the data to give each country-time cell an equal weight. Moreover, a clustering approach along the same dimension is used to correct for possibly downward-biased standard errors. A negative correlation between equal treatment laws and the gender wage residual could also be caused by endogeneity of the political variables. Therefore, in the next section, we use instrumental variables (IV) techniques to control for this problem. Finally, we have to address a major problem of meta-regression-analysis: are all data points equally reliable? So far we treated all data points alike; however, one might want to account for the different quality of the underlying research by using an appropriate weighting scheme. We suggest several such schemes in Section 4.3. Finally, we apply a battery of specification checks concerning the used indicators for competition equal treatment laws and include additional institutional variables to probe the validity of our results.

4.1. The effect of laws and competition on the gender wage gap

As the ratification of the ILO conventions C100 and C111 are strongly collinear (with a correlation coefficient of 0.75), we present results based on C111 only in Table 1 and results based on an 'equal treatment law index' which adds up the ratification of CEDAW, ILO C100 and C111 in Table 2.

The first column in each of these tables presents a base specification, where we include only the meta-regression variables describing the characteristics of the individual gender wage gap study i (i.e., method, data characteristics etc.), our variables for equal treatment law and competition as well as a time trend. In the next two columns we incrementally include other variables, dummies for continents, socio-economic indicators like fertility rate, GDP per capita and female activity rates as well as indicators for the religious composition of the population.[6] In Columns (4) and (5) we run fixed-effects models by additionally including a set of country dummies.

As can be seen from Table 1 we find that countries having signed the CEDAW convention or the ILO convention C111 prohibiting discrimination have significantly

Table 1. The impact of competition and equal treatment laws on the gender wage residual I[a]

	(1)	(2)	(3)	(4)	(5)
CEDAW	−0.054	−0.040	−0.034	−0.040	−0.044
	(0.019)**	(0.024)	(0.014)*	(0.026)	(0.023)
ILO C111	−0.068	−0.082	−0.093	−0.262	−0.239
	(0.023)**	(0.016)**	(0.014)**	(0.042)**	(0.050)**
Work ban index (0–2)	0.036	0.037	0.036	0.064	0.043
	(0.015)*	(0.010)**	(0.014)*	(0.056)	(0.053)
Economic freedom index (0–10)	−0.014	−0.024	−0.027	−0.043	−0.116
	(0.006)*	(0.011)*	(0.011)*	(0.012)**	(0.028)**
(Economic freedom index)^2					0.007
					(0.003)*
Fertility rate		0.004	−0.010	0.012	0.003
		(0.018)	(0.024)	(0.023)	(0.026)
Female activity rate		−0.000	0.000	0.001	−0.001
		(0.001)	(0.001)	(0.004)	(0.004)
GDP per capita		0.000	−0.001	−0.003	−0.004
		(0.002)	(0.002)	(0.004)	(0.003)
Continent fixed effects	No	Yes	Yes	No	No
Religious composition	No	No	Yes	No	No
Country fixed effects	No	No	No	Yes	Yes
Observations	1530	1530	1530	1530	1530
Adjusted R^2	0.38	0.44	0.46	0.59	0.60

Notes: Robust standard errors in parentheses.
[a] All regressions in the tables (except Table 5) also include the variables enumerated in Box 4, including a time trend.
* significant at 5%; ** significant at 1%.

[6] These data are only cross-sectional data relating to the late 1980s and were taken from Sala-i-Martin (1997).

lower gender wage residuals as has been hypothesized. The effects are rather large: signing CEDAW reduces the wage residual by 3–5 log points, signing ILO C111 reduces it by 7–26 log points. Labour standards, on the other hand, that try to protect women by prohibiting women's night and underground work have a counterproductive effect as expected. As these work bans reduce access to jobs for females, they lead to occupational crowding and lower wages: the wage residual rises between 4 and 11 log points if the country signed one 'protective' ILO convention. Also the effect of higher economic freedom goes in the expected direction. A higher rate of economic freedom reduces the gender wage residual significantly; if the country is ranked one point higher in the ten-point scale on economic freedom the gender wage residual drops between 1.4 and 4.4 log points. The standard deviation of economic freedom is 1.7, so observed differences in this indicator have a rather large effect on the gender wage residual. In Column (5) we include a quadratic term and find that the negative effect of economic freedom on discrimination is particularly strong for low levels of economic freedom, and ceases to exist at a value of 8.3 (8.8 in Table 2) of the Economic Freedom Index (the mean of which is 7.2).

Size of government is one component in the construction of the Economic Freedom Index. The larger the government sector, the lower economic freedom. However, previous research has shown consistently that wage differentials in the public sector are lower than those in the private sector of an economy. As a result,

Table 2. The impact of competition and equal treatment laws on the gender wage residual II

	(1)	(2)	(3)	(4)	(5)
Equal treatment law index (0–3)	−0.037	−0.037	−0.044	−0.068	−0.67
	(0.008)**	(0.006)**	(0.006)**	(0.021)**	(0.019)**
Work ban index (0–2)	0.036	0.036	0.031	0.042	0.018
	(0.014)*	(0.010)**	(0.016)	(0.026)	(0.042)
Economic freedom index (0–10)	−0.013	−0.022	−0.027	−0.043	−0.124
	(0.005)*	(0.011)*	(0.015)	(0.011)**	(0.032)**
(Economic freedom index)^2					0.007
					(0.003)**
Fertility rate		0.001	−0.015	0.013	0.003
		(0.016)	(0.023)	(0.024)	(0.027)
Female activity rate		−0.000	0.001	0.002	−0.001
		(0.001)	(0.002)	(0.004)	(0.004)
GDP per capita		0.000	−0.001	−0.004	−0.005
		(0.003)	(0.002)	(0.004)	(0.004)
Continent fixed effects	No	Yes	Yes	No	No
Religious composition	No	No	Yes	No	No
Country fixed effects	No	No	No	Yes	Yes
Observations	1530	1530	1530	1530	1530
Adjusted R^2	0.37	0.43	0.45	0.59	0.60

Notes: Robust standard errors in parentheses.
* significant at 5%; ** significant at 1%.

the quantitative impact of competition is even underestimated by using the Economic Freedom Index, because the impact of public sector employment would go in the opposite direction than that of competition as such.

All measured effects of law and competition are fairly robust across specifications, interestingly the biggest effects for all of these variables can be found in the fixed-effects model. The inclusion of additional socio-economic variables does not change our results considerably. Fertility rates and female participation rates do not seem to influence the gender wage residual once legal issues and economic freedom are controlled for: the coefficients are generally insignificant and their signs change often.[7] Countries with a high proportion of Confucians (which is mainly South Korea and Taiwan) have relatively low gender wage residuals, those with high Muslim and Jewish percentages relatively high gender wage residuals (not shown in the tables).

Table 2 presents the same specifications using the 'equal treatment law index'. The results corroborate the aforementioned conclusions: this composite index always has a significantly negative sign, leaving the other variables practically unchanged.

The evidence so far confirms that countries that ratify international conventions combating discrimination have lower gender wag gaps, that those signing international protective laws have higher gender wage gaps, and that competition decreases gender wage differentials. We now proceed to probe the direction of causality in these correlations and, especially, their robustness. As regards the latter, we investigate issues that are potentially relevant to our meta-data, and we see whether our results hold for different data and specifications, e.g. for different available measures of competition, for the inclusion of potentially missing variables, as well as for different country groups.

4.2. On possible endogeneity of international convention signing

A causal interpretation of the impact of signing an equal treatment law is unwarranted at this stage because ratification may simply measure the predisposition of a country towards gender equality. For example, a country may sign such a law if the gender wage gap is low in the first place because in such a case the 'costs' of signing – in terms of having to change policies involuntarily – would be low. Another potential problem would be that the signing of an international law is domestically not binding and therefore inconsequential. Our measured (negative) coefficients would reflect something else then. Chau and Kanbur (2001) strongly argue that this is not the case and that the signing of such international laws is not costless. Samson and Schindler (1999) also make the case that states, today, do not ratify conventions for 'window-dressing' purposes because they 'are aware that they will be held to account

---

[7] There is an argument that participation rates as well as fertility are endogenous to female wages, which is well taken. However, given focus on the competition and equal treatment laws variables, we cannot go deeper into this issue – finding instruments for these variables for such a large set of countries seems rather impossible. Suffice it to say that results for our variables of interest do not change markedly, whether the control variables are included or not.

through the supervisory system' (p. 214). However, in order to address this issue of causality, we need to find instruments that can predict the signing of such laws, but which do not directly affect the countries' gender wage gaps.

Two different IV strategies will be implemented. Chau and Kanbur (2001) explain the signing of International Labour Standards by – amongst others – peer group effects: 'if our peers do sign this international law, we will also sign'. To implement this idea for each country we use the ratification standard for CEDAW, ILO C100 and C111 of its geographic neighbours. Insofar as the immediate neighbours can proxy peer groups, an impact on the ratification of the international laws should be given. On the other hand, an equal treatment law in the neighbouring country is highly unlikely to influence the gender wage gap in the original country.[8]

The second instrumental strategy uses a state's willingness to bind itself by international treaties: if a state is generally willing to sign international agreements, it may also be more inclined to sign the ILO conventions on equal treatment. As indicators for the willingness to bind oneself internationally, we used the ratification of the other five ILO core conventions on forced labour, freedom of association, the right to organize and minimum working age (C29, C87, C98, C105 and C138).[9] As these conventions have nothing to do with equal treatment of men and women, they should exert no separate influence in the wage gap equations.

Results of the instrumented regressions are reported in Table 3 for the equal treatment law index. The IV regressions shown use the most complete specifications from Table 2, that is, Column (3) including all control variables as well as a fixed-effects approach corresponding to Column (4). The IV procedure does not change the main message: Columns (1) and (2) present results using the neighbouring countries instruments, in Columns (3) and (4) we present results using other ILO conventions. Signing of an international convention reduces the gender wage residual considerably: the more so in the fixed-effects estimates. Whereas endogeneity problems would call for an upward bias in the OLS estimates, high(er) estimates in the IV regressions can be rationalized by a measurement error problem in the OLS regressions with the equal treatment law indicator as we do not measure national laws but only the signing of an international convention. This measurement error will under most circumstances lead to an attenuation effect of the associated coefficients. IV methods will correct for this downward bias as far as the instrument is uncorrelated with the error in the original measurement, which is highly probable. Precision in the fixed effects models is somewhat lower, because of the unbalanced panel aspect of the data: in some countries there are very few observations. The other variables do not change much. Statistics like a marginal R^2 and an F-test for the inclusion of the

[8] An argument could be made that the instrument is invalid, because it falls prey to a missing variables problem: geographical neighbours might share the same *Zeitgeist*, or social attitudes, and therefore a correlation between gender wage gaps in neighbouring countries may exist.

[9] These, together with the two equal treatment conventions and the convention on child labour (C182 in 1999), are considered the eight core ILO conventions.

Table 3. Instrumental variables estimates

Instrument used	(1) Neighbouring countries	(2) Neighbouring countries	(3) Other ILO conventions	(4) Other ILO conventions	(5) Other ILO 'non-union' conventions	(6) Other ILO 'non-union' conventions
Equal treatment law index (0–3)	−0.049 (0.019)*	−0.106 (0.063)	−0.055 (0.011)**	−0.148 (0.028)**	−0.047 (0.015)**	−0.049 (0.078)
Work ban index (0–2)	0.031 (0.016)	0.024 (0.056)	0.031 (0.017)	−0.048 (0.041)	0.031 (0.016)	0.008 (0.057)
Economic freedom index (0–10)	−0.028 (0.016)	−0.045 (0.013)**	−0.030 (0.013)*	−0.034 (0.011)**	−0.028 (0.013)*	−0.032 (0.011)**
Continent fixed effects	Yes	No	Yes	No	Yes	No
Country fixed effect	No	Yes	No	Yes	No	Yes
Marginal R² in first stage	0.052	0.003	0.173	0.019	0.045	0.013
F-test in first stage	95.5	28.4	357.7	321.1	81.2	292.3
Observations	1530	1530	1530	1530	1530	1530
Adjusted R²	0.48	0.62	0.48	0.51	0.48	0.53

Notes: Robust standard errors in parentheses.
* significant at 5%; ** significant at 1%.

instruments in the first stage regression are very big, showing a big influence of the instruments on the endogenous regressors.

Both strategies might be somewhat problematic due to not completely satisfactory exclusion restrictions. Therefore, we use another instrument in Columns (5) and (6), where we use again the propensity of a country to sign other ILO conventions; but we exclude conventions which are related to freedom of association and the right to organize (C87 and C98), because these conventions might be related to unionization, which might also have effects on wages and wage inequality. Using only other ILO conventions (freedom of forced labour and minimum age convention) as more convincing instruments we are able to replicate our results very clearly: in the cross-section as well as the fixed effects specification the results are closer to each other and corroborate the OLS results from Table 2.

4.3. Robustness and problems of meta-regression analysis

Since our analysis is based on a meta-regression, in the following we tackle one potential problem of meta-regression analysis to test for the robustness of our results. A meta-analysis typically covers a large amount of studies of very different quality. Some studies may be methodologically outdated or simply be conducted poorly. While a careful qualitative review might point out such cases – even if only in a very casuistic way, this procedure is impossible within a meta-regression analysis. Hence, one has to find other ways to control the quality of the underlying study. One way is to take the econometric procedure explicitly into account. This has been done in the standard versions of our meta-regression models where we accounted for the major methodological discussions in the literature: we considered whether or not possibly endogenous human capital variables, like work experience, were instrumented in a particular research paper, whether panel data methods were used to control for unobservable individual effects or whether sample selection problems were duly considered. All these methodological subtleties can easily be captured by introducing dummy variables into the meta-regression analysis.

A further possibility is to treat (weight) studies at hand differently according to their assessed quality. So far our analysis has treated all studies found in the literature alike, that is, all data points in our meta-regression analysis get equal weight in the regressions. In Table 4 now, we suggest four different weighting schemes[10] to account for the quality of the underlying studies and to check for robustness of our results. Columns (1)–(4) present the different weighting schemes using all control variables, whereas Columns (5)–(8) additionally use country fixed-effects.

Any researcher in the field of gender wage differentials probably has his or her own priors regarding which studies are good or bad, but for our study we had to look for

---

[10] The proposed weighting schemes are always in addition to the appropriate weighting for time and country which has been used already above.

Table 4. Robustness check using weights for quality of underlying study

Weighting schemes	(1) Journal rank	(2) No. of obs.	(3) No. of regressors	(4) R²	(5) Journal rank	(6) No. of obs.	(7) No. of regressors	(8) R²
Equal treatment law index (0–3)	-0.029	-0.055	-0.053	-0.042	-0.002	-0.035	-0.054	-0.052
	(0.005)**	(0.008)**	(0.006)**	(0.009)**	(0.023)	(0.020)	(0.013)**	(0.022)*
Work ban index (0–2)	0.063	0.063	0.037	0.032	0.007	0.028	0.020	-0.168
	(0.017)**	(0.019)**	(0.017)*	(0.010)**	(0.053)	(0.059)	(0.038)	(0.060)**
Economic freedom index (0–10)	-0.025	-0.014	-0.033	-0.013	-0.013	0.001	-0.036	-0.016
	(0.014)	(0.009)	(0.010)**	(0.013)	(0.016)	(0.009)	(0.014)*	(0.014)
Fertility rate	-0.008	-0.020	-0.020	-0.002	-0.034	0.005	0.012	0.030
	(0.032)	(0.009)*	(0.013)	(0.024)	(0.025)	(0.024)	(0.018)	(0.028)
Female activity rate	-0.004	0.006	-0.000	0.001	-0.008	0.005	-0.002	0.001
	(0.003)	(0.002)**	(0.002)	(0.002)	(0.006)	(0.007)	(0.005)	(0.005)
GDP per capita	-0.002	-0.004	-0.002	-0.002	-0.001	-0.005	-0.004	-0.003
	(0.002)	(0.003)	(0.002)	(0.002)	(0.002)	(0.004)	(0.003)	(0.005)
Continent fixed effects	Yes	Yes	Yes	Yes	No	No	No	No
Religious composition	Yes	Yes	Yes	Yes	No	No	No	No
Country fixed effects	No	No	No	No	Yes	Yes	Yes	Yes
Observations	1530	1223	1530	909	1530	1223	1530	909
Adjusted R²	0.68	0.80	0.52	0.44	0.74	0.84	0.61	0.56

Notes: Robust standard errors in parentheses.
* significant at 5%; ** significant at 1%.

general indicators for 'quality', which are operational and can be replicated. First, we looked at journal quality and applied the citation-based journal rankings from Laband and Piette (1994) as weights (Columns (1) and (5)). This scheme is agnostic about our own priors of study quality, but assumes that the peer-review process does a good gatekeeping job in letting the most reliable studies be published in the best journals. We assigned the lowest weight to non-journal publications like chapters in books or working papers. A drawback of this approach is that non-US and non-UK studies often find it much harder to get access to top-notch international journals. Therefore US and UK studies implicitly get a higher weight in this procedure. Another quality or precision indicator is the number of observations an estimate of the gender wage residual is based on. Consequently, we use sample size in the log wage regressions as a weighting scheme in Columns (2) and (6). Since a higher number of control variables for individual productivity in a wage regression reduces the problem of unobserved heterogeneity, the quality of a gender wage gap estimate should increase with the number of controls used.[11] In Columns (3) and (7), therefore, the number of regressors in the underlying wage equations is used as a weighting scheme. Finally, the coefficient of determination, R^2, is an obvious quality indicator for a wage regression. Therefore in Columns (4) and (8) we use the average R^2 of the male and female wage regressions as weights.[12]

The results in Table 4 present a fairly robust picture and corroborate the afore-mentioned results. With one exception, the effect of equal treatment laws as well as of competition lies within a similar range as in the non-weighted models. The effect of work bans is very consistent compared to the non-weighted scheme; in some specifications it is even higher.

Moreover, meta-analysis is subject to publication bias which occurs when journal editors tend to publish papers with significant results only (see, e.g., Ashenfelter et al., 1999). It can seriously harm meta-regression analysis when studies with low or insignificant results are systematically missing, because the numerical size of the effect will be overestimated. However, for the unexplained residual of the gender wage gap this is less of a problem, since typically no standard errors are reported. While this might be unfortunate for the general quality of this research stream, it reduces the possibilities for publication bias considerably, because both researchers and editors cannot judge a paper according to the statistical significance of the result. Also the sign of the gender wage gap should not cause a 'file drawer problem', as Stanley and Jarrell (1998) have pointed out. According to them, most researchers accept the fact that gender wage differentials exist; therefore a study finding no or reverse discrimination is of particular interest and, as a result, not less likely to be published (Stanley and Jarrell, 1998, p. 954). Stanley (2005) calls 'type II selection' the fact that strong effects,

[11] This approach could have the disadvantage, that some studies use too many or inappropriate control variables, like e.g. professional position, which might be caused by unequal treatment itself.

[12] An obvious candidate for such a weighting scheme would be the standard error of the calculated Blinder--Oaxaca wage differential. However, this is calculated only by Silber and Weber (1999).

no matter in which direction, are more likely to be published, and concludes 'Fortunately, if there is type II selection without any noticeable directional selection, it is
unlikely to materially affect the overall assessment of either conventional narrative
reviews or meta analyses' (Stanley, 2005, p. 319).

Finally, we consider the robustness of the constructed gender wage differential as
such. If one does not trust meta-regression analysis, one may prefer to use original
wage data of the different countries. As there is no internationally comparable data,
e.g. a household survey on wages, available for such a broad spectrum of countries
for such a long time period, one may want to use the original wage data from the
studies underlying the meta-regression instead. Most studies report the aggregate
wage differential of their original data.

In the following, we use these total gender wage differentials, instead of the meta-
residuals, as our dependent variable and regress them on our indicators for competition and equal treatment laws. The sample size is somewhat smaller, because not all
studies report aggregate statistics on the data used. As the studies concern data from
different demographic groups, we use 14 explanatory variables controlling for sample
selection – as in Tables 1–4 – but refrain from including our meta-variables relating
to methods used in the wage regressions in the underlying studies, because we are
only using the raw data here. The results in Table 5 – using raw wage differentials –
show qualitatively very similar effects compared to Table 2, where we used the
Blinder-Oaxaca unexplained meta-residuals. Clearly, these results do not take into
account the problem that raw wage differentials might also arise because of different

**Table 5. Robustness check: The impact of competition and equal treatment laws
on the total wage differential**

	(1)	(2)	(3)	(4)
Equal treatment law index (0–3)	−0.064	−0.053	−0.050	−0.073
	(0.006)**	(0.008)**	(0.006)**	(0.008)**
Work ban index (0–2)	0.030	0.036	0.045	0.005
	(0.010)**	(0.013)*	(0.018)*	(0.016)
Economic freedom index (0–10)	−0.017	−0.021	−0.012	−0.017
	(0.005)**	(0.015)	(0.020)	(0.010)
Fertility rate		−0.001	0.021	−0.016
		(0.014)	(0.021)	(0.009)
Female activity rate		0.001	0.003	0.001
		(0.001)	(0.003)	(0.000)*
GDP per capita		−0.001	−0.001	−0.004
		(0.004)	(0.004)	(0.001)**
Continent fixed effects	No	Yes	Yes	No
Religious composition	No	No	Yes	No
Country fixed effects	No	No	No	Yes
Observations	1202	1202	1202	1202
Adjusted R²	0.39	0.42	0.46	0.65

Notes: Robust standard errors in parentheses.
* significant at 5%; ** significant at 1%.

human capital of males and females. We are therefore not in favour of such a procedure but instead plead for the use of meta-regression analysis; nevertheless it is reassuring that the general tendency of the results is very similar.

4.4. Robustness checks

4.4.1. Different measures of competition.
The Economic Freedom Index, as compiled by the Fraser Institute, is a conglomerate of items which are supposed to capture the main elements of economic freedom in a society, that is, the lack of government intervention in markets in general. It is a weighted average of five sub-components, the sub-components themselves are constructed with several indicators each (38 indicators in total). The indicators are: (1) size of government (expenditures, taxes, tax rates, etc.), (2) legal structure and security of property rights (rule of law, protection of intellectual property, etc.), (3) access to sound money (money supply, inflation, freedom to own foreign currency accounts, etc.), (4) freedom to trade internationally (tariffs, non-tariff trade barriers, capital market controls, etc.) and (5) regulation of credit, labour and business.

Some of these sub-components are directly related to competition on product markets, like property rights and regulation or freedom of international trade, others are not. For example, low inflation rates and low money supply growth rates will have only a second-order effect on the degree of competition in a society, if they have any effect at all. Likewise, the size of the public sector can be seen as neutral with respect to competition as long as higher tax rates do not inhibit the formation of new businesses. However, it is a standard finding that gender wage gaps are generally lower in the public sector. As a result, including the public sector as one indicator of the Economic Freedom Index (a higher public sector contributes negatively to the index), our results may underestimate the negative correlation between economic freedom and gender wage differentials – as has been pointed out before.

In Table 6 we therefore disaggregate the Economic Freedom Index into its components and perform the same analysis as before. In accordance with our expectations we find that the absence of business regulation has the highest impact on gender wage gaps (Column (6)), followed by freedom with respect to international trade (Column (5), not significantly so) and the legal structure/property rights component in Column (3). Interestingly, the access to sound monetary policy (Column (4)) has no measurable impact on the gender wage gap, whereas a higher public sector (Column (2)) reduces the gender wage gap considerably, as expected, because of its predetermined pay scales and more stringent application of equal pay legislation. Column (7) includes all the components of the Economic Freedom Index separately. While the point estimates remain very much the same, their significance levels fall because of multicollinearity of the components.

While the Economic Freedom Index from the Fraser Institute is only an imperfect indicator for competition in product markets, there are no alternative worldwide

Table 6. Different components of the Economic Freedom Index

	(1) Base Economic Freedom Index	(2) Only government size component	(3) Only legal structure and property rights	(4) Only access to sound money	(5) Only freedom to international trade	(6) Only business regulation	(7) All components separately
Equal treatment law index (0–3)	−0.068 (0.021)**	−0.065 (0.018)**	−0.055 (0.014)**	−0.062 (0.020)**	−0.065 (0.019)**	−0.070 (0.017)**	−0.068 (0.017)**
Work ban index (0–2)	0.042 (0.046)	0.032 (0.046)	0.041 (0.055)	0.025 (0.043)	0.038 (0.031)	0.016 (0.044)	0.061 (0.046)
Economic freedom index (0–10)	−0.043 (0.011)**						
– Government size component		−0.023 (0.009)*					−0.015 (0.013)
– Legal structure component			−0.022 (0.008)*				−0.016 (0.009)
– Sound money component				−0.007 (0.007)			−0.005 (0.010)
– Free trade component					−0.029 (0.025)		−0.022 (0.029)
– Business regulation component						−0.042* (0.021)	−0.019 (0.035)
Observations	1530	1518	1489	1518	1502	1506	1483
Adjusted R²	0.59	0.59	0.59	0.59	0.60	0.59	0.59

Notes: Robust standard errors in parentheses, fixed effects estimates, comparable to Column 4 in Table 2.
* significant at 5%; ** significant at 1%.

indicators which are consistently calculated for a longer time period. There are two international indicators focusing explicitly on product market regulation: the OECD Product Market Regulation Index (Nicoletti and Scarpetta, 2003) and the World Bank Doing Business Data Base. Both indicators are available only for a subset of countries and for a much shorter time period. We can therefore use these indicators only in a cross-sectional manner.

The OECD Product Market Regulation Index can be broken down into inward-oriented policies, like state controls and barriers to entrepreneurship, outward-oriented policies – for example, barriers to trade and foreign direct investment – and administrative regulation (Nicoletti and Scarpetta, 2003, pp. 55f.). It is available only from 1998 on. Figure 3 shows the correlation between the different components of the Market Regulation Index and the country mean of the gender wage residual from our data, which is possible only for a set of 20 countries. It shows a consistently positive relation: product market regulation is positively related to the gender wage differential. This applies likewise to inward- and outward-oriented policies as well as for the index of administrative regulation; the strongest relation exists for outward-oriented policies.

The Doing Business Data Base from the World Bank is a benchmark set of indicators for the ease of running and establishing businesses in 155 countries. Unfortunately, the data do not start before 2004 – for some countries even later – which is already outside our data base for the gender wage gaps. Again, we use a graphical tool to see if there is an association between the mean gender wage gap in a country and the ease of running or starting a business there. We have chosen some indicators

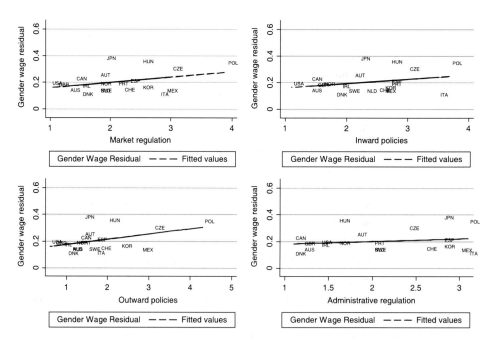

Figure 3. Market regulation and wage residuals

which are related to product market competition to see if our results using the Economic Freedom Index can be corroborated using the World Bank data set. Figure 4 shows that all chosen indicators (of higher regulation) show a positive relation with the country's average gender wage gap: this is true for the costs to start a business, the costs to register property, the rigidity of employment regulation as well as the easiness to import (number of documents required for a typical import); less so for the cost to get a licence or the number of documents required for exports.

These graphical exercises are not entirely convincing; they rely on cross-sections only, no other variables are controlled for and the time periods are not matching. Still, the message from all these different indicators is the same: economies characterized by more regulation in product markets have higher gender wage differentials, which corroborates the results from the Economic Freedom Index.

4.4.2. Lagged impact of equal treatment laws. New laws do not change economic behaviour immediately. This can be particularly so in the case of the ratification of an international convention, which requires a subsequent transformation into national law or other changes at the national level in order to be able to influence pay scales and the like. For this reason we rerun our analysis from Table 2, but use indicators for equal treatment laws which are lagged by 2 years (Table 7). The results are very much the same as those with contemporaneous legal indicators: periods in countries where international equal treatment laws have been in effect for some time are characterized by substantially lower gender wage gaps. The results are very similar if one-year or three-year lags for the laws are used.

4.4.3. Missing variables that might explain gender wage gaps. So far, we have concentrated on the impact of competition and equal treatment laws on the gender wage gap, but have left other important potential influences out of consideration. Blau and Kahn (2003) argue that institutions play a very big role in explaining gender pay differences across countries. They show that general principles of wage formation which will materialize in the form of inequality in a country will also shape wage differentials by gender to a substantial amount. Such institutions consist of union strength, bargaining rules, minimum wages and the like. Insofar as these bargaining institutions are correlated with our variables of interest – competition and equal treatment laws – we have misspecified our regression equations with resulting spurious correlation results.

In Table 8 we include some of these institutional indicators, which is only possible for a subset of our data – mostly OECD countries. Here, general inequality in the economy is captured by male inequality only (the male 50th/10th percentile earnings ratio), because otherwise gender wage differentials would be a part of the explanatory variable thus leading to an endogeneity problem. Moreover, we include union density, an OECD index for the strictness of employment protection as well as an index for wage bargaining centralization.

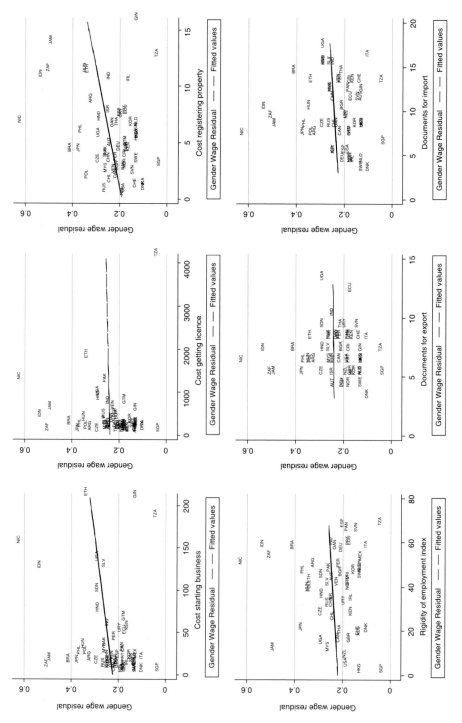

Figure 4. Doing business regulation and wage residuals

Table 7. Lagged impact (2 years) of equal treatment laws

	(1)	(2)	(3)	(4)
Equal treatment law index (0–3)	−0.030	−0.031	−0.038	−0.063
	(0.005)**	(0.004)**	(0.004)**	(0.015)**
Work ban index (0–2)	0.038	0.036	0.034	0.052
	(0.016)*	(0.009)**	(0.016)*	(0.046)
Economic freedom index (0–10)	−0.010	−0.020	−0.023	−0.037
	(0.005)	(0.009)*	(0.010)*	(0.010)**
Fertility rate		−0.000	−0.016	0.001
		(0.015)	(0.021)	(0.024)
Female activity rate		−0.000	0.001	0.001
		(0.001)	(0.002)	(0.004)
GDP per capita		0.000	−0.001	−0.002
		(0.002)	(0.002)	(0.004)
Continent fixed effects	No	Yes	Yes	No
Religious composition	No	No	Yes	No
Country fixed effects	No	No	No	Yes
Observations	1530	1530	1530	1530
Adjusted R^2	0.36	0.42	0.45	0.60

Notes: Robust standard errors in parentheses.
* significant at 5%; ** significant at 1%.

Column (1) in Table 8 replicates our prime results from Table 2 for our restricted sample; results are comparable with exception of the Economic Freedom Index, which is negative but insignificant now, most probably due to the reduced variation in this narrow sample. Unfortunately, this severe restriction of our sample does not allow us to seriously test the hypothesis that the impact of competition is hiding some influence of bargaining institutions. However, including institutional variables does not change our main message about signing international conventions: signing an international convention on equal treatment of females consistently reduces the gender wage gap, both for the OLS as well as for the fixed effects case. The results are less consistent with the work ban index: the effects are very consistent across the OLS specifications, but practically zero for the fixed effects specifications. We assume this is again due to the reduced variation of this variable in the restricted sample.

The results of the institutional variables are according to expectations: general inequality in a country is positively associated with a higher gender wage gap (Column (2)). If we include also union density, employment protection and an index for the centralization of wage bargaining in Column (3), we see that only centralization of wage bargaining has a dampening influence on the gender wage gap, the effect of unionization is economically (and statistically) insignificant, and stricter employment protection even has an increasing effect on gender wage differentials (although not statistically significant). The latter might be due to a well-known phenomenon that marginal groups tend to be hit by employment protection measures the most. Since general inequality can be seen as a product of these institutional regulations, we

Table 8. Other indicators influencing the gender wage residual

	(1) OLS	(2) OLS	(3) OLS	(4) OLS	(5) Fixed effects	(6) Fixed effects	(7) Fixed effects
Equal treatment law index (0–3)	−0.038 (0.009)**	−0.035 (0.009)**	−0.025 (0.013)	−0.014 (0.009)	−0.054 (0.021)*	−0.039 (0.017)*	−0.036 (0.017)*
Work ban index (0–2)	0.042 (0.011)**	0.045 (0.011)**	0.050 (0.032)	0.051 (0.026)	−0.000 (0.043)	0.004 (0.046)	0.001 (0.050)
Economic freedom index (0–10)	−0.001 (0.017)	−0.007 (0.017)	−0.011 (0.027)	−0.009 (0.022)	0.008 (0.025)	0.003 (0.024)	0.016 (0.023)
Male earnings inequality 50th/10th percentile ratio		0.076 (0.025)**	0.054 (0.029)		−0.083 (0.073)	−0.123 (0.052)*	
Union density			−0.002 (0.002)	−0.002 (0.001)		−0.005 (0.003)	−0.003 (0.003)
Strictness of employment protection (0–2)			0.047 (0.025)	0.030 (0.018)		0.043 (0.045)	0.034 (0.042)
Index of wage bargaining centralization			−0.034 (0.013)*	−0.043 (0.019)*		0.011 (0.017)	0.012 (0.019)
Observations	956	956	920	1035	956	920	1035
Adjusted R^2	0.51	0.52	0.56	0.53	0.59	0.60	0.58

Notes: Robust standard errors in parentheses.
* significant at 5%; ** significant at 1%.

produce Column (4), where we leave out general inequality: the results are very similar to Column (3), but the effect of wage bargaining centralization is somewhat larger.[13] It is interesting to see that these well-established effects of wage bargaining institutions do not survive the introduction of country fixed effects; general wage inequality is even (significantly) negative in Columns (5) and (6).

Certainly, there may still be other variables that could be of potential relevance for our analysis but are not available for the long list of countries and time periods included in our study. One example is the provision of daycare facilities in a country. If mothers cannot obtain sufficient daycare, they may be forced to 'buy' more flexible hours in the form of reduced wages from their employers which would not be observable in our data. As a result, flexible hours of women could explain part of the gender wage residual and a provision of more sufficient public daycare could reduce the gender wage gap. It should be noted, though, that McCrate (2005) has found only very small compensating differentials for flexible hours in the United States. Moreover, public daycare does not necessarily reduce the gender wage gap. Indeed, it could encourage female workers with little qualifications to enter the market and thereby increase the wage gap between the genders. Furthermore, the fertility decision of women may be based on the provision of daycare facilities and thereby further complicate the picture. While public daycare is positively correlated with the size of the public sector, included in our freedom index, the effect of daycare on the gender wage residual seems ambiguous.[14]

4.4.4. Effects in different country groups.

Finally, we split our sample into data from Europe, North America and Australia and the rest[15] to see if our relations hold as well in different regions of the world (Table 9). It turns out that the results are fairly robust with the exception of the economic freedom index which only holds for less developed countries: we suspect that this is due to less variation in OECD countries in the economic freedom index, in particular over time. These results also confirm our quadratic effects shown in Tables 1 and 2: economic freedom has the strongest impact the less economic freedom there is. OECD countries already seem to be above the critical level of economic freedom necessary. Case studies like Jolliffe and Campos (2005) for transformation countries find that discrimination has indeed substantially declined during Hungary's transition to a competitive market economy.

5. CONCLUSIONS

In this paper we investigated the effect of competition and equal treatment law on the gender wage residual. For our test we used a new international data set

---

[13] This corresponds with the results by Blau and Kahn (2003) who find an inverse relation between the gender wage gap and male wage inequality as well as a negative effect of collective bargaining coverage.

[14] For a survey on the determinants of motherhood and work status see Del Boca and Locatelli, 2006.

[15] Former communist countries were coded under 'Rest of the World'.

Table 9. Impact in different countries

	(1) All countries	(2) Europe, North America and Australia	(3) Rest of the world
Equal treatment law index (0–3)	−0.037	−0.018	−0.022
	(0.006)**	(0.008)*	(0.014)
Work ban index (0–2)	0.036	0.038	0.052
	(0.010)**	(0.011)**	(0.021)*
Economic freedom index (0–10)	−0.022	0.003	−0.027
	(0.011)*	(0.015)	(0.014)
Observations	1530	1066	464
Adjusted R^2	0.43	0.45	0.48

Notes: Robust standard errors in parentheses.
* significant at 5%; ** significant at 1%.

constructed by meta-analysis which is substantially richer and covers a longer time span than any other data set available. Not only are internationally comparable micro data for a similarly large number of countries non-existent, also national micro data for such a vast number of different countries would not be obtainable or manageable for any individual researcher. Our meta-data consist of all published estimates of previously conducted studies on the national level with the best data locally obtainable. The estimates for the gender wage residuals were made comparable by using all the relevant information on research methods and data quality of the respective study as control variables.

We then used this extensive information to examine the reasons for the gender wage differential on an international level. Do market forces and equal treatment laws successfully combat discrimination? The answer to both of these questions is yes: Countries with a higher economic freedom have a lower gender wage residual than others. This confirms Becker's theory, that increased competition reduces discrimination, and supports the results of recent industry-specific papers at the country-level. Even though the Economic Freedom Index does not aim at measuring Becker's concept of competition, it does approximate the relevant notion of conditions under which market forces are allowed to work more freely in an economy – which we showed to result in lower gender wage residuals.

It also seems that the ratification of international conventions supporting equal treatment of men and women has a strong and significant impact on the gender wage residual. While one might suspect that equal treatment laws are signed by societies with a general tendency towards equal treatment of the sexes, IV estimates – taking care of possible endogeneity of the signing of international conventions – are supporting our conclusion that it is the ratification of anti-discrimination laws which causes equal treatment. It should be noted that our measure of the impact of signing an international convention should not be attributed to the sole impact of such a convention: typically such conventions trigger other national policies which are fostering integration of females in the workforce, such as national equal treatment laws, measures facilitating the compatibility of work and family duties and so on. In an econometric sense, our estimates also cover impacts of induced national policies.

Moreover, another result speaks against the hypothesis that the signing of international conventions is just a consequence of a national stance towards equal treatment rather than being causal for gender wage gaps: whenever a country has signed 'protective conventions' – which were designed to protect women against unpleasant working conditions – gender wage residuals increase. This is exactly what is implied by crowding of female workers in the remaining more pleasant occupations, but is not implied by the alternative hypothesis that societies with a generally women-friendly climate have lower gender wage residuals. The welfare implications of a ratification of these protective conventions are clear. Not only do they reduce job-opportunities of women, they also reduce their earnings. The welfare effects of the conventions prohibiting discrimination are less clear: they decrease the gender wage gap, but may also have negative effects on employment.

In our analysis we applied a battery of specification tests to look at the possible endogeneity of the ratification of conventions, we used different indicators for product market competition, and introduced institutional variables to consider the influence of wage bargaining on gender wage differentials. From the obtained results we conclude that by and large our results hold also under these circumstances. As we have to use internationally comparable indicators for equal treatment laws just as for competition, we cannot go into the details of actual equal treatment or affirmative action legislation and draw conclusions about which kind of implementation of an anti-discrimination law would be better. There is no substitute for a detailed country- or sector-specific study starting from first principles. Nonetheless, we consider our paper to provide complementary and convincing evidence that these laws do matter, either in a direct way by restricting unequal treatment by employers or by setting up and fostering a general climate in a country favourable for gender equality. While there have been some industry studies showing that more competition is detrimental to gender discrimination, our paper is the first to show this relation on a large international scale: it seems that more competition in an economy means more opportunities for females and subsequently less discrimination. However, it should be noted that policies favouring product market competition will not only affect the gender wage gap, but also wages in general, female employment and economic growth. The clearest conclusion concerning women's welfare can be made with respect to paternalistic 'female-protecting' measures. Our results show for the first time that countries that restrict female work in terms of restrictions of time or type of work not only limit women's employment opportunities; crowding women in a limited set of jobs and occupation, also reduces their equilibrium wages.

Discussion

Lans Bovenberg
Tilburg University, CentER, Netspar, and CEPR

I enjoyed studying this paper for a number of reasons. First of all, it employs a very rich data set to explore the gender wage gap. In particular, it employs studies on no less than 62 countries during the extensive time period of 35 years ending in 1997. Another nice aspect of the paper is that it conducts a large number of robustness checks involving econometric methods, explanatory variables, sample size and schemes for weighing the results from various studies.

The paper is also a good application of meta-analysis, which formally summarizes the results from a large number of empirical studies. This is a great service to economic policymakers. As regards policy, the paper considers the impact of both economic and legal institutions on the gender wage gap by considering the effects of both competition and international laws mandating equal treatment of men and women. As it turns out, both competition and legal instruments appear effective in reducing the gender wage gaps. The effects are in fact quite substantial. Signing an international treaty forbidding the discrimination of women and increasing the competition index by one standard deviation can each narrow the wage gap by as much as 7 percentage points. In other words, both lawyers constructing international treaties and economists encouraging competition can help in this respect.

As an economist, however, I should hasten to point out that the study also finds that some legal measures, such as prohibiting women from doing some types of work, is counterproductive in reducing the wage gap. The same holds true for strict employment protection. Hence, the impact of legal measures on the gender wage gap depends very much on the type of measure we are considering.

Theory

The paper starts with a discussion of the theory on the wage gap, starting with Becker's observation that competition will tend to weed out employers with discriminatory tastes. The paper focuses on the effects of competition on the commodity market, but also briefly considers the impact of labour-market imperfections. The theoretical section argues that competition on commodity markets tends to reduce the wage gender gap. Imperfections in the labour market, in contrast, exert ambiguous effects. Search frictions may widen wage gaps, whereas centralized wage setting compressing wage schedules may actually have the opposite effects. This suggests that the devil is often in the detail. To really do justice to relevant international differences in labour-market institutions, one has to explore the specific features of these institutions – something that is beyond the scope of this study.

Another complication in investigating the impact of labour-market institutions on gender discrimination is that institutions may exert different impacts on gender wage gaps, on the one hand, and gender employment gaps, on the other. For example, efficiency wage considerations may boost the wages of women compared to men, but at the same time may cause the equilibrium unemployment rate for women to exceed that of men. This suggests that one should look at gender wage and employment gaps together. The study of Weichselbaumer and Winter-Ebmer considers only gender wage gaps as a dependent variable since this is what the underlying studies report. Nevertheless, it sometimes includes the female activity rate as an explanatory variable in the meta-analysis regressions. The sign in this explanatory variable is not the positive one that one would expect if more abundant female labour supply depresses female wages and increases the wage gap. This does indeed suggest that the wage gap and the employment gap are somehow determined simultaneously.

Also, wage-compressing institutions (such as centralized wage bargaining) may exert opposite effects on the gender wage gap and the gender employment gap. High minimum wages, for example, may contain the gender wage gap but at the same time reduce employment opportunities for women, as only women with high productivity levels find work. In such an environment, the observed gender wage is likely to underestimate gender discrimination. This is because only high productivity women select into employment, so that we do not observe the wages of other women. This may explain why in several European countries observed wage gaps for low-skilled women tend to be smaller than for high-skilled women.

Some legal measures prohibiting gender wage discrimination may face a similar trade-off. If the government prevents employers from paying lower wages to women, these employers may shift the discrimination of women towards other areas – for example, by hiring fewer women. In contrast to legal measures, competition on commodity markets is likely to boost both female wages and female employment. Compared to legal measures, economic measures may thus be more effective in combating gender discrimination. In any case, all this suggests that the gender wage gap studied in the paper is only a partial measure for gender discrimination, and may have to be complemented by data on employment.

Factors behind gender wage residuals

The main body of the paper rightly points out the gender wage residuals computed in the paper do not necessarily indicate discrimination, but may rather measure gender differences in productive features that are observed by the employers but not by the researchers. Married women with children may have to put substantial time and energy into housework, limiting their ability to work long and inflexible hours. Moreover, cultural factors may limit their career orientation. The substantially higher detrimental wage gap for married women compared to single women (of about 20 percentage points) suggests that there may be something in this argument: that non-observed productivity differences may exist that explain the wage gap. In this respect, it would be of interest to know whether women with children suffer large wage penalties.

The gender wage residuals may indicate unobserved differences not only in productivity and human capital but also in preferences for the composition of compensation for work. Women tend to prefer larger fringe benefits in the form of childcare, paid leave benefits or flexible working hours (allowing them to care for sick children or parents). Indeed, women tend to select occupations and sectors that offer these types of benefits. In the Nordic countries, for example, women tend to work more for the public sector, in which powerful unions give priority to high-quality family-friendly schemes and working conditions rather than high wages, while men go for private employment with higher paid jobs.

Whether gender wage residuals are due to discrimination or unobserved heterogeneity determines whether more competition will reduce gender wage residuals. Competition weeds out only discrimination, but not the unobserved differences in human capital. In this context, it is of interest that in a smaller sample with mostly OECD countries more competition (as measured by the freedom index) does not seem to reduce the gender wage residual. This suggests that gender discrimination in these countries is limited, and that most gender wage gaps originate in unobserved differences in productivity and preferences. In this connection, it should be noted that the decrease in gender wage gaps has stagnated during the last 25 years in the Nordic countries. In an environment without discrimination, legal measures may be ineffective or even counterproductive in that they reduce wage gaps at the expense of wider employment gaps. This is one reason why wage gaps should be studied together with employment gaps.

Omitted variables

One measure for unobserved productivity measures between men and women may be policies that help parents combine work and family. Some policies, such as high-quality childcare, may help women to focus more on their career and to work longer, more inflexible hours, thereby enhancing their productivity. Indeed, one of the concerns I have with the paper is that the international treaties prohibiting gender discrimination may pick up some of the impact of these family-friendly policies.

In this respect, it would be of interest in further meta-analysis to include, at least for OECD countries, indicators of family-friendly policies. International treaties might lose some of their significance if these indicators for family-friendly policies were added, and the coefficients for these latter indicators and their various components would be of interest in and of themselves. In particular, compared to paid-leave policies (especially when they last for an extensive period beyond a few months), childcare facilities would be expected to have a larger negative impact on gender wage residuals.

Causality

The neglect of the impact of polices for family-work reconciliation in the meta-analysis brings me to the important issue of causality. The authors interpret the signing of equal treatment laws as the cause of a lower gender wage gap. But is the signing of the law not more the endogenous result of an increased disposition of a country towards gender equality, rather than the cause of a smaller wage gap?

The authors recognize this potential objection and use two alternative instruments for the endogenous signing of international treaties. One is the signing of international laws by neighbouring countries, and the other is a state's willingness to bind itself by other ILO conventions. However, the attitude of neighbouring countries may simply reflect similar cultural trends towards gender equality.

In any case, it is of interest that the IV estimates yield an even stronger impact of the legal variables. This does indeed suggest that the signing of the international treaties imperfectly measures something else, which is better represented by the signing behaviour of neighbouring countries or the signing behaviour of the country itself on other ILO conventions. This other factor may indeed be a cultural trend towards the value of the individual and opposition against discrimination in general. Indeed, as an economist, I have to confess that I am rather sceptical of the impact of legal measures, since the courts can use only verifiable information. I tend to believe much more in the power of implicit, cultural contracts than that of legal, explicit contracts.

At the same time, I must admit that one of the important results in the paper – that legal prohibition of certain occupation choices for women raises the wage gap – is quite strong. This result does indeed suggest that legal measures have a bite and are not simply the endogenous response to wider cultural trends that limit discrimination of women. However, a prohibition of occupation choices may be easier to police (and verify) than an obligation to pay women the same wage as men. Thus, at the end I remain a bit sceptical about the impact of legal measures.

Other econometric issues

Also, other explanatory variables may be endogenous. Market deregulation, for example, may be an endogenous response to a more open attitude towards outsiders. Indeed, economic liberalization tends to go together with cultural liberalization. Hence, market deregulation may pick up some of the impact of these other effects. Controls like the female participation rate and the fertility rate are also likely to be jointly determined with the gender wage gaps.

Another econometric issue is the selection of low-productivity women into non-participation or unemployment in societies with compressed wage differentials. This may cause observed overall wage residuals to understate gender discrimination.

A problem with meta-analysis is that the researcher may want to use several observations from the same study. That is in fact also what the authors do. This violates the assumption in the estimation that observations are independent. The authors may in part deal with that by weighing and clustering observations, but this involves studies pertaining to the same country or time period rather than data points originating in the same study.

Functional forms

The estimations assume that the impact of both competition and legal measures is constant across countries. However, legal measures may be particularly powerful in non-competitive countries in which competition has not weeded out discrimination. Similarly, competition is effective in countries with ineffective legal measures. In other words, the impacts of legal and economic factors are not independent but interact. The empirical result that international treaties have less impact in high quality studies, which tend to involve the competitive economies of the United States and the United Kingdom, are consistent with this.

Conclusion

In conclusion, this paper employs a rich set of data, applies meta-analysis in a nice way, and comes up with important policy conclusions: both competition and legal instruments appear effective in reducing the gender wage gaps. In my role of discussant, I was hard pressed to uncover some of the inevitable weak points of the paper. The gender wage residuals are in my view not a good measure for gender discrimination. In OECD countries, they are rather likely to represent unobserved gender differences in productivity and preferences. This explains why competition seems rather ineffective in these countries. It may also make legal measures counterproductive by harming the employment prospects of women. I remain somewhat sceptical about the causality of the impact of the legal measures. Finally, I would like the authors to study the impact of policy measures reconciling work and family and have them do more robustness tests on interaction effects and the functional form.

This paper uses the techniques of meta-analysis to investigate the role of product market competition and international equal treatment conventions in influencing the residual gender wage gap across a large number of countries. My comments focus mainly on the causal relationship between conventions and the gender wage gap. I suggest that other country characteristics (including time-varying ones) may lie behind both trends in the gender wage gap and the signing or 'denouncing' of international conventions.

Wendy Carlin
University College London and CEPR

In an earlier paper (2005) reporting the basic meta-analysis results, Weichsel-baumer and Winter-Ebmer (henceforth WWE) find that the total wage gap is 0.33

and the residual wage gap – that is, once account has been taken of productive characteristics – is 0.20. For the sample as a whole, the residual wage gap declines very slowly at an annual rate of 0.17%. The United States contributes 40% of the observations to the meta-analysis sample and the residual wage gap there declined by 0.30% (although it did not fall after the mid 1990s). It fell faster (by 0.80%) in Australia, Canada and New Zealand whereas there was no significant trend in Europe or in the less developed countries in the sample (for which the number of observations was small). From the data presented in the current paper, it appears that there is no clear correlation between the residual wage gap and GDP per capita – Nicaragua has the highest gap at 0.63 and Tanzania the lowest at 0.05. Two questions that are not addressed in the paper are whether such a correlation is to be expected and more fundamentally whether the residual wage gap is measuring the same thing in Guinea and Sweden, where there is a gap of 0.14 in each case.

The authors motivate their focus on the role of product market competition and international conventions by reference to Becker's model of discrimination. Employers who have a taste for discrimination, if it is not profitable, would not survive in a competitive market (unless non-discriminating employers are absent). This leaves room for increased competition and direct anti-discrimination regulation or legislation to affect the gender wage gap. The mechanisms through which conventions could affect the wage gap are not spelled out but presumably they could operate either by making bad taste more costly or by directly influencing attitudes.

The use of meta-analysis in their empirical design is an attractive one – there are a very large number of studies of the gender wage gap and meta-analysis raises the prospect of gaining additional insight from combining them. Once the results have been standardized using meta-analysis, the international dimension of the data opens up the possibility of uncovering the role of competition and conventions. WWE report that meta-analysis estimates are different from the reported wage residuals in the papers that form their sample: whereas there is a slight upward trend in wage residuals in the latter, once meta-analysis is applied, a slow decline is revealed. Their results underline the importance of using this technique when studies vary widely especially in terms of sample selection (e.g. a well-known result from gender wage gap studies is that the gap is smaller for 'never married' people, which implies that the comparison of the never married gender wage gap with that from a sample of the population at large will be misleading).

An appealing feature of WWE's empirical strategy is to make use of two types of international convention that have opposite predictions for the gender wage gap. The equal treatment conventions (CEDAW and ILO C111) should reduce the gender wage gap whereas the work ban conventions (ILO C89 and C45), which prevent women from night and underground work, should increase the gender wage gap by restricting the access of women to particular occupations and jobs. They find that these predictions are supported by the data.

Whilst it is plausible that the signing of an international convention could influence behaviour, it seems equally likely that the causality runs in the other direction – or indeed that other more fundamental features of economic or political development lie behind both conventions and the gender wage gap. To explore this a little further, I looked at the work ban conventions. It turns out that the night work convention (C89) was only ever signed in 23 out of the 62 countries in the sample and was subsequently 'denounced' in nearly 50% of the cases of ratification. The underground work convention was denounced in eleven cases. The frequent denunciation of these two conventions suggests that the variation at work in the regression may be picking up the association between a fall in the gender wage gap and the decision to denounce the convention. The causality the authors rely on is that denunciation would open up these activities to women and reduce the gender wage gap. However, it seems equally plausible that the more equal treatment of women (reflected in a narrowing of the gender wage gap) led to pressure to get rid of anomalous discriminatory treaties such as the work ban conventions.

The comments of the Dutch trade unions (CNV) in support of the government's denunciation of the underground working convention (C45) in 1998 are consistent with that alternative interpretation:

> 'The CNV considers that the question is whether such a Convention is still compatible with the General Equal Treatment Act which provides that there must be no discrimination with regard, inter alia, to access to the employment market for men and women except where such discrimination is objectively justified.'[16]

In order to test for possible reverse causality or omitted variables, WWE use IV estimation. They use two instrumental variables for the signing of conventions: the signing by geographical neighbours and the propensity of countries to sign conventions in general. The validity of these instruments depends on their relevance for the signing of the equal treatment and work ban conventions and the absence of a direct channel from the instrumental variables to the gender wage gap. Although the former requirement is easily satisfied, the authors themselves point out that it is difficult to rule out the latter (see footnote 8, for example, and also the discussion in Lans Bovenberg's comment). Moreover, it is not entirely clear how the denunciation of conventions is handled in the first stage regressions. The work ban conventions are not significant in the IV regressions, which may reflect some of these problems. In addition it is rather hard to see that the effect of work bans for night and underground working would in themselves have a sufficiently large influence on labour market behaviour to show up as a determinant of the residual wage gap.

In an empirical study of the determinants of the ratification of international conventions, it appears that both political variables and economic ones that shape

---

[16] See ILO archive CEACR 1996/67th session:

http://webfusion.ilo.org/public/db/standards/normes/appl/index.cfm?lang=EN

political pressures are relevant (Boockmann, 2006). These results are salient to the claim in WWE's paper that they establish causality from the signing of conventions to the gender wage gap. One variable of interest is the share of public sector workers in the economy. In Boockman's study in a fixed effects estimation, this is associated with a higher tendency to sign conventions and it may well have an indirect effect on gender wage gaps (in addition to its direct effect via the narrower gap for public sector workers themselves, which is controlled for in the meta-wage regression). Such political pressures could also lead to the denouncing of restrictive conventions such as those covering underground and night work.

Turning to the second theme of the paper – that competition in the product market reduces gender wage gaps by narrowing the scope for employers to indulge their taste for discrimination – WWE use the Fraser Institute Economic Freedom index as their proxy. More convincing than the use of the aggregate index of economic freedom are the results in Table 6 where the components are analysed individually. These results suggest that better legal structure and property rights and less business regulation lead to a lower gender wage gap, which is in line with the underlying hypothesis. WWE also provide some indicative results for the OECD countries using cross-sectional data. As Boockman's study shows, groups of countries within the OECD differ markedly in their tendency to sign conventions with the sharpest contrast being between the southern European countries (France and Italy) and Scandinavia on the one hand with high rates of ratification and the Anglo-Saxon countries on the other with low rates. Setting aside my doubts about whether conventions do lead to a narrowing of the residual wage gap, there seems to be an interesting opportunity to explore whether competition acts as a substitute for conventions – for example, in the Anglo-Saxon countries. The authors could extend their analysis of competition for the OECD countries by using the OECD's regulatory reform indicators, which are available from 1975 to 2003.

In conclusion, I think the authors are right to emphasize that residual gender wage gaps are not especially informative about the issue of labour market discrimination broadly defined. Employment gaps matter as well. The fact that residual gender wage gaps become very small or even disappear among men and women with similar family roles underlines that the priority for policy is to understand the determinants of women's opportunities for combining work and family.

Panel discussion

Tim Hatton wondered whether the fact that females are more often part-time employed, or not at all employed, is fully accounted for by the paper's data and procedures. Part-time employees tend to earn lower hourly wages, and not only participation rates but also the incidence of part-time work is likely to be affected by gender wage discrimination. Hans-Werner Sinn remarked that while from the economic point of view 'discrimination' occurs when wages deviate from marginal productivity, in policy debates the term is sometimes applied to all sorts of wage differentiation. Some non-economists seem to think that wages should be the same regardless of individual productivity differences, that market mechanisms 'discriminate' against low productivity people. Such views lead to misguided wage equalization policies that, by requiring women or other workers to be paid more than their marginal productivity, reduce their chances to be employed and, ultimately, their welfare.

DATA APPENDIX

- Published papers used in the meta-analysis: http://www.econ.jku.at/weichsel/work/meta_papers.pdf
- Fertility rates, economic activity rates, CEDAW ratification from Wistat, Women's Indicators and Statistics Database, Version 4, United Nations.
- CEDAW (Convention on the Elimination of All Forms of Discrimination against Women). Coding:

CEDAW not ratified:	0
CEDAW ratified, reservation Art. 2:	1
CEDAW ratified, reservation Art. 4, 5, 7, 9, 11, 13, 15, 16:	2
CEDAW ratified, reservation Art. 29(1):	3
CEDAW ratified without reservation:	4

- ILO (International Labour Organization) conventions: data on ratification of ILO conventions from the ILO website: http://webfusion.ilo.org/public/db/standards/normes/

  ILO C100: Equal Remuneration Convention 1951
  ILO C111: Discrimination (Employment and Occupation) Convention 1958
  ILO C45: Underground Work (Women) Convention 1935
  ILO C89: Night Work (Women) Convention 1948
  ILO C29: Forced Labor Convention 1930
  ILO C87: Freedom of Association and Protection of the Right to Organize Convention, 1948
  ILO C98: Right to Organize and Collective Bargaining Convention 1949
  ILO C105: Abolition of Forced Labor Convention 1957
  ILO C138: Minimum Age Convention 1973
- Journal Ranking from Laband and Piette (1994), rankings based on impact adjusted citations per character in 1990, citations to articles published 1985–89.
- Economic Freedom Index Fraser Institute, Gwartney *et al.* (various years).
- Religion from Sala-i-Martin (1997).
- Male earnings inequality, union density, employment protection indicator, index of wage bargaining centralization: OECD Labor market indicators.
- Doing business regulation: World Bank (www.doingbusiness.org).

Table A1. Descriptive statistics on gender wage gaps, economic freedom and equal treatment laws

	Country-code	CEDAW signed	ILO C100 signed	ILO C111 signed	ILO C45 signed	ILO C89 signed	Mean Economic Freedom Index	Mean Gender Wage Residual
Argentina	ARG	1985	1956	1968	1950	Not ratified	3.9 (0)	0.33 (0.04)
Australia	AUS	1983	1974	1973	1953, denounced 1988	Not ratified	7.73 (0.38)	0.14 (0.09)
Austria	AUT	1982	1953	1973	1937	1950, denounced 2001	6.75 (0.13)	0.25 (0.09)
Barbados	BRB	1980	1974	1974	Not ratified	Not ratified	6.0 (0)	0.21 (0.01)
Bolivia	BOL	1990	1973	1977	1973	1973	5.8 (0)	0.38 (0.03)
Brazil	BRA	1984	1957	1965	1938	1957	4.06 (0.63)	0.42 (0.26)
Bulgaria	BGR	1982	1955	1960	1949	Not ratified	4.38 (0)	0.22 (0)
Canada	CAN	1981	1972	1964	1966, denounced 1978	Not ratified	8.14 (0.18)	0.22 (0.11)
Chile	CHL	1989	1971	1971	1946, denounced 1997	Not ratified	6.64 (0)	0.25 (0.15)
China	CHN	1980	1990	2006	1936	Not ratified	4.24 (0.36)	0.25 (0.09)
Colombia	COL	1982	1963	1969	Not ratified	Not ratified	4.84 (0.25)	0.11 (0.04)
Costa Rica	CRI	1986	1960	1962	1960	1960	6.84 (0)	0.18 (0.06)
Cote d'Ivoire	CIV	1995	1961	1961	1961	Not ratified	5.18 (0)	-0.03 (0.13)
Cyprus	CYP	1985	1987	1968	1960	1965, denounced 2001	6.05 (0.35)	0.30 (0.10)
Czech Republic	CZE	1993	1993	1993	1993	1993, denounced 2001	4.96 (0)	0.30 (0)
Denmark	DNK	1983	1960	1960	Not ratified	Not ratified	6.81 (0.46)	0.11 (0.08)
Ecuador	ECU	1981	1957	1962	1954	Not ratified	4.96 (0)	0.18 (0.02)
El Salvador	SLV	1981	2000	1995	Not ratified	Not ratified	5.25 (0.38)	0.27 (0.10)
Ethiopia	ETH	1981	1999	1966	Not ratified	Not ratified	—[a]	0.34 (0.15)
Guatemala	GTM	1982	1961	1960	1960	1952	5.98 (0)	0.18 (0.03)
Guinea	GIN	1982	1967	1960	1966	1966	5.6 (0)	0.14 (0.01)
Honduras	HND	1983	1956	1960	1960	Not ratified	5.96 (0)	0.30 (.)
Hong Kong	HKG	Not ratified	Not ratified	Not ratified	1936, denounced 1998	Not ratified	9.39 (0.14)	0.14 (0.07)
Hungary	HUN	1980	1956	1961	1938	Not ratified	4.86 (0.19)	0.35 (0.09)
India	IND	1993	1958	1960	1938	1950	4.29 (0.23)	0.25 (0.15)
Indonesia	IDN	1984	1958	1999	1950	Not ratified	5.95 (0.80)	0.54 (0.13)
Ireland	IRL	1985	1974	1999	1936, denounced 1988	1952, denounced 1982	6.85 (0.18)	0.17 (0.11)
Israel	ISR	1991	1965	1959	Not ratified	Not ratified	4.39 (0.40)	0.26 (0.07)
Italy	ITA	1985	1956	1963	1952	1952, denounced 1992	7.14 (0.22)	0.11 (0.05)
Jamaica	JAM	1984	1975	1975	Not ratified	Not ratified	5.39 (0.09)	0.50 (0.25)
Japan	JPN	1985	1967	Not ratified	1956	Not ratified	7.47 (0.35)	0.38 (0.15)
Kenya	KEN	1984	2001	2001	1964	1965	4.84 (0.26)	0.17 (0.17)

Table A1. *Continued*

	Country-code	CEDAW signed	ILO C100 signed	ILO C111 signed	ILO C45 signed	ILO C89 signed	Mean Economic Freedom Index	Mean Gender Wage Residual
Malaysia	MYS	1995	1997	Not ratified	1957	Not ratified	7.00 (0.28)	0.27 (0.22)
Mexico	MEX	1981	1952	1961	1938	Not ratified	6.06 (0.71)	0.13 (0.11)
Netherlands	NLD	1991	1971	1973	1937, denounced 1998	1954, denounced 1972	7.91 (0.08)	0.14 (0.11)
New Zealand	NZL	1985	1983	1983	1938, denounced 1987	1950, denounced 1981	8.4 (0)	0.20 (0)
Nicaragua	NIC	1981	1967	1967	1976	Not ratified	5.98 (0)	0.63 (0.12)
Norway	NOR	1981	1959	1959	Not ratified	Not ratified	7.52 (0.32)	0.18 (0.08)
Pakistan	PAK	1996	2001	1961	1938	1951	3.7 (0.61)	0.27 (0.13)
Panama	PAN	1981	1958	1966	1959	1970	6.92 (0)	0.19 (0.00)
Peru	PER	1982	1960	1970	1945, denounced 1997	Not ratified	2.78 (0.64)	0.22 (0.17)
Philippines	PHL	1981	1953	1960	Not ratified	1953	5.12 (0.28)	0.37 (0.07)
Poland	POL	1980	1954	1961	1957	Not ratified	5.28 (0)	0.35 (0)
Portugal	PRT	1980	1967	1959	1937	1964, denounced 1992	6.11 (0.27)	0.18 (0.08)
Russia	RUS	1981	1956	1961	1961	Not ratified	3.40 (1.03)	0.27 (0.10)
Singapore	SGP	1995	2002	Not ratified	1965	Not ratified	8.88 (0)	0.04 (0.10)
Slovenia	SVN	1992	1992	1992	1992	1992	—	0.15 (0.)
South Africa	ZAF	1995	2000	1997	1936	1950	5.9 (0)	0.51 (0.22)
South Korea	KOR	1984	1997	1998	Not ratified	Not ratified	6.02 (0.29)	0.16 (0.10)
Spain	ESP	1984	1967	1967	1958	1958, denounced 1992	6.44 (0.14)	0.21 (0.08)
Sudan	SDN	Not ratified	1970	1970	Not ratified	Not ratified	0 (0)	0.30 (0.27)
Sweden	SWE	1980	1962	1962	1936, denounced 1967	Not ratified	6.48 (0.72)	0.14 (0.06)
Switzerland	CHE	1997	1972	1961	1940	1950, denounced 1992	8.37 (0.09)	0.14 (0.10)
Taiwan	OAN		Not ratified	Not ratified	Not ratified	Not ratified	7.07 (0.28)	0.24 (0.12)
Tanzania	TZA	1985	2002	2002	1962	Not ratified	4.14 (0.06)	0.05 (0.09)
Thailand	THA	1985	1999	Not ratified	Not ratified	Not ratified	6.14 (0.39)	0.22 (0.03)
Trinidad & Tobago	TTO	1990	1997	1970	Not ratified	Not ratified	6.54 (0)	0.34 (0.04)
Uganda	UGA	1985	2005	2005	1963	Not ratified	3.87 (0.49)	0.30 (0.10)
UK	GBR	1986	1971	1999	1936, denounced 1988	Not ratified	7.47 (0.88)	0.18 (0.13)
Uruguay	URY	1981	1989	1989	1954, denounced 1978	1954, denounced 1982	6.74 (0)	0.20 (0.03)
USA	USA	Not ratified	Not ratified	Not ratified	Not ratified	Not ratified	8.39 (0.34)	0.19 (0.13)
Venezuela	VEN	1983	1982	1971	1944	Not ratified	5.86 (0.09)	0.23 (0.01)
West Germany	DEU	1985	1956	1961	1954	Not ratified	7.78 (0.17)	0.22 (0.11)

^a For Ethiopia and Slovenia, no Economic Freedom Index was available; we introduced 'missing variable dummies' to control for this.

REFERENCES

Altonji, J.G. and R.M. Blank (1999). 'Race and gender in the labor market', in O. Ashenfelter and D. Card (eds.), *Handbook of Labor Economics*, Vol. 3, North-Holland, Amsterdam, 3143–259.

Arrow, K.J. (1980). 'Models of job discrimination', in A.B. Atkinson (ed.), *Wealth and Income Inequality*, Oxford University Press, Oxford [1971], 389–407.

Ashenfelter, O., C. Harmon and H. Oosterbeek (1999). 'A review of estimates of the schooling/earnings relationship, with tests for publication bias', *Labour Economics*, 6(4), 453–70.

Ashenfelter, O. and T. Hannan (1986). 'Sex discrimination and product market competition: The case of the banking industry', *Quarterly Journal of Economics*, 101(1), 149–73.

Azmat, G., M. Güell and A. Manning (2006). 'Gender gaps in unemployment rates in OECD countries', *Journal of Labor Economics*, 24(1), 1–37.

Basu, K. and A.J. Felkey (2005). 'A theory of efficiency wage with multiple unemployment equilibria: How a higher minimum wage can curb unemployment', Working Paper, Cornell University.

Basu, K., H. Horn, L. Román and J. Shapiro (eds.) (2003). International Labor Standards, Blackwell Publishing, Malden and Oxford, 2003.

Becker, G.S. (1957). *The Economics of Discrimination*, University of Chicago Press, Chicago.

Berik, G., Y. van der Meulen Rodgers and J.E. Zveglich, Jr (2004). 'Does trade promote gender wage equity? Evidence from East Asia', *Review of Development Economics*, 8(2), 237–54.

Bertola, G., F.D. Blau and L.M. Kahn (2005). 'Labor market institutions and demographic employment patterns', mimeo, Università di Torino.

Black, D. (1995). 'Discrimination in an equilibrium search model', *Journal of Labor Economics*, 13(2), 309–34.

Black, S. and E. Brainerd (2004). 'Importing equality? The effects of increased competition on the gender wage gap', *Industrial and Labor Relations Review*, 57(4), 540–59.

Black, S. and P.E. Strahan (2001). 'The division of spoils: Rent-sharing and discrimination in a regulated industry', *American Economic Review*, 91(4), 814–31.

Blau, F.D. and L.M. Kahn (1992). The Gender Earnings Gap: Learning from International Comparisons, American Economic Review, Papers and Proceedings, 82/2, 1992, 533–38.

— (1996). 'Wage structure and gender earnings differentials: An international comparison', *Economica*, 63(250), Suppl. S29–62.

— (1997). 'Swimming upstream: Trends in the gender wage differential in the 1980s', *Journal of Labor Economics*, 15(1), 1–42.

— (2003). 'Understanding international differences in the gender pay gap', *Journal of Labor Economics*, 21(1), 106–44.

— (2004). 'The US gender gap in the 1990s: Slowing convergence', NBER-Working Paper.

Blinder, A.S. (1973). 'Wage discrimination: Reduced form and structural estimates', *Journal of Human Resources*, 8(4), 436–55.

Boockmann, B. (2001). 'The ratification of ILO conventions: A hazard rate approach', *Economics and Politics*, 13, 281–309.

— (2004). 'The effect of ILO minimum age conventions on child labour and school attendance', ZEW Discussion Paper 04-52.

— (2006). 'Partisan politics and treaty ratification: The acceptance of International Labour Organisation conventions by industrialised democracies', *European Journal of Political Research*, 45, 153–80.

Bowlus, A.J. and Z. Eckstein (2002). 'Discrimination and skill differences in an equilibrium search model', *International Economic Review*, 43(4), 1309–45.

Brown, D.K. (2001). 'Labor standards: Where do they belong on the international trade agenda?', *Journal of Economic Perspectives*, 15(3), 89–112.

Brown, R.S., M. Moon and B.S. Zoloth (1980). 'Incorporating occupational attainment in studies of male-female earnings differentials', *Journal of Human Resources*, 40(1), 3–28.

Chang, M.L. (2000). 'The evolution of sex segregation regimes', *American Journal of Sociology*, 105(6), 1658–701.

Chau, N.H. and R. Kanbur (2001). 'The adoption of labour standards conventions: Who, when and why?', CEPR Discussion Paper No. 2904, London.

Cotton, J. (1988). 'On the Decomposition of Wage Differentials', *Review of Economics and Statistics*, 70(2), 236–43.

Del Boca, D. and M. Locatelli (2006). 'The determinants of motherhood and work status: A survey', IZA Discussion Paper No. 2414.

Edgeworth, F. (1922). 'Equal pay to men and women for equal work', *Economic Journal*, 32(128), 431–57.

Engerman, S.L. (2003). 'The history and political economy of international labor standards', in K. Basu *et al.* (eds.), *International Labor Standards*, Blackwell, Oxford, 9–83.

Frankel, J. and A. Rose (2001). 'An estimate of the effect of common currencies on trade and income', mimeo, Haas School of Business, Berkeley.

Gneezy, U. and A. Rustichini (2004). 'Gender and competition at a young age', *American Economic Review*, 94(2), 377–81.

Gneezy, U., M. Niederle and A. Rustichini (2003). 'Performance in competitive environments: Gender differences', *Quarterly Journal of Economics*, 118(3), 1049–74.

Goldberg, M.S. (1982). 'Discrimination, nepotism, and long-run wage differentials', *Quarterly Journal of Economics*, 97(2), 307–19.

Gunderson, M. (1994). *Comparable Worth and Gender Discrimination: An International Perspective*, International Labour Office, Geneva and Washington, DC.

—— (2006). 'Viewpoint: Male-female wage differentials: How can that be?', *Canadian Journal of Economics*, 39(1), 1–21.

Gwartney, J., R. Lawson, W. Park and C. Skipton (various years). *Economic Freedom of the World*, Fraser Institute, Vancouver, BC.

Heckman, J.J. (1998). 'Detecting discrimination', *The Journal of Economic Perspectives*, 12(2), 101–16.

Hellerstein, J.K., D. Neumark and K.R. Troske (2002). 'Market forces and sex discrimination', *Journal of Human Resources*, 28(2), 353–80.

Holzer, H.J. and K.R. Ihlanfeldt (2001). 'Customer discrimination and employment outcomes for minority workers', *Quarterly Journal of Economics*, 113(3), 835–67.

Jolliffe, D. and N.F. Campos (2005). 'Does market liberalisation reduce gender discrimination? Econometric evidence from Hungary, 1986–1998', *Labour Economics*, 12(1), 1–22.

Kahn, L.M. (1991). 'Discrimination in professional sports: A survey of the literature', *Industrial and Labor Relations Review*, 44(3), 395–418.

Kevane, M. (2003). 'Ratification of CEDAW (Convention for the Elimination of Discrimination Against Women)', mimeo, Santa Clara University.

Laband, D.N. and M.J. Piette (1994). 'The relative impacts of economics journals: 1970–1990', *Journal of Economic Literature*, 32(2), 640–67.

McCrate, E. (2005). 'Flexible hours, workplace authority, and compensating wage differentials in the US', *Feminist Economics*, 11(1), 11–39.

Mulligan, C.B. and Y. Rubinstein (2005). 'Selection, investment, and women's relative wages since 1975', NBER Working Paper 11159.

Neumark, D. (1988). 'Employers' discriminatory behavior and the estimation of wage discrimination', *Journal of Human Resources*, 23(3), 279–95.

Neumark, D. and W.A. Stock (2001). 'The effects of race and sex discrimination laws', NBER Working Paper 8215.

Nicoletti, G. and S. Scarpetta (2003). 'Regulation, productivity and growth: OECD evidence', *Economic Policy*, 36, 9–72.

Niederle, M. and L. Vesterlund (2005). 'Do women shy away from competition? Do men compete too much?', NBER Working Paper 11474.

Oaxaca, R. (1973). 'Male-female wage differentials in urban labor markets', *International Economic Review*, 14(3), 693–709.

Olivetti, C. and B. Petrongolo (2006). 'Unequal employment? A cross-country analysis of gender gaps', IZA-Discussion Paper 1941.

Oostendorp, R.H. (2004). 'Globalization and the gender wage gap', World Bank Policy Research Working Paper 3256, April.

Reimers, C.W. (1983). 'Labor market discrimination against Hispanic and black men', *Review of Economics and Statistics*, 65(4), 570–79.

Rodrik, D. (1996). 'Labor standards in international trade: Do they matter and what do we do about them?' in R.Z. Lawrence, D. Rodrik and J. Whalley (eds.), *Emerging Agenda for Global Trade: High Stakes for Developing Countries*, The Johns Hopkins University Press, Baltimore, 35–80.

Rosén, A. (2003). 'Search, bargaining, and employer discrimination', *Journal of Labor Economics*, 21(4), 807–29.

Sala-i-Martin, X. (1997). 'I just ran two million regressions', *American Economic Review Papers and Proceedings*, 87(2), 178–83.

Samson, K. and K. Schindler (1999). 'The standard-setting and supervisory system of the ILO', in R. Hanski and M. Suksi (eds.), *An Introduction to the International Protection of Human Rights*, Abo Akademie University, Turku/Abo, 185–216.

Schöpp-Schilling, H.B. (1998). 'Das Frauenrechtsübereinkommen – ein wirksames Instrument für die weltweite Gleichberechtigung und Gleichstellung von Frauen?', in G. Baum, E. Riedel and M. Schaefer (eds.), *Menschenrechtsschutz in der Praxis der Vereinten Nationen*, Nomos, Baden-Baden, 15–65.

Schwieren, C. (2003). 'The gender wage gap – due to differences in efficiency wages or discrimination?', Working Paper, Universiteit Maastricht.

Silber, J. and M. Weber (1999). 'Labor market discrimination: Are there significant differences between the various decomposition procedures?', *Applied Economics*, 31, 359–65.

Singh, N. (2001). 'The impact of international labor standards: A survey of economic theory', Working Paper, University of California, Santa Cruz.

Stanley, T.D. (2001). 'Wheat from chaff: Meta-analysis as quantitative literature review', *Journal of Economic Perspectives*, 15(3), 131–50.

— (2005). 'Beyond publication bias', *Journal of Economic Surveys*, 19(3), 309–46.

Stanley, T.D. and S.B. Jarrell (1998). 'Gender wage discrimination bias? A meta-regression analysis', *Journal of Human Resources*, 33(4), 947–73.

Strang, D. and P.M.Y. Chang (1993). 'The International Labor Organization and the welfare state: Institutional effects on national welfare spending, 1960–1980', *International Organization*, 47(2), 235–62.

Weichselbaumer, D. and R. Winter-Ebmer (2005). 'A meta-analysis on the international gender wage gap', *Journal of Economic Surveys*, 19(3), 479–511.

— (2006). 'Rhetoric in economic research: The case of gender wage differentials', *Industrial Relations*, 45, 416–36.

Winter-Ebmer, R. (1995). 'Sex discrimination and competition in product and labor markets', *Applied Economics*, 27, 849–57.

WTO agricultural reforms

SUMMARY

Rich countries' agricultural trade policies are the battleground on which the future of the WTO's troubled Doha Round will be determined. Subject to widespread criticism, they nonetheless appear to be almost immune to serious reform, and one of their most common defences is that they protect poor farmers. Our findings reject this claim. The analysis conducted here uses detailed data on farm incomes to show that major commodity programmes are highly regressive in the US, and that the only serious losses under trade reform are among large, wealthy farmers in a few heavily protected sub-sectors. In contrast, analysis using household data from 15 developing countries indicates that reforming rich countries' agricultural trade policies would lift large numbers of developing country farm households out of poverty. In the majority of cases these gains are not outweighed by the poverty-increasing effects of higher food prices among other households. Agricultural reforms that appear feasible, even under an ambitious Doha Round, achieve only a fraction of the benefits for developing countries that full liberalization promises, but protect the wealthiest US farms from most of the rigors of adjustment. Finally, the analysis conducted here indicates that maximal trade-led poverty reductions occur when developing countries participate more fully in agricultural trade liberalization.

— *Thomas W. Hertel, Roman Keeney, Maros Ivanic and L. Alan Winters*

Economic Policy April 2007 Printed in Great Britain
© CEPR, CES, MSH, 2007.

Distributional effects of WTO agricultural reforms in rich and poor countries

Thomas W. Hertel, Roman Keeney, Maros Ivanic and L. Alan Winters

Purdue University; Doha; World Bank

1. INTRODUCTION

'Trade theory is about whose hand is in whose pocket and trade policy is about who should take it out.' (Finger, 1981)

This paper is about some well-known hands in well-known pockets but in new combinations and at a level of detail that has not previously been possible. For the first time it considers the trade-offs in global agricultural trade reform between farmers in rich and poor countries making use of farm-level and household-level data. It delves further into the distributional consequences of reform than previous research and in doing so lays bare some of the political economy that has made agricultural trade reform so tortured.

A common apology for preserving agricultural support is that it supports low income farmers in the North and that liberalization would benefit only the rich land

This article is a revision of the paper prepared for the 44th Panel Meeting of *Economic Policy*, Helsinki, Finland, 20–21 October 2006. The authors thank Gilles Duranton, Philippe Martin, Reinhilde Veugelers and other members of the Panel for valuable comments and suggestions. Annexes are available from: www.economic-policy.org

The Managing Editor in charge of this paper was Philippe Martin.

Economic Policy April 2007 pp. 289–337 Printed in Great Britain
© CEPR, CES, MSH, 2007.

owners in the South. While these assertions contain a few grains of truth, this paper shows that the net effects are the very opposite: it is the wealthiest of rich country farmers who predominantly gain from protection and farm households in poor countries who pay the price.

The Doha Development Agenda (DDA) of the World Trade Organization (WTO), which is in the process of being restarted after its collapse in mid-2006, has an explicit mandate to improve welfare and reduce poverty in developing countries (WTO, 2004). The bulk of the global gains from merchandise trade reform derive from reforms in agriculture (Hertel and Keeney, 2006; Anderson and Martin, 2006), and most of these gains are predicted to accrue to rich countries as they reduce outlays on farm programmes and reduce protection for agricultural products. But such reforms also benefit many households in developing countries – particularly those in the farm and rural sectors, which comprise a majority of the world's poor – so it would seem that such reforms should be an easy sell to policy-makers in rich and poor countries alike. Experience suggests the opposite.

While agricultural reforms in industrial countries are indeed likely to benefit large and diffuse groups of taxpayers and consumers, they will hurt some of the farm sector – with the impact concentrated on some of the most powerful and well-organized interest groups in that sector. By contrast, farmers in developing countries – the potential beneficiaries of reform – have little or no influence in the political process, while their urban counterparts have some interest in maintaining the status quo.

The political economy of trade policy has long recognized the greater effectiveness of concentrated lobbies – see, for example, Winters (1987) or Anderson (1995) and Orden *et al.* (1999) on agriculture – and 70 years ago Schattschneider (1935) recognized that one needs to evaluate such concentration at a fine level of disaggregation. Thus, in this paper we argue that the interesting issue in agricultural reform is not the potential global welfare gains, although these can be substantial (Anderson *et al.*, 2006), but rather, the medium run (2–3 years) *distribution* of the benefits and costs of reform across households in rich and poor countries. Given the ambition of this exercise, we can consider only the United States among rich countries, and 15 developing countries for which we can assemble household survey data on income sources on a relatively uniform basis.

While we are interested in the impacts of agricultural reforms previously deemed possible under the DDA, we also want to advance the policy-making agenda and so devote considerable attention to reforms that are not currently under consideration. Notably, we consider greater-than-Doha liberalization by developed and developing countries, which turns out to be pro-poor – and some compensation mechanisms which might reduce rich country opposition to agricultural trade reforms. There is a tendency at present to doubt that the WTO could ever deliver the sorts of reforms we discuss here. The immediate prospects are not auspicious, but we do not entirely despair for the longer run. Moreover, we believe that if developing countries cannot collectively persuade developed countries to reform agriculture in the context of the

WTO, they certainly will not be able to do so in the context of bilateral negotiations for regional trade arrangements such as are currently absorbing so much effort around the world.

This analysis contains four key steps: the specification of a plausible DDA agreement including its translation into cuts in actual agricultural support; calculating the impacts of such reforms on global trade, prices and production; tracing these global impacts back to different classes of farm households within the United States; and tracing them back to households in our focus developing countries. The combination of these steps into a holistic framework represents a significant contribution of this work, which brings together data and modelling components to conduct global scale analysis.[1]

1.1. DDA specification

There have been many studies of WTO trade reforms in the context of the DDA, but few of these bear close relationship to the actual negotiations undertaken in Geneva or to actual trade barriers in the world at the time the DDA will be implemented. In contrast, recent studies based mostly on the GTAP 6 database, recognize the significance of trade preferences for developing countries' exports (Bchir *et al.*, 2005; Bouët *et al.*, 2004) and also that the DDA will be implemented in a world where China has acceded to the WTO and the EU has been enlarged.[2] This is the approach taken here. We build on two recent World Bank projects which begin with tariff line data and specify agricultural market access scenarios based on detailed analysis of tiered formula cuts in current levels of tariff bindings (Anderson *et al.*, 2006b; Hertel and Winters, 2006). In cases where post-reform bindings fall below currently applied tariff levels, liberalization is predicted to occur. If this is not the case, no actual liberalization occurs despite the reduction in tariff bindings. This detailed analysis is particularly critical for analyzing developing countries, where bound tariffs are high and reductions in these bindings are modest due to special and differential treatment (Jean *et al.*, 2006). Similar detail is necessary for prospective reductions in domestic support (Jensen and Zobbe, 2006).

Given a set of plausible liberalizations, we need to translate these into a set of changes in prices, outputs, inputs, etc. around the world. Since reforms are widespread sectorally and geographically, this requires a global, multi-sectoral, general equilibrium approach as epitomized in global computable general equilibrium (CGE) models. Many such models have been used to analyze trade reforms, each emphasizing different features according to the authors' purpose. Box 1 offers a brief introduction to the essential features of CGE analysis.

---

[1] We also offer modest methodological advances on the previous literature in two of the four steps.

[2] Studies dated prior to 2004 typically miss these features.

Box 1. Computable general equilibrium (CGE) modelling

General equilibrium, which dates back to Leon Walras (1834–1910), is one of the crowning intellectual achievements of economics. It recognizes that there are many markets and that they interact in complex ways so that, loosely speaking, everything depends on everything else. Demand for any one good depends on the prices of all other goods and on income. Income, in turn, depends on wages, profits and rents, which depend on technology, factor supplies and production, the last of which, in its turn, depends on sales (i.e., demand). Prices depend on wages and profits and vice versa.

To make such an insight useful, economists have to be able to simplify it sufficiently to derive predictions and conclusions. Theorists typically do this by slashing the dimensionality, say, to just two goods, two factors and two countries, and often focusing on just a few parts of the system. An alternative approach is to keep the complex structure but to simplify the characterization of economic behaviour and solve the whole system numerically rather than algebraically. This is the approach of computable general equilibrium (CGE) modelling.

CGE models specify all their economic relationships in mathematical terms and put them together in a form that allows the model to predict the change in variables such as prices, output and economic welfare resulting from a change in economic policies, given information about technology (the inputs required to produce a unit of output), policies and consumer preferences. They do this by seeking prices at which supply equals demand in every market – goods, factors, foreign exchange. One of the great strengths of CGE models is that they impose consistency on one's view of the world, e.g., that all exports are imported by another country, that the sum of sectors' employment does not exceed the labour force, or that all consumption be covered by production or imports. This consistency can often generate empirical insights that might otherwise be overlooked in complex policy analysis – such as the fact that import protection gives rise to an implicit tax on exports.

The mathematical relationships assumed are generally rather simple, and although 'many' markets are recognized, they still have to be very aggregated – particularly for global economic analysis. For example, the global CGE model used in this paper has 31 sectors, so, for example, 'transport and communications services' appear as a single industry. In principle, all the relationships in a model could be estimated from detailed data on the economy over many years. In practice, however, their number and parameterization generally outweigh the data available. In the model used for this paper, only the most important relationships have been econometrically estimated. These include the international trade elasticities (Hertel *et al.*, 2005), the agricultural factor supply and demand elasticities (OECD, 2001), and consumer preferences (estimated specially for this paper, based on the methods outlined in Cranfield *et al.*, 2003 and Reimer and Hertel, 2004). The remaining economic relationships are based on literature reviews, with a healthy dose of theory and intuition. An important limitation of CGE models is that very few of them are tested as a whole against historical experience – although ours is one such (Valenzuela *et al.*, 2007; Liu *et al.*, 2004).

Having specified most of the relationships, the CGE modeller manipulates a subset of parameters so that the model will replicate detailed data for one 'base' year – this is known as 'calibration'. To calculate the effects of a policy change the model is solved once without the change and once with it in an otherwise identical universe and the difference in outcome calculated. Often the 'without' scenario is just the database year, although in our case we project key features of the global economic policy environment economy forward to 2005 in order to facilitate our analysis of the Doha Round.

In summary, CGE modelling is a very powerful tool, allowing economists to explore numerically a huge range of issues on which econometric estimation would be impossible; in particular to forecast the effects of future policy changes. The models have their limitations, however. First, CGE simulations are not unconditional predictions but rather 'thought experiments' about what the world would be like if the policy change had been operative in the assumed circumstances and year. The real world will doubtless have changed by the time we get there. Second, while CGE models are quantitative, they are not empirical in the sense of econometric modelling: they are basically theoretical, with limited possibilities for rigorous testing against experience. Third, conclusions about trade policy are very sensitive to the levels assumed for trade restrictions in the base data. One can readily do sensitivity analysis on the parameter values assumed for economic behaviour (as we have done in this paper), but less so on the data because altering one element of the base data requires compensating changes elsewhere in order to keep the national accounts and social accounting matrix in balance. Of course, many of these criticisms apply to other types of economic modelling and, therefore, while imperfect, CGE models remain the preferred tool for analysis of global trade policy issues.

1.2. Distributional impacts for US farm households

US farm household data are taken from the Agricultural Resource Management Survey (ARMS) (USDA-ERS, 2005). This comprehensive survey of US farm households is conducted over a sample of around 15 000 households using economic and geographic sampling frames. These data distinguish farm households' places in the wealth distribution, commodity sources of farm income, and detailed information on off-farm income so that changes in total income and welfare can be calculated in the wake of agricultural reforms. Keeney (2005) uses these data to analyze the distributional consequences of stylized WTO scenarios, representing the only previous analysis of US farm household impacts of a Doha agreement. The ARMS data have served as the source for other disaggregate analyses (most notably Hanson and Somwaru's (2003) work on the WTO acceptability of counter-cyclical payments) but in these cases the distributional character has been focused on farm structure rather than the welfare focus of Keeney (2005), and global reforms have not been considered.

1.3. Distributional impacts for poor country households

Winters (2002) and Winters *et al.* (2004) provide an analytical framework and evidence on tracing the effects of trade policy through to individual households and poverty. Hertel and Reimer (2005) develop this framework in the context of CGE modelling. We believe that the impact of trade reform on individual households will vary widely depending on their sector of primary employment, their endowments and their consumption patterns. Therefore for each of our 15 focus developing countries we utilize household survey data to divide households into seven classes (strata) according to their principal income source and estimate factor-specific poverty elasticities for each country and stratum combination. These elasticities are incorporated directly into our global CGE model and embody information about the shape of income distribution and income sources in the neighbourhood of the poverty line. When combined with estimates of consumption behaviour at the poverty line, those estimates allow for accurate assessments of how poverty headcounts will likely change in the wake of WTO trade reforms. Drawing on the results for the 15 developing countries in our sample, we seek to arrive at some general conclusions about the poverty impacts of trade policy reforms in rich and poor countries.

The remainder of the paper is organized as follows. We proceed with discussion of the unique analytical framework created for this study's analysis of the distributional impacts of WTO reforms in both rich and poor countries. Following that, we outline the policy scenarios to be applied in this framework. The results section begins with discussion of changes in macroeconomic indicators for trade, prices and national welfare as well as changes in US farm household welfare and in developing country poverty focusing on the impacts of agricultural reforms undertaken in rich countries. We extend this analysis to global reforms and non-agricultural sectors, separately identifying the contributions of these reforms to the poverty headcount results. The concluding section summarizes our findings and offers policy recommendations.

2. ANALYTICAL FRAMEWORK

Figure 1 provides an overview of the analytical framework used in this paper. The boxed items in the top rows represent inputs to the framework, and the double boxes

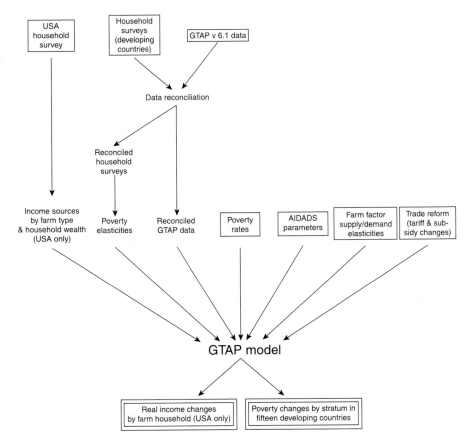

Figure 1. Overview of the analytical framework

at the bottom of the figure represent outputs of particular relevance to this study. The other entries represent intermediate steps in the analysis. As can be seen, we begin with three fundamental sources of data: household survey data from the United States, household survey data from the 15 focus countries, and the GTAP database. Agricultural earnings data in the latter two sources are reconciled, as the GTAP data are notoriously weak when it comes to the estimation of returns to self-employed labour in the farm sector (see Annex III for details). The reconciled survey data are used to compute the poverty elasticities discussed in Box 2, while the revised GTAP data are used to specify agricultural technology in the global CGE model. Other inputs to the global modelling exercise include: farm income sources by farm type for the United States, the poverty headcounts, by region, for $1/day and $2/day, the estimated parameters for our consumer demand system, estimates of farm factor supply and demand elasticities from the OECD, as well as the trade reform scenarios (see Table 6). These inputs are combined with a modified version of the GTAP CGE model of the global economy.

With this overview in mind, a bit more needs to be said about the aspects of this analytical framework that are key to our analysis. Our starting point is the GTAP version 6.1 database (Dimaranan, 2007). Virtually all contemporary analyses of the Doha Development Agenda start at this same point. Data availability is easily the most limiting resource for global analysis and GTAP version 6 represents the only database covering global economic activities with bilateral trade and protection data that reflects tariff preferences. This also permits us to draw on the carefully constructed Doha reform scenarios developed and utilized in the recent books by Anderson and Martin (2006), and Hertel and Winters (2006).[3] These scenarios also involve a pre-experiment in which key trade policies are updated to 2005, and it is from that new benchmark that the trade liberalization experiments proceed.

Our modifications to the standard GTAP model focus on features that enhance analysis of agricultural reforms and simulation of distributional impacts. We retain the simplistic yet empirically robust assumptions of constant returns to scale and perfect competition typically featured in agricultural trade studies.[4] Our modifications are aimed at permitting us to shed new light on the distributional consequences of WTO reforms – focusing particularly on the seemingly intractable problem of agriculture liberalization in the industrial countries. We turn now to these modifications.

2.1. Factor markets

Since the work of T.W. Schultz (1945), economists have recognized the importance of off-farm factor mobility in determining farm incomes. Significant wage differentials between farm and non-farm employment persist in the United States and other high income economies (Gardner, 1992; Kilkenny, 1993). The limitations of agricultural labour markets have also been prominently featured in the development economics literature, as an explanation for the very low level of agricultural supply response (de Janvry *et al.*, 1991). The common CGE assumption of perfect mobility of labour and capital from agriculture to non-agriculture forcing wages to equalize at each point in time for farm and non-farm workers, with comparable skills, is at odds with historical observation.

Effectively modelling the complex processes leading to limited farm/non-farm, rural/urban mobility for the full range of countries in our model would be a lifetime project. Instead, we specify a constant elasticity of transformation function which 'transforms' farm-labour into non-farm labour and vice versa. This transformation

---

[3] These tariff-cutting scenarios are now available on the GTAP website to those wishing to replicate this work. For the purposes of this paper, we have used scenarios S0 (pre-simulation with China's WTO accession, EU enlargement, etc.) and S8: the central Doha scenario used in the Hertel–Winters volume.

[4] Francois *et al.* (2005) introduce monopolistic competition in the manufacturing sector into their analysis of WTO reforms. The resulting variety and scale effects generally boost the gains to rich countries and dampen the gains to poor countries from rich country reforms. However, the predominance of variety gains and losses in this framework can be questioned, and this feature also makes their model less stable; given our focus on agricultural reforms, we have chosen to exclude this feature from our analysis.

function permits wages to diverge between the farm and non-farm sectors, a key driver in our distributional analysis. With segmented labour markets, the impact of reduced subsidies to agriculture in the rich economies will not be shared equally between the farm and non-farm labour forces. Similarly, the benefits from higher farm prices in developing countries following rich country reforms will not be shared as widely with non-farm households in the presence of factor market segmentation.

Much of the reasoning behind differing agricultural and non-agricultural labour rewards similarly applies to returns to agricultural investment. Therefore, we also introduce a constant elasticity of transformation function governing capital movements between agriculture and non-agriculture, with full capital mobility (a unique rental rate on capital) only applying across uses within these two broad sectors.

The extent of burden shifting between farm and non-farm labour and capital will depend on the size of the associated factor supply elasticities. In order to calibrate these key parameters, we draw on the OECD's (2001) parameterization of agricultural factor markets which derive from comprehensive econometric reviews for the EU (Salhofer, 2001) and for North America (Abler, 2001) as well as a modelling panel's assumptions for the Japanese economy. These elasticities are intended to represent medium-term adjustment possibilities (i.e., 2–3 years). Thus we gear our analysis around medium-term outcomes from trade reform. (This is appropriate, since our CGE model does not take into account the impact of trade reforms on investment, productivity and economic growth.)

We assume a constant aggregate level of land, labour and capital employment reflecting the belief that the aggregate supply of factors is unaffected by trade policy. This is not the 'full employment' assumption sometimes derided by advocates of structuralist models of development; rather it assumes that aggregate employment is determined by factors such as labour market norms and regulation that are largely independent of trade policy in the long run. Absent sufficient detail on these employment drivers, we look to wage changes to clear farm and non-farm labour markets in each country.[5]

2.2. Rich country farm household impacts

The potential for adverse impacts on rich country farm household incomes has received far less attention than the distributional impacts in poor countries, yet it represents a key component of the political economy of WTO trade reform. A primary factor in determining the impact of agricultural reforms on farm household welfare in rich countries is the share of their income that currently comes from the farm sector. If farm income is only 10% of total household income, then a 10% drop in farm income translates into just a 1% drop in overall household income (for

[5] This market clearing assumption means that our model does not generate the large changes in competitiveness that Polaski (2006) finds when real wages become misaligned.

constant non-farm income). Recent OECD (2003) statistics report the on and off-farm income split for farm households in numerous member countries – see Annex Table A.6.1. Farm income provides only 8% of the total income of US farm households and 10% and 12% in Canada and Japan respectively. In Europe the share is larger, in the 60–70% range.

In the global CGE model, we model a representative farm household for each region and explicitly track the allocation of its labour and capital between the farm and non-farm sectors (recall the factor supply elasticities above) and the allocation of its land across agricultural uses. As returns in agriculture fall when subsidies are removed, farm households reallocate some farm-owned resources to the non-farm sector as well as adjusting the output composition to changes in relative land returns. Total farm household income in the model is then determined as the sum of returns on their endowments employed in agriculture, plus the returns on those employed in non-agriculture.

While the average farm household's welfare change is an important component in assessing WTO outcomes for any given country, greater detail on the distribution around this average is required to develop insight into the political economy of agricultural reform. This requires more disaggregate data. We have obtained these data for the United States, and we use a 'micro-simulation' approach in which the general equilibrium changes in product and factor prices are combined with disaggregated household data to evaluate the welfare impact on different groups of farm households in this country. These different groups are defined first by their product specialization and then by their place in the wealth distribution of similarly specialized producers. The households and their initial income sourcing are benchmarked using the ARMS annual survey data of the US farm household population for 2004. The ARMS survey data has no longitudinal component. Hill (1996) argues that in such cases wealth provides a suitable substitute for multi-period averages necessary to accurately gauge the income position of farm households. Accordingly, we group households by wealth decile.

Table 1 identifies the disaggregate US farm households of our study. They represent income specialized households in four highly protected sub-sectors: dairy, cotton, rice and sugar, and a residual category of non-specialized farm households. The specialization criterion is that at least one-third of farm revenue be derived from rice, cotton or dairy (to be specialized in those products), and one-fifth of farm revenue from sugar (to be specialized in sugar). The second line of delineation among households distinguishes eleven intervals in the wealth distribution of each specialization group. The farm income share for the specialized groups ranges from 0.22 to 0.92 with larger dependencies for wealthier farms. The residual category 'Other', is by far the largest in the population and mirrors the aggregate distribution of US farm households. Its low farm income shares contrast sharply with those of the specialized farms.

The choice of dairy, sugar, rice and cotton as focus households is driven by the level of support and protection these products enjoy in the United States: about 50%

Table 1. US farm income shares by household type and wealth group

Wealth group (percentile)	Rice	Sugar	Cotton	Dairy	Other
10	0.39	0.22	0.67	0.56	−0.01
20	0.39	0.22	0.67	0.47	0.03
30	0.58	0.22	0.75	0.72	0.01
40	0.58	0.78	0.64	0.48	−0.01
50	0.84	0.78	0.82	0.59	0.07
60	0.55	0.78	0.59	0.57	0.07
70	0.76	0.31	0.64	0.71	0.11
80	0.80	0.31	0.63	0.61	0.12
90	0.75	0.66	0.83	0.81	0.20
95	0.74	0.91	0.68	0.83	0.21
100	0.74	0.91	0.91	0.92	0.41

Source: USDA-ERS, *Agricultural Resource Management Survey* 2004.

of total producer revenue for US milk, sugar and rice is attributable to farm programmes (OECD, 2002) while government programmes provide about 35% of revenue for cotton producers (Sumner, 2006). Other products like maize and oilseeds
receive less support in the United States (25%) as do livestock products (less than 5%).
In addition, maize, oilseed and livestock producers in the United States tend to be
much more product-diversified in farm revenue. Thus, the focus of our analysis is
squarely on those households specialized in highly protected products. In particular,
we believe that high levels of support foster income specialization and specialization
enhances interest group formation and lobbying around a specific agricultural product.
Our results will provide insight into this dynamic that disfavours policy reforms in the
most needed areas.

2.3. Poverty assessment

There are many dimensions through which rich country reforms affect developing
countries. Here we focus on the poverty headcount – that is, the proportion of the
population that falls below the poverty line. This is the most widely cited figure in
the literature, and, by considering two different poverty criteria ($1/day and $2/day),
we explore the sensitivity of our findings to the choice of poverty line. We do this for
15 focus countries for which we have been able to assemble comparable household
survey data. These countries are listed in Table 2 and together they span the continents
of Africa, Asia and Latin America. In the aggregate, they account for nearly 1 billion
people, and more than 400 million poor (measured at the $2/day poverty line; 150
million poor when evaluated at the $1/day poverty line). While they are not a ran-
dom sample, they do span a wide range of per capita income levels as well as differing
degrees of industrialization. Therefore, as we will see, the location and earnings
patterns of the poor in these 15 countries vary greatly.

There are many alternative approaches to estimating the poverty impacts of trade reforms (Annex II). The analytical approach used here builds on that of Hertel *et al.* (2004), which employs a sequential, macro-micro modelling strategy in which results from the global model are passed on to a series of micro-simulation models. In this paper we summarize the key characteristics of these micro-simulation models using *highly disaggregated* poverty elasticities – describing the impact of a change in various components of earnings on poverty within a given population group, or stratum. This permits us to present and analyze our results for all 15 focus countries in a compact and easy to understand manner while maintaining the diversity of poverty outcomes under global trade reform.

A key finding in the work of Hertel *et al.* (2004) is the importance of stratifying households by their primary source of income. Unlike some of the rich countries (and particularly the United States, as discussed above), farm households in developing countries often rely on the farm enterprise for virtually all of their income and are likely to be highly diversified in the products grown on the farm. Furthermore, the share of national poverty concentrated in these agriculture-specialized households is quite high in the poorest countries in our sample – between one-quarter and one-half of the $1/day headcount in Chile, Colombia, Indonesia, Malawi, Mozambique and Zambia. On the other hand, this share is relatively small in Mexico, Peru and Thailand, where a much smaller proportion of the households are engaged in farming, as well as Vietnam, where rural households are more likely to have substantial off-farm income.

Not only are farm households in the poorest countries more likely to be specialized in farming, these specialized farm households also tend to be poorer, on average, than the rest of the population. This point is evident from Figure 2 which plots the poverty headcount in the entire population (horizontal axis) against the poverty rate in the agriculture-specialized group (vertical axis). With the exception of Peru, Mexico and Venezuela, which lie slightly below the 45 degree-line, it is clear that agriculture specialized households have a higher poverty rate – indeed, in the case of Brazil, this is about six times the national poverty rate. The implication of this pattern of farm income specialization is that the poorest households in the poorest countries are more concentrated on agriculture and therefore more likely to benefit from producer price increases engendered by multilateral trade reforms.

We follow Hertel *et al.* (2004) in identifying five household groups that rely almost exclusively (95% or more) on one source of income: agricultural self-employment, non-agricultural self-employment, rural wage labour, urban wage labour, or transfer payments. The remaining households are grouped into rural and urban diversified strata, leading to seven strata in total. Table 2 reports the share of the total national poverty headcount ($1/day) arising in each stratum, for each of our 15 focus countries. Agriculture specialized households and rural diversified households tend to dominate the poverty headcount, although exceptions are Colombia, Venezuela and Peru, where self-employed, non-agriculture households contain a large share of the poor.

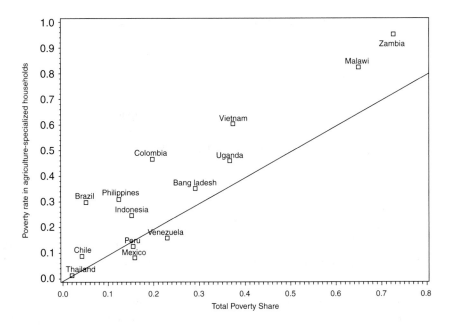

Figure 2. Total poverty rate versus poverty rate among agricultural specialized households (line denotes locus of points with equal poverty rates)

Source: Authors' calculations.

The change in the national poverty rate is calculated from the changes in the poverty headcount in each stratum. The latter depend on the density of the income distribution in the neighbourhood of the poverty line. This can be usefully captured by the stratum-specific poverty elasticities which have been computed numerically based on the cumulative income distribution taken from the household survey data for each of the focus countries (Box 2). These are reported in Table 3, and they answer the question: If incomes in a given stratum rise by 1%, what percentage reduction in the poverty headcount will be achieved? They range from a low of 0.0006 in the self-employed agriculture stratum in Zambia, where nearly all of the population is well below the poverty line, to a high of 3.63 in the urban diversified stratum of Brazil, where the population density at the poverty line is quite high.

However, all income sources are not equally important for households in poverty. In most cases these households own few assets, and have few skills, so their primary endowment is unskilled labour. Increased returns to capital in the wake of trade reforms will do little to reduce poverty. However, a rise in the unskilled wage will make a great deal of difference. This fact is captured in our work by disaggregating the poverty elasticities by income source, as shown in Table 4 for the case of Peru. These elasticities measure the percentage change in stratum poverty headcount, in response to a 1% increase in returns to different types of household endowments.

So, for example, from the first entry in row 2 of Table 4, we see that a 1% increase in unskilled wages in Peruvian agriculture reduces the $1/day poverty headcount in

Table 2. Stratum contributions to the $1/day poverty population in each country

Country	Strata							
	Agr.	N-Agr.	Urb. Lab.	Rur. Lab.	Trans.	Urb. Div.	Rur. Div.	Total
Bangladesh	0.15	0.13	0.04	0.22	0.03	0.07	0.37	1.00
Brazil	0.14	0.09	0.24	0.15	0.32	0.04	0.03	1.00
Chile	0.26	0.01	0.09	0.09	0.28	0.15	0.12	1.00
Colombia	0.28	0.43	0.03	0.04	0.12	0.05	0.04	1.00
Indonesia	0.42	0.12	0.02	0.07	0.04	0.06	0.28	1.00
Malawi	0.54	0.11	0.00	0.03	0.07	0.01	0.25	1.00
Mexico	0.05	0.06	0.05	0.12	0.28	0.14	0.29	1.00
Mozambique	0.41	0.13	0.01	0.05	0.14	0.06	0.19	1.00
Peru	0.07	0.35	0.01	0.02	0.22	0.11	0.23	1.00
Philippines	0.12	0.06	0.03	0.05	0.03	0.23	0.49	1.00
Thailand	0.06	0.02	0.00	0.06	0.11	0.07	0.68	1.00
Uganda	0.10	0.04	0.00	0.03	0.02	0.07	0.75	1.00
Venezuela	0.08	0.24	0.17	0.10	0.28	0.08	0.05	1.00
Vietnam	0.04	0.11	0.00	0.00	0.05	0.10	0.70	1.00
Zambia	0.34	0.23	0.10	0.07	0.07	0.09	0.11	1.00

Notes: Column headings are specializations for each household: Agr. = agricultural, N-Agr. = non-agricultural, Urb. Lab. = urban labour, Rur. Lab. = rural labour, Trans. = transfer, Urb. Div. = urban diversified, Rur. Div. = rural diversified.

Source: Household surveys for each country.

Table 3. Elasticity of poverty headcount ($1/day) with respect to total income

Country	Strata						
	Agr.	N-Agr.	Urb. Lab.	Rur. Lab.	Trans.	Urb. Div.	Rur. Div.
Bangladesh	1.64	2.02	1.58	0.63	0.56	1.74	1.09
Brazil	0.75	1.28	1.94	2.19	0.34	3.63	2.69
Chile	1.90	2.24	2.06	1.55	2.45	2.29	2.60
Colombia	0.79	0.60	1.73	1.72	0.93	1.14	1.00
Indonesia	2.35	2.14	2.38	2.89	1.17	2.58	2.87
Malawi	0.49	0.30	2.26	1.97	0.43	1.04	0.76
Mexico	1.73	1.90	3.33	2.08	2.28	1.63	1.80
Mozambique	0.28	0.94	0.97	0.76	0.48	1.58	0.99
Peru	1.50	1.32	2.37	1.73	0.44	1.09	1.05
Philippines	2.25	1.96	2.98	2.44	1.69	2.42	1.98
Thailand	2.30	2.42	2.98	2.45	2.78	2.42	2.59
Uganda	0.28	0.40	1.71	0.34	0.01	0.36	0.21
Venezuela	0.69	1.16	2.57	2.17	0.01	1.72	1.53
Vietnam	0.48	1.12	2.81	8.98	0.84	0.86	1.01
Zambia	0.00	0.64	2.28	0.91	0.45	1.29	0.37

Notes: Column headings are specializations for each household: Agr. = agricultural, N-Agr. = non-agricultural, Urb. Lab. = urban labour, Rur. Lab. = rural labour, Trans. = transfer, Urb. Div. = urban diversified, Rur. Div. = rural diversified.

Source: Authors' calculations, based on household survey data.

Box 2. Estimating poverty impacts in the focus countries

The unifying theme of our results is that different households are affected differently by trade reforms. Thus, how we derive and treat differences among households is central to the analysis. The most consistent approach embeds household behaviour fully within the national CGE model, but this is computationally burdensome (Rutherford *et al.*, 2006) and would add significant complexity to an already complex global analysis. A popular simplification involves solving a national CGE model and combining the resulting changes in commodity prices, factor prices and possibly quantities and employments with household data on earnings and expenditures to estimate a (first-order) approximation of the welfare effects on households. Chen and Ravallion (2004) apply this to 80 000 households to estimate the poverty effects of Chinese accession to the WTO. Hertel and Winters (2006) are conceptually similar in their estimates of the poverty implications of the Doha Round, but with up to three levels of modelling: a global multi-country CGE model to calculate the effects of the Round on each country's prices of imports and export demand; more detailed national CGE models for 12 country case studies to estimate the effects of these on local prices etc., and, in the cases where the national models do not embed households directly, household modules to calculate the first order welfare approximations by household.

A further simplification is again to solve a CGE model with a single representative consumer, but now to consider the effects of a shock on only a few summary statistics such as average incomes, unskilled wages and food prices. Then, applying 'poverty elasticities' to these statistics allows one to estimate the implied change in poverty. (The poverty elasticity relates the proportionate change in poverty to the proportionate change in *per capita* GDP – see, for example, Ravallion, 1997). This is the approach in Cline (2004), and Anderson *et al.* (2006b) among others. These studies differ *inter alia* in the base poverty levels to which they apply the elasticities.

For the purposes of this paper, we adopt a hybrid of the alternatives. For a global model of the size we have used to explore the DDA, it is not computationally feasible to embed households or even many representative household groups into the CGE model. And neither do we have the requisite data on factor earnings by household for the majority of developing countries. However, we believe that the impact of trade reform on individual households will vary widely depending on their primary sector of employment, their endowments, as well as their consumption patterns. Therefore we reject the single poverty elasticity approach. Instead we utilize the factor earnings and income distribution data for our 15 target developing countries, where this has been obtained and processed in a uniform manner, and we estimate country-stratum-factor price-poverty line specific poverty elasticities. These elasticities embody information about the shape of the income distribution as well as the composition of household earnings in the neighbourhood of the poverty line for key subgroups (strata) of the population.

The specifics of our approach are as follows: for each of our 15 countries we have household surveys that identify sources of income. As described in the Annex, we first adjust the earnings data in order to ensure that the composition of factor incomes in agriculture match those reported in the National Accounts. (A comprehensive reconciliation of these two, mutually inconsistent, sources of income would be a monumental, so we focus on the sector most central to our analysis, which also happens to be the easiest to reconcile.) We then divide households into seven strata, or groups of households, according to their predominant source of income and location: for five the criterion is that 95% or more of income comes from the named source – agricultural self-employment, non-agricultural self-employment, urban wages, rural wages and transfers; for the remaining two we distinguish urban diversified and rural diversified. Each stratum is then ordered by total income and divided into 20 vigntiles to create a total of 140 classes of households in each of the 15 focus countries.

For each stratum we calculate poverty elasticities with respect to each source of income, where the shares of income come from the vigntiles in which the poverty line falls, and the density of households around the poverty line from the overall distribution. The density determines the change in headcount poverty resulting from a given change in stratum income, while the earnings shares determine how a change in (e.g.) unskilled wages change stratum income in the neighbourhood of the poverty line. Once the CGE model has been solved for a new set of factor prices, we can use these poverty elasticities to determine the change in stratum poverty – and, given the relative importance of stratum poverty in national poverty – the change in the latter may also be obtained.

Of course, a rise in factor earnings is only meaningful from a poverty perspective if commodity prices do not also rise by the same amount. Therefore we must deflate the factor price changes by the change in the real cost of living at the poverty line. This is obtained by solving the AIDADS demand system for the expenditure necessary to achieve the poverty level of utility at the post-reform prices.

Table 4. Poverty elasticities, by stratum and income source, $1/day: Peru

Factor	Agr.	N-Agr.	Urb. Lab.	Rur. Lab.	Trans.	Urb. Div.	Rur. Div.
Land	0.04	0.00	0.00	0.00	0.00	0.01	0.03
Agr. Unskilled Labour	1.41	0.00	0.00	0.00	0.00	0.25	0.21
Agr. Skilled Labour	0.00	0.00	0.00	0.00	0.00	0.01	0.00
Non-Ag. Unskilled Labour	0.00	1.08	0.00	0.01	0.00	0.31	0.32
Non-Ag. Skilled Labour	0.00	0.14	0.00	0.00	0.00	0.05	0.07
Wage Labour Unskilled	0.00	0.00	2.19	1.58	0.00	0.21	0.13
Wage Labour Skilled	0.00	0.00	0.16	0.12	0.00	0.01	0.00
Agricultural Capital	0.05	0.00	0.00	0.00	0.00	0.01	0.03
Non-agricultural Capital	0.00	0.09	0.00	0.00	0.00	0.05	0.12
Transfers	0.01	0.01	0.02	0.02	0.44	0.18	0.15
Total	1.50	1.32	2.37	1.73	0.44	1.09	1.05

Notes: Column headings are specializations for each household: Agr. = agricultural, N-Agr. = non-agricultural, Urb. Lab. = urban labour, Rur. Lab. = rural labour, Trans. = transfer, Urb. Div. = urban diversified, Rur. Div. = rural diversified.

Source: Authors' calculations based on household survey data.

the agriculture stratum by 1.41%. It also contributes to poverty reductions in the diversified households. Indeed, the elasticity is slightly higher for urban diversified households than for rural diversified ones, indicating that these households earn a non-negligible share of their income from agriculture self-employment, despite their urban status in the survey. Labour income is also dominant in the other strata, although in the case of non-agriculture, it is non-agricultural self-employed labour, and in other cases it is wage labour. Note also that the non-agriculture and wage labour specialized households receive income from both skilled and unskilled labour.

Returning to the agriculture stratum poverty elasticities in the first column of Table 4, we see that, in addition to unskilled labour, there are also small elasticities for land, agriculture capital and transfers. If returns to all of these income sources were to rise by 1%, then stratum income would rise by 1% for all households, including the households at the poverty line. Therefore, the elasticities in Table 4 sum (column-wise) to the same figure displayed in Table 3 for this particular stratum.

As noted in Table 2, in addition to the agriculture stratum, the rural diversified stratum is a very important repository for the poor in most of our focus countries. For this reason, it is interesting to examine the poverty elasticities for this particular stratum across the full range of focus countries. These are reported in Table 5. To facilitate comparison across countries, we have normalized these elasticities, by dividing by their total (e.g., 1.05 for the rural diversified households in Peru, as taken from the last column of Table 3). So the elements in each row of Table 5 represent the contribution of each endowment to the total poverty elasticity for the rural diversified stratum in a given country. Clearly the composition of the aggregate poverty elasticity for the rural diversified stratum varies considerably across countries – further evidence of the great variety of developing countries included in our sample.

As expected, unskilled earnings are generally dominant in the rural diversified households' earnings profile, with the type of earnings depending on the sector in which the labour is employed. Land rents are generally unimportant for the poor, excepting in the case of the Philippines, and, to a lesser degree, Uganda. Skilled labour also plays a small role in earnings at the poverty line in these countries, and hence contributes little to the poverty elasticities. Agriculture and non-agriculture capital plays a more important role in some countries – most notably non-agriculture capital in Vietnam, where it accounts for 55% of the poverty elasticity for the rural diversified households. Transfer payments are quite significant at the poverty line in the wealthier countries – most notably Brazil, Chile and Thailand, where they account for more than a third of the total poverty elasticity for the rural diversified households.

The ten different income sources in Table 5 must be mapped to factor earnings in the general equilibrium model. For example, agricultural labour and capital receive the corresponding farm factor returns from the general equilibrium model, as do non-agricultural labour and capital. Wage labour reported in the survey presents a problem, since we don't know how much of this is employed in agriculture versus non-agriculture activities. For this reason, we simply assign to it the economy-wide average wage – a blend of the farm and non-farm wages. Finally, transfer payments are indexed by the growth rate in net national income (Annex V offers elaboration on this choice).

Of course our evaluation of household welfare depends not only on earnings, but also on what happens to consumer prices. With food prices likely to rise in the wake of rich country agricultural reforms, and with the poorest households potentially spending the bulk of their income on food, this could have adverse consequences for poverty. Therefore, we turn next to our treatment of consumer preferences.

2.4. Household preferences and welfare

Given the emphasis in this paper on household welfare – in both rich and poor countries – it is important that we pay close attention to the specification of household preferences and the resulting pattern of demands across the income spectrum. The approach used here follows closely that of Hertel *et al.* (2004) insofar as we begin with an econometrically estimated, international, cross-section demand system, which is then systematically adjusted to reproduce national per capita demands. These national preferences are then used to predict demands across the income spectrum within each country; in particular they are used to assess the impact of consumer price changes on households at the poverty line in our 15 focus countries. In the United States, the national demand system is used to evaluate welfare for each of the farm household groups discussed above.

Table 5. Poverty elasticities for rural diversified stratum, $1/day

Country	Land	Agr. Unskilled Labour	Agr. Skilled Labour	Non-Agr. Unskilled Labour	Non-Agr. Skilled Labour	Wage Labour Unskilled	Wage Labour Skilled	Agr. Capital	Non-Agr. Capital	Trans.	Total
Bangladesh	0.01	0.18	0.00	0.20	0.00	0.43	0.04	0.01	0.03	0.10	1.00
Brazil	0.00	0.10	0.04	0.12	0.00	0.32	0.01	0.01	0.00	0.41	1.00
Chile	0.05	0.16	0.00	0.02	0.00	0.35	0.00	0.07	0.00	0.35	1.00
Colombia	0.00	0.22	0.00	0.30	0.00	0.22	0.02	0.00	0.02	0.21	1.00
Indonesia	0.06	0.32	0.00	0.20	0.00	0.26	0.00	0.04	0.08	0.04	1.00
Malawi	0.03	0.38	0.00	0.07	0.00	0.08	0.00	0.06	0.11	0.27	1.00
Mexico	0.01	0.14	0.00	0.06	0.00	0.48	0.00	0.01	0.01	0.30	1.00
Mozambique	0.01	0.43	0.00	0.07	0.00	0.07	0.00	0.02	0.20	0.20	1.00
Peru	0.02	0.20	0.00	0.30	0.07	0.13	0.00	0.03	0.11	0.14	1.00
Philippines	0.22	0.00	0.02	0.14	0.01	0.30	0.01	0.12	0.08	0.11	1.00
Thailand	0.04	0.21	0.03	0.03	0.01	0.24	0.07	0.02	0.02	0.35	1.00
Uganda	0.14	0.15	0.00	0.06	0.00	0.09	0.06	0.26	0.14	0.10	1.00
Venezuela	0.00	0.10	0.00	0.32	0.01	0.28	0.04	0.00	0.00	0.26	1.00
Vietnam	0.01	0.09	0.00	0.14	0.00	0.00	0.00	0.00	0.55	0.21	1.00
Zambia	0.01	0.03	0.00	0.20	0.00	0.43	0.05	0.03	0.13	0.12	1.00

Notes: Column headings are earnings sources: Trans. = transfers.

Source: Authors' calculations based on household survey data.

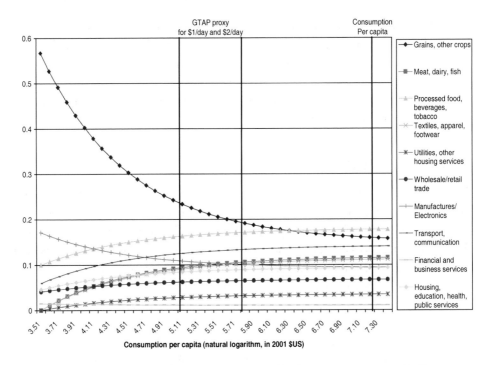

Figure 3. Estimated budget shares across the income spectrum in Peru

Source: Authors' calculations.

   The demand system chosen for this task must be flexible enough to explain the broad pattern of consumption in Malawi, on the one hand, and the United States on the other. Accordingly, we follow Hertel *et al.* (2004) in using a demand system – nicknamed AIDADS – which features highly non-linear Engel curves and has been shown to perform very well in out-of-sample predictions of per capita international demand behaviour (Cranfield *et al.*, 2003; see Annex IV for a detailed discussion). For our purposes, the key feature is that the chosen demand system allocates two-thirds of its parameters to predicting behaviour at extremely low income levels, which is what we need to predict the consumption impacts on the poor. Estimation of this demand system for this paper is undertaken using the 80-country, per capita consumption data set offered by GTAP, version 6.1, and it is subsequently nationally calibrated to reproduce observed demands in each country; the resulting parameters are reported in Annex IV.

   The best way to understand the implications of the estimated demand system is to view the results for a particular country. Figure 3 plots the predicted household budget shares for Peru, across the income spectrum. These show how the pattern of consumer expenditures are predicted to vary from the subsistence level (origin of horizontal axis), where expenditures on food and clothing are dominant (budget share of nearly 60%), to the national per capita expenditure level where the household budget is more diversified (the horizontal axis reports the natural logarithm of consumption expenditure, per capita, and extends only to the national average income level). Vertical lines denote the $1/day, $2/day and national per capita expenditure levels. Note that at the $1/day poverty line, 49% of the budget is devoted to food, with the bulk of this spent on crops. The initial levels of utility at the two poverty lines are each fixed, and the estimated demand system is used to determine the change in the cost of attaining this exogenous poverty level of utility when prices and demands change following trade liberalization.

3. POLICY SCENARIOS

Our attention in this paper is on the distributional impacts of WTO reforms in agriculture. Since such reforms are most contentious in the rich countries, we focus initially on impacts of liberalizing agricultural policies in the rich countries alone. The OECD produces annual estimates of the producer support estimate for its member countries. Rice is far and away the most protected commodity by this measure; on average OECD rice producers receive more than 80% of their revenue as a result of some policy intervention. Both sugar and milk producers in the OECD receive over 40% of their revenue from some combination of market intervention and direct government support, while other grains and oilseeds lie below that level.

Across countries, the producer support for OECD member countries varies widely ranging from a low value of 1% of producer revenue in New Zealand to a high value of 69% of producer revenue in Switzerland (Annex Table A.6.2). For the OECD in aggregate, transfers to producers account for 31% of revenues. Producer support in the EU is near the OECD-wide average. In Western Europe and East Asia producer support is considerably above the OECD average, while that in North America and Central and Eastern Europe is somewhat below. Australia and New Zealand provide minimal support to producers through agricultural policies.

The OECD producer support estimate is a combined measure of all support to producers capturing the transfer of treasury monies paid to farmers as well as the transfers from commodity sales at prices supported above world market levels. Thus this subsidy measure can be broadly decomposed into market price support (i.e. border policies) and farm policy transfers including output and input subsidies, area- and livestock headage-based payments, and the various payments tied to land use, farm income and historical payments. The relative importance of these differs across countries but in most instances the division between market price and other support is roughly equal. The primary exception is in East Asia (Japan and Korea) where producer support is provided nearly entirely as market price support.

The WTO separates support policies into three groups, with separate negotiating modalities for each of them. Translating from the OECD producer support measure to the WTO's aggregate measure of support framework is not straightforward. The market price support component captures both the market access and export subsidy pillars of the WTO agricultural negotiations. The remaining portion of the OECD measure poses a significant challenge for quantifications in the context of the WTO

Table 6. Overview of scenarios

Instrument	Rich Agriculture		Global (all countries and merchandise)	
	Doha (%)	Full (%)	Doha (%)	Full (%)
Agr. Tariffs Rich	−45, −70, −75[c]	−100	−45, −70, −75	−100
Agr. Tariffs Poor (Non-LDC[a])	n.a.	n.a.	−35, −40, −50, −60[d]	−100
Agr. Export Subsidies	−100%	−100	−100	−100
Amber Box Subsidies[b]	−75 Group 1 −60 Group 2	−100	−75 Group 1 −60 Group 2	−100
Non-Agr. Tariffs Rich	n.a.	n.a.	−50	−100
Non-Agr. Tariffs Poor (Non-LDC[a])	n.a.	n.a.	−33	−100
Green Box Subsidies	n.a.	n.a.	n.a.	n.a.

[a] Least developed countries (LDCs) are not required to make any tariff reductions under Doha scenarios.

[b] Group 1 countries have amber box subsidies accounting for more than 20% of producer revenue. Group 2 countries have support less than 20% of producer revenue. A third grouping exists for developing countries where 40% reductions are required, but adequate data on amber box subsidies is available to model this.

[c] These three percentage cuts are applied in a tiered formula whereby higher portions of the tariff are more deeply cut. Tiers are defined over the tariff rate and the reductions increase at 15% and then 90%.

[d] These four percentage cuts are applied in a tiered formula whereby higher portions of the tariff are more deeply cut. Tiers are defined over the tariff rate and the reductions increase at 20%, 60%, and 120%.

domestic support negotiations, as these are differentiated according to 'traffic light' designations (amber, blue and green boxes) that intend to characterize the level of distortion created by a particular policy implementation. This complexity of moving from the OECD's comprehensive domestic support database to the WTO domestic support framework is the reason we draw on the published study by Jensen and Zobbe (2006) for our Doha agricultural scenarios. These authors consider in detail not only the WTO designations of support, but also the associated binding overhang versus actual support levels that we cannot evaluate by looking at the OECD producer support estimates in isolation.

The Doha scenario considered in this paper derives from the so-called July 2004 Framework Agreement (WTO, 2004) as embodied in the core scenario from the Hertel and Winters volume (2006) and is summarized, along with the other policy scenarios considered in this paper, in Table 6. The first column of this table highlights the implications for cuts in support in the rich countries' agricultural sectors – the main focus of this paper. This Doha scenario assumes that industrial countries with domestic support in excess of 20% of production cut their bound commitments by 75%, while others cut by 60%. However, even with these ambitious reductions, the gap between bindings and applied policies, as well as the inclusion of market price support concepts mean that effectively only five WTO members would be required to reduce actual support, based on 2001 notifications: Australia, EU, Iceland, Norway, and US (Jensen and Zobbe, 2006). Export subsidies are the one area where bold cuts (full elimination) are on the table, and we assume this outcome in our Doha scenario. When it comes to developing countries (see Column 3) domestic subsidy bindings are cut by 4%. In this case, Jensen and Zobbe (2006) estimate that only Thailand's subsidies would be affected.

Agricultural tariffs in the rich countries are reduced using a tiered formula, with marginal cuts changing at 15 and 90% initial bound tariff rates. The marginal cuts are 45% on the first 15 percentage points of the tariff, 70% for the range between 15 and 90%, and 75% on the remainder.[6] For developing countries, the inflection points are placed at 20, 60 and 120% bound tariff levels in agriculture, with marginal cuts of 35, 40, 50 and 60%, respectively.

Of course, cross-sector trade-offs are at the heart of the WTO negotiations, so we also consider the impact of non-agricultural elements of a prospective Doha Development Agenda on both rich and poor countries. Given the importance of non-agricultural income to farm households in many of the rich countries, this also could have a direct bearing on farm household welfare. In the case of poverty impacts in developing countries, improved access to rich country manufactures markets, as well as access to the markets of other developing countries can have an important impact on the demand for unskilled labour, and hence poverty rates.

Following Hertel and Winters (2006), we focus the attention of our non-agricultural shocks on market access (see Column 3 of Table 6), since barriers to services trade and investment remain difficult to quantify and these parts of the WTO negotiations appear unlikely to yield significant changes in the near term. Specifically, non-agriculture tariffs are subjected to proportional cuts of 50% for developed and 33% for developing countries. The least developed countries are not required to cut tariffs under this central scenario (see Anderson and Martin, 2006). As a consequence of these relatively ambitious tariff cuts in both farm, and non-farm trade, average world-wide tariffs for all merchandise trade drop from 4.7% in the baseline to 3.2%.

In order to establish a benchmark set of liberalization results from which to make comparisons, we begin by examining the distributional consequences of the complete elimination of rich country support for agriculture. We then consider the portion of this impact that would be delivered under the particular Doha scenario discussed above. After this we add, in turn, non-agricultural reforms in the rich countries, and liberalization in the developing countries (both agricultural and non-agricultural).

Finally, we consider the likely scenario that governments in rich regions will opt to compensate adversely affected farm households through WTO green-box means. These green-box payments are tied to land use, not output, and are designed to be neutral across farm products (i.e. the subsidy is not contingent of a specific use of the land). As such they generate minimal distortions in world markets and so are in line with WTO guidelines as their primary effect is simply the transfer of income from taxpayers (including farmers) to farmers.

---

[6] For example, a tariff of, say, 100% is cut by 66.95%: = [15%*0.45 + (90 − 15)%*0.70 + (100 − 90)%*0.75]. By applying the cuts at the margin we avoid the discontinuities implied by the July Framework.

Throughout our analysis, we employ a macroeconomic closure which fixes the ratios of government spending, tax revenue, net national savings, and the trade balance, all relative to net national income. This closure facilitates linking the aggregate and disaggregate welfare impacts of trade reform (see Annex V for an extended discussion of our closure assumptions and their implications).

4. RESULTS

4.1. Agricultural liberalization by the rich economies

Before discussing the farm household impacts, we consider briefly the macroeconomic impacts of these policies. Complete liberalization of rich country farm policies generates some very large trade volume increases for rice, sugar and beef products where border protection is dominant, whereas world trade in coarse grains and cotton actually falls, as rich country subsidies are eliminated and exports are reduced. Under the Doha scenario, which emphasizes trade volume-reducing export subsidy elimination, as opposed to trade volume-increasing tariff reductions, the global trade volumes for wheat and dairy products also fall. Details are available in Annex Table A.6.3.

We begin our discussion of model results by looking at the national macroeconomic impacts of the reforms. These are reported in Table 7 using two key national indicators: the percentage change in the regional terms of trade (ToT; an index of export prices relative to import prices), and the percentage change in real aggregate consumption (national welfare derived from the private consumption of goods and services). For this first table of model results we report mean (in bold) as well as upper and lower bounds from a 95% confidence interval for each result. This allows us to evaluate whether a particular result is significantly different from zero (we note the cases where they are not with a hash mark: #) as well as evaluate when confidence intervals for two scenarios overlap (meaning we cannot say with 95% confidence that one scenario produces a different result than another).[7] These sensitivity results refer to the robustness of results to the uncertainty inherent in our estimated trade, factor demand and supply elasticities, as these are the crucial parameters in our model. They have been generated using the Gaussian Quadrature method of numerical integration. This procedure shares many properties with the common Monte Carlo simulation sensitivity process of drawing from a set of parameter distributions, but is considerably more efficient due to the intelligent selection of evaluation points.[8]

---

[7] In subsequent tables of results we only note when a result cannot be distinguished from zero with 95% confidence.

[8] Because of the quadrature-based intelligent selection of evaluation points, our model results needs to be well-approximated by a third-order polynomial. Arndt (1996) has tested and developed the procedure for the GTAP model finding that a third-order polynomial does provide a good approximation to GTAP model results and that GQ results are quite consistent with those generated from Monte Carlo simulations. Our particular implementation of Gaussian Quadrature (GQ) also requires that we assume parameter distributions are symmetric and that parameters are independently distributed.

Table 7. Welfare and terms of trade results

	Full ToT Lower	Full ToT Mean	Full ToT Upper	Doha ToT Lower	Doha ToT Mean	Doha ToT Upper	Full Welf. Lower	Full Welf. Mean	Full Welf. Upper	Doha Welf. Lower	Doha Welf. Mean	Doha Welf. Upper
Rich countries												
Aust. and New Zlnd.	2.21	**2.80**	3.39	0.92	**1.10**	1.28	0.58	**0.72**	0.86	0.22	**0.26**	0.30
Japan	−1.47	**−1.25**	−1.03	−0.47	**−0.39**	−0.31	0.50	**0.95**	1.40	0.23	**0.47**	0.71
Canada	−0.11	**−0.07**	−0.03	−0.04	**−0.02#**	0.00	0.23	**0.27**	0.31	0.08	**0.10**	0.12
US	0.29	**0.35**	0.41	0.12	**0.14**	0.16	0.02	**0.02**	0.02	0.01	**0.01**	0.01
Europe FTA	−0.40	**−0.30**	−0.20	−0.10	**−0.06**	−0.02	0.12	**0.22**	0.32	0.12	**0.18**	0.24
Focus countries												
Bangladesh	−0.80	**−0.60**	−0.40	−0.25	**−0.21**	−0.17	−0.36	**−0.28**	−0.20	−0.12	**−0.10**	−0.08
Brazil	3.31	**5.27**	7.23	0.82	**1.94**	3.06	0.41	**0.72**	1.03	0.08	**0.26**	0.44
Chile	0.55	**0.77**	0.99	0.13	**0.15**	0.17	0.09	**0.15**	0.21	−0.01	**0.01#**	0.03
Colombia	1.06	**1.26**	1.46	0.52	**0.60**	0.68	−0.04	**0.00#**	0.04	−0.01	**0.01#**	0.03
Indonesia	−0.27	**−0.23**	−0.19	−0.12	**−0.10**	−0.08	−0.30	**−0.26**	−0.22	−0.09	**−0.09**	−0.09
Malawi	1.94	**2.55**	3.16	−0.23	**0.12#**	0.47	1.41	**1.82**	2.23	−0.10	**0.17#**	0.44
Mexico	−0.38	**−0.14#**	0.10	−0.13	**−0.11**	−0.09	−0.30	**−0.24**	−0.18	−0.08	**−0.08**	−0.08
Mozambique	−0.50	**−0.40**	−0.30	−0.17	**−0.15**	−0.13	−0.65	**−0.53**	−0.41	−0.16	**−0.14**	−0.12
Peru	1.70	**3.25**	4.80	0.05	**0.15**	0.25	0.22	**0.53**	0.84	−0.03	**−0.01#**	0.01
Philippines	−0.07	**0.01#**	0.09	−0.10	**−0.08**	−0.06	−0.25	**−0.21**	−0.17	−0.11	**−0.11**	−0.11
Tanzania	−0.31	**−0.02#**	0.27	−0.35	**−0.23**	−0.11	−0.17	**−0.09**	−0.01	−0.10	**−0.08**	−0.06
Thailand	0.64	**1.11**	1.58	0.17	**0.23**	0.29	0.42	**0.71**	1.00	0.11	**0.15**	0.19
Uganda	−1.04	**−0.59**	−0.14	−0.81	**−0.65**	−0.49	−0.33	**−0.23**	−0.13	−0.23	**−0.19**	−0.15
Venezuela	−0.47	**−0.41**	−0.35	−0.25	**−0.23**	−0.21	−0.13	**−0.11**	−0.09	−0.06	**−0.06**	−0.06
Vietnam	0.07	**0.27**	0.47	−0.14	**−0.12**	−0.10	−0.09	**0.07#**	0.23	−0.20	**−0.18**	−0.16
Zambia	−0.26	**−0.18**	−0.10	−0.05	**−0.01#**	0.03	−0.24	**−0.20**	−0.16	−0.05	**−0.05**	−0.05

Note: Model results at mean values differ from model results evaluated at the point estimate due to non-linearity of the model.

Result can *not* be distinguished from zero change at the 95% confidence level.

Source: Authors' simulations.

Turning to the results reported in Table 7, we first note from these results that agricultural liberalization is good for the rich countries (welfare rises). Furthermore, these changes are statistically significant from zero (no # marks next to them). The fact that reform of this highly distorted sector will benefit the rich countries should come as little surprise, and it is well-established in the literature (Anderson *et al.*, 2006a; Francois *et al.*, 2005; Dimaranan, Hertel and Keeney, 2004). The roadblock to agricultural reform has to do with the concentration of losses among key interest groups – a point to which we will turn shortly. Note also that the Doha reforms capture a significant share of total gains available to Europe under full agricultural reform, and a little under half in other rich countries. In fact, for Europe we cannot even establish with 95% certainty that the welfare gains from Doha reform will be lower than those from full reforms based on the confidence interval bounds (i.e., they overlap).

A somewhat more controversial point has to do with the impact of rich country agricultural reforms on the developing countries. Here, the key mechanism for transmission of economic welfare is through the ToT. If a country is a net importer of food products and the world price of food products rises, then the ToT might be expected to deteriorate. This is the case of Bangladesh, for example, which, according to Table 7, experiences a 0.60% ToT deterioration under Rich-Agr-Full Liberalization, and a 0.25% ToT decline under the Rich-Agr-Doha scenario – both of which are statistically significant. This is primarily due to higher prices for cotton, wheat and oilseeds. With a deteriorating ToT, Bangladesh can afford fewer imports for a given amount of exports and real consumption is expected to decline. On the other hand, Brazil, with a 5.48% ToT appreciation, can now consume more imports, or export less and consume more domestic production, so its welfare rises.

Of course, the story is a bit more complex for two reasons. First of all, in a world of differentiated products, there is no single 'world price' for a good. Even a commodity like rice is differentiated and many different prices can co-exist in the world market at one point in time. So it can matter whether you source your rice from a country whose price is rising, for example due to the elimination of an export subsidy. This is the case with dairy imports into Venezuela from the EU and United States. Venezuela also suffers from higher import prices for manufactures from Brazil, since the latter country experiences a real appreciation. In short, Venezuela is an example of a country that experiences ToT and consumption losses due to its specific pattern of imports. (A full decomposition of the ToT results is available in Annex Table A.6.5.) Overall, we find that the ToT deteriorate in 8 of the 15 focus countries in the case of full agricultural reform in the rich countries, with the number being somewhat larger (10 of 15) in the case of the Doha reforms. The latter result follows from the greater emphasis of Doha on export subsidies as opposed to market access.

The second complication to the simple 'ToT drive welfare' story described above arises from the presence of domestic tax and subsidy distortions. Note in particular, that in the case of the Philippines (Rich-Agr-Full) and Peru (Rich-Agr-Doha), the

Table 8. Percentage change in farm income for rich regions by source (on/off-farm)

Region	Rich Region Doha Ag. Reforms			Rich Region Ag. Full Reform		
	On-farm	Off-farm	Total	On-farm	Off-farm	Total
Australia and New Zealand	7.3	$-0.0^{\#}$	4.4	17.3	$-0.0^{\#}$	10.5
Japan	-15.5	0.6	-1.4	-28.2	1.2	-2.5
Canada	3.5	0.0	0.4	6.3	0.1	0.7
US	$-0.3^{\#}$	$0.0^{\#}$	$-0.0^{\#}$	-4.4	0.1	-0.3
EU and other Europe	-5.8	0.3	-3.5	-12.7	0.5	-7.7

$^{\#}$ Result can *not* be distinguished from zero change at the 95% confidence level.

Source: Authors' simulations.

ToT improve, but welfare falls. This stems from the fact that both countries have domestic tax policies that favour agriculture relative to industry. Therefore an expansion of agriculture at the expense of industry has an adverse effect on economic efficiency and overall welfare. However, neither the ToT change for Philippines (Rich-Agr-Full) nor the welfare change for Peru (Rich-Agr-Doha) is statistically significant in light of our parametric sensitivity analysis.

Now let us turn to the distributional results of rich country agricultural reforms. Table 8 reports the percentage change in real on-farm income and off-farm household income, as well as the implied change in real household income for the aggregate farm household in each of the rich economies. From the on-farm income results, it is clear why there is so much opposition to these reforms. The average decline in Japan is 16% under the Doha scenario and 28% under the Full Liberalization scenario and 6% and 13% respectively in the EU. On-farm income losses in the United States are much smaller – indeed they are not distinct from zero under the Doha scenario, while Canadian and Australia/New Zealand producers see gains in real on-farm income.

However, as noted above, farm households in many of these countries are quite diversified in their earnings. If we factor in the change in real, off-farm income, which tends to rise (albeit modestly, since there are no reforms outside of agriculture), the total impact on real farm household income is considerably moderated. Indeed, in Japan, the losses drop by a full order of magnitude – from -15.5% to just -1.4% under the Doha scenario. In the United States, the losses become negligible, even under full liberalization. The dampening factor is less prevalent in Europe, where the role of off-farm income is smaller than in Japan and the United States.

Given the very modest aggregate farm household losses in the United States, the question arises: Why is the farm-based opposition to reform so strong in that country? This becomes quite clear when we delve more deeply into the US impacts. Table 9 reports the welfare impacts on representative households in each of the 11 wealth classes across the five US producer groups. It is clear that under the Rich-Agr-Full-Lib scenario, the losses to the richest, and likely most influential, producer groups are

Table 9. Disaggregate US farm household income impacts of Ag. Reforms

Income group (percentile)	Rice Hhld.		Sugar Hhld.		Cotton Hhld.		Dairy Hhld.		Other Hhld.	
	Doha	Full	Doha	Full	Doha	Full	Doha	Full	Doha	Full
10l	1.36[#]	−5.08	−0.12[#]	−0.97	−2.09	−8.31	−0.30[#]	−2.44	0.02	0.08
20	1.37[#]	−5.11	−0.12[#]	−0.97	−2.09	−8.31	−0.30[#]	−2.00	−0.03	−0.12
30	1.89[#]	−6.55	−0.34[#]	−2.64	−1.63	−7.03	−0.43[#]	−2.94	0.00[#]	0.00[#]
40	1.89[#]	−6.57	−0.87	−4.80	−2.13	−8.14	−0.32[#]	−2.11	0.01	0.08
50	6.32[#]	−16.63	−0.87	−4.80	−1.60	−7.64	−0.41[#]	−2.56	−0.08	−0.35
60	1.63[#]	−7.68	−0.87	−4.80	−1.18	−5.00	−0.44[#]	−2.74	−0.08	−0.34
70	4.64[#]	−14.92	−0.37	−1.98	−1.47	−6.66	−0.66	−3.74	−0.17	−0.70
80	5.53[#]	−17.08	−0.37	−1.98	−1.15	−5.13	−0.47	−2.92	−0.18	−0.78
90	5.60[#]	−17.79	−0.65	−3.73	−1.81	−8.94	−0.71	−4.26	−0.31	−1.31
95	5.33[#]	−18.91	−1.33	−6.49	−1.61	−6.77	−0.46[#]	−3.56	−0.30	−1.31
100	5.31[#]	−18.83	−1.33	−6.49	−3.53	−12.68	−0.50[#]	−4.04	−0.56	−2.39

[#] Result can *not* be distinguished from zero change at the 95% confidence level.

Source: Authors' simulations.

very large – nearly 20% of income in the case of the wealthiest rice producers. The wealthiest sugar producers are also hard-hit, as are cotton producers across the board.

One surprising thing about the results in Table 9 is the impact on rice producers under the Doha scenario. Here, they switch from being the biggest losers to the biggest gainers (based on this particular five-way producer grouping). To further investigate this result we have performed a decomposition (using the methodology of Harrison, Horridge and Pearson, 1999) that separately identifies the partial impact of US rice reforms, US non-rice reforms, Japanese rice reforms, and the residual category of all other agricultural reforms on US farm household welfare. The results (available in Annex Table A.6.6) show that the US agricultural reforms contribute negatively to rice producer welfare. The initial level of support for rice production is very high and even the modest reduction of the Doha scenario would generate an average real income loss of −4.5% for rice producers if applied in isolation. Other US agricultural reforms have a lesser impact (−2% average income change) since rice households lose support on any other crops they might produce and non-rice reforms lower returns to labour and capital in agriculture. Therefore, the positive Doha welfare impact derives from non-US policy reforms.

The US rice producer gains under Rich-Agr reforms are dominated by the gains from increased access to the lucrative Japanese market. Cuts in Japanese rice protection increase average US rice producer welfare by 8%, with the average contribution of other countries liberalizing adding an additional 1%. So US producers gain under Rich country reforms, following the Doha Agenda, since their cuts in domestic support are modest (28%), while the improvement in market access to Japan is substantial. Of course, Japanese negotiators will strive to have rice treated as a sensitive product, thereby limiting the increase in market access, and this will obviously limit the final gains under any agreement.[9] A further qualification of these results is that they show a very large standard deviation. This is because they are extremely sensitive to the size of the substitution elasticity between rice sourced from different countries – and this has itself been estimated with a fairly large standard deviation (Table A.1.1). Therefore, it is hardly surprising that the US rice household welfare gains under Doha, are not significantly different from zero at the 95% confidence level.

Given the very large amount of household wealth tied up in agriculture, it is also important to consider the impact of these trade reforms on the wealth position of farm households in the US – again by the 11 wealth categories. These results are reported in Table 10 for the three most severely affected household groups: rice, sugar and cotton producers. This table decomposes the total change in household wealth (final column) into its component parts under the Rich-Agr-Full scenario. The first three columns of Table 10 deal with the asset side of farm wealth, giving the share of land in farm assets, and the percentage change in farm asset value associated with farm land and farm capital (they are share-weighted so that the sum of these two entries gives the percentage change in farm assets). We see that farm households differ considerably in the share of land in their farm asset portfolio which typically increases with wealth class. Therefore, the contribution of farmland losses to the total change in farm asset values also tends to rise with wealth. Thus, for the 95–100 wealth percentile of rice households, the total decline in farm asset values is $-(23.96 + 1.44) = -25.40\%$. Since these households are also somewhat leveraged (10% debt to asset ratio – see Column 4 in Table 10), and since the cost of servicing the farm debt declines very little, the decline in farm wealth (-28.25%) is larger than the decline in asset values.

The final three columns detailing the Rich-Agr-Full scenario concern changes in *total* household wealth. In order to move from the change in farm wealth to total household wealth, we need to know the share of farm wealth in total household wealth, as well as the change in non-farm wealth. These are reported in the columns preceding the change in total household wealth. Note that the changes in non-farm wealth are small, since the scenarios here consider only agricultural liberalization. When we look at the farm share in total wealth, we see that it tends to be quite high – and is often highest for the wealthiest households. Thus, the detrimental impact on land rents from the reductions in support carry through as the dominant component of aggregate household wealth change with larger effects on wealthier households.

Comparing these wealth results from Rich-Agr-Full to those in Table 9 for household income, we see that the relatively greater importance of agricultural assets in household wealth, as compared to the share of farm income in household income, coupled with non-negligible debt/asset ratios, leads to a magnification of the losses

---

[9] Jean *et al.* (2006) provide a systematic analysis of the case in which sensitive and special commodities are exempted from steep tariff cuts, facing instead a modest 15% cut in bound rates (the Doha scenario considered in this paper). In the case where just 2% of industrial country tariff lines and 4% of developing country tariff lines in agriculture are exempted, the overall average tariff cuts are greatly reduced. Furthermore, Anderson *et al.* (2006a) find that such exemptions erase any potential for poverty reduction under our Doha scenario.

Table 10. Disaggregate US farm household wealth impacts of Ag Reforms

Percentile	Farm Assets Land Shr.	Farm Assets Land.	Farm Assets Capital	Farm Wealth Debt/ Asset	Farm Wealth Value	NFarm Wealth Value	HHLD Wealth Farm Shr.	HHLD Wealth Value
Rice								
10	0.27	−10.93	−2.88	0.19	−17.13	−0.07	0.72	−12.38
20	0.27	−10.93	−2.88	0.19	−17.13	−0.07	0.72	−12.38
30	0.17	−5.98	−3.30	0.07	−9.99	0.01	0.72	−7.15
40	0.17	−5.98	−3.30	0.07	−9.99	0.01	0.72	−7.15
50	0.34	−17.27	−2.60	0.19	−24.42	0.00	0.63	−15.40
60	0.27	−10.20	−2.88	0.21	−16.59	−0.03	0.74	−12.29
70	0.43	−17.22	−2.27	0.18	−23.78	−0.02	0.80	−18.95
80	0.46	−19.14	−2.15	0.15	−25.01	−0.37	0.91	−22.85
90	0.50	−21.73	−1.98	0.14	−27.71	0.01	0.69	−19.07
95	0.64	−23.96	−1.44	0.10	−28.25	−0.03	0.91	−25.59
100	0.64	−23.96	−1.44	0.10	−28.25	−0.03	0.91	−25.59
Sugar								
10	0.30	−1.17	−2.77	0.19	−4.91	−0.06	0.88	−4.34
20	0.30	−1.17	−2.77	0.19	−4.91	−0.06	0.88	−4.34
30	0.30	−1.17	−2.77	0.19	−4.91	−0.06	0.88	−4.34
40	0.40	−3.07	−2.37	0.28	−7.63	−0.01	0.84	−6.42
50	0.40	−3.07	−2.37	0.28	−7.63	−0.01	0.84	−6.42
60	0.40	−3.07	−2.37	0.28	−7.63	−0.01	0.84	−6.42
70	0.52	−3.56	−1.92	0.21	−6.95	−0.01	0.89	−6.19
80	0.52	−3.56	−1.92	0.21	−6.95	−0.01	0.89	−6.19
90	0.48	−2.93	−2.05	0.11	−5.64	0.00	0.83	−4.69
95	0.52	−4.65	−1.91	0.16	−7.85	0.00	0.89	−7.02
100	0.52	−4.65	−1.91	0.16	−7.85	0.00	0.89	−7.02
Cotton								
10	0.60	−10.39	−1.60	0.10	−13.30	−0.18	0.96	−12.83
20	0.60	−10.39	−1.60	0.10	−13.30	−0.18	0.96	−12.83
30	0.44	−6.51	−2.21	0.12	−9.87	−0.01	0.84	−8.29
40	0.60	−10.58	−1.59	0.08	−13.23	−0.02	0.88	−11.66
50	0.36	−5.92	−2.53	0.14	−9.89	−0.02	0.76	−7.55
60	0.49	−5.49	−2.02	0.08	−8.17	0.01	0.69	−5.62
70	0.39	−6.93	−2.41	0.20	−11.67	0.01	0.76	−8.89
80	0.45	−5.38	−2.20	0.07	−8.14	0.02	0.29	−2.31
90	0.49	−7.82	−2.03	0.15	−11.68	0.00	0.74	−8.60
95	0.63	−7.62	−1.45	0.11	−10.17	−0.02	0.89	−9.04
100	0.91	−13.66	−0.38	0.02	−14.31	−0.28	0.98	−14.02

Notes: First column is land share in farm assets and second two columns are share weighted value changes in farm land and capital assets. Farm debt to asset ratio is computed from the USDA-ERS ARMS database for each household type and is used for calculating the percentage change in household wealth change from farming (sixth column). The next to last column provides the share of farm wealth in the total household wealth (from the same ERS database) and is used to share weight farm and non-farm wealth changes to the total in the final column.

Source: Authors' simulations.

in wealth, relative to the income losses. While rice, cotton and sugar households stand to lose a substantial percentage of their income under the full liberalization scenario, they lose an even larger percentage of their wealth.

Having considered the impact of rich country agricultural reforms on farm households in the rich economies, we now turn to the impact of these reforms on the poorest farm households in some of the poorest countries in the world. As noted previously, we do this via a set of disaggregated poverty elasticities – each of which relates to one of the income sources for the poor. We focus our analysis on the Rich-Agr-Full-Lib results, subsequently comparing these to the Doha impacts.

Table 11 reports the change in cost-of-living deflated factor returns, by country under the $1/day poverty line assumption. With the exception of Uganda, which is the only focus country to experience a real depreciation in the face of rich country agricultural liberalization,[10] these returns rise for all agricultural factors in all regions – a simple consequence of the higher world prices for farm products. The biggest increases are in land prices (the least mobile factor of production) – with very substantial increases (from 15–39%) in Brazil, Mexico, Peru and Thailand. This is followed by unskilled agricultural labour and capital. Note that the poverty-deflated earnings fall for non-agricultural labour and capital in most countries. This will translate into higher poverty rates for the self-employed, non-agriculture households. However, the economy-wide average wage for unskilled labour rises in Brazil, Chile, Malawi, Peru, Philippines, Thailand and Vietnam, so that modest poverty reductions in the wage-labour households are expected. The final column of Table 11 shows that transfers, which are assumed to be indexed by net national income, generally do not rise fast enough to offset the higher cost of living at the poverty line. So we expect poverty in the transfer strata to rise.

Table 12 reports the consequent changes in $1/day poverty, by stratum. As expected, poverty rates in the agriculture stratum fall in all countries, excepting Uganda. Due to its relatively higher poverty elasticities, the largest percentage reductions in poverty are in Thailand. However, there are also double-digit percentage reductions in poverty among the self-employed agricultural households in Brazil, Chile and Peru. Clearly the same reforms that reduce the incomes of the richest farm households in the United States, and other developed countries boost those of the poorest farm households in some of the poorest countries in the world. Obversely, the very policies that assist the richest farmers in the rich countries create poverty among poor country farm households. The diversified household strata (both urban and rural) also show substantial poverty reductions in a number of cases – particularly Brazil, Chile and Thailand. On the other hand, higher food prices consistently push more of the non-agriculture, self-employed and the transfer dependent households into poverty.

Figure 4 offers a useful summary of the differential impact of rich country agricultural liberalization on different types of poor households in developing countries. The vertical axis reports the 'sign consistency' of poverty impacts across the 15 focus countries. This is computed as the ratio of the average to the average absolute value of the poverty change. When this reform lowers poverty for a given stratum in all

---

[10] In the case of Uganda, the impact of preference erosion in the EU market is particularly severe.

Table 11. Percentage change in cost of living adjusted factor returns: $1/day poverty

Country	Land	AgUnskl	AgSkl	NagUnskl	NagSkl	WgUnskl	WgSkl	AgCap	NagCap	Transfer
Bangladesh	1.64	0.77	0.57	-0.38	-0.46	-0.06[#]	-0.46	0.53	-0.55	-0.33
Brazil	39.28	16.06	14.73	-1.68	-1.99	0.46	-1.82	14.63	-2.31	-0.69
Chile	12.55	6.13	5.44	-0.96	-1.19	0.12	-1.18	5.42	-1.29	-0.72
Colombia	9.75	4.41	3.74	-1.70	-1.84	-0.58	-1.84	3.68	-2.19	-1.13
Indonesia	2.56	1.22	0.81	-0.75	-0.95	-0.12	-0.94	0.82	-0.94	-0.57
Malawi	1.78	1.37	1.13	0.78	0.53	1.02	0.54	1.22	0.61	1.35
Mexico	16.73[#]	4.82	4.13	-1.20	-1.50	-0.18[#]	-1.50	4.13	-1.60	-1.11
Mozambique	1.38	0.51	0.31	-0.61	-0.65	-0.26	-0.64	0.32[#]	-0.72	-0.46
Peru	14.61	7.90	6.34	-1.53	-1.88	1.30	-1.61	6.19	-2.05	-0.71
Philippines	2.20	1.07	0.65	-0.79	-0.90	-0.03[#]	-0.86	0.54	-1.16	-0.57
Thailand	22.67	10.93	8.28	-1.66	-2.70	2.41	-2.42	7.83	-3.27	-1.27
Uganda	-0.14[#]	-0.16	-0.19	-0.15	-0.22	-0.16	-0.22	-0.18	-0.21	-0.19
Venezuela	2.02	0.90	0.78	-0.39	-0.43	-0.20	-0.43	0.79	-0.45	-0.33
Vietnam	4.23	2.03	1.61	-0.66	-0.86	-0.04[#]	-0.86	1.68	-0.76	-0.32
Zambia	1.56	0.75	0.60	-0.32	-0.38	-0.07	-0.38	0.59	-0.54	-0.21

Note: All earnings have been deflated by the country-specific cost of living at the poverty line.

[#] Result can *not* be distinguished from zero change at the 95% confidence level.

Source: Authors' simulations.

Table 12. Percentage change in the poverty headcount ($1/day) across developing country strata, when rich countries undertake full agricultural reform

Country	Agr.	N-Agr.	Urb. Lab.	Rur. Lab.	Trans.	Urb. Div.	Rur. Div.
Bangladesh	−1.27	0.78	0.09[#]	0.05	0.18	−0.05[#]	0.02[#]
Brazil	−10.45	2.21	−0.57[#]	−0.79	0.23	−7.10	−4.81
Chile	−12.53	2.24	−0.22[#]	−0.14[#]	1.78	−4.65	−4.25
Colombia	−3.37	1.04	1.04	1.03	1.06	0.13[#]	0.01[#]
Indonesia	−2.86	1.62	0.45	0.46	0.66	−0.56	−0.80
Malawi	−0.67	−0.22	−2.10	−1.88	−0.57	−1.20	−0.92
Mexico	−7.83	2.35	0.77	0.37[#]	2.57	−0.29[#]	−0.52[#]
Mozambique	−0.15	0.62	0.25	0.20	0.22	0.21	0.06[#]
Peru	−10.83	2.14	−2.53	−1.82	0.32	−1.61	−1.32
Philippines	−3.52	1.68	0.22[#]	0.15[#]	0.97	−0.55	−0.54
Thailand	−22.04	4.35	−6.68	−5.49	3.43	−7.69	−7.90
Uganda	0.05	0.07	0.34	0.06	0.00	0.06	0.04
Venezuela	−0.61	0.45	0.54	0.46	0.00	0.37	0.31
Vietnam	−0.99	0.78	0.13[#]	1.87	0.26	−0.64	0.36
Zambia	0.00	0.26	0.40	0.12	0.09	0.19	0.06

Notes: Column headings are specializations for each household: Agr. = agricultural, N-Agr. = non-agricultural, Urb. Lab. = urban labour, Rur. Lab. = rural labour, Trans. = transfer, Urb. Div. = urban diversified, Rur. Div. = rural diversified.

[#] Result can *not* be distinguished from zero change at the 95% confidence level.

Source: Authors' simulations.

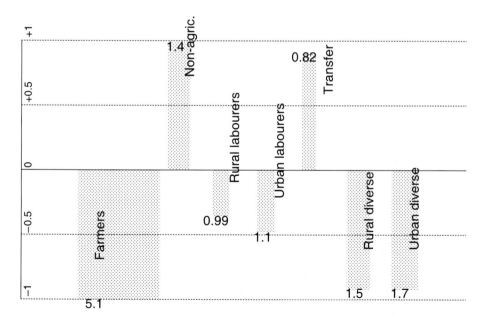

Figure 4. Sign consistency (y-axis) and average absolute value (area of rectangle) of percentage poverty changes, by stratum, 15 focus countries: Rich-Agr-Full scenario

Table 13. National poverty impacts due to rich country liberalization of agriculture: Full versus Doha reform

Country	Rich Agriculture Full Reform				Rich Agriculture Doha Reform			
	$1/day		$2/day		$1/day		$2/day	
	%	1000s	%	1000s	%	1000s	%	1000s
Bangladesh	−0.06[#]	−27[#]	0.06	62	0.00[#]	0[#]	0.02	21
Brazil	−1.88	−431	−2.61	−958	−0.73	−167	−0.96	−352
Chile	−3.99	−12	−2.48	−35	−0.99	−3	−0.57	−8
Colombia	−0.29	−12	−0.67	−59	−0.17	−7	−0.46	−40
Indonesia	−1.18	−177	−0.20	−210	−0.13	−20	0.00[#]	0[#]
Malawi	−0.72	−31	−0.32	−25	0.41	17	0.15	12
Mexico	0.34	32	−0.10	−25	0.15	14	0.03	7
Mozambique	0.09	5	0.06	8	0.05	3	0.02	3
Peru	−0.43	−19	−1.71	−157	0.04	2	−0.18	−17
Philippines	−0.66	−75	−0.41	−143	0.03[#]	3[#]	0.00[#]	0[#]
Thailand	−7.10	−84	−4.15	−806	−1.43	−17	−0.83	−161
Uganda	0.04	7	1.12	220	0.04	7	1.58	310
Venezuela	0.24	8	0.18	13	0.11	4	0.09	6
Vietnam	0.25	4	−0.24	−62	0.14	2	0.12	31
Zambia	0.13	8	0.03	2	0.03	2	0.01	1

[#] Result can *not* be distinguished from zero change at the 95% confidence level.

Source: Authors' simulations.

countries, its sign consistency reaches its minimum value of −1.0. On the other hand, when it raises poverty in all countries, this measure reaches its maximum value of 1.0. From the figure it is clear that the impact on poverty amongst agriculture specialized households is consistently favourable (i.e. a reduction). On the other hand, poverty amongst non-agriculture self-employed households consistently rises in the wake of rich country agriculture reforms. On balance, the rural and urban wage dependent and diversified households also tend to experience poverty reduction, while transfer dependent households show consistent poverty increases across this sample of countries.

The other important piece of information summarized in Figure 4 is the average absolute value of the poverty changes for each stratum. This is captured by the relative areas of each shaded rectangle, with the associated value recorded as well. Thus, the average absolute value of the poverty changes for the agriculture stratum is 5.1%. This is considerably larger than the next largest entries: 1.5% and 1.7% for the rural and urban diverse poverty changes, respectively. Overall, Figure 4 gives a picture of relatively broad-based poverty reduction, with some important exceptions in the case of self-employed non-farm, and transfer-dependent households.

The net effect of Rich-Agr-Lib on the national poverty headcount is reported in the first set of columns in Table 13. National poverty at the $1/day level falls in 10 of the 15 countries, with small percentage increases in Mozambique (unskilled wages fall), Uganda (factor prices fall), Venezuela (high share of poor in the non-agriculture stratum), Vietnam (large poverty elasticity for non-agricultural capital) and Zambia (negligible poverty elasticity in agriculture stratum). The next column of Table 13 converts these percentage changes in national poverty into thousands of people. Here, the reductions in Brazil, Indonesia, Philippines and Thailand are clearly dominant. When we move to the $2/day poverty line with Rich-Agr-Lib (next two columns of the table), the national poverty picture is reversed in two cases: Bangladesh (small decrease becomes a small increase) and Vietnam (small insignificant increase becomes a small decrease), so once again poverty falls in two-thirds of the 15 countries. On balance, the largest changes involve poverty reductions, with Brazil, Indonesia, Philippines and Thailand standing out.

We can contrast these outcomes with those that would be achieved under the prospective Doha reforms (Rich-Agr-Doha reforms only), and this is done in the final four columns of Table 13. More modest rises in agriculture earnings and lesser increases in the unskilled wage rate (adjusted for the cost of living at the poverty line) mean that now poverty rises (albeit slightly) in more than half the countries (8 of 15) in the case of $1/day poverty. Clearly, even the ambitious Doha Development Agenda under examination here is less poverty friendly than would be a proportionately scaled back version of full liberalization in rich country agriculture. The latter would presumably show poverty reduction in all the same countries – just to a lesser degree. Yet the Doha scenario results in fewer countries showing poverty reductions than under the full liberalization of Rich Agriculture.

4.2. Global liberalization scenarios

We now turn to a set of liberalization scenarios that involve tariff cuts in both agriculture and non-agriculture sectors and in both the rich and the poor countries. Developing country agricultural tariffs are quite high, so abolishing them increases world agricultural trade volumes relative to Rich-only liberalization. Reforming them on Doha terms, however, makes little difference because the large binding overhangs and modest cuts in developing country bound tariffs (no cuts for LDCs) translate into little additional market access. Adding tariff cuts in manufactures on the other hand leads to significant increases in manufacturing trade under both full and Doha scenarios and for both developed and developing countries (see Annex Table A.6.3 for detailed results).

Table 14 reports the aggregate welfare and ToT impacts of these global reforms. Comparing Rich Agriculture (Table 7) with Global reforms (Table 14); the most striking change in the rich countries is the improvement in the ToT for Japan, which benefits from manufacturing tariff cuts. On the other hand, the Canadian ToT deteriorate more as a result of preference erosion in the US manufactures market. However, despite the ToT loss, Canadian welfare rises by more under global full liberalization than under Rich-Agr-Lib alone.

Turning to the focus countries, we see very different ToT and welfare impacts than those stemming from Rich-Agr reforms only. The ToT for these developing countries

Table 14. Macroeconomic impacts of liberalization: global scenarios

| | Global (all countries and merchandise) | | | |
| | Full | | Doha | |
	ToT	Welfare	ToT	Welfare
Rich countries				
Aust. and New Zlnd.	2.30	0.76	1.09	0.28
Japan	0.28	1.29	0.04	0.54
Canada	−0.64	0.39	−0.23	0.06
US	0.29	0.06	0.01	0.01
Europe FTA	−0.12	0.42	−0.12	0.20
Focus countries				
Bangladesh	−5.66	−0.65	−0.04	−0.04
Brazil	3.72	0.67	2.03	0.31
Chile	0.58	0.32	0.18	0.01
Colombia	−1.52	−0.54	0.33	−0.07
Indonesia	1.11	0.51	0.23	0.07
Malawi	3.56	3.83	0.34	0.32
Mexico	−2.02	−0.20	−0.43	−0.12
Mozambique	0.00	1.19	−0.13	−0.08
Peru	0.66	0.60	0.11	−0.02
Philippines	−0.33	0.49	0.12	0.12
Tanzania	−2.05	−0.66	−0.29	−0.08
Thailand	1.50	2.08	0.54	0.51
Uganda	−0.99	−0.32	−0.64	−0.18
Venezuela	−2.19	−0.26	−0.68	−0.03
Vietnam	−1.25	5.73	−0.85	−1.17
Zambia	−0.46	0.28	0.04	−0.03

Notes: No sensitivity analysis is conducted for global scenarios.

Source: Authors' simulations.

fall in about the same number of cases (9 of 15), due to the expansion of poor country exports in the wake of own and other developing country tariff cuts and the erosion of preferences in manufacturing. However, welfare only falls for six of these countries, with efficiency gains dominating the ToT losses in the other three cases (Philippines, Vietnam and Zambia). In contrast, under Global Doha, there are fewer ToT losses, but also fewer (and smaller) welfare gains. These mixed aggregate welfare effects for developing countries from global trade reforms are quite comparable to those reported in other studies of the aggregate impacts of global trade reforms on developing countries (Francois *et al.*, 2005; Anderson and Martin, 2006; Hertel and Winters, 2006; Bouet *et al.*, 2006).

The changes in real farm income under global reforms are dominated by the Rich-Agr reforms previously discussed. Liberalizing rich country non-agricultural merchandise trade is slightly beneficial to the farm households – by lowering the price of non-agricultural goods, but tariffs on most of these products are already quite low

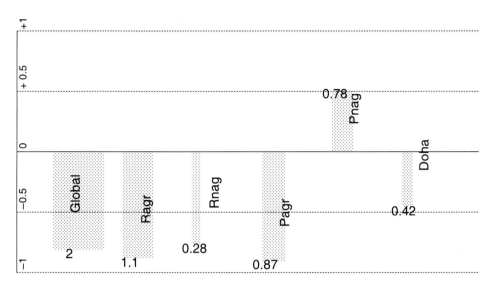

Figure 5. Sign consistency (y-axis) and average absolute value (area of rectangle) of percentage national poverty changes, by policy scenario, 15 focus countries

and so the impact is minimal. On the other hand, trade reforms in the poor countries as a group tend to be slightly adverse for the welfare of rich country farm households. This is due to a complex set of factors, including the tendency for tariff cuts to encourage labour and capital to shift back to the food and agriculture sector, as well as the impact of increased demand on the general price level in rich countries. But these effects are very small, relative to the primary impact of the Rich-Agr policies themselves.

Given these results for the average farm household in the rich countries, it is hardly surprising that the impacts of global reforms on individual US farm households are quite similar to that reported previously in the Rich-Agr reform scenario (Table A.6.8). Welfare for the wealthiest farm households is driven first and foremost by their own national policies, with the largest international interactions occurring among the world's richest (and largest) markets – as in the case of US–Japan rice trade.

However, when it comes to the poverty impacts of global trade reform, agricultural policies in the rich countries are only part of the story – trade policies in the developing countries themselves assume much greater prominence. Figure 5 uses the sign consistency and average absolute value measures developed in Figure 4 to summarize the national poverty impacts of the different types of trade policy reform. Specifically, we decompose the impact of global trade reform into its constituent parts: Rich-Agr, Poor-Agr, Rich-Nagr, and Poor-Nagr, using the numerical technique of Harrison *et al.* (1999). As noted previously, Rich-Agr reforms contribute to poverty reduction in the majority of countries (negative sign consistency). The large average absolute value of these poverty impacts (1.1%) is also the largest of any of these policies. This is followed in importance by agricultural trade reforms in the poor countries (AAV =

0.87%), which show an equally consistent pattern of poverty reduction. The average impact of non-agriculture reforms rich countries is of lesser magnitude, although generally poverty-reducing, whereas the non-agriculture tariff cuts in the poor countries are poverty-increasing, on balance, in our 15 country sample. (Individual country results are reported in Annex Table A.6.9.)

The final rectangle in Figure 5 reports the sign consistency and average absolute value of the national poverty changes under the Doha scenario. This should be compared to the Global result at the beginning of the figure. Here, we see that, not only does the Doha scenario have a smaller average absolute value than global full liberalization (hardly surprising), the Doha scenario is also less poverty friendly than the global liberalization scenario, with a sign consistency of less than -0.5. (Individual country results are reported in Annex Table A.6.10.) Hertel and Ivanic (2006) emphasize that qualitatively less favourable impact of Doha on poverty is due to the heavy weight given to export subsidy elimination (which raises import prices for food), while the developing countries make only mild cuts to their applied tariffs under the Doha scenario and the least developed countries are not required to cut tariffs at all.

4.3. Compensation for rich country farmers

The farm household welfare impacts in rich countries are dominated by liberalization of the agricultural pillars. Inclusion of agriculture and developing country reforms do little to make up the lost income as the scope of reforms is broadened. With this in mind we consider a final scenario that asks what compensation would be required to hold aggregate farm income unchanged under the global full liberalization experiment.[11] This requires solving for an endogenous green-box subsidy to land in the following rich regions where aggregate farm income declines: Japan (-28.4%), Europe (-11.5%), and the United States (-3.7%). The choice of aggregate farm income as a compensation target reflects the expectation that the policy process will continue to focus on this readily available measure to gauge the well-being of the farm population. In an alternative compensation simulation we investigate the cost savings generated in these three countries by compensating on the basis of aggregate farm household income (inclusive of off-farm income).

Farm income compensation at the level of a representative farm household in each of these countries leads to sizable increases in WTO green-box outlays in each country. In Japan, agricultural land is subject to net taxation initially, and compensation requires an increase in expenditure to produce net subsidization at the level of $9.1 billion in land-based payments. Both the EU and the United States have significant land-based payments initially and the compensation scheme here indicates that the EU

---

[11] We are not asserting that compensation for OECD farmers is justified, nor even necessary to achieve the reforms, although a case for the latter could certainly be made.

would need a 63% increase over that initial level at a cost of $11.8 billion. For the United States, the percentage increase is smaller at 27.4%, coming at a cost of $3.3 billion.

As discussed previously, the use of farm income as a welfare indicator for the population of farm households in wealthy countries is incomplete and in this case would lead to considerable over-compensation in welfare terms. Using the full farm household welfare criterion as opposed to solely farm income, we find that Japanese and US policy-makers need only compensate these farmers with $6.3 billion and $2.4 billion, nearly a one-third reduction. The reduction in the EU is much smaller (only $300 million less than when compensating based on losses in farm income alone). This follows directly from the small share of income obtained from non-farm activities by farm households in the EU as well as the less favourable developments in off-farm wages.

5. CONCLUSIONS

This paper has sought to identify the impacts of WTO reforms on farm households in rich and poor countries. It has done so via innovative use of newly available household survey data that identify the income sources and degree of earnings specialization of households. This proves to be a critical factor in assessing the household welfare impacts of trade reforms. In the rich countries, we focus our attention on the United States, where survey data permit us to assess the impacts of trade reforms by wealth decile and commodity specialization. In the poor countries, we analyse changes in the poverty headcount – among both farm and non-farm households.

Our findings highlight the fact that, in the medium run (2–3 years), wealthy farmers are the main beneficiaries of current trade policies aimed at protecting agriculture in the rich countries. Furthermore, these benefits tend to be concentrated in a few products that receive very high levels of support presently. In the United States, rice stands out – followed by cotton, sugar and dairy. When we look at aggregate farm household welfare in the United States, it is little affected by agricultural trade policy reforms. This is because many of the farm products receive little or no support and improved market access in other countries benefits export-oriented producers. Indeed, this is why the average farm household in Australia, Canada and New Zealand is expected to gain from rich country agricultural trade reforms. A second reason why the average farm household in the US is not more severely affected by trade policy reform stems from the degree of earnings diversification in that country. On average, only 8% of farm household income in the US is derived from farming. This income diversification is also critical in Japan where just 12% of farm income is obtained from on-farm earnings. As a consequence, while Doha trade reforms cause on-farm incomes to drop by 16% in Japan, the average farm household impact is just 1.4%.

The finding of generally modest medium-run impacts on the average farm household stands in sharp contrast to the strong opposition from agricultural lobbies in the rich countries. This opposition can be better understood when we use our household survey data for the US to show that the degree of earnings diversification diminishes for the wealthiest farms in the highly protected commodities, and this provides them with strong incentives to prevent the very substantial drop in household welfare that can be expected under trade reform. Furthermore, since these households have most of their assets tied up in agriculture, the percentage drop in household wealth is even greater than the income decline. Consequently, some compensation mechanism may prove necessary to solve the political impasse currently plaguing the Doha talks. We explore one such mechanism by which payments are aimed at neutralizing the loss in average on-farm income for each commodity group. This programme would introduce around $25 billion of new agricultural subsidies into global agriculture from the three countries where farm income declines (Japan, EU and the United States) and would undoubtedly make the Doha scenario much more palatable to the farm lobbies.

In the poorest countries, we find that, with one minor exception, rich country agriculture reforms benefit low-income farm households. Regardless of the poverty line considered, the poverty headcount in this part of the developing world falls. However, the impact on non-farm population groups is mixed. In those countries where agriculture makes up a large share of the unskilled labour force, rich country reforms tend to increase the demand for labour sufficiently to benefit unskilled workers throughout the economy. But self-employed households in the non-agricultural economy, as well as those dependent on transfer payments, systematically lose. Therefore the national poverty outcome inevitably depends on the relative weights of these different groups in the national poverty picture. Since a large share of the poor reside in agriculture, national poverty falls in two-thirds of the focus countries in the wake of rich country agricultural liberalization.

Reviving the DDA in the WTO offers one way – we would argue almost certainly the only way – of starting to reap these benefits in the near term. The WTO could reform the privileges of the richest farmers of the North for the sake of the poor farmers in the South. And, if policy-makers were really serious about poverty reduction, they would push for more poor country farm and food tariff cuts, as these products loom large in the household budgets of the poor. Giving the latter access to food at world market prices (adjusted for marketing margins) is a sure way to reduce poverty. Yet this is precisely the component that is mostly omitted under the current Doha proposals. Indeed, global trade liberalization is the policy configuration with the most favourable poverty outcomes across the 15 developing countries examined in this study.

━━━━━━

Discussion

Gilles Duranton
University of Toronto

One may wonder about the interest of a paper assessing the hypothetical effects of the Doha Round only months after its negotiation entered a state of what may turn out to be terminal coma. To help us understand what happened and pave the road ahead, this paper offers three main insights. First, it gives a clear-cut explanation regarding why the Doha negotiations collapsed in 2006 without the US or the EU making any significant attempt to salvage it.

Before going deeper into these issues, it is helpful to comment briefly on the approach taken by the authors. In a nutshell, they use a computable general equilibrium (CGE) model and assess the distributional effects of trade liberalization (Doha and a number of variants) within a major developed country (the United States) and a (diverse) bunch of developing countries. The tag 'CGE with distribution' that summarizes the paper may be both deceptive and off-putting. The deception comes from the fact that this simple label actually hides a very sophisticated mechanics. The core of the work is the standard computable general equilibrium model (GTAP) that prevails in the literature. It is combined with the US Agricultural Resource Management Survey and 15 developing country household surveys. The main idea is that trade liberalization will have some aggregate effects on the prices and quantities produced and in turn these will affect the income of individual US farmers as well as the income and consumption of households in developing countries.

A lot of hard work is involved here. GTAP is an unruly beast which is hard to domesticate. Then, the authors had to make a number of changes to this model. First, it had to be more sophisticated on the factor side to allow for some imperfect mobility of factors across sectors (instead of perfect mobility) to generate meaningful distributional effects. Using the trade jargon, a Heckscher–Ohlin framework had to be transformed into something closer to a factor-specific model. Trade costs also had to be incorporated because sourcing matters a lot for agricultural imports. A farming income function for US farmers had to be constructed. Many poverty estimates also had to be meticulously calculated for developing country households. Finally, plugging the effects of a CGE model into such surveys requires a tremendous amount of work. The authors should be praised for all this.

However, many in the economics profession are deeply uncomfortable with CGE modelling. This type of exercise reminds us too much of the big macro models of the 1970s that turned out to be misleading and were eventually abandoned. Without doubt, large models with many equations and even more ad-hoc assumptions are more akin to cooking than serious economic research as we would define it nowadays. This being said, the authors have made a noteworthy effort with respect to the quality of the estimates generated by their model. First, they have kept the wiring of the CGE framework into the household surveys simple to limit their degrees of freedom and avoid transforming the CGE black-box into an even larger black-box. Second, they have checked the predictions generated by their parameters for a number of (independent) outcomes against the *ex-post* realizations of these outcomes. This is certainly something. One may regret that the CGE methodology lags behind the state of the art in modern macroeconomic calibration. Such much-needed contribution is however beyond the scope of the current paper. Finally, note that despite the important caveats mentioned above, CGE models are (nearly) the only tool we have to put some much-needed numbers behind proposed changes in trade policy. Absent the numbers from CGE, we would be left with the quantitative claims made by various advocacy groups. The quality and seriousness of the CGE estimates such as those offered here are certainly light-years above the numbers produced by farmers unions or ideologically motivated NGOs.

Returning to the conclusions of the paper, why did Doha collapse without any major player trying to prevent this? The paper offers a simple answer. As many of us suspected, farmers in Europe, the United States and Japan are part of this answer. As we also suspected, the aggregate effects of Doha were going to be quite small since the proposal that died was rather minimal. However, the major new insight delivered by the paper is that most farmers in North America would lose very little. It is only a tiny fraction of them (particularly those producing sugar, cotton, rice and dairies) that stood to lose really a lot from Doha. However, these farmers wield considerable political power in North America, Europe and Japan, through both their geographically concentrated single-issue votes and their unions that lobbied very effectively to derail the Doha Round. The last key result of the paper is that Doha would have reduced poverty even in the poorest agriculture-importing countries, contrary to many claims to the contrary.

This brings me to the second major lesson from the paper. The Doha Round was sold as 'trade liberalization to reduce poverty'. A key selling point was that developing countries as a whole had a comparative advantage in agriculture while protection from rich countries in that sector prevented them from exploiting their comparative advantage. This pro-poor rhetoric backfired badly. Opponents to Doha were quick to point out that trade liberalization for agricultural goods would lead to an increase in agricultural prices on the world markets. Since the poorest countries in the world tend to be net importers of agriculture, Doha was thus bound to hurt them according to the counter-claim. This counter-claim possibly killed much of the initial popular support for Doha. What the paper does here is to show that Doha (and *a fortiori* stronger forms of trade liberalization) was indeed pro-poor. The reason is that the poorest of the poor tend to be farmers in the poorest countries and they stood to gain from higher prices for agricultural goods resulting from trade liberalization. This sets the record straight but it is also quite clear that 'selling Doha' as a poverty-alleviation scheme will always be difficult since such counter-counter claim is unlikely to settle the debate in the public opinion.

At this stage, there are good reasons to be very pessimistic about the future of trade liberalisation. What was on the table in 2006 for the Doha Round was extremely modest but got derailed nonetheless.

On this issue, the paper is clearly in a traditional 'public interest' perspective and attempts to assess what sort of compensation could be offered to the 'losers' from the liberalization of agricultural trade. This perspective is understandable given the institutional affiliation of some of the co-authors of the paper. Let me take a different route in this comment. Before going any further, note first that giving a huge lump-sum to very small and extremely well-organized vested interests that have managed to extract great rents from their governments is hard to justify on moral grounds. This is of course assuming that any amount of compensation will ever be enough to satisfy these vested interests, which is itself in doubt.

The first suggestion (of a long-run nature) would be to foster 'farming dilution'. The main opponents to Doha are rich farmers from rich countries for whom farming represents most of their income. 'Marginal' farmers stand to lose only a small fraction of their overall income. Favouring the diversification of the activities of farming households is certainly a possibility. This could weaken the 'hard core' of the opposition to agricultural trade liberalization. On the other hand, this could also paradoxically strengthen the anti-liberalization coalition by making it more homogenous. Besides, this is a potentially extremely costly solution that is likely to take a very long time. Previous attempts at farming diversification policies do not seem very encouraging either.

A second suggestion would be to use the fact that, at least in North America, the hard core of the coalition against agricultural trade liberalization is tiny. It might be possible to bring on board small farmers through a compensation scheme and isolate the others. Whether this is a feasible solution depends on how easy it would be to split the farming opposition to liberalization and in turn this is very sensitive to the details of how the farming lobbying works. The third suggestion would be to replace the positive pro-poor stance of agricultural trade liberation by much negative publicity around those that benefit the most from protection and subsidies. Put differently, trade liberalization could be sold as a way to finish with unfair subsidies received by very small coalitions of vested interested. Naming and shaming the 'profiteers' may go some way towards isolating some lobbies from their friends in Congress or in the executive. The latter may start to find it inconvenient being associated with deeply unpopular groups. Finally, at least in the United States, it may also be possible to play winners against losers of trade liberalization. Unilateral liberalization of, for instance, cotton trade is not politically feasible since it will have Louisiana up in arms and other members of Congress will moderately support Louisiana in exchange for future reciprocity. At the opposite end, broad trade liberalization measures may also run into trouble for the same reason but this time compounded by the fact that there will be a complete coalition of potential losers. Such broad proposals, like the Doha proposal, seem to be doomed. Instead, a trade deal that includes, say, software and cotton will pitch California against Louisiana and some progress might be achieved. This type of argument suggests that the future of trade liberalization may not be about broad deals but instead about small packages that can go around binding political constraints.

In conclusion, this paper by Thomas Hertel and his co-authors suggests that the political constraints should be at the heart of any further thinking about trade liberalization. Rather than lay down what should be done from a first-best perspective and then worry about how it can go through, economists should think about the politics right from the start. The second departure that is suggested here is that the standard approach of trying to compensate the losers is unlikely to work well. These potential losers have played their game in a very nasty (but very effective) way. It is probably time that proponents of trade liberalization in agriculture started to think about less nice strategies as well. This may not be something we enjoy but this is about the plight of hundreds of millions of people in the developing world after all.

Panel discussion

Panel members were broadly in agreement with the main conclusions of the paper and in fact thought that the political message should be more forcefully trumpeted. The discussion focused on some elements that are still missing in the CGE models and that may be important for the impact of trade reforms. Omer Moav, for example, noted that price changes affect farmers behaviour also because they affect the decision of entry and exit. A related comment by Steve Redding is that the heterogeneity of producers is not integrated in CGE models. It may be crucial in our understanding of the effect of trade reforms because reallocation from least to most productive farmers may lead to larger efficiency gains. Christian Gollier commented the distributional effect of trade reforms on price volatility is overlooked and may in practice be very important in poor countries.

WEB APPENDIX

Available at: www.economic-policy.org

REFERENCES

Abler, D.G. (2001). 'Elasticities of substitution and factor supply in Canadian, Mexican, and US agriculture', Appendix A.2 in *Market Effects of Crop Support Measures*, OECD, Paris.

Adelman, I. and S. Robinson (1978). *Income Distribution Policy in Developing Countries: A Case Study of Korea*, Oxford University Press, Oxford and World Bank, New York.

Anderson, K. (1995). 'Lobbying incentives and the pattern of protection in rich and poor countries', *Economic Development and Cultural Change*, 43, 401–24.

Anderson, K. and W. Martin (eds.) (2006). *Agricultural Trade Reform and the Doha Development Agenda*, Palgrave Macmillan and World Bank, New York.

Anderson, K., W. Martin and D. van der Mensbrugghe (2006a). 'Market and welfare implications of Doha reform scenarios', Chapter 12 in K. Anderson and W. Martin (eds.), *Agricultural Trade Reform and the Doha Development Agenda*, Palgrave Macmillan and World Bank, New York.

— (2006b). 'Global impacts of the Doha scenarios on poverty', Chapter 17 in T.W. Hertel and L.A. Winters (eds.), *Poverty and the WTO: Impacts of the Doha Development Agenda*, Palgrave Macmillan and World Bank, New York.

Arndt, C. (1996). *An Introduction to Systematic Sensitivity Analysis via Gaussian Quadrature*, GTAP Technical Paper No. 24, Center for Global Trade Analysis, Purdue University, http://www.agecon.purdue.edu/gtap/techpapr/tp-2.htm.

Bchir, M.H., L. Fontagné and S. Jean (2005). 'From bound duties to actual protection: Industrial liberalisation in the Doha Round', paper presented at the 8th Annual Conference on Global Economic Analysis, Lubeck, Germany, available online at www.gtap.org.

Bouët, A., C. Bureau, Y. Decreux and S. Jean (2004). 'Developing countries faced with multilateral agricultural liberalization: Contrasted fortunes', paper presented at the 7th Annual Conference on Global Economic Analysis, Washington, DC, available online at www.gtap.org.

Bouët, A., D. Orden and S. Mevel (2006). 'More or less ambition in the Doha Round?', paper presented at the 9th Annual Conference on Global Economic Analysis, Addis Ababa, available online at www.gtap.org.

Bourguignon, F., and L.A. Pereira da Silva (2003). *The Impact of Economic Policies on Poverty and Income Distribution: Evaluation Techniques and Tools*, World Bank, New York and Oxford University Press, Oxford.

Chen, S. and M. Ravallion (2004). 'Welfare impacts of WTO accession to the World Trade Organization', *World Bank Economic Review*, 18, 29–57.

Cline, W.R. (2004). *Trade Policy and Poverty*, Institute for International Economics, Washington, DC.

Cranfield, J.A.L., J.S. Eales, T.W. Hertel and P.V. Preckel (2003). 'Model selection when estimating and predicting consumer demand using international, cross-section data', *Empirical Economics*, 28, 353–64.

Cranfield, J.A.L., P.V. Preckel, J.S. Eales and T.W. Hertel (2004). 'Simultaneous estimation of an implicit directly additive demand system and the distribution of expenditure – an application of maximum entropy', *Economic Modeling*, 21, 361–85.

De Janvry, A., M. Fafchamps and E. Sadoulet (1991). 'Peasant household behavior with missing markets: Some paradoxes explained', *Economic Journal*, 101, 1400–17.

Dimaranan, B. (2007). *Global Trade Assistance and Production: The GTAP 6 Data Base*, Center for Global Trade Analysis, Purdue University.

Dimaranan, B., T.W., Hertel and R. Keeney (2004). 'OECD domestic support and the developing countries', in B. Guha-Khasnobis (ed.), *The WTO, Developing Countries and the Doha Development Agenda: Prospects and Challenges for Trade-led Growth*, Palgrave-Macmillan, London.

Emini, C.A., J. Cockburn and B. Decaluwe (2006). 'The poverty impacts of the Doha Round in Cameroon: The role of tax policy', Chapter 13 in T.W. Hertel and L.A. Winters (eds.), *Poverty and the WTO: Impacts of the Doha Development Agenda*, Palgrave Macmillan and World Bank, New York.

Finger, J.M. (1981). 'Policy research', *Journal of Political Economy*, 89, 1270–71.

Francois, J., H. van Meijl and F. van Tongeren (2005). 'Trade liberalization in the Doha Development Round', *Economic Policy*, 20, 349–91.

Gardner, B.L. (1969). 'Determinants of farm family income inequality', *American Journal of Agricultural Economics*, 51, 753–69.

— (1992). 'Changing economic perspectives on the farm problem', *Journal of Economic Literature*, 30, 62–101.

— (2000). 'Economic growth and low incomes in agriculture', *American Journal of Agricultural Economics*, 82, 1059–74.

Golub, A., T.W. Hertel, H. Lee and N. Ramankutty (2006). 'Modeling land supply and demand in the long run', paper presented at the Ninth Annual Conference on Global Economic Analysis, Addis Ababa, 15–17 June, also available at: http://www.gtap.agecon.purdue.edu/resources/download/2628.pdf

Hanson, K. and A. Somwaru (2003). 'Distributional effects of US farm commodity programs: Accounting for farm and non-farm households', paper presented at the 6th Annual Conference on Global Economic Analysis, June, The Hague, The Netherlands.

Harrison, W.J., J.M. Horridge and K. Pearson (2000). 'Decomposing simulation results with respect to exogenous shocks', *Computational Economics*, 15, 227–49.

Harrison, G., T. Rutherford and D. Tarr (2002). 'Trade policy options for Chile: The importance of market access', *World Bank Economic Review*, 16, 49–79.

Harrison, G., T. Rutherford, D. Tarr and A. Gurgel (2003). 'Regional, multilateral and unilateral trade policies of MERCOSUR for growth and poverty reduction in Brazil', Policy Research Working Paper 3051, World Bank, Washington, DC.

Hertel, T.W. and M. Ivanic (2006). 'Understanding the poverty implications of the Doha Development Agenda', mimeo, Center for Global Trade Analysis, Purdue University, W. Lafayette, IN.

Hertel, T.W., M. Ivanic, P.V. Preckel, and J.A.L. Cranfield (2004). 'The earnings effects of multilateral trade liberalization: Implications for poverty', *World Bank Economic Review*, 18, 205–36.

Hertel, T.W. and R. Keeney (2006). 'What is at stake: The relative importance of import barriers, export subsidies, and domestic support', Chapter 2 in K. Anderson and W. Martin (eds.), *Agricultural Trade Reform and the Doha Development Agenda*, Palgrave Macmillan and World Bank, New York.

Hertel, T.W. and J.J. Reimer (2005). 'Predicting the poverty impacts of trade reform', *Journal of International Trade and Economic Development*, 14, 377–405.

Hertel, T.W. and L.A. Winters (eds.) (2006). *Poverty and the WTO*, Palgrave Macmillan and World Bank, New York.

Hill, B. (1996). *Farm Incomes, Wealth, and Agricultural Policy*, Ashgate, Brookfield, VT.

Jean, S., D. Laborde and W. Martin (2006). 'Consequences of alternative formulas for agricultural tariff cuts', Chapter 4 in K. Anderson and W. Martin (eds.), *Agricultural Trade Reform and the Doha Development Agenda*, Palgrave Macmillan and World Bank, New York.

Jensen, H.T. and F. Tarp (2005). 'Trade liberalization and spatial inequality: A methodological innovation in a Vietnamese perspective', *Review of Development Economics*, 9, 69–86.

Jensen, H.G. and H. Zobbe (2006). 'Consequences of reducing limits on aggregate measurements of support', Chapter 9 in K. Anderson and W. Martin (eds.), *Agricultural Trade Reform and the Doha Development Agenda*, Palgrave Macmillan and World Bank, New York.

Keeney, R. (2005). 'Decoupling and the WTO: Farm sector and household impacts in the United States', Unpublished PhD dissertation, Purdue University.

Keeney, R. and T.W. Hertel (2005). 'GTAP-AGR: A framework for assessing the implications of multilateral changes in agricultural policies', GTAP Technical Paper No. 24, Center for Global Trade Analysis, Purdue University, available at: http://www.gtap.agecon.purdue.edu/resources/tech_papers.asp

Kilkenny, M. (1993). 'Rural/urban effects of terminating farm subsidies', *American Journal of Agricultural Economics*, 75, 968–80.

Liu, J., T.C. Arndt and T.W. Hertel (2004). 'Parameter estimation and measures of goodness of fit in a global general equilibrium model', *Journal of Economic Integration*, 19(3), 626–49.

Orden, D., R. Paarlberg and T. Roe (1999). *Policy Reform in American Agriculture: Analysis and Prognosis*, University of Chicago Press, Chicago.

OECD (Organization for Economic Cooperation and Development) (2001). *Market Effects of Crop Support Measures*, OECD Publications, Paris.

— (2002). OECD PSE/CSE database, www.oecd.org.

— (2003). *Farm Household Income: Issues and Policy Responses*, OECD Publications, Paris.

Polaski, S. (2006). *Winners and Losers: Impact of the Doha Development Round on Developing Countries*, Carnegie Foundation, Washington DC.

Ravallion, M. (1997). 'Can high-inequality developing countries escape absolute poverty?', *Economics Letters*, 56, 51–57.

Reimer, J.J. and T.W. Hertel (2004). 'Estimation of international demand behavior for use with input-output based data', *Economic Systems Research*, 16, 347–66.

Rimmer, M. and A. Powell (1996). 'An implicitly additive demand system', *Applied Economics*, 28, 1613–22.

Rutherford, T., D. Tarr and O. Shepotylo (2006). 'The impact on Russia of WTO accession and the DDA: The importance of liberalization of barriers against foreign direct investment in services for growth and poverty reduction', Chapter 16 in T.W. Hertel and L.A. Winters (eds.), *Poverty and the WTO: Impacts of the Doha Development Agenda*, Palgrave Macmillan and World Bank, New York.

Salhofer, K. (2001). 'Elasticities of substitution and factor supply elasticities in European agriculture: A review of past studies', Annex A.2 in *Market Effects of Crop Support Measures*, OECD Publications, Paris.

Schattschneider, E.E. (1935). *Politics, Pressure, and the Tariff*, Prentice Hall, New York.

Schultz, T.W. (1945). *Agriculture in an Unstable Economy*, McGraw Hill, New York.

Sumner, D.A. (2006). 'Reducing cotton subsidies: The DDA cotton initiative', Chapter 10 in K. Anderson and W. Martin (eds.), *Agricultural Trade Reform and the Doha Development Agenda*, Palgrave Macmillan and World Bank, New York.

Surry, Y. (1990). 'Econometric modeling of the European compound feed sector: An application to France', *Journal of Agricultural Economics*, 41, 404–21.

USDA-ERS (US Department of Agriculture Economic Research Service) (2005). *Agricultural Resource Management Survey Briefing Room*. USDA-ERS website: http://www.ers.usda.gov/Briefing/ARMS/

Valenzuela, E., T.W. Hertel, R. Keeney and J.J. Reimer (2005). 'Assessing global CGE model validity using agricultural price volatility', GTAP Working Paper No. 33, Center for Global Trade Analysis, Purdue University, available at: http://www.gtap.agecon.purdue.edu/resources/working_papers.asp

Van der Mensbrugghe, D. (2006). 'Estimating the benefits: Why numbers change', Chapter 4 in R. Newfarmer (ed.), *Trade, Doha, and Development: Window into the Issues*, World Bank, Washington DC.

Winters, L.A. (1987). 'The political economy of the agricultural policy of industrial countries', *European Review of Agricultural Economics*, 14, 285–304.

— (2002). 'Trade liberalisation and poverty: What are the links?', *World Economy*, 25, 143–71.

Winters, L.A., N. McCulloch and A. McKay (2004). 'Trade liberalization and poverty: The evidence so far', *Journal of Economic Literature*, 27, 481–506.

World Bank (2001). *Global Economic Prospects*, World Bank, Washington DC.

— (2003). *Global Economic Prospects*, World Bank, Washington DC.

WTO (World Trade Organization) (2004). *Decision Adopted by the General Council on 1 August 2004*, WT/L/579, WTO Secretariat, Geneva.

International migration

SUMMARY

The international movement of labour remains much more restricted than movement of goods or capital, and the worldwide economic gains to liberalizing migration are large. This paper asks whether those gains could be realized through better international cooperation on migration along the lines of the WTO for trade. Although public opinion is marginally more negative towards the liberalization of migration than of trade, the key impediment is the lack of a basis for reciprocity in negotiations over migration. And this is because migration is largely driven by absolute advantage rather than by comparative advantage as in the case of trade. Consequently there is no basis for WTO-style negotiations over migration and therefore no grounds for reforming the international architecture in the hope of fostering liberalization.

— Timothy J. Hatton

Economic Policy April 2007 Printed in Great Britain
© CEPR, CES, MSH, 2007.

Should we have a WTO for international migration?

Timothy J. Hatton

University of Essex, Australian National University and CEPR

1. INTRODUCTION

We live in a world where policies towards international trade are very liberal while policies towards international migration are very restrictive. During the last half century economic globalization has been fostered and underpinned by policy liberalization in trade, capital markets and a number of other areas. In trade, the GATT/WTO has promoted liberalization through multilateral negotiation but no such forum exists for international migration. Thus, international migration remains less globalized than international markets in goods and capital and, as a result, it is the field in which the gains to liberalization are likely to be the largest. As Dani Rodrik puts it:

> The gains from liberalising labour movements across countries are enormous, and much larger than the likely benefits from further liberalisation in the traditional areas of goods and capital.
> If international policymakers were really interested in maximising worldwide efficiency, they

An earlier version of this paper was presented as the Julian Simon Lecture at the third Annual Migration Meeting at IZA, Bonn, 20–21 April 2006. I am grateful for comments from participants at the IZA and for comments on earlier drafts from seminar participants at the Australian National University, Carlos III University, Trinity College, Dublin and University of Essex, and from participants at the conference on 'Immigration: Impacts, Integration and Intergenerational Issues', University College, London, 29–31 March 2006. This version has also benefited from constructive comments from four referees, as well as from discussants Neil Gandal and Manuel Arellano, and other participants at the 44th Panel meeting of *Economic Policy* in Helsinki, 20–21 October 2006. I am also grateful for support for this research from the Australian Research Council under grant no. DP0557885.

The Managing Editor in charge of this paper was Paul Seabright.

Economic Policy April 2007 pp. 339–383 Printed in Great Britain
© CEPR, CES, MSH, 2007.

would spend little of their energies on a new trade round or on the international financial architecture. They would all be busy at work liberalising immigration restrictions. (2002, p. 314)

Recently, new thinking about enhanced co-operation over migration has been reflected in a number of policy forums, the most notable of which is the United Nations.[1] In 2003 the UN set up a Global Commission on International Migration, which produced a report calling for greater international cooperation. One of its 'principles for action' is that:

The governance of international migration should be enhanced by improved coherence and strengthened capacity at the national level; greater consultation and cooperation between states at the regional level, and more effective dialogue and cooperation among governments and between international organisations at the global level. (UN, 2005, p. 4)

This report formed the background for the High Level Dialogue at the UN General Assembly in September 2006, which focused for the first time on international migration. It followed earlier international consultations in calling for greater international co-operation, but all have stopped short of recommending a forum for multilateral negotiation along the lines of the WTO.[2]

So, should we have a WTO for international migration? If it has been successful for trade, then why couldn't the same principles be adapted to migration? To answer this question we need to have a better understanding of why these two strands of policy differ so much in the first place. Only then is it possible to suggest how such reforms might proceed and to evaluate whether they are likely to be successful.

2. MIGRATION AND TRADE POLICIES

2.1. Globalization and liberalization

Most people would acknowledge that barriers to international migration are much higher than barriers to the international movement of goods. In most countries the ratio of imports to GDP far exceeds the ratio of immigrants to total population. Across the world the average share of immigrants in the population is about 3%; by contrast the ratio of imports to GDP is 10%. Across OECD countries the average share of immigrants to population is about 6% while the share of imports to GDP is 27.5%. Furthermore, the trends in openness are very different; since the 1960s the worldwide ratio of immigrants to population has increased only modestly while the ratio of imports to GDP has doubled.[3]

---

[1] Other prominent initiatives include the International Organization for Migration's Dialogue on Migration, the so-called Berne Initiative, and the International Labour Organization's efforts to develop a non-binding framework for international migration. Newland (2005, p. 1) documents various initiatives and conventions since 1999 and comments that 'suddenly migration was everywhere one looked in the UN system and beyond.' A summary of UN resolutions and recommendations since 1990 is provided by the United Nations (2006).

[2] However, some writers have suggested setting up such a forum, for example Ghosh (2000), Straubhaar (2000), and most prominently, Bhagwati (2003).

[3] According to the UN's figures, the share of the world's population that is foreign-born increased from 2.2% in 1965 to 2.9% in 2000. However, much of this increase is accounted for by the re-drawing of national boundaries as a result of the break up of the Soviet Union (Hatton and Williamson, 2005a, p. 205).

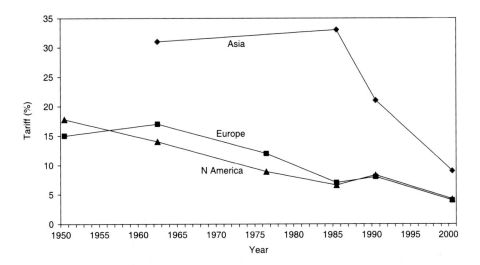

Figure 1. Average tariffs, three regions, 1950–2000

Source: Findlay and O'Rourke, 2007, Table 9.1, as represented by Baldwin 2006, Tables 2–4. North America is Canada and the US; Europe is the EU-15 excluding Ireland and Luxembourg but including Norway and Switzerland; Asia is represented by Indonesia, Philippines, Taiwan, Thailand, China, Korea and Japan. Not all countries are represented in all years.

Immigration polices certainly appear to have remained a lot tougher than restrictions on trade, particularly in the developed world, and indices of policy support that view. Figure 1 shows the average (unweighted) tariff for three world regions from 1950 to 2000. On this measure, average tariffs in Europe and North America fell from more than 15% in 1950 to about 4% in 2000. In Asia they declined more steeply, more recently, and from higher levels. While a variety of non-tariff barriers still exist, the trend towards more liberal policy is clear.

Barriers to migration are even harder to measure. The best we can do is to use the data periodically collected by the UN from governments about whether their policy aim is to reduce immigration, increase it, or keep it the same. Table 1 shows that the proportion of developed country governments aiming to reduce migration has increased from less than 20% in the mid-1970s to more than 40% in recent years. Among less developed countries, restrictiveness has also increased but from a much lower base. Of course this is not a measure of actual immigration policies and its interpretation is open to question. But for what it is worth, it suggests that policy intentions were becoming more restrictive, particularly up to the mid-1990s.

2.2. International policies

The correlation between policy liberalization and globalization is clear enough. But have reduced restrictions on trade actually been the cause of the rising trade to income ratios? And have international negotiations played an important part?

Table 1. Government Immigration Polices, 1976–2001 (percentage of governments aiming to restrict immigration)

Year	1976	1986	1996	2001
All countries	7	20	40	40
More developed countries	18	38	60	44
Less developed countries	3	15	34	39

Source: United Nations (2002, p. 18).

Table 2. Most favoured nation tariff cuts by industrial countries

Implementation period	Round	Weighted tariff reduction (%)	Implied tariff at period beginning
1948–63	First five GATT rounds (1947–62)[1]	36	15.4
1968–72	Kennedy Round (1964–67)[2]	37	11.3
1980–87	Tokyo Round (1973–79)[3]	33	8.3
1995–99	Uruguay Round (1986–94)[4]	38	6.2

Notes: These are for tariffs on industrial goods excluding petroleum. (1) US only; (2) US, Japan, EC(6) and UK; (3) US, EU(9), Japan, Austria, Finland, Norway, Sweden and Switzerland; (4) US, EU(12), Japan, Austria, Finland, Norway, Sweden and Switzerland.
Source: Subramanian and Wei (2005, p. 27).

Turning to the first question, Table 2 shows the percentage reductions in industrial tariffs in various negotiating rounds of the GATT/WTO since 1948. These only apply to industrial goods and they fail to pick up changes in non-tariff barriers. But they are dramatic indeed and they surely account for much of the secular fall in trade barriers – particularly in recent decades as the number of participating countries has increased from 23 in the Geneva round of 1947 to 117 in the Uruguay round of 1986–94.

Given that the GATT/WTO does seem to have been associated with lower tariffs, is it also associated with increased trade? Recent studies suggest that it is. Baier and Bergstrand (2001) find that membership of the GATT increased trade by 25% between 1956–8 and 1986–8 (or by three times as much as the fall in transport costs). Although two-thirds of the growth in world trade was due to the growth in per capita income, tariff declines account for three-quarters of the increase in trade to GDP ratios. More recently Subramanian and Wei (2005) used a gravity model of international trade to assess the effect of membership of the GATT/WTO. They found that, over successive rounds, it increased industrial country imports by 175% and world trade as a whole by 120% between 1950 and 2000.[4] Nevertheless it is important to note that a significant share of trade liberalization took place outside of the GATT/WTO framework, and that growing incomes and falling transport costs also contributed to the expansion in world trade (Findlay and O'Rourke, 2007, Ch. 9).

---

[4] These results effectively overturn the earlier findings of Rose (2004) who found very little effect of WTO membership on trade volumes.

2.3. The gains from liberalization

How much could reducing barriers to trade and migration increase world welfare? And how would those gains be shared across the different regions of the world? A number of studies have calculated the benefits from specific trade liberalizations using multi-region, multi-sector computable general equilibrium (CGE) models. Using this approach, Harrison *et al.* (1997) put the worldwide gains from all of the measures included in the Uruguay Round at 0.5% of world GDP ($93 billion at 1992 prices) in the short run and up to 0.8% of world GDP ($171 billion) in the long run. The larger long-run gains are principally due to the realization of increasing returns to scale and capital accumulation. Although only a third of the gains accrue to developing countries, they are a larger proportion of GDP for them than for the industrialized countries.[5] Other studies produce rather similar orders of magnitude (e.g. Francois *et al.*, 1996).

What would be the benefits of total trade liberalization? On the basis of 1997 when most of the provisions of the Uruguay Round were in place, and using a variant of the same (GTAP) model Cline (2004, p. 180) estimates that moving to complete free trade would increase world GDP by 0.93% ($228 billion at 1997 prices), with nearly 40% of the gains going to developing countries. One scenario for the outcome of Doha suggests that it could achieve about 40% of the gains from total liberalization (Cline, 2004, p. 185).

How do the gains from freeing up international migration compare with those from moving to free trade? One early estimate came to the astonishing conclusion that eliminating all barriers to migration could as much as double world GDP (Hamilton and Whalley, 1984). This estimate is based on allowing labour to move until real wages are equalized worldwide, and it implies a massive transfer of population from poor to rich countries. More recent studies have produced more modest estimates. Using a similar methodology, but with different data and assumptions, Moses and Letnes (2004) estimate the gains at about 10% of world GDP in 1998 ($3,390 billion). This estimate is much more modest, largely because workers in the developing world are assumed to be inherently much less productive than those in developed countries, and hence there is substantially less gain in shifting them from poor to rich countries. Even so, they imply that the gains from moving to free migration are ten times as large as those from moving to free trade.[6]

[5] The model used by Harrison *et al.* (1997) has four factors of production (skilled labour, unskilled labour, capital and land), 22 product groups and 25 countries or country groups. Producers maximize profits subject to a constant elasticity of substitution (CES) production function for factors and fixed coefficients for intermediates; consumers maximize a multi-level utility function in which domestically produced and foreign goods are combined using a CES-Armington structure and imports from different regions are similarly combined into a composite import good at a lower level. The market clearing general equilibrium model is calibrated to the data from the Global Trade Analysis Project (GTAP) database. Variants of this model are used by Cline (2004) and Winters *et al.* (2003) cited below.

[6] The models of Hamilton and Whalley (1984) and Moses and Letnes (2004) assume that a single homogenous good is produced in each of seven regions using capital and (homogenous) labour that are combined in a CES production function. Capital is immobile and counterfactual outputs are calculated under the assumption that efficiency adjusted wage rates are equalized across the regions. Hamilton and Whalley assumed the labour efficiency of workers in less developed regions was a half or a third that of the developed world. With this and other adjustments the gains to liberalization are reduced to around a fifth to a third of worldwide GDP. Moses and Letnes assume efficiency ratios of one-third for regions with medium human development and one-fifth for regions with low human development. Some calculations reviewed below in Box 3 suggest that the labour efficiency ratios are greater than some have assumed and thus the gains to migration are somewhat larger.

Other studies use multi-region CGE models that allow for trade and include two types of labour: skilled and unskilled. Using this approach Iregui (2005) finds that full liberalization would increase world GDP by between 15% and 67%. Of particular interest is the study by Winters *et al.* (2003) who use a model (GTAP) similar to that used to evaluate the gains from liberalizing trade. They consider a partial liberalization that would involve a transfer of labour from developing countries to the OECD equivalent to 3% of its existing labour force and composed of equal numbers of skilled and unskilled workers. The total gain is about 0.6% of world income ($156 billion at 1997 prices).[7] Thus a 'modest' liberalization – one that would raise the OECD's foreign labour force by about a quarter – would deliver static gains that are comparable with those of removing all remaining restrictions on trade.

One further point to note is that Winters *et al.* (2003, p. 1145) find that the gains to the migrants themselves are roughly equal to the total gain in world welfare (see Box 1). Assuming that a large proportion of this is sent back in the form of remittances (possibly for consumption on return), this could more than offset the income loss that would otherwise be experienced by the source regions in the absence of remittances.

3. PUBLIC OPINION TOWARDS IMPORTS AND IMMIGRANTS

In democratic countries governments must heed public opinion, and some observers see this as the reason why, in the developed world, trade has been liberalized more than migration. One possibility is that the average voter sees immigration as much more of a 'threat' than imports of goods that embody foreign labour. In that case policies that are more liberal towards trade than to migration simply reflect voter attitudes. An alternative view would be that opposition towards trade and towards immigration reflect a very different balance of social and economic considerations and that these concerns are held by different groups of voters. As a result they may translate into different policy outcomes.

Box 1. The gains from liberalizing migration

The figure illustrates the framework used by Hamilton and Whalley (1984) and Moses and Letnes (2004) to measure the worldwide gains from free migration. Here there are two regions, the rich region (R), with labour demand curve D^R sloping down from left to right and the poor region (P) with labour demand curve D^P sloping down from right to left. The labour demand curves are downward sloping because other factors (such as capital) are fixed, and their elasticities depend on assumptions about the elasticities of factor substitution. The total labour supply is the width of the box, T. The initial allocation of

---

[7] Winters *et al.* (2003) also make an adjustment for differential labour efficiency, such that a migrant's productivity increases by half the gap between source and host countries' labour productivity.

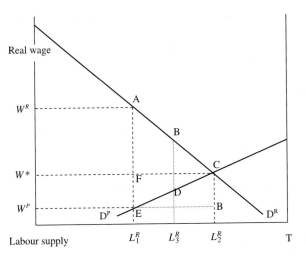

labour is L_1^R in region R, and $T - L_1^R$ in region P, producing wage rates W^R and W^P respectively. Under free migration, labour migrates from P to R until wage rates are equalized at W^*; labour supply in R expands to L_2^R while in P it shrinks to $T - L_2^R$.

This simple blackboard model provides a number of useful insights. First, since total income is the sum of the areas under the two demand curves, the gains to liberalization are measured as the area of the triangle ACE. Letting the slope of D^R be $-\beta$ and the slope of D^P be α, the welfare gain is measured as $(\alpha + \beta)(L_1^R - L_1^P)^2/2$. Note that, because the gains to full liberalization are proportional to the square of the labour transfer, a partial liberalization, say from L_1^R to L_3^R, captures most of the gains: area ABDE. If we set $L_1^R - L_2^R$ equal to one, and if L_3^R is halfway between L_1^R and L_2^R, then partial liberalization yields 75% of the gains, because it leaves $0.5 \times 0.5 = 0.25$ of the total gains unrealized (the triangle BCD). Similarly, going 10% of the way yields 19% of the gains leaving 0.9×0.9, or 81%, unrealized.

Second, there are major distributional effects. Liberalization reduces the wage and increases profits (the area under the demand curve down to the wage) in R and raises wages and reduces profits in P. Notice that much of that gain accrues to the migrants themselves: area FCBE, which is measured as $\alpha(L_1^R - L_2^R)^2$. Thus the ratio of migrant gain to total welfare gain is $2\alpha/(\alpha + \beta)$, and if $\alpha > \beta$ the gain to the migrants exceeds the aggregate net gain. Note also that the original residents of R gain area ACF and non-migrants in P lose area CBE. Thus the gain to P can only be positive if it includes that accruing to the migrants.

Third, the size of the gains depends crucially on the labour demand elasticities. In the illustration the total gain can be expressed as $(W^R - W^P)^2/2(\alpha + \beta)$. Thus, for a given initial wage gap, $W^R - W^P$, the more elastic are the demand curves (the smaller are α and β) the further to the right will be L_2^R, the more labour will move from P to R, and the larger is the area of the triangle ACE. If demand curves are more elastic in the long run, say because capital adjusts, then the long-run gains to liberalization will be greater than the short-run gains.

Table 3. Questions in the ISSP National Identity Surveys 1995/6

Limit Imports:
(Respondent's country) should limit the import of foreign products in order to protect the national economy.
Immigrants Good
Immigrants are generally good for (respondent's country).
Immigrant Jobs
Immigrants take jobs away from people who were born in (respondent's country).
Reduce Immigration
Do you think the number of immigrants to (respondent's country) should be (increased/reduced)?

Coding of responses to the first three questions listed is: (1) agree strongly, (2) agree, (3) neither agree nor disagree, (4) disagree, (5) disagree strongly. Coding of responses to the last question is: (1) increased a lot, (2) increased a little, (3) remain the same as it is, (4) reduced a little, (5) reduced a lot.

Source: Codebooks for the 1995/6 International Social Survey Module on National Identity.

3.1. Survey data on public attitudes

Opinion surveys make it possible to measure the intensity of attitudes towards trade and immigration across a range of countries. One such survey is the National Identity module of the International Social Survey Program (ISSP) that was conducted for 24 countries in 1995/6. Besides its multi-country coverage, the main advantage of the survey is that it contains questions on attitudes towards both trade and migration. Thus it is possible to compare the responses to each across the same group of individuals.

There are three questions on attitudes towards immigration and one question on attitudes towards imports. These questions are displayed in Table 3. The response to each question is on a five-point scale representing the intensity of agreement or opposition to the statement. The questions on whether immigrants are generally good for the economy and whether immigrants take jobs from natives do not relate directly to policy. But the final question asks whether immigration should be increased or decreased. This may be compared with the question that asks whether the country should limit imports. These questions are not quite the same in that the imports question asks specifically about the national economy while the question on immigration asks how *much* immigration should be increased or reduced (Box 2). Nevertheless they both relate to the country's policy stance and the responses are each graduated on a five-point scale.

The average survey responses to these questions are presented in Table 4, where each question is scaled so that the most negative response takes the value 5 and the most positive response takes the value 1. According to these responses, average attitudes are mildly anti-immigration and anti-imports, with rather stronger opposition for the policy-related questions. Comparison of the two policy-related questions suggests that opposition to immigration is only slightly more intense than opposition to imports. On this basis it is hard to see why, over the last decade or so, trade policy has been so much more liberal than immigration policy. A further point is that the correlation between the responses to these two questions is positive but not particularly strong. Across the whole sample the correlation coefficient is 0.22. This suggests that there may be systematic differences between those who are opposed to immigration and those who are opposed to trade. If so, then this might help to explain how attitudes towards trade and immigration that are apparently similar on average nevertheless translate into very different policy outcomes.

Box 2. Different questions, different answers?

It is often argued that the responses to opinion questions depend on the precise way that the question is framed. As noted above, the ISSP questions on attitudes to imports and to immigration are framed differently, which could create the illusion that attitudes to imports are only a little less negative than attitudes to immigration. Unfortunately there appears to be no dataset in which the identical question is asked for both imports and immigration. However, it is possible to conduct some sensitivity analysis using surveys from a single country, in this case Australia.

The ISSP question on increase/reduce immigration in Table 4 produces an average value (on an increasing anti-immigration scale) of 3.77. In 1999 the Australian Constitutional Referendum Survey asked if the number of migrants allowed into Australia had: (1) gone much too far, (2), gone too far, (3) about right, (4) not gone far enough, (5) not gone nearly far enough. This question did not ask how much immigration should be increased/reduced and it presented the options in a different order. When placed on an increasing anti-immigration scale, the 3,350 responses produce an average of 3.53. But this still does not specifically ask about jobs or the economy. In 1995 the World Values Survey asked a question if the government should (1) let anyone come who wants to, (2) let people come as long as jobs are available, (3) place strict limits on the numbers, or (4) prohibit people coming here. Placing these on an equivalent five-point anti-immigration scale (applying the values 1.2, 2.4, 3.6, 4.8) gives an average value for 2,029 respondents of 2.90.

The ISSP question on limiting imports produced an average value of anti-import sentiment of 4.05. Another question in the same survey for Australia asked how strongly the respondent agreed with the statement 'Opening up Australia's economy to foreign competition has a bad effect on job security in this country.' This question is closer to the one on immigration, which asked specifically about jobs (see Table 3) and it produced an average of 3.93 (as compared with 3.01 for the immigration-jobs question).

A 2005 survey on Public Opinion and Foreign Policy asked a question on imports that was framed more positively and not related to jobs: 'We should allow entry into Australia of the goods and services we import regardless of what other countries do because we benefit from having them available at the cheapest prices'. Asked if they were for or against, 63% of respondents were against. These responses are consistent with the 63% who answered in favour of 'restricting the goods and services that we import from overseas so that they don't sell more cheaply than Australian goods and services'. However, when asked whether 'we should try to negotiate international agreements that open other countries' markets for our exports in return for their goods coming into Australia', 90% answered in the affirmative. Thus, for trade opinion, it is not the difference between the benefits to consumers and potential job losses that seems to matter, but rather the issue of reciprocal arrangements with other countries. This is important to what follows below.

Note: The figures quoted here exclude the 'don't know' or no answer, but they differ slightly from those in Table 4, which exclude non-responses to either question.

Source: All the surveys referred to here are available from the Australian Social Science Data Archive at: http://assda.anu.edu.au/

3.2. Explaining individual attitudes

A number of recent studies have analysed opinion surveys in order to identify and measure the socio-economic basis of attitudes towards trade and migration. For my purposes the most interesting ones are those that have used the cross-country data summarized in Table 4 to study the determinants of public opinion towards immigration (Bauer *et al.*, 2000; Mayda, 2006; O'Rourke and Sinnott, 2006) and towards trade (O'Rourke and Sinnott, 2001; Mayda and Rodrik, 2005). The regressions in Table 5 follow the spirit of the specifications used in these studies, by using similar variables and including a full set of country dummies. Not surprisingly, the results are consistent with their findings. The dependent variable is on the one to five scale, either to limit imports or reduce immigration. These are ordered probit regressions and they do not take into account any correlation between the equation errors arising from unobserved heterogeneity. Bivariate probit regressions in Appendix 1 indicate a significant residual covariance, but this has little effect on the estimated coefficients.

Following O'Rourke and Sinnott (2006), I characterize prejudice against things foreign in two variables labelled 'patriotism' and 'chauvinism'. Patriotism is measured as the average response to three questions that capture the individual's sense of loyalty to his or her country. Chauvinism is the average response to four questions that elicit the extent to which the individual believes that his or her country is

Table 4. Attitudes towards imports and immigration, 1995/6

Country	Imports limit	Immig bad	Immig jobs	Immig reduce	No. Obs
Australia	4.01	2.47	2.97	3.77	2291
Germany W	3.10	2.94	2.81	4.22	981
Germany E	3.56	3.15	3.43	4.36	485
United Kingdom	3.76	3.28	3.36	4.06	891
United States	3.76	3.01	3.32	3.88	1049
Austria	3.89	2.82	3.02	3.82	841
Hungary	4.08	3.81	3.85	4.41	889
Italy	3.61	3.59	2.92	4.16	985
Ireland	3.67	2.59	2.96	3.06	892
Netherlands	2.92	3.28	2.87	3.83	1730
Norway	3.13	3.52	2.68	3.87	1182
Sweden	3.19	3.25	2.54	3.95	980
Czech Rep	3.43	3.86	3.24	4.16	905
Slovenia	3.49	3.41	3.60	3.99	801
Poland	3.88	2.98	3.56	3.86	921
Bulgaria	4.33	3.93	3.92	4.19	592
Russia	3.78	3.48	3.44	3.74	862
New Zealand	3.38	2.66	3.13	3.73	909
Canada	3.28	2.41	2.62	3.30	1270
Philippines	3.63	3.09	2.99	3.79	1117
Japan	2.89	2.83	2.29	3.33	895
Spain	3.87	3.13	3.12	3.39	947
Latvia	4.13	3.69	3.58	4.23	746
Slovakia	3.57	3.80	3.53	4.00	1025
U Mean	3.60	3.21	3.16	3.88	24 186
W Mean	3.57	3.15	3.10	3.85	

Source: Based on data from the 1995/6 International Social Survey (ISSP) module on national identity. These figures are the average attitude towards imports and immigration on a scale of increasing opposition from 1 to 5. The sample used here excludes cases where, for any of the four questions, there was a non-response or where the response was 'don't know'.

superior to others.[8] As the first two columns of Table 5 illustrate, these variables each contribute strongly and positively to an individual's sentiment, both against immigration and against imports. And they provide compelling evidence that prejudice is an important component of individual attitudes.

Among individual characteristics, being female is particularly associated with anti-trade opinion while being a first- or second-generation immigrant is particularly associated with pro-immigration opinion. Being employed reduces anti-imports sentiment but is not significant for immigration opinion. Consistent with most other studies, those with more than secondary education are less opposed to liberalization

[8] These clusters of variables are those identified by O'Rourke and Sinnott (2006, p. 24) using principal components analysis. The components that comprise the patriotism index (appropriately scaled) are the responses (e.g. for a British respondent) to the questions: (1) 'Generally speaking, Britain is a better country than most other countries', (2) 'The world would be a better place if people from other countries were more like the British', and (3) 'I would rather be a citizen of Britain than of any other country in the world'. The components that comprise the chauvinism index are the (again, appropriately scaled) responses to: (1) 'People should support their country even if the country is in the wrong', (2) 'Britain should follow its own interests, even if this leads to conflicts with other nations', (3) 'How important do you think each of the following is for being truly British' . . . 'to have been born in Britain', and (4) 'It is impossible for people who do not share British customs and traditions to become fully British'.

Table 5. The determinants of anti-imports and anti-immigration attitudes

Variable	(1) Reduce immigration	(2) Limit imports	(3) Reduce immigration	(4) Limit imports
'Patriotism'	0.080	0.181		
	(3.77)	(11.32)		
'Chauvinism'	0.396	0.378		
	(7.58)	(13.84)		
Second generation	−0.317	−0.050	−0.428	−0.183
immigrant	(8.02)	(1.36)	(11.58)	(4.84)
Female	0.056	0.249	0.032	0.209
	(1.94)	(9.23)	(1.04)	(9.42)
Age	0.001	0.001	0.005	0.005
	(0.76)	(1.10)	(3.68)	(5.39)
Employed	−0.014	−0.052	−0.047	−0.086
	(1.24)	(2.77)	(2.85)	(5.10)
High educated	−0.246	−0.256	−0.612	−0.325
	(9.67)	(9.05)	(2.47)	(1.52)
High educated ×			0.804	−0.187
Inequality			(1.66)	(0.39)
High educated ×			−0.013	−0.002
GDP per capita			(0.21)	(0.06)
Cut 1	−0.865	−0.409	−2.187	−2.035
Cut 2	−0.111	0.599	−1.455	−1.085
Cut 3	1.181	1.208	−0.222	−0.513
Cut 4	2.025	2.260	0.577	0.474
Pseudo-R^2	0.088	0.094	0.056	0.057
No. of obs	19 850	19 850	19 850	19 850
Country dummies	Yes	Yes	Yes	Yes

Note: Ordered probit with z statistics in parentheses based on robust standard errors clustered by country. The Philippines has been excluded.

Source: Data from the 1995/6 International Social Survey (ISSP) module on national identity.

of both imports and immigration. One interpretation is that those with more education are more enlightened and therefore less xenophobic. But an alternative view is that those with higher skills are less threatened by direct competition from immigrants or by indirect competition from imports with high skill content.[9]

O'Rourke and Sinnot (2006) suggest that the effect of education on attitudes should vary with economy wide characteristics. In addition the patriotism and chauvinism may reflect unobserved characteristics that are correlated with the other explanatory variables. The second and third columns drop patriotism and chauvinism and interact education with two economy wide variables. The first is inequality as measured by the Gini coefficient of household income.[10] In the context of immigration

---

[9] See, for example, Scheve and Slaughter (2001) and Dustmann and Preston (2004a). One suggestion is that the effects of patriotism and chauvinism might vary with other characteristics. However the effect of interacting the patriotism variable with second generation or with high educated in the immigration opinion equation did not give significant coefficients on the interaction. The interaction of chauvinism with high educated gave a significant positive coefficient, but with little effect on the other variables.

[10] The Gini coefficients are taken from World Bank (2003, Table 2.8, pp. 64–66). Figures for Germany (East and West), Bulgaria, Russia and the Philippines were taken from the WIDER World Inequality Database WIIB2Beta (2004) at http://www.wider.unu.edu/wiid/wiid.htm.

this represents the Roy model: the greater is inequality (and the return to education) relative to the rest of the world, the greater the incentive to high-skilled immigrants, and therefore the greater the threat to high-skilled locals. It can also be interpreted in the context of import competition as reflecting the relative scarcity of skills: the greater is inequality, the greater the skill scarcity and the greater the threat from skill intensive imports. This interaction effect takes the expected positive coefficient in the immigration opinion equation (thus the highly educated are more against immigration the more unequal the income distribution) but it is not significant in either.

The second interaction is between high education and the country's (PPP adjusted) GDP per capita.[11] This has also been given a factor scarcity interpretation: specifically that higher GDP largely reflects a greater abundance of skill and human capital (Mayda, 2006; O'Rourke and Sinnott, 2006). Hence the higher is GDP per head the lower is the threat to the highly skilled from skilled immigration and from imports that embody this abundant factor. As others have found, the interaction between education and GNP per head is negative as predicted for both immigration opinion and trade opinion but not significant for either.

Two things stand out about these regressions. First, the signs of the coefficients are the same for every variable in columns (1) and (2). So, whatever interpretation we place on the individual coefficients, it appears that the same *sorts* of people are opposed to both imports and immigration. It is important to stress, however, that a great deal of the variation remains unexplained by these variables and that the correlation across individuals between the two types of opinion is modest. Second, the coefficients on the variables representing patriotism and chauvinism are negative and significant, indicating that such prejudice has a larger influence on anti-import sentiment than on anti-trade sentiment. If, as is sometimes argued, immigration policy is dominated not by economic considerations but by nationalism and prejudice, then, according to these results, the effects on trade policy should be even greater.

3.3. Country-level effects

Across a broad range of countries attitudes are on balance against both imports and immigration, and the same types of people are against imports as are against immigration. If such attitudes map into policy, one would naturally predict that most countries would adopt policies that were restrictive towards both immigration and imports. And if nationalistic sentiments drive policy, one might even predict that trade policies would be tougher than immigration policies. However, this takes no account of the actual stance of policy upon which these attitudes are conditioned. If actual immigration policies were more liberal then opposition to immigration might be more

---

[11] Real GDP per capita at constant 1996 US dollars, purchasing power parity adjusted, from A. Heston, R. Summers and B. Aten, Penn World Table version 6.1, Center for International Comparisons at the University of Pennsylvania, October 2002, at: http://pwt.econ.upenn.edu./php_site/pwt61_form.php.

Table 6. Country effects on anti-imports and anti-immigration attitudes

Variable	(1) Reduce immigration	(2) Limit imports	(3) Reduce immigration	(4) Limit imports
Percentage of	0.036		0.044	
foreign nationals	(1.84)		(2.49)	
Import percentage		−0.006		−0.007
of GNP		(1.33)		(1.30)
Govt welfare	0.033	−0.016	0.032	
expenditure/GNP	(3.03)	(1.44)	(2.89)	
Unemployment	−0.020	0.031		0.027
rate	(2.23)	(2.25)		(2.15)
GDP per capita	0.112	0.061	0.113	
	(3.51)	(1.53)	(2.41)	
Eastern Europe	0.649	0.412	0.655	0.395
	(4.24)	(3.47)	(3.89)	(2.88)
Pseudo-R^2	0.035	0.032	0.034	0.030
No. of obs	19 850	19 850	19 850	19 850
Individual effects	Yes	Yes	Yes	Yes
Country dummies	No	No	No	No

Note: OLS with *t* statistics in parentheses based on robust standard errors clustered by country. The Philippines has been excluded.

Source: Data from the 1995/6 International Social Survey (ISSP) module on national identity.

intense. Similarly, if barriers to imports were higher then perhaps opposition to imports would be less intense. This suggests that we should look at differences between countries rather than at differences between individuals within a country.

The regressions in Table 6 include the individual characteristics that appeared in the second two columns of Table 5 (not reported in Table 6), excluding the interactions but including country-level variables rather than country dummies. Since there are only 23 countries the list of explanatory variables has to be kept to a minimum. The key question is whether higher levels of immigration or imports lead to public opinion becoming more negative. Column (1) shows that a higher percentage of foreign nationals in the population makes opinion more negative towards immigration, although the coefficient is only significant at the 10% level. Another key variable is the size of the welfare state. The larger is the share of welfare expenditures in GDP the greater is opposition to immigration, presumably because of the belief that immigrants are likely to raise the cost of welfare.[12] One might also have expected that higher unemployment would make attitudes towards immigration more negative, but the coefficient on the national unemployment rate is negative and significant. When this variable is excluded as in column (3) the coefficient on the share of foreign nationals becomes slightly stronger. The effect of GDP per capita is positive, suggesting

---

[12] A number of recent studies have emphasized the importance of welfare state implications in shaping attitudes towards immigration; see, for example, Dustmann and Preston (2004b), Hanson *et al.* (2005), Facchini and Mayda (2006).

that immigration is seen as more of a threat in richer countries. Finally, a dummy for Eastern Europe indicates that opinion is significantly more anti-immigration in those countries. This perhaps reflects the fact that these countries have only recently emerged into the global economy.

Column (2) introduces the share of imports in GNP as an explanatory variable for attitudes towards limiting imports. If attitudes harden as import penetration increases then the coefficient should be positive. In fact, it is negative but small and insignificant. Similarly, the variable for welfare expenditures to GDP produces a negative but insignificant coefficient while GDP per capita is weakly positive. Leaving out the welfare state variable makes little difference to the coefficient on the import share. The two variables that do matter are the national unemployment rate which gives a coefficient that is positive and significant and, as for immigration opinion, the dummy for Eastern Europe.

The country-level variables are limited, but they do suggest one thing: that anti-immigration opinion hardens when there are more immigrants but the same effect cannot be found for imports. The result for immigration is not particularly strong, but is consistent with other research, which finds that attitudes to immigrants become more negative as the proportion of immigrants increases (Dustmann and Preston, 2001; Boeri et al., 2002, Ch. 5). In the present dataset the average percentage of foreign nationals across the 23 countries is 4.3%. If that figure were doubled to 8.6% then opinion would become more negative by 0.16 points. By contrast the percentage of imports in GNP over the 23 countries is 34.7%. If the immigration share were raised to even half that level then anti-immigration opinion would increase by half a point – a substantial amount.[13]

4. NATIONAL POLITICS AND INTERNATIONAL POLICIES

We have seen that attitudes to restricting imports and immigration are somewhat similar in intensity, although they are conditioned on the current situation. Clearly they could look very different under different policy counterfactuals. But what is the relationship between opinion and policy? How far are policy outcomes shaped by domestic politics and partisanship? And what shapes the differing styles of political discourse that seem to apply to trade and to migration?

4.1. Public opinion and policy

Let us assume, consistently with the results reported above, that opposition to immigration is an upward sloping function of the liberalness of policy. And suppose that there is a similar function relating opposition to imports to policy liberalness, but that the latter is much flatter. This situation is depicted in Figure 2. Suppose, further, that

---

[13] This is based on the estimated coefficient from an ordinary least squares equation equivalent to column (3) of Table 6.

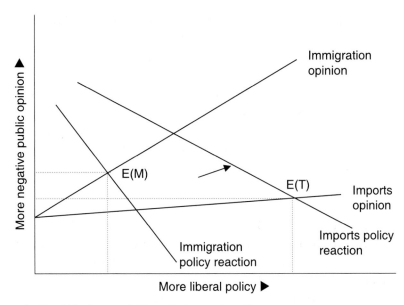

Figure 2. Equilibrium public opinion and policy

there is a downward sloping policy reaction function. It seems reasonable to think that this function is downward sloping – it simply says that governments respond to more negative public opinion with tougher policies. In Figure 2 there are two policy reaction functions, with the one for imports much further to the right. This gives rise to two equilibrium points, *E(M)* for immigration and *E(T)* for imports. Opinion is slightly more negative towards immigration than towards imports but immigration policy is much tougher than import policy. This seems to be a reasonable characterization of the current situation in the typical developed country. But why should the equilibrium for imports be so much further to the right? And why have the two branches of policy drifted apart over the last 40 or 50 years, with migration policies becoming tougher and trade policies becoming more liberal?

In principle we could decide which set of curves – public opinion or policy reaction functions – moved apart the most by looking at trends in public opinion. This is difficult to do with any confidence. For the United States the evidence suggests that the percentage wanting immigration to be reduced is the same in 2004 as it was in 1977 (42%), but with temporary increases in the early 1980s and in the early 1990s (Simon, 2004, p. 21). For imports the picture is rather less clear because of lack of consistency over time in the questions asked. For the United States the impression is one of hardening attitudes towards free(er) trade at least up to the 1990s (Phelps, 1993). The most that can be said on the basis of this evidence is that there are no particularly strong trends in public opinion. The best guess, therefore, is that opinion and policy curves for imports *both* shifted to the right relative to those for immigration.

Study of very long-run trends suggests a number of reasons why immigration policies have become tougher relative to import policies (Hatton and Williamson, 2005b).

One relates to government budgets. When social security, public health and pensions were in their infancy, immigrants could not become a fiscal burden. But with the rise of the welfare state, public opinion and government policies have become much more concerned with keeping out immigrants who could potentially become a welfare burden. Between 1910 and 1970 social transfers (health, welfare, unemployment, pensions, housing subsidies) as a share of GDP rose from 0.6 to 10.4% in the US and from 0.7 to 14.8% in the median OECD country (Lindert, 2004, pp. 12–13). On the other hand, until well into the twentieth century tariffs were a major source of tax revenue. In the 1890s the share of customs revenue in total tax revenue averaged 58% for seven labour-scarce countries and it was particularly high in Latin America and in other New World countries such as the US and Australia. By the 1970s the customs share of tax revenue in OECD countries was only about 4%. As the sources of tax revenue widened, the 'need' for tariffs as a revenue raising device has declined. Hence the evolution of tax systems has increased the pressure for immigration controls but has eased the pressure for high tariffs.

Second, the spread of democracy that gathered pace in the twentieth century was a process in which the franchise percolated down the hierarchy of class an income, first to middle class and skilled workers and then to the urban unskilled. In most of the developed world the percentage of adults voting was less than 30% until it underwent a steep ascent beginning in the 1920s. The result was a progressive increase in political voice among those who were most likely to be hurt by labour market competition from relatively low-skilled immigrants. This was heightened by a third factor, which was the growing proportion of migrants coming from low income countries. Economic development and rising incomes, combined with falling transport costs and improved communication has progressively enlarged the potential for long-distance migration from the poorest parts of the world. The gap between the average immigrant's source country income and that of New World host countries was already increasing before the First World War but this trend was arrested from then until the 1950s. Between the 1950s and the 1990s the ratio of immigrant-weighted source country GDP per capita to destination GDP per capita fell from 49% to 22% in the US, from 65% to 31% in Canada and 96% to 45% in Germany (Hatton and Williamson, 2005b, Table 1). Hence the 'threat' of unskilled migration has progressively increased. Thus immigration barriers have risen, in part, because there is more migration pressure to hold back.

History also suggests that macroeconomic crises lead to sudden shifts in policy towards protectionism of one sort or another. For example, the Great Depression witnessed an enormous increase in tariffs worldwide *and* a parallel increase in immigration controls (Hatton and Williamson, 2005a, Ch. 8). Similarly, when the world economy moved into recession after the first oil shock of 1973/4, immigration policy became tougher in a number of countries, particularly in Europe, where guestworker policies abruptly ended. But tariff barriers continued to fall, and this despite the fact that higher unemployment seems to harden public opinion towards imports. Since

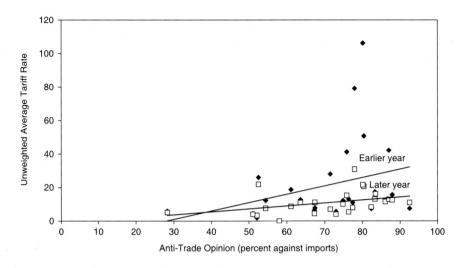

Figure 3. Trade opinion and tariffs

the 1960s there appears to have been a rightward shift in the import policy function that cannot easily be accounted for.

What evidence is there to suggest that the import policy function has shifted to the right? Unfortunately data to examine the link between public opinion and policy outcomes is scarce. However, it is possible to compare opinion data such as that examined above with a measure of trade policy, the average tariff rate. Here I use a different survey, the World Values Survey, which covers a wide range of countries for 1995/6.[14] The proportion expressing anti-import opinion is plotted along the horizontal axis. On the vertical axis is the unweighted average tariff calculated by the World Bank. Two tariff rates are included, one about five years earlier than the opinion data and one about five years later. On the assumption that opinion does not vary wildly from one year to another, this should give some indication of the changing relationship between anti-trade opinion and tariff policy.

There are only 23 countries for which we have both policy and opinion data and so any inference must be tentative. But the evidence from the plots in Figure 3 is suggestive. First, it suggests that the relationship between anti-trade opinion and the tariff rate (an inverse measure of liberalness) is positive, consistent with the policy reaction function in Figure 2. Second, the relationship between opinion and the tariff rate is steeper for the earlier year tariff than for the later year tariff. Although the difference is not statistically significant, the result is consistent with the notion that

[14] The WVS data are available at http://www.wotldvaluessurvey.org. One reason for preferring the WVS to the ISSP survey for the purposes of this comparison is that it is less weighted towards EU countries that share a common external tariff. The WVS question asked: Do you think it is better if (1) Goods made in other countries can be imported or sold here if people want to buy them; or that (2) There should be stricter limits on selling foreign goods here, to protect the jobs of people in this country. The percentage answering (2) above is plotted on the horizontal axis of Figure 2; EU countries are omitted.

tariff rates have become less responsive to domestic public opinion over time.[15] Tariff rates were already relatively low in most countries by 1990 and we might speculate that the relationship would be steeper if we could go further back in time.

4.2. The domestic politics of trade and migration

Is the politics that surrounds immigration policy somehow different than that which provides the setting for debates over import restrictions? If so, that might explain why the latter has become so much more liberal over the last 30 years or so. One possibility is that governments see that immigration and imports are substitutes to some (possibly increasing) extent and therefore that there are economic gains from relaxing one of them, but that there is more political gain in limiting immigration than in limiting imports. As we have seen, similar sorts of people oppose both immigration and imports, and so freeing up the latter but not the former may represent a politically successful strategy. This could be because trade policy and immigration policy play out very differently in the political arena. Thus, for the United States, Greenaway and Nelson see trade policy as characterized by 'group politics' while immigration policy is characterized by 'democratic politics'. According to them, 'The public politics of trade and immigration are distinctive . . . trade is seen as national and essentially economic, while immigration is local and essentially social' (2006, p. 25).

This is an important insight, but it is only a partial explanation. The main reason that trade is characterized by group politics is that there are clearly identifiable groups on both sides. Exporters (and their employees) stand to gain from greater access to foreign markets, while import competing firms (and their employees) stand to lose, and a political balance must be found between them.[16] Although some groups, such as employers as a whole, stand to gain directly from immigration they simply do not have the votes, and those who stand to gain indirectly, such as consumers, are too dispersed.[17]

The differences in the political frameworks that apply to trade policy and migration policy can be related directly to two key differences in the economic fundamentals. The first is that, to a first approximation, trade is based on comparative advantage while migration is based largely on absolute advantage. Thus for relatively rich countries immigration is much more of a one-way street than trade (see further below). While exporters often constitute a strong lobby group pressing for better access to foreign markets, open immigration policy fails to gain political support because there is no clearly identified group lobbying for better access to foreign labour markets. The

---

[15] The earlier year slope remains steeper than the later years slope even if the two extreme observations (Bangladesh and India) are eliminated.

[16] Following Grossman and Helpman (1994) most models of endogenous trade policy use a framework involving industry-level lobby groups.

[17] In a widely cited paper Freeman (1995) argued that those who favour immigration are relatively concentrated and well organized compared with the more diffuse groups that suffer the costs. According to him this explains why policy in countries such as the US is less restrictive than it would otherwise be.

second fundamental difference is that (as Box 1 illustrated) the largest gains from migration accrue to the migrants themselves. Even though the gains from free(er) migration are greater than the gains to free(er) trade, those who stand to gain the most are not part of the political process in the destination country, at least *ex ante*.

This suggests that there are good reasons why trade policy is more often characterized by group politics. But it does not necessarily follow that group politics, by itself, will lead to trade liberalization. After all, there are powerful lobbies on both sides, and the balance could go either way. In the United States the political balance gradually swung away from protectionism:

> From the days of the early American republic through the 1980s, US trade politics was dominated by economic interests and producer interests in particular. This gave policy a distinctly protectionist tilt up to the 1930s. But it also provided the foundation for the 'system' of antiprotectionist counterweights, which turned the policy around from the Roosevelt administration onward. Reciprocal trade negotiations energized export interests that would gain from reducing overseas barriers. This balanced the power of import-threatened industries, which were also bought off in part by trade remedy procedures and special deals for the strongest sectors, particularly textiles. (Destler, 2005, pp. 253–54)

Thus, at least in the modern era, group politics is as much the *result* of the clash of interests over trade as its cause (Rogowski, 1989). As Gilligan (1997) shows, the Reciprocal Trade Agreements Act (RTAA) of 1934 gave the political edge to exporters by delegating the authority for trade negotiations away from Congress to the President.[18] This was an attempt to escape from beggar-thy-neighbour tariff polices of the underemployed 1930s.[19] For exporters, the benefits of liberalization were not seen as cheaper imports and lower costs (in which case unilateral liberalization would have sufficed) but as improved access to foreign markets. The RTAA was important, not just because it tilted the balance of power in the United States, but because by giving the President powers to negotiate reciprocal agreements, it paved the way for American leadership of GATT in the period after the Second World War.

The histories of trade politics have played out somewhat differently in other countries. But in most of them policy has been influenced by the interplay between industry-based groups or associations and political parties or coalitions. As Hiscox (2002) shows, the degree to which policy is debated between industrial/sectoral groups or emerges from broader, class based, politics depends on the size and structure of the economy and the degree of internal factor mobility. The greater is internal mobility and the less specific are factors of production the more the style of politics resembles the class-based model proposed by Rogowski (1989). But whatever is the structure of

[18] In particular it led to the establishment of the post of Special Trade Representative (later the United States Trade Representative) located in the White House. This removed much of the political bargaining from the floor of the House to series of advisory committees in which export and import-competing interests were more evenly balanced. However, the authority vested in the president was temporary and was subject to renewal for each round of GATT negotiations.

[19] In particular it was a reaction from the Hawley Smoot tariff, which was introduced in 1930 and is seen by many as having led to widespread retaliation, which in turn contributed to the collapse of international trade in the 1930s.

the groups, they seem to be more evenly balanced for trade policy than for policy over migration.

In a number of countries, the balance of power in domestic trade politics gradually shifted in favour of free(r) trade. A key element is the shifting balance within peak associations representing business interests. Thus, in their respective countries, the Confederation of British Industry, the Conseil National du Patronat Français, the Canadian Manufacturers' Association and the Australian Manufacturing Council gradually became less protectionist. In some cases their views softened as the least competitive sectors were bought off. In Britain and France the least competitive sectors such as textiles, iron and steel shipbuilding and coal mining enjoyed continuing protection or were given special industry assistance. In addition, small business and newer sectors gained ascendancy as traditional manufacturing sectors declined. These trends interacted with the growing influence of neo-liberal ideas in different layers of government.[20] Thus Canada shifted to towards free trade with the US and away from the so-called National Policy in the wake of the pro-trade MacDonald Commission Report. But as Lusztig (2004, p. 119) notes 'it is no exaggeration to claim that without the support of the business community, the Mulroney government could not have been persuaded to take its free-trade gamble'. In Australia, the government's traditionally protectionist Tariff Board shifted cautiously towards freer trade in the mid 1960s by giving compensating concessions to the textiles and motor vehicles sectors. It became radically more free trade in the 1980s, gradually gaining the support of industrial lobby groups such as the Australian Manufacturing Council (Lusztig, 2004, pp. 170–72).

The shift toward free trade in opinion and in policy fed on itself, both at the domestic level and at the international level. At the domestic level, steps towards free trade eliminated or sidelined the least import-competitive firms, weakening their resistance to further tariff reforms. On the international level the growth of trade agreements in and outside of the GATT and the growth in multilateralism underpinned the potential gains to exporters of further trade liberalization (Baldwin, 2006). This virtuous cycle did not embrace the developing world because domestic politics in the developed world ruled out significant liberalization in key areas such as agriculture and textiles. In middle income countries such as Chile and Mexico where protectionist interest groups dominated, liberal reforms occurred only in the aftermath of economic crises and seismic political realignments. Among poorer countries such as India liberalization was also contingent on alignments between liberal politicians and pro-trade interests but for many the inducement of the gains offered by the Uruguay round and China's accession to the WTO were important catalysts. Thus the locomotive effect of trade reforms led by the GATT/WTO gradually (and incompletely) diffused from rich to poor countries.[21]

[20] According to Gourevitch (1986) this trend occurred in most developed countries regardless of the particular political party in power, and it was one reason why the macroeconomic turmoil of the 1970s and 1980s did not result in a retreat to protectionism.

[21] On developing countries and the GATT/WTO, see Hoekman and Kostecki (1995, Ch. 10); India's trade reforms are described by Panagariya (2004).

5. DO INTERNATIONAL INSTITUTIONS MAKE A DIFFERENCE?

We have seen that while trade has been gradually liberalized over the last half century, international migration has not, and the question is why? One obvious answer
is that tariff reductions have been largely achieved through multilateral negotiations
in the GATT and the WTO while there have been no such organizational arrangements devoted to the multilateral lowering of barriers to migration. That leads to two
questions. First, why has no such forum emerged for migration? And second, is there
a basis for an organization similar to the WTO, say, a World Migration Organization?

5.1. A case of institutional failure?

It might be suggested that the particular historical circumstances that led to the creation of
the GATT simply did not coalesce for international migration. Yet a variety of organizations
have emerged for international cooperation on issues related to migration. The International
Organization for Migration (IOM) has been in existence under various different names
since 1951, but the IOM has not established a track record anything like that of the GATT.[22]
The IOM has assisted some 11 million migrants (mainly refugees) since its creation but
its mission has never been to broker multilateral migration agreements or to establish an
architecture for reducing immigration controls on a global level. The same might be said
of the International Labour Organization (ILO), which was founded in 1919 and became
an agency of the United Nations in 1946. The focus of the ILO is industrial relations, social
justice and human rights and although it has developed an interest in global governance
it has not provided a forum for multilateral negotiations over immigration controls.

Appealing to accidents of history is not a very satisfying explanation for the fact
that the 'right' institutional structure has failed to emerge. After all, the origins of the
GATT were inauspicious. The GATT agreement of 1947 was originally linked to the
Havana Charter that proposed the establishment of an International Trade Organization (ITO). Although the ITO was stillborn because it was never ratified by the
United States, the GATT survived.[23] And it took on a life of its own, gaining in
authority and widening in influence, despite its lack of organizational status and weak
legal foundations.[24] Thus the GATT seems to have succeeded despite, rather than

[22] It began as the Provisional Intergovernmental Committee for the Movements of Migrants from Europe and it quickly evolved into
the Intergovernmental Committee for European Migration (ICEM). It changed its name again to the Intergovernmental Committee
for Migration in 1980 and then, with the amendment and ratification of the 1953 constitution, it became the IOM in 1989.

[23] The main sticking point was the unwillingness of the UK to abolish its system of Imperial Preference that embraced most
of the British Commonwealth and that had been erected in the wake of the 1931 tariff. For this reason multilateralism was not
a prominent feature of the GATT negotiations until the Kennedy round. Truman withdrew the ITO charter from Congress in
December 1950. According to Milner, had the ITO gone to Congress in 1945 when the Democrats were in power and when
the Bretton Woods agreement was ratified, the outcome might have been different. Thus accidents of history probably affected
the form of the GATT more than its substance.

[24] As one contemporary observer put it: 'In legal and institutional patrimony, the GATT is one of the most humble, if not
deprived, of the multitude of international bodies on the current world scene. But in positive accomplishments, the GATT must surely
rank near the top' (Dam, 1970, p. 335). For more recent histories of the GATT/WTO see Beane (2000) and Brown (2003).

because of, the international legal architecture.[25] It could hardly be argued that a similar organization for migration would have been impossibly ambitious. After all, the earliest GATT negotiations included only 23 countries, a number that had risen to 117 for the Uruguay Round of 1986–94.

The crucial period of international institution building in the immediate postwar years that also gave birth to the United Nations, the International Monetary Fund and the World Bank can be read as an attempt to restore the liberal international order that was destroyed in the interwar period. It also spawned a number of agreements relating to migration including the ILO convention on migration in 1949, the antecedent of the IOM in 1951, and the Refugee Convention in 1951. Surely there was sufficient momentum in those early postwar years to generate a framework for multilateral agreements over immigration controls. Nevertheless it did not happen, then or subsequently, and the question is: why?

5.2. The basis for multilateral negotiations

In order to answer this last question it is necessary to look at the basis for multilateral negotiations under the GATT/WTO. Some would argue that the need for multilateral negotiations is far from obvious in the first place, since countries stand to gain almost as much from unilateral trade liberalization as from multilateral trade liberalization. As Paul Krugman puts it:

> If we nonetheless have a fairly liberal world trading system, it is only because countries have been persuaded to open their markets in return for comparable market-opening on the part of their trading partners. Never mind that the 'concessions' that trade negotiators are so proud of wresting from other nations are almost always actions that these nations should have taken in their own interest anyway; in practice countries seem willing to do themselves good only if others promise to do the same. (1997, p. 13)

On the other hand Bagwell and Staiger (2002) argue that the various provisions of the GATT/WTO can be better understood by abandoning the small country assumption and assuming that countries have some influence over their terms of trade. They interpret the central features of the GATT as motivated by governments' attempts to escape from a terms of trade-driven prisoner's dilemma.

It is useful to summarize the key principles that underlie the multilateral negotiations under the GATT/WTO to see if the same principles could be applied to international migration. These are reciprocity, non-discrimination and national treatment. Reciprocity means negotiating access to foreign markets in exchange for concessions of approximately equal value to foreign suppliers in domestic markets. Non-discrimination – the Most Favoured Nation clause – means that a concession granted to one party

---

[25] Irwin has argued that the failure of the ITO with its multifaceted agenda may have been a blessing in disguise. As he puts it: 'The GATT was formed by carving out and implementing the commercial-policy sections of the Havana Charter that was to have guided the ITO. The narrow focus of the GATT served the process of trade liberalization (and the institution itself) well because the GATT's mission was simple and straightforward' (1995, p. 325).

must be granted to all parties to the negotiations. And national treatment means that foreign firms must be able to sell in the domestic market on the same terms as domestic firms. Whether or not some rational economic basis can be found to explain these elements, could they nevertheless be applied to negotiations over international migration?

Turning first to non-discrimination, most countries already have immigration policies that do not discriminate among potential immigrants by country of origin. Among the major immigrant-receiving countries, policies that discriminated in favour of certain origins and against others largely disappeared in the 1960s and 1970s. In the United States, the national origin quotas were abolished by the 1965 Amendments to the Immigration Act. Similarly in Canada and Australia preferences for European, and specifically British, immigrants were replaced by points systems that applied regardless of the immigrant's origin country. And the European guestworker schemes that provided opportunities to migrants from specific source countries were largely abandoned in the 1970s. Of course, family reunification schemes, skilled worker pro- grammes and points systems do implicitly favour immigrants from some countries over others. Nevertheless, the principle of non-discrimination does not seem to be a major stumbling block to the setting up of a multilateral framework for immigration policy.

Secondly, permanent immigrants are accorded largely the same rights in receiving country labour markets as native-born workers, even before they become citizens. And in most countries that also includes equal access to public welfare, health and education systems.[26] Of course there are many forms of discrimination against immi- grants, but they are not part of the legal framework. Indeed, most developed countries have equal opportunities legislation that expressly forbids it. Thus the equivalent of national treatment (that immigrants can sell their labour on the same terms as the native-born) is a well-established principle in most immigration countries and it would not seem to be an impediment to international agreement over immigration policy.

The missing element is reciprocity. And the reason is that migration is much more of a one-way street than is trade. While, in a multilateral context, trade balances have to add up roughly to zero, net migration balances do not. If rich and poor countries were gathered around the negotiating table, it is difficult to see how improved terms of access to the labour markets of the poor(er) countries could be of equal value to similar conditions of access granted by rich(er) countries in return. Indeed, even the poorer countries may have little incentive to come to the bargaining table. Those in poor countries who have the greatest incentive to support such negotiations are precisely those who wish to leave.

The adding up condition that applies to trade but not to migration is not a trivial point. It is the reason why, in the absence of barriers, comparative advantage is the most important determinant of trade flows, while absolute advantage is the most important determinant of migration (see Appendix 2). Thus labour productivity differences between countries that are not simply due to the endowments of other

---

[26] It is notable that California's Proposition 187 of 1994, which sought to remove these benefits from illegal immigrants, was subsequently declared unconstitutional by a US District Court.

factors are a much more serious impediment to reaching reciprocal agreements over migration than over trade. As Box 3 shows, international wage gaps are largely due to differences in total factor productivity. Thus even if relative endowments were the same across countries, thus eliminating trade based on comparative advantage, the remaining wage gaps would still provide a basis for one-way migration. Migration would only be eliminated by forcing the net migration balance to zero, which is essentially what restrictive immigration policies aim to do.

Box 3. Relative wages, endowments and productivity

How far are differences in real wages across countries accounted for by differences in factor endowments as compared with differences in total factor productivity? A number of studies have shown that a large share of the gap is accounted for by productivity. In a recent study, Hendricks (2002) calculated the ratio of a given country's real wage to that for the US and then estimated the contributions of physical capital, measured skills and unmeasured skills to that gap. The remainder is therefore due to the differences in technology or total factor productivity.

Real wage and total factor productivity (TFP) ratios to the US for 67 countries

	Real wage ratio to US (%)		TFP ratio to US (%)	
	Mean	Coefficient of variation	Mean	Coefficient of variation
Poorest countries	13.5	1.9	30.2	6.4
Middle income countries	34.0	1.5	53.8	4.7
Richest countries	72.7	2.1	75.3	2.4
All 67 countries	39.7	17.1	52.8	10.4

Source: Calculated from Hendricks (2002, pp. 204–05).

As the table shows, the poorest third of countries (ranked by GDP per capita) have real wages that average only 13.5% of the US. But some of that difference is attributable to lower skills and less physical capital per worker. Giving the workers in these countries the same capital and skill endowments as the US would raise their wages to 30.5% of the US level. Thus, some of the difference is due to lower endowments of skill and capital. But even with identical factor proportions, labour productivity in poor countries still averages less than a third that of the US, and even for middle-income countries, TFP is little more than half.

This has important implications for trade versus migration. If factor proportions were the same the world over there would be no basis for trade (insofar as trade is based on relative factor scarcity). But the remaining wage differences still provide a basis for migration.

It is important to recognize also the consistency between domestic policies and international policy. In democratic countries, agreements made at the international level must also command sufficient political support at home – giving rise to what has sometimes been labeled a 'two-level game' (Putnam, 1988; Milner, 1997). The reciprocal element in trade agreements must ensure that the gains to export interests are sufficiently large for the package as a whole to gain overall acceptance at home. By contrast with the situation for trade, in most developed countries there is no coherent group petitioning its political representatives to support negotiations for better access to the labour markets in the Third World. Thus there is little to bargain over in the international arena that would command support at home.[27] It follows that failure to establish an international framework for migration that plays the same liberalizing role that the GATT/WTO plays for trade is not simply an accident of institutional history.

5.3. Is reciprocity the key?

Experimental evidence suggests that reciprocity is fundamental to human interactions, the best-known example being the ultimatum game. In that situation individuals are often observed to turn down an offer that they perceive to be insufficiently generous, even though it is not in their narrow economic interest to do so. Similarly, individuals are often willing to inflict punishments on those who act selfishly, even though it is costly to do so. Fehr and Gächter (2000) observe that some element of reciprocity is important in a variety of economic settings where contracts cannot be fully specified and where an element of trust is required. The evidence suggests that it is also important in people's perceptions of trade negotiations. As noted in Box 2 above, a majority of Australian respondents to a survey on foreign policy were against unilateral opening of the domestic market, even if it made goods cheaper, and they supported restricting cheap foreign imports. But an overwhelming majority supported reciprocal trade negotiations. Thus, even if we adopt Krugman's view that unilateral liberalizations are (almost) always in a country's best economic interest, that is clearly not the perception of the majority of voters.

It was argued above that the shape of domestic politics surrounding reciprocal trade agreements reflects the fact that there are clearly identifiable groups of gainers and losers. But the importance of reciprocity goes deeper than that because governments in democratic societies need to heed public opinion in general, as well as to strike a balance between interest groups. Thus public attitudes towards reciprocity help governments to mobilize popular support for trade liberalization. Indeed, this may be a reason why governments have sometimes seized opportunities for reciprocal liberalization, even when the balance of interest group power still favours restriction.

---

[27] Of course there may be other reasons why international agreements on immigration policies may be more or less acceptable in domestic politics (see Hollifield, 2000), but the purpose here is to focus purely on the economic fundamentals.

It may also help to explain the observed tendency for democratic countries more often to enter reciprocal trade agreements, even controlling for a variety of other observable characteristics (Mansfield *et al.*, 2002).

Reciprocity, of course, can mean many things. At one level it may be little more than direct exchange: tit for tat, or quid pro quo. At the other extreme it may mean a form of gift exchange; offering something the benefits of which are indirect at best and which reflect behavioural norms rather than narrow self-interest. In the context of international trade agreements, Keohane (1986) distinguishes between 'specific reciprocity' and 'diffuse reciprocity'. The former characterizes conditional MFN agreements, normally bilateral deals where there is a rough equivalence of concessions on both sides. While such agreements may be easier to reach, they are also easier to unravel. The latter is associated with unconditional MFN agreements and with multilateralism. Besides being more complex to negotiate, the equivalence is much less direct and the potential to free ride is much greater. These features underpin the introduction since the Kennedy Round of across the board tariff cuts (rather than item by item negotiations), simultaneous (rather than sequential) agreement, and the formalization of sanctions through a dispute settlement mechanism.

There are examples of unilateral trade liberalization, the most famous of which is Britain's abolition of the Corn Laws in 1846. But from the time of the 1860 Cobden-Chevalier treaty between Britain and France, most trade liberalizations were based on negotiated treaties that included MFN clauses.[28] In the US the trade agreements made between the introduction of the RTAA and the 1960s were mainly bilateral deals that reflect specific rather than diffuse reciprocity. According to Keohane (1986, p. 26) multilateral negotiations were built upon this foundation:

> The successful synthesis of specific and diffuse reciprocity in the Kennedy and Tokyo rounds exemplifies the significance of institutional innovation in world politics. The forms of reciprocity made a difference. As the social exchange literature suggests, sequences of action, both within the negotiating rounds and between them, help to create obligations and solidify ties among the participants. Yet the resulting norms remain weak enough that specific reciprocity persists as an essential element of the tariff reduction process.

Thus reciprocity has been a key underpinning to agreements over tariffs, both in the WTO and in the context regional trade agreements as well as the recent proliferation of bilateral free trade deals (Baldwin, 2006). Unilateral liberalizations, from the Corn Laws to the Asian Tigers, have been the exception rather than the rule. Reciprocity is also a key feature of many other spheres of international cooperation and if agreements on migration are to work then they must proceed on this basis.

Since migrants predominantly flow one way (at least those that move between poor and rich countries), the scope for reciprocity seems to be limited. But are there elements associated with migration over which bargains could be struck? One which

---

[28] There were also a number of trade wars that reflect negative reciprocity, such as that between France and Italy in 1887–90.

is often mentioned is the sizeable flow of remittances that are sent from rich to poor countries; another is development aid. But it is important to stress that these are benefits that flow *to* the poorer countries and thus they do not provide the basis for 'concessions' that poor countries could make in return for labour market opening in the developed world. If reciprocity is the foundation for international agreement then the key is to find something that the poorer countries can offer to the rich counties and not the other way around.

6. IS THERE A WAY FORWARD?

What are the prospects for future multilateral agreements on international migration? The argument advanced here suggests that it will be hard, if not impossible, to reach the sorts of global agreements for migration as have been negotiated for trade. The fundamental reason is that while trade is driven largely by comparative advantage, migration is driven largely by absolute advantage. This is why the gains to freeing up migration are so much greater than the gains to liberalizing trade. But it is precisely because migration is more of a one-way street than trade that agreements based on reciprocity will be hard to reach. And this is unlikely to change as long as the enormous gaps in economic development persist.

Yet recent developments have led some observers to the view that a global framework for liberalizing migration could be within reach. This optimism is reflected in the objectives of the Global Commission on International Migration, one of which is to 'provide the framework for the formulation of a coherent, comprehensive and global response to migration issues'.[29] There have been a number of suggestions about the appropriate forum for carrying this forward, for example whether it should be part of the UN system, what should be the basis of representation, whether it should focus on deal-making, on rule-setting or simply provide a focus for debate. What has been lacking is any serious consideration of whether any of these organizational arrangements would actually work to liberalize immigration controls. Indeed commentators have often concentrated on the form rather than on the function of such organizations. I would argue that form should follow function and that more thought should be given to precisely what the negotiations should be about. Four possibilities are worth considering.

The first is the explicit linking of immigration policy to some other policy issue. If the lack of basis for reciprocity is the fundamental impediment to negotiating a more liberal migration regime then the solution could be to throw something else into the bargain. One possibility would be to link migration and trade. Issue linkage has arisen in the GATT/WTO with the inclusion of provisions for trade-related intellectual property (TRIPS) and trade-related investment measures (TRIMS). Environmental protection issues have emerged in the context of the dispute settlement mechanism

---

[29] See http://www.gcim.org/en/.

and there has been strong pressure to build environmental protection and labour standards more explicitly into the bargaining process. On the whole economists have argued against issue linkage, (a) because it further complicates the negotiations, which may impede trade liberalization, and (b) because it may not deliver greater cooperation on the linked issue, except under very special conditions.[30]

Nevertheless, the idea of linking migration to trade has been fostered by the advent of Mode 4 of the General Agreement on Trade in Services (GATS) that came into effect in 1995. This provides for the 'temporary movement of natural persons' as a means of effecting trade in services. The fact that the only genuinely global agreement relating to migration has been engineered by the WTO, which has been so successful at liberalizing trade, invites the idea that the 'right' international framework could do the same for migration.[31] But that would be misleading. Mode 4 does not cover migrants seeking access to employment abroad, nor does it provide a route to permanent residence or citizenship. It is not an agreement on migration *per se*, and its application remains very limited.[32] One reason for its lack of success is that it does not require reciprocity – and this is because it has proved so difficult to agree upon.

What about a grand bargain that linked a deeper liberalization of migration to trade or some other issue? For this to happen there must be an approximate matching of the gains received on one policy with the concessions given on another (assuming that international agreements are underpinned largely by specific reciprocity rather than by diffuse reciprocity, to use Keohane's terms). This implies that the more multilateral are the negotiations the less close the match is likely to be for any individual country and hence the stronger the underlying correlation needs to be between the concessions offered and the benefits received. It also implies that some measure of equivalence must be found. This is difficult because immigration policies are based on rationing by quantity while import controls are based on rationing by price. In the Tokyo round quantity restrictions were converted to tariff equivalents as a prelude to an across-the-board tariff reduction, but it is difficult to see how this could be effected for migration. The same applies to other grand bargains that might be considered, such as exchanging more open immigration policies in the developed world for tougher environmental controls in the less developed countries.[33] Other proposals such as linking more open developed country labour markets with aid, investment or other support for development fail even more badly because the costs fall only on the rich countries, leaving no scope at all for reciprocity.

[30] Limão (2005) shows that in order for interlinking to enhance cooperation, the issues must be interdependent in the government's objective function and they must be strategic complements.

[31] For an optimistic assessment of the potential development of Mode 4, see UN (2004, pp. 136–38); and for a comparison with other migration agreements see International Organization for Migration (2006).

[32] One reason for this is that countries are permitted to apply admission criteria based on economic needs, labour market tests or qualifications. In other words it is constrained by the same policies that limit immigration.

[33] Lodefalk and Whalley (2002) provide a survey of proposals for a World Environmental Organization. They conclude that such a forum would need to be given enough teeth to engineer bargains such as exchanging cash for environmental commitments, but they argue that a WTO style organization would not be an appropriate structure to deal with market failures or with improved rule making.

While it might be possible to find some policy concession that would be valued by developed countries in exchange for access to their labour markets, any such proposals have an even more fatal flaw. This is that those countries that send migrants do not on the whole place any value on seeing more of their citizens emigrate. According to the UN's periodic survey, only 5% of developing country governments in 2001 thought that the level of emigration from their country was too low, while 23% thought that it was too high. Similarly, only 6% stated that their policy aim was to increase emigration while 22% said that their aim was to reduce it (UN, 2002, p. 19). Given that most of the benefit from international migration flows to the migrants themselves, this is easy to understand. If the benefits of liberalization go to those who leave the country, why should a source country government regard this as a gain worth giving concessions for?[34] Indeed many such governments express concerns that further liberalization would exacerbate the brain drain. The only significant gain seems to be from remittances, which amounted in 2001 to $72.3 billion or 1.3% of developing country income, a sum that exceeded official development assistance (Ratha, 2003, p. 158). But if this is so valuable to developing countries why do so few of them wish to encourage emigration?[35]

A second possibility is to build upon existing regional agreements that involve cooperation in a variety of other dimensions but particularly trade. The best-known and most advanced example is the European Union where the principle of free migration among member states is deeply embedded. In Africa, the Economic Community of West African States (ECOWAS) and the Common Market for Eastern and Southern Africa (COMESA) have agreed protocols on free movement, but these have never been fully implemented. Similarly in South America, the Andean Community and the Southern Common Market (MERCOSUR) have agreements in principle to facilitate cross-border movement and residence (UN, 2004, p. 194). Such agreements have the potential to work because they are between countries at similar income levels and hence there is the prospect of two-way traffic. In cases such as these, where development gaps between the countries are small by world standards, migration is driven more by comparative advantage, making two way flows a more realistic prospect and offering some potential for building agreements based on reciprocity.

Could such regional agreements provide the building blocks for wider agreements, either by expanding the regional groups or by negotiations between regional groups? The evidence suggests not. A good illustration is the North American Free Trade Agreement (NAFTA), which has not been extended to embrace free migration. This is because Mexico is so much poorer than the United States.[36] Another illustration is

---

[34] In source countries that are undemocratic and unequal, where autocratic rulers rely on the support of rich capitalists and property owners, there seems even less reason why the government would want to encourage the abundant factor to leave.

[35] One important exception is the Philippines which has an active emigration programme, supported by two agencies that are attached to the Department of Labour.

[36] One of the explicit motivations of the NAFTA agreement was to reduce the pressure of illegal migration from Mexico to the United States on the hypothesis that trade and migration are substitutes. This view was supported prior to the agreement by the US Commission for the Study of International Migration and Cooperative Economic Development, which suggested that NAFTA would increase migration pressure in the short run but reduce it in the long run (Martin et al., 2000, pp. 146–54). Evidently, after 12 years, the long run has not yet arrived.

the refusal of most of the EU-15 countries to open their labour markets to the countries that acceded to membership in 2004 and the likelihood that even more of them will remain closed for as long as possible to the future accession states, Bulgaria, Romania and perhaps Turkey. So, on the one hand regional agreements among neighbouring countries at similar income levels seems the most feasible path to freeing up migration. As with the EU, they may eventually expand to embrace a somewhat more hetero-geneous group. But on the other hand such agreements will not exploit the largest worldwide gains: those that arise from migration from the poorest to richest countries.

A third possibility that has been canvassed is to promote agreements for temporary migration, especially from poor to rich countries. Two well-known examples are the *Bracero* programme of 1942–64 that brought temporary migrants to the US from Mexico, and the *Gästarbeiter* system of 1955–73 that recruited temporary migrants to Germany from a number of Mediterranean countries.[37] Other such examples include the temporary worker programmes of the Gulf States, Israel, Singapore and Korea. While these have been out of fashion in the West, interest in them has recently revived. One advantage to the host country of short-term migrant employment contracts is that the numbers can be adjusted to employment conditions. Another is that they restrict access to welfare state benefits – something that is clearly an issue of public concern. These agreements also appear to be attractive to the source countries that have signed up to them. One reason is that remittances are much larger for migrants who intend to return. Another is that, to the extent that migrants gain human capital abroad, there is less of a brain drain and more of a brain gain. And third, if their families stay at home, and the migrants return, they are much more likely to exert political leverage in the source country in favour of such agreements.

Guestworker agreements went out of fashion because of two side effects. One is that many of the guestworkers became permanent. In Germany the number of resi-dent foreigners rose from 4 million at the time of the *arbeitstopp* in 1973 to 4.4 million in 1985. Another is that many of them became illegals and generated even further illegal immigration when the guestworker programmes were wound down. However, it has been suggested that such side effects can be avoided if the right incentives are provided and if there is adequate enforcement (Boeri *et al.*, 2002, Ch. 6; Schiff, 2004). These incentives include the employer posting a bond that is returnable when the migrant leaves at the end of the contract and deferring some of the migrant's pay until he or she returns to the source country. Existing agreements often include one of these but not both and it is argued that, in addition, source country cooperation is needed in order to avoid generating new waves of illegal immigration. Some observers see scope for agreements in which the central focus is expanding guest-worker programmes in exchange for cooperation in controlling illegal immigration, although it is not clear how effective such schemes would be.

---

[37] These agreements were made with Italy in 1955, Greece and Spain in 1960, Turkey in 1961 and 1964, Morocco in 1963, Portugal in 1964, Tunisia in 1965 and Yugoslavia in 1968.

Whatever their shape, most guestworker-type schemes are bilateral agreements. That seems almost inevitable for agreements that attempt to thwart illegal immigration through strengthening border controls. It is far from clear that such programmes could or should form the basis for multilateral agreement. One recent report lists 176 bilateral agreements currently in existence (OECD, 2004). These are typically agreements for the temporary migration of contract workers, seasonal workers, working holiday-makers and trainees. For the most part they are bespoke agreements that are tailored to the needs of specific sectors in the host country; others involve elements of training or cultural exchange. It therefore seems unlikely that a multilateral negotiation over temporary migrant numbers would succeed, and it does not provide the foundation upon which a serious liberalization of migration could be built.

Following from this, a fourth possibility is to consider agreements on issues other than immigration quotas or the number of immigrants. Most observers who have thought about what a global agency should do have suggested a range of activities that does not explicitly include the striking of grand bargains over migrant numbers. An illustrative example is the list of functions suggested by Newland (2005, p. 7), which includes: data collection, dissemination and analysis; policy research and development; technical assistance and training; provision of services; a platform for discussion; support for negotiations; anti-trafficking initiatives; promotion of migration-related development initiatives; coordination. This list and others like it illustrate two things. One is that many of the functions are, at least in principle, covered by existing organizations. The other is that the central mission is not well defined. Phrases such as 'a platform for discussion' or 'coordination' fail to specify clearly enough what the core functions would be.

To be fair, those who contemplate some supra-national organization often have in mind issues such as controlling illegal migration, combating migrant trafficking, upholding the legal rights of migrants, and assisting refugees. But the evidence is that governments are reluctant to come to the negotiating table on these issues. Only a minority have signed up to the ILO and UN conventions that focus on the rights of migrants, and there is a distinct lack of enthusiasm for discussing deeper global collaboration.[38] Another strand of thought in the aftermath of 9/11 focuses on linking migration concessions in the developed world with enhanced security measures in source countries (Koslowski, 2004). However, international cooperation on security is a much wider problem of which migration is only a small part.[39] Collaboration on these issues might lead to confidence building and it could help to provide conditions that would

[38] The two major ILO instruments are the Migration for Employment Convention (Revised (No. 97) of 1949), which has 42 signatories, and the Migrant Workers (Supplementary Provisions) Convention (No. 143), which has 18 signatories. The UN Convention on the Rights of All Migrant Workers and Members of their Families took 13 years to come into force and has so far been ratified by 25 countries (Newland, 2005, p. 4). When a questionnaire was circulated to UN member states in 2003 about convening a global conference on migration, 47 were in favour, 26 were against and 111 did not reply (Koslowski, 2004, p. 3).

[39] There exists a UN Convention on Transnational Organized Crime, which came into effect in 2003 and to which several protocols have been added. In considering a General Agreement on Migration, Mobility and Security, Koslowski (2004) acknowledges that poor countries have neither the incentive nor the resources to implement hi-tech security measures within their borders.

expand the scope for bilateral migration programmes. But it does not create a *prima facie* case for a new international institution (or even for a radical modification of existing institutions). Creating a new institution for migration would only be justified if it had the central mission of expanding world migration and if it could be endowed with the means of reaching that end. So far that case remains unproven.

7. CONCLUSION

There has recently been much political chatter about reforming the international migration regime, but it has not been very well focused. At one level headlines in the *Economist* such as 'Let in the Huddled Masses' (cover, 31 March 2001) completely lack *realpolitik*. Why should governments unilaterally change immigration policies that presumably they find to be politically optimal? Yet at the same time, most economists sympathize with the sentiments underlying the *Economist's* headlines, given that the global gains from liberalizing migration seem to be so large. It is common to assume that this apparent global market failure can be put down to some mix of bigotry and prejudice in domestic politics and a lack of international institutions that can overcome coordination failures. The argument put forward here suggests that neither of these arguments is as strong as it appears at first sight.

Clearly migration differs from trade in a variety of dimensions. Migration affects societies and their cultures in ways that trade does not; migration is typically more permanent than trade, it is a stock rather than a flow, and migrants eventually get the vote. While these are valid considerations, the fact is that public opinion is not very much more hostile to letting in more immigrants than it is to letting in more imports. Nevertheless resistance to immigration goes up as the numbers increase. One reason for this is that there is no well-defined group that has the economic interest and the political power to press developed country governments into more open immigration policies. Those who have the most to gain, the migrants themselves, do not have a vote *ex ante*. More important still, residents of the developed world have little interest in opening up opportunities to migrate to poorer countries. This asymmetry means that there is no basis for the kind of reciprocity that underpins the WTO, and this in turn is because migration is driven largely by absolute advantage rather than by comparative advantage.

There are very good reasons why no organization resembling the WTO exists for international migration. And it seems pointless to conjure up a World Migration Organization without a clear idea about what it would do. Any new organization would need to have a well-defined objective (much as free trade is the overarching goal of the WTO) rather than being a talking shop, of which there is currently no shortage. It would need the capacity to create binding commitments, to which its members could be held. And in order to bring governments to the negotiating table it would have to be based on a form of reciprocity that would be meaningful in a multilateral context.

So, should we have a WTO for international migration? On the arguments presented in this paper, the answer is clearly no.

Discussion

Manuel Arellano
CEMFI and CEPR

This paper puts together evidence and discussion aimed at understanding why trade policies are so liberal whereas migration policies are so restrictive, despite the fact that migration is the field where the expected gains from liberalization are largest. A focus for the paper is provided by the question in the title, which helps to organize the material and motivates additional discussion at both ends.

Many of the arguments developed are interesting and compelling. I also appreciate the effort (and difficulty) in finding empirical evidence to back them. Many of my comments are on empirical aspects, even if they are not necessarily central to the paper's arguments.

How much more trade than migration?

The paper begins by checking that there is indeed more trade than migration. This is done by comparing imports to GDP ratios with immigrants to total population ratios.

I suppose these are natural measures for each concept, but I am not sure how informative are direct numerical comparisons, given that GDP is a flow measure whereas population is a stock. In fact, one problem with linking immigration and trade policies is the difficulty in finding some measure of equivalence.

How large is the causal effect of GATT/WTO on trade?

Next, there is some discussion and evidence on the effects of trade policies and GATT/WTO membership on trade, which is suggestive and useful. However, worries of reverse causality persist.

Did membership of GATT increase trade or was the willingness to trade causing GATT expansion? Even if empirical resolution may be difficult, progress on this question could be made by analyzing the determinants of GATT membership.

Are the same types of people really opposed to both imports and immigration?

The paper reports regression results from cross-sectional survey data for multiple countries on the determinants of individual attitudes towards protection and immigration. The motivation for these estimates is finding out to what extent the anti-migration and the anti-trade groups overlap, given small differences in aggregate attitudes.

The conclusion is that opposition to immigration is not much more intense than to imports and that the same sorts of people are opposed to both, so that policy differences cannot be explained by differences in public attitudes.

The force of this conclusion is limited by the fact that regressors explain less than 10% of the variability in responses to the policy questions. So we cannot really say from these estimates that the 'same' people are opposed to both. We just do not know.

Since most of the variation is in the errors, we might say that the same people are opposed to both if we observe a large positive correlation between the unobservables determining opposition to immigration and imports. However, the correlation between probit errors (Appendix) is between 0.2 and 0.3, which is of the same magnitude as the correlation found across country averages (described as not particularly strong, and suggestive that there may be systematic differences between those who are opposed to immigration and those who are opposed to trade).

Prejudice against things foreign or economic motive?

I am not sure that the evidence in Table 5 on prejudice as a determinant of attitudes is so compelling. The effects of 'patriotism' and 'chauvinism' will be upward biased if they are positively correlated with unobserved determinants. This is potentially relevant because the low R^2s leave much room for unobserved heterogeneity bias in the effects of 'patriotism' and 'chauvinism'.

I have in mind heterogeneity in individual exposure to competition from immigration or trade (e.g. working in an industry threatened by imports). Or maybe I am just prejudiced in favour of economic motives.

It is interesting that the effect of 'patriotism' on imports is more than twice the size of the effect on immigration. I wonder if there is a differential effect for second-generation immigrants. That is, that patriotic feeling in the descendants of immigrants may produce less opposition to immigration than to imports.

Country-level effects

The left-hand side variables should be understood as measuring sentiment towards limiting imports or immigrants relative to existing conditions, which vary across countries. To some extent this is taken care of by country dummies in the regression.

The purpose of Section 3.3 is to go inside the dummies to check if their variation can be associated with country differences in fractions of imports or foreign born, and the size of the welfare state. This is a useful but limited exercise. One limitation is that the change in conditions in a given country may matter more than cross-sectional differences in the levels. Another limitation is that country-level effects need not be restricted to an additive term.

Equilibrium policy outcomes

Section 4 discusses the association between opinion and policy in a supply and demand framework. That is, regarding equilibrium policy outcomes as intersections of public opinion and policy reaction functions, then thinking of shifters of these functions. This is a useful way of organizing the discussion in spite of lack of empirical content.

I do not see a basis for saying that the plots in Figure 3 are 'consistent with the policy reaction function of Figure 2', just because they are upward sloping. This would be the case if we knew *a priori* that regression lines have to be one curve or the other, but the only presumption is that they are just some combination of both. Maybe one could argue that anti-trade opinion functions are relatively flat.

Much of the material in this section is of an expository nature, but nevertheless central to the paper. This includes a review of the arguments in Hatton and Williamson (2005b) and the discussion on the different natures of politics of trade and migration (as in Greenaway and Nelson, 2006).

Back to the international institutions: lack of reciprocity?

The lack of an international forum for migration is not regarded as an accident of history, but the result that reciprocity, which is key under GATT/WTO, is missing in migration. The conclusions are that it will be hard to get global agreements for migration and that regional agreements may be a realistic way forward.

Falling transport costs have enlarged the potential for long-distance migration, but they have also increased the potential for temporary movements, recurrent and return migration. Overall, there seems to be a widening array of migration arrangements.

Migrant remittances have become an important source of development finance for some countries. This fact may induce governments in developing countries to regard liberalization of migration as a gain worth giving concessions for, even if they find it difficult to admit to their own citizens an interest in active emigration policy as a solution to their economic problems.

Because of the two previous considerations, agreements on new forms of migration may become a more important ingredient of liberalization of migration than they have been in the past.

Panel discussion

Philippe Martin asked what differences there were between the political reactions to migration during the nineteenth-century globalization wave, and those today. He suggested this might be because of the productivity benefits that migrants brought with them. He also pointed out that migration could not be considered a solution to the demographic problems caused by ageing, as migrants would age too in their turn.

Thomas Hertel pointed out that temporary migration is indeed a subject included in the WTO and is fundamentally different from permanent migration, especially in terms of gains for the source country. Furthermore, he thought there was value for developing countries in including temporary migration, particularly as a way to make up for the lack of progress on some other issues such as agriculture. Lans Bovenberg agreed, and argued that the benefits to host countries facing adverse demographic changes could be valuable in the short term (even if the long-term demographic benefits were less clear). Likewise, the benefits to sending countries in terms of remittances could also be a significant incentive. In reply the author accepted that temporary migration could indeed help negotiations, if it could really be sure to be temporary (migrants tend to defect into the informal sector, and may retire in the destination country). That, he said, was more likely to be feasible on a bilateral basis; developing countries tend not to like emigration much, so it is not a bargaining chip for the WTO.

Wendy Carlin said that the evidence that immigration leads to a fall in wages is not very strong. The author agreed, but said this was because of poor data; he was sceptical that this meant that the true effect was unimportant.

Gian Maria Milesi-Ferretti thought it was worth looking at the example of countries in the Arabian peninsula with up to 60% immigrants. Is immigration really a one-way street? The benefits and costs (brain drain, remittances) appear to indicate a two-way relationship. Many emigrants are high-skilled and can afford the cost (he cited the example of Malawian doctors going to the US).

Rudolf Winter-Ebmer suggested that the EU-level process of setting up a single immigration policy is similar to the WTO measures under consideration, but aims at reducing not fostering migration. Agreement to do so across the EU is likely because there is a lot of uncertainty about the distributional impact: it seems that earlier immigrants are those hurt most by new immigration, so it is strange to see in the data that they are in favour of further immigration.

Finally, Hans-Werner Sinn suggested it was a mistake to think that the issue was one of comparative versus absolute advantage. Worries about migration arise rather from two factors. The first is distributional concerns: there may be gains from trade, but autarky-scarce factors are likely to lose out. The second is concerns about sharing public goods (the welfare state, and lots of infrastructure, would have to be privatized or fenced in). Free migration is not efficient when there are open-access public resources. Those externalities are not present in the case of trade.

APPENDIX 1

Table A1. Bivariate probit estimates of the determinants of anti-imports and anti-immigration attitudes

Variable	(1) Reduce immigration	(2) Limit imports	(3) Reduce immigration	(4) Limit imports
'Patriotism'	0.075	0.169		
	(3.68)	(10.18)		
'Chauvinism'	0.400	0.387		
	(7.45)	(12.93)		
Second generation immigrant	−0.311	−0.022	−0.424	−0.159
	(6.03)	(0.55)	(9.46)	(3.57)
Female	0.064	0.259	0.038	0.218
	(2.14)	(9.23)	(1.20)	(8.86)
Age	0.001	0.002	0.005	0.007
	(0.91)	(2.23)	(3.90)	(6.35)
Employed	−0.020	−0.049	−0.053	−0.084
	(1.33)	(2.41)	(2.68)	(4.65)
High educated	−0.261	−0.283	−0.579	−0.449
	(9.76)	(8.82)	(2.21)	(1.62)
High educated × Inequality			0.724	−0.143
			(1.35)	(0.23)
High educated × GDP per capita			−0.023	−0.009
			(0.36)	(0.15)
Rho	0.188		0.281	
	(12.77)		(15.09)	
No. of obs	19 850	19 850	19 850	19 850
Country dummies	Yes	Yes	Yes	Yes

Note: These estimates are comparable with those in Table 4 except that here the left-hand side variable is reduced to a dummy taking the value 1 for opinion ratings 4 or 5 and zero otherwise. Bivariate probit coefficients are reported with z statistics in parentheses based on robust standard errors clustered by country. Rho is the adjusted correlation coefficient between the equation errors.

APPENDIX 2

Comparative and absolute advantage: a Cobb–Douglas illustration

An important theme in this article is that, when there are substantial economy-wide differences in productivity between countries, then incentives for trade and for migration diverge. This can be illustrated most clearly in the two-country, two-good, two-factor case in which production technology is Cobb–Douglas with constant returns to scale.

In each country goods A and B are produced with the following technologies:

$$Q_A = v_i L_A^{\alpha} K_A^{1-\alpha}; \quad Q_B = v_i L_B^{\beta} K_B^{1-\beta} \tag{1}$$

where Q is output, L is labour, K is capital and v_i is an economy-wide efficiency term specific to country i. Minimizing the cost of producing good A, we find from the first order conditions that the shares of labour and capital in total cost are:

$$\frac{wL_A}{TC} = \alpha; \; \frac{rK_A}{TC} = 1 - \alpha \tag{2}$$

where w is the wage rate, r is the user cost of capital and TC is a given total cost. Substituting for L and K in the production function gives average cost equations:

$$AC_A = \frac{TC_A}{Q_A} \frac{1}{v_i} w^\alpha r^{1-\alpha} z_A; \; AC_B = \frac{TC_B}{Q_B} \frac{1}{v_i} w^\beta r^{1-\beta} z_B \tag{3}$$

where z_A and z_B are constants that depend only on α and β respectively. Applying the zero profit conditions $AC_A = p_A$ and $AC_B = p_B$, and taking the ratio gives:

$$\left[\frac{w}{r}\right]^{\alpha-\beta} = \frac{p_A/z_A}{p_B/z_B} \tag{4}$$

Assuming they each produce both goods, two countries i and j facing the same relative price, as under free trade, will have the same factor price ratio, which does not depend on absolute productivities v_i and v_j. Eliminating r using the price equation for p_A gives an expression for the wage in country i as:

$$\frac{w}{p_A} = \frac{v_i}{z_A} \left[\frac{p_A/z_A}{p_B/z_B}\right]^{\frac{1-\alpha}{\alpha-\beta}} \tag{5}$$

If p_A and p_B are identical in both countries, nominal (and real) wages differ in proportion to the differences in country-specific productivities, providing an incentive to migrate.

Under autarky, relative prices will be determined by factor endowments. Country i's factor allocation can be expressed, using the cost share equations (2), as:

$$L = L_A + L_B = \alpha \frac{TC_A}{w} + \beta \frac{TC_B}{w}; \; K = K_A + K_B = (1-\alpha)\frac{TC_A}{r} + (1-\beta)\frac{TC_B}{r} \tag{6}$$

And using the average cost equations (3) we obtain outputs Q_A and Q_B as:

$$Q_A = \frac{v_i}{(\beta - \alpha)z_A} \left[\frac{w}{r}\right]^{-\alpha} \left[K\beta - L(1-\beta)\frac{w}{r}\right];$$

$$ \tag{7}$$

$$Q_B = \frac{v_i}{(\alpha - \beta)z_B} \left[\frac{w}{r}\right]^{-\beta} \left[K\alpha - L(1-\alpha)\frac{w}{r}\right]$$

The domestic utility function is assumed to be Cobb–Douglas:

$$U = Q_A^\gamma Q_B^{1-\gamma} \tag{8}$$

From the first order conditions for utility maximization we obtain:

$$\frac{p_B}{p_A} = \frac{(1-\gamma)}{\gamma}\frac{Q_B}{Q_A} \tag{9}$$

Substituting for outputs using (7) and eliminating w/r using (4) gives:

$$\frac{p_B}{p_A} = \frac{z_B}{z_A}\left[\frac{xK}{yL}\right]^{\beta-\alpha} \tag{10}$$

where x and y are functions of α, β and γ. The autarky price ratio depends on the ratio of factor endowments. And since trade accounts must balance, the potential for trade depends on comparative advantage as reflected by differences across countries in factor intensities and not on absolute productivity differences. Using (4) and (10) the wage for country i can be written as:

$$\frac{w}{p_A} = \frac{v_i}{z_A}\left[\frac{xK}{yL}\right]^{1-\alpha} \tag{11}$$

Alternatively, since prices now differ between countries, we can write the real wage using the geometric price index derived from the indirect utility function:

$$\frac{w}{p_A^\gamma p_B^{1-\gamma}} = v_i\left[\frac{xK}{yL}\right]^{1-\beta-\gamma(\alpha-\beta)} z_A^{\frac{\beta-1}{\alpha-\beta}} z_B^{\frac{1-\alpha}{\alpha-\beta}} \tag{12}$$

The real wage difference between countries i and j depends on the factor endowment ratios that drive trade but it also depends on the economy-wide efficiency parameter v_i and v_j. As illustrated in Box 3, real wage differences between rich and poor countries are largely due to differences in overall total factor productivity rather than in relative factor endowments. Thus the incentive to migrate depends mainly on absolute advantage as reflected in the efficiency terms rather than on comparative advantage as reflected in factor endowments.

REFERENCES

Bagwell, K. and R.W. Staiger (2002). *The Economics of the World Trading System*, MIT Press, Boston, MA.

Baier, K. and J.H. Bergstrand (2001). 'The growth of world trade: Tariffs, transport costs and income similarity', *Journal of International Economics*, 53, 1–27.

Baldwin, R. (2006). 'Multilateralising regionalism: Spaghetti bowls as building blocs on the path to global free trade', CEPR Discussion Paper 5775, CEPR, London.

Bauer, T., M. Lofstrom and K.F. Zimmermann (2000). 'Immigration policy, assimilation of immigrants and natives' sentiments towards immigrants: Evidence from 12 OECD countries', *Swedish Economic Policy Review*, 27, 11–53.

Beane, D.G. (2000). *The United States and GATT: A Relational Study*, Pergamon, Amsterdam.

Bhagwati, J.N. (2003). 'Borders beyond control', *Foreign Affairs*, 82, 98–104.

Boeri, T., G.H. Hanson and B. McCormick (2002). *Immigration Policy and the Welfare System*, Oxford University Press, Oxford.

Brown, A.G. (2003). *Reluctant Partners: A History of Multilateral Trade Cooperation*, University of Michigan Press, Ann Arbor, MI.

Cline, W.R. (2004). *Trade Policy and Global Poverty*, Center for Global Development, Washington DC.

Dam, K.W. (1970). *The GATT: Law and International Economic Organization*, University of Chicago Press, Chicago.

Destler, I.M. (2005). *American Trade Politics* (4th edn), Institute for International Economics, Washington.

Dustmann, C. and I. Preston (2001). 'Attitudes to ethnic minorities: Ethnic context and location decisions', *Economic Journal*, 111, 353–73.

— (2004a). 'Racial and economic factors in attitudes to immigration, CReAM Discussion Paper 01/04, University College, London.

— (2004b). 'Is immigration good or bad for the economy? Analysis of attitudinal responses', CReAM Discussion Paper 06/04, University College, London.

Facchini, G. and A.M. Mayda (2006). 'Individual attitudes towards immigrants: Welfare-state determinants across countries', 12A Discussion Paper 2127, 12A, Bonn.

Fehr, E. and S. Gächter (2000). 'Fairness and retaliation: The economics of reciprocity', *Journal of Economic Perspectives*, 14, 159–81.

Findlay, R.E. and K.H. O'Rourke (2007). *Power and Plenty: Trade, War and the World Economy in the Second Millenium*, Princeton University Press, Princeton (forthcoming).

Francois, J.A., B. McDonald and H. Nordström (1996). 'The Uruguay Round: A numerically based qualitative assessment', in W. Martin and L.A. Winters (eds.), *The Uruguay Round and the Developing Countries*, Cambridge University Press, Cambridge.

Freeman, G.P. (1995). 'Modes of immigration politics in liberal democratic states', *International Migration Review*, 29, 881–902.

Ghosh, B. (2000). 'New international regime for orderly movements of people: What will it look like?' in B. Ghosh (ed.), *Managing Migration: Time for a New International Regime?* Oxford University Press, Oxford.

Gilligan, M.J. (1997). *Empowering Exporters: Reciprocity, Delegation and Collective Action in American Trade Policy*, University of Michigan Press, Ann Arbor, MI.

Gourevitch, P. (1986). *Politics in Hard Times: Comparative Responses to Economic Crises*, Cornell University Press, Ithaca, NY.

Greenaway, D. and D. Nelson (2006). 'The distinct political economies of trade and migration policy through the window of endogenous policy models', in F. Foders and R.J. Langhammer (eds.), *Labor Mobility and the World Economy*, Springer Verlag, Berlin.

Grossman, G.M. and E. Helpman (1994). 'Protection for sale', *American Economic Review*, 84, 833–50.

Hamilton, B. and J. Whalley (1984). 'Efficiency and distributional implications of global restrictions on labor mobility', *Journal of Development Economics*, 14, 61–75.

Hanson, G.H., K.F. Scheve and M.J. Slaughter (2005). 'Public finance and individual preferences over globalization strategies', NBER Working Paper 11028, NBER, Boston.

Harrison, G.W., T.F. Rutherford and D.G. Tarr (1997). 'Quantifying the Uruguay Round', *Economic Journal*, 107, 1405–30.

Hatton, T.J. and J.G. Williamson (2005a). *Global Migration and the World Economy: Two Centuries of Policy and Performance*, MIT Press, Cambridge MA.

— (2005b) 'A dual policy paradox: Why have trade and immigration polices always differed in labor scarce economies?' NBER Working Paper 11866, NBER, Boston.

Hendricks, L. (2002). 'How important is human capital for development? Evidence from immigrant earnings', *American Economic Review*, 92, 189–219.

Hiscox, M.J. (2002). *International Trade and Political Conflict: Commerce, Coalitions, and Mobility*, Princeton University Press, Princeton, NJ.

Hoekman, B.M. and M.K. Kostecki (1995). *The Political Economy of the World Trading System: From GATT to WTO*, Oxford University Press, Oxford.

Hollifield, J.F. (2000). 'Migration and the "new" international order: The missing regime', in B. Ghosh (ed.), *Managing Migration: Time for a New International Regime?* Oxford University Press, Oxford.

International Organization for Migration (2006). *International Dialogue on Migration No. 7: Managing the Movement of People*, IOM, Geneva.

Iregui, A.M. (2005). 'Efficiency gains from the elimination of global restrictions on labour mobility: An analysis using a multiregional CGE model', in G.J. Borjas and J. Crisp (eds.), *Poverty, International Migration and Asylum*, Palgrave Macmillan, London.

Irwin, D.A. (1995). 'The GATT in historical perspective', *American Economic Review*, 85 (Papers and Proceedings), 323–28.

— (2002). *Free Trade under Fire*, Princeton University Press, Princeton, NJ.

Keohane, R.O. (1986). 'Reciprocity in international relations', *International Organization*, 40, 1–27.

Koslowski, R. (2004). 'Possible steps towards and international regime for mobility and security', Global Migration Perspectives No. 8, United Nations, Geneva.

Krugman, P. (1997). 'What should trade negotiators negotiate about?' *Journal of Economic Literature*, 35, 113–120.

Limão, N. (2005). 'Trade policy, cross-border externalities and lobbies: Do linked agreements enforce more cooperative outcomes?' *Journal of International Economics*, 67, 175–99.

Lindert, P.H. (2004). *Growing Public: Social Spending and Economic Growth since the Eighteenth Century*, Cambridge University Press, Cambridge.

Lodefalk, M. and J. Whalley (2002). 'Reviewing proposals for a world environmental organisation', *World Economy*, 25, 601–17.

Lusztig, M. (2004). *The Limits of Protectionism: Building Coalitions of Free Trade*, University of Pittsburgh Press, Pittsburgh.

Mansfield, E.D., H.V. Milner and B.P. Rosendorff (2002). 'Why democracies cooperate more: electoral control and international trade areements', *International Organization*, 56, 477–513.

Martin, P., B.L. Lowell and E.J. Taylor (2000). 'Migration outcomes of guestworker and free trade regimes: The case of Mexico-US migration', in B. Ghosh (ed.), *Managing Migration: Time for a New International Regime?* Oxford University Press, Oxford.

Mayda, A.M. (2006). 'Who is against immigration? A cross-country investigation of individual attitudes towards immigrants', *Review of Economics and Statistics* (forthcoming).

Mayda, A.M. and D. Rodrik (2005). 'Why are some people (and countries) more protectionist than others', *European Economic Review*, 49, 1393–430.

Milner, H.V. (1997). *Interests, Institutions and Information: Domestic Politics and International Relations*, Princeton University Press, Princeton, NJ.

Moses, J.W. and B. Letnes (2004). 'The economics costs to international labor restrictions: Revisiting the empirical discussion', *World Development*, 32, 1609–26.

Newland, K. (2005). 'The governance of international migration: Mechanisms, processes and institutions', UN Global Commission on International Migration Discussion Paper.

OECD (2004). *Migration for Employment: Bilateral Agreements at a Crossroads*, OECD, Paris.

O'Rourke, K.H. and R. Sinnott (2001). 'What determines attitudes towards protection?' in S.M. Collins and D. Rodrik (eds.), *Brookings Trade Forum 2001*, Brookings Institute Press, Washington DC.

— (2006). 'The determinants of individual attitudes towards immigration', *European Journal of Political Economy*, 22, 787–808.

Panagariya, A. (2004). 'India's trade reforms: Progress, impact and future strategy', Unpublished paper, Columbia University.

Phelps, R. (1993). 'International perspective: American public opinion on trade, 1950–1990', *Business Economics*, 28, 35–41.

Putnam, R.D. (1988). 'Diplomacy and domestic politics: The logic of two level-level games', *International Organization*, 42, 427–460.

Ratha, D. (2003). 'Workers' remittances: An important and stable source of external development finance', in *Global Development Finance*, World Bank, Washington DC.

Rodrik, D. (2002). 'Final remarks', in T. Boeri, G. Hanson and B. McCormick (eds.), *Immigration Policy and the Welfare System*, Oxford University Press, Oxford.

Rogowski, R. (1989). *Commerce and Coalitions: How Trade Affects Domestic Political Alignments*, Princeton University Press, Princeton, NJ.

Rose, A.K. (2004). 'Do we really know that the WTO increases world trade?' *American Economic Review*, 94, 98–114.

Scheve, K.F. and M.J. Slaughter (2001). 'Labor market competition and individual preferences over immigration policy', *Review of Economics and Statistics*, 83, 133–45.

Schiff, M. (2004). 'When migrants overstay their legal welcome: A proposed solution to the guest-worker program', IZA Discussion Paper 1401, IZA, Bonn.

Simon, R.J. (2004). 'Immigration and crime across seven nations', Paper presented to the IZA Annual Migration Meeting, IZA, Bonn.

Straubhaar, T. (2000). 'Why do we need a New General Agreement on Movements of People?'

in B. Ghosh (ed.), *Managing Migration: Time for a New International Regime?* Oxford University Press, Oxford.

Subramanian, A. and S.-J. Wei (2005). 'The WTO promotes trade, strongly but unevenly', CEPR Discussion Paper 5122, CEPR, London.

Winters, L.A., T.L. Walmsley, Z.K. Wang and R. Grynberg (2003). 'Liberalising temporary movement of natural persons: An agenda for the development round', *World Economy*, 26, 1137–61.

World Bank (2003). *World Development Indicators 2003*, World Bank, Washington DC.

UN (2002). *International Migration Report 2002*, United Nations, New York.

— (2004). *World Economic and Social Survey, 2004: International Migration*, United Nations, New York.

— (2005). *Migration in an Interconnected World: New Directions for Action. Report of the Global Commission on International Migration*, United Nations, New York.

— (2006). *Compendium of Recommendations on International Migration and Development: The United Nations Development Agenda and the Global Commission on International Migration Compared*, United Nations, New York.

Tax competition

SUMMARY

The debate on tax competition lacks due attention when it comes to the provision of public goods used by firms in their production process. Indeed, firms may accept higher corporate taxation provided they enjoy good infrastructure and public services. We quantify such trade-off, i.e. the extent to which a 'high tax, high public goods' strategy is attractive to capital as compared to a 'low tax, low public goods' combination. We revisit and develop the popular model of tax competition introduced by Zodrow and Mieszkowski (1986) in a way that allows for the testing of its main prediction. The under-provision of public inputs can be tested econometrically by estimating and comparing two simple elasticities: capital with respect to the tax rate, and capital with respect to public inputs. We regress US foreign direct investment in 18 EU countries over 1994–2003 on several variables, including the corporate tax rate and the stock of public capital, used as a proxy for public input. Based on these estimations (−1.1 for the tax elasticity and +0.2 for the public input elasticity), we conclude that raising public input through an increase in the corporate tax rate reduces inward FDI, and that tax competition may indeed lead to an under-provision of public inputs. Furthermore, a 'high' equilibrium (high taxation and high level of public input) is not attainable for a country starting from a 'low' equilibrium unless households have a strong preference for public inputs. On the whole, the impact of tax competition may be more diverse than a mere 'race to the bottom'.

— Agnès Bénassy-Quéré, Nicolas Gobalraja and Alain Trannoy

Economic Policy April 2007 Printed in Great Britain
© CEPR, CES, MSH, 2007.

Tax and public input competition

Agnès Bénassy-Quéré, Nicolas Gobalraja and Alain Trannoy

CEPII, Paris, and Université Paris X; Université Paris X; Ecole des Hautes Etudes en Sciences Sociales, IDEP-GREQAM

1. INTRODUCTION

The debate on tax competition has been gaining momentum in the EU since the beginning of the new century, particularly since the EU enlargement of 2004. Indeed, within the last ten years (1996–2006), statutory corporate tax rates declined by an average of 9 percentage points in the EU15 and an average of 11 percentage points for the new member states (NMSs) (Figure 1). Due to the broadening of the tax base, the decrease in the *effective* tax rates was less significant in the EU15[1] than in the new member states, where the decline was nearly one percentage point a year on average.[2] These figures support the existence of a 'race to the bottom' which, when defined in this context, describes any series of competitive and non-cooperative tax cuts made by national governments with the ambition of attracting more foreign capital.

We are grateful to Michael Overesch for providing a complete EATR data set, to Brigitte Dormont for a useful suggestion, to Donna Henry-Norker, Michel Le Breton, Philippe Martin, Thierry Mayer, Cecilia Garcia Penelosa, Pierre Pestieau, Stephen Redding, Fred Rychen, Laurent Simula and Tanguy Van Ypersele for useful comments, and to the participants in the *Economic Policy* panel in Vienna on 21–22 April 2006 for additional comments. The usual disclaimer applies.

The Managing Editor in charge of this paper was Philippe Martin.

[1] See Devereux *et al.* (2002).

[2] The fact that tax revenues did not converge downwards (see recent evidence by Stewart and Webb, 2006), can at least be partially explained by increased profitability and higher incentive for firms to incorporate (see Griffith and Klemm, 2004; Krogstrup, 2004; Devereux and Sorensen, 2005; Weichenrieder, 2005).

Economic Policy April 2007 pp. 385–430 Printed in Great Britain
© CEPR, CES, MSH, 2007.

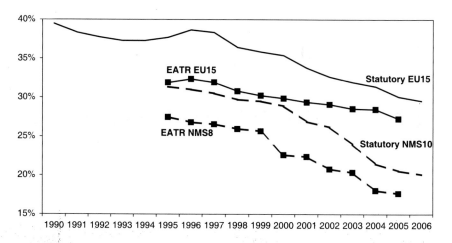

Figure 1. Corporate tax rates in the EU25, 1990–2006 (unweighted averages)

Source: Devereux, Griffith and Klemm (2002), Eurostat, KPMG for statutory rates; Overesch (2005) for EATR (effective average tax rates).

1.1. A puzzle

A contradiction seems to emerge regarding the perceived importance of the corporate tax rate: at odds with the 'race to the bottom' scenario are a number of business surveys revealing that corporate taxation is not a primary criterion for location decisions. For instance, corporate taxation is only one of the 18 criteria listed by Ernst & Young (2005), along with domestic market, transportation, infrastructure, telecommunication networks, labour costs, flexibility and skills, R&D, etc. However, European policy debates regarding tax competition between member states have primarily focused on *corporate* taxation; other issues and policy instruments (e.g. infrastructure, education, public R&D) have been to a large extent overshadowed.

The present paper aims at breaking with the truncated debate in favour of a more balanced approach which considers the impact of both sides of government activity on location choices. In this respect, Figure 2 suggests that such bi-dimensional competition does exist in the EU. Figure 2 positions 18 EU member states according to their combined level of corporate tax rate and stock of public capital per square kilometre, as measured in 2002. We note that the countries with high corporate tax rates provide a high level of infrastructure, which could mitigate the disadvantages of high taxation. Our data is bounded by the Netherlands and Hungary: the former exhibits both a high tax rate and high public capital, while the latter displays a low combination of both. Interestingly, we observe that Ireland is somewhat of an outlier and positioned close to Hungary, while the majority of EU 15 governments display a relatively high combination of taxation and public capital.

The race to the bottom and the bi-dimensional competition suggested by Figures 1 and 2 could be regarded as contradictory. At a first glance, the very nature of

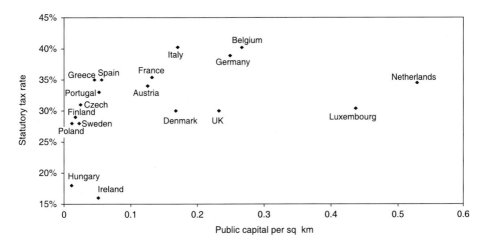

Figure 2. Public capital and statutory tax rate in 2002

Note: In some countries, several tax rates are applied. In Estonia, for instance, retained profits are not taxed. In France, small and medium size firms face a reduced rate. Here we use top statutory corporate tax rates, which, in the absence of tax optimization, are those applying to multinationals. For the calculation of public capital, see Section 3, Box 6.

Source: Kamps (2004a), World Development Indicators (2005) and same as Figure 1.

bi-dimensional competition seems to render any race to the bottom impossible. Indeed, high tax countries could remain attractive to foreign capital through the provision of public goods, such as infrastructure, which are useful to firms. In keeping with this argument, it follows that high tax countries should have little or no incentive to take the 'race-to-the-bottom' route. However, many EU countries seem to be tempted by the prospect of lowering their corporate tax rates. For instance, Germany, a high tax and high spending country according to Figure 2, plans on cutting its statutory tax rate by almost 10 percentage points by 2007, and envisages further cuts in the long term.

1.2. The purpose of the paper

The aim of the paper is to cast light on the existence of a 'race to the bottom' in the EU in spite of the importance of public goods in corporate location choices. It is even more important to solve this puzzle given that two opposite economic policies can be defended, depending on whether the message conveyed by Figure 1 or that conveyed by Figure 2 is favoured. On the one hand, from a normative standpoint tax coordination within the EU can be justified on equity grounds (Figure 1). On the other hand, from a positive standpoint Figure 2 illustrates an impressive diversity of tax and spending profiles, which can be attributed to history, political preferences, or the pressure and lobbying exerted by firms. Judging from this diversity, a normative argument could be made for a *laissez-faire* policy: unnecessary at best, tax coordination may even be harmful since it precludes each nation from expressing its own choice of tax level and public spending.

To gain further insight into these contending views, we provide a theoretical framework which captures both the bi-dimensional (or 'dual') conception of competition as well as 'race to the bottom' competition. With this in mind, we revisit and develop the simple and popular model of tax competition introduced by Zodrow and Mieszkowski (1986), with the ambition of testing its predictions. In their model, capital taxation enables the government to provide public goods, such as infrastructure, which are in turn used as factors of production by the firms. In our framework, we call such 'productive' public goods *public inputs*. Their positive impact on marginal productivity mitigates the negative impact of capital taxation on after-tax private return. Consequently, an increase in capital taxation induces less capital outflow.

Under reasonable assumptions providing for a 'well-behaved' production function, our theoretical model lends credence to the idea that benevolent governments looking to attract foreign capital should either (1) cut taxes while reducing public input, or (2) rely on immobile tax bases in order to fund the public input. Our main methodological contribution is to emphasize that the incentive for 'a race to the bottom' is an empirical question that can be econometrically evaluated: it requires comparing the elasticities of capital with respect to the tax rate and with respect to the public input. We then estimate the elasticities of foreign capital with respect to corporate taxation rates and public capital on the basis of US foreign direct investment in 18 EU countries between 1994 and 2003. Standard control variables are used, such as the size of the economies under investigation, the existence of agglomeration effects, and unit labour costs.

1.3. The key findings

The dual and 'race to the bottom' conceptions of competition are nothing but the two sides of the same coin.

On the one hand, inward foreign direct investment is significantly affected in a negative manner by corporate taxation and positively affected by public capital stock. On average, a higher tax rate must be compensated by a higher stock of public capital at the equilibrium. Low-equilibrium and high-equilibrium countries can coexist when the two elasticities are opposite in sign. This supports the evidence of Figure 2.

On the other hand, our estimates confirm that funding a *marginal* increase in public capital through corporate taxation, induces a capital out-flow. Public capital is in fact not productive enough to compensate for the required increase in corporate taxation. This conclusion holds unless labour taxation bears an increasing share in the financing of public inputs.

Consequently, even if public infrastructure is appealing to firms, the threat of a race to the bottom being triggered cannot be dismissed. The magnitude of this threat largely depends on the (un)willingness of voters to bear an increase in taxes destined to benefit firms. Figure 1 suggests that voter reluctance has decreased in the recent past.

In contrast with the attractiveness of public inputs, household-oriented public goods, such as health or social security spending, seem to be unappealing to foreign investors. Competition could therefore lead to a distortion in the structure of public spending, in favour of firms and at the expense of households.

These findings bear important policy implications. National governments are caught in a vice with firms demanding competitive tax cuts on one end, and households making their voices heard by way of the ballot box. From this perspective, tax co-ordination in the EU is justified on both political and social grounds.

An underlying argument for coordination is that it may allow citizens to influence the distribution of the tax burden and that of spending, while at the same time mitigating the risk that divergent national preferences create too large a gap between societies and political leadership at the EU level. However, minimum tax rates may not provide the appropriate solution. We suggest that tax coordination should instead consist in agreeing on the minimum share of public inputs to be funded by corporate taxation. Each country would remain free to decide which should be the nature, quantity and quality of its public input.

The paper is organized as follows. Section 2 develops the theoretical model, Section 3 provides econometric support for its main implications, Section 4 derives policy implications and Section 5 concludes.

2. A CONCEPTUAL FRAMEWORK FOR TAX AND PUBLIC INPUT COMPETITION

It has been acknowledged at least since Tiebout's celebrated paper (1956) that both local and national jurisdictions compete on taxes and public inputs to attract economic agents. The driving force behind this competition is the mobility of agents (be they households or firms) which leads each jurisdiction to vie for the most attractive combination of tax-level and public spending. Zodrow and Mieszkowski's (1986) paper is the cornerstone of a wide literature on tax competition,[3] which examines the implications of differential mobility between different production factors, with capital being mobile while land or labour is not.

In their seminal paper, a public good (which can be either consumed or used as an input) is financed by a distorting source tax on capital. It is shown that the relative cost of providing the public good is greater under perfect capital mobility than in closed economy. Consequently, when capital taxation is the only viable option, capital mobility leads to the under-provision of public goods, as compared to the autarky case.

---

[3] See reviews by Wilson (1999) and Krogstrup (2002).

This under-provision result has been challenged by Noiset (1995), Sinn (1997, 2003), and Dhillon *et al.* (2006) when dealing with the case of public inputs. Noiset emphasizes that under-provision comes from an assumption about the impact of the public input on the marginal productivity of capital. Specifically, Zodrow and Mieszkowski (1986) assume that an extra unit of public good raises the marginal productivity of private capital by less than its marginal cost for private investors in terms of additional taxation. When this assumption is relaxed, tax competition can (1) be efficient or (2) can also result in a 'race to the bottom' or (3) may even result in a 'race to the top', characterized by an over-provision of public goods and excessive tax rates (Dhillon *et al.*, 2006). Naturally, such indeterminacy is a cause for concern because it calls for conflicting policy implications. For instance, if tax competition leads to a 'race to the top', then tax co-ordination should consist in capping tax rates rather than introducing a minimum rate.

It is shown in this section that the case for under- or over-provision of public goods basically depends on the relative values of two elasticities which can be econometrically estimated: (1) the elasticity of capital with respect to the tax rate, with the level of public input held constant; and (2) the elasticity of capital with respect to the public input, with the level of the tax rate held constant. Estimates of these elasticities are presented in the empirical section. It is also argued that the conventional wisdom about under-provision of public goods is confirmed under reasonable assumptions regarding the production process. All proofs are relegated to Appendix A.

2.1. A model with testable implications

Let us now consider an extension of Zodrow and Mieszkowski's (1986) model in which public goods are used by *both* consumers and firms. In practice, this is true of many public goods, such as transport infrastructure, public education, justice and police, among others. These are to be distinguished from other public goods such as sports, 'cultural infrastructure', health expenditures and inter-individual redistribution, which target households rather than firms.

For the sake of clarity, a *public input* is defined herein as a public good used both by firms and households. It is also taken to be a pure public good *à la* Samuelson within the country's borders.[4] More specifically, for a given output level, the quantity available to each firm is independent of the number of firms. This assumption seems reasonable when considering most public inputs, such as public infrastructure, education or research. In addition, congestion in the use of this public input is ruled out.[5]

In our simple model, presented in Box 1, all firms are identical. Production for each firm depends on its capital stock and employment, as well as on the public

---

[4] From an international point of view, it is a local public good.

[5] The marginal productivity and the marginal utility of public inputs do not depend on the number of users. Clearly, this is a simplifying assumption. For a more nuanced approach to congestion, see Sinn (1997, 2003).

Box 1. The model

Let $F(K, L, G)$ be the production function, where K stands for capital, L for (fixed) labour and G for public input. If x denotes the consumption of the private good, the government maximizes the utility of a representative household:

$$\text{Max } U(x, G) \tag{1.1}$$

under the three following constraints:

(i) Public budget constraint: a fraction α $(0 \leq \alpha \leq 1)$ of the public input G is funded by capital taxation tK:

$$tK = \alpha G \tag{1.2}$$

(ii) Balanced current account: net exports are equal to net capital income receipts (long-run national budget constraint):

$$F(K, L, G) - x - G = r(K - \bar{K}) \tag{1.3}$$

where $\bar{K}$ denotes households' wealth and r is the world rate of return.

(iii) International arbitrage condition: after-tax return $(F_K - t)$ is equal to world return r (profit maximization constraint):

$$F_K - t = r \tag{1.4}$$

In a closed economy, constraint (1.3) reduces to $F(\bar{K}, L, G) = x + G$ and constraint (1.4) is replaced by: $K = \bar{K}$.

---

input. The private good and the public input are produced by the same production process, and the gross opportunity cost of producing one extra unit of public input in terms of the forgone production of the private good is equal to one. Capital is assumed to be internationally mobile, as opposed to labour, which is not. Consequently, under the small open economy assumption, arbitrage implies that the after-tax return of capital is equal to the exogenous world return.[6]

Public input is *partially* financed through a source tax t on the capital stock available in the country, K, either owned locally or internationally. Hence, other taxes are levied to finance its provision. Since labour is assumed to be immobile, a tax on this

---

[6] Two alternative assumptions are usually considered in the literature. Under the small country hypothesis, the world capital after-tax return is exogenous whereas it is endogenous in the large country case (cf. Wildasin, 1988; Laussel and Le Breton, 1998; Wooders and Zissimos, 2005). Here, it is assumed that the return of capital in the country has no feedback effect on the world return of capital. This seems a realistic assumption for each European country taken separately.

factor induces no distortions and is therefore lump-sum. For a basic model in which the government is completely free to set both labour and capital tax rates to reach efficiency, the outcome is quite predictable: the efficient government would indeed rely entirely on labour taxation. A more realistic and nuanced model might help us gain further insight by introducing a binding constraint on the tax rates, which might for instance capture the government's concern for fairness between labour and capital taxation. Let $0 \leq \alpha \leq 1$ be the proportion of public input funded by the corporate tax. The two extreme cases correspond to pure capital taxation ($\alpha = 1$) and to lump-sum taxation ($\alpha = 0$).

The rate of capital taxation is chosen to maximize households' utility,[7] which depends on their private-good consumption and on the public input. In particular, households benefit from public inputs both directly, since they consume it, and indirectly, since it helps firms in producing more private goods. Each household's wealth endowment can either be invested in local or foreign capital. In each case, it follows from international arbitrage that the after-tax return is the world return. Households also receive labour income equal to the production surplus once the world capital return have been paid by firms. The optimal provision of public good in this open economy is contrasted with the optimal provision under autarky, where capital is immobile.

The *closed economy* case serves as a benchmark, and is therefore presented first. In such an economy, capital and labour resources are fixed. In particular, the domestic capital stock is equal to households' wealth endowment. Hence, a tax on either factor is equivalent to a lump-sum tax and efficiency of resource allocation is independent of the means by which the public good is financed. An efficient allocation, where household utility is maximized, is characterized by equality between the marginal rate of substitution and the marginal rate of transformation. Here, the marginal rate of substitution is the amount of private good the consumer is willing to give up to consume one extra unit of public input. The marginal rate of transformation is the net opportunity cost of producing one additional unit of public input instead of producing the private good. In our economy, the latter is equal to 1 minus the marginal productivity of the public input. Therefore, in closed economy (G_{closed}), the efficient provision of public inputs is reached when the marginal rate of substitution between the public and private goods ($MRS_{G/x}$) is equal to 1 net of the marginal productivity of the public input (F_G). Formally this reads as follows:

$$MRS_{G/x} = 1 - F_G \tag{1}$$

In an *open economy*, capital is assumed to be perfectly mobile between countries, while labour remains immobile. Thus, a tax increase to fund additional public input may lead capital to flow in or out of a given country. This adds a new constraint, or pressure, on government decision-making. At first glance, and all other things being

---

[7] Hence, we do not consider the case of a Leviathan government. See Edwards and Keen (1996).

equal, we expect capital to flow out since a tax increase depreciates the domestic return of capital (direct effect). However, *the 'all other things being equal' clause is not satisfied here.* Indeed, more corporate tax receipts translate into more public input, which raises the marginal productivity of capital and thus the domestic return of capital (indirect effect). If the indirect effect prevails, capital may flow in. Consequently, the optimal provision of public goods when opening up the economy depends on the direction in which capital reacts subsequent to a marginal increase in taxation. Specifically, the optimal public-input provision G_{open} requires the following condition to hold (see Appendix A):

$$MRS_{G/x} = 1 - F_G - \alpha\frac{e_{K/t}}{1 + e_{K/t}}, \tag{2}$$

where $e_{K/t}$ is the elasticity of private capital with respect to the tax rate, accounting for the fact that higher taxation means higher public-input provision. This tax elasticity, formally defined in Box 2, is the percentage change in capital generated by a percentage

---

Box 2. The adjusted tax elasticity of capital

The adjusted tax elasticity of capital is defined as:

$$e_{K/t} = \left.\frac{dK/K}{dt/t}\right|_{G=\frac{1}{\alpha}tK} \tag{2.1}$$

As shown in Appendix A, $e_{K/t}$ can be detailed in the following way:

$$e_{K/t} = \frac{e^0_{k/G} + e^0_{k/t}}{1 - e^0_{k/G}}. \tag{2.2}$$

with:

$$e^0_{k/t} = \frac{dK/K}{dt/t} < 0 \tag{2.3}$$

and:

$$e^0_{K/G} = \frac{dK/K}{dG/G} > 0 \tag{2.4}$$

It follows from (2.2) that at the optimum of an open economy, $e_{k/t} \leq 0$ if and only if

Either: $|e^0_{k/t}| \geq e^0_{k/G}$ Or: $e^0_{k/G} \geq 1.$

(This second possibility is ruled out by one of our assumption of decreasing returns.)

change in the tax rate, with the provision of public input *adjusted* accordingly. Henceforth, it is referred to as the *adjusted tax elasticity of capital*.

The optimal rule adopted by the government in an open economy (2) differs from that which is adopted in a closed economy (1). The two rules only coincide when the elasticity is zero, that is, when the tax rate has little or no influence on the level of capital, or when there is pure lump-sum funding.[8] Comparing these two optimal policies reveals that solving the under-provision issue only requires determining the sign and magnitude of this elasticity.

The sign of $e_{K/t}$, depends on whether capital flows in or out following a tax increase. In the conventional 'race-to-the-bottom' scenario, the adjusted tax elasticity is negative, so a tax increase invariably leads to capital outflows. If, in addition, the elasticity's absolute value is less than 1, the marginal rate of substitution between private and public goods in the country at hand is higher under tax competition than under autarky. Since the MRS is a decreasing function of the public good, a shift against the provision of the public input at the margin is obtained. This may be interpreted as an inverse elasticity rule *à la* Ramsey: the more elastic the capital, the less taxed it must be, resulting in a lower provision of public inputs. Consequently, in a second-best setting, it is efficient to provide less public inputs because it is funded by a distorting tax. This remains true for whatever fraction of the public input is financed by corporate taxation. If a government intent on attracting foreign capital were to spend one extra euro towards the provision of public inputs, corporate taxation would have to be raised by less than α euros, meaning that corporate taxation is increasingly substituted by labour taxation. Indeed, the model predicts an outflow of capital whenever the relative contribution of the corporate tax towards this extra euro of public goods is greater than or equal to α%.

However, if an extra unit of public input has a large positive impact on the marginal productivity of private capital, then the adjusted tax elasticity may be positive. In this case, the positive impact of an additional unit of public input may outweigh the negative impact of extra taxation on the domestic rate of return. Thus, the conclusion is reversed provided $e_{K/t} < 1$: opening up the economy results in a shift towards more public input at the margin ('race-to-the top' scenario).

Under any scenario, a heavier reliance on capital taxation (i.e. the higher α), results in a larger gap between the closed-economy and open-economy variables.[9] Conversely, if the public input is funded exclusively through labour taxation ($\alpha = 0$), then opening up the economy is neutral as regards resource allocation between private and public goods.

The issue of under- or over-provision at the margin may be settled by separating $e_{K/t}$ into two elasticities, both of which can be econometrically estimated: (1) the tax

---

[8] This case corresponds to $\alpha = 0$. Note that it is not the openness of the economy *per se* which induces inefficiency but the fact that a distorting tax is used.

[9] The term $\alpha\dfrac{e_{K/t}}{1 + e_{K/t}}$ is increasing in α. $e_{K/t}$ itself depends on α. It has been omitted in the notation for convenience.

elasticity of capital *holding public input constant* $e^0_{K/t}$ on the one hand; and (2) the elasticity of capital with respect to public input *holding the tax rate constant* $e^0_{K/G}$ on the other hand. These two elasticities provide a clear advantage over the *adjusted tax elasticity of capital*, since each of them can be estimated because the other element is held constant. The former (1) is the standard tax elasticity of capital which gives the relative variation of the capital stock following a 1% increase in the tax rate. The latter (2) is the percentage change in capital in response to a 1% increase in the public input.

Intuitively, it is natural to expect the former to be negative and the latter to be positive. However, their relative magnitude is an empirical issue with major consequences. Indeed, as shown in Box 2, the adjusted tax elasticity is negative if $|e^0_{K/t}| > e^0_{K/G}$. As is made explicit in the econometric section (3.3), this condition is satisfied. Ultimately, our findings corroborate the view that tax competition leads to under-provision of public input at the margin.

However, it is worth re-emphasizing that Equations (1) and (2) are *marginal* conditions. Comparing them allows us to determine the direction in which resource allocation is distorted by capital openness at the margin. It does not, however, provide a clear indication on the level of public input provision: this level can increase or decrease under autarky, depending on whether the country is a net capital importer or exporter. Global results are obtained under the assumption of certain decreasing returns, as is made more precise in the next section.

2.2. A case for under-provision

It is first argued that, at the optimum of an open economy, plausible assumptions on the production function require that the *adjusted tax elasticity of capital* is negative, which in turn implies the under-provision of public inputs. A global scenario for the under-provision of public inputs is then derived under the same assumptions and further qualifications.

Our assumptions concerning the production function all amount to some form of diminishing returns (Box 3): the marginal productivity of each production factor is positive and decreasing, and when both capital and public input grow at the same rate, the marginal product of capital exhibits diminishing returns to scale. In addition, the marginal productivity of capital increases with public input, which is a complement to private capital. However, this effect is lower the greater the level of capital or public input. The plausibility of this assumption – which is crucial for our results – merits illustration. Consider a road network. Without a doubt, adding one extra kilometre of road would increase the productivity of one additional truck. However, intuitively the higher the initial number of trucks or the higher the initial length of the road network, the lower the positive effect. As shown in Box 4, these reasonable assumptions imply that for small, open economies relying solely on the corporate tax, the *adjusted tax elasticity of capital* must be negative at the optimum. A closer look at the implications of the arbitrage condition on the capital market illuminates this result.

Box 3. Assumptions on the production function

Let $F(K, L, G)$ be an increasing function of all three of its arguments (F_K, F_L, $F_G > 0$) and let the marginal productivity of each factor be decreasing (F_{KK}, F_{LL}, $F_{GG} < 0$). The marginal product of capital exhibits decreasing returns to scale in capital and public input, i.e. $F_K(L, K(1 + \lambda), G(1+ \lambda)) < F_K(L, K, G)$ for any $\lambda > 0$. (This assumption is confirmed by Kamps (2004b) on the basis of estimated augmented Cobb–Douglas functions for OECD countries.) In addition, K and G are complements in the sense that the marginal productivity of capital increases with G ($F_{KG} > 0$). However, such complementarity declines at higher levels of capital or public input (F_{KGK}, $F_{KGG} < 0$). F_{KG} tends to infinity when $G = 0$, and tends to 0 when G approaches infinity. The widely used augmented Cobb–Douglas production function, $F(K, L, G) = AL^{1-\gamma}K^{\gamma}G^{1-\beta}$ with $0 < \gamma < \beta < 1$, satisfies these conditions.

Box 4. The sign of the adjusted tax elasticity of capital

Differentiating the arbitrage condition (1.4) and the public budget constraint (1.2) yields the adjusted tax elasticity of capital:

$$e_{K/t} = \frac{t}{K} \frac{\alpha - KF_{KG}}{\alpha F_{KK} + tF_{KG}} \qquad (4.1)$$

The fact that the marginal product of capital exhibits decreasing returns to scale as a function of capital and public input ensures that the denominator is negative (see Appendix A, Claim 6). Hence, $e_{K/t}$ and $KF_{KG} - \alpha$ must be of the same sign. It is negative if the gain in the marginal capital productivity following a marginal increase in public input (F_{KG}) is lower than the corresponding tax increase (α/K): here, a capital tax increase with a corresponding rise in public input leads to capital outflows. It is shown in Appendix A that this scenario accurately captures an open economy's equilibrium under the assumptions outlined in Box 3 when $\alpha = 1$. As depicted in Figure 3, the optimum must thus lie in the downward-sloping section of the graph, which traces the after-tax return of capital as a function of public input.

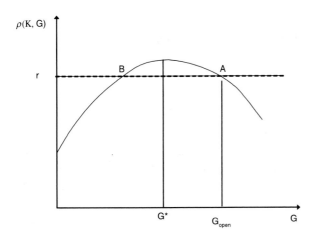

Figure 3. Capital return as a function of public input for a given capital level

By definition, the after-tax domestic capital return ρ is the difference between the marginal productivity of capital F_K and the budget-balanced tax rate t:

$$\rho(K, G) \equiv F_K(L, K, G) - \frac{G}{K}. \tag{3}$$

The after-tax domestic capital return is graphed as a function of public input in Figure 3. As emphasized in Appendix A, this graph is hump-shaped for any stock of capital K; an open economy at equilibrium is of no exception and also exhibits an inverted-U shape. Namely, ρ rises with G up to a threshold of public input G^*, at which point ρ decreases. Given a fixed level of capital stock, this shape serves to illustrate the diminishing impact of an extra unit of public input on private return, bearing in mind that the cost of an extra unit of public input in terms of additional taxes remains constant for the firm. In general, two levels of public input satisfy the arbitrage condition: a low one and a high one (i.e. points B and A, respectively, where the after-tax domestic return of capital is equal to the world return r). It can be shown that the level of public input chosen by the government turns out to be greater than G^*, and corresponds to point A (Appendix A). Seeing as this equilibrium lies in the downward-sloping segment of the graph, it follows that a marginal increase in public spending reduces the after-tax domestic return of capital.

The following policy implication arises. In an open economy, *it is not possible for a government to attract capital by raising corporate taxes* even when spending all of the extra revenues *on public input*. In sum, although public services are productive, they are not productive enough to raise the after-tax capital return.

The different *levels* of public input provided by a closed and an open economy can now be contrasted. Three possible scenarios are examined in turn.

We first investigate a case in which the capital stock is equal to domestic wealth ($K = \bar{K}$). Here, the level of public input in an open economy G_{open} is strictly lower than that of a closed economy G_{closed}. G_{open} is therefore on the left of G_{closed}, which implies that opening up the economy results in the under-provision of public inputs.

The focus is now on a capital exporting country $(K < \bar{K})$. The after-tax return under autarky is thus below the world return, and capital flows out when opening up the economy. If the demand for public inputs increases with income (i.e. if it is a normal good), public input provision increases with capital. Therefore, it follows that a 'global' version of the under-provision result is valid as well.

We now turn to a capital-importing country $(K > \bar{K})$, i.e. a country whose after-tax return under autarky is higher than the world return. The inflow of private capital allows public input provision to increase. However, the inflow of capital must be above a certain threshold to ensure a greater provision of public inputs than under autarky.[10] Below this threshold, public input is still under-provided. However, the 'provision gap' between the autarky and open economy equilibria is smaller here than under the two other scenarios developed above.

The above analysis does not take into account the possibility of agglomeration economies, which would preclude marginal capital productivity from declining when capital accumulates. A number of recent models have indicated that 'centrally located' countries may benefit from a geographic rent, which allows them to keep their capital tax rates above those of 'peripheral countries'.[11] These models cogently suggest that geographic diversity is as a source of tax diversity. Additionally, they emphasize that public investment in infrastructures or R&D can favour agglomeration effects. As a result, the agglomeration dimension of the 'tax & spend' choice has to be acknowledged and taken into account in the empirical testing of the model.

3. ECONOMETRIC ANALYSIS

3.1. Empirical determinants of US foreign direct investment in Europe

As argued in the previous section, the incentive for a 'race to the bottom' depends on the relative magnitudes of two simple elasticities: (1) the elasticity of capital with respect to the corporate tax rate, and with public input held constant, and (2) the elasticity of capital with respect to public input, taking the corporate tax rate as constant. These elasticities can be estimated on the basis of direct foreign investment allocation in Europe. We use data issued by the US Bureau of Economic Analysis that provides a measure of US foreign direct investment in EU countries. This database, widely used in the literature (see Hines, 1999), is well suited for our exercise because of its large size (US FDI in 18 EU members for ten sectors over the span of

---

[10] Beyond the threshold, the marginal result remains robust, i.e. the provision of public input is reduced at the margin, compared with autarky, but we cannot conclude that the amount of public input provided is lower.

[11] Such models are part of the growing 'new economic geography' literature. See Krugman, 1991; Ludema and Wooton, 2000; Andersson and Forslid, 2003; Baldwin and Krugman, 2004.

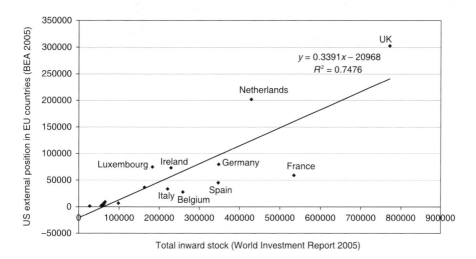

Figure 4. Total inward FDI and US position in the European Union, in 2004 (US$ million)

Source: Bureau of Economic Analysis, and UNCTAD, *World Investment Report.*

$1994-2002)^{12}$ and its consistency (only one reporting country, one methodology, one taxation scheme of repatriated profits). In addition, the country distribution of US FDI does not contradict that of total inward FDI in EU countries (Figure 4).

Our dependent variable is the capital expenditure by US majority-owned affiliates in 18 EU countries in ten industries, during the time span of 1994 to 2003. Capital expenditure is defined as an expenditure 'made to acquire, add to, or improve property, plant, and equipment' (Bureau of Economic Analysis, 2003, p. 88). Hence, the stock of capital expenditures corresponds to productive capital, i.e. the foreign component of K in our theoretical model.[13] For convenience, it is herein called FDI, although FDI actually includes some intra-group capital flows which may be unrelated to physical investment.

Both flows and stocks of FDI have been studied in the literature. Working with stocks has several advantages. First, it is coherent with our theoretical framework which models decision-making on the basis of capital levels. Second, stocks are much less volatile than flows, which are sometimes dependent on one or two large takeovers, especially in relatively small countries. Lastly, stocks are never negative or nil in our database. This allows us to work with logarithms and estimate elasticities.

To date, the extensive literature on the determinants of FDI[14] has not devoted much attention to the impact of public inputs (see Box 5). This silence may partly be

---

[12] The 18 EU countries are the EU15 plus the Czech Republic, Hungary and Poland. The ten sectors are chemical, electric and electronic goods, food, metals, machinery, finance (except banking), wholesale trade, transport equipment, other industries, and services.

[13] Wheeler and Mody (1992), among a number of other authors surveyed in Hines (1999) use the same dependent variable.

[14] See, for instance, Eaton and Tamura (1996), Wei (2000), or Bloningen and Davies (2002), Head and Mayer (2004), Bloningen (2005).

Box 5. The empirical literature

The combined impact of tax rates and the provision of public inputs on capital location has not yet been extensively explored in the empirical literature. This combined impact can be tested either at the local or international level. At the local level, Gabe and Bell (2004) study the influence of public expenditures and property tax rates on corporate location choices in Maine (US) from 1993 to 1995. They find that raising education spending by 10% leads to a 6% increase in the number of firms settling there. Their study confirms that firms take the provision of public factors into consideration when choosing their location. According to Gabe and Bell, a strategy combining low taxation and a low provision of public factors is less successful than the opposite strategy that couples high taxation with a high provision of public goods.

At the international level, there is an extensive literature with the ambition of assessing the impact of corporate taxation on FDI (see the surveys by Hines, 1999 and Devereux and Griffith, 2002). The meta-analyses proposed by de Mooij and Ederveen (2003, 2005) show that, on average, a 1% decline in the corporate statutory tax rate raises inward FDI by 3–4% (a result gleaned from 371–427 recorded semi-elasticities of FDI with respect to corporate tax rates). In their overview of the differences arising in the literature, de Mooij and Ederveen account for differences in data, methodology, and control variables, but without including public factors as routine controls.

The impact of public infrastructure has been investigated much less often. Wheeler and Mody's (1992) index of infrastructure quality (drawn from the Country Assessment Service of Business International) reveals a positive and significant impact on US capital expenditures in majority-owned affiliates during 1982–88. Loree and Guisinger (1995) use two composite infrastructure indicators to assess their relationship with US foreign direct equity investment in 1977 and in 1982. Mody and Srinivasan (1998) obtain a positive and statistically significant relationship between a given country's production of electricity per dollar of GDP and the level of US FDI in that country.

due to the challenging task of identifying an appropriate measure of public infrastructure. In our study we use the stock of public capital per square kilometre as a proxy for public infrastructure. This variable is in agreement with our theoretical model which assumes the absence of congestion in the use of public capital.[15] It is denoted $LPUBK_{ijt}$ in logarithm for country i, sector j and year t.

[15] As a robustness check, we also performed some estimations with public capital per capita as a measure of public input. Due to collinearity between this measure of public capital and external distance, the results were weakly significant but still consistent with the results presented in the paper.

The impact of public capital on FDI is to be contrasted with that of household-specific public goods as measured by (1) the logarithm of the ratio of social public expenditures to GDP ($LSOCEXP_{it}$) and that of (2) the logarithm of the ratio of health public expenditures to GDP ($LHEAL_{it}$). As these two variables are unlikely to have a direct impact on private capital productivity, they are not expected to attract FDI. They could even deter foreign direct investors from investing if they anticipate higher tax pressure resulting from higher social expenditures.

Two measures of corporate tax rates are used: statutory rates ($LSTATUT_{it}$) and effective average tax rates ($LEATR_{it}$), both expressed in logarithms. While in theory the EATR provides a more accurate measure of corporate taxation, its computation relies on a number of assumptions concerning: the type of investment (share of real estate, machinery, intangibles, inventories and financial assets in the investment project); the source of financing (the share of retained earnings, equity and debt); a fixed inflation rate; a fixed interest rate; and a fixed, pre-tax rate of return on investment.[16] In particular, the way investment is financed could be thought of as endogenous to the tax rate (thin capitalization strategy). The EATRs used here were calculated by the ZEW[17] on the basis of a 20% pre-tax return and a 2% inflation rate. The difficulty is that this calibration may not apply to every EU country. In particular, we expect the EU15 countries to have lower pre-tax returns and lower inflation rates than the new member states. However, as argued by Overesch (2005), the main source of difference in EATR across countries pertains to statutory rates. Consequently, we have included these statutory rates in our baseline estimations, and robustness checks are performed with EATRs. In keeping with the literature, two sets of control variables are introduced: economic geography and costs.

The economic geography literature (see Baldwin *et al.*, 2003) maintains that market size, distance to markets, and agglomeration economies influence inward FDI because of the combination of returns to scale and trade costs.[18]

For instance, using these two factors (returns to scale and trade costs) we can formulate an alternate definition for market potential (which is generally defined as the weighted sum of domestic and foreign GDP). In particular, one such definition has been applied in the context of the EU, and involves weighing the two factors according to internal and external distances (see Harris, 1954; Head and Mayer, 2004).

Internal distance is taken into account to mirror internal transportation costs. External distance reflects the transportation costs borne when supplying European foreign markets from a given, reference country. However, there is no reason to suspect that FDI should react to GDP, internal and external distances in the same manner. Thus, GDP remains separate from distance in our estimations.

---

[16] The methodology was first proposed by King and Fullerton (1984) and applied to OECD countries by Devereux and Griffith (2002).

[17] Zentrum für Europäische Wirtschaftsforschung. We are grateful to Michael Overesch for kindly providing the data.

[18] Market access is not considered here because all target countries are part of the EU.

Both the dependent variable (FDI) and the market size variable (GDP of the host country in logarithm, $LGDP_{it}$) are expressed at constant domestic prices but in current dollars. So, when currency i appreciates against the US$, the GDP of country i rises in US$. If the volume of FDI stays constant, FDI in current US$ rises by the same proportion as the domestic exchange rate. Nevertheless, US investors may be tempted either to reduce the volume of FDI, because local costs are higher once converted into US$, or to increase it, because of the target market's higher purchasing. As this is an empirical issue, the nominal exchange rate ($LEXCH_{it}$ in logarithm) is added to the GDP as a separate explanatory variable, which is lagged one year to avoid reverse causality.

Conventionally, internal distance is considered as the sum of town to town distances. It is therefore a measure of market density. Indeed, for a given GDP, a larger country is less attractive because of higher internal transportation costs.

As for external distance, it corresponds to the log of the sum of distances from country i to each other destination country in the sample. In order to avoid multicollinearity, one of the two distance variables must be omitted in our estimations. Due to border effects, external distance is expected to matter more than internal distance. Therefore, the former ($LDISTE_i$) is included rather than the latter.

Finally, agglomeration economies are difficult to disentangle from market potential since they also rely on size. Head and Mayer (2004), for instance, use the number of firms in the same sector originating from the same country and which are already located in the region of destination. However, they work on a specific, firm-level dataset of Japanese firms. In our study, the share of employment in the destination country of a given sector ($AGGLO_{it}$) is used as a proxy for agglomeration economies, an approach that is consistent with Braunerhjelm and Svensson (1996) and Braunerhjelm et al. (2000). The intuition is that we expect US multinationals to be attracted by countries specialized in their sector. The underlying assumption is that they will benefit from agglomeration economies, irrespective of the nationality of the firms already in place.

Turning to cost variables, we include the logarithm of sector-level unit labour costs ($LULC_{ijt}$) in the estimations. As detailed in Box 6, unit labour costs are expressed in current dollars and we ensured that this sector-specific variable was not collinear with the nominal exchange rate (see Appendix B). A measure for labour market flexibility, which captures hiring and firing practices, is also taken into account in the set of controls ($FLEX_{it}$). The definitions and sources of dependent and explanatory variables are detailed in Box 6.

3.2. Econometric methodology

The following equation is estimated:

$$LFDI_{ijt} = a_0 + a_1 LGDP_{it} + a_2 LDISTE_i + a_3 AGGLO_{ijt} + a_4 LEXCH_{it} + a_5 LULC_{ijt}$$
$$+ a_6 FLEX_{it} + a_7 LTAX_{it} + a_8 LPUBK_{it} + u_{ijt} \tag{4}$$

Box 6. The variables used in the regressions

LFDI_{ijt} denotes the logarithm of the stock of capital expenditures by US majority-owned companies located in country i, sector j, year t (with at least 50% ownership), deflated by the local investment price index in current US$ (100 in 2000). *Source*: Bureau of Economic Analysis (FDI in US$) and OECD (investment price index in local currency).

LPUBK_{it} is the logarithm of the net stock of public capital measured in US$ millions at constant prices per square km. *Source*: areas are from the World Bank, public capital is from Christopher Kamps (2004a), updated for 2002 using Eurostat public investment figures. For the Czech Republic, Hungary and Poland, which are missing in Kamps' database, we use the index of public infrastructure constructed by Ayalp *et al.* (2004) for 2002, which we rescale by using the ratio of public capital to public infrastructure in Germany during the same year. We then recover the whole series of public capital in the four countries using Eurostat public fixed capital investment series and the same depreciation factor as in Kamps (2004a). For Luxembourg, which is also omitted in Kamps' database, the public capital ratio is assumed to be the average between that of the Dutch and the Swiss in 2002. The whole series is then obtained in the same way as for the three NMS. This capital stock is that of 'the government' in the traditional sense. It includes public hospitals, education infrastructure, administration offices, public lands and buildings, gross fixed capital of public firms and public equipment, but excludes military capital.

LSOCEXP_{it} is the logarithm of social expenditures by public institutions as a share of GDP in country i at time t. *Source*: Eurostat.

LHEAL_{it} denotes the logarithm of health expenditures as a share of GDP in country i at time t. *Source*: OECD.

LTAX_{it} is the logarithm of the corporate tax rate in country i and in year t. Two measures are used for this rate: statutory rates (*Sources*: Michael Devereux's webpage and Eurostat) and effective average tax rates (EATR; *Source*: Overesch, 2005).

LGDP_{it} is the logarithm of GDP in country i and in year t at year-2000 prices, converted into US$ using current exchange rates. *Source*: OECD.

LDISTE_{i} is the logarithm of the sum of distances from country i to each of the other destination countries in the sample. *Source*: CEPII's web page.

AGGLO_{ijt} is the share of sector j in total employment of country i in year t. *Source*: STAN-OECD (rev3) database. Due to differences in sector coverage between STAN and BEA databases, some approximations had to be made and the shares do not sum to unity in each country over our sectors.

LEXCH$_{it}$ denotes the current nominal exchange rate index with respect to US$, base 100 in 2000. *Source*: OECD. For EMU countries, the exchange rate prior to 1999 is re-calculated with fixed conversion rates between each currency and the euro (conversion rates are available on ECB's website). The nominal exchange rate is lagged one year to avoid reverse causality from inward FDI to the exchange rate. A rise denotes an appreciation of the domestic currency against the US$.

LULC$_{ijt}$ is the unit labour cost in country i, sector j, year t, in current US$. Unit labour cost indices in US$ (100 in 2000) are multiplied by each country's real exchange rate with respect to US$ in 2000 (100 = PPP, > 100 if domestic currency is overvalued compared to PPP, <100 in the reverse case). *Sources*: STAN-OECD database for unit labour costs, World Bank-WDI for real exchange rates with respect to US$. Missing data were filled by using the growth rate of unit labour cost indices for the whole economy (OECD). The latter index was also used to construct unit labour cost levels for the whole economy (used in the aggregate equation).

FLEX$_{it}$ measures hiring and firing practices on labour market. *Source*: Fraser variable 5bii. The original data set is provided at five-year intervals before the year 2000, after which it is provided on a yearly basis. It is interpolated here to get annual data for our entire time span. A higher value points to more flexibility.

where the i, j and t subscripts designate the host country, the sector and the year, respectively. The variables are described in detail in the previous section and in Box 6. It is expected that: $a_1 > 0$, $a_3 > 0$, $a_2 < 0$, $a_5 < 0$, $a_6 > 0$, $a_7 < 0$, $a_8 > 0$, while a_4 is *a priori* ambiguous. More specifically, a_7 stands for the elasticity of capital with respect to the corporate tax rate, with public capital held constant. It corresponds to $e^0_{K/t}$ in the theoretical model (Section 2, Box 3). a_8 is the elasticity of private capital with respect to public capital density, with the tax rate held constant, i.e. it represents $e^0_{K/G}$.[19]

Two difficulties arise when estimating Equation (4). The first one stems from potential collinearity among the regressors. Fortunately, the correlation matrix reported in Appendix B provides evidence against multicollinearity: the highest Pearson correlation coefficient is 53% in absolute terms, which is generally considered to lie within acceptable limits (see Cohen *et al.*, 2003).

The second difficulty pertains to endogeneity. Some explanatory variables may be affected by inward FDI. This is especially the case regarding the exchange rate because capital inflows are expected to lead to an exchange-rate appreciation. However, other variables such as GDP, unit labour costs, agglomeration, tax rates or public capital,

---

[19] Additional estimations performed on semi-elasticities provide the same order of magnitude for the elasticity of the average tax rate (the results are available from the authors on demand).

could also be involved. To resolve this problem, the exchange rate is lagged one year in all regressions and robustness checks are performed by lagging the variables already mentioned. Nevertheless, this is not sufficient since both FDI and explanatory variables could be affected by some other omitted variables.

To deal with this unobserved heterogeneity, fixed effects are introduced. Since our panel is three-dimensional, three types of fixed effects have to be considered: time, sector and country. The three types of fixed effects are introduced successively rather than simultaneously, lest we leave too little variance to be explained by economic variables. The variance under scrutiny is different in the three exercises. In the time dimension, a group is defined by the average of the dependent variable for a given year. Then, time-fixed effects capture the between-group variance (variance across the years), which represents a small fraction of the total variance of the dependent variable (11.5%). Therefore, the regression with time-fixed effects is expected to generate approximately the same result as the OLS regression. It should be likewise for the regressions with sector-fixed effects, since they reflect the between-sector variance, which only amounts to 11.8% of the total variance. However, introducing country-fixed effects changes the perspective dramatically since they absorb the variance of the dependent variable across the countries, which represents 64.7% of the total variance.

Our FDI data does not depict a large intra-country dispersion. It is all the more so for explanatory variables and obviously for geographic distance. In Austria, Spain and Sweden, the statutory tax rate does not show any variation across time. Moreover, GDP, labour market flexibility and public capital are relatively smooth over time in all countries. As regards public capital, the coefficient of variation over time is often very low (below 5%). Only in new member states does it reach relatively high levels (22% in Poland). By contrast, the cross-country dispersion exceeds 100% in 2002. So, country-fixed effects are likely to be collinear with some explanatory variables. To address this difficulty, external distance, which is both time and sector invariant, is omitted at first. Unsurprisingly, the bulk of our sample's variance is absorbed by country-fixed effects and the impact of tax and public capital variables cannot be measured, calling for another approach.

We adopt a different strategy that involves running two kinds of regressions.[20] First, in order to account for the within-sector × country variance (which only represents 8% of the dependent variable's overall variance), Equation (4) is estimated using first-differentiated variables. The purpose of running this regression is to evaluate how changes in the explanatory variables over time influence FDI flows into and out of a given country-sector. Not much explanatory power is expected due to the low time variance of our explanatory variables.[21] Second, Equation (4) is estimated using time averages in hopes of accounting for the remaining variance (the between sector × country variance which represents the bulk of the total variance, 86.5%). From a statistical viewpoint, an observation is now the time average of a country-sector. This

---

[20] We are grateful to Brigitte Dormont for this suggestion.

[21] Mody and Srinivasan (1998) face the same problem when performing a within-estimation.

second type of regression casts light on the impact of cross-sector, cross-country or cross-sector × country differences within the explanatory variables on average inward sector-country FDI. In this regression, country and sector-fixed effects are introduced. When country-fixed effects are taken into account, the regression correctly measures the impact of fiscal variables on inward FDI while controlling for cross-country heterogeneity. In all cases, standard errors are clustered at the country level, (see Moulton, 1990) and the residuals are corrected for heteroscedasticity.

3.3. Econometric results

A first set of estimation results is provided by Table 1 below, where the corporate tax variable is the statutory tax rate. Columns (1) to (4) report the results obtained by

Table 1. Benchmark results

Fixed effects	OLS					Panel	
	Aggregate FDI	Sector-level	Sector-level balanced	Sector-level lags[a]		Baseline	
	(1) No	(2) No	(3) No	(4) No	(5) Time	(6) Sectors	(7) Countries
LGDP	1.145***	1.185***	1.153***	1.187***	1.143***	1.173***	−0.907
	0.052	0.062	0.069	0.061	0.058	0.054	0.654
LDISTE	−1.148***	−0.609	−1.008*	−0.725	−0.718	−0.625	−
	0.234	0.453	0.486	0.443	0.425	0.464	
AGGLO	−	0.033***	0.037***	0.034***	0.032***	0.031**	0.032***
		0.008	0.010	0.008	0.008	0.012	0.007
LEXCH$_{(-1)}$	0.067	1.062**	0.955**	1.128**	−1.425*	0.741*	−0.063
	0.378	0.476	0.332	0.498	0.704	0.384	0.564
LULC	1.382***	−0.071	−0.146	−0.185	−0.161	−0.007	−0.409
	0.328	0.316	0.324	0.384	0.387	0.373	0.266
FLEX	−0.146***	−0.002	−0.024	0.005	−0.053	0.001	0.072
	0.039	0.102	0.102	0.104	0.092	0.083	0.074
LTAX	−2.044***	−1.479***	−1.321***	−1.463***	−1.446***	−1.505***	−0.223
	0.115	0.179	0.196	0.177	0.169	0.179	0.495
LPUBK	0.181***	0.277***	0.171**	0.237***	0.240**	0.293***	0.624
	0.068	0.085	0.080	0.079	0.088	0.080	0.938
CONS	−0.583	−2.456	1.965	−0.881	0.128	−3.241	0.542
	2.809	4.603	5.078	4.725	4.448	4.783	3.105
No. obs	165	1346	1800	1231	1346	1346	1346
R-squared	0.8511	0.6217	0.6097	0.6211	0.6325	0.7356	0.6694
Root MSE	0.6465	1.206	1.1899	1.2063	1.1925	1.0116	1.1342
Hausman test[b]	−	−	−	0.04 (0.92)	−	−	−

[a] LGDP, LEXCH, LTAX, LPUBK, LULC and AGGLO are lagged one year.

[b] Statistics and p-value. The null of the Hausman test is non-endogeneity (equal coefficients in columns (4) and (2)).

*** significant at 1%; ** significant at 5%; * significant at 10%. Standard errors below coefficients are clustered at country level.

OLS, that is, on pooled data. In Column (1), data are aggregated by countries, and consequently the sector dimension of the data is omitted.[22] In all other columns, the sector dimension is included, which raises the number of observations from 165 to 1346. In Column (3), the qualitative values of the dependent variable are replaced by their conditional mean[23] so that the number of observations rises to 1 800 to obtain a balanced panel. Finally, Column (4) is the same as Column (2), except that a number of explanatory variables are lagged.

According to these four columns, inward FDI increases by slightly more than 1% for countries that experience a 1% increase in GDP, whereas a country which is 1% more peripheral suffers from approximately 1% less inward FDI. These orders of magnitude are relatively standard.[24] Furthermore, a sectoral employment increase equal to 1% of total employment in a given country leads to a 3.5% increase in inward FDI in this sector/country. We find substantial evidence for the existence of an agglomeration effect, as did Braunerhjelm and Svensson (1996) and Braunerhjelm et al. (2000), who used the same variable for explaining Swedish location choices.

In OLS sector-level estimations, the coefficient on the (lagged) nominal exchange rate is positive and significant at least at the 5% level. An exchange-rate appreciation is therefore positively correlated with an increase in inward FDI. One way of interpreting this result is to say that the demand-side effect (higher purchasing power in the target country) prevails over the supply-side effect (higher costs). Conversely, the coefficient estimated for the sector-level unit labour cost is not significant. Moreover, in the estimation performed on aggregate FDI, the exchange rate coefficient is not significant, but the unit labour cost variable (which accounts for the whole economy in this context) is significant and of positive sign. All in all, there is no evidence suggesting that higher costs serve as a deterrent to inward FDI in the EU. While this may at first run against our intuition, these results are not isolated in the literature (see Loree and Guisinger, 1995; Wei, 2000; Head and Mayer, 2004; Bénassy-Quéré et al., 2005). They can be explained by demand effects or by the mismeasurement of labour productivity (see Devereux and Griffith, 1998 who also find unit labour costs to be non-significant determinants of US FDI in Europe). It should also be noted that the labour flexibility variable is either non-significant or of the wrong sign in this first set of estimations.

The coefficient on the statutory tax rate is negative and significant at the 1% level in all four estimations (Columns (1) to (4)). The elasticities obtained (−2.0 on aggregate data, −1.3 to −1.5 on sector-level data) are consistent with the meta-analysis

[22] The agglomeration variable is omitted since it is the share of each sector in the employment of each country. For unit labour costs, we use country data.

[23] There are in fact 454 values of the dependent variable which are expressed as a qualitative variable. We know that FDI has been positive but no aggregate amount is reported. We then replace the unknown amount by the sector-country mean on observable data.

[24] Note that the distance variable does not measure distance from the origin country (the United States), but average distance between the host country and the other European countries.

proposed by de Mooij and Ederveen (2005). As is consistent with theory, more public capital attracts FDI, and the coefficient is significant at least at the 5% level in all four regressions. This strongly suggests that, all things (and in particular the corporate tax rates) being equal, public capital attracts FDI. A 10% increase in public capital will, on average, translate into a 2% increase of FDI inflow. However, the latter elasticity is significantly lower than for the statutory tax rate, and less than 1. This implies that the condition for the under-provision of public capital is met (see Box 2 in Section 2): a 1% drop in corporate taxes with a corresponding decrease in public capital leads to a foreign capital *inflow* (the elasticity $e_{K/t}$ is negative). These results are not altered by balancing the panel (Column 3) or introducing lags (Column 4). The Hausman test reveals that the null hypothesis of non-endogeneity cannot be rejected at the 1% level (see the bottom of Table 1, Column (4)).

The results obtained from panel data estimations are reported in Columns (5) through (7). The regressions with fixed effects on time (Column (5)) or on sectors (Column (6)) lead to similar results as the OLS estimations. The sole difference is that the regression with time-fixed effects yields a negative exchange rate coefficient, that is, a currency appreciation leads to lower inward FDI. Indeed, countries whose currencies appreciate relatively more than others tend to receive less FDI, probably because of a relative loss in cost-competitiveness. When country-fixed effects are introduced (Column (7)), only agglomeration, which is a country × sector × time variable, remains significant. Even GDP fails to be significant in this last regression of Table 1. As already mentioned, one prominent feature and difficulty that characterizes our dataset is the limited variance of most explanatory variables in the time dimension – especially when compared to the larger variances found in the sector dimension and, above all, in the country dimension. Hence, panel data analysis with country-fixed effects is unlikely to provide very useful results about the nature or existence of dual competition on tax rates and public inputs. In our estimates from Table 3, the regression using sector-fixed effects is taken as our baseline specification.

The results obtained from running regressions on reduced dimensions of the panel are presented in Table 2. In the first column, all variables are in first-difference. As expected, the model is unable to explain the changes in FDI for each sector-country over time, due to the very low variance of explanatory variables. In the other columns, all variables are averaged over time and the OLS regressions are performed on averages. Columns (2) and (3) first present the results without fixed effects under two different specifications. We note that in this case both the tax rate and public capital become significant, of correct sign and close to the benchmark estimation. In Column (4), country-fixed effects are introduced. The software then automatically drops redundant fixed-effects or explanatory variables. Both fiscal variables remain significant and of correct sign, but the impact of labour flexibility is surprisingly negative and significant. In Column (5), this variable is excluded and the results are unchanged for taxation and public capital. In the last column, both country and sector fixed

Table 2. Regressions on reduced dimensions of the panel

Fixed effects	First differences			Time averages		
	(1) No	(2) No	(3) No	(4) Countries	(5) Countries	(6) Countries and sectors
LGDP	0.230	1.161***	1.130***	1.036***	1.124***	1.032***
	0.537	0.078	0.071	0.007	0.010	0.011
LDISTE	–	–	−0.954***	–	−0.201**	–
			0.243		0.089	
AGGLO	0.024	0.036***	0.034***	0.036***	0.036***	0.013
	0.047	0.009	0.009	0.010	0.010	0.012
LEXCH$_{(-1)}$	−0.031	1.189	−0.123	–	–	–
	0.160	1.566	1.811			
LULC	0.011	0.023	0.253	−0.992	−0.992	−1.131
	0.123	0.694	0.622	0.722	0.687	1.016
FLEX	−0.003	0.007	−0.069	−0.241***	–	−0.241***
	0.031	0.127	0.110	0.010		0.015
LTAX	0.053	−1.408***	−1.483***	−1.225***	−1.187***	−1.213***
	0.140	0.257	0.198	0.059	0.036	0.087
LPUBK	−0.367	0.316***	0.180**	0.144**	0.179**	0.144*
	0.312	0.086	0.077	0.056	0.064	0.080
CONS	0.001	−8.763***	–	−2.508	−1.772	−2.922
	0.016	2.710		2.983	3.854	4.501
No. obs	1620	180	180	180	180	180
R-squared	0.0006	0.6552	0.7734	0.7183	0.7183	0.8425
Root MSE	0.6176	1.0935	1.07	1.0248	1.0248	0.7889

*** significant at 1%; ** significant at 5%; * significant at 10%. Standard errors below coefficients are clustered at country level.

effects are introduced. The results are basically unchanged, except for the agglomeration variable which fails to be significant. Columns (4) to (6) correspond to our preferred specifications since they account for unobserved countries heterogeneity.

The elasticity of FDI with respect to the tax rate is lower when country-fixed effects are included, which is in line with de Mooij and Ederveen's (2005) findings.[25] It is worth mentioning that the elasticity of FDI with respect to the tax rate is again significantly higher than unity in absolute value. Therefore, raising the corporate tax rates while keeping the stock of public capital constant *reduces* tax revenue, which would be inconsistent with a government's optimal decision' in an open economy.[26] It is equally important to note that the coefficient on public capital is lower when country-fixed effects are introduced but remains significant at least at the 10% level

[25] De Mooij and Ederveen find a typical semi-elasticity of −1.92 for panel data, compared to −7.81 on a cross-section basis. In a recent paper, Razin and Sadka (2006) obtain a −3.6 semi-elasticity using a Heckman estimation on flow FDI data with country-fixed effects. In Columns (4) and (5), a −1.19 to −1.23 elasticity is found. With an average corporate tax rate of 33%, a semi-elasticity ranging from −3.6 to −3.7 is obtained.

[26] See Appendix A. Values for tax elasticity found in the literature are quite high and it is not uncommon to find figures above 1 in absolute value (see the previous footnote).

Table 3. Panel estimations, robustness checks

	Baseline (1)	1994–1999 (2)	1998–2003 (3)	EATR (4)	Lagged EATR (5)	Social expend. (6)	Health expend. (7)
LGDP	1.173***	1.166***	1.179***	1.192***	1.189***	1.205***	1.201***
	0.054	0.041	0.070	0.055	0.054	0.041	0.072
LDISTE	−0.625	−0.100	−1.049**	−0.494	−0.581	−0.980***	−0.582*
	0.464	0.446	0.462	0.469	0.474	0.320	0.455
AGGLO	0.031**	0.033**	0.028**	0.032**	0.031**	0.027**	0.031**
	0.012	0.014	0.011	0.013	0.013	0.011	0.012
LEXCH	0.741*	−0.454	1.090***	0.858*	0.978**	0.914***	0.769*
	0.384	0.442	0.346	0.434	0.447	0.313	0.390
LULC	−0.007	0.275	−0.181	−0.062	−0.211	−0.151	−0.093
	0.373	0.303	0.496	0.368	0.457	0.296	0.366
FLEX	0.001	−0.061	0.017	−0.001	0.013	0.015	−0.005
	0.083	0.059	0.100	0.089	0.092	0.061	0.075
LTAX	−1.505***	−1.686***	−1.460***	−1.841***	−1.811***	−0.996***	−1.442***
	0.179	0.188	0.180	0.326	0.309	0.150	0.163
LPUBK	0.293***	0.496***	0.165*	0.307***	0.268***	0.176**	0.297***
	0.080	0.073	0.087	0.079	0.073	0.069	0.089
LSOCEXP	–	–	–	–	–	−1.470***	–
						0.427	
LHEAL	–	–	–	–	–	–	−0.590
							0.580
CONS	−3.241	−7.542	1.515	−4.942	−3.847	5.042	−2.105
	4.783	4.678	4.688	4.966	5.311	4.019	5.066
No. obs	1346	718	889	1346	1231	1346	1346
R-squared	0.7356	0.7567	0.7558	0.7289	0.7302	0.7498	0.7369
Root MSE	1.0116	0.9993	0.960	1.0243	1.0217	0.98448	1.0096
Hausman test	–	–	–	–	0.78 (1.000)	–	–

*** significant at 1%; ** significant at 5%; * significant at 10%. Standard errors below coefficients are clustered at country level.

in all specifications. Consequently, this step of our econometric methodology corroborates the qualitative predictions offered by our theoretical model, and we can safely conclude that the *adjusted tax elasticity* ($e_{K/t}$ in the theoretical model) is negative.

Table 3 presents several robustness checks for our baseline estimation, and this latter estimation is reported for convenience in the first column. Columns (2) and (3) report the results from the same panel estimation with sector-fixed effects on two sub-samples: 1994–1999 and 2000–2003. The corporate tax rate and public capital coefficients are of correct sign and significant at least at the 10% level in the two sub-samples, although we note that both coefficients decline over time. In contrast, the distance coefficient is only significant in the second sub-sample, which is consistent with a trade literature showing that, in spite of decreasing transportation costs, distance is becoming increasingly important (see, for instance, Brun *et al.*, 2005). In Column (4), the statutory tax rate is substituted by the EATR. The elasticity of FDI with respect to the EATR is higher than with respect to the statutory tax rate, which is standard in the literature (see de Mooij and Ederveen, 2005). Similar results are obtained when the EATR is lagged (Column (5)). Finally, the last two columns of Table 3 include social expenditures and healthcare expenditures as additional controls. It is remarkable to note that the coefficients on both variables are negative, which suggests that higher household-specific expenditures have a negative impact on inward FDI. That said, the social expenditure coefficient is the only statistically significant one. In this regression, the public capital coefficient declines to slightly less than 0.2, while the tax rate elasticity decreases to a unitary value. Introducing health expenditures, however, does not affect the regression.

The final step of the analysis involves assessing how the impact of taxation depends on such country characteristics as: (1) size, (2) trade openness, (3) the existing stock of public capital and (4) the tax rate. The rationale for examining (1) and (2) can be found in the traditional tax competition literature; the standard argument proposes that small open countries have a greater incentive to cut taxes than their larger, relatively closed counterparts because the perceived elasticity of capital with respect to taxation is higher. In turn, justification for including (3) can be found in our theoretical model, which yields a tax elasticity of capital that is a declining function of public capital stock.[27] Hence, capital is less elastic with respect to the tax rate in countries that spend more on public input. The sign for the tax elasticity derivative with respect to the tax rate (4) cannot be *a priori* determined, but applying a Laffer curve argument suggests that high tax countries are likely to exhibit a higher elasticity than low tax countries.

In order to study such heterogeneity, dummy variables are introduced. Each of them divides the sample into two groups of countries, according to their size, openness, public capital and corporate taxation, successively. These dummies are then included with tax rates in the estimations. The list of countries found in each group is provided in Appendix C.[28] The results are reported in Table 4. The elasticities obtained when grouping the countries according to their size (Columns (2)) or openness (Column (3)) are all significantly negative, but not significantly different from one another. In contrast, the tax elasticity for 'high public capital' countries is not significant, as opposed to 'low public capital' countries.[29] This result suggests that a tax cut is more likely to attract FDI in low public capital countries.[30] The final column of Table 4 shows that the elasticity of FDI with respect to the statutory tax rate is higher in high-tax countries than in low-tax countries, but the difference is not significant. In other words, from an econometric point of view we cannot safely claim anything

---

[27] $\dfrac{\partial e_{K/t}^{0}}{\partial G} = \dfrac{t}{K}\dfrac{F_{KGK}}{F_{KK}^{2}} < 0$ under the assumptions detailed in Box 3.

[28] Trade openness is defined here as the sum of exports and imports over GDP in 2003, source OECD. Size is based on our GDP variable. Public capital is based on our *PUBK* variable (public capital per square kilometre) and tax on our *STATUT* variable.

[29] See the Wald test on the bottom-most line of Table 4. Only in Column (4) does the test reject the null of equal coefficients on both groups of countries.

[30] We have tried to test the robustness of this result by introducing two dummy variables in the multiplicative form in the specification reported in Table 2. The results are inconclusive due to one of these variables being dropped by Stata.

Table 4. Panel estimations, country groupings

Dependent variable: LFDI	Baseline (1)	Country size (2)	Trade openness (3)	Public expenditure (4)	Statutory tax level (5)
LGDP	1.173***	1.168***	1.143***	1.230***	1.236***
	0.054	0.092	0.054	0.069	0.067
LDISTE	−0.625	−0.619	−0.765	−1.174**	−0.595
	0.464	0.435	0.489	0.512	0.467
AGGLO	0.031**	0.031**	0.031**	0.031**	0.032**
	0.012	0.012	0.011	0.012	0.011
LEXCH	0.741*	0.741*	0.797*	0.438	0.802**
	0.384	0.385	0.387	0.374	0.354
LULC	−0.007	−0.007	−0.040	−0.090	−0.086
	0.373	0.375	0.356	0.356	0.323
FLEX	0.001	0.002	−0.002	0.082	0.056
	0.083	0.081	0.079	0.065	0.079
LTAX	−1.505***	−	−	−	−
	0.179				
Small size	−	−1.503***	−	−	−
		0.179			
Large size	−	−1.522***	−	−	−
		0.350			
High openness	−	−	−1.564***	−	−
			0.231		
Low openness	−	−	−1.703***	−	−
			0.412		
High public cap	−	−	−	−0.207	−
				0.471	
Low public cap	−	−	−	−1.359***	−
				0.158	
High tax rate cap	−	−	−	−	−2.051***
					0.430
Low tax rate	−	−	−	−	−1.680***
					0.193
LPUBK	0.293***	0.292***	0.306***	0.614***	0.233***
	0.080	0.084	0.085	0.112	0.078
CONS	−3.241	−3.284	−1.641	3.605	−4.291
	4.783	4.510	4.713	5.631	5.032
No. obs	1346	1346	1346	1346	1346
R-squared	0.7356	0.7356	0.7361	0.7479	0.7395
Root MSE	1.0116	1.012	1.011	0.9880	1.004
Wald test, Prob>F[a]	−	0.9508	0.5303	0.0104	0.2163

[a] H_0: 'the coefficients on *LTAX* are equal for both groups'.

*** significant at 1%; ** significant at 5%; * significant at 10%. Standard errors below coefficients are clustered at country level.

about the importance of tax decisions in high tax countries, but we *can* assert that tax decisions are of *relatively less* importance in high public capital countries than in low public capital countries. To summarize, the main assumptions underpinning our model are not rejected by the data. Public capital does indeed attract foreign capital, but financing an increase in public capital through an increase in the corporate tax rate leads to an outflow of foreign capital. Therefore, in an open economy, the under-provision of public inputs at the margin may be deemed a valid result.

4. POLICY IMPLICATIONS

The theoretical results obtained in Section 2, and their empirical validation in Section 3, yield several policy implications. The first one addresses the under-provision of public goods in an open economy.

> **Policy implication 1.** Tax competition leads to resource allocation being shifted away from public goods to private goods, irrespective of whether the country is a net exporter or a net importer of capital.

This is the main implication from our finding of a *negative adjusted tax elasticity of capital*, which demonstrates that capital flows out when the receipts generated from an increase in the corporate tax rate are spent on public inputs. It is difficult to provide an illustration for the under-provision result because it applies at the margin. That said, this marginal shift in resource-allocation can be seen in Figure 5. Similar trends have been observed in average public and private capital-to-GDP ratios up to 1986. After 1986, a downward trend is observed, much steeper for public than for private capital. This divergence coincides with the implementation of the EU Single European Act. Although it could be attributed to a rise in the marginal productivity of private capital due to corporate reengineering and restructuring initiatives, the divergence remains consistent with the resource-allocation shift predicted by our model.

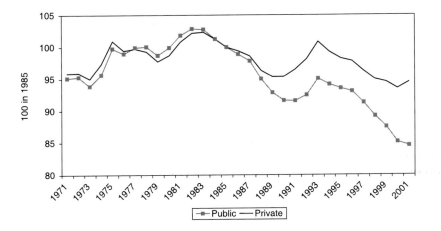

Figure 5. Public and private (non-residential) capital, % GDP, weighted EU average[a]

[a] Unweighted averages deliver similar results.

Source: Kamps (2004a), own calculations.

This shift in resource allocation is valid for each EU member but also for the EU as a whole. It is, however, mitigated at the EU level because the latter may have an impact on the world return.

Our model, however, does not lend credence to the idea that corporate taxation should be increased in the EU in order to raise the so-called 'Lisbon expenditures' on higher education, infrastructures, or R&D. Lest private capital should flow out of the EU, our findings suggest that the public expenditures required to achieve the Lisbon agenda should at least be partially funded through another, less mobile tax base.

Policy implication 2. Countries seeking to provide more public inputs must rely more heavily on immobile tax bases.

This call for a shift in the tax base is justified on account of our theoretical model, and the negative adjusted tax elasticity of capital that we estimated. Namely, a capital outflow results whenever the additional provision of public inputs is not financed through a greater reliance on labour taxation. The ratio between the revenue levied by the value added tax versus the corporate income tax for the EU15 is shown in Figure 6. There has been a steep rise in this ratio since 2000, with a leap in the median ratio from 2 in 2001 to 3 in 2004. The tax reforms announced in Germany in 2006, which consist of a 3 percentage point increase in the VAT rate and a near 10 percentage point decrease in the statutory corporate tax rate, give us reason to suspect that this trend is unlikely to change in the near future.

In addition, our theoretical model gives credence to the fact that the higher the positive impact of one extra unit of public input on the marginal productivity of capital, the lower the distortion in favour of the private good.

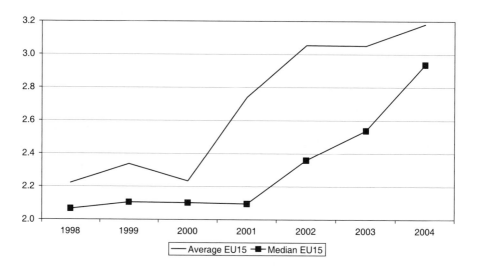

Figure 6. VAT/corporate tax receipt ratio

Source: IMF Government Finance.

Policy implication 3. Any policy which increases the marginal private return of public input can reinforce the country's attractiveness vis-à-vis foreign investors.

Our econometric analysis reveals that increasing public capital has a positive impact on inward FDI, as opposed to extra social expenditures. In addition, more public capital tends to make foreign capital less elastic to a rise in corporate taxes. Hence, governments are facing incentives prompting a gradual move away from unproductive public expenditures towards public inputs.[31] In other words, one way of raising the marginal private return of public input is to reallocate public resources towards expenditures bearing the strongest positive on the marginal productivity of public capital. This involves increasing budgets devoted to building infrastructure, schooling or R&D while simultaneously reducing those used for social security and redistribution. The consequence is an *expenditure shift*.

Policy implication 4. Tax competition distorts the composition of public expenditures away from unproductive public goods towards more productive public inputs.

Illustrating this policy implication requires distinguishing public expenditures defined as public inputs from those that are household-specific. With this in mind, we use the IMF's *Government Finance Statistics* database. We take 'public input expenditures' to mean general government expenditures likely to have a positive impact on private capital productivity, which includes expenditures regarding 'economic affairs' (including transportation), education, public order and defence. Defence is included because its related expenditures are often believed to have positive externalities on upstream or downstream private industries.[32] On the other hand, 'household-specific expenditures' cover social protection, health, housing and community amenities, recreation, culture and religion. The remaining public spending – general public services, environmental protection, debt service – are excluded from the analysis.[33]

Figure 7 is constructed on the basis of the above classification. Even if composition effects due to missing observations cannot be ruled out, the figure suggests that a slight shift from household-specific expenditures to public inputs has taken place in the EU25 starting in 1998. This figure also reveals a discrepancy between the ways expenditures are allocated in the EU15 countries and how they are allocated within the new member states. The difference may be partly explained by the latter group of countries needing public infrastructure, notably transportation networks.

---

[31] This expenditure-shift implication of tax competition can also be shown theoretically by introducing two public goods in our model, one being a household-specific good, hence not a public input. This variant is not developed here but available from the authors upon request (see also Keen and Marchand, 1997).

[32] Removing defence from public input expenditures does not change the results.

[33] In our analysis, education and public-order expenditures, which are likely to raise households' utility, are classified as public inputs because they are not *specifically* directed to households.

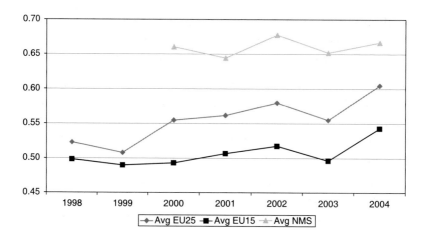

Figure 7. Expenditure shifting: public input/household-specific expenditures

Source: Government Finance Statistics 2006.

However, increasing the efficiency of the public sector in each of its tasks is an alternative way for the governments to remain competitive with respect to neighbouring tax rates and public spending. For example, governments can change the incentive structure faced by civil servants or delegate the detailed allocation of public budgets to those who are responsible for the results.[34] With these types of improvements, the same level of public inputs would have more impact on private return, because of the efficiency gains in the public sector.[35]

Policy implication 5. Tax competition is expected to provide incentives for governments to raise the efficiency of the public sector.

Tax competition could act as a form of yardstick competition in which voters compare their government's performance with that of others (Schleifer, 1985). While yardstick competition may be significant within the United States (Besley and Case, 1995a, 1995b), cultural and linguistic differences constitute large impediments for this type of mechanism to apply in the EU. Tax competition may in fact appear as a substitute, prompting governments to either reduce public expenditures or make them more efficient. These two ways of increasing the private return of public expenditures – expenditures shifting and efficiency enhancing – interact in a non-neutral way with respect to the balance between household public goods and public inputs. Interestingly, we note that for firms (but perhaps less so for households), the bias in favour of public inputs may be more pronounced when efficiency of the public sector is increased.

---

[34] The French reform introduced in 2006 (*Loi Organique relative aux Lois de Finances*) is an attempt in this direction.

[35] A precise way to show this is to introduce a public-sector specific inefficiency which raises the transformation rate between the private and public goods above one in the model. If this inefficiency can be reduced through additional effort of the public sector, which itself is costly, then capital openness raises the optimal effort level. This variant of the model is available from the authors upon request.

Policy implication 6. The public sector's tax competition-led efforts to reduce inefficiency increase the composition bias of public expenditures in favour of public input and to the detriment of household-specific public goods.

Indeed, the opportunity cost of providing an unproductive public good is higher when the impact of the productive public good on private return is greater.[36] The flip-side of this argument is that countries failing to reduce public-sector inefficiency are likely to see their provision of household-specific public goods maintained, while their attractiveness in the eyes of public-input intensive firms is likely to decline.

For reasons including history, geography or social preferences, not all EU countries are equally equipped to efficiently produce public inputs with high private return, to fight existing inefficiency, or to abandon expenditures on unproductive public goods.

Policy implication 7. Countries can adopt different strategies in the setting of their tax rate and public input combination: they should set this combination according to their marginal private rate of return on public input. The higher this return, the more sustainable a high corporate tax rate is.

This return can be influenced by the size of the country, its market potential, its wealth, the kind of goods produced and the quality of public input. Thus, a positive correlation between corporate taxation and public input is observed, as illustrated in Figure 2. The question then becomes whether high tax, high public capital countries will have an incentive to adopt a lower tax and lower public capital strategy. The answer remains ambiguous according to our econometric analysis. Indeed, although a high stock of public capital serves as a shield against capital outflow subsequent a tax increase, high tax and low tax countries alike still face the same incentive to decrease their corporate tax rate at the margin.

5. CONCLUSION

The idea that capital flees from high tax to low tax countries is as widespread as it is popular. It can, however, be misleading. This paper emphasizes that focusing solely on the tax side of countries' competition for multinational location destinations is unduly restrictive. In particular, coupled with tax rates, geography, market size and agglomeration effects, *public infrastructure* plays a part in the firms' location decision: all other things being equal, increasing public capital by 10% induces a 2% inflow of foreign direct investment.

High-tax member states are undoubtedly facing strong pressure to cut corporate taxation. Nevertheless, it is far from clear that corporate taxation will necessarily vanish over time, or that tax rates will necessarily converge to the same lower bound for all countries. As we have argued, tax spending can indeed improve public infrastructures, education and more generally public services, which may in turn

---

[36] A formal proof of this result may also be obtained upon request.

improve private capital productivity. Consequently, rational investors may choose to stay in a relatively high-tax country if they deem that the level and quality of public inputs (more than) compensates for higher taxes.

However, drawing from both our theoretical and empirical analyses, we note that increasing public capital through corporate taxation is harmful to a country's attractiveness. Public capital is thus bound to decline if it is not at least partially funded by other taxes. Basically, our study indicates that a 'high tax/high public input' equilibrium is sustainable only if households are willing to bear an increasing share of the financing of public inputs. This condition is more likely to be met in countries like France or Germany, which have traditionally invested in public inputs for a long period of time. In addition, countries characterized by a high level of public capital accumulation are unlikely to react to the pressures of tax competition as readily as their counterparts: this is because public capital accumulation lowers the elasticity of FDI with respect to taxation. Ultimately, our results suggest that tax competition between countries is being undertaken on a competitive playing field that is complex and likely to yield more diverse results than the oft-cited 'race to the bottom'.

Our results also suggest that tax co-ordination focusing solely on the setting of tax rates is misguided, and that comparing the financing of public inputs by mobile and immobile taxpayers is likely to be more fruitful.

Discussion

Stephen Redding
London School of Economics and CEPR

This paper addresses an important policy question. Fiscal competition is the subject of a lively policy debate among economists and politicians inside and outside Europe. A particular concern in this debate is the possibility of a 'race to the bottom', where in order to attract private-sector investments, governments competitively lower their tax rates, thereby eroding the ability to finance welfare states and other areas of public-sector activity.

The low rates of corporate taxes in some of the new members of the European Union, such as Latvia and Lithuania, have featured prominently in the European debate. In 2004, they prompted Nicolas Sarkozy to declare with a high-handed air that if the new members are 'rich enough' to forgo high taxes, they can hardly ask the European Union for development funds.

This paper makes an important point, which dates back to at least Tiebout (1956), that governments do not only compete in taxes but also in terms of the public goods that they offer. Some of these public goods enter private consumption, but others affect the productivity of private-sector activity. The authors exposit this point within a theoretical model, which builds on Zodrow and Mieszkowksi (1986), and present empirical evidence using a panel of data on 18 current EU members for 11 industries during the period 1994–2002.

I have two general comments on the paper. First, the model assumes that the public input to production is financed by the corporate tax on mobile capital. However, this behaviour is not optimal within the context of the model. The optimal behaviour for the government would be to charge a zero rate of tax on the mobile factor and finance public inputs through a tax on immobile labour. In the model, a tax on labour is equivalent to a lump-sum tax, but even if one allowed for distortionary effects of a tax on labour, governments would still have an incentive to shift taxation towards the immobile factor.

Second, the econometric analysis in the paper seeks to empirically disentangle the relationship between foreign direct investment, taxation and the provision of public capital. This is a challenging endeavour. All three sets of variables are endogenously determined. For example, it is not difficult to think of unobserved heterogeneity across locations (including but not limited to differences in natural endowments and the policy environment) which raise productivity in the private sector, thereby increasing production activity and the tax base, facilitating a combination of either lower tax rates and/or higher levels of public capital. If the unobserved heterogeneity across locations is time-invariant, this suggests exploiting time-series variation in the data through differencing or the inclusion of location dummies. But time-series changes in tax rates and public capital may be limited and are certainly also endogenous.

The authors are therefore to be commended for addressing this difficult problem, and the paper reports a number of interesting empirical findings. Thinking about these empirical findings raises a number of questions. Is there a way of more tightly connecting the exact econometric equation estimated with the theoretical model? Would the results look similar for total inward foreign direct investment (FDI) rather than inward FDI from the US? Is inward FDI the most appropriate left-hand side variable or should one exploit net investment positions (outward FDI may also be influenced by fiscal competition)? Variation in tax rates across locations will introduce incentives for transfer pricing, as examined for example by Bernard et al. (2006), and such transfer pricing will introduce a relationship between financial measures of FDI and tax rates. The discussion in the paper emphasizes the increase in the number of observations achieved through the use of industry-level data, but many of the right-hand side variables only vary at the country-level. Some specifications report clustered standard errors, but it is not clear at what level the standard errors are clustered. Finally, given the endogeneity concerns raised above, how should we interpret the coefficients on variables such as the agglomeration and public capital measures? Do these coefficients capture the causal effect of the variables on FDI? Or are there other omitted variables which result in both a high-level of FDI and a high level of public capital?

In short, the paper raises many interesting and topical questions that will be the subject of ongoing debate for years to come. Notwithstanding the paper's empirical findings of a connection between FDI and public capital, the success of low-tax European countries such as Ireland and the Baltic states in attracting FDI, and the fears embodied in the public pronouncements of politicians in high-tax European countries such as France and Germany, suggest that competition over tax rates will remain an important and enduring policy issues.

Panel discussion

Much of the discussion focused on some of the assumptions in the theoretical model and identification issues in the empirical section of the paper. For example, Duranton questioned the assumption that the government was benevolent – a malevolent government may want to increase taxes and lower spending and in this case, tax competition may be beneficial. Anne Sibert pointed that in the model, even when labour supply is endogenous, it is less mobile than capital and therefore labour rather than capital should be taxed to avoid double distortion. Sinn argued that the Zodrow–Mieszkowski results had been proven wrong in the context of infrastructure (while the results might have been right on the consumption of public goods, which are under-provided). Sinn also warned about the assumptions of congestion externalities; some should be present in the case of a public good, but the paper's equations lacked the relevant term and assumed away all such externalities. Duranton suggested that the opposite signs on the rate of tax and capital could be evidence of a missing variable such as another tax rate. In a related comment, Kotsogiannis suggested that empirically there should be account taken for substitutability across taxes. Further-more, in several EU countries, much of the infrastructure is paid for by EU funds and Kotsogiannis asked how this would bear on the results. Moav raised some doubt over whether it was possible to distinguish between investment in public capital and the quality of institutions. The authors said that they did not have the data to distin-guish between different types of investment. Konrad indicated that there may be some issues with the time structure of the model; FDI is typically based on expecta-tions of *future* taxation and the *current* level of infrastructure. This could change the nature of the (non-simultaneous) competition. Mody brought up the issue of differ-ences between old and new EU members; and questioned the idea that new members charge low rates of tax and older ones provide a higher public input. Rather, tax competition may now work more broadly than just through corporate taxes and to attract FDI, new EU members will also need to invest in public goods.

APPENDIX A: PROOFS

Claim 1. At the optimum of the closed economy, the FOC reads:

$$MRS_{G/x} = 1 - F_G \tag{1}$$

Proof. In a closed economy, the resource constraint writes:

$$F(\bar{L}, K, G) - x - G \geq 0. \tag{A.1}$$

The utility function of the representative agent is:

$$U(x, G) \tag{A.2}$$

which satisfies Inada's conditions. We have:

$$\bar{K} - K \geq 0. \tag{A.3}$$

where $\bar{K}$ is the domestic capital stock. In a closed economy, the first best allocation is given by the maximization of (A.2) under (A.1) and (A.3). Let $MRS_{G/x}$ denote the marginal rate of substitution between the private good x and the public good G ($MRS_{G/x}$ is a decreasing function of G). The first-order condition is:

$$0 < MRS_{G/x} = 1 - F_G < 1 \tag{A.4}$$

and $K = \bar{K}$. Let G_{closed} be the solution. From (A.4), we deduce:

$$F_G(\bar{L}, \bar{K}, G_0) < 1. \quad \blacksquare$$

Claim 2. At the optimum of the open economy, the FOC reads:

$$MRS_{G/x} = 1 - F_G - \alpha \frac{e_{K/t}}{1 + e_{K/t}}. \tag{2}$$

Proof. A direct proof goes as follows. At the optimum, the marginal utility of one additional unit of public good must be exactly compensated by the marginal disutility of the foregone quantity of private good. Differentiating the budget constraint of the public sector ($\alpha G = tK$) provides the variation in public input that is obtained through a marginal tax increase, dt:

$$dG = \frac{1}{\alpha}(Kdt + tdK) = \frac{K}{\alpha}dt\left(1 + t\frac{dK}{K}dt\right) = \frac{K}{\alpha}(1 + e_{K/t})dt \tag{A.5}$$

Now, the quantity of private good the household has to give up in order to obtain the quantity of public good financed by an increase dt is given by differentiating the national budget constraint (1.3) written as a function of t:

$$dx = F_K dK + F_G \frac{\partial G}{\partial t}dt - \frac{\partial G}{\partial t}dt - rdK \tag{A.6}$$

Using the arbitrage condition and the partial derivative $\dfrac{\partial G}{\partial t} = \dfrac{1}{\alpha}\left(K + t\dfrac{\partial K}{\partial t}\right)$, we get:

$$dx = \left(1 + \frac{F_G - 1}{\alpha}\right)tdK + \frac{F_G - 1}{\alpha}Kdt = \left[\left(1 + \frac{F_G - 1}{\alpha}\right)(1 + e_{K/t}) - 1\right]Kdt \tag{A.7}$$

Equalizing the marginal utility of (A.5) with the marginal disutility of (A.7) we get:

$$U_G \frac{(1 + e_{Kt})}{\alpha} K dt = -U_x \left[\left(1 + \frac{F_G - 1}{\alpha} \right)(1 + e_{K/t}) - 1 \right] K dt \qquad (A.8)$$

This yields the FOC: $MRS_{G/x} = \dfrac{1 - \left(1 + \dfrac{F_G - 1}{\alpha}\right)(1 + e_{K/t})}{1 + e_{K/t}} \quad \alpha = 1 - F_G - \alpha \dfrac{e_{K/t}}{1 + e_{K/t}}$ ∎

Claim 3.

$$e_{k/t} = \frac{e_{k/t}^0 + e_{k/G}^0}{1 - e_{k/G}^0} \qquad (2.2)$$

Proof. We have:

$$e_{K/t} = \frac{t}{K}\frac{\alpha - KF_{KG}}{\alpha F_{KK} + tF_{KG}}, \quad e_{k/t}^0 = \frac{t}{KF_{KK}} \leq 0 \quad \text{and} \quad e_{k/G}^0 = -\frac{G}{K}\frac{F_{KG}}{F_{KK}} \geq 0.$$

Substituting $e_{k/G}^0 / K e_{k/t}^0$ for F_{KG} in the expression of $e_{k/t}$, using $tK = \alpha G$, and rearranging, we obtain (2.1) ∎

Claim 4. At the optimum of an open economy, $e_{k/t}^0 \geq -1$.

Proof. The government maximizes $U(x, G)$ under the public input constraint (1.2), the resource constraint (1.3) and the arbitrage condition (1.4). The FOC with respect to K includes the Lagrange multiplier of the arbitrage condition, γ, and reads:

$$U_x F_K + \gamma \left(F_{KK} + \frac{\alpha G}{K^2} \right) - U_x r = 0 \qquad (A.9)$$

or, equivalently using the public input constraint:

$$U_x F_K + \gamma \left(F_{KK} + \frac{t}{K} \right) - U_x r = 0$$

and finally:

$$U_x t + \gamma F_{KK}(1 + e_{k/t}^0) = 0$$

since $U_x > 0$ and $F_{KK} < 0$, the FOC cannot be met when $1 + e_{k/t}^0 < 0$ ∎

To sum up, finding $e_{k/t}^0 > 1$ would mean that the government does not maximize household utility in the open economy.

Claim 5. At the optimum of an open economy, $e_{k/t} \leq 0$ if and only if either: $|e_{k/t}^0| \geq e_{k/G}^0$ or: $e_{k/G}^0 > 1$.

Proof. $e_{k/t} \leq 0$ if $e_{k/t}^0 + e_{k/G}^0 \leq 0$ and $1 - e_{k/G}^0 > 0$ or $e_{k/t}^0 + e_{k/G}^0 \geq 0$ and $1 - e_{k/G}^0 < 0$. Using Claim 4, the first case results in the condition $|e_{k/t}^0| \geq e_{k/G}^0$ and the second case results in $e_{k/G}^0 > 1$ ∎

Claim 6. If a proportional increase in capital and public input reduces the marginal productivity of capital, then

$$\alpha F_{KK} + t F_{KG} < 0. \qquad (A.10)$$

Proof. By assumption, $F_K(L, K(1 + \lambda), G(1 + \lambda)) < F_K(L, K, G)$ for any $\lambda > 0$. For $dK/K = dG/G > 0$, this assumption translates into:

$$F_K\left(\bar{L}, K\left(1 + \frac{dK}{K}\right), G\left(1 + \frac{dG}{G}\right)\right) < F_K(\bar{L}, K, G).$$

Omitting labour, which is constant,

$$F_K(K + dK, G + dG) - F(K, G + dG) + F_K(K, G + dG) - F_K(K, G) < 0$$

Divide this inequality by dK and note that $\frac{1}{\alpha}dK = dG/t$ for (1.2) to hold.

$$\frac{F(K + dK, G + dG) - F(K, G + dG)}{dK} + \frac{t}{\alpha}\frac{F(K, G + dG) - F(K, G)}{dG} < 0$$

Then, taking the limit we obtain (A.10)   ■

Claim 7. Under the assumption of Claim 6, $e_{k/G}^0 < 1$.

Proof. (A.10) can be written $\alpha F_{KK}(1 + e_{k/G}^0) < 0$ ■

In an open economy, the arbitrage condition reads:

$$\rho = F_K(\bar{L}, K, G) - t = r. \tag{A.11}$$

where ρ is the domestic, after-tax rate of return and r is the exogenous world interest rate. The domestic return as a function of G is given by:

$$\rho(G) = F_K(\bar{L}, K, G) - \alpha G/K. \tag{A.12}$$

Claim 8. For any K, for any α, $\rho(G)$ is single-peaked.[37]

Proof. Follows from an application of the intermediate value theorem and from assumptions

$$F_{KGG} < 0, \lim_{G \to +\infty} F_{KG} = 0, \quad \text{and} \quad \lim_{G \to 0} F_{KG} = +\infty. \quad ■$$

We now define $G^*(K)$ as the level of G which maximizes the after-tax domestic return for a given K. This level is given by differentiating (A.12) w.r.t. G:

$$F_{KG}(\bar{L}, K, G^*(K)) = \alpha/K \tag{A.13}$$

Claim 9. For any K, for any α, $F_G(\bar{L}, K, G^*(K)) \geq \alpha$

Proof. Since $F_G(\bar{L}, 0, G) = 0$ for any G,

$$\int_0^K F_{KG}(\bar{L}, \kappa, G^*(K))d\kappa = F_G(\bar{L}, K, G^*(K)).$$

Because F_{KG} is a decreasing function of K $(F_{KGK} \leq 0)$, one obtains

$$F_{KG}(\bar{L}, \kappa, G^*(\kappa)) \geq \alpha/\kappa \quad \text{for every } \kappa < K.$$

---

[37] Zodrow and Mieszkowski assume that $\rho(k, G)$ is a decreasing function whatever the level of G, whereas Dhillon *et al.* (2004) assume a hump-shape curve.

Integrating $F_{KG}(\bar{L}, \kappa, G^*(\kappa))$ between 0 and K, we find the desired result ■

In an open economy, the government maximizes $U(x, G)$ under the public input constraint (1.2), the resource constraint (1.3) and the arbitrage condition (1.4). The FOC with respect to G writes:

$$U_x(F_G - 1) + U_G + \gamma\left(F_{KG} - \frac{\alpha}{K}\right) = 0 \tag{A.14}$$

Let K_{open} and G_{open} be the solution of the two FOC (A.9) and (A.14). For $K = K_{open}$, at most two values of G satisfy the arbitrage condition (see Claim 8). The first one is such that $F_{KG} \geq \alpha/K_{open}$ and the second is such that $F_{KG} \leq \alpha/K_{open}$.

Claim 10. For $\alpha = 1$, $F_{KG} \leq 1/K_{open}$ for $G = G_{open}$, which means that G_{open} is on the decreasing section of the hump-shaped curve of $\rho(G)$.

Proof. Suppose G_{open} is such that $F_{KG}(\bar{L}, K_{open}, G_{open}) > 1/K_{open}$. By Claim 8, $G_{open} < G^*(K_{open})$. By Claim 9, $F_G(\bar{L}, K_{open}, G^*(K_{open})) \geq 1$. Since F_G is decreasing in G, $F_G(\bar{L}, K_{open}, G_{open}) > F_G(\bar{L}, K_{open}, G^*(K_{open})) \geq 1$. As $F_{KG}(\bar{L}, K_{open}, G_{open}) > 1/K_{open}$ and $F_G(\bar{L}, K_{open}, G_{open}) > 1$, (A.14) cannot be satisfied. Hence, $F_{KG} \leq 1/K_{open}$ ■

APPENDIX B

Table B1. Correlation matrix (balanced sample)

	LGDP	LDISTE	AGGLO	LEXCH	LULC	FLEX	LSTATUT	LPUBK	LSOCEXP	LHEAL	LEATR
LGDP	1										
LDISTE	-0.14	1									
AGGLO	0.03	-0.01	1								
LEXCH	-0.21	0.02	-0.04	1							
LULC	0.04	0.03	0.13	0.25	1						
FLEX	-0.37	-0.18	0.013	0.22	0.23	1					
LSTATU	0.38	-0.20	-0.02	0.10	0.05	-0.29	1				
LPUBK	0.38	-0.53	-0.00	-0.21	-0.12	-0.15	0.37	1			
LSOCEXP	0.25	-0.14	-0.02	0.11	-0.01	-0.11	0.41	-0.04	1		
LHEAL	0.51	0.01	0.01	-0.11	-0.16	-0.38	0.39	0.31	0.29	1	
LEATR	0.44	-0.16	-0.02	0.08	0.03	-0.35	0.95	0.40	0.35	0.33	1

APPENDIX C

Table C1. Country groupings

	Low	High
Size	Czech Rep., Denmark, Finland, Greece, Hungary, Ireland, Luxembourg, Poland, Portugal	Austria, Belgium, France, Germany, Italy, the Netherlands, Spain, Sweden, the UK
Openness	Finland, France, Germany, Greece, Italy, Poland, Portugal, Spain, the UK	Austria, Belgium, Czech Rep., Denmark, Hungary, Ireland, Luxembourg, the Netherlands, Sweden
Public capital per sq metre	Czech Rep., Finland, Greece, Hungary, Ireland, Poland, Portugal, Spain, Sweden	Austria, Belgium, Denmark, France, Germany, Italy, Luxembourg, the Netherlands, the UK
Statutory tax	Austria, Denmark, Finland, Hungary, Ireland, Poland, Spain, Sweden, the UK	Belgium, Czech Rep., France, Germany, Greece, Italy, Luxembourg, the Netherlands, Portugal

REFERENCES

Ayalp, T., D.O. Baykaler and Y. Özgünel (2004). 'FDI attractiveness of Turkey: A comparative analysis', Tüsiad/Yased mimeo, February.

Andersson, F. and R. Forslid (2003). 'Tax competition and economic geography', *Journal of Public Economic Theory*, 5(2), 279–304.

Baldwin, R.E. and P. Krugman (2004). 'Agglomeration, integration and tax harmonization', *European Economic Review*, 48, 1–23.

Baldwin, R.E., R. Forslid, G. Ottaviano, P. Martin and F. Robert-Nicoud (2003). *Economic Geography and Economic Policy*, Princeton University Press, Princeton, NJ.

Bénassy-Quéré, A., L. Fontagné and A. Lahrèche-Révil (2005). 'How does FDI react to corporate taxation?', *International Tax and Public Finance*, 12(5), 583–603.

Bernard, A.B., J.B. Jensen and P.K. Schott (2006). 'Transfer pricing by U.S.-based multinational firms', Tuck School of Business at Dartmouth, mimeo.

Besley, T. and A. Case (1995a). 'Incumbent behavior: vote seeking, tax setting and yardstick competition', *American Economic Review*, 85(1), 25–45.

—— (1995b). 'Does electoral accountability affect economic policy choices? Evidence from gubernatorial term limits', *Quarterly Journal of Economics*, 150, 769–98.

Bloningen, B.A. (2005). 'A review of the empirical literature on FDI determinants', NBER Working Paper No 11299.

Bloningen, B.A. and R.B. Davies (2002). 'Do bilateral tax treaties promote foreign direct investment?', NBER Working Paper No. 8834, March.

Braunerhjelm, P., R. Faini, V. Norman, F. Ruane and P. Seabright (2000). 'Integration and the regions of Europe: How the right policies can prevent polarization', *Monitoring European Integration* 10, CEPR report, ch.3.

Braunerhjelm, P. and R. Svensson (1996). 'Host country characteristics and agglomeration in foreign direct investment', *Applied Economics*, 28(7), July.

Brun, J.F., C. Carrère, P. Guillaumont and J. de Melo (2005). 'Has distance died? Evidence from a panel gravity model', *The World Bank Economic Review*, 1, 99–120.

Bureau of Economic Analysis (2003). *Survey of Current Business*, November.

Cohen, J., P. Cohen and S.G. West (2003). *Applied Multiple Regression/Correlation Analysis for the Behavioral Sciences* (2nd edn), Lawrence Erlbaum Associates, Hillsdale, NJ.

Devereux, M.P. and R. Griffith (1998). 'Taxes and location of production: Evidence from a panel of US multinationals', *Journal of Public Economics*, 68, 335–67.

—— (2002). 'The impact of corporate taxation on the location of capital: a review', *Swedish Economic Policy Review*, 9, 11–33.

Devereux, M., R. Griffith and A. Klemm (2002). 'Corporate income tax reforms and international tax competition', *Economic Policy*, October, 450–95.

Devereux, M.P. and P.B. Sorensen (2005). 'The corporate income tax: International trends and options for fundamental reform', paper prepared for the Work Party No. 2 of the Committee on Fiscal Affairs of the OECD, October.

De Mooij, R. and S. Ederveen (2003). 'Taxation and foreign direct investment: A synthesis of empirical research', *International Tax and Public Finance*, 10, 673–93.

—— (2005). 'Explaining the variation in empirical estimates of tax elasticities of foreign direct investment', Tinbergen Institute Discussion Paper 108/3.

Dhillon, A., M. Wooders and B. Zissimos (2006). 'Tax competition reconsidered', WP 0602 Vanderbilt University, forthcoming in *Journal of Public Economic Theory*.

Eaton, J. and A. Tamura (1996). 'Japanese and US exports and investment as conduits of growth', in T. Ito and A.O. Kueger (eds.), *Financial Deregulation and Integration in East Asia*, University of Chicago Press, Chicago, 51–72.

Edwards, J. and M. Keen (1996). 'Tax competition and Leviathan', *European Economic Review*, 40, 113–34.

Ernst & Young (2005). *European Attractiveness Survey 2005*.

Gabe, T.M. and K.P. Bell (2004). 'Tradeoffs between local taxes and government spending as determinant of business location', *Journal of Regional Science*, 44, 21–41. *Regional Science and Urban Economics*, 25, 655–73.

Griffith, R. and A. Klemm (2004). 'What has been the tax competition experience of the last 20 years?', *Tax Notes International*, 1299–1314.

Harris, C. (1954). 'The market as a factor in the localization of industries in the United States', *Annals of the Association of American Geographics*, 64, 315–48.

Head, K. and T. Mayer (2004). 'Market potential and the location of Japanese investment in the European Union', *The Review of Economics and Statistics*, 86(4), 959–72.

Hines, J. (1999). 'Lessons from behavioral responses to international taxation', *National Tax Journal*, 52(2), 305–23.

Kamps, C. (2004a). 'New estimates of government net capital stocks for 22 OECD countries, 1960–2001', IMF Working Paper 04/67.

—— (2004b). *The Dynamic Macroeconomic Effects of Public Capital: Theory and Evidence for OECD Countries*, Springer, Heidelberg.

Keen, M. and M. Marchand (1997). 'Fiscal competition and the pattern of public spending?', *Journal of Public Economics*, 66, 33–53.

King, M.A. and D. Fullerton (1984). *The Taxation of Income from Capital*, University of Chicago Press, Oxford.

Krogstrup, M.A. (2004). 'Are corporate tax burdens racing to the bottom in the European Union?', EPRU Working Paper 2004-04.

Krogstrup, S. (2002). 'What do theories of tax competition predict for capital taxes in EU countries? A review of the tax competition literature', HEI Working Paper No. 05/2002.

Krugman, P. (1991). 'Increasing returns and economic geography', *Journal of Political Economy*, 99, 483–99.

Laussel, D. and M. Lebreton (1998). 'Existence of Nash equilibria in fiscal competition models', *Regional Science and Urban Economics*, 28, 283–96.

Loree, D. and S. Guisinger (1995). 'Policy and non-policy determinants of U.S. equity foreign direct investment', *Journal of International Business Studies*, second quarter, 281–99.

Ludema, R.D. and I. Wooton (2000). 'Economic geography and the fiscal effects of regional integration', *Journal of International Economics*, 52(2), 331–57.

Mody, A. and K. Srinivasan (1998). 'Japanese and U.S. firms as foreign investors: do they march to the same tune?', *The Canadian Journal of Economics*, 31(4), 778–99.

Moulton, B.R. (1990). 'An illustration of a pitfall in estimating the effects of aggregate variables on micro units', *The Review of Economics and Statistics*, 72(2), 334–38.

Noiset, L. (1995). 'Pigou, Tiebout, property taxation, and the underprovision of local public goods: comment', *Journal of Urban Economics*, 38, 312–16.

Overesch, M. (2005). 'The effective tax burden of companies in Europe', CESifo DICE Report 4, 56–63.

Razin, A. and E. Sadka (2006). 'Vying for foreign direct investment: A EU-type model of tax competition', NBER Working Paper 11991.

Schleifer, A. (1985). 'A theory of yardstick competition', *Rand Journal of Economics*, 16, 319–27.
Sinn, H.W. (1997). 'The selection principle and market failure in systems of competition', *Journal of Public Economics*, 66, 247–74.
— (2003). *The New Systems Competition*, Blackwell, Oxford.
Stewart, K. and M. Webb (2006). 'International competition in corporate taxation: evidence from the OECD time series', *Economic Policy*, January, 153–201.
Tiebout, C. (1956). 'A pure theory of local expenditures', *Journal of Political Economy*, 64, 416–24.
UNCTAD (2005). *World Investment Report 2005*.
Wei, S.-Ji. (2000). 'How taxing is corruption on international investors?', *The Review of Economics and Statistics*, LXXXII(2), 1–11.
Weichenrieder, A.J. (2005). '(Why) do we need corporate taxation', mimeo, Goethe Universität Frankfurt and CESifo, April.
Wheeler, D. and A. Mody (1992). 'International investment location decisions: The case of U.S. firms'. *Journal of International Economics*, 33(1/2), 57–76.
Wildasin, D.E. (1988). 'Nash equilibria in models of fiscal competition', *Journal of Public Economics*, 35, 229–40.
Wilson, J.D. (1999). 'Theories of tax competition', *National Tax Journal*, 52(2), 269–304.
Wooders, M. and B. Zissimos (2005). 'Relaxing tax competition through public good differentiation', Cesifo, Working Paper No. 932.
Zodrow, G.R. and P. Mieszkowski (1986). 'Pigou, Tiebout, property taxation and the underprovision of local public goods', *Journal of Urban Economics*, 19, 356–70.

Economics of Transition

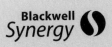

3795 025

Doris **weichselbaumer** is Assistant Professor at the University of Linz, Austria. Her area of interest is labour economics with a particular focus on the economics of minorities, issues of discrimination, as well as feminist and behavioural economics.

Rudolf **winter-ebmer** is Professor for Labour Economics at the University of Linz, Austria and the Institute for Advanced Studies (IHS), Vienna. His research interests are unemployment, education, discrimination and aging as well as policy evaluation in general.

Thomas **hertel** is Distinguished Professor at Purdue University and the founder and Executive Director of the Global Trade Analysis Project (GTAP). His recent research has focused on the impacts of developed country trade policies on poverty in developing countries.

Maros **ivanic** is Senior Expert and Economic Consultant at the Economic Analysis and Industrial Research Department (EAIR) at GOIC where he analyzes issues related to international trade and the WTO.

Roman **keeney** is an Assistant Professor in the Department of Agricultural Economics at Purdue University. His research interests are US farm policy and the economics of farm and rural households.

L. Alan **winters** is Director of the Development Research Group of the World Bank, and is currently on leave from the University of Sussex where he is Professor of Economics. He is one of the world's leading specialists on the empirical and policy analysis of international trade.

Tim **hatton** is Professor of Economics at the University of Essex and at the Australian National University. He has written extensively on the economic causes and effects of international migration from the nineteenth century to the present.

Agnès **bénassy-quéré** is the Director of CEPII, Professor at University Paris X and a Lecturer at Ecole Polytechnique. Her main research interests are monetary and fiscal policy, and the international monetary system.

Nicolas **gobalraja** is currently a PhD student at Université Paris X. His research focuses on econometrics and tax competition at both state and local levels.

Alain **trannoy** is currently Director of Research at EHESS in Marseilles. His main research line studies inequalities both from a theoretical and empirical point of view.

CEPR

CES

pse

ISBN 978-1-4051-5545-8

0266-4658(200704)22:02;1-K

9 781405 155458